The organic gardener's complete
guide to
VEGETABLES
and FRUITS

from the Editors of Rodale Press

 Rodale Press, Emmaus, Pennsylvania

Editor: **Anne M. Halpin**
Vegetables Editor: **Suzanne L. Nelson**
Editorial Staff: **Marilyn Hodges, Deborah Fry, Nancy Lee Maffia**
Copy Editor: **Jane Sherman**
Art Director: **Karen A. Schell**
Book Design: **Kim E. Morrow**
Layout: **Daniel M. Guest**
Illustrations: **Jack Crane, Kathi Ember**

Library of Congress Cataloging in Publication Data
Main entry under title:

The organic gardener's complete guide to
  vegetables and fruits.

  Bibliography: p.
  Includes index.
  1. Vegetable gardening. 2. Organic
gardening. 3. Fruit-culture. I. Rodale Press.
SB324.3.073   635′.0484   81-17857
ISBN 0-87857-386-0 hardcover   AACR2

  4 6 8 10 9 7 5 3   hardcover

Contents

Acknowledgments

The editors wish to thank everyone who contributed their time and talents to the preparation of this book. Special thanks to the following: Herb S. Aldwinckle, Dr. Michael J. Balick of the New York Botanical Garden, Steve Ganser and Skip Kauffman of the Organic Gardening and Farming Research Center Brian Goldman, M. C. Goldman, Jamie Jobb, Klaus Neubner, George Park, Jr., and Tim White.

Introduction

Where does the motivation come from to lug countless shovels full of manure, to endure the ache of winter-lazy muscles called upon to till soil in the spring, to patiently pick cabbage loopers from each broccoli plant in a 10-foot row? Ask one person why he gardens, and he may tell you he does it for the pleasure of plucking warm, vine-ripened tomatoes bursting with juice as he needs them, and for the almost sinful pleasure of sinking his teeth into hot, succulent kernels of corn that just ten minutes before were still out on the stalk. Pose the question to another person, and she'll tell you in dollars-and-cents terms that gardening is an effective way to shave money off the family food bill. Ask a third person, and she will stress her concern about a consumer's dependence on chemically treated produce shipped from miles away, and tell you how she is seeking to break away from this precarious, wasteful system of food distribution to become more self-reliant. And then there are those who will tell you that they garden as a form of relaxation and recreation. All these reasons underscore the fact that home gardening is becoming an increasingly popular and increasingly important activity.

And, as people become increasingly aware of the ramifications the use of chemical fertilizers and pesticides have on the environment as well as on the food they eat, the more organic gardening methods appear as a gentle and sane approach to safeguarding diminishing resources, the earth's water supply, the health of the soil, and ultimately, the health of people themselves.

Between the covers of this book, you will find all the information you need to grow a wide range of vegetable and fruit crops by tried and true organic methods in your home garden. To help you make the best use of this book, here is a brief description of how the information is presented and how you can find exactly what you need to know.

The book is divided into two main sections, one dealing with vegetables, the other with fruits. Each of these sections is broken down into several chapters providing general information on such topics as garden planning, basic planting methods, and basic cultural techniques. If you're new to organic gardening, you'll probably want to read through the chapters in their entirety. If you've got some experience under your belt, you can skip the basic chapters on planning and zero in on intensive gardening, espalier and cordon training, and other techniques which may be new to you.

The heart of the book is its detailed coverage of 57 vegetable and 45 fruit crops. These are gathered together under the headings "A Guide to Vegetables for the Home Garden," and "A Guide to Fruits for the Home Garden," which follow the general chapters in their respective sections. In these Guides you'll find specific advice on soil needs, spacing and planting methods, culture through the season, potential pest and disease problems, harvest and storage. To aid you further in your gardening endeavors, many of the fruits and vegetables discussed have an accompanying chart giving recommended varieties and their pertinent characteristics.

This book was designed so that the general chapters would supplement the information given under the individual vegetable and fruit listings. For example, when you look under Beets in the Vegetable Guide, you'll find a 6-inch spacing given for planting in a raised bed. If you are unfamiliar with raised beds, check back with the general chapters, Preparing the Soil and Planting (chapters 2 and 3), to find out how to prepare and plant a raised bed.

As a prelude to the vegetable and fruit gardening sections of this book, this portion presents a brief discussion of various aspects of a long-range soil management program—the keystone of the organic approach, whether you're growing apples or radishes. It's an old organic gardening maxim that if you feed the soil (instead of the plants), and take care to build and maintain its organic matter content, then everything else in the garden will take care of itself. It's no coincidence that gardeners who have employed sound organic gardening methods for many seasons find that their soil's texture improves dramatically, that their garden's productivity increases with only minimal, if any, supplemental fertilization throughout the season, and that their encounters with insect pests and soilborne diseases decline in frequency. There is nothing magical about all of this—it's just the gardener's reward for attending to the soil's needs.

Your main concern as an organic gardener should be to continually work organic matter into the soil so that it can be broken down by soil microorganisms into a crumbly, dark substance known as humus. For a soil to be considered in prime condition, it should have a humus content of at least 5 percent. Humus is a critical ingredient in your soil because it combats leaching by holding nutrients in the root zone, counteracts the effects of a drought by holding water where plant roots can get to it, and keeps the soil well aerated. A soil rich in humus is the best possible medium for plant roots, and the most hospitable environment for beneficial soil microorganisms and earthworms. A humusy, well-nourished soil encourages large numbers of these microorganisms to become active, which in turn helps control and ultimately eliminate soilborne diseases caused by fungi and other pathogens. Organic matter also has been found to act as a buffer between these helpful soil microorganisms and any toxic chemicals which may be present in your soil, as well as reducing the activity and movement of pesticides that may have seeped into your soil from elsewhere. And finally, humus encourages healthy plant growth, which keeps insect damage down.

Organic matter, referred to as the storehouse of the soil's nutrients, also benefits the soil's fertility level as it is broken down by microorganisms. One of the end products of decomposition is nitrogen in a form that can be used by plants. Organic matter also plays a key role in keeping phosphorus and potassium available in the soil in forms that can be used for plant growth. In this way, crops get the proper nutrients in the forms they can absorb, as they are needed. With a careful soil maintenance program, there is no feast-or-famine cycle of nutrients—they are always present, being released gradually.

As you can see, organic matter plays the starring role in maintaining a healthy, fertile growing medium for your fruit and vegetable crops. And healthy, abundant crops are nothing more than an extension of soil in good condition. Highlighted in the following pages are several aspects of a long-range soil management program that you should become familiar with. Once you understand these basic concepts or techniques, you're well on your way to growing fruits or vegetables successfully the organic way.

Determining Your Soil Type

The first step in managing your soil is understanding its basic character, and where it falls among the four main soil types: clay, loam, muck, and sand. All soil is made up of four main ingredients, and the actual mix of sand, clay, silt, and organic matter determines the water- and nutrient-holding capacity of the

Getting to Know Your Soil

Soil Type	Texture	Characteristics	How to Improve or Maintain
Clay	Feels rock hard when dry, and sticky, greasy, or rubbery when moist. When you squeeze it in your hand, it forms a sticky, compact mass that doesn't break apart easily.	The very small clay particles pack together, discouraging good drainage and aeration. Clay soil is slow to absorb water, but once it does, it is very slow to dry out. It stays cold and wet well into the planting season, but does retain the sun's warmth well into the fall. If worked when too wet, the soil will form rocklike lumps and clods which are very difficult to break apart. Because nutrients don't leach out readily, this soil tends to be rich in nutrients. While a high proportion of clay particles is undesirable, they are necessary to some degree, to give strength and water-holding capacity to the soil. Clay soil is hard to work.	Massive infusions of organic matter are needed to loosen up the soil and to form a crumbly, friable structure that will promote good drainage and root zone aeration. Good materials to add are compost, manure, leaf mold, rice hulls, peat moss, coarse sand, sawdust, and wood chips. Lime helps upgrade the texture and makes the soil nutrients that are present available to growing plants. Green manure crops are very effective in improving clay soils, especially legume crops. Work organic matter into the soil in fall and leave the soil surface in a rough condition over the winter to allow frost action to break up large clods. Don't always dig to the same depth, for this will encourage a hardpan layer to form. As this layer of soil that is never penetrated becomes harder, drainage is hindered and salt concentrations may build up to harmful levels.

(continued)

Getting to Know Your Soil—*continued*

Soil Type	Texture	Characteristics	How to Improve or Maintain
Loam	Soil appears to be made of various-sized crumbs. When you squeeze it in your hand, it molds readily into a ball, which falls apart easily when squeezed.	Generally speaking, a loam consists of 50% sand, 40% silt (gritty particles halfway between clay and sand), and 10% clay with supplemental organic matter. Soils with a higher proportion of clay are termed clay loams, and those with a higher proportion of sand are called sand loams. Loam retains water well, with the excess free to drain away. Nutrients are not quickly leached out of this soil. Easy to work and very productive.	Keep this "ideal" soil in top shape by continually adding organic matter to maintain fertility and good structure.
Muck and Peat	Appears very dark brown in color. When you squeeze it in your hand, it may feel like peat moss.	This soil is rich in organic matter like mosses, grasses, and ferns in various stages of decay. The term "peat soil" is used to describe a soil in which the organic matter is not fully decomposed; a muck soil is this same soil at an advanced stage of decay. Muck soils tend to be waterlogged and somewhat deficient in lime. They are rich in nutrients (especially nitrogen), although the proper balance of minerals may not be present for good plant growth. Suited mainly for vegetable crops like celery, lettuce, and onions.	Encourage adequate drainage by adding layers of gravel or drainage tiles. Add lime as needed.
Sandy	Feels grainy and gritty. When you try to squeeze it into a ball, it may be so loose and crumbly that it holds no shape, or if it does, it will crumble apart easily.	Large, irregular particles create open spaces through which water and soluble nutrients quickly flow. Dries out and warms up rapidly, so it is especially suited for early spring crops. Easy to work and well aerated. Because nutrients leach out so quickly, sandy soils commonly have deficiencies of calcium, nitrogen, potassium, and phosphorus. The poor water-retaining capacity of this soil means there is little moisture reserve for plants to draw upon in times of drought.	Continually work in organic matter to hold water and nutrients in the soil where plants can draw upon them. Work manure in deeply in the fall or winter, and add plenty of peat moss, compost, leaf mold, or sawdust to the top layer to help build a fertile, well-structured topsoil. A green manure program will also improve the soil structure.

soil, and whether it is a well-structured growing medium for plant roots. A lab analysis can give you the exact proportions of these ingredients and pinpoint your soil type, but you don't actually need to be that precise. You can find out all you need to know about your soil's basic identity by bending over and picking up a handful. Rub it between your fingers and compare its texture with the descriptions given in the chart on Getting to Know Your Soil. Once you've identified your soil type, you can read about its basic characteristics, both good and bad, and what you can do to improve or maintain it.

Checking Your Soil's pH

You can work copious amounts of organic matter into your garden and add appropriate amounts of rock powders in the belief that you are bringing your soil to the peak of fertility and good structure, but end up sabotaging your own efforts by a simple omission—failure to test your soil's pH.

Soil pH is the term used to express the degree of acidity or alkalinity, and it is based on a scale of 0 (acid) to 14 (alkaline) with the midpoint of 7 indicating a neutral soil condition. The pH is an important element in the overall health and well-being of your garden, for it influences bacterial action, soil structure, nutrient availability and leaching, and the toxicity of certain elements.

In very acid soils (below pH 5), phosphorus becomes locked up in a form that is unavailable to plants. Nutrients such as calcium, potassium, and magnesium have an increased tendency to leach out of overly acid soils. In addition, beneficial soil bacteria begin to slow down their work of turning organic matter into humus, adversely affecting soil structure. An acid condition can even prompt earthworms to move out of your garden to more hospitable ground. The incidence of the disease clubroot, which often strikes brassicas, increases in acid soils.

An overly alkaline soil (above pH 7.5) is no better. A high degree of alkalinity causes most of the trace elements, which are necessary for good plant growth, to be locked up and made unavailable to plants. An alkaline condition also breaks apart humus and in some cases causes a concentration of salts to build up to such levels that they become toxic to plants.

To find out where your soil stands along the pH scale, you must test it. There are a number of ways you can do this, ranging from commercially available do-it-yourself test kits to sophisticated test meters. For a fee you can send soil samples to an agricultural experiment station (through your local extension agent) or to a private soil laboratory for a complete analysis.

Your soil pH can change from season to season, and vary from one place to another in the garden. Pine needles or oak leaves falling on a certain area will gradually cause the soil to become more acid. Acid rains caused by industrial pollution can also serve to lower the soil pH. To safeguard the health of your garden soil, it is wise to test the pH three times a year—before planting, midway through the season, and after harvest. When you are collecting a soil sample, take small amounts from at least three or four locations in the garden so you get a good representation of your garden's current pH status. Make sure the soil doesn't come in contact with your hands, since natural oils secreted by the skin can affect the results of the tests.

Soils generally register a pH between 4.5 and 8.5. Most vegetables and fruits grow best in soils with a pH between 6 and 7 (see the Vegetable Guide and the Guide to Fruits for specific crop preferences). Depending on what your soil test shows, you can either grow those crops that are suited to that particular pH, or incorporate certain materials to change the pH to bring it to a level that accommodates a wider range of fruits and vegetables.

If your soil is too acid, you work in natural ground limestone (especially crushed dolomite), bone meal, pulverized eggshells, clamshells, oyster shells, or wood ashes to raise the pH. If your soil is too alkaline, you would want to add pine needles, cottonseed meal, acid peat moss, leaf mold, sawdust, or wood chips.

There is no hard and fast rule about how much of what material you must add to raise and lower the pH by so many units. The best plan is to work in a pound of the material you have chosen, then test the soil in a couple of weeks. If you need to make further adjustments, do them in two or three more applications, spaced several weeks apart. Be sure to till the material into the soil as deeply as possible.

Composting

As you embark on a soil-building program, you'll find no better source of organic matter than compost. A serious organic gardener would no sooner be caught without a good source of compost than a serious cook would be caught with an empty canister of flour. Compost is the lifeblood of a thriving organic garden, where it serves the dual purpose of enriching the soil and creating a light, porous structure conducive to good plant growth. In its finished form it contains roughly two parts nitrogen, one part phosphorus, and one part potassium, with a pH of 7. It releases its nutrients slowly, and they aren't easily leached away by water seeping through the root zone. Thus, compost is a slow but steady source of basic nutrients. In addition to its fertility value, compost is a first-class soil amendment that can help turn hopelessly clayey or sandy soils into rich, crumbly, productive loam.

Composting is a relatively simple process, as long as you meet certain basic needs: you must assemble the proper blend of organic matter, nitrogen, and humus-forming bacteria, and make sure that there is adequate air and moisture present so the pile heats up and the process of decomposition gets under way.

The granddaddy of composting methods is known as the Indore Method. With this classic method and its variations, you build up layers of organic matter, interspersed with a layer of manure or other high-nitrogen substance, and a layer of soil. The pile should measure 6 to 7 feet wide, 3 to 5 feet high, and 6 to 7 feet long (or longer).

There are several ways you can start out: build an unconfined pile on the ground, start a pile in a 2- to 3-foot-deep pit, or build your pile in a bin. Gardeners out in the country with plenty of room tend to prefer the unconfined pile, while suburban gardeners usually opt for the more visually appealing bin.

To get your compost pile going, lay down a layer of brush to form the base. Add a 6-inch layer of green or dry vegetable matter (see the chart on Compost Ingredients), then a 2-inch layer of manure (or other nitrogen-rich substance such as blood meal or cottonseed meal), followed by a ⅛-inch layer of topsoil. If you wish, you can add a sprinkling of lime and other materials like phosphate rock, granite dust, or wood ashes to fortify your final compost. Repeat these layers until the pile stands 3 to 5 feet tall. As you are layering, dampen the materials slightly, but only enough so that they are as moist as a damp sponge. To aid the aeration of the completed pile, insert some poles or pipes down into the pile.

Compost Ingredients

What to Use	What to Avoid	Sources of Nitrogen (to increase bacterial activity)
Coffee grounds Eggshells Ground corncobs Hedge trimmings Kitchen wastes (vegetable and fruit peels) Lawn clippings Pine needles Sawdust Shredded leaves Shredded twigs Straw Tea leaves Weeds and disease-free plant debris Wood shavings	Material thicker than ¼ inch (shred or chop large pieces to speed up decomposition) Diseased or pest-laden materials Plant debris carrying pesticides or herbicides Meat, bones, grease, other fatty substances (these are slow to decompose and attract undesirable creatures) Seeds and fruit pits (attractive to rodents) Cat or dog manure, bird droppings (handling fresh manure and droppings and subsequent use of compost may transmit parasites harmful to humans)	Blood meal Bone meal Cottonseed meal Manure Tankage

If you've provided the right mix of organic matter, nitrogen, bacteria, moisture, and air, the pile should begin to heat up and begin to shrink in size within a couple of days. You'll need to turn the pile twice to help the decomposition process along. Two to three weeks after the pile was built, turn it with a spading fork or pitchfork. Turn once again about three weeks later. As you turn the pile, move the outer portions to the inside (where the heat is the greatest) so the organic matter will be uniformly decomposed. Within three months, the material should be reduced to a crumbly, black substance, ready to add to your garden.

If you'd like quicker results and have access to a shredder, you can try the 14-day California Method. For this method, you will need a bin of some sort to contain the material, which should be a mix of green garden debris or garbage, and dry garden debris. Begin by layering 2 to 4 inches of green materials, then 2 to 4 inches of dry materials. This organic matter should be shredded into pieces no larger than 6 to 8 inches. Moisten each layer so that the particles glisten, but don't overwater so you end up with a sodden mess. A good size for a bin is 3 feet square, and the pile should range in height from 3 to 4 feet.

Frequent turning is the key to success with this method, for it provides the aeration necessary for the aerobic bacteria to do their breakdown work. You can turn it as frequently as your muscles can stand (not more than once per day), but don't allow more than two to three days to go by without turning. Effective turning involves removing the material from the bin in such a way that the material from the outside (top and sides) ends up on the inside of the new pile. Fluff up the material as you fork it back in the bin. If the pile seems dry, add a

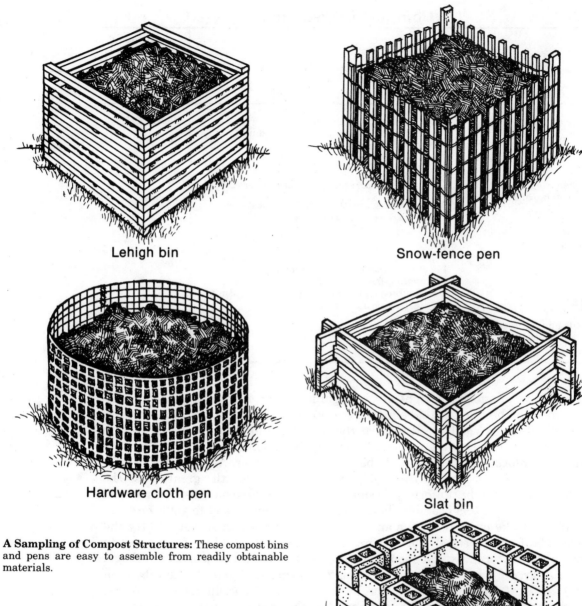

Lehigh bin

Snow-fence pen

Hardware cloth pen

Slat bin

A Sampling of Compost Structures: These compost bins and pens are easy to assemble from readily obtainable materials.

Block bin

little water as you turn it. A well-built, frequently turned pile can be ready in as few as 14 days, or with less frequent turnings, in a month. The compost is ready to use when the pile has stopped generating heat and the material looks dark and crumbly.

You never need to worry about overapplying compost, or about it burning tender plants. As a general guide, apply at least a half-inch layer to your garden each year. You can make a general application and work it into your garden plot before planting, add it to furrows before sowing or transplanting vegetables, or work it into the soil before planting a fruit tree or berry bush. Screened compost is a good seed-starting medium, and it can also be sprinkled over newly sown seeds in the garden to keep the soil from crusting. Use it as a top-dressing or as a mulch in the vegetable garden. Build a mulch ring around fruit trees, 1 to 2 inches thick, starting 2 feet away from the trunk, extending out to the drip-line. Or work 3 to 4 inches of compost into the top couple of inches of soil around the tree, or around berry plants.

Mulching

Mulching your fruit or vegetable garden figures into a sound soil management program, and in addition can help cut down on the time you must spend on garden upkeep.

A mulch is nothing more than a layer of organic, or in some cases inorganic, material that you spread on the soil surface. It will keep soil moisture from evaporating by protecting the soil from the direct effects of the wind and the hot sun. A mulch serves you well during any long dry spells, since you can get by with fewer waterings and make a limited water supply go further.

In terms of soil structure, mulches provide the immediate benefit of guarding against soil erosion. Organic mulches in particular play an important part in the long-range care of your soil's structure and fertility. While the mulch is on the soil surface, certain nutrients break down gradually and work their way into the soil with the help of heavy rains. At the end of the season, when you turn the mulch into the soil, it will be broken down further and eventually enrich the soil's humus content. Examples of particularly nutrient-rich mulching materials are straw, seaweed, various hays, corncobs, peat moss, wood chips, grass clippings, and sawdust.

Mulch (especially the black plastic type) is a weed deterrent of good repute. It also acts as an insulating blanket to guard against temperature extremes, thus keeping the soil warm in winter and cool in summer. The exceptions to this are the plastic sheeting mulches, which tend to magnify the rays of the sun and to raise the soil temperature. A thick, fluffy mulch is an effective way to protect asparagus beds, berry bushes, strawberry plants, and other hardy vegetables from the effects of low winter temperatures.

A fine-textured mulch can lend a tidy, uniform, well-tended air to any vegetable or fruit patch. And it can help keep the harvest clean by sparing it from mildew, mold, rot, and mud splatters that result when crops like cucumbers,

A Guide to Mulching Materials

Mulch Material	How to Use	Helpful Tips
Organic		
Alfalfa hay	Spread 2–3 in. deep; add extra nitrogen before you spread it; good for winter protection.	Easy to handle and long-lasting, since it breaks down slowly.
Bark chips	Spread layer of polyethylene first, before adding chips; generally used in decorative gardens rather than in vegetable gardens or around fruit trees.	Small chips scatter easily, larger chips stay in place; both turn gray as they age.
Buckwheat hulls	Spread 1–2 in. thick in summer; use deeper layer in winter.	Clean, attractive, lightweight mulch; good potassium content; lasts for several years.
Cocoa bean hulls or shells	2-in. layer is effective; 4 cu. ft. bag covers 60 sq. ft. with a 2-in. layer.	Chocolate odor fades after mulch is spread; hulls or shells absorb 2½ times their weight in water; lasts around 1 year.
Compost	Spread 2–4-in. layer in the vegetable garden and around fruit trees and berry bushes.	You can use the partially decomposed matter as a mulch, and save the crumbly, humusy part of the compost pile to work directly into the soil.
Corncobs	Should be ground into pieces 1 in. or smaller; use a 3–6-in. layer; apply extra nitrogen before laying down mulch.	As cobs decay, their sugar content helps increase the soil microorganism population.
Cornstalks	Chop or shred before using; spread 2 in. deep; apply extra nitrogen before spreading mulch.	Relatively inexpensive and readily obtainable.
Grass clippings	Spread a 1–2-in. layer; generally used in vegetable gardens; problems with fresh clippings can be avoided by composting them briefly or by combining them with lighter materials like wood chips or compost.	As inexpensive and accessible as they come; use grass clippings that haven't gone to seed to keep from introducing undesirable plant growth into the garden; too thick a layer of fresh clippings may create problems by compacting, thereby blocking soil aeration and causing water to run off; too thick a layer of fresh clippings can also give off a bad odor, build up excessive heat, and serve as a breeding ground for flies and gnats.
Leaves	More effective in shredded form; spread shredded leaves about 4 in. deep; mix unshredded leaves with straw or wood chips to keep them from compacting into a soggy mat; use 8–12-in. layer of this mixed mulch for winter protection.	Oak leaves are acidic in nature, and prolonged use can lower soil pH; dry leaves tend to blow away easily; unshredded leaves decompose more slowly than shredded leaves; no extra nitrogen is necessary.
Manure	Must be well rotted (composted); apply about 2–3 in. deep.	Avoid fresh manure since it will burn plants; manure can be a source of excess salts and weed seeds in the garden.
Mushroom compost	Lay down a 4-in. layer.	A good soil conditioner; available from commercial mushroom growers; at times may give off an unpleasant odor.

Mulch Material	How to Use	Helpful Tips
Newspaper	Use layer of 6–8 sheets and overlap neighboring layers; anchor with thin layer of soil, rocks, or wood chips; add extra nitrogen.	Newsprint ink contains no harmful chemicals, but coated glossy paper used in magazines can release substances harmful to soil microorganisms; breaks down completely in about 1 year's time; leaves gray, telltale clumps in the soil.
Peat moss	Spread 4-in. layer among acid-loving plants like blueberries and potatoes; moisten thoroughly and knead water through material before spreading.	If allowed to dry out, is easily carried off by the wind; once it's dry, peat moss is very difficult to moisten, since water tends to run off the surface without being absorbed.
Pecan shells	Spread 1–2 in. thick.	Inexpensive in areas where growers are abundant; long-lasting; harmless orange mold may appear on shells; rake moldy shells under and mold will disappear.
Pine needles	Use 2–4-in. layer around acid-loving plants (see Peat moss); good year-round mulch for strawberries.	Good-looking mulch, inexpensive and easy to obtain; can be a fire hazard when dry; acidic nature can lower soil pH after prolonged use.
Salt hay	In general, use 3-in. layer; on strawberry beds, use 1½–2-in. layer; very good year-round mulch.	Good source of trace minerals; doesn't mat down.
Sawdust	Add extra nitrogen to soil before applying, or compost the material first; spread about a 2-in. layer; for blueberries, use sawdust from softwoods, which will afford better aeration and promote an acid soil condition; hardwood sawdust can act as an elixir of youth for old apple trees.	Tends to blow away when dry and also forms a crust if allowed to dry out.
Seaweed	Use 1–2-in. layer.	Good source of potassium.
Stones	Permanent-type mulch; place stones in areas between beds or rows, or around fruit trees; set stones as close together as possible, and level firmly in the ground.	Warms the ground, keeps down weeds, and conserves moisture; heat absorbed during the day protects tender plants on cool nights.
Straw	Add extra nitrogen to soil before laying down 8–10 in.; material will eventually compact down to 4 in.	Easy to work with; long-lasting and slow to break down; clean and contains no weed seeds; where appropriate, leave on all season long and work into the soil in the fall to break down over the winter.
Wood chips, shavings	See Sawdust	
Inorganic		
Aluminum foil	Spread strips of foil alongside growing plants; anchor edges with soil or rocks; lift at end of the season and reuse the following year; recycle when too ragged to use in the garden.	Although foil does not enhance the soil fertility or break down into humus, it protects the ground from erosion and conserves moisture; reflected light helps control aphids; increases amount of sunlight available to plant leaves, which can hasten fruit ripening; foil can lower soil temperature by 10 degrees, so it is useful when growing cool-season plants.

(continued)

A Guide to Mulching Materials—*continued*

Mulch Material	How to Use	Helpful Tips
Inorganic (*continued*)		
Black plastic sheeting (polyethylene film)	1½-mil-thick sheeting is the simplest to handle and most durable for repeated use; lay over rows or beds and make slits to insert seeds or seedlings; anchor in soil-filled ditches or with rocks; use around hard-to-weed crops and vining vegetables.	Warms soil to a lesser degree than clear sheeting; soil temperatures rise only 1–3 degrees in the first inch; the advantage is its weed control factor, its tendency to reduce water loss, and its ability to create a clean, disease-resistant environment for crops.
Clear plastic sheeting (polyethylene film)	1½-mil-thick sheeting is the simplest to handle and most durable for repeated use; use for vining, heat-loving plants like melons, pumpkins, squash, tomatoes; can also be used to hasten early germination of cool-season crops like lettuce and spinach; lay over rows or beds and make slits to insert seeds or seedlings; anchor in soil-filled ditches or with rocks.	The mulch to use if you want to warm the soil; soil temperatures in the top 6 in. are raised 8–10 degrees; one drawback—weeds flourish; can be used to solarize the soil to get rid of soilborne disease organisms.

melons, squash, strawberries, and tomatoes sprawl on unmulched ground.

Problems usually occur when mulching materials are not understood or have been improperly applied. As with any garden practice, mulching is not entirely foolproof, and it certainly won't solve all your garden headaches. Where soil is heavy and poorly drained, a thick mulch could do more harm than good. It would prevent the soil from drying in the spring, might sharply diminish aeration, and would increase the chances of crown-rot problems. Gardeners who must work with cold clay soils would be advised to incorporate all available organic matter into the soil, thereby raising their beds and improving soil structure, rather than using it as a mulch. A mulch is best suited to soils that are light to average or only slightly heavy in texture.

The Guide to Mulching Materials gives you a handy rundown of mulching materials and general tips on how to use them. For the beginning organic gardener in particular, and wherever soils are still low in organic matter, a good organic mulch is the best choice. Almost any organic material will do, provided it is disease-free and does not form too heavy a mat. Although you will want to use the cheapest, most easily obtainable material, understand its specific qualities before you apply it. Consider potentials for disease, nutrient tie-up, pH problems, and excessive compaction or heat. Woody materials such as sawdust or wood chips tend to utilize soil nitrogen when they first decompose, so extra fertilization would be necessary in order to guarantee sufficient nitrogen supplies for crop use. If you don't have lots of manure or dried blood on hand to apply along with the woody mulch, seaweed, fresh grass clippings, or another mulch with a lower carbon content would be worthwhile. Acidity becomes a problem in some gardens when oak leaves or pine needles are used as a mulch. These tend to lower soil pH, making them fine materials for blueberries, potatoes, or tomatoes, but devastating to many other crops. Finally, some fresh mulches might become so compacted as they decompose that soil aeration would be limited and excessive heat would become a problem. Fresh grass clippings and unchopped leaves may create this dilemma unless they are composted for a brief period before being applied, or are combined with a lighter material such as wood chips or compost.

And even though you're an organic gardener, don't ignore the benefits of certain inorganic mulching materials. Although plastics, aluminum foil, and similar substances do not build soil or contribute nutrients, they do protect the ground from erosion and conserve moisture. While rainwater does not penetrate these materials, moisture already held in the soil cannot escape, giving plants a constant supply of water throughout the season. If watering should be necessary, it can be supplied from beneath the mulch. The initial cost of these mulches can be offset by the fact that they can be recycled from year to year.

Fertilizing the Organic Way

In the organic garden, your basic objective is to feed the soil, not necessarily the individual crops that are growing in it. When you incorporate a wide variety of natural materials you ensure that the proper nutrients will always be present in the soil, where they will be released slowly as the plants need them, rather than in a single massive dose, as occurs with chemical fertilizers.

The basic materials that boost and maintain your soil's fertility fall into two categories: organic matter and rock powders. Organic matter encompasses such materials as animal and green manures, compost, leaf mold, bone meal, dried blood, and wood ashes. Organic matter supplies the major nutrients—nitrogen, phosphorus, and potassium—in varying amounts, and also plays an important role in making these nutrients available in forms that can be used by plants.

Crops in an organic garden get most of their nitrogen as an end product from the decomposition of organic matter caused by soil bacteria and earthworms. In order for the decomposition process to continue, you must add regular infusions of organic matter. However, you must pay attention to the type of material you are adding. If, for example, you were to add some dry plant matter that was high in carbon but low in nitrogen, the bacteria would have to draw upon the nitrogen present in the soil to fuel their breakdown of the carbon material. Although decomposition of this woody material would eventually release nitrogen to the soil as an end product, there would be a temporary deficiency of nitrogen available for plant growth. To counteract this drain on the soil's nitrogen, you should add a high-nitrogen substance such as blood meal or manure whenever you add woody plant matter to the soil.

Organic matter contains considerably less phosphorus than nitrogen, but its value lies more in making soil phosphorus already present from other sources available to growing plants. A soil rich in organic matter is rich in soil bacteria, which secrete acids that promote the breakdown and availability of phosphorus. Without ample organic matter, phosphorus in the soil would be locked up in insoluble compounds.

Organic matter also makes potassium available to plants. Most of the soil's potassium is bound up in mineral form and therefore unavailable to plants; some

tricks of the trade

Compost and Manure Teas

These are nothing more than enriched water which can be added to give a midseason fertility boost to heavy-feeding crops. This supplemental feeding will come in particularly handy in gardens where organic methods have not been in practice long, and where the soil hasn't achieved a high level of ongoing fertility. Compost and manure teas are also widely used as starter solutions for vegetable transplants, and when berry bushes and fruit trees are set in the ground. You'll find that these liquids are easy and inexpensive to make and convenient to use.

For compost tea, fill a burlap bag with finished compost and suspend it in a bucket or watertight barrel filled three-quarters of the way with water. Stir the contents several times over the course of two weeks. You can also make the tea by simply filling the container one-quarter full of loose compost, adding water to fill, and stirring as directed above. Tea made this way will need to be strained before using.

The mixture will bubble and deepen in color as bacterial activity and nutrient leaching take place. When the bubbling has stopped and the liquid is brown in color, the compost tea is ready to use. You should dilute it until it reaches a light amber color, and apply about 1 pint per vegetable plant, and more for bushes and trees. You can store the extra brewed tea in jars or bottles with loosely fitting aluminum foil caps. Tight-fitting caps are not appropriate, for they would hinder the release of gases which may occur over time.

For a smaller batch of compost tea, fill a sprinkling can halfway with finished compost and add water to fill to the top. Stir briskly, about 12 times, then pour it on. You can use the same compost several times before its nutrient value is leached away, and even then it is still of value to the garden. You should dig it into the soil where it will benefit the structure.

Manure tea is made in the same manner as compost tea. Fill a burlap bag full of fresh manure, then suspend it in a garbage can full of water. Let the manure/water mixture steep for several days before using. When you do apply it to the garden, dilute it as needed with water, so that it has the color of weak tea.

---

potassium appears in soluble form which plants can use, but there is the danger that it can be quickly leached from the soil before plants can draw upon it. Organic matter helps hold soluble potassium in the root zone, and helps change mineral potassium into a form acceptable to plants as they need it. In short, organic matter helps balance the potassium level in the soil.

Rock powders are substances derived from natural materials which complement the use of organic matter. Commonly used rock powders are phosphate rock, granite dust, and greensand; the first is rich in phosphorus, while the last two are good sources of potassium.

By using rock powders, you build the natural phosphorus and potassium reserves in the soil; by working in plenty of organic matter you boost the soil's nitrogen level and ensure that the soil nutrients will be readily available in the form that plants can use as they grow.

VEGETABLES

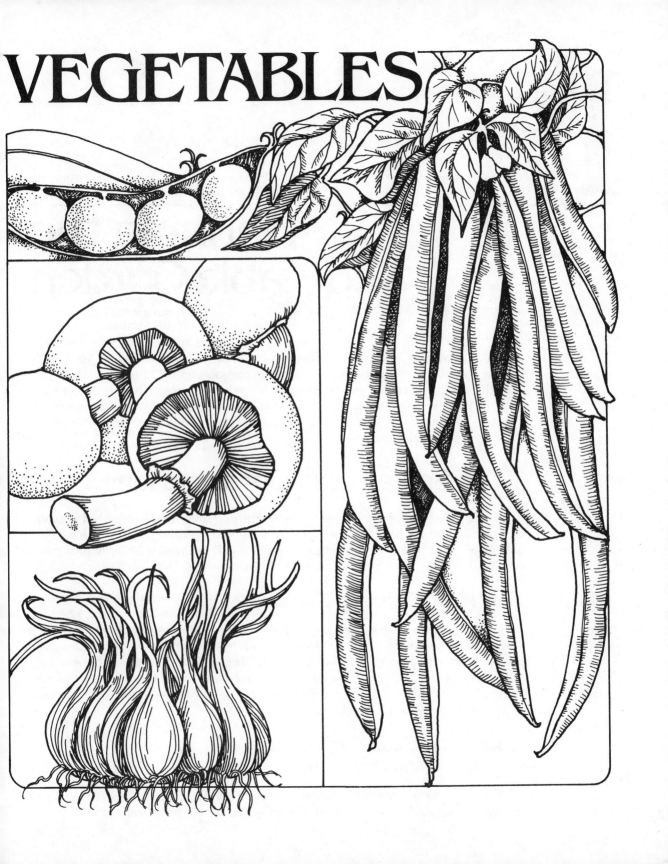

1

Planning the Vegetable Garden

Whether you're gardening to help ease the pinch on the family food bills, to attain a greater degree of self-sufficiency, to ensure that the food on your table is untainted by harmful chemicals, or any combination of these reasons, a well thought-out garden plan can enable you to make the most efficient use of your garden space. Whatever you reap from your garden will directly reflect how much effort has gone into it, both during the initial planning process and later on, as the growing season progresses.

Some Basic Considerations

Long before the shovel slides into your garden soil and a single seed is sown, you should already have a clear vision of what your garden is going to look like, both in terms of its size and of what vegetables will be found within. A good place to start is to ask yourself the following questions.

How Much Space Is Available?

A homesteader with several acres obviously has more space to work with than a suburban dweller who is limited to a 5-by-10-foot garden patch along the driveway. But no matter whether you're dealing in feet or acres, both are viable gardening spaces. Apartment and city dwellers can transform a variety of containers on a sunny roof or patio into a garden plot. (See the section on Gardening in Containers, later in this chapter.)

How Much Space and Time Do You Want to Devote?

You may have 1,000 square feet at your disposal, but that doesn't mean you should immediately plan to plant the entire area; that may be more of an investment in time than you are ready to make. There's no way around it—gardening does take time, if you want to do it well. There are ways to cut down on maintenance, but the truth of the matter is that every square foot of garden is going to require your attention at some point in the course of preparing the soil, planting seeds, mulching, watering, and so on throughout the season. If the time you can spend on a garden is limited, keep this in mind as you plan the dimensions. It's better to err on the small side the first year than to prepare a larger area only to watch it become overgrown and unkempt due to neglect as the season progresses. Even if time is no problem, if this is your first garden don't let your enthusiasm carry you into planning more than you can handle. After successfully managing a small garden for one season, you can add on as your gardening experience grows.

What Is the Purpose of Your Garden?

The garden size and amount of vegetables you plant will also depend on how you expect your garden to meet your family's food needs. A salad garden is a small patch, usually situated right outside the kitchen door, where the cook can step out and gather an assortment of fresh greens, radishes, scallions, baby carrots or beets, and a few tomatoes. A 3-by-3-foot patch, with closely spaced rows and a succession of plantings, can produce an adequate supply of salad fixings.

A soup or summer garden is meant to meet the family's fresh vegetable needs throughout the growing season, with no surplus intended for winter storage or processing. Staggered small plantings which mature in sequence over a period of time will provide just the right amount at a single harvest to be eaten fresh, without spoilage and waste.

A surplus garden will meet the family's needs during the growing season, plus produce enough vegetables for storage and processing to feed the family throughout the winter. Such a garden decreases your dependence on outside sources of food and gives you year-round control over how the food you will eat is grown and processed. Vegetables especially suited for storage such as onions, potatoes, pumpkins, winter radishes, winter squash, and late cabbages would be found in this garden. Also, when two plantings of crops like beets, carrots, peas and turnips are made, the later planting would be intended for storage and the earlier planting used fresh. To make processing easier, plantings should be made in large blocks so that a sizable quantity of each vegetable matures at one time.

What Are Your Family's Likes and Dislikes?

It is a waste of time, money, and garden space to plant a vegetable your family doesn't like, unless you plan on marketing it somehow. It's only common sense to concentrate your efforts on vegetables that will be used, and not to tie up garden space with crops that won't be eaten. If you're trying out a new vegetable, plant sparingly. If it's a success, you'll know to increase your planting next season; if it doesn't go over well, you haven't invested a large amount of productive space on a failure.

Deciding Which Varieties to Grow

Before you purchase seed, whether you do it by mail after leafing through a catalog from a seed company, or whether you buy it off the rack at the local hardware store, you should give careful thought to the vegetable varieties you will grow. Flipping through any seed catalog will reveal the range of varieties available. For instance, the catalog of one large, nationally known seed company lists 23 varieties of sweet corn, 21 varieties of cucumbers, and 34 varieties of tomatoes.

Don't be confused by this assortment; rather, take advantage of the opportunity this selection offers to choose those varieties which are best suited to your growing conditions and the way you intend to use the harvested crop. To help you with your selection, consider the following points.

Size and Growth Habit

The size of your plot has an effect on which vegetable varieties you can grow. A large garden can accommodate rambunctious, sprawling vine crops like pumpkins and squashes, while a smaller garden planted with the same vegetables would become a choked, snarled mess. However, successful attempts in breeding smaller, more compact bush forms of vine crops which bear standard or near-standard sized vegetables have made growing these plants in a small area more feasible than it used to be. Dwarf forms of nonvining crops, which are perfect for small gardens, are available, too. If you are working with a small garden area, pay attention to those varieties labeled "dwarf" and "compact" as you read catalog descriptions or seed packets.

Disease Resistance or Tolerance

Many varieties are being bred with resistance or tolerance to certain diseases, an important safeguard for the organic gardener. Each term, resistance and tolerance, implies a different response to disease. A disease will not attack a variety which has been specially bred to be resistant to that disease. On the other hand, a tolerant variety will be attacked by the disease, but is able to withstand the damage and continue to grow and bear. There are many resistant or tolerant varieties available now, and you should choose from among them the varieties that are best suited to your gardening area. To be sure which varieties are adapted to your growing conditions, contact the local extension agent (in the United States, listed in the phone book also under the titles County Agent, Agricultural Agent, or Farm Advisor; in Canada, listed in the phone book under "Provincial" government, Department of Agriculture).

Resistance or tolerance have been bred into varieties of the following vegetable crops against the corresponding diseases. (Information taken from Colorado State University Extension Service Bulletin No. 7.218, "Plant Pests in the Organic Garden," by Charles W. Basham.)

Bushy Space Savers: Traditionally space-grabbing crops like cucumbers and squash are no longer off-limits to small gardens, thanks to the advent of bush varieties. As demonstrated here by cucumber plants, the compact bush variety takes up much less space than the standard vining type. Even if you have a large garden with plenty of room, bush varieties are still a good alternative to vining types. The extra space formerly reserved for vine crops can be planted in another crop to further increase your garden's productivity.

Crop	Disease
Beans, lima	Downy mildew
Beans, snap	Mosaic
Cabbage	Yellows
Cucumbers	Anthracnose, downy mildew, mosaic, powdery mildew, scab
Onions	Pink rot
Peas	Wilt
Peppers	Tobacco mosaic
Spinach	Blight, downy mildew
Squash	Cucumber mosaic, squash mosaic
Tomatoes	Early blight, fusarium, gray leaf spot, leaf mold, verticillium

Time to Maturity

The time it takes to grow a seed or transplant to the point where the crop is ready for harvesting is a point to consider, especially if you are faced with a short growing season, or if you want to use techniques like succession planting and interplanting. Certain vegetables are quick to mature, and will be in and out of your garden in a relatively short period of time. (See the chart on Quick-Maturing Vegetables.) Of the vegetables which require a longer time to mature, there are often early-, mid-, or late-season varieties available. Based on the length of your particular growing season, you can choose among varieties with differing times to maturity to find the ones best suited to your garden.

Quick-Maturing Vegetables

Among the vegetables listed here, the longest wait you'll have from garden to table is 60 days, and the shortest a mere 20 days. The numbers in this chart indicate the average number of days to maturity from the time seeds are sown.

Beans, bush snap varieties: 50	Peas, early varieties: 55
Beets: 60	Radishes: 25
Garden cress: 20	Scallions (green or bunching onions): 40
Kale: 60	Spinach: 50
Kohlrabi: 60	Squash, summer: 48
Lettuce, leaf: 45	Swiss chard: 60
Mustard: 45	Turnips: 60
Okra: 55	Watercress: 50

Intended Use or Storage

The description of each vegetable variety in a seed catalog or on the seed packet often mentions whether that variety is recommended for canning or freezing, or whether it is best used fresh. Varieties specifically bred for canning or freezing (particularly in beans, cucumbers, squashes, and tomatoes) are not always as succulent, sweet, or tender for fresh consumption as other varieties. Instead, they have been developed for their firm textures and lasting flavors when preserved. The information on individual vegetables which appears in A Guide to Vegetables for the Home Garden often includes listings of noteworthy varieties, with comments on whether they can, freeze, or store well.

Vitamin Content

Selecting vegetable varieties with the highest nutritive value assures you that your family is harvesting the best possible health benefits from the garden. While all vegetables provide essential minerals and vitamins in varying amounts, the following vegetables can be dubbed the "Top Ten" since they provide substantial amounts of important nutrients like vitamins A and C, calcium, niacin (B_3), riboflavin (B_2), thiamine (B_1), iron, and potassium. Ranked in descending order (based on the combined amount of the above nutrients each vegetable contains) these nutritional powerhouses are broccoli, spinach, Brussels sprouts, lima beans, peas, asparagus, artichokes, cauliflower, sweet potatoes, and carrots. See the chart on The Best Vegetable Sources of Important Nutrients for a closer look at the nutritional character of these vegetables.

The Best Vegetable Sources of Important Nutrients

Vitamin A   Recommended adult daily minimum: 5,000 IU
    Carrots   11,000 IU/3½ oz.
    Sweet potatoes 8,800 IU/3½ oz.
    Spinach   8,100 IU/3½ oz.

Vitamin C   Recommended adult daily minimum: 60 mg.
    Broccoli   113 mg./3½ oz.
    Brussels sprouts 102 mg./3½ oz.
    Cauliflower 78 mg./3½ oz.

Calcium   Recommended adult daily minimum: 800 mg.
    Broccoli   103 mg./3½ oz.
    Spinach   93 mg./3½ oz.
    Lima beans 52 mg./3½ oz.

Niacin (B_3)   Recommended adult daily minimum: 13–18 mg.
    Peas 2.9 mg./3½ oz.
    Asparagus 1.5 mg./3½ oz.
    Lima beans 1.4 mg./3½ oz.

Riboflavin (B_2)   Recommended adult daily minimum: 1.2–1.6 mg.
    Broccoli 0.23 mg./3½ oz.
    Asparagus 0.20 mg./3½ oz.
    Spinach 0.20 mg./3½ oz.

Thiamine (B_1)   Recommended adult daily minimum: 1.0–1.4 mg.
    Peas 0.35 mg./3½ oz.
    Lima beans 0.24 mg./3½ oz.
    Asparagus 0.18 mg./3½ oz.

Iron   Recommended adult daily minimum: 10–18 mg.
    Spinach 3.1 mg./3½ oz.
    Lima beans 2.8 mg./3½ oz.
    Peas 1.9 mg./3½ oz.

Potassium No recommended adult minimum, but healthy adults need about 2,500 mg. daily
    Lima beans 650 mg./3½ oz.
    Spinach 470 mg./3½ oz.
    Artichokes 430 mg./3½ oz.

Other Considerations

There are several ways you can find out which vegetable varieties do well in your particular area. First, talk to neighboring gardeners. You may find veteran vegetable growers who have done variety tests in their gardens, or who save their own seeds from year to year. Often, these people are eager to offer advice and share both their findings and their plants or seeds with a novice or newcomer.

When you are purchasing seed, check whether the seed has been treated. Very often bean, corn, and pea seed is treated with fungicide, which is intended to keep the seed from rotting while germinating in cold soil in early spring. You can tell chemically treated seed by its appearance; it is usually brightly colored and coated with a chalky substance. Some seeds are treated with hot water to kill the organisms causing anthracnose, black leg, and black rot in a number of important vegetable crops. Hot water treatment is completely safe, and seeds treated this way can be used by organic gardeners. Seed catalogs will usually mention if the seed has been treated, and some seed companies offer untreated seed especially for organic gardeners. Untreated seed sown too early in the spring when the soil is cold will not germinate well. To ensure that a good percentage of the seed germinates, sow bean seed when the soil temperature reaches 65°F, corn seed when the soil temperature is over 60°F, and pea seed when the soil temperature ranges between 55° and 60°F.

To find out what's available in vegetable varieties, some seed searching is necessary, not to mention fun. The selection of seeds on display racks in hardware and grocery stores is not nearly as complete as the selection offered by a seed catalog. Most large seed companies advertise in national gardening magazines, newspapers, and journals, and will send their catalogs to you for free or for a

behind the scenes

All-America Selections and the Story of a Winner

In the case of vegetable breeding, it isn't necessarily true that there's nothing new under the sun. New, in the sense of improved, vegetable varieties for the home gardener are continually being introduced, and the research behind these varieties is spurred on to a large degree by the lure of winning a prestigious award given out by an all-volunteer organization known as All-America Selections.

All-America Selections (established in 1932) makes awards on a yearly basis for the new vegetable and flower varieties that it feels exhibit qualities that are superior to contemporary varieties. The awards are based on the votes of a council of professional judges, who have studied the new varieties at more than 50 trial sites scattered across the United States and Canada.

An average of six to ten awards are given out each year, in the form of bronze, silver, or gold medals. A gold medal is the highest possible accolade, designating a significantly superior variety, and is rarely awarded.

Seed entries pour in from around the world, representing years of breeding research done by seed companies, university breeders, government breeders and even individuals. Each new variety is entered with the name of a comparison variety against which its performance can be judged. The choice of a comparison variety is critical, since the merit of the new variety is based on how superior it is to the comparison. If no comparison were used, the only thing the trials would prove is that the new variety can indeed be grown. But when matched up and judged against the best-to-date variety of its type, the value of the new variety is readily apparent. The comparison variety suggested by each entrant is reviewed by a panel of experts from All-America Selections, and this panel either adopts it or proposes a better one.

In each of the trial grounds scattered throughout North America, the new varieties are planted side by side with their comparisons, then grown and observed under the same conditions. The criteria for judging include taste, texture, yield, disease resistance, fruit size, climatic adaptability, and novelty or uniqueness. The designated judge at each trial ground rates the new variety on a scale from 0 to 10, based on how the variety is perceived to benefit the home gardener. In order to win, a variety must receive points from

nominal charge. A number of interesting specialty seed companies also publish catalogs and newsletters, but you must do a bit more digging to find these.

Selecting the Site

No gardener, or at best only a select few, will be blessed with the ideal garden site—a loamy, fertile, well-drained plot of land which slopes gently toward the south, where it soaks up eight to ten hours of sunlight, and which is sheltered from the wind but not hemmed in by encroaching tree roots or buildings.

If your potential plot doesn't measure up to this fantasy site, don't abandon all hope. Rest assured that each gardener will be faced with a unique situation and will have to compensate for some flaws in his or her chosen garden site. By keeping in mind the following points you can select the best location within the context of your own geographical limitations.

at least three-quarters of the trial grounds. This rule ensures that the winning varieties are highly adaptable to different soil and climatic conditions.

A prime example of the excitement a new, award-winning variety can generate is the Sugar Snap Pea, the recipient of a Gold Medal in 1979. Dr. Calvin Lamborn, Research Director at Gallatin Valley Seed Company in Twin Falls, Idaho, is credited with making a vegetable breeding breakthrough in the creation of the pea. Dr. Lamborn in turn credits a co-worker, Dr. M. C. Parker, for laying the important groundwork for the research.

The breeding effort began as a curiosity and offshoot of his central work developing peas and beans suitable for commercial canning and freezing. His goal was to eliminate the distorted pod characteristic of standard edible-podded peas and to boost yields. To this end, he crossed a common shell pea mutant having thicker-fleshed pods than usual with a common edible-podded type, and spent the next ten years further developing the cross. What this breeding effort yielded was a new variety that blended plump, sweet peas with a crunchy, edible pod that actually tastes better as it reaches full maturity. This early-season vegetable makes a sweet, tender and juicy addition to bowls of salad greens, at a point in the garden season when there aren't a lot of other

salad fixings besides greens and radishes available. And to heighten their appeal, they're equally tasty eaten raw or lightly steamed. In short, the Sugar Snap Pea possesses many qualities that appeal to the home gardener.

Dr. Lamborn recognized this appeal, and entered his new pea in the All-America Selections. What happened next is history. The Sugar Snap Pea and Dr. Lamborn won worldwide acclaim, but this is one breeder who is not content to rest on his laurels. He is developing dwarf types of Sugar Snap Peas that will produce earlier and later than the original Sugar Snap, and he is also at work on a stringless variety. It's not too hard to visualize, in the not-too-distant future, another All-America Selection Gold Medal being awarded to an early, dwarf, stringless Sugar Snap Pea.

Throughout this book, the abbreviated letters AAS will be used to designate a variety which has won an All-America Selection award. When reading the variety charts in the chapters and those that accompany individual vegetables in the Vegetable Guide, the AAS is your cue that this designated variety was widely tested on a variety of soils, and under a variety of climatic conditions. Although the All-America Selection varieties are not perfectly adapted to all gardens, your chances of success are decidedly greater when you select an award-winning variety.

Location

Before digging up part of an established lawn or other grassy area for your garden, scout around first and use your eyes before you start using your shovel. It makes sense that the spot where the grass looks greenest and healthiest will be a good place for growing things—namely vegetables. Also, you will ultimately save time and energy if you site the garden in close proximity to the compost pile, toolshed, kitchen door, and water source.

If you're strapped for space and are considering using a strip of ground along the walls of your home, garage, or other building, be sure to allow a margin of 2 feet between vegetable plants and the wall. Any concrete, stucco, or plaster used in construction may have introduced a large amount of lime into the soil

tricks of the trade

Shady Gardening

The home gardener who is used to hearing about a minimum daily requirement of six hours of sunlight may have trouble believing that it is possible, and sometimes even preferable, to garden in the shade. But a partially shaded garden plot can indeed be advantageous, if the right crops are grown. Vegetables grown for their leaves and roots don't require as much direct sun to produce a crop as fruiting vegetables. In fact, leafy salad greens like lettuce and spinach, along with cabbage and celery, prefer to grow in partial shade and do poorly in constant sun.

Defining what exactly constitutes "partial shade" is a tricky exercise in semantics. At the deepest end of the shade spectrum is a garden that receives no direct sun, and very little, if any, reflected sunlight. A "deeply shaded" garden such as this is not a hospitable site for vegetables. Continuing along the spectrum, a "lightly shaded" garden is one that receives no direct sun, but is illuminated by reflected or indirect light for a good portion of the day. Leafy greens like lettuce and spinach can get by in this type of location, but most shade-tolerant vegetables need at least several hours of direct sun daily. This leads us to the definition of a "partially shaded" garden. This is one which receives at least two hours of sun daily, and is in shade or indirect light for the balance of the daylight hours.

Where there is no naturally occurring shade and you wish to grow shade-loving leafy greens, celery, and cabbage during the hot stretch of midsummer, you must take measures to provide the partial shade. To keep these crops from wilting or bolting, prop shingles, boards, house screens, or lengths of snow fence alongside the crop to cast a shadow over the plants. To cover an entire raised bed, construct a lath frame, and support it on rocks or cement blocks. An inexpensive alternative is to suspend a piece of cheesecloth over the plants in the bed, held in place by stakes set along the bed perimeter. When the sun is particularly scorching and the temperatures soar, sprinkle a little water on the cheesecloth to help keep the plants cool.

Don't keep these shading devices up all day—even the shade lovers need some sun to keep them growing. The best practice is to keep them up for several hours during the hottest, brightest portion of the day.

which could be detrimental to your plants. Your best insurance is to leave the 2-foot margin and to replace the top 3 to 4 feet of the bed with fresh soil.

Light

In order for most vegetables to grow properly, the garden should receive at least six hours of direct sun daily (eight to ten hours are ideal).

It's helpful to remember as you are deciding where individual vegetables will be planted that the southern and western sides of the garden will receive the most light and heat. Vegetables that will benefit from the extra sun, such as beans and tomatoes, should be planted there, while the crops preferring coolness and shade, like lettuce, should be grown on the northern and eastern sides.

There are advantages to gardening in the shade. Leafy greens grown in partial shade will be extra succulent, and free from the bitterness that can mar their flavor when the temperatures climb too high. A partially shaded garden also provides a longer growing period for cool-season crops, since they can continue to produce right on through the summer in their "cool" haven (cool in relation to the areas receiving direct sun for most of the day). This prolonged productivity is especially noticeable in the cut-and-come-again crops like broccoli, cabbage, endive, kale, leaf lettuce, mustard, and spinach. There are other bonuses, too—like fewer weeds to contend with, longer intervals between watering, and less sweat to wipe from your brow as you work among the plants.

The disadvantages have to do with scaling down your expectation of size and tempering a certain amount of impatience. Vegetables (excepting shade-loving salad greens) grown in partial shade won't reach full size, as compared to those grown in higher light intensities. They will also mature more slowly—which means you'll have to wait a little longer for your crops to reach harvestable size. But this factor can be offset by starting the plants indoors, or by sowing them as early as possible outdoors, before leaves on the trees have developed fully and block the sun. You'll also want to allow a little extra room when spacing plants in a shady garden. Plants tend to sprawl and compete for the available sun, and can impede each other's growth if set too close together.

Don't let a lack of direct sun put a damper on your gardening enthusiasm. Take that partially shaded spot of land and use it to your advantage by planting any of the following vegetables:

Beets	Hamburg parsley	Onions, bunching
Broccoli	Herbs–angelica, chervil, chives, mint, parsley	Peas
Cabbage		Sorrel
Carrots	Kale	Spinach
Chinese cabbage	Lettuce, leaf	Swiss chard
Endive and Escarole	Mustard	Turnips
Garden cress	New Zealand spinach	Watercress

If you are stuck with a spot that is shaded by buildings, trees, shrubbery or any other tall objects, you'll have to adapt to the situation by concentrating on shade-tolerant vegetables in your garden. You may not be able to grow the sun worshippers like corn, squashes, or tomatoes, but you'll make up for their absence by most likely harvesting a bumper crop of crisp and succulent salad greens. (See the box on Shady Gardening.)

Slope

A garden located on a piece of land that gently slopes to the south or southwest will receive more direct sun than a nonsloping plot. The benefit of this arrangement is apparent in the spring when the soil warms up more quickly and in the fall when it stays warmer slightly longer. A slight slope where the air circulates freely will reduce the chances of frost damage in early spring and late fall. Cold air is heavy air, and will move down to the lowest area and settle. A garden located on a slope and not at the bottom of a hill will not be caught in a pocket of cold air and can thus escape the ravages of late spring and early fall frosts. Another plus is that the soil on a slope drains well.

While a little slope with the right exposure is beneficial, too much of a slope (when your land drops more than 1 foot in 50 feet) can pose problems. If you have no choice but to contend with a hilly area, terraces and contour rows which run across the slope can help you catch rainfall and prevent erosion from stealing away your valuable garden soil. (See the box, Create a Garden with Terraces.)

Drainage

The drainage of your prospective garden site is another important aspect to consider. Poorly draining soil will hamper the plants' growth and cause them to yellow, since the water which collects interferes with the necessary interaction of air with plant roots and soil microorganisms. Steer clear of low areas where water can collect, or areas which receive the runoff from adjacent pieces of property. If you have no alternative but to plant in a low-lying area, try using raised beds. A slight drainage problem can be alleviated by increasing the amount of organic matter in the soil. But if you have a serious drainage problem caused by a hardened, compacted layer beneath the soil, a more involved system involving drainage tiles and gravel may be necessary. Your local extension service is the best source of information on how to improve drainage in your garden. The cooperative extension service of Rutgers University in New Brunswick, New Jersey, puts out a very helpful pamphlet, "Soil Drainage Affects—You, Your Home, and Your Plants," which you may wish to consult. (See the Bibliography.)

Trees or Shrubs Adjacent to the Garden

Trees are a particular nemesis of vegetable plants. The outstretched leafy branches that provide a shady haven for sweaty gardeners, also, unfortunately, block out the sun needed for vegetable growth. In addition, trees cause underground interference with their roots, which take nutrients and water from the soil in their drip-line, a circular area extending out from the trunk as far as the branches reach. If you do plant your garden near a tree, you may find that the crops grow splendidly for about the first two months and then suddenly seem to lose their vigor. That's because the tree roots are taking up a major share of the water and nutrients, robbing the vegetables of their share. You must compensate for this by giving extra doses of food and water.

It's a good idea to give black walnut trees a wide berth, since their roots secrete a substance known as juglone which is harmful to certain vegetables, especially tomatoes. If space allows, provide a margin of 80 feet between the garden and any black walnut trees. If that's not possible, at least plant your vegetables outside the drip-line.

Wind Exposure

If your region is often buffeted by winds, they may knock your plants over, uproot them, and otherwise retard their growth. Constant winds also have a drying effect on soil, robbing it of moisture. An effective means of prevention is a windbreak located on the windward side of the garden. Windbreaks can be fences, hedges, trees, or even a sheet of light-admitting fiberglass. Trees and hedges planted as a windbreak should of course be located far enough away so they don't interfere with vegetable growth.

Making a Working Diagram of the Garden

In order to set the garden plan on paper, you must first pull together some basic information. Once you've pinpointed where the best location for your garden is, you will have an idea of what its largest dimensions can be, as dictated by the space available. Your answer to the question of how much time you can devote should be factored in with the kinds of vegetables you have decided to plant. Add to this an approximate idea of the amount of each vegetable you want to harvest to meet your needs, and you arrive at the final garden size. (See the chart on How Much of Each Vegetable to Plant for help with your planning.)

Once you've assembled all this information, you are ready to draw up a scale model of your garden. Measure off the dimensions of your garden using a scale of ½ inch per foot or the premarked grid on graph paper (having each square correspond to a round number of feet or inches of garden space makes the planning easier). Within the perimeter you can now plan where each crop will be grown (see the section on Planning the Layout, which follows, for a more detailed discussion). Based on the growing system you will use (conventional rows, raised beds, wide-row plantings), note the spacing requirements for each vegetable. These may be found in the individual vegetable entries in the Vegetable Guide or on seed packets. Mark off the spaces to be occupied by each crop, and jot down the date each is to be planted. It is also helpful to include any succession crops in parentheses along with their projected planting dates.

make your own

Create a Garden with Terraces

For centuries farmers and gardeners in Asia have terraced their hillsides so that land that is less than ideal for cultivation is not wasted. Maybe your yard has some sloping ground that you can make into tiers of productivity with a little work and some imagination. Instead of struggling with your lawn mower to keep a hilly section of your yard neat and trim, why not cooperate with Mother Nature? A properly terraced slope is easy to tend and attractive to look at. In addition to being a productive growing space, terraces help to reduce soil erosion.

Terraces are essentially little walls that form steps up a hillside. The differences in height between terraces can be several feet or just a few inches. The width of each terrace can vary, too. There are several ways you can go about terracing your land, depending on the amount of time, money, and materials you want to invest.

Retaining walls of bricks, stones, or cement blocks, built using standard masonry techniques, often serve as the foundations for terraces. A small amount of earth can exert a terrific amount of pressure, but a properly built retaining wall can keep this pressure in check. These walls should be thicker at the base than at the top for greater strength and support. If you're planning a masonry wall, make sure a concrete footing is poured below the frost line so the wall is unaffected by frost heaving. To avoid the buildup of water pressure, provide small holes at the bottom of the retaining wall to allow water to drain out. You should arrange the stones in a dry stone wall so that they slant downward into the hillside. This keeps the soil from eroding out from between them during heavy rains.

Building a masonry wall is a labor-intensive construction project that many people will be inclined to pass up. There can even be red tape involved because some municipalities require building permits for this kind of construction. An easier way to build terraces is to use recycled railroad ties. Usually, railroad ties come in 8-foot or 14-foot lengths, but you can occasionally find them in shorter pieces. You'll need lots of muscle and a couple of friends to help heave them around because the larger ones can weigh up to 250 pounds, while the smaller ones weigh between 100 and 200 pounds. Be sure to find out what the ties have been treated with. Older ties treated with creosote should be safe to use, but newer ties treated with creosote will be toxic to plants.

To make a terrace of railroad ties, first determine how many terraces you want. For ex-

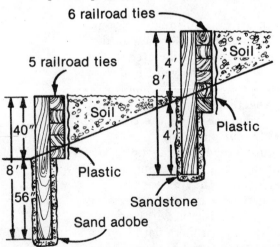

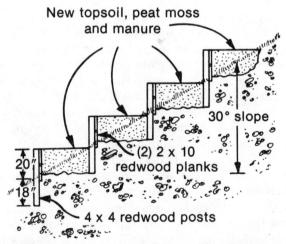

Terracing Options: All three of these terrace gardens are effective ways to tame a hillside and turn it into a productive growing space. The two-level terrace, far left, is made from recycled railroad ties. Ties anchored vertically into the ground act as supports for the hrizonal stacks of ties set on the uphill side. The center terrace shows four levels created by vertical posts and horizontal planks. Plants get off to a good start when you provide them with

ample, if you want two terraces and you have 8-foot ties, make two rows of vertical ties to function as the support for the terraces. Dig holes at just less than 8-foot intervals, sink the ties 4 feet deep into these holes and pour concrete around their bases to anchor them firmly. The number of ties you place on the uphill side of the support ties will determine the height of the terrace. Unlike a masonry wall, a wall of railroad ties will allow soil and water to seep through the spaces between ties. To prevent this, line the inside of the wall with heavy plastic, or stuff plastic into these spaces. Some gardeners grow plants between the ties to help to control erosion.

If you can't find railroad ties, you can build a similar terrace with 4 × 4 posts and 2 × 10 planks. Preserve and waterproof the posts and planks with a nontoxic substance such as copper napthenate. Sink the posts vertically at least 18 inches into the ground at intervals along each terrace to form the support structure. Pour concrete around them, and then place 2 × 10s on the uphill side of the posts to form the terrace.

In 1976, Ray Wolf, an avid do-it-yourselfer and executive editor of the Plans Department of Rodale Books, built two terraces in his backyard using railroad ties. He reports that they are still holding up well several years later. He did not use vertical posts because his grade was not severe, and the terraced area was small—just 16 feet long and 5 feet wide. Besides, he feels that putting in posts is a lot of hard work that most people can't or won't do. "Anyone who has played with Lincoln Logs as a child can build terraces like mine," he says. He leveled each area to be terraced and built the support structure of railroad ties into the hillside. The ties overlap from one terrace to the other to make a strong support, and the entire structure is held together with concrete reinforcing rods.

Ray admits that there was a lot of work involved in building his terraces. After he assembled the structure, he drilled the holes for the rods layer by layer. As each layer was drilled, he removed it and drilled the next. He then restacked the structure as he had previously assembled it and inserted the rods. He cautions others building a similar terrace to mark each piece so that it is reassembled correctly.

Ray's terrace served him well, but he does admit to the disadvantages of using railroad ties. They are expensive and bulky, and they take up a lot of growing space. He is now further refining his terrace design by using 16-foot-long 2 × 6s to build terraces in the backyard of his new home.

No matter which terrace design you decide to use, build the lowest terrace first and work your way up the hill. It's easier to loosen soil and move it downhill than to carry it uphill. More likely than not, you'll have to get additional soil to fill in the terraces. Most gardeners use a mixture of soil, compost, and manure. Slope the soil in each terrace upward toward the front wall to prevent water from running off, and allow the soil to settle for a few weeks before planting. Many gardeners make walkways of grass or planks in their terraces to make tending their tiers of plenty easier. Terraces are convenient gardening areas, and they will last for years if you build them carefully.

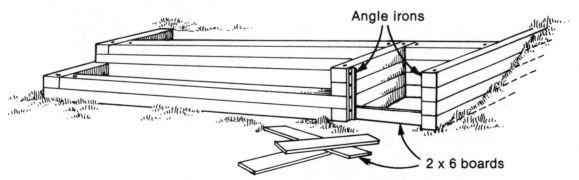

a rich growing mix made of equal parts fresh topsoil, peat moss, and well-rotted manure. The terrace on the right is a good option for gardeners with only a gentle slope to contend with. In this design, overlapping railroad ties and concrete reinforcing rods take the place of vertical posts in supporting the structure.

How Much of Each Vegetable to Plant?

When your garden is still in the planning stages, you may be unsure of how much of each type of vegetable to plant to keep your family supplied throughout the growing season. If you're a long-time gardener and have kept track of your plantings, you probably know from trial and error how many feet of beets you should plant for your family of five. But what if you're planning your first garden, or planting some new vegetables in your plot? How can you keep from overplanting and underplanting? One way to gauge the amount is to take the planting-per-person amount (given below) and multiply it by the number of people in your family. This will give you an estimate of how many plants will meet your family's needs. Then, depending on which growing system you use (conventional rows, raised beds, or wide rows) you can figure out the appropriate space needed to accommodate that number of plants and proceed with your planning. Of course, the amount to plant per person can at best be a rough guideline, so you should make allowances for your family's likes and dislikes and plant more or less accordingly. Also, if you plan to store or process your harvest, you should double the amount planted per person.

Vegetable	Amount to plant per person	Vegetable	Amount to plant per person
Artichoke, globe	2–4 plants	Kale	7 plants
Artichoke, Jerusalem	3–5 plants	Kohlrabi	8 plants
Asparagus	10 crowns	Lettuce, head	7 plants
Beans, lima bush	30 plants	Lettuce, leaf	15–20 plants
Beans, lima pole	6 plants	Malabar spinach	4–6 plants
Beans, snap bush	10–15 plants	Mustard	7 plants
Beans, snap pole	3–5 hills or 10 plants	New Zealand spinach	4–6 plants
Beets	10–15 plants	Onion plants	37 plants
Broccoli	3–6 plants	Parsnips	25 plants
Brussels sprouts	5 plants	Peanuts	16 plants
Cabbage, early	4–5 plants	Peas	37 plants
Cabbage, late	10–12 plants	Peppers	2–3 plants
Carrots	30 plants	Potatoes, early	4–6 plants
Cauliflower	4–6 plants	Potatoes, late	10–15 plants
Celeriac	12 plants	Pumpkins	3 hills or 6 plants
Celery	9 plants	Radishes	30 plants
Celtuce	6–9 plants	Rhubarb	2–3 roots
Chinese cabbages	3–6 plants	Rutabaga	10–13 plants
Collards	3–6 plants	Salsify	30 plants
Corn	30–40 stalks	Soybeans	37 plants
Cowpeas	37 plants	Spinach	25 plants
Cucumbers	2–3 hills or 6–9 plants	Squash, summer	2–3 hills or 4–6 plants
Eggplant	2–3 plants	Squash, winter	2–3 hills or 4–6 plants
Endive and Escarole	3–4 plants	Sweet potatoes	10–18 plants
Florence fennel	10 plants	Swiss chard	3–5 plants
Garlic	5–9 plants	Tomatoes	3–5 plants
Horseradish	3–5 plants	Turnips	30 plants

This garden diagram serves many purposes. By seeing how many plants of each vegetable you have allotted space for, you know how much seed to purchase. When you take it along to your garden site, you have a handy planting guide, showing when and where each crop will go into the garden, and it acts as your seasonal reminder for succession plantings. This diagram will also be a point of reference for future planning. If the 50 feet of carrots you planted this year just weren't enough, next season you'll know by refreshing your memory with the diagram that you need to plant more than 50 feet. And keeping a permanent record of which vegetables grew where will help you plan crop rotations.

Planning the Layout

As you're working on your garden diagram, there are certain points you should consider when deciding where to plant each vegetable. No matter which growing system you use, be it conventional rows, raised beds, or wide rows, the following items deserve special attention in the layout.

Growth Habit

Take note of the growing characteristics of the vegetables to be planted. Vine crops such as cucumbers and squashes that ramble over a wide area should occupy spots along the border, so they have room to roam outside the garden.

Tall-growing crops like corn, or those that are trellised and staked, such as pole beans and tomatoes, should be planted along the northern side of the garden so that as the sun passes overhead they will not shade any adjacent low-growing crops which need full sun.

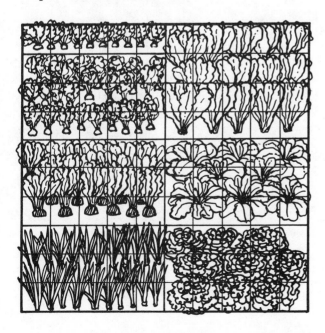

Salad Garden: A 5-by-5-foot plot can provide an abundance of salad fixings to please any palate. This garden is divided into seven sections, each with a different salad crop. In the top right is a planting of Swiss chard which will last all season. The center and lower right hold cool-season crops of spinach and various leaf lettuces. These will be replaced by staked tomatoes when the weather warms up. From top to bottom on the left are radishes, baby carrots, baby beets, and scallions.

Orienting Garden Rows and Beds

You may find conflicting advice on which way garden rows should run. Some sources advocate running rows north to south, while others advocate east-west rows. The fact is that there is no definitive answer. The way you run the rows depends on the lay of the land and how much sun your particular crops need. If your garden plot slopes, plan your rows so that they will run across the slope to

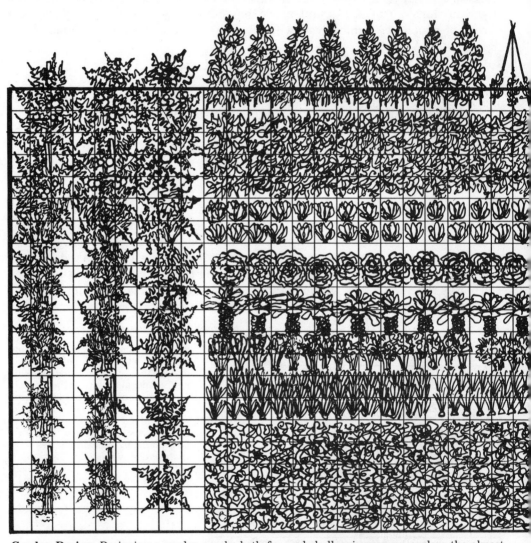

Garden Design: Designing a garden can be both fun and challenging as you explore the almost unlimited possibilities for laying out your vegetable crops. This particular 20-by-50-foot garden employs the conventional row system. Each square foot (represented by one square) is used to its fullest potential to yield bountiful harvests of vegetables for fresh use, as well as a surplus for winter storage. The secret of high yields is to never let any garden space lie idle. For example, in this garden succession crops of lettuce will follow cauliflower, carrots will follow spinach, and pepper transplants will be set in the space vacated by an early harvest of beets. Plantings of early-, mid-, and late-season

thwart any erosion problems. If your land is flat and you are growing mainly tall to medium height, sun-loving vegetables, run the rows east to west to maximize the sun's benefits. A north-south orientation works for shade-loving crops when they are grown adjacent to a row of tall plants, which will throw their shadows on their lower neighbors as the sun passes overhead.

Unless your ground slopes, the all-purpose orientation for your beds is east to west. Of course, if your land slopes, you'll want to run them across the slope.

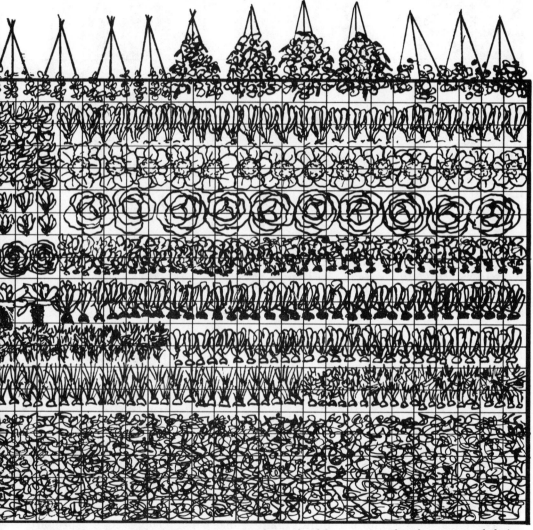

varieties of potatoes and tomatoes ensure a steady supply of these crops, rather than an overwhelming glut of produce. Staggered plantings of pole beans and cucumbers also help disperse the harvest over a period of time. These crops are trellised along the edge of the plot where they will not shade any sun-loving crops. Along the lower edge of the garden, a strip of ground is occupied by a green manure crop. When these soil-building plants are tilled under, they will help increase the fertility and tilth of that portion of the garden. With careful planning, you can grow and till under a green manure crop and still have time to raise summer crops like squash and pumpkins.

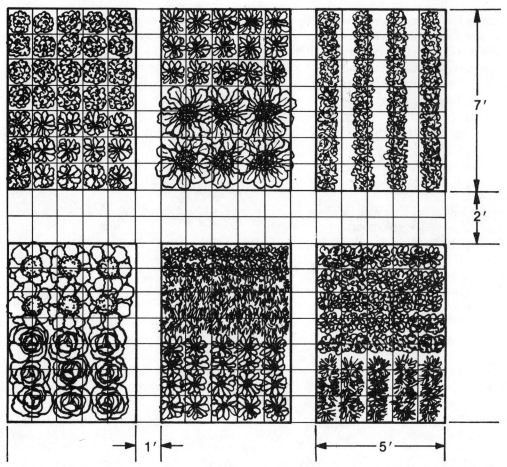

Raised Beds: This intensive gardening technique is a neat and orderly way to organize your garden. It's especially helpful when you group crops with similar growing needs together to streamline their care. Seasonal rotations are easy to keep track of, too, when you can simply alternate which crops grow in each bed.

Season Length

Grouping plants according to their season length can be a big help when the time comes to make succession plantings. When crops that mature early are grown together in a group, harvesting opens up a block of space ready to accommodate the next crop. Grouping long-season crops together means that they will be out of the way as you harvest the early maturers and are busy replanting.

Setting aside a bed for perennials makes sense when it comes time to prepare the soil each season for annual vegetables. By concentrating the perennials in one area, you won't have to worry about dislodging them as you proceed with your plowing or spading of the garden. Biennial crops, which take two seasons to complete their growth cycle, usually warrant no special consideration, since most are simply raised and harvested in a single season, before they reach maturity. However, some gardeners wish to leave beets, cabbage, carrots, or onions in the ground for two seasons so that flowering occurs and seeds can be gathered. When seed-saving is planned, you should group these vegetables in an area of the garden where they will be undisturbed.

Gardening System

The nature of your layout will depend on whether you are using conventional rows, raised beds, or wide rows. A further discussion of all of these growing systems appears in chapter 3. If you're using conventional rows (where seeds or transplants are set in a single row, with specific spacing between plants in the row and between the rows themselves), consider whether you will be cultivating by hand or by machine. If you use machinery like a rotary tiller, you will need to allow extra space between rows and a space for turning at the row ends. When it comes to spacing your vegetables, refer to the distance requirements listed on seed packets or given under individual vegetables in the Vegetable Guide, and plan accordingly, row by row. You'll find the spacing described in terms of "inches between plants within the row" and "distance between rows," which makes planning the layout of a garden of this type relatively straightforward.

Whether you're planning to plant your garden in wide rows (a band of closely spaced plants, about 18 inches wide, as opposed to a conventional narrow row) or raised beds (specially prepared growing areas in which plants are spaced closely together without conventional row spacings between them), remember to leave sufficient pathways so you have easy access to the planting areas. A path 1 foot or wider between beds is adequate, and it's a good idea to allow for a wider path down the center of the garden to allow room for maneuvering wheelbarrows and setting down large tools. There are various spacing patterns you can use when planting wide rows and raised beds, and these are examined in more detail in chapter 3, in the section on Seed-Planting Techniques.

Plant Rotation

The time when you're planning the layout is also the time to concern yourself with plant rotations. This is an important part of responsible garden management, for at the same time rotation is helping to replenish the soil nutrients used by the growing vegetables, it is also helping to control soilborne diseases and insect pests. Alternating the types of vegetables you plant in the same spot in your garden from one year to the next requires a system, but once you understand the basic principle of plant rotation, it is a simple thing to incorporate into your garden planning. And no garden is too small for you to practice rotation—in fact, small gardens demand it. Because of the concentration of plants within a small area, allowing the same vegetable to occupy the same spot season after season puts an undue strain on the already limited soil resources.

Crops vary as to the type and amount of nutrients they draw from the soil. By growing the same vegetable in the same spot, year after year, you risk depleting the soil of those particular nutrients which the plant uses. Rotating

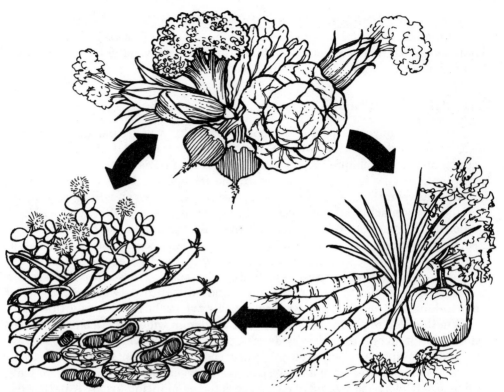

Crop Rotations: Plants, like people, have different appetites. Some like to consume more than others, and some are even kind enough to replace almost everything they remove from the soil. To keep nutrient levels balanced within your garden, try not to grow the same vegetables (or those with similar appetites) in the same spot year after year. A good rotation cycle to use is to follow heavy feeders (top) by light feeders (lower right) by soil builders (lower left); or, follow heavy feeders by soil builders by light feeders. The only limitation is that heavy feeders should not follow light feeders.

vegetables with differing nutrient needs equalizes the drain on the soil's available nutrients. Vegetables can be divided into three groups based on what they give back and take from the soil: heavy feeders, light feeders, and soil builders. The rotations you should use involve following heavy feeders by light feeders by soil builders; or following heavy feeders by soil builders by light feeders. You should never follow light feeders by heavy feeders without some form of soil replenishment. Use the chart on Vegetables with Similar Nutrient Needs to help you plan your rotations.

Rotations also keep a check on soilborne diseases and insects. A vegetable can be host plant to a certain soilborne disease which will continue unabated if the host is continuously grown in the same spot. However, when you remove the host plant and set an unrelated or nonsusceptible plant in its place, you have taken an effective step toward controlling the disease (especially if three or four years pass before the host plant is planted again). Some fungi, bacteria, and viruses which can be countered by plant rotation include: bean blight, black rot, cabbage black leg, clubroot, cucumber anthracnose, fusarium wilts, and scab.

Vegetables with Similar Nutrient Needs

Heavy Feeders		Light Feeders	Soil Builders
Asparagus	Kohlrabi	Carrots	Alfalfa
Beets	Lettuce	Garlic	Beans, broad
Broccoli	Okra	Leeks	Beans, lima
Brussels sprouts	Parsley	Mustard	Beans, snap
Cabbages	Pumpkins	Onions	Clover
Cauliflower	Radishes	Parsnips	Peanuts
Celery	Rhubarb	Peppers	Peas
Collards	Spinach	Potatoes	Soybeans
Corn	Squash, summer	Rutabaga	
Cucumbers	Squash, winter	Shallots	
Eggplant	Tomatoes	Sweet potatoes	
Endive and Escarole		Swiss chard	
Kale		Turnips	

In addition to countering diseases, rotation may also reduce your pest problems. Each type of insect tends to feed on a very narrow range of plants. So, for instance, one type of insect will zero in on your broccoli, feast away throughout the season, lay its eggs, and die. If you plant broccoli in the same spot the following season, when the eggs hatch, the succeeding insect generation will find a ready-made food supply and you'll have to fight the bugs for your broccoli. But the simple act of alternating what you grow from season to season in the same spot of ground can help reduce your pest problems. When you alternate crops, keep in mind that insects and diseases tend to attack plants in the same family. Since broccoli belongs to the mustard family, don't plant another family member like cabbage or kale in its place. Instead, choose an unrelated alternate, such as the broad bean from the pea family, or eggplant from the nightshade family. To check which vegetables are related, refer to the listings in the Vegetable Guide.

There are several ways you can accommodate rotation in your garden plan. First of all, dividing your garden into sections will help you get a rotation system going. A garden sectioned into beds allows you to work with already clearly defined units of soil, among which you can move the appropriate crop groupings. If you're working with rows, it may help to divide your entire plot into thirds; in the rows of the first third you will plant the heavy feeders, in the second the light feeders, and in the final third the soil-building crops.

The entire plant rotation cycle takes place over three years. However, if you are practicing succession cropping, you are in a sense rotating plants within the same season. You can guard against soil depletion during these seasonal rotations as well, by alternating root crops (such as beets, carrots, and parsnips) with leafy foliage crops (such as lettuce, spinach, and Swiss chard), or by alternating fruiting crops (eggplants, peppers, squashes, tomatoes) with leafy crops. You can also alternate shallow- and deep-rooted crops to vary the soil levels from which the nutrients are drawn. If a problem develops with soilborne diseases, you can help control them during succession planting by not following a host plant with a plant that is also susceptible to the disease.

Tips for Small Gardens

When your gardening expectations exceed the available space, you must try in every possible way to get maximum use out of a minimum of space. Judge every vegetable you plant according to its space/yield ratio, opting for those which produce a high yield in proportion to the space they occupy. The vegetables you want for maximum production are those which keep producing over a period of time so you get a high yield from only a few plants (peppers and tomatoes), and those which yield up a bumper crop from a small space (beets, bush squashes, radishes). You'll also reap a mighty harvest from a minuscule space by planting "cut-and-come-again" crops, such as cabbage or lettuce. See the accompanying charts on Space/Yield Ratio, Cut-and-Come-Again Crops, and Space-Saving Vegetable Varieties for more examples.

Whatever you may be lacking in horizontal gardening area you may be able to gain in vertical space. Gardens don't always have to stretch out toward the horizon—they can reach for the sky as well. By erecting a fence or trellis that measures 5 feet tall and 30 feet long, you've gained 150 feet of gardening space. Within the plot itself, you can save space by training vine crops to grow upward instead of sprawling along the ground—making room for more vegetables. Cu-

Space/Yield Ratio

These vegetables produce the most in the least amount of space.

Beans (bush and pole)	Mustard	Summer squash (bush varieties)
Beets	Onions	Tomatoes
Carrots	Peppers	Turnips
Lettuce	Radishes	

Cut-and-Come-Again Crops

More than one harvest is possible if you cut the outer leaves of certain leafy green plants before they fully mature, when they are about 3 to 4 inches long. You can safely pick down to about the six centermost leaves. Take care not to harm the growing point of the plant so that leaf production can continue. With cabbage and broccoli, cutting the main head will stimulate a second crop of sprouts.

Broccoli	Escarole	New Zealand spinach
Cabbage (early varieties)	Kale	Swiss chard
Chinese mustard cabbage	Lettuce, leaf	
Endive	Mustard	

Space-Saving Vegetable Varieties

Variety Name	Sources
Beans, Bush Shell	
French Dwarf Horticultural	Widely available
Taylor's Dwarf Horticultural	Gurney Seed and Nursery Co.
	Stokes Seeds, Inc.
Beans, Bush Snap and Lima	
Any bush variety is suitable.	
Beets	
Little Ball	W. Atlee Burpee Co.
Little Mini Ball	Stokes Seeds, Inc.
Cabbage	
Baby Head	Stokes Seeds, Inc.
Cabbage Darkri	Geo. W. Park Seed Co., Inc.
Morden Dwarf	Farmer Seed and Nursery
Carrots	
Little Finger	W. Atlee Burpee Co.
Ox-Heart	Widely available
Short N Sweet	W. Atlee Burpee Co.
Cauliflower	
Garant	Thompson and Morgan, Inc.
Predominant	Thompson and Morgan, Inc.
Corn	
In general, early varieties are smaller than main crop varieties and can be more closely spaced.	Farmer Seed and Nursery
Faribou Golden Midget	
Golden Midget	Widely available
Golden Miniature	Stokes Seeds, Inc.
Mini Max Hybrid	Gurney Seed and Nursery Co.
Cucumbers	
Bush varieties take up only ⅓ the space of regular vining types and still produce a heavy crop.	
Bush Champion	W. Atlee Burpee Co.
Cucumber Bush Whopper	Geo. W. Park Seed Co., Inc.
	L. L. Olds Seed Co.
Patio Pik	Widely available
Pot Luck	Widely available
Spacemaster	Widely available
Eggplant	
Black Beauty	Widely available
Morden Midget	Geo. W. Park Seed Co., Inc.
Slim Jim	Geo. W. Park Seed Co., Inc.

(continued)

Space-Saving Vegetable Varieties—*continued*

Variety Name	Sources
Lettuce	
Any variety is suitable as a space saver. These midget varieties are noteworthy because each head yields a single serving, and they grow very well in container gardens.	
Midget Lettuce	Earl May Seed and Nursery Co.
	Gurney Seed and Nursery Co.
Tom Thumb	Widely available
Peas, Edible-Podded	
Dwarf Gray Sugar	Widely available
Little Sweetie	Stokes Seeds, Inc.
Snowbird	W. Atlee Burpee Co.
Peppers, Hot	
Red Chili	Widely available
Small Red Cherry	Widely available
Peppers, Sweet	
Calwonder	DiGiorgi Co., Inc.
	Joseph Harris, Co., Inc.
Pepper Pot	Geo. W. Park Seed Co., Inc.
Vinedale	Stokes Seeds, Inc.
Pumpkins	
Cinderella	Widely available
Funny Face	Widely available
Jackpot	Joseph Harris Co., Inc.
Spirit	Widely available
Squash, Summer	
Early Golden Summer Crookneck	Widely available
Early White Bush (also called White Patty Pan)	Widely available
Gold Rush	Gurney Seed and Nursery Co.
Squash Creamy	Geo. W. Park Seed Co., Inc.
Squash, Winter	
Burpee's Butter Boy	W. Atlee Burpee Co.
Burpee's Butterbush	W. Atlee Burpee Co.
Bush Table Queen	W. Atlee Burpee Co.
	DiGiorgi Co., Inc.
Early Butternut Hybrid	Gurney Seed and Nursery Co.
Emerald	Joseph Harris Co., Inc.
Gold Nugget	Widely available
Table Ace	Joseph Harris Co., Inc.
	Gurney Seed and Nursery Co.
Table King (also called Bush Acorn)	Widely available

Variety Name	Sources
Sweet Potatoes	
Bush Porto Rico	Geo. W. Park Seed Co., Inc.
	W. Atlee Burpee Co.
Tomatoes	
Patio Hybrid	Widely available
Pixie	W. Atlee Burpee Co.
Presto	Joseph Harris Co., Inc.
Small Fry Hybrid	Widely available
Tiny Tim	Widely available
Tomato Goldie	Geo. W. Park Seed Co., Inc.

cumbers, pole beans, Malabar spinach, melons, peas, vining varieties of summer and winter squash, and tomatoes can all be trained to grow vertically. (See the box, Supporting Your Vegetables in Style, in chapter 4 for some helpful tips on building fences, trellises, and other supports.)

Raised beds, in conjunction with intensive gardening techniques, can turn even the smallest garden into a gardener's delight with their outpouring of vegetables. The rich, prepared soil serves as a fertile base for the closely spaced plants. (For more information on preparing and planting raised beds, see the sections on Shaping Your Garden: Rows and Raised Beds in chapter 2, and Seed-Planting Techniques in chapter 3.)

Other intensive gardening techniques can help you make the most efficient use of your space. The use of wide rows (also called band plantings) is one method that can increase the yield of a small garden while at the same time cutting down on chores like weeding and mulching. Production from these bands, as in raised beds, is four times the yield taken from the same area planted in conventional rows. (This technique is discussed further in chapter 3, in the section on Seed-Planting Techniques.)

Interplanting or intercropping is an intensive technique by which you can fit more plants into the garden at the same time and increase the yield per square foot. The basic idea is to match up two compatible plants to grow on the same space. These pairings include fast- and slow-growing vegetables, small plants nestled under taller ones, and shade lovers growing in the shadow of taller sun seekers.

Succession planting is another intensive technique that can net you a continuous supply of vegetables by making sure that your garden is working nonstop, without any nonproductive gaps in the season. This involves planting the same vegetable at two- to three-week intervals to stagger the harvest, or planting early-, mid-, and late-season varieties of the same vegetable at the same time, or replacing a crop with another as soon as it is harvested. (Both interplanting

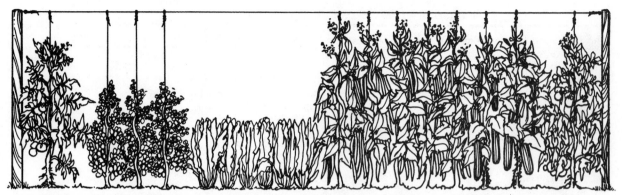

Growing Up with a Vertical Garden: Many overlooked pieces of land can be used to produce fresh vegetables by going up, not out, with a vertical garden. The garden shown here is supported by two 6-foot poles set 20 feet apart, giving the equivalent of about 180 square feet of growing area. Two support wires run horizontally from post to post, and a series of vertical strings are suspended from the top wire to the bottom wire. From left to right, this garden holds a tomato plant, three Malabar spinach plants, five Swiss chard plants, five scarlet runner beans, two oriental cucumbers, and another tomato. The garden's capacity goes beyond even the plants pictured here. Early in the season, lettuce and radishes can be grown in the spots earmarked for the tomatoes and cucumbers, and likewise, Sugar Snap peas can precede the Swiss chard.

and succession planting are discussed in detail in chapter 3 in the section on Techniques for Highest Continual Yield.)

A cold frame or hotbed is a good investment to use in conjunction with a small garden. In addition to growing early and late crops of salad greens, you can also raise transplants which will be ready to pop in as soon as garden space opens up. This shortens the time in which this second crop matures, which can even allow you time, depending on the length of your growing season, to slip in a third, hardy crop. (Refer to the section on Extending the Garden Season in chapter 3 for more details.)

Gardening in Containers

Apartment and condominium dwellers, inner-city residents, mobile-home owners, and other would-be gardeners whose ground space is limited or non-existent don't have the luxury of thinking in terms of conventional garden plots. They must improvise and adapt their gardening endeavors to their particular situation. Container gardening is a multi-faceted solution—it encompasses everything from windowboxes to various containers scattered on doorsteps, patios, and balconies, from elaborate high-rise rooftop layouts to hanging baskets. As long as you can provide the basics—a container full of growing medium, light, water, and fertilizer—you can grow fresh vegetables for your table.

The trend in vegetable breeding toward compact, bush varieties expands the realm of vegetables suitable for container gardening. The availability of dwarf and midget varieties of garden favorites like cabbages, carrots, eggplants, lettuce,

A Container Gardening Guide

The following list gives you an idea of which vegetables grow well in containers, along with the container size appropriate for each vegetable. Vegetables with a * alongside are featured in the chart on Space-Saving Vegetable Varieties that appears earlier in this chapter. Refer to that chart for the names of specific varieties with dwarf or otherwise compact growth which make them perfect for container gardening. Vegetables listed below without a * indicate that any variety is suitable for container gardening.

Container Crop	Container Size for One Plant
Beans, bush	8 in. wide/8–10 in. deep
Beans, pole	12 in. wide/8 in. deep
Beets*	6–12 in. deep
Broccoli	12 in. wide/12 in. deep/5 gal. capacity
Brussels sprouts	12 in. wide/12 in. deep/5 gal. capacity
Cabbage*	8–10 in. wide/12 in. deep/3–5 gal. capacity
Carrots*	10–12 in. deep
Corn*	21 in. wide/8 in. deep (plant no less than 3 plants per container; these measurements apply to a group of 3 plants)
Cucumbers*	8 in. wide/12 in. deep/1–2 gal. capacity
Eggplant*	12 in. wide/12 in. deep/3–5 gal. capacity
Endive and Escarole	6 in. wide/6 in. deep
Kale	8 in. wide/8 in. deep
Lettuce*	8 in. wide/6–8 in. deep
Mustard	8 in. wide/6–8 in. deep
Onions	2–3 in. wide/10–12 in. deep
Peas*	4 in. wide/12 in. deep
Peppers*	24 in. wide/12 in. deep/2 gal. capacity
Radishes	2 in. wide/4–6 in. deep
Spinach	8 in. wide/4–6 in. deep
Squash, summer and winter*	24 in. wide/24 in. deep/5 gal. capacity
Swiss chard	12 in. wide/8–12 in. deep
Tomatoes, dwarf*	6 in. wide/6 in. deep/1 gal. capacity
Tomatoes, standard	12 in. wide/24 in. deep/2–3 gal. capacity
Turnips	6 in. wide/10–12 in. deep

peppers, and tomatoes means that the container gardener's selection isn't limited, even if his space is. See the chart, A Container Gardening Guide, for a list of suitable container crops. To help get your container garden under way, here is a rundown of the basics that you'll need to know.

Finding Suitable Containers

There's no need to rush out and purchase brand spanking new containers. You can easily scavenge and recycle containers that you find in your home or neighborhood. The main thing to remember is that the containers must be large enough and durable enough to accommodate the vegetables you want to grow. Most vegetables need 12 inches or less of soil, so your containers need not be extremely deep. Give leaky buckets, dented garbage cans, discolored dishpans, rejected wastebaskets, less than watertight aquariums, and pock-marked Styrofoam coolers a new life. Pay a visit to the local produce market and latch onto wooden crates, fruit boxes, and bushel baskets. If you are willing to make an outlay of cash for a touch more elegance, you can purchase giant-sized clay pots, cedar tubs, plastic pots, or half-barrels from garden supply centers or hardware stores. There are also lightweight paper pulp pots on the market, made from compressed, recycled paper. If you are handy with a hammer and nails and have access to scrap lumber, you can slap together some quick and inexpensive boxes. Note that any wooden containers should be covered on all surfaces with a nontoxic wood preservative (such as copper naphthenate, sold under the name Cuprinol) which will keep the wood from rotting, which in turn keeps it serviceable for three to five years.

Consider adding wheels to the bottom of your container or building a simple dolly on which a container may rest. A mobile container allows you to move the plant to the best light, out of reach of buffeting winds, and indoors when frost threatens.

Some people recommend the use of large, heavy-gauge plastic bags filled with a lightweight soilless mix. These bags have holes poked in the bottom for drainage and slits cut in the top where seedlings or seeds are set in place. This is an inexpensive container alternative, but keep in mind that these bags are unattractive, difficult to move around, and will leak water and soil which can damage wooden surfaces.

Some plants with trailing growth like dwarf cucumbers and tomatoes look very attractive when grown in hanging baskets or hanging redwood planters.

Homemade Vertical Garden: An empty corner by a sunny window or a vacant spot on the patio is just the place for this vertical gardening cylinder filled with vegetable plants. The base is an 18- to 24-inch plywood circle with several drainage holes. Chicken wire stapled to the base forms a cylinder that is lined with a sheet of plastic or sphagnum moss and filled with a soilless mix.

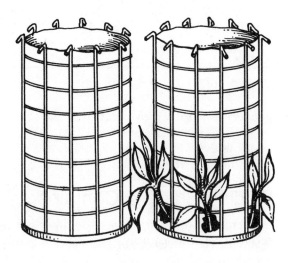

Planting the Cylinder: When it comes time to plant, just poke your finger through the plastic and push the soilless mix around to make a hole for the seedling roots. Set the seedling in the hole and make sure its roots are covered and gently firmed in place. The grid of the chicken wire serves as a convenient spacing pattern as you plant.

Just make sure to firmly secure the basket with appropriate hardware at the outset—always remembering that when you water, the soil will become wet, and wet soil is extremely heavy.

No matter what type of container you use, providing proper drainage is imperative, since no vegetables like to grow with their roots surrounded by soggy soil. The best way to provide drainage is to drill or poke ¼-inch holes along the lower edge of the container, near the bottom, but not directly in the bottom.

In addition to these drainage holes, you should add ½ inch of drainage material to the bottom of the container, such as gravel, pebbles, pieces of crushed brick, or bits of broken clay pots. If there are no drainage holes in your container, increase this drainage layer to a depth of 1 inch.

Growing Mixes

The growing medium you provide for your vegetable crops will determine to a large degree the success of your container garden. Since the plants will be growing and maturing in a confined space, what fills that space must be rich and of the proper texture to support their needs.

Container gardeners have the option of using a growing medium containing soil, or one that is completely soilless. The soilless mixes have the advantage of being lightweight (roughly half the weight of an equal amount of garden soil), and are especially recommended for rooftop gardeners. A downstairs neighbor can become justifiably nervous when floorboards start sagging and groaning, especially if he or she knows that a cubic foot of soil weighs roughly 25 pounds.

There are countless recipes for mixes containing soil. There is no such thing as a "best" recipe—it's up to you to decide which one is best for you in terms of accessibility of ingredients and cost. One good mix consists of seven parts rich garden soil, one part peat moss, one part vermiculite, and one part perlite. (This soil mix was developed by experimental container gardeners at McGill University in Montreal in 1975, under the direction of Prof. Witold Rybczynski.) Another reliable soil mix contains equal parts garden soil, compost, and sand.

Soilless mixes are available commercially under a wide variety of trade names. They are all composed of vermiculite, peat moss, fertilizers, and trace elements in varying proportions. You can mix up your own with little trouble and at little expense. Just blend together three parts peat moss and one part coarse sand, perlite, or vermiculite. Add 6 ounces of ground dolomitic limestone per bushel of this mix to neutralize the acidity of the peat moss. A soilless mix will release all the nutrients it has absorbed at once as compared to releasing them over a long period as mixes with soil do. This means that you must be diligent and faithful in replenishing the nutrients on which the vegetables depend for their best growth.

Planting and Culture in Containers

You can start your container garden by either seeding directly in the containers or transplanting seedlings you've started indoors. See chapter 3 for information on growing transplants, and refer to individual vegetable entries in the Vegetable Guide for planting dates.

Container-grown vegetables need the same amount of light as those grown in the backyard plot. All vegetables need at least six hours of light daily to grow well. As a rule, leafy greens and some root crops can get by with less light and still produce, but fruiting plants need nearly full sun for a successful harvest.

Containers equipped with wheels or set on a dolly can be moved around to take advantage of the available light. If your containers are too heavy to move or for some other reason must remain stationary, you can increase their light ration by making use of reflected light. Place the containers against light-colored walls or, for a portable reflective backdrop, take boards and paint them white or cover them with aluminum foil. Position these on the east and west sides of the container and you'll note a marked increase in light made available to your plants. If you're a high-rise rooftop gardener, you'll find that these boards also serve the function of windbreaks to protect your plants from the frequent gusting winds.

Soil in containers dries out more quickly than soil in the garden. In fact, your containers may need one watering a day, and even two in very warm weather. Check them daily and if the top inch of soil feels dry, water thoroughly—until you see the water draining out the bottom. (City gardeners should let the chlorine and fluoride in their tapwater dissipate by drawing the water the night before they plan to use it.) By applying a mulch of wood chips, pebbles, shredded leaves, or peat moss you can help conserve soil moisture.

If you're going to be away for several days, the best bet is to get a reliable friend to come in and tend your garden. In the absence of such a friend, there are steps you can take to slow down moisture loss. Before you go, water your vegetables either early or late in the day, but not in the midday heat. Take a large plastic bag or sheet of plastic and encircle each pot, covering as much of the soil surface as possible, but not the plant. Finish by securing with a piece of twine.

Frequent waterings rapidly leach nutrients out of the containers. This means you must feed frequently throughout the season to replace what is lost. You should feed at every third watering or at least once a week, with dilute solutions of manure tea, compost tea, or fish emulsion. Or, as recommended by experimental container gardeners at McGill University in Montreal, you can feed every third week with a nutrient-rich solution of equal parts bone meal, granite dust, flaked seaweed, blood meal, and either fish emulsion or manure tea.

Tips for Large Gardens

Wasted space and poor management are just as critical in a large garden as they are in a small one. Even with more space at your disposal, you should strive to make efficient use of the whole area. Remember, more area means that more mulch, water, and compost will be needed. It's important to keep in mind that a large, unkempt garden can be outproduced by a smaller but better managed one. Don't try more than you can handle—even if the space is available.

Continue to set aside space for perennial beds, and consider growing a not-so-common perennial such as Jerusalem artichokes. A larger garden allows you to grow vegetables well suited for winter storage, such as potatoes, pumpkins, and winter squash, which demand a lot of growing space for a long period of time. More garden area also means you can grow plenty of food for canning and freezing. You can also accommodate a block of corn rows, something which isn't always feasible in a smaller garden. Intensive techniques like interplanting and succession planting, as well as the use of raised beds, are still appropriate in the larger garden. You may also want to devote a strip, several feet wide, along one edge to an outdoor seedbed, where you can start midsummer crops to be transplanted when the early crops are done.

2

Preparing the Garden Soil

All higher plants in the plant kingdom have certain elemental needs that must be met by the soil. In the vegetable garden where most crops have just a few months to develop from seed to edible harvest, soil composition and quality are particularly important. The soil must provide a steady supply of nutrients in order to promote rapid, uninterrupted plant growth. Crop yields, appearance, and even taste are affected by the balance and availability of these nutrients. Soil gases and water also play essential roles in the production of vegetables: if they are not available at the right times or in the right amounts, then reduced yields, improper development, or even disease could result.

As the growing medium for roots, soil must also provide structural support for all shapes and sizes of vegetable plants, from tomatoes to lettuce to Brussels sprouts. At the same time, it must be loose enough for air and water to penetrate, for germinating seeds to break through, and for root and tuber crops such as carrots, parsnips, and potatoes to expand and grow. Its physical properties, then, become as important as its chemical ones, for both affect the vegetable garden's health and productivity. Recognizing this, the wise gardener tries to determine the character of his or her soil, examines its strengths and weaknesses, and finally devises an appropriate program of preparation and management.

Judging Your Soil: What Do You Have to Work With?

Although an experienced botanist or soil expert can often judge a soil's chemical nature simply by studying the natural vegetation it supports, most gardeners rely on periodic chemical tests. The agricultural extension service of your state or province will test soil samples for a minimal charge, or you can use a do-it-yourself kit. (See the Introduction.) Home nitrogen, phosphorus, and potassium tests aren't 100 percent reliable and their results should be considered only very rough estimates of the actual levels of available nutrients in the soil. Results from the extension service are much more accurate, but even these should be interpreted broadly. Furthermore, their recommendations for a chemical fertilization program are of little or no use to the organic gardener. Although pound-for-pound conversions can be made from chemical to organic materials, such factors as variations in soil, quality of the organic material, and time and method of application make the mathematics inaccurate.

The pH test, whether done professionally or by the gardener, is extremely valuable. It tells the acidity or alkalinity of the soil so that you can figure out how much lime or other neutralizing material must be added. (See the Introduction for a discussion of the types of materials and quantities to add.) This is most important, for if the pH is either too low or too high the plants will not be able to absorb all the nutrients you add to the soil. Most vegetable crops prefer a slightly acidic soil with a pH roughly between 6.0 and 6.8. Beans, broccoli, cabbage, corn, cucumbers, peppers, radishes, squash, sweet potatoes, tomatoes, and turnips can tolerate a pH as low as 5.5, but not much lower.

A simple "squeeze" test, in which you mold the soil in your hands and feel its texture, will help you to determine the physical nature of your soil. Follow the guidelines for this test as described in the Introduction, and decide in what general class your soil belongs. Few soils will be entirely clay, loam, or sand, but rather some combination of these. The technical names are not important to the home gardener, just the general classifications. Knowing whether the soil tends to be mostly clay or mostly sand is important in deciding how and when to cultivate, what organic materials to add, and even what to plant. All soil types can sustain some vegetables, but only with proper care and management can they be altered and amended to continuously support a variety of vegetable crops. The following is a rundown of the basic soil types and the kinds of vegetable crops that are best suited to each.

Sandy soils do not hold moisture, so they can be planted in early spring and worked throughout even the wettest seasons. Cole crops such as broccoli, cabbage, and kohlrabi, as well as short-season crops like lettuce and radishes, do well on these soils. If enough organic matter is added and the plants are watered frequently, sandy soils also produce fine root crops such as carrots, parsnips, and salsify.

Clay soils have the opposite problem of sandy types. Because they retain moisture so well, very often they may stay wet into the early summer months, delaying cultivation and planting. Adding organic matter improves these soils by increasing drainage and by reducing the tendency to form hard clods. Early crops like peas and root crops like carrots and radishes probably will not do well in native clay soils until organic matter has been added over a period of several years.

Muck or peat soils are very rich in organic matter at various stages of decomposition, and are dark brown in color. If well drained with well-decomposed organic matter, these soils are considered excellent for growing celery, lettuce, onions, and other heavy-feeding vegetables. They have a high nitrogen content of 1 to 2½ percent, but are usually low in potassium and need special fertilization and management programs in order to produce a diversified harvest.

Loams are considered best for general vegetable production since they are both naturally fertile and retentive of moisture. Fortunately, most home garden soils are partly loam. Loosely textured enough for small-growing vegetables and root crops, these soils can also support larger plants such as beans and tomatoes. Loams consist of about equal proportions of clay, sand, and silt, so they are neither sticky like the clay soils nor coarse like the sandy ones.

Improving Your Soil's Structure and Fertility

Given the choice, what is the "ideal" soil every gardener would hope to find in his or her patch? The soil in the ideal vegetable garden is a deep silt loam with about 5 percent or more humus and a pH of about 6. It has a crumbly texture, and is coarse enough to drain off excess water, yet fine enough to hold moisture throughout the hot and dry part of the season. It is well fortified with readily accessible reserves of nitrogen, phosphorus, and potassium.

Alas, this ideal garden soil is seldom found just waiting to be planted. Rather, it needs to be made, and remade each year through an ongoing soil management program. If you are lucky enough to have a garden plot of silt loam, or even sandy or clay loam, then your initial gardening work will be much simpler than that of gardeners with predominantly sandy or clay plots.

Since soil changes as new materials are added and plants, insects, earthworms, and rodents remove and release nutrients, samples should be chemically tested every few years. Structural changes will be obvious as you work the soil, but chemical alterations may be less noticeable. Results from the tests will serve as guidelines for replenishing the supply of organic matter and the microorganisms that go with it. Any soil, no matter how rich and fertile it is initially, will soon be depleted of its nutrients if it is not continually replenished and built up.

The Introduction outlines the elements of a good organic soil management program, including such techniques as composting and mulching. To complement these basic procedures, there are a number of other techniques particularly useful in building vegetable garden soil, such as adding natural fertilizers and animal manures and starting a green manure program. No one method is going to solve all your soil's problems, and some of the practices discussed here may not be at all practical in your situation. The best program for your garden soil will probably incorporate several different techniques which make use of the materials and equipment available to you.

Natural Fertilizers

Organic soil enhancers like compost, green manure, and animal wastes solve many nutrient deficiencies while improving soil structure. However, these are not balanced fertilizers and continued use could promote certain nutrient deficiencies in the soil. Fully decomposed compost and cow manure each have a chemical analysis showing a high percentage of nitrogen. They will take care of the nitrogen needs of most vegetable plants, and even supply the necessary micronutrients, but they will not supply the large amounts of phosphorus and potassium needed by so many vegetable crops like beets, carrots, and tomatoes. This is where natural fertilizers enter the picture. Natural fertilizer supplements are needed to supply phosphorus and potassium and to add extra nitrogen to crops with high nutrient needs.

The secret to successful fertilization in the organic vegetable garden is timing. Natural fertilizers rely on microorganisms to break them down to forms plants can use, and this process takes time. As a gardener, you must be able to anticipate the plants' nutrient needs and apply fertilizers accordingly. To help you in your task, refer to the chart on Percentage Composition of Common Organic Materials and Their Relative Availability that appears later in the chapter. If you apply certain materials after you spot deficiency symptoms, the plants may not receive the nutrients in time. If you apply others too early, nutrient value of the fertilizer may be reduced by leaching. Luckily, a soil rich in organic matter tends to minimize these fertility problems. A properly conditioned soil promotes a pH good for fertilizer solubility, cuts down on leaching, and supplies the microorganisms necessary for the breakdown of natural fertilizers.

Just when fertilizers should be applied depends mostly on the nature of the specific material itself, as well as soil type, pH level, when you are going to plant, and what you are going to plant. Most nitrogenous substances are highly soluble and lose their nutrient value through leaching. Therefore, dried blood, bat guano, and animal tankage, which release their nitrogen relatively quickly, should not be applied until just before planting time.

Potassium fertilizers have different rates of release, and you must keep this in mind when deciding when to apply a given fertilizer. Mineral fertilizers like granite dust and greensand (found in undersea deposits) take a long time to break down and become available to plants. Apply these in the fall to benefit spring crops, or in the spring for crops to be grown later in the season. Other potassium sources, including green plant residues, seaweed, and wood ashes, release their nutrients relatively quickly, making them susceptible to leaching. Don't apply these materials to the garden until spring, just before planting time, or until they are needed through the course of the season.

A word of caution when using wood ashes: because they have a very rapid release rate, they can burn seeds, stems, and root hairs of young plants on direct contact. Make sure they are dispersed well throughout the top 8 inches of soil before planting. (They can also be used as a side-dressing or mulch later in the season, allowing a margin of safety between ashes and plants.) Wood ashes contain 20 to 53 percent lime, so they serve to raise the pH. Go easy on their use in areas where acid-loving crops such as potatoes will grow. Under no circumstances should you add coal ashes to your garden, for they are high in sulfur and can be harmful to growing plants.

Vegetable Crops and Their Relative Nutrient Needs*

Nitrogen (N)

High (3 or more lbs./1,000 sq. ft.)	Medium (1–3 lbs./1,000 sq. ft.)	Low (less than 1 lb./1,000 sq. ft.)
Celery	Broccoli	Beans
Corn	Cabbage	Beets
Okra	Cucumbers	Carrots
Tomatoes	Eggplant	Cauliflower
	Lettuce	Horseradish
	Onions	Parsnips
	Potatoes	Peppers
	Pumpkins	Radishes
	Squashes	Rutabaga
	Sweet potatoes	Turnips
	Swiss chard	

Phosphorus (P)

High (¾ lb. or more/1,000 sq. ft.)	Medium (⅜–¾ lb./1,000 sq. ft.)	Low (less than ¼ lb./1,000 sq. ft.)
Celery	Beans	Beans
Corn	Beets	Peas
Cucumbers	Broccoli	Peppers
Potatoes	Brussels sprouts	
Pumpkins	Cabbage	
Squashes	Carrots	
Tomatoes	Cauliflower	
	Onions	
	Parsnips	
	Peas	
	Sweet potatoes	

Potassium (K)

High (2 or more lbs./1,000 sq. ft.)	Medium (1–2 lbs./1,000 sq. ft.)	Low (½–1 lb./1,000 sq. ft.)
Brussels sprouts	Beans	Corn
Cabbage	Beets	Peppers
Carrots	Cauliflower	
Celery	Corn	
Kale	Cucumbers	
Parsnips	Eggplant	
Potatoes	Kale	
Salsify	Lettuce	
Sweet potatoes	Onions	
	Peas	
	Spinach	
	Tomatoes	

*Needs based on the amount of the nutrient each crop removes from the soil, provided no part of the plant is returned to the soil after harvest.

Commonly used phosphorus fertilizers, such as phosphate rock and bone meal, require time to become soluble, so they are less subject to leaching. They must be applied in fall in order to supply phosphorus to spring plants, and in early spring to benefit summer plants. Because these materials require a pH above 5 in order to break down efficiently, it may be necessary to add some lime at the same time you add the phosphorus-rich material.

The best way for you to get these fertilizers into the garden soil is to broadcast them before the crops are planted. Pulverize mineral substances like greensand and phosphate rock and chop plant matter or wastes like compost, grass clippings, and leaves, so that they may be spread evenly over the soil surface. With mineral substances, the finer the texture, the more quickly the nutrients will be released. With a rotary tiller, plow, or garden rake, work the fertilizers into the top few inches of soil.

You can determine just how much fertilizer is needed through chemical soil testing, and knowledge about your soil and the vegetable plants you want to grow. During the initial soil preparation, what you want to do is replace the approximate amounts of nitrogen, potassium, and phosphorus removed by the vegetables during the previous growing season. (This fertilization is simply replacing the nutrients that were taken from the soil, and does not take into account a soil that is deficient in the first place.) Here are the amounts of the major nutrients used by the vegetables which you must replace:

Nitrogen	1 to 3 lbs. per 1,000 sq. ft.	50 to 120 lbs. per acre
Phosphorus	¼ to ¾ lb. per 1,000 sq. ft.	15 to 30 lbs. per acre
Potassium	2½ to 4 lbs. per 1,000 sq. ft.	100 to 150 lbs. per acre

To determine within these ranges the appropriate amount of each nutrient that was taken from your soil and must be replaced, check the chart on Vegetable Crops and Their Relative Nutrient Needs. If you grew mostly medium nitrogen-feeding crops, the chart will tell you that you should replace 1 to 3 pounds of nitrogen for every 1,000 square feet of garden space planted. If you grew mostly root crops (low-nitrogen feeders) and few high-nitrogen crops, then you only need to replace less than 1 pound for every 1,000 square feet. This same reasoning applies to phosphorus and potassium.

Once you have calculated the general amounts of these soluble nutrients that need to be replenished to the soil, you must figure out how much natural fertilizer to apply to furnish the right amounts of nitrogen, phosphorus, and potassium. The rate is determined by the percentage of a particular nutrient a natural fertilizer contains. The general formula you use to determine how much of a particular fertilizer to apply is this: Multiply the percentage of the nutrient (N, P, or K) contained in the fertilizer by the amount that must be replaced to the soil. Thus, a garden encompassing 1,000 square feet needs: 15 to 45 pounds of blood meal (15 percent nitrogen); 7½ to 22½ pounds of phosphate rock (about 30 percent phosphorus); and 17½ to 28 pounds of wood ashes (7 percent potassium). Refer to the chart on Percentage Composition of Common Organic Materials and Their Relative Availability for a listing of the nutrient contents of various organic fertilizers.

Percentage Composition of Common Organic Materials and Their Relative Availability

Organic Material	Nitrogen	Phosphorus	Potassium	Relative Availability
Activated sludge	5.0	3.0	0	Medium
Alfalfa hay	2.5	0.5	2.1	
Animal tankage	8.0	20.0	0	Medium
Apple leaves	1.0	0.2	0.4	
Basic slag	0	0.8	0	Rapid
Blood meal	15.0	1.3	0.7	
Bone meal (steamed)	4.0	21.0	0.2	Slow
Brewer's grains (wet)	0.9	0.5	0.1	
Castor pomace	5.5	1.5	1.3	Slow
Cattle manure (dried)	2.0	1.8	2.2	Medium
Cattle manure (fresh)	0.3	0.2	0.4	Medium
Cocoa shell dust	1.0	1.5	2.7	Slow
Coffee grounds (dried)	2.0	0.4	0.7	
Colloidal phosphate	0	18–24	0	Slow
Cornstalks	0.8	0.4	0.9	
Cottonseed	3.2	1.3	1.2	
Cottonseed meal	7.0	2.5	1.5	Slow to medium
Dried blood	12–15	3.0	0	Medium to rapid
Fish emulsion	5.0	2.0	2.0	Medium to rapid
Fish meal	10.0	4.0	0	Slow
Fish scrap	7.8	13.0	3.8	Slow
Granite dust	0	0	5.0	Slow
Greensand	0	1.5	5.0	Very slow
Guano	12.0	8.0	3.0	Medium
Hoof meal and horn dust	12.5	1.8	0	Slow
Horse manure (composted)	0.7	0.3	0.6	Medium
Horse manure (fresh)	0.4	0.2	0.4	Medium
Leaf mold (composted)	0.6	0.2	0.4	Medium
Mushroom compost	0.4–0.7	57–62	0.5–1.5	Slow
Oak leaves	0.8	0.4	0.2	Rapid
Peach leaves	0.9	0.2	0.6	
Phosphate rock	0	30–32	0	Very slow
Pig manure (fresh)	0.6	0.4	0.1	Medium
Pine needles	0.5	0.1	0	
Poultry manure (fresh)	2.0	1.9	1.9	Medium to rapid
Rabbit manure (fresh)	2.4	0.6	0.1	Medium
Roses (flower)	0.3	0.1	0.4	
Sawdust	4.0	2.0	4.0	Very slow
Seaweed	1.7	0.8	5.0	Slow to medium
Sheep manure (fresh)	0.6	0.3	0.2	Medium
Soybean meal	6.7	1.6	2.3	Slow to medium

Organic Material	Nitrogen	Phosphorus	Potassium	Relative Availability
Tankage	6.0	8.0	0	
Tobacco stems	2.0	0	7.0	Slow
Wood ashes	0	1.5	7.0	Rapid

Animal Manure

At one time, animal manure was considered the foundation of good garden fertilization. Where they can still be obtained without a long haul or great expense, horse, pig, cattle, sheep, and poultry manures remain some of the best all-purpose amendments you can add to your soil.

Depending on the animal source, what the animal was fed, its stage of growth and general health, the fresh manure can contain from 11 to 22 pounds of nitrogen per ton, as well as moderate amounts of potassium and phosphorus. The way the fresh manure is handled affects its nutrient content as well. If it is stored unprotected from the elements, rain and melting snow will steal away the water-soluble nutrients before the manure is applied to the garden. The same thing happens when it is left exposed to the air; the volatile nutrients evaporate into the air, reducing the amount of nutrients that will find their way into the soil. But manure remains an excellent source of organic matter and food for soil microorganisms. Animal manure is available in three forms: fresh or green, rotted or composted, and dried. The first two forms are the least expensive.

In its fresh state, manure is potent stuff, and should never be applied directly to plants or soon before planting to avoid burning seeds, seedlings, and delicate plants. Spread it on the soil the fall before spring planting and plow it under immediately to make sure the nutrients are incorporated into the soil instead of released to the air. The latest fresh manure can safely be applied and turned under is two to three months before planting. If you wait too long or don't incorporate it well, fresh manure can cause root crops to grow rapidly into large, tough vegetables, or fork at the ends.

The general rate of application in the garden is a 2- to 3-inch layer spread over the soil, which works out to about 10 to 15 pounds per square yard. If you apply it during cold weather, the manure should first be allowed to cool in the stable or some other protected area. This will reduce evaporative losses once it is added to the garden. Dress the soil with approximately 10 pounds phosphate rock per 25 pounds manure to make up for the relatively low phosphorus content. Poultry manure, extremely high in available nutrients, should not be overapplied, particularly in spring or summer months. In relative terms, you need apply only half as much chicken manure as other animal manures.

Composted or "well-rotted" manure is manure that has been set aside in a pile and allowed to decompose into a moist and relatively odor-free product. Some stables sell this material, or you can oversee the process yourself if you have a quantity of fresh manure available. The easiest way to do this is to layer manure into a standard compost pile, along with green plant matter and dirt. (See the Introduction for basic composting procedures.) If the amount of manure you're dealing with is large, you can leave it in a pile and cover it with a layer of dirt, peat moss, or sawdust. Keep the pile moist, not soggy, and turn it every few weeks. Within several months, you'll find your manure has turned to a soft, crumbly, earthy-smelling material. The heat of the decomposition process destroys many harmful bacteria and weed seeds, and diminishes its potency, so you can work rotted manure into the soil up to two weeks before sowing seeds. Decomposition also condenses the pile of manure, due to the breakdown of fibrous material. Although some nutrients are lost through this process, because of the weight loss, composted manure is higher in nutrients pound for pound than fresh manure.

When well rotted, manure will not burn plants and can be applied safely at any time during the growing season as a nutritional side-dressing. It can even be used as a soil-improving garden mulch, applied 1 to 2 inches thick, then incorporated into the soil at the end of the season.

Dried manure is the pulverized, odor-free, bagged product sold through garden centers and nurseries at a steep price. To reach this state, the fresh manure has been dried in an oven to reduce the percentage of water, thereby increasing the percentage of nutrients and humus per unit of weight. As an example, one ton of fresh hen manure that contains 20 pounds of nitrogen, 16 pounds of phosphorus, and 10 pounds of potassium will contain 40 pounds of nitrogen, 30 pounds of phosphorus, and 19 pounds of potassium when dried.

Given the cost of this dried manure, you could end up spending a bundle if you were to depend on this as the mainstay of your soil-conditioning and fertilizing program. Fresh and composted manures are preferred over the dried form, to keep the cost of gardening down. Use dried manure only if you are gardening in a very small area, or in containers, or if no other soil amendment is available or practical to use.

Green Manure

Animal wastes are not the only or even the best source of nutrient-rich organic matter. In fact, some first-rate organic vegetable gardeners manage to build rich soil without any animal wastes, not to mention chemical fertilizers.

Composting is one way to do this; the cultivation of green manure crops is another. In this process, legume or nonlegume (grass or grain) crops are sown and cultivated right on the garden plot, then plowed under while still green. When growing, these crops protect soil from wind and water erosion. When plowed under, all the various nutrients that went to produce the crop are returned to the soil, along with added organic matter and, in some cases, added nutrients.

Green manuring is most useful to farmers or to gardeners with vegetable plots too large for conventional mulching or composting. Since they are usually grown during at least part of the same season as the vegetable crops, green

Green Manuring in the Garden: An excellent way to improve soil texture and fertility is to grow green manure crops. If you have a large plot you can incorporate green manuring into your garden planning without having to sacrifice the harvest. Instead of tying up the whole garden all season with a green manure crop, compromise by dividing it into two sections and growing vegetables in one section and a green manure crop in the other. The presence of green manure plants during the growing season can offer an unexpected benefit for vegetables; some green manure crops produce flowers that can lure honeybees into your garden to pollinate the squash and cucumbers. Each year, alternate the crops that grow in each section, so that the vegetable plants can capitalize on the increased fertility of the soil where the green manure crop grew the year before.

manures make the land unavailable for growing vegetables. Often, gardeners divide the available land into two sections, planting one with vegetable crops and the other with green manure crops, then alternating the crops in each plot in successive seasons.

The best green manure crops for most areas are legumes, especially alfalfa and the various clovers. These plants produce strong, deep roots that can bring up nutrients from as far as 30 feet below the surface. They are good forage and honey crops and some have leaves, flowers, or seeds that may be harvested for use as tea, flour, or as a potherb. Most importantly, legumes harbor bacteria that can harness nitrogen from the air and convert it into forms available to plant roots. The bacteria, known as *Rhizobia,* live in tiny nodules formed on legume roots. Using energy stored in the roots, they "fix" gaseous nitrogen from the air in the surrounding soil, giving it to the plant in a usable form. This provides a built-in source of nitrogen and makes nitrogen fertilization unnecessary. When the legume is plowed under, this nitrogen is left for successive crops.

If your soil is too acid, wet, or infertile to support a healthy vegetable crop, or if you simply want to build organic matter content, then a nonlegume is the best choice. In fact, under the conditions of intensive gardening where as much land as possible should be kept in production, nonlegume green manures such as brome, buckwheat, millet, oats, rye, sudangrass, and wheat may be the best soil-improving crops, no matter what the soil conditions. They produce consid-

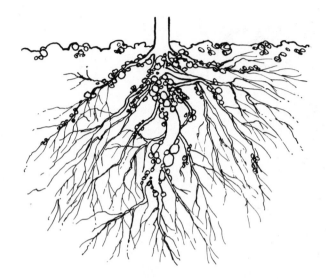

Nitrogen Storehouses: The roots of the soybean shown here house many beneficial bacteria in tiny knoblike structures known as nodules. Soybeans, along with other nitrogen-fixing legumes like peas and beans, enjoy a near-perfect symbiotic relationship with the bacteria *Rhizobia*. The bacterium receives the carbon it needs for its life processes from the legume host and in turn provides the legume with nitrogen in a form the plant can use.

erably more succulent top growth than most legumes, and in shorter periods of time. Some are quite hardy and can be grown through the winter in northern areas. (Canadian gardeners and those in the northern tier of the United States will have success with crops like barley, bluegrass, rye, and winter wheat.) When tilled under while still green, they create humus and eventually provide some boost to the soil's fertility.

Planting and tilling schedules for green manure crops depend upon the crop rotation plan in the garden (incorporating both vegetable and green manure crops), the green manure crop's needs, and of course, local climate and soil factors. Seed may be sown in spring for summer tillage, in summer for fall tillage, or in fall for winter or spring tillage. In order to increase nitrogen levels and root growth, certain crops may even be left for several seasons, if periodically mowed to prevent blossoming and to encourage top growth.

Before planting, prepare soil as thoroughly as you would for any vegetable crop. Apply compost, manure, lime, phosphate rock, wood ashes, and other ma-

A Guide to Green Manure Crops

Crop	Soil	Climate	Planting and Harvesting Dates	Comments
Legumes				
Alfalfa	Well drained, loamy; neutral pH	Any	Summer (North)—Early fall Late summer (South)— Summer of second year	Lime if pH is below 6.
Alyce clover	Any	South, Gulf Coast	Summer—Early fall	Summer annual; could cause nematode infestation in soil.
Cowpeas	Any	South	Midsummer—Anytime	Good rotation crop in Southwest.
Crimson clover	Sandy loam	Any	Summer (North)—Early fall Late summer (South)— Summer	Sow with rye grass.

Crop	Soil	Climate	Planting and Harvesting Dates	Comments
Legumes *(continued)*				
Crotolaria	Any	South	Early spring—Early fall	Requires very hot weather.
Florida beggarweed	Rich, sandy loam	South, Gulf Coast	Summer—Early fall	Summer annual; may turn into a garden nuisance, since plants appear without reseeding the following year.
Hairy indigo	Poor, sandy	South	Late winter to early spring—Fall	Summer annual; certain strains suitable for use as far north as Georgia.
Hairy vetch	Sandy	Any but extreme North	Early fall—Summer	Winter annual; sow with rye; good winter cover crop in the North.
Lupine	Sandy loam	Varied, according to species	Summer (North)—Early fall Early fall (South)—Early spring to summer	Does well on acid soils; blue lupine could cause nematode infestation.
Red clover	Loam	North	Summer—Fall	No inoculation needed; good summer green manure crop; cut early growth for hay, later growth for green manure.
Sesbania	Any	South	Midsummer—Early fall	Thrives in wet, acid soils; requires hot weather to produce.
Soybeans	Loamy; neutral pH	Central, East	Summer—Fall	Use late-maturing variety; drought-resistant.
Sweet clover	Any, well drained	Any	Fall or spring—Late summer to fall of second year	Easily adapted to all locales as a biennial or annual; especially good in the North.
Velvet beans	Sandy	South	Summer—Fall	Deep rooted; good choice for poor soils.
Nonlegumes				
Barley	Loamy; neutral to alkaline	North, Central	Summer—Early fall Fall—Summer (winter varieties)	Good choice for northern winter cover crop.
Brome grass	Any	North, Central	Early fall—Summer	Hardy winter cover crop.
Buckwheat	Any	North, Central	Midsummer—Early fall	Attracts bees; good choice for acid soils; sensitive to cold weather.
Oats	Any	Any	Early fall (Deep South)—Summer Midsummer—Early fall	Good nurse crop for various legume green manures; good forage.
Rye	Any	Any	Summer—Early fall Fall—Early spring to summer	Good winter cover crop; choose winter rye for extreme North; can be cut for hay in fall and tilled under in spring.
Winter wheat	Loamy	North	Fall—Early spring to summer	Good forage crop, can be cut for hay or mulch.

terial as needed. If legumes are to be planted, avoid excessive nitrogen fertilizing. However, in order to guarantee that the legumes have enough *Rhizobia* to fix adequate quantities of nitrogen, inoculate the seeds with the bacteria before planting. (See chapter 3 for more information on how to inoculate legumes.) Broadcast seeds evenly on the smoothed soil surface and cover with a fine sifting of soil. The green manure crop should need little care during the growing season, except perhaps some weeding during the early stages and occasional watering.

You can turn the crop under at any time between its greening and blossoming. As a general rule, till it under just before the first buds emerge. If the green

tricks of the trade

Choosing Your Garden Tools and Making Them Last

Like all consumer goods, hand tools for the garden are available in a wide range of prices and workmanship. A garden tool that you will use constantly throughout the season, year after year, should be the very best quality that you can afford. A cheaper tool may not lighten your wallet as much initially, but it will end up costing you plenty by making the gardening task harder, and by wearing out sooner.

Here is a checklist of details to look for as you examine a tool that indicate good design, good materials, and good workmanship:

• Among the sturdiest and most durable tools are those made of high-carbon steel. There are also stainless steel spades and forks on the market that add a whole new dimension of beauty and durability to gardening tools, but they are very expensive. What you get for your money are blades and prongs that glide almost effortlessly through the soil, and seem to clean themselves by shedding dirt easily.

• Lightweight and well-balanced tools make rearranging soil less of a chore.

• Handles should be of a thickness that is comfortable when gripped in your hand. Sheet metal handles are standard fare on most garden tools. A distinguishing characteristic of a superior tool is a handle made of a single piece of smooth-grained hardwood such as hickory or ash. Handles come in various shapes. You should look for a handle that provides good leverage and a firm grip, and for extra strength, one that has a piece of wood filling in the base of the Y-shape.

• Check the height of the tool in relation to your height; a handle that is too short can easily mean sore back muscles after a session in the garden.

• The fewer connecting joints there are on the tool, the better. A joint commonly appears on spades and digging forks where the head of the tool is stuck into the bottom end of the handle and the point where they connect is wrapped with a piece of metal. Higher-quality tools have no soft spots like this; instead, a solid socket extends up from the head and completely encloses the lower end of the handle shaft for about 6 inches. This overlapping of handle shaft and connecting socket serves to reinforce this stress point, which results in a long-lasting tool.

Once the tools have been purchased and put to use, it's a good idea to take the time to keep them in top shape. A wire brush or wooden scraper is handy to scrape away any sticky, clayey residue from shovel and spade blades. Going one step further, you can plunge the working end of the tool into a container of sand, and then wipe

manure crop is to be followed by early vegetables, the best time to turn it under is fall or winter. This allows plenty of time for decomposition during wet, cold months. Summer green manure crops decompose more rapidly and do not need to be tilled under until two or three weeks before planting the midsummer or fall vegetables. Of course, if the crop is woody, then decomposition will require more time. If you miss the chance to till before the crop matures, then either mow it for hay and wait until it grows back to green manuring stage before incorporating it into the soil, or go ahead and till under the mature crop, add manure, and wait at least one season before planting the garden.

down with an oily rag (use cooking oil rather than motor oil, since the latter will harm beneficial microorganisms in the soil).

And don't ignore the cutting edges of shovels and spades—these are the critical points that can either hinder or help your digging efforts. Check them periodically and keep these edges sharp with the aid of a file. The best setup for sharpening is one where you can clamp your tool in a vise, leaving both hands free to work the file. With a smooth motion, push the file away from you across the beveled edge of the tool, and simultaneously move it sideways. Lift the file from the blade as you bring it back for another stroke.

Before you put your tools away for the year, check them for any loose screws and bolts. And before they go into hibernation, clean off the entire surface and bury the working end in a container of sand mixed with oil.

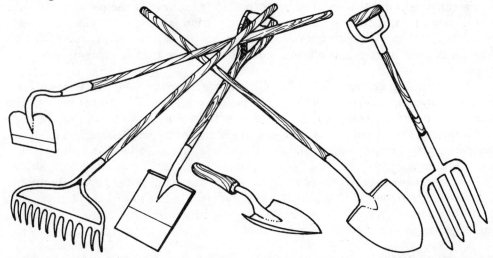

Basic Tools for the Garden: The act of gardening calls for certain tools in addition to those that are the most fundamental—your hands. A few basic tools can make the activities of digging and preparing the soil, fine-tuning the seedbed, planting, and cultivating go smoothly and effectively with less effort on your part. The basic complement of gardening equipment should include (from left to right) a hoe, rake, spade, trowel, shovel, and spading fork. Items like rotary tillers, wheelbarrows, and wheel cultivators are useful too, but generally only in large gardens.

A plow, disc, or rotary tiller may be used to incorporate plant matter into the soil. You may find that a very dense crop might need scything or mowing before it can be tilled, and even then could require several tillings to break it up. Hand digging, even in a fairly small plot, is inefficient and doesn't really do a complete job. On poor soil, or where you need to speed decomposition, it may be helpful to add manure, blood meal, or other nitrogen-rich materials during the tillage. This is not always necessary, however, and as long as the green manure is well chopped and mixed in with the soil, it will form humus.

No matter how succulent the green manure, allow at least two or three weeks between tilling and planting. Warm soil temperatures and rain will speed humus formation, but still it is best to wait at least several weeks in order to avoid problems with temporary nitrogen shortage in the soil. By planting time, most of the plant debris should have decomposed to the point of being indistinguishable from the rest of the soil.

Working the Soil

The purpose of working the soil every year—of spading, hoeing, turning, and raking—is threefold: to promote good fertility, drainage, absorption, and soil atmosphere; to remove woody plant residues or diseased debris; and to create a firm seedbed. Usually, preparations are done at two stages before planting. In the fall, diseased plant matter is removed, certain fertilizers added, and soil broken up and loosened. In the spring, other fertilizers are added, undecomposed debris removed, and the seedbed smoothed for planting. If factors outside your control don't permit this two-stage soil preparation, all the work can be done in the spring, but it will be much harder. Also, spring soil preparation allows less time for organic materials to break down into a form that is accessible to your crops.

By beginning cultivation in the fall, you further improve soil in two ways; first, by exposing overwintering insect pests to birds, cold temperatures, and wind, and second, by leaving the ground open to frost action. The work to be done in the spring is minimal and since less time is needed to get the seedbed in shape, you can start planting much earlier, a real advantage in boosting the yield of your garden.

The best time to cultivate is when the soil is damp but not soggy, and crumbly in texture. If too wet, it will compact and eventually form hard clods; if too dry, it will be reduced to a fine powder. By starting in the fall, you can afford to wait until the soil is exactly right for turning.

Cleaning Up

The first step of cultivation, whether the ground is to be worked by machine or by hand, in the fall or in the spring, is to remove the diseased and woody plant materials left over from the previous vegetable garden. (In the interest of disease control, remove all diseased plant debris in the fall, to give harmful organisms

tricks of the trade

Solarizing Your Soil

Sterilizing soil to get rid of harmful fungi and pathogens requires elaborate steam machines and chemicals, but a process devised by University of California professor Gerald Pullman is safe, simple, and nearly as effective. Soak the bare soil with water, then cover it with sheets of clear plastic (not the black plastic used to control weed growth). After several weeks in the sun, the soil will be "solarized"—almost 100 percent free of harmful organisms in the top 12 to 18 inches. But be ready to begin weeding, for that clear plastic acts as a greenhouse, providing a near-perfect environment for some pesky plants.

less time to become established.) Pull up cabbage, cauliflower, and broccoli stalks, tomato vines, and bean plants. When this work is done in the fall, some clean plant matter should be left in place as it will add bulk and will probably decompose during the winter. If you're doing this preliminary work in the spring, clear the plot of all plant matter, since there is not sufficient time for it to break down before planting. Add wastes to the compost heap, and bury them deeply in the pile to eliminate any pests.

Digging

After rough plant material and undecayed matter have been cleared away, turn the soil and add pH adjusting materials and fertilizers. (See the Introduction for guidelines on altering soil pH, and earlier sections in this chapter for guidelines on adding fertilizers.) If you are working your soil in the fall, you can safely add natural fertilizers that require a long period of time to break down and release their nutrients. If you are working your soil in the spring, you should concentrate on fast-acting fertilizers, those that make their nutrients available relatively quickly. (See the chart on Common Organic Materials and Their Relative Availability that appears earlier in the chapter.)

Depending on how large your garden is, you can turn the soil by hand or by rotary tiller. If you are using a rotary tiller, simply pass over the garden once the lime and fertilizer have been spread on the soil, following either a row-by-row or a circular pattern, spiraling in toward the center of the plot. Although the process consumes a lot more time and energy when done by hand, in some instances it is the only way to get the soil into the best shape possible for planting. Hand digging may be carried out in several different ways.

Probably the most common way of preparing fairly good, ordinary garden soil by hand involves digging a series of trenches. This "trenching and turning" method is the simplest way to prepare a garden plot, whether you are cutting through sod for a first-time garden or working a previously planted plot.

Trenching and Turning: This simple method of soil preparation is useful for either new or established garden plots. Using a keen-edged spade, dig a trench at one end of the plot and transport the soil to the other end. Then fill the first trench with soil from the adjacent trench by simply turning the soil into the empty one. Repeat this process until you work your way to the final trench. Fill this one with the soil that was set aside from the first trench.

Begin by digging a trench about 1 foot wide and just 8 inches deep along one end of the garden. If you are slicing through sod, a keen-edged spade will make the job much easier. There is no need to dig deeper than 8 inches unless you will be growing deep-rooted crops, and then you can go down 12 inches. If you dig too deeply you will turn up the poor subsoil, which has little nutrient value and virtually no organic matter.

Using a wheelbarrow, move this top layer of soil you have just removed from the trench to the far end of the garden patch, where it will be used to fill in the last trench. Next, dig a trench parallel to the first one, turning the dirt you lift from this second trench into the first trench. Continue this process, filling each trench with the soil from the succeeding one. Try to keep the edge of your trench straight up and down and the garden edges clean. Although a spade is the perfect tool for this edging work, a spading fork seems to work best when the soil is fairly heavy. Be sure to chop up any plant matter you uproot as you go, and bury it at various depths in the soil, particularly if you are spading sod. Fertilizers and lime may be added trench by trench, or you can broadcast them, raking the materials lightly into the soil after the entire plot has been turned.

For a garden that is being turned in the fall, do not smooth the surface too much. A rough soil surface benefits most from the twin actions of freezing and thawing, which serve to loosen the soil structure and create beneficial air pockets. However, sandy soil does not hold water, and freezing and thawing have little effect on its structure. Sandy soil can be raked smooth in fall and covered with a heavy mulch.

In the two-step, double-digging system, the soil is not turned, but transferred gently so that the soil layers aren't disturbed, and the subsoil is loosened to

Double-Digging: This method takes you down deep, beyond the top layer of soil, to break up the subsoil which often forms a hardpan impermeable to probing roots. To start, dig a trench and transport the topsoil to the other end of the plot. Loosen the subsoil in the bottom of the trench by plunging a spading fork into the soil and pushing it back and forth. Work your way along the trench with the spading fork, inserting it and using a pushing and pulling motion, until all the subsoil is loosened. Dig a second trench and transfer the topsoil to the first trench. Try to maintain the original top-to-bottom arrangement of the soil layers by sliding the soil into place instead of simply turning the shovel over and dumping. What you will end up with after the final trench is loosened and filled is a garden plot slightly higher than when you started, filled with loosened, almost fluffy soil.

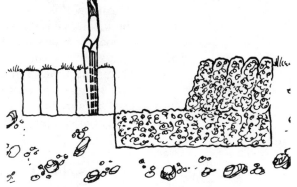

improve drainage and aeration. Begin by cutting away sod from the surface of the garden plot. Roll it up for composting or other uses. If a garden was planted there the previous year, simply clear away all woody plant debris. Next, dig a 2-foot-wide trench along one end of the bed, about 8 to 12 inches deep. Transport this soil to the far end of the plot, where it will be used to fill in the final trench. Instead of simply filling in the first trench with soil from the next one, loosen the subsoil at the bottom of the trench by pushing the fork deeply into it and working the fork back and forth. If the subsoil is very heavy, showing mottling with lots of clay, then you may need to remove at least some of it and add a bed of gravel and/or drainage tiles. Otherwise, just loosen it and leave it in place.

After the subsoil has been loosened, use the spade to remove the top 8 to 12 inches of soil in sections from the next 2-foot-wide trenching area. Soil should be slid off the spade so that the top of the soil slice stays on top and the bottom soil remains on the bottom. Continue trenching, loosening the subsoil, and sliding new topsoil into place until the whole bed has been dug and the last trench filled with soil from the first one. The result is a slightly raised bed of loose, friable soil.

Enhancing a Double-Dug Bed: Lighten up heavy soil or fortify otherwise good-textured soil in a double-dug bed by alternating layers of organic material with soil in the trenches. The addition of compost or well-rotted manure is especially important in intensively planted beds which must support a heavy concentration of crops.

If the garden soil is extremely heavy or otherwise in poor condition, or if you will be using intensive plant spacing, you can modify this double-digging method to create a looser, more fertile planting bed. Instead of simply filling in the trenches with soil from the succeeding trench, add alternate layers of well-rotted manure or compost. Place 3 inches of the manure or compost on top of the loosened subsoil, then 3 inches of topsoil, continuing until the garden surface is 4 to 5 inches above the surrounding ground level. Fill in the rest of the trenches with the same layers of compost or manure and soil.

Shaping Your Garden: Rows and Raised Beds

When most people imagine a vegetable garden, they picture a rectangular plot of ground, almost level with its surroundings, and planted in a series of straight and narrow rows—in short, a sort of miniature farm field. While this system seems to work fine on large farms where mechanical planting and harvesting are required, it isn't necessarily the best plan for the home gardener. First of all, with the soil nearly level to the surrounding yard, drainage is poor and the soil takes longer to warm in spring. Also, you must devote a large portion of the cultivated ground to paths that run between the planted rows. And, when you walk upon them during the season, they become compacted and all the more unsuitable for cultivation the following year.

Gardeners of old, both on this continent and in Europe and the Orient, had a much more sensible method for raising garden vegetables—in beds. These beds were raised some 6 to 12 inches above ground level, and were about 3 to 5 feet wide, an easy reach for an outstretched arm during weeding and planting. Because the gardeners didn't need to step into the beds to work, the soil remained loose and friable. Drainage and aeration were much improved, allowing the growing season to begin quite early in spring. By using sound organic soil-care techniques, they were able to grow many different high-quality crops in a seemingly limited space.

Today, these raised bed systems survive as integral parts of the intensive method of gardening. In this section, in addition to conventional rows, three types of raised beds are described—the growing bed, the structured-side bed, and the Chinese mound.

Rows

You can easily plan for the conventional row garden on paper in early spring. When the time comes to prepare the soil, you do your work in one large rectangular or square area, turning the soil, incorporating the appropriate organic matter, and adding the necessary fertilizers. This is where rowed gardens have their one possible advantage. The large, single area allows easy access for rotary tillers, plows, and other mechanical equipment. Not only is this a help in preparing the soil for a large garden area, but also for weeding and cultivating where mulching is not desired or practical. When you are ready to plant, you define the rows by following the recommendations for in-row spacing and between-row spacing given in the individual vegetable entries in the Guide to Vegetables for the Home Garden or on the seed packets themselves.

Growing Beds

The keystone of French Intensive gardening, the growing bed, was revived and improved by Alan Chadwick, a British horticulturist. Chadwick combined the best organic gardening techniques with techniques for maximum production to create a dynamic, successful gardening system.

Growing Beds: In addition to being the most efficient way to utilize garden space, these beds are neat and attractive showplaces for your vegetables. Once they are prepared, they save you time and labor, while providing four times the yield of the same area planted in conventional rows. Growing beds are easy to design and can be modified to suit any garden plan.

In this system, the garden area is divided into rectangular beds, intersected by narrow paths. These beds are slightly raised, narrow areas that are never walked upon once they have been prepared. For this reason, they should be no wider than 3 to 5 feet—3 feet where there is access from only one side, up to 5 feet where the bed can be reached from both sides. Length depends on your own tastes and the available space. Allow for paths 1 foot or wider between beds, and consider running a wider central path of 2 to 3 feet the length of the garden area, to make room for wheelbarrows and garden tools.

Growing beds are double-dug, according to the instructions given earlier in the chapter. This is hard work, but the results are well worth the effort. As you work the soil, you are loosening it to a depth of 20 to 24 inches, which improves drainage and aeration considerably. Unless your soil is in excellent condition, as you dig you should add rotted manure and other organic materials. With these infusions of organic material the level of the beds should be some 4 to 5 inches above ground level. This further improves drainage, and tends to create a warmer soil for growing plants. The high organic matter content (at least 20 percent for best results), helps the garden support heavy, intensive crop production. With careful planning, a variety of crops may be planted close together, with plenty of nutrients and moisture for all. Yields are generally as much as four times that of the same square footage planted in conventional rows.

Structured-Side Beds

One variation of the raised bed often brings even higher yields, particularly where native soil is quite heavy or otherwise of poor quality. By adding structured

Structured-Side Bed: Gardening problems caused by poor soils and inadequate drainage can be remedied by building a structured-side bed. The sides are made of sturdy materials like wood or concrete and the beds are filled with soil "made to order." You can mix topsoil with organic materials like compost, leaf mold, or peat moss to arrive at a soil possessing all the qualities needed for optimum vegetable growth.

sides to the beds, you can raise the soil as much as 2 or 3 feet above ground level. This enables you to improve your own soil by piling compost, loamy soil, rotted manure, and other organic matter on top of a double-dug bed. Railroad ties, masonry "walls," cement blocks, stones, bricks, or wooden frames may be used as side supports. Where drainage is extremely poor, first lay down a layer of gravel or sand, then bring in a load of topsoil from outside the bed. Layer rich compost or well-rotted manure with the topsoil to provide the best soil consistency.

Drawbacks to this system are minor in comparison to the problems you would face gardening with your native soil in traditional ways. Slugs and snails may hide in the rock walls or railroad ties. Also, the soil tends to remain fairly wet in early spring because the sides prevent air circulation. However, you'll probably be able to plant earlier than if you were working in a traditional vegetable patch that is level with the surrounding soil. As a bonus, these high-rise beds tend to be easy to maintain and require less stooping and straining on your part. As long as the beds are kept fairly small and manageable, you can create excellent soil conditions in just one or two seasons.

Chinese Mounds

Gardeners who wish to avoid the hard work of double-digging will find the Chinese mound system a practical alternative to growing beds. Fully described in Peter Chan's book, *Better Vegetable Gardens the Chinese Way* (see the Bibliography), Chinese mounds are the traditional beds of oriental gardening. Like the growing beds described above, these are narrow, slightly raised areas with a series of permanent paths connecting them. However, unlike growing beds, these are only single-dug, saving both time and labor. Studies at the University of Maine indicate that, where soil is not excessively compacted, double-digging will not make a significant difference over single-digging or rotary tilling. If your soil is basically in good shape, you can simply turn it, and incorporate plenty of compost, manure, and other materials into the first 12 inches. This procedure will raise the bed and sufficiently loosen most soils. If you're planning on building a series of mounds, you should have an ample supply of organic matter on hand.

The exact dimensions of your Chinese mounds will vary according to your particular gardening space. You can make them any length you desire, but they should be about 4 feet wide at the base and 3 feet wide at the surface, with gently sloping sides. After adding the organic matter, the soil in the mound should extend about 6 inches above the surrounding ground level. As with growing beds, you must allow room for dirt paths alongside the beds, or if you prefer, lay stones for permanent paths. These mounds can be easily prepared and planted year after year without ever being stepped upon, thus keeping the ground light and friable. Since they are open to air and sun, like the growing beds, you'll find that the mounds dry out very quickly in spring so you can begin to plant quite early in the season. As with growing beds, if you lay the mounds out in an east-west direction they can take full advantage of the sunshine, making planting possible still earlier.

Preparing the Seedbed

Before seeds can be sown or plants set out in the garden bed, soil must be raked smooth and leveled. This is best done on a dry day, just before planting. If final preparations are made too far in advance, a hard crust may form on the soil surface, making further cultivation necessary before seeds can be planted.

Clear away any undecayed green manure or woody plant debris still remaining in the garden. By allowing such materials to remain in the soil, you are simply inviting disease and insect damage. Rocks brought to the surface through winter frost heaving should also be removed, and large clods broken apart with your fingers, hoe, or rake. Don't pound the soil, for this will compact it. If a clod doesn't break apart with a light tap of the hoe or rake, then just rake it aside. The goal is to have a perfectly smooth, light, fine soil to a depth of 8 to 12 inches, or even slightly deeper for root crops such as long carrots or parsnips. To keep the soil as loose as possible, avoid walking on it. If you have opted for a gardening system like the growing bed or Chinese mound, then this will be no problem. However, if you are working in a standard one-plot vegetable patch with rows, then you will be unable to avoid walking in it and compacting some of the soil. The best solution is to lay down boards to walk on, or at least to walk only in the places where paths will be laid out at planting time.

Next, rake the garden area smooth so that the tops of any raised beds are level, with only a gradual slope on the sides. If the slope is too great, wind or rain will cause the beds to collapse. Furrows, pits, and small irregularities in the soil surface will result in puddling or drying out and will cut down on the germination of your seeds. The smoother the seedbed, the better the germination and initial growth will be. When the bed is completely raked and clean, water it lightly with a fine mist, not a heavy stream, and allow it to rest a few hours before planting. This brief waiting period gives the water a chance to percolate into air pockets in the soil and lets the ground firm up.

A Calendar of Soil Care

The following calendar offers a "plan of attack" of sorts for managing your vegetable garden soil on a year-round basis. Notice that most of the work is best done during spring and fall, conveniently leaving summer free for plant care.

Fall: This is the season of renewal—organic matter and certain nutrients removed by plants during summer months are now returned to the soil for breakdown during the fall and winter months.

Clean Up: Remove diseased plant material and woody stalks and shoots. If you are planning a first-year garden, cut away sod.

Green Manure: In the North, work in any summer green manure crop and/or plant a hardy winter cover crop. In the South, cut legume green manure crops and leave as a mulch or till under and plant a nonlegume cover crop.

Soil-Care Cycle: Tending the soil is a year-round process, as shown in this simple cycle. The arrival of each season brings a reminder to take care of certain needs the soil has, in order to ensure its ongoing health.

Test: Send soil samples to the local county agent for testing or follow instructions for a do-it-yourself chemical soil test. Also, take note of the physical properties of your soil and any signs of change from previous years.

Fertilize: Apply lime, phosphorus fertilizers, and organic matter as dictated by the soil test.

Dig: Prepare the soil by trenching and turning, double-digging, or any other procedure you choose. Add drainage material such as gravel and/or tiles, if necessary. Leave a rough surface, particularly if you are gardening in the North with a fairly heavy soil.

Mulch: Mulch may be applied now for winter protection from frosts and erosion, but this is not necessary and may not even be advised if soil is in poor condition and would benefit from frost heavage.

Winter: The garden soil does most of its own work during winter months, provided you have supplied all the necessary microorganisms and materials for soil enhancement.

Mulch: Many gardeners wait until midwinter to apply a mulch since, by this time, harmful grubs and other organisms will have been exposed to freezing temperatures. A thick mulch, applied along with hot (fresh) manure on a cold day in late winter will encourage the soil to warm up that much earlier in the spring.

Spring: During early spring months, soil must be aired out, and allowed to dry before plants and seeds are started. Final fertilization is done.

Clean Up: Remove large pieces of undecayed plant matter and rake away winter mulch, unless permanent mulching is being practiced. Clear away rocks and clods of soil.

Green Manure: Incorporate winter green manures at least two to three weeks before planting seeds. Summer green manures can be planted for early tillage in late spring, or for summer or fall tillage.

Test: Make a final pH test of the soil to be sure that any problems were corrected by the fall liming or organic matter amendments.

Fertilize: Apply potassium and nitrogen fertilizers, along with additional organic matter, as necessary. Lime if tests show pH deficiency.

Rake: Level the soil and rake smooth.

Water: Gently water the soil in preparation for seed planting.

Summer: After mulching, soil usually requires little care other than occasional watering (see chapter 4) and fertilizing.

Mulch: After plants have developed several sets of leaves, apply a heavy mulch of organic matter or choose from such inorganic materials as black plastic, aluminum foil, or rocks.

Water: Periodically, check soil moisture with a moisture gauge (see chapter 4). If soil seems wet, consider drainage ditches.

Inspect: If plants show signs of disease or insect damage, check soil for signs of hiding pests. Rake back mulch as necessary or apply organic insecticides if absolutely unavoidable. "Solarize" garden spots infested with damping-off or other fungal or bacterial diseases. (See the box on Solarizing Your Soil earlier in this chapter.)

3

Planting

In order to make maximum use of the growing season with minimum risk to the garden's health, gardeners in all regions need patience and planning. They also need to be aware of their particular soil type, local climate, and the needs of crops they intend to raise. Before planting the garden, learn when to expect the last frost in your area, which plants can handle that freeze, and how to manage the idiosyncracies of your particular garden climate. Decide which crops should be direct-seeded in the garden and which will be raised from transplants. Then, when the safe planting time finally arrives, use the best techniques to assure top yields throughout the entire growing season.

Deciding When to Plant

Garden guides almost always include planting charts or maps showing the "mean" or "average" dates of the last spring frosts throughout the country. While these may help you decide when to plant, they are misleading. First of all, mean dates of last frost are just that—the mean, or middle, dates taken from a long list of last frost dates as they occurred over the years. It's easy to overlook the fact that such charts are only predictions, and are wrong as often as they are right. Crops planted on the appropriate mean date of last frost stand a 50–50 chance of being hit with subfreezing temperatures. It is not until two or three weeks after this date, the "frost-free" date, that chances of a killing frost are minimal.

Determining the Frost-Free Date

A fairly sound prediction of the last frost date, and hence the frost-free date, is necessary in planning just when to start certain seeds indoors, transplant other crops, and direct-seed in the garden. One way to make more accurate predictions is to keep your own records. Your backyard climate may be quite different from that of the surrounding locale. A large lake or nearby pond will tend to act as a kind of stabilizer of temperature shifts, lowering spring temperatures and raising fall temperatures. Temperatures are generally lower in higher elevations or on northern exposures, but some low-lying areas are colder than higher slopes because cold air masses tend to settle in the lowest areas. Windbreaks, protective buildings, and southern exposures can act as buffers in the immediate area against a drop in temperature. Thus, it is important to become familiar with your garden's particular microclimate.

Each year, note the date of the last spring frost as it occurs in your garden area. If you are new to the area, find out about its general climatic history from

Plant Hardiness and Outdoor Seed-Sowing Dates

Cool-Season Crops		Warm-Season Crops	
Hardy: withstand subfreezing temperatures. Plant 4 to 6 weeks before frost-free date.	*Half-Hardy:* withstand some light freezing (short-term exposure to subfreezing temperatures). Plant 2 to 4 weeks before frost-free date.	*Tender:* fruit and leaves injured by light frosts. Plant on frost-free date.	*Very Tender:* need warm temperatures (above 70°F) for growth. Any exposure to temperatures just above freezing will damage fruit or leaves. Plant 1 week or more after frost-free date.
Broccoli	Beets	Asparagus peas	Beans, lima
Brussels sprouts	Carrots*	Beans, shell	Corn (depending on variety planted
Cabbage	Cauliflower	Beans, snap	
Chinese cabbage	Celeriac	Corn (depending on variety planted)	Cucumbers
Chives	Celery		Eggplant
Collards	Cresses	Cowpeas	Luffa
Garlic	Endive	Malabar spinach	Peanuts
Horseradish	Escarole	New Zealand Spinach	Peppers
Kale	Lettuce*	Okra	Pumpkins
Kohlrabi	Mustard	Soybeans	Squash, summer
Leeks	Parsnips	Tomatoes	Squash, winter
Onions	Potatoes, white		Sweet potatoes
Peas	Radishes*		
Rhubarb	Swiss chard		
Rutabaga			
Salsify			
Scallions			
Spinach			
Turnips			

*These plants are classed as half-hardy because they withstand only light freezing; however, they can be planted at the same time as hardy crops and protected from extreme cold.

the local weather service office (there are 300 of these offices in the United States listed in the phone book under U.S. Government, Department of Commerce; gardeners in Canada should contact a local independent weather station and request the information). Then speak with neighboring gardeners to find out when they start to plant, harvest fall crops, and the like. After several years of first-hand observation, you will begin to see a pattern and will know just how your garden's climate differs from the weather service description of that latitude. Make a mental note of the approximate date of the last frost, add two to three weeks, and you will know the frost-free date for your area.

Sowing Seeds Outdoors

You can gauge the best time to sow your crops outdoors by relating this frost-free date to the cold-resistance capacities of your plants. Vegetable crops are classified according to four levels of cold tolerance: hardy, half-hardy, tender, and very tender. The Plant Hardiness and Outdoor Seed-Sowing Dates chart places common vegetables in their appropriate hardiness category. Along with each category, the general time for planting in relation to the frost-free date is given.

Another point of reference you should use in conjunction with plant hardiness and the frost-free date is soil temperature. Each vegetable has an optimum temperature range at which its seed will germinate, and for best results, you should plant only when the soil temperature is within that range. For example, crops like beans and corn will rot if the soil isn't warm enough. Germination temperatures are given in individual entries in the Vegetable Guide. A soil thermometer is a relatively inexpensive garden tool available in many garden centers or through mail-order catalogs. With a thermometer, it's easy to pinpoint the soil's temperature and determine when the time is right to plant.

Sowing Seeds Indoors

For judging when to start seeds indoors and when to set young plants outdoors, use the frost-free date, the number of weeks it takes to grow a seedling to transplant size, and air temperature as your guidelines. These procedures are discussed in detail later in this chapter.

The Daylength Factor

One other factor that can influence planting time and crop development is daylength. For certain crops, flowering and fruiting are induced by daylength (or photoperiod) as well as by temperature. There are even a few crops that are entirely governed by daylength. Fortunately, most crops are day-neutral, which means their flowering and fruiting are brought on more by temperature and moisture conditions than by daylength, so they are easily adapted to a variety of latitudes and planting dates.

However, when you are planting spinach, potatoes, and onions, you must keep their daylength requirements in mind. Both spinach and potatoes are long-day plants that require short nights to flower or form tubers, and these processes are inhibited if nights are longer than a certain critical length (which differs among plants). Since flowering signals the end of spinach's usefulness as an edible crop, you want to plant it in early spring when the days are short (nights are long) to inhibit the natural cycle of flowering and seed production. But if you misjudge your planting date and your crop is growing when temperatures rise and nights become shorter than eight hours, your spinach will bolt to seed and turn bitter.

Conversely, with potatoes, you are growing them specifically for their tubers, so you want to plant them with respect to their need for long days (longer than 10 hours) and short nights (less than 14 hours).

The onion is another vegetable with a performance that is affected by day-length. Certain varieties form bulbs under short-day conditions, while others require long days to form bulbs.

With all these vegetables—spinach, potatoes, and onions—it is important to select varieties appropriate to your latitude and to carefully plan planting dates. (See the individual entries in the Vegetable Guide for varieties recommended for various latitudes and information on when to plant.)

Taking and Minimizing Risks

A number of different propagation techniques can be used to minimize weather risks. If all vegetables had to be started from seed sown directly in the garden, many crops of tropical origin could not be raised in the United States and Canada. Even with the use of mulches, hotcaps, and cold frames, the growing season is just too short for eggplants, tomatoes, and certain other crops to develop in the garden from seed to fruition. Fortunately, while many vegetables are best grown from seed planted outdoors, many do well when started inside for later transplanting to the garden, which gives the plants a jump on the season. Others, like horseradish, onions, and rhubarb, are best started by root, tuber, corm, or bulb, rather than from seed. When you are selecting a mode of propagation, consider both the climate in your area and the plant's physiological characteristics (hardiness, days to maturity, life cycle) to help find the technique that will give you the best results. Don't be afraid to experiment, either. For instance, while most gardeners in your area start their squash indoors, you may find that by starting yours directly outdoors, the plants will be healthier and more prolific.

Storing and Testing Seeds

All vegetables can be propagated by seed, and for most, this is the simplest method. You can purchase seeds from mail-order suppliers, or from local garden, grocery, and hardware stores. Many gardeners believe that stock bought from the grower is fresher than that purchased at the hardware or grocery store, but this is not necessarily true. Reputable merchants will not try to sell last year's seed, and seed suppliers will not distribute it. Each packet is usually stamped with an expiration date, indicating when seeds can no longer be depended upon for high performance. Just to be sure, read packets before you purchase them, and speak up if you do find outdated seeds on display.

Storing Seeds

Seeds can survive almost indefinitely in a more or less suspended state when given the proper environment. Although optimum storage life varies among species, most seeds will survive at least two years, with some lasting for centuries. With a little care and thought, it is a simple enough task to save seeds for use in next year's garden, whether they are leftovers from the seed you purchased, or seeds you have gathered from your own plants. (See the individual entries in the Vegetable Guide for specifics on how long unused seed is good.)

The most important storage factor is low moisture content. Seed growers dry vegetable seeds in order to lower the moisture content as much as possible. Most seeds readily absorb water and, if stored in a damp atmosphere, will increase their respiration and enzyme action. In a proper planting environment, this would lead to germination and growth. In storage, it leads to molding and rot. For that reason, you should store your seeds at a relative humidity of less than 65 percent.

Each species of seed differs in its temperature requirements. For most, the best temperature is between 0° and 32°F. Temperature is interrelated with humidity, so that the higher the humidity, the higher the temperature must be. A good rule of thumb is that combined temperature and humidity should be kept at less than 100.

Seed life can be further extended by placing seeds in a sealed container. This reduces the oxygen content and creates a controlled atmosphere. The best containers for seed storage are metal tins or sterile glass jars with tight-fitting lids sealed with freezer tape. To avoid identification problems, leave seeds in their labeled packets or envelopes. Powdered milk, cornstarch, or silica gel can be added to absorb excess moisture and maintain low humidity. Containers may then be kept in an unheated garage or attic, a refrigerator, or in any other cool, dark, dry place.

Testing for Germination Rate

Any seeds which have been stored over the winter should be tested for their viability, or germination rate. Seeds coming directly from the grower to the gardener usually have a tested rate of about 80 to 95 percent, meaning 80 to 95 out of every 100 seeds will germinate under proper conditions. Rates naturally decline as seeds are stored. By testing before you plant, you can determine how many seeds must be sown in order to guarantee a certain number of mature plants.

To test seeds, place 20 to 50 seeds on a moistened blotter of paper towels or a piece of cotton fabric. You can either cover the seeds and blotter with a bell jar, or place a damp towel on top. The idea is to keep the seeds moist and to protect them from cool, drying drafts. Lift the jar or towel each day in order to air seeds, add water, and check for germination. Wait the average number of days to germination (given on seed packets), and preferably one week longer, before counting the results. Count the number of seeds germinated, then divide by the number tested to get the germination rate in percentage form. If it is below 60 percent, consider purchasing new seed. If it is between 60 and 80 percent, just plant the seeds more thickly in order to assure an adequate number of plants.

Starting Seeds Indoors

Starting seeds inside in flats not only speeds up the harvest date, but ultimately saves money on transplant costs and increases the variety and range of the crops grown in the outdoor garden. Greenhouse transplants typically sell for 2 to 20 times the cost of the seed needed to produce them. Often they have been chemically fertilized and sprayed with insecticides, or may be diseased, damaged, or too far along in their own growth cycle by the time you are ready to plant them. In the end, a moderate investment of time and money will let you produce healthier transplants at home.

Most gardening guides suggest starting cole crops, eggplants, peppers, and

Plant Response to Transplanting

Group A: plants that suffer little or no damage from proper transplanting.		Group B: plants that tolerate careful transplanting when roots are not disturbed in the process. (Start seeds in individual containers; handle seedlings as little as possible, and thin by cutting instead of lifting.)		Group C: plants that don't take transplanting well. Extra care will yield some survivors. (Treat as for Group B. Any disturbance to roots will check growth.)	
Artichoke, Jerusalem (dormant only)	Garlic	Artichoke, globe	Spinach	Beans	Peanuts
Asparagus (dormant only)	Kale	Beets	Squash, summer and winter	Corn	Peas
Broccoli	Kohlrabi	Carrots	Swiss chard	Okra	
Brussels sprouts	Leeks	Cucumbers	Turnips		
Cabbage	Lettuce	Parsnips			
Cauliflower	Mustard	Pumpkins			
Celery	Onions				
Collards	Parsley				
Eggplant	Peppers				
Endive	Rhubarb (dormant only)				
Escarole	Shallots				
	Tomatoes				

Guide to Figuring Indoor Planting and Setting-Out Dates

Vegetable	Column I Weeks to Transplant Size (from time of sowing)	Column II Spring Setting-Out Dates (in relation to frost-free date)	
		Weeks Before	Weeks After
Asparagus	12–14	—	4
Beans, lima	3–4	—	1–2
Beans, snap	3–4	—	1–2
Beets	4	4	—
Broccoli	6–8	4	2–3
Brussels sprouts	6–8	4	2–3
Cabbage	6–8	5	2–3
Carrots	5–6	4	—
Cauliflower	6–8	4	2
Celery	6–8	3	3–4
Collards	6–8	4	2
Corn	4	—	2–3
Cucumbers	2–3	1	—
Eggplant	8–10	—	2–3
Endive and Escarole	4–5	4	2
Garlic	4–6	2–4	1
Kale	6–8	5	2
Kohlrabi	6–8	5	2
Leeks	4–6	5	2
Lettuce	4–6	2	3
Mustard	4–6	5	2
Okra	6–8	—	3–4
Onions, bulbing	4–6	6	2
Onions, bunching	4–6	4–5	2
Parsley	4–6	4–6	4–6
Parsnips	4–6	4	3–4
Peanuts	4–6	Plant on	frost-free date
Peas	4	4	2–3
Peppers	6–8	—	2–3
Spinach	4–6	3–6	—
Squash, summer	4	—	4
Squash, winter	4	—	3–4
Sweet potatoes	6–8	—	2–3
Swiss chard	4	3–4	—
Tomatoes	6–10	—	4
Turnips	3–4	4	—

tomatoes indoors. Although these are the vegetables most commonly started early from seed, you aren't limited to only these—there are many more vegetables that can be treated this way with good results. However, you should be aware that some vegetables respond to transplanting better than others, and that plants such as beans, corn, and peas can be very difficult to move into the garden successfully. Consult the chart on Plant Response to Transplanting before deciding which of your vegetables will benefit from a head start indoors.

The next thing you must do is determine when to start your seeds indoors. This is easy to figure out by taking the setting-out date (when seedlings can be safely moved to the garden) and counting back the number of weeks it takes to grow the vegetable to transplant size. Timing is important because if you start your seeds too soon, the plants will outgrow their pots and become tall and gangly. It's better to err on the side of lateness when starting seeds, for young plants transplant more successfully than old ones.

Use the chart, Guide to Figuring Indoor Planting and Setting-Out Dates, and a calendar to help you with your calculations. The spring setting-out dates for the various vegetables are given in terms of weeks before and after the frost-free date. To pinpoint these dates for your own area, start by determining the frost-free date (two to three weeks after the local last frost date). Make a note of the frost-free date in the appropriate spaces on your calendar. Depending on the hardiness of your crops, you will then either subtract or add the weeks given in Column II to this date, to arrive at the precise setting-out date for each vegetable. Mark the setting-out date on the calendar also.

Now use this setting-out date as your starting point and count back the number of weeks it takes to grow your particular vegetable seed to transplant size (given in Column I). This date is when you can start your seed indoors.

As a working example, here's the way to figure the indoor planting date for cabbage seeds in an area where the last frost date is April 20.

1. Add 2 to 3 weeks (in this case, 2½ weeks have been added) to the last frost date of April 20, to arrive at a May 8 frost-free date.

2. Count back five weeks (see Column II, Cabbage) from the frost-free date to find the setting-out date—April 3.

3. From this setting-out date, count back six to eight weeks (see Column I, Cabbage) to settle on the indoor seed-planting dates of Feb. 7 to 21.

Germinating Media

Germinating seeds, young seedlings, and maturing plants all have slightly different needs, and the same mix should not be used for all three stages of growth. From the sowing to thinning stage, the growing medium should be quite loose, fine, and able to hold moisture without becoming soggy. It must also be firm enough to hold a tiny seedling upright, particularly after watering. Because newly germinated seedlings have their own food supply, the starter mix should not be too rich. Most seedlings are usually transplanted to individual containers or flats holding a richer growing medium before they have exhausted the food stored in their seeds.

Gardeners quibble over the best soil to use for seed starting, but all generally

Seed-Starting Mixes

2 qt. sphagnum peat moss	1 qt. loamy soil, pasteurized	1 qt. sphagnum peat moss	1 qt. peat moss
1 qt. vermiculite	1 qt. peat moss	1 qt. vermiculite	1 qt. soil, pasteurized
1 qt. perlite	1 qt. sharp sand	1 qt. perlite	1 qt. perlite
1 tbsp. dolomite lime			

agree that it must be sterile, or at least pasteurized, so it is free from disease-carrying organisms, harmful insects, and viable weed seeds. Sterile soil or planting mix can be bought at most garden stores; pasteurized soil can be made by placing your own garden soil in a 180°F oven for 30 to 45 minutes. This will not produce absolutely weed-free, organism-free material, but it will virtually eliminate the chances of damping-off or other soilborne problems. If you were to heat the soil to kill all weed seeds and organisms, you would run the risk of creating an intolerably high salt level in the soil.

Whether you select soil or one of the artificial soilless media now on the market will depend mostly on cost and intended use. If your soil is poor, you can buy an artificial mix, but be aware that many of these contain chemical fertilizers. You can easily make organically acceptable germinating mixes right at home from a number of inexpensive, readily available ingredients. Perlite, vermiculite, sawdust, or peat moss may all be used alone or in combination to start seeds. Since the only requirement is that the medium be well drained, clean, and able to hold moisture, the possibilities are endless. Unless you plan on leaving some or all of the seedlings in this medium until planting out, fertility need not be a concern. Several formulas are suggested in the chart on Seed-Starting Mixes, some containing soil and some without, but experience will help you develop your own recipe.

Containers

There are all kinds of seed-starting containers for sale, and many others you can make or "recycle" from household throw-aways. Practically anything will do, provided it has drainage holes, is sufficiently deep to allow for adequate root growth, and has been sterilized. Select containers at least 2½ to 3 inches deep, and use deeper ones for larger transplants. Wash used containers in a 10 percent bleach solution, boil them for 10 to 12 minutes, or clean them with rubbing alcohol.

The most common planting containers are plastic or wooden flats sold in garden shops. These rectangular shallow boxes are used for starting large numbers of plants, and are especially good for easily transplanted crops such as cabbage, lettuce, and tomatoes. A foil roasting or loaf pan will serve the same purpose, provided you have cut drainage slits in the bottom. You can also construct your own flat from scrap lumber. (See the box on Building a Customized Flat.)

Some gardeners prefer to sow seeds in individual pots so that seedling roots do not have to be untangled during transplanting. This is especially critical when

Seed Starters: Despite their dissimilar appearances, these containers have several things in common. They allow for good drainage, are spacious enough to accommodate seedlings, and where practicable, have been thoroughly cleaned or sterilized. From left to right, the containers shown here include plastic pots, trimmed milk cartons, peat pots, peat discs (compressed and expanded), a cast-off muffin tin, newspaper cuffs, and an egg carton.

starting any temperamental crops that don't tolerate disturbance of their roots. (See the chart on Plant Response to Transplanting, Groups B and C.) To avoid serious setbacks when these plants are transferred to the garden, grow them in individual containers which can be gently peeled away from the root mass, or which will decompose in the ground, thus eliminating the need for separating container and plant. Any biodegradable containers like milk cartons, sections of rolled newspapers, or peat pots will do. Since no transplanting will be done as the seedlings are maturing, start these crops in a rich growing medium which will nourish their growth until they are set out in the garden. (See the chart on Rich Mixes for Seedlings, later in this chapter.)

Peat pots are often recommended for seed starting, but they are expensive and tend to dry out, draining water away from plant roots. If you do use them, moisten the pots at least half an hour before filling them with soil (six to eight hours before is even better). Place them in flats, filling spaces between the pots with moist peat moss or soil. Keep the whole setup well watered.

Garden centers and nurseries usually carry compressed peat discs wrapped in plastic netting, marketed under the names "Jiffy-Seven" or "Plant Pellets." These cubes and pellets are soil and container all in one, and they provide a perfect environment for germinating seeds. They are usually inexpensive and more easily handled than the standard peat pots; however, the plastic netting which encases the pellets may constrict roots. Before you set these peat discs into the garden, snip open the plastic netting to make it easier for the roots to work their way out into the garden soil.

Probably the simplest, most reliable individual containers are the round or square plastic pots which may cost a bit more, but can usually be recycled for several seasons. These come in varying sizes, from very small ones suitable for initial plantings to 4-inch pots for eggplant, pepper, or tomato seedlings. Yet

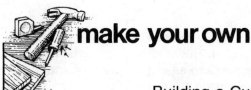

make your own

Building a Customized Flat

A flat is one of the best friends a seed starter can have. It cradles the germinating medium and seeds in place until that magical moment when leaves have sprouted, roots have developed, and the seedlings are sturdy enough to be moved into individual containers.

If you've ever inherited a flat from a nursery or greenhouse, no doubt it fit these standard measurements—2½ inches deep, 22 inches long, and 12 inches wide. These dimensions evolved as a convenient size for use in the greenhouse, but as a home gardener, you don't need to be concerned with how a flat fits between the cramped aisles of a greenhouse. This frees you to deviate from the standard measurements and build functional flats from pieces of scrap wood.

Depth is the only critical dimension. Your flat should be at least 2½ inches deep because at least that much soil is needed to accommodate the quick, probing growth of seedling roots. A 3-inch-deep flat holds the right amount of soil and allows a margin between the soil surface and the top of the flat. As for length and width, they vary according to the number of seedlings you want to start in each flat. You should plant one type of seed per flat, and allow ½ to 1 inch between seeds in all directions. (Use the lesser distance for small to medium-sized seed, and the greater distance for large seed.) Based on these spacings and the number of seedlings that you want, you can calculate the dimensions of your flat.

Any type of wood can be used. Pine, recycled wooden crates, and exterior plywood are the sturdiest materials and will hold up the longest. Hardboard (Masonite) and interior plywood will rot quickly and cut short the life of your flat.

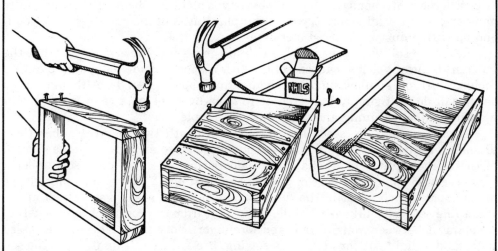

Do-It-Yourself Flat: With some scrap lumber and a little know-how, you can build a first-rate seed-starting container in nothing flat. Start with two equal sides and two equal ends and nail the frame together. Set the frame down and nail random-width pieces of wood across the bottom, leaving a slight space between adjacent pieces (to promote good drainage). What you've got when you're done is a low-cost, no-frills container ready for seasons of use.

another option are the lightweight plastic trays with attached individual growing compartments, which allow you to easily push the seedlings from the compartments without damage to the roots. Clay pots are a good sturdy choice, and like the plastic ones, they can be reused from season to season. You can press milk cartons into duty by trimming them down to within 3 or 4 inches of the bottom and adding drainage slits. Paper cups make good individual containers, and so do cylinders of newspaper which you slice into 4- to 5-inch sections and secure around the circumference with a piece of string. You must set these newspaper rings into a flat or plastic tray before planting since they have no bottoms of their own to support the soil and seedlings.

Sowing the Seeds

Usually seeds will germinate within one to two weeks of being planted in a warm, moist medium, but a few vegetables are slow sprouters. Some vegetable seeds have very hard coats which must be scarified (scratched or softened) before germination can take place. There are several ways you can scarify seed to hasten germination. Cover beet, carrot, celery, and parsnip seeds with boiling water and allow them to soak for several hours (or until the seed coat splits) before planting. Encourage early germination of New Zealand spinach by scratching the seed coat with a sharp knife, file, or sandpaper.

Prepare flats and pots by placing a layer of perlite, fine gravel, coarse sand, sphagnum moss, or other light material on the bottom. This promotes good drainage. If container holes are large, cover the bottom with damp paper towels before you add drainage material. Fill with moistened soil or germinating mix to within ½ inch of the container's rim. If peat moss or vermiculite is being used, thoroughly moisten the material before trying to fill planting containers. Otherwise, you'll end up with a dusty, scattered mess.

Level the soil with your hand, a shingle or a stick. Press gently so that the medium is firm, yet not packed solid. With a spoon handle, stick, or planting dibble, mark off shallow furrows, about 1 inch apart, in flats. Although small seeds will do well simply scattered at random over the surface of the flat, row planting makes thinning and transplanting simpler.

As a general rule, seeds are buried at a depth two to three times their diameter. Seeds ordinarily planted deeply outdoors to avoid frost damage may, of course, be planted more shallowly indoors. In individual pots, sow at least three seeds so you can be sure of getting one good plant. In the flats, place large seeds about 1 inch apart in the furrows, and medium seeds just ½ inch apart. Plant fine seed as thinly as possible, shaking it from the corner of the packet, or dropping it between your thumb and forefinger. Very fine seed may be mixed with sand or light soil for more even sowing. Press the seeds lightly into the soil surface, then cover with the proper amount of soil or mix. Do not plant fine seed too deeply; just cover very lightly with peat moss, sand, or soil.

Once you have sown the seeds in pots and along the marked furrows in flats, water very gently with a mister. Too strong a stream of water will disrupt the spacing and perhaps flood the containers, so go slowly. Let the water fall from above, like rain. Next, label, date, and cover the containers with burlap, cheese-

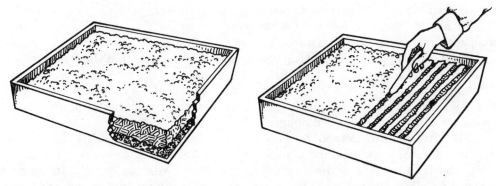

Preparing a Flat: The first step calls for adding a layer of drainage material, to keep the seedlings from becoming waterlogged. This flat has a drainage layer of coarse sand and perlite. Next pour in the growing mix, then level and firm it gently. A Popsicle stick is the perfect tool with which to draw evenly spaced shallow furrows across the surface.

cloth, or plastic in order to maintain a moist soil surface. Do not allow any covering to rest on the soil, and be sure to leave a small opening for air to enter and escape. Place the container in a warm spot, preferably where air temperatures will not fall below 65°F. For a more precise temperature guide, turn to individual crops in the Vegetable Guide to find the best soil temperature for germination. To keep soil temperatures sufficiently high during germination, you can set containers on top of the refrigerator or television, above a fluorescent light ballast, or on a plate warmer. If warmth is going to be a problem for the entire time the plants are indoors, and you are using flats as opposed to individual pots, consider buying some heating cables or coils at the local garden shop. Place these in the bottom of each flat, bury them in several inches of vermiculite or perlite, and then cover with a screen before adding the soil mixture. A thermostat and timer allow for easy control.

Most seeds will germinate in total darkness, so there is no need to worry about light levels until germination has occurred and seedlings have broken the soil surface. The one common exception to this rule is lettuce, which does need some light for germination. You can make sure lettuce receives enough light by not covering the seeds with growing medium.

As water collects on plastic coverings, shake it off, letting the droplets fall back onto the soil surface. During these early days before the seeds have sprouted, it is important to maintain moist conditions without allowing mold to form. If mold or fungal growth does develop, remove the covering, and watch the container carefully for further signs of infestation. You have probably failed to provide adequate drainage; as long as sterile or pasteurized medium has been used, there should be no serious problems.

Caring for Seedlings

As soon as you see green shoots appearing on the soil surface, remove all coverings. This period just after sprouting, until seedlings are moved to the garden, is one of the most crucial in the plants' lives, and requires close attention if good results are to be obtained. You must make sure that the plants are neither chilled nor overheated, neither overwatered nor allowed to dry out. Household temperatures are usually satisfactory. Slow, steady growth is preferable to quick, succulent growth; if plants shoot up too rapidly, this is a sign that the temperature is too high. Ventilation is important, but make sure your seedlings are located away from cold drafts, heaters, and air vents. Do not make mini-greenhouses of flats by covering them with plastic tents. At this stage, such high humidity only promotes disease and insect damage.

Moisture must be supplied to all levels of the soil, particularly during the first few days of growth. Until plants are well established, keep the soil surface fairly moist, but don't allow any puddles to form. Mist daily with lukewarm water, and allow the moisture to soak in gradually. Apply enough water so that the entire flat is moistened at all levels, even though roots only penetrate into the first inch or two. If the flat bottom dries out, soil compaction and poor root development result.

As plants grow, they will search out water at lower levels. When they are 2 or more inches tall and have developed their first two sets of leaves, they should be watered less frequently, with the soil surface allowed to dry between soakings. Since they are strong enough to withstand heavier streams, you can use a watering can. Continue using only warm water until the hardening-off process begins, and water early enough so that leaves have a chance to dry before nightfall.

Lots of "automatic" watering systems have been devised by inventive gardeners over the years. These setups allow you to go away for a few days without wondering whether your plants will survive the drought. To borrow a method used by greenhouse operators, set pots and flats on an old table covered with a thick blanket which has been thoroughly soaked in warm water. Bunch one end

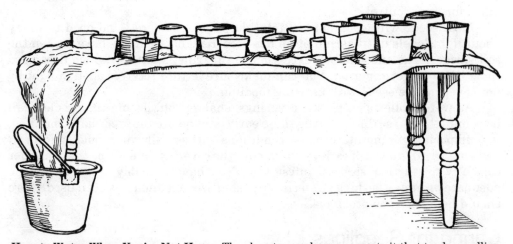

How to Water When You're Not Home: The absentee gardener can see to it that tender seedlings don't dry up while he is away. This setup calls for an old table, a thick blanket, and a bucket of water. Capillary action draws the water up into the blanket where it is absorbed by the soil that is exposed in the drainage holes of the seedling containers.

of the blanket into a bucket of water on the floor. Capillary action draws water from the bucket into the blanket where it is absorbed through holes in the pot bottoms. Use thin-bottomed plastic flats and pots so that soil poking through the drainage holes will come in contact with the wet blanket. You can achieve the same effect by burying a long strip of burlap, cotton, or cheesecloth in each container so that one end extends from the drainage hole. Place this free end of the material into a reservoir of water much lower than the bottom of the container. Although both systems will work, they are really no substitute for daily or weekly waterings carried out as necessary.

Light, too, is important in early growth stages, essential from the moment a first bit of green shows above the ground. Proper light produces thick-stemmed, leafy plants easily able to withstand the shock of transplanting. Seedlings need much more intense light than mature plants do, and suffer markedly if they do not receive it. A minimum of 6 hours of full sunlight is necessary, with most young plants benefiting from 12 to 15 hours a day. Although it is possible to supply the necessary light through a sunny, southern window, more often than not the sporadic, rather dim light of late winter proves inadequate for developing plants.

A more reliable light source is fluorescent lighting. Regular, industrial-type hanging fixtures of the sort used in basements and garages are perfect for lighting seed flats and pots. Suspended by chains, they can easily be raised or lowered as plants grow. They can be used to supplement window light or to provide all the

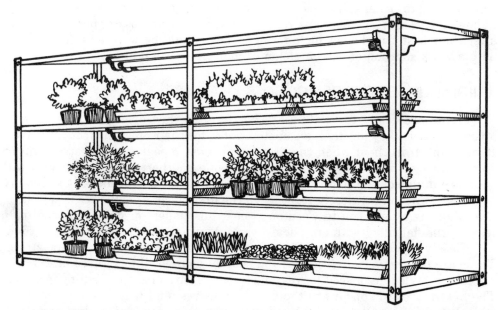

Light Garden for Seedlings: Young plants need 12 to 15 hours of light a day to get off to a good start. You can make sure they get ample light by constructing a light garden like this in your basement or a spare room. The triple-decker arrangement uses space efficiently and provides plenty of room for trays and pots of vegetable seedlings destined for the garden.

light seedlings need. Thus, you can grow transplants in a dark basement or even a closet, providing there is an electrical outlet nearby and temperature and humidity are adequate.

A two-tube, 4-foot-long fixture will provide adequate light for a 1-by-4-foot area. Three fixtures, hung 8 inches apart, create a 3-by-4-foot "mini" garden easily able to house all the vegetable seedlings you'll need for a small vegetable garden.

Special fluorescent tubes emitting light from the red end of the spectrum have been developed specifically for indoor plant growth. These "grow-light" tubes are certainly very good for raising transplants, but the ordinary "cool white" or "warm white" tubes will also do nicely. The best combination is often said to be one of the special plant tubes alongside a cool white tube. This gives a broad balance of red and blue light and is less expensive than some other setups may be.

Since these lamps remain cool, you can set the flats very close to the fluorescent lights without worrying about scorching leaves or even drying out the soil. Start with flats just 3 inches beneath the tubes, and gradually raise the lights, or lower the flats, as seedlings grow. Since most light is produced in the center of the tubes, rearrange containers every once in a while so all the seedlings get their fair share.

Although most young plants are light hungry, some darkness is necessary for proper growth, so don't let the lights run constantly in the hope of speeding growth. As a convenience, set a timer to turn the fixture on and off each day.

Nourishment is rarely a problem for very young seedlings since they are transplanted to richer soil as soon as they have depleted their stored seed energy. If, however, seedlings must remain in a vermiculite, peat moss, or perlite medium after their first true leaves have formed, they should be watered twice a week with a weak solution of fish emulsion or manure or compost tea.

Thinning Seedlings Indoors

Plants are ready to be thinned shortly after they emerge. Spaced 1 inch apart or closer, they hardly have enough room for their emerging sets of leaves. If you don't thin them when the first true leaves appear, or separate them for transplanting, the roots will begin choking one another, stems and leaves will become entangled, and competition for light and water will eventually kill many of them. Why plant so closely together in the first place? The answer is selection. Overplanting allows you to weed out weak, misshapen, or damaged seedlings, leaving the flat filled with only healthy plants worthy of moving to the garden.

Closely check over the seedlings just as the first true leaves are appearing. These are not the very first leaves you spot on your seedlings; those first leaves are called cotyledons or seed-leaves, and they will shrivel as the seedling matures. The next leaves to appear are the first true leaves, and will be recognizable as miniature versions of the mature leaves. Once this set of leaves has appeared, you can begin thinning. Prime candidates for thinning are seedlings with distorted leaves, mechanical injuries, or those that are overcrowding their neighbors. Weak plants can be easily removed without damaging surviving plants. Simply

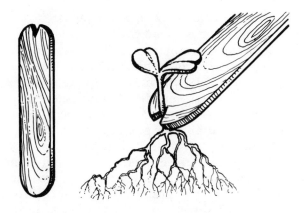

Thinning Tool: If there's a Popsicle stick, tongue depressor, or other flat stick around, transform it into a handy thinning aid. Cut a notch in one end and use the stick to lift seedlings out of pots and flats.

cut off their stems with a small pair of scissors, clipping just at the soil surface, leaving roots in the soil. Some tall, slender seedlings can be pulled out of the soil by hand, too.

Another way to thin plants is to prick them out, using a pronged, flat wooden stick to remove them. Simply insert the stick into the soil alongside the seedling to be thinned, then lift up to remove the plant, taking as little soil as possible. Water the flat after all thinning has been completed.

Transplanting Seedlings

Unless seeds are sown in deep, individual containers or spacious flats of rich soil, transplanting is necessary even before the plants are moved to the garden. Left in a shallow flat for too long, seedlings will "bottom-out," with their roots forced to grow along the base of the container. This hinders their absorption of water and nutrients and causes growth distortion. Seedlings need richer soil for growth than they do for germination. By transplanting them just after their first true leaves appear, you can supply seedlings with the correct type of soil for this stage of growth. Also, by transplanting them while they are at this young, resilient stage the seedlings will recover most rapidly from the shock of the move.

All plants suffer some initial shock from transplanting, but most will recover if handled carefully. Growth is usually halted for a few days after the move, and water absorption is significantly diminished. A few crops, including beans, corn, cucumbers, peas, and squash, are easily injured by even the most delicate transplanting operation, and for that reason should be started in individual pots and

Rich Mixes for Seedlings

1 qt. compost	1 qt. leaf mold	4 qt. loamy soil	1 qt. sand
1 qt. loamy soil	2 qt. loamy soil	2 qt. peat moss	1 qt. vermiculite
1 qt. sand, perlite, or vermiculite	1 qt. compost or well-rotted manure	2 qt. leaf mold	1 qt. loamy soil
		2 qt. vermiculite	1 qt. sphagnum moss
		6 tsp. dolomite lime	1 qt. perlite

kept there until they are set out. (See the chart that appears earlier in this chapter, Plant Response to Transplanting, Groups B and C.)

Before you begin, assemble fresh containers, a batch of rich, moist growing medium, and drainage material such as sand, gravel, or perlite. Be sure to select flats or pots at least 3 inches deep so that roots will have adequate room for growth. The medium you use must be packed with nutrients to fuel the growth of seedlings at this formative stage in their development. Refer to the chart on Rich Mixes for Seedlings to find soil mixes suitable for seedlings from the time they are thinned to the time they are planted out.

Start by thinning flats of all weak or malformed seedlings. Place a damp paper towel over the bottom of any fresh container with very large drainage holes, and line all containers with a thin layer of drainage material. Fill the containers to within ½ inch of the rim with the soil mix. Firm the soil in the corners and along the sides of flats, then use a leveling strip such as a ruler or stick to smooth the surface. Where a large number of flats are being prepared, you can use a "spotting board," a special pegboard sold in some garden stores, to make evenly spaced holes over the surface of the flat. Otherwise, use your finger, a sharp stick, or a dibble to poke holes every 3 to 4 inches in staggered rows in flats, and to make individual holes in pots. The holes should be deep enough to adequately accommodate the roots of the seedlings.

Remove seedlings from flats by using a dibble or pointed stick. If roots are extremely entangled, you may find it easiest to cut around each seedling with a sharp knife, although if they are quite close together, this could damage all the plants. Whatever you do, avoid pulling to untangle roots, for this will tear them. Try to separate them gently using a pencil or dibble, always remembering that roots will do best if protected by soil. When it comes time to lift the plant, hold it by the leaves, not by the stem or the fragile growing point, both of which are easily bruised.

As each seedling is lifted from the flat, gently place it in a hole deep enough so that it can be buried up to its first set of true leaves. As the soil is packed down around the stem and water is added, the soil level will end up slightly lower than this. Planted too shallowly, the seedling will grow sideways along the soil surface.

You want to make sure that the seedling roots are in firm contact with the surrounding soil. Use your forefingers to press the soil around the stem, forming a saucerlike depression. Press down toward the roots, not against the plant. Water slowly, allowing moisture to gradually seep downward to the roots. This will compact the soil so that it may be necessary to add some more in order to adequately cover the roots.

After transplanting, don't water again for several days. The plants are in shock and should be allowed to rest out of direct sunlight or strong artificial light. Wilting may occur, but this will usually pass in a day or two as the plants become established. When they are well rooted and seem to be standing upright again, resume normal care by watering whenever the soil dries out, and fertilizing with a weak solution of manure tea or fish emulsion every week or two. If a rich planting medium has been used, plants won't need much fertilizing.

The Delicate Job of Transplanting: Treat the seedlings tenderly as you transfer them to a larger container. Lift them by their leaves to keep from crushing the fragile stems. Try to handle only the tips of the leaves to avoid bruising the growing point that lies at the base of the leaves where they join the stem.

Hardening-Off

Before being moved outdoors, seedlings must be "hardened-off," or adjusted to the harsher environment of the garden. Used to the constant, comfortable temperatures and frequently supplied water of an indoor environment, they must be made to withstand frost, wind, insect injury, sun, drought, and other unfavorable conditions.

Any treatment that checks plant growth increases hardiness. For this reason, most hardening-off programs begin with very slight changes in plant care. About two weeks before seedlings are to be transplanted to the garden, you should allow slightly more time between waterings. Do not let the plants wilt, but do force their roots to reach down for water. At the same time, discontinue all fertilizing.

A few days after this drying out has begun, start placing flats outside on a shaded porch or in a well-ventilated cold frame during the warmest part of each day. Begin by leaving them out for an hour or two, and gradually increase the period until, within ten days, they are able to stay outside all day. Bring them in at night to prevent frost damage.

Seedlings planted in flats can be further hardened by a process known as "blocking." About ten days before planting out, cut between plants so that each seedling has a block of soil at least 3 inches by 3 inches. Use a sharp knife, and make clean, straight cuts. This severs the large lateral roots and forces new branch roots to form. Blocking checks growth momentarily, but ultimately strengthens the plant.

A note of caution: It is possible to overharden plants, particularly through overexposure to cold temperatures at this early stage of growth. Overhardening

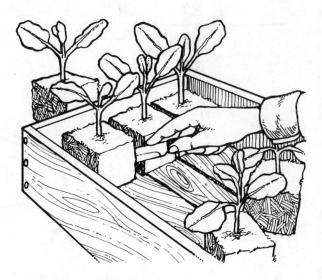

Strengthen Your Plants by Blocking: About 10 days before planting your seedlings outside, block them off in the flat. With a sharp knife, make even cuts between the rows of plants so that each one has about a 3-inch-square block of soil around it. This severing causes new branching roots to form which contribute to the plants' ability to grow and thrive in the outdoors. Blocking makes the planting task easier, too, since the blocks will separate with little difficulty, as shown here.

could significantly delay growth or cut down on early yield, so care must be taken to harden plants gradually, giving seedlings plenty of time to become accustomed to the changes in water and temperature. Particular care should be taken with celery and cabbage, which could flower prematurely if exposed to temperatures below 45°F for prolonged periods. Be careful with eggplants, peppers, and tomatoes, all of which will not fruit on time if overhardened.

Direct-Seeding in the Garden

Although some garden crops might be started indoors or purchased for transplanting, most are probably started from seed planted right in the garden. As long as the growing season is not too short, most crops can be grown in this manner. Direct-seeding requires less work and planning on your part and avoids the initial shock of transplanting for the plant.

However, there are a number of drawbacks to direct-sowing, even beyond the limitations it sets on growing season. Birds, insects, wind, and weather are all enemies of newly planted seed and, as any farmer will tell you, some early seed loss is inevitable in the garden. Cold spring soil may slow germination, and seedling care in the out-of-doors is less than adequate. Fortunately, you can offset all of these potential problems with a variety of cultural measures. Although the outdoor environment will never be as predictable as the indoor one, a well prepared seedbed, good seed, proper attention to depth and rate of planting, and special care in thinning, watering, and early cultivation can ensure a good stand of direct-seeded plants.

Follow the suggestions given earlier in the chapter in the section on Deciding When to Plant to determine when seeds should first be sown outdoors. Remember, too, that not all crops need to be, or even should be, planted at the same time and

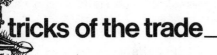

tricks of the trade

Inoculate Legumes for a Better Harvest

For top yields and optimum soil benefits from legume plantings, you should treat your bean and pea seeds with a bacteria inoculant before sowing. Available at garden centers and through mail-order seed catalogs, these inoculants are nothing more than a mixture of soil and active nitrogen-fixing bacteria (called *Rhizobia*). Garden soils alone do not always contain large amounts of these *Rhizobia* bacteria, needed to fix the nitrogen from the air to the nodules on the roots of the legumes. That is why this supplemental bacteria is very important in boosting yields and helping plants utilize atmospheric nitrogen. Simply sprinkle the dry granules over the seeds as you sow, or put the seeds in a paper bag, add some inoculant, and shake to dust the seeds.

that successive sowings are best for dispersed harvests of a number of crops. Make sure you allow enough time for succession crops to mature before the end of the season.

When the seedbed has been properly prepared according to the steps outlined in chapter 2, and the soil has reached the appropriate temperature for the crop you are planting (see the Vegetable Guide), choose a calm, sunny day to begin planting. Rows and raised beds should be carefully marked off according to the garden plan you have drawn up. Measure and follow the plan closely so that all the vegetables you intend to grow will fit into the garden. Don't feel you must fill every inch of the available garden space with seeds. Remember that when thinning time comes, you may want to transplant some seedlings to other parts of the patch. Leave a section of some rows or part of a bed unseeded for this purpose, or for the subsequent sowing of other crops.

Seed-Planting Techniques

There are two basic ways to plant seeds by hand. Where entire beds or blocks of space within a bed are to be planted in the same crop, the seeds may be broadcast—scattered randomly over the soil surface. For conventional rows and intensive plant spacing patterns in raised beds, seeds are sown individually, which gives you more control over spacing and placement. Wide-row plantings can be made using either technique.

Broadcasting: This a good method for sowing cover crops, herbs, greens, or other small-seeded crops for which spacing is not terribly important in the early stages. Some gardeners choose to plant carrots, onions, radishes, and turnips this way as well since it guarantees a good stand of these delicate, weak plants. Thinning is inevitable when seed is broadcast and it can be a rather messy operation if you want to try transplanting some seedlings to another area. When seed is broadcast too thickly, seedlings form a dense, tangled bed, a veritable lawn of young plants. However, if the job is done right, it can be an excellent technique for quick, even planting.

Scatter seeds over the prepared seedbed by flinging them outward in even motions. The idea is to scatter the seeds in midair so that they fall evenly on the soil. Fine seeds may broadcast more easily if mixed with sand or dry peat moss before spreading. When the entire area has been seeded, broadcast a covering of fine soil or peat moss, so that the seeds are covered to a depth appropriate to the type of seed planted (planting depths for all vegetables are given in individual entries in the Vegetable Guide). Water with a gentle spray from a sprinkler or watering can, being particularly careful not to flood the soil surface or wash away seeds.

Conventional Rows: For row seeding, mark off furrows by using the corner of a regular hoe blade for large ones, and a stick or garden tool handle for shallow ones. Rows can be placed as close together as the recommended in-row distance between plants for that variety, provided the soil is in excellent condition. Remember the general rule that seeds are sown about two to three times as deep as they are wide. Too deep a furrow could result in a poor germination rate, too shallow a furrow in malformed seedlings.

Small seeds can be sown directly from the packet, or by dropping them in pinches from between your forefingers. Or, you can mix them with fine sand and spread the sand/seed mixture. You can also rig up a seed spreader from household cast-offs like salt and pepper shakers. At the completion of a row, cover seeds

tricks of the trade

Tips for Midsummer Seed Sowing

Your garden soil is going to be a lot warmer and drier in midsummer than it was in the spring when you made your first plantings. There are a number of things you can do to compensate for these conditions to ensure good germination.

• Moist soil is a must for good germination. The best time to sow seed is after a rain.

• If the rains don't arrive conveniently around planting time, you must provide the moisture yourself. When you prepare the soil, dig a furrow or hole 3 to 4 inches deep, add a ½-inch layer of compost to the bottom, cover by another ½ inch of garden soil, and water well. Onto this wet bed, lay your seeds and cover with a thin layer of dry soil. Don't fill the furrow to make it even with the garden surface—this depression will shield the row from drying winds, help collect rainfall, and eliminate runoff.

• Seeds can be planted slightly deeper than usual in order to take advantage of available soil moisture.

• A sprinkling of dry grass clippings or straw over newly planted rows or beds will help keep the soil surface from crusting.

with compost or rich, fine soil to prevent loss of moisture from the ground, and press seeds into the soil.

Larger seeds, from spinach- to pumpkin-sized, are easy to handle, so uniform spacing in rows is no problem. However, don't be tempted to plant farther apart in order to avoid later thinning or transplanting; birds, bugs, and environmental factors will keep some seeds from ever coming up. Where the soil is rich and well prepared, or where a poor germination rate is expected, you can plant even closer than is generally recommended on seed packets and in the Vegetable Guide. With large seeds, as with small, it is important to cover them adequately, press them firmly into the soil, and water gently unless rain is expected. Seeds sown later in the gardening season, from midsummer to fall, should be planted in slightly deeper furrows to help conserve moisture. (See the box on Tips for Midsummer Seed Sowing.)

Hill Planting: Certain crops, including beans, corn, cucumbers, melons, pumpkins, and squash, are often planted in hills or mounds to provide seeds with a warmer germinating area. In the case of corn, it also creates good pollinating conditions. To prepare a hill in a garden with loamy, fertile soil, form a 2- to 3-inch-high mound, about 12 inches square. The higher the mound, the warmer it will be, but also the drier it will be during hot summer days. If the soil is poor, or if the crop being grown is a heavy feeder, dig a hole 12 inches deep and 12 inches square before you form the mound. Add 8 inches of well-rotted compost, manure, or other organic material, then cover this with 8 inches of soil. This lode of nutrients is strategically placed to give young plants an early boost.

Depending on the crop being grown, plant three to six seeds in the mound, evenly spaced along the top and sides, and buried at the correct depth. Later, after seedlings have developed their first true leaves, thin the hills to about three vine crop seedlings or four corn seedlings.

Raised Bed Systems: There are a number of seeding patterns you can use when planting raised beds that will space plants closer together than is normally

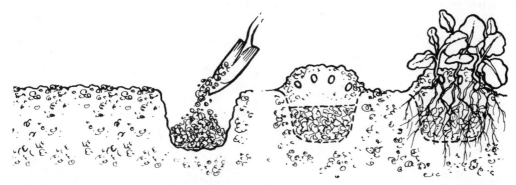

Hill Planting: The idea behind this technique is to plant seeds in a mound of soil slightly higher than the surrounding soil. This "hill" provides a warm germinating area for heat-loving crops like beans, corn, cucumbers, pumpkins, and squash. To nourish heavy-feeding crops, fill the bottom of a 12-inch-deep hole with 8 inches of well-rotted manure or compost, then add 8 inches of soil. Space seeds evenly along the top and sides of the hill. After they have germinated, thin to the strongest seedlings to allow adequate room for growth.

recommended in gardening guides. These closer spacings allow you to grow more plants within the concentrated area of the bed. If the soil has been well prepared and enriched with plenty of organic matter, these dense plantings will not stunt the plants or in any way hinder their growth. These seeding patterns call for a certain amount of precision as individual seeds are planted. Large seeds are the easiest to handle this way, and should be covered, tamped down, and watered as described above. Small seeds are nearly impossible to plant individually, so your best bet is to pinch a few seeds between your thumb and forefinger and drop them in the appropriate spacings. Later on, when the seeds have germinated, you'll have to go back and thin out these clusters.

The bed row system is easy to plan and set up. In a row-planted bed, crops are placed in closely spaced rows, with a different crop in each row. This allows for a diversified crop mix, and takes advantage of interplanting and companion planting techniques.

The trick to planning bed rows is to determine distances between individual rows of different crops. To calculate this distance, average the recommended planting distances for the two neighboring crops given in the chart on Vegetable Spacing for Intensive Culture or the in-row spacings for vegetables not given in

Vegetable Spacing for Intensive Culture

Crop	Inches	Crop	Inches
Asparagus	18	New Zealand spinach	12
Beans, lima	9	Okra	18
Beans, snap	6	Onion, bulb-type	6
Beets	6	Onion, bunching	3
Broccoli	18	Parsley	6
Brussels sprouts	18	Parsnips	6
Cabbage	18	Peanuts	18
Carrots	3	Peas	6
Cauliflower	18	Peppers	15
Celery	9	Potatoes	12
Chinese cabbage	12	Pumpkins	36
Collards	15	Radishes	3
Corn	18	Rhubarb	36
Cucumbers	18	Rutabaga	9
Eggplant	24	Salsify	6
Endive and Escarole	18	Spinach	6
Garlic	6	Squash, summer	24
Kale	18	Squash, winter	36
Kohlrabi	9	Sweet potatoes	12
Leeks	6	Swiss chard	9
Lettuce, head	12	Tomatoes	24
Lettuce, leaf	9	Turnips	6
Mustard	9		

Bed Planting Systems: All three of these planting systems are departures from the conventional row garden. Their aim is to space plants as closely and efficiently as possible, without hampering plant growth. Bed rows (left) allow a mix of different vegetables to be grown in the same bed. The recommended planting distances for different crops to be grown in adjacent rows are averaged to arrive at the new plant spacing. Square-center spacing (below left) is based on a grid pattern, allowing the same spacing between plants in a row as between the rows themselves. Equidistant spacing (below right) shrinks the actual distance between rows by staggering the rows of plants. Both square-center and equidistant spacing are intended for single-crop beds.

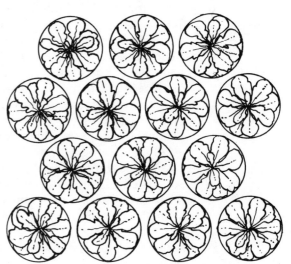

the chart. According to the chart, snap beans require 6 inches between plants, and carrots require 3 inches. Therefore, by a simple calculation you can determine that these crops should be spaced approximately 4 to 5 inches apart.

You can plant anywhere from two to six different crops in a bed. You might try placing tall plants in the central rows, with shorter ones flanking the sides, or intersperse tall crops with short crops. However, as you plan, be wary of shading problems and pay close attention to the other limitations of various companion planting and interplanting combinations.

Square-center spacing is a grid-type pattern that is useful in beds planted with a single crop. With this spacing, the plants are treated as if they were individual squares which together form a gridlike pattern across the surface of the bed. With the center of each plant acting as the center of a square, the distance from the center to each of the square's sides is the distance given in the spacing chart. This means that when you are planting, you allow the same distance between the plants in a row as between the rows themselves.

Equidistant plant spacing is an even more efficient spacing pattern for single-crop beds. In this pattern, the plants are treated as circles, with the result that the rows will fit more closely together. Here, it is the distance between plant centers that corresponds to the spacing on the chart, while the actual distance between rows shrinks. This is done by planting staggered rows so that the plant centers are not perpendicular.

Wide-Row Planting: This is a useful arrangement for small and large seeds alike. Also called band planting, it involves sowing seeds in several very close rows that together form a single 18-inch-wide band of one crop. A similar effect can be obtained by simply broadcasting or scattering seeds evenly across the 18-inch-wide strip. Individual bands are spaced about 24 to 30 inches apart.

The most striking advantage of these wide bands is their high yield, sometimes as much as four times the yield produced by the same area planted in single rows. Individual plants produce less, but the overall yield of the area goes up. Weeds tend to be crowded out by the close-growing crops, and, because of the dense, leafy canopy shading the ground, cool-season crops perform especially well. Beans, beets, lettuce, onions, radishes, and most other compact plants do well in wide rows. Furthermore, any vegetables needing special soil will benefit since fertilizers can be easily incorporated into the wide strips.

You can broadcast seeds in the 18-inch strips, or plant them individually in staggered, closely spaced rows. The latter is preferable as long as seeds are large enough to handle in this manner. Sow seeds as close together as your soil and seedlings can bear, remembering that the main idea of this arrangement is to start seeds right where they will remain until harvest time. Some gardeners have succeeded with rows spaced as closely as 3 inches, but 4 to 5 inches is probably a better minimum, with much larger areas needed for many crops. Plant one row, then stagger the next so that each seed is opposite an empty space in the first row. Cover seeds, firm the soil, and water as for any type of planting arrangement.

Through trial and error you may find that too close a spacing pattern will encourage dampness (from shade thrown by overlapping leaves), which in turn can cause rotting to occur in crops like beans and onions. Once you see this problem developing, it's easy enough to stop; simply remove a plant here and there so enough light can enter to dry the area out a bit.

Thinning and Transplanting Outdoors

Weak or overcrowded seedlings need to be thinned in the outdoor garden, just as they do when grown indoors in flats or pots. Whether or not the seedlings are saved, they must be removed with a certain amount of care in order to spare remaining plants. Choose a cloudy, calm day for thinning and transplanting. Late afternoon is usually a good time, for it allows plants to become established while the sun is low in the sky. If you are planning on transplanting some of the thinnings, prepare a weak manure or compost tea and bring along a putty knife or hand fork, a trowel, some compost or rich soil, and a sharp stick or pencil.

Begin by watering the row so that the soil is loose and easy to handle. Use the hand fork or putty knife to separate a section of soil and plants. How many plants you remove depends on the desired spacing for that particular crop. Check the individual vegetable entries in the Vegetable Guide to determine how many inches to allow between plants when thinning. For plants to be transplanted, be sure to dig deeply enough so that roots pull away with only minimal tearing. If the day is very hot, place the soil and plant mass in a pan with a little warm water, or on a damp towel.

In transplanting the seedlings, carefully disentangle the roots of adjacent seedlings by gently combing through the soil with the sharp stick. Keep as much soil as possible around the roots of individual seedlings. Hold the seedlings by their leaves, not by their stem or growing point. Use a dibble or the sharp stick to poke a hole in the new growing area, lower the plant into it, then replace and firm the soil. Water slowly and gently with the manure or compost tea.

Wilting will probably occur the next day, and perhaps for several days afterward. This is to be expected since plants have been traumatized by the move. As long as you have planted them at the right depth and firmed the soil around them, daily waterings should help them recover without any significant setbacks. Where the sun is particularly harsh, cover newly transplanted seedlings with a paper cone or bushel basket.

Buying Transplants

Not all gardeners are able to or even want to start all their own crops from seed planted indoors or directly in the garden. Limited time and space make it necessary for many gardeners to rely on professional growers for at least some of their spring and fall transplants. Since growers differ in their plant-raising methods—in the soils and fertilizers and pest control measures they employ—and ultimately in the quality of their product, it is worth your while to be on guard when choosing seedlings. Ask questions about the varieties available. Find out whether plants have been raised organically. The single best way to ensure that your purchased seedlings are of good quality is to buy from a local nurseryman.

Do not be lured into buying the largest plants out of hope that they will produce bushels of early fruit. These are the most expensive plants, but they are not always the strongest. Very large plants will be sharply set back by transplanting, and although they may already show a few fruits or blossoms, they could turn out to be far behind others in producing the main crop. Tall, gangly plants in small pots will prove top-heavy and may grow abnormally when moved to the garden.

Instead, choose short, sturdy seedlings with healthy green leaves that show no signs of insects or diseases. Scrape away the soil surface around cabbage and other cole crops to check for clubroot. Roots that appear very yellow, soft, or extremely woody indicate unhealthy plants that you don't want in your garden.

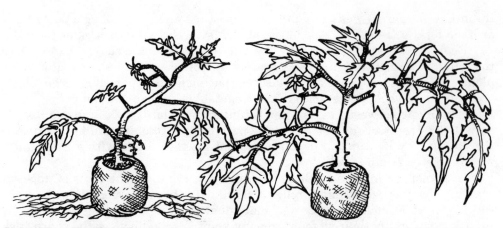

Sizing Up a Seedling: No matter what the price tag says, the seedling on the left is no bargain. When purchasing seedlings to set out in your garden, look for plants like the one on the right that are stocky, not leggy, with healthy green foliage. Give them a thorough going-over to check for pests and signs of disease. Inferior seedlings seldom turn out to be much more than inferior plants.

Seedlings growing in individual containers, or widely spaced and blocked off in flats, are superior to those crowded into flats. This is especially true with hard-to-transplant crops such as beans and cucumbers. Check to be sure that seedlings have been given adequate rooting depth, and that roots have not grown out several inches from the bottom of the pot or flat. Some root growth should be visible from the drainage holes, but too much may indicate a rootbound plant which will have serious developmental problems.

Ask the grower about hardening-off procedures for your purchased plants so that you may continue whatever program he has begun. Chances are, seedlings you pick up in a greenhouse have not yet been thoroughly hardened, and will require very gradual hardening, beginning with cessation of fertilizers and watering. If plants have already spent time outside, store them on a shady porch or in an open cold frame, being sure to provide frost protection as needed. Water only to prevent wilting, and don't fertilize plants at all until they are set out.

Planting Out

Purchased seedlings, as well as those raised in the home or cold frame, may be planted in the garden as soon as they have been hardened and outside conditions permit. See the earlier chart, Guide to Figuring Indoor Planting and Setting-Out Dates, for references on when it is safe to set your plants out. Specific soil and air temperature requirements differ from crop to crop. To guide you in your planting, see individual entries in the Vegetable Guide. It is best to set out plants on a cloudy, damp day. If you must work on a sunny day, hold off until late afternoon or early evening when the sun is low in the sky.

Following the garden plan, dig a hole for each transplant. A transplanting trowel, narrower than the ordinary garden trowel, is excellent for this, for it

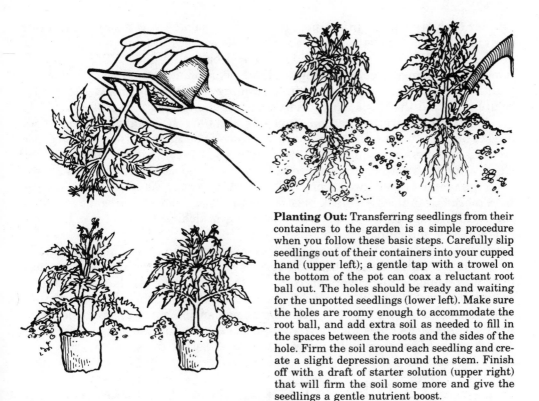

Planting Out: Transferring seedlings from their containers to the garden is a simple procedure when you follow these basic steps. Carefully slip seedlings out of their containers into your cupped hand (upper left); a gentle tap with a trowel on the bottom of the pot can coax a reluctant root ball out. The holes should be ready and waiting for the unpotted seedlings (lower left). Make sure the holes are roomy enough to accommodate the root ball, and add extra soil as needed to fill in the spaces between the roots and the sides of the hole. Firm the soil around each seedling and create a slight depression around the stem. Finish off with a draft of starter solution (upper right) that will firm the soil some more and give the seedlings a gentle nutrient boost.

allows you to make deep, straight-sided holes without disturbing other nearby seedlings already in place. Most seedlings should be planted at least at their potted depth, and up to 1 inch deeper. Members of the cabbage family must be planted deeply to prevent the center stalk from growing crookedly. Make sure the holes are deep enough so these plants can be covered with soil up to their first set of true leaves.

Once all the necessary holes have been dug in the proper places, transplanting can begin. In beds, work from the center out, so that you do not have to reach across just-planted seedlings. Keep the following items close by: a trowel, a pencil or stick for separating seedling roots, a starter solution of manure or compost tea in a watering can, and some sort of mulch.

Potted seedlings will easily slip out of their containers if they are turned upside down and softly tapped on the bottom. With your hand cupped gently over the top of the pot and two fingers spread to accommodate the seedling, the root and soil mass should drop into the palm of your hand. As long as the roots are protected by a large mass of moist soil, there is no reason to handle the seedling itself or to expose the roots while transplanting. Seedlings in flats should have been blocked off as described earlier to make them easier to remove. As bare-rooted seedlings are removed, dip them into a slurry of mud and compost to keep the roots from drying out.

Set each transplant into a prepared hole as soon as you remove it from its container. Double check to make sure that the hole is deep enough to accommodate all the roots. Pat extra soil in around the soil ball if needed to fill up the hole completely. Firm the soil, leaving a slight depression around the base of the plant. This hollow will keep water from running off. Pour warm water or starter solution around the transplant to settle the roots and firm the soil further.

In all but the wettest seasons, you should mulch the plants as soon as they are set out in the garden. (Note, however, that if you are planting warm-season crops like peppers and tomatoes a little early, you should hold off from mulching right away, to give the soil a chance to warm up some more.) Mulch heavily, but keep the material well away from stalks until the plants have been established. If an inorganic mulch like black plastic is being used, it should be set down before the seedlings are planted. (See the section on Mulching in chapter 4 for more guidelines on mulching transplants.)

Transplanted seedlings may need some additional protection from the elements, particularly during the first few days after planting out. Use cloches, hotcaps, or plastic row covers on cold nights to prevent frost damage. (See the section on Extending the Garden Season that follows in this chapter.) On the first one or two hot, sunny days following transplanting, place a newspaper "hat" with several large holes for ventilation over each seedling to shade it from the sun. A bushel basket or slotted row or bed cover serves the same purpose.

Roots, Tubers, and Bulbs

A few garden vegetables are best propagated by actual plant tissue, rather than by seed. This is generally a faster method, and one that involves less transplanting. Asparagus, globe artichoke, horseradish, and rhubarb are propagated

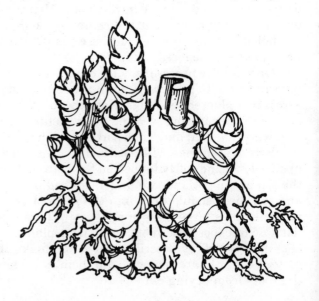

Dividing a Rhubarb Crown: Carefully uproot the dormant rhubarb plant in early spring or fall, and cut off the top growth to expose the large crown. Cut away old portions that appear shriveled or rotten, then cut the remaining crown into as many pieces as possible, being sure to leave at least two "eyes" or stem buds and substantial roots on each part.

by root cuttings or entire root crowns. Potatoes and Jerusalem artichokes are started by tubers, the fleshy portion of underground stems. Garlic, onions, and shallots are all started from bulbs, "sets," or bulb sections called "cloves." Instructions for planting specific crops by these methods are found in the individual plant entries in the Vegetable Guide.

Techniques for Highest Continual Yield

In order to guarantee top yields all year long, you may wish to use two intensive gardening methods—succession planting and interplanting. Succession planting is the raising of new crops in spaces just vacated by others. The new crop may be a repeat of the earlier one, or an entirely different vegetable crop. Thus, a bed of early lettuce might be followed by beans, and these by fall turnips or spinach. Each is planted as soon as, or just before, the other has been harvested. Occasionally, crops with different rates of maturity are planted at the same time. The result of all types of succession planting is a garden that always produces at top capacity, with continuous harvests throughout the entire season.

Interplanting, on the other hand, is the planting of different crops within the same garden area. Timing is still an important consideration, but other plant needs and growth patterns are also important factors. Tall plants are grown beside short ones, and deep-rooting ones with shallow-rooting ones. The result is a thickly planted bed or patch which yields far more produce per square foot than the same area planted in conventional rows.

Both succession planting and interplanting take full advantage of the garden soil, light, and other factors. They are excellent ways not only to increase yields, but also to control insects and diseases, improve soil structure, and generally improve the health of the garden.

Succession Planting

Virtually every beginning gardener has practiced a kind of haphazard succession planting, raising new crops whenever or wherever garden space is available. Often the results are successful, but sometimes these crops aren't as healthy or productive as they might be. When you plan carefully according to maturity dates and local conditions, succession planting almost always succeeds. In fact, the successive plantings can be even healthier and more productive than the early ones.

Productive succession planting depends on the right timing, so you must know the estimated days to maturity of the crops you grow. In addition, you need a sound, firsthand knowledge of the garden's specific climate—its soil, typical air temperatures, rainfall, and the like. With these in mind, you can plan successions correctly.

One way to succession plant is to sow long- and short-season crops together in a row or bed. You can space plants more closely together than usual since the short-term crop will be removed by the time the long-term one needs its full complement of growing space. This enables you to fill in some of the nooks and crannies left after certain transplants are set out or seeds are sown. Typical plantings of this sort are radishes and cabbage; early cabbage and tomatoes;

behind the scenes

Bumper Crops from Cramped Quarters

For transplanted gardeners who take root in an urban or suburban setting, as well as for those who have always lived there, the biggest problem is finding a place to garden in. Postage-stamp-sized yards and balconies or terraces are often the only areas available, falling far short of the ideal 25-by-30-foot plot envisioned by most garden texts.

The trend in population movement of the past few decades has found more and more people congregating in urban and suburban areas. Add to this trend the slow but steady increase in home gardening since the early 1970s, and the stage is set for the emergence of intensive and container gardening on a grand scale.

Klaus Neubner, the senior vice-president and chief horticulturist of George W. Park Seed Company in Greenwood, South Carolina, assessed these simultaneous trends and realized that what was needed to make gardening in small spaces a successful venture were vegetable varieties that would take up little garden space, yet produce bumper crops.

Neubner saw that bush, or dwarf, vegetables were the answer to the home gardener's dilemma of making do in a small space, and he set about promoting these space-saving vegetables and introducing them to the home gardening market.

He contacted a plant breeder and described the cucumber variety he envisioned for the small-space gardener—a bushy plant with short vines and no runners that at the same time would be a vigorous plant, producing good-tasting, salad-sized fruit.

What emerged from this breeding effort was the cucumber variety offered as Bush Whopper in Park's 1977 seed catalog. This marked the first time a bush variety was made available to the home garden market. Looking back on the over-whelming response to this introduction, Neubner feels that Park Seed broke the ice, and that home gardeners had been waiting for smaller plants that would be easier to manage in a small garden. What has developed since the first bush cucumber is a clearly discernible trend toward the breeding and marketing of bush vegetables. Today, all you need to do is flip through a seed catalog to see how many varieties have been developed to fill this need for good producers that take up a minimum of space. And although they were developed with small gardens in mind, Neubner says that they are used just as often in large gardens: "After all, saving space is good for anyone." Neubner foresees further refinements such as a burpless bush cucumber and a seedless bush watermelon, as well as traits like early maturity and disease resistance bred into other bush vegetables.

In an interview, George Park, Jr., assistant vice-president in charge of seed selection, elaborated on several reasons why bush varieties are such a hit with home gardeners. First of all, they give a gardener control over the available space, and their compact growth allows for a more precise garden design. Second, they require less maintenance once they're planted—there's no need to stake or trellis vines, or constantly move vines out of the way as you work in the garden.

What makes a bush plant bushy was also explained by Park. Bush varieties are actually dwarf plants, which doesn't imply that they are weak or in any other way inferior. Rather, they vary from the standard-sized varieties in the length of their internodes (the distance between leaves along a stem). In a dwarf variety, the internodes are shorter, which creates denser growth. But other than the internodes, little else varies between bush and standard varieties. If you compare the leaf of a bush variety with one from a standard variety, you will find that they are close in size, if not the same size. And because fruit size is genetically independent of plant size, most dwarf varieties bear fruit of the same size as standard varieties.

Chinese cabbage and eggplant; lettuce and turnips; and radishes and beans. In all cases, the first vegetable of the pair is harvested before the second achieves full growth. As long as the short-season crop is given its minimum required intensive gardening space (see the chart on Vegetable Spacing for Intensive Culture), it can be grown between or beside the long-term crop. When you are beginning, choose the early varieties that mature most rapidly so that you can be sure they will be harvested in time for long-term crops to mature.

A variation of this succession planting is relay planting. Relays are the successive plantings of the same vegetable over a period of time. This guarantees a dispersed harvest over the course of several weeks or months. It is especially useful for crops which are desired continuously but in small quantities such as beans, lettuce, green onions, and radishes, or for popular crops that are needed in full supply all summer long, such as corn and potatoes. The only requirement for a relayed crop is that it be one with a broad tolerance of daylength and temperature, otherwise ripening problems may occur. You must also see to it that your soil's nutrient content is up to the steady drain of the same nutrients. To ensure that enough nutrients are present for successive relay crops, add supplemental feedings throughout the season.

Plant relays every seven to ten days, in the same row or bed. You may wish to combine the technique with standard succession plantings by sowing one batch of, say, radish seeds along with carrots, while a later sowing of radishes is made with beans.

A similar relay effect may be achieved by simply planting early-, middle-, and late-maturing varieties of the same crop at the same time. Although differences are usually slight with most crops, certain vegetables (such as cabbage, corn, squash, and tomatoes) do have a wide range of maturity rates among their varieties.

Finally, probably the most commonly practiced sort of succession planting is the planting of one crop in the space recently vacated by another. This technique is a must with short-season crops such as cabbage, peas, or spinach which are soon harvested and must be replaced with another crop. Do not let the garden lie fallow—every square foot should be filled throughout the summer if you are to achieve high yields. Plan successive plantings of this type by considering the soil nutrient benefits of the first crop and the needs of the second one. (For a complete discussion of how nutrient needs figure into plant rotations, see chapter 1.) Beans, for instance, tend to improve soil nitrogen reserves. Since cabbage is a heavy nitrogen feeder, it is a good successor crop. Consider also the structural improvements crops make on soils. Deep-rooted crops tend to loosen soil and improve aeration; they draw nutrients from low levels, leaving the topsoil fairly fertile. Thus, following a deep-rooted crop with a shallow-rooted one, or vice versa, makes sound gardening sense.

Interplanting

Interplanting, or intercropping, takes advantage of certain plant needs and growth characteristics to increase the yield per square foot of garden space. With this system, several different vegetables are grown close together in the same planting area, such as tall crops near short ones, or deep-rooted with shallow-rooted. It is a situation readily found in nature where plants grow together in diversified patterns with many varieties sharing the same field, patch of woods, or streamside, each benefiting in some way. Farmers often copy this by alternating rows of beans and corn or cabbages and radishes. In the home garden, you can carry the idea one step further by interplanting within each row or bed. This not only makes your garden space more productive, but it may also improve the health of your crops.

To interplant successfully, take advantage of the crops' different aboveground growth habits, their rooting depths, nutrient needs, and light requirements. Examine potential negative effects plants may have on one another, as well as positive ones. Consider all aspects of plant growth and then plan accordingly, making the most of what the garden and the plants have to offer. The result will be a dense planting of healthy crops forming a kind of living mulch, a perfect microclimate, over the garden bed.

Small, compact crops such as beets, onions, parsley, and radishes can be planted among almost any larger upright plants. Taller plants may help shade, and therefore cool, the smaller ones, aiding in moisture conservation. Vining crops might be trained to crawl around bushy ones, thereby making good use of all available space. Sometimes, crops are even grown on others, as with a pole bean/corn interplanting. Pole beans, planted after the corn has become well established, climb up the cornstalks, making double use of soil and space. For some more compatible vegetable pairings, see the chart on Aboveground Growth Patterns.

Root patterns are another important component of interplanting. Plants can be categorized by the depth to which their root systems reach: shallow-rooting vegetables reach 18 to 36 inches deep; medium-rooting vegetables extend 36 to 48 inches into the soil; and deep-rooting crops probe more than 48 inches down.

Aboveground Growth Patterns

These vegetable combinations represent plants that may be interplanted successfully because of their complementary physical growth patterns.

Bean–celery	Corn–Chinese cabbage	Melon–radish
Bean–corn	Corn–lettuce	Onion–cabbage
Bean–corn–squash, melon, cucumber	Corn–potato	Onion–carrot
Bean–radish	Corn–squash, melon, cucumber	Onion–eggplant
Bean–tomato (staked)	Cucumber–okra	Onion–pepper
Cabbage–chive	Kohlrabi–beet	Onion–spinach
Cabbage–pepper	Leek–carrot	Pea on trellis–cole crops, turnip, lettuce, carrot, kohlrabi, spinach; radish
Cabbage–squash, melon, cucumber	Leek–parsley	
Cabbage–tomato	Lettuce–carrot–onion	Sweet potato–pumpkin
Cole crops–carrot	Lettuce–onion	
Corn–cabbage	Lettuce–radish	

Characteristic Rooting Depth

Shallow Rooting (18 to 36 inches)	Medium Rooting (36 to 48 inches)	Deep Rooting (more than 48 inches)
Broccoli	Beans, snap	Artichokes
Brussels sprouts	Beets	Asparagus
Cabbage	Carrots	Beans, lima
Cauliflower	Cucumbers	Parsnips
Celery	Eggplant	Pumpkins
Chinese cabbage	Mustard	Squash, winter
Corn	Peas	Sweet potatoes
Endive	Peppers	Tomatoes
Garlic	Rutabaga	
Leeks	Squash, summer	
Lettuce	Swiss chard	
Onions	Turnips	
Parsley		
Potatoes		
Radishes		
Spinach		

The idea is to match shallow-rooting crops with medium or deep-rooting ones, and medium-rooting with deep-rooting crops. Shallow roots absorb water and nutrients from upper soil zones, while larger, longer roots draw moisture and food from lower levels, thus eliminating any competition for these important elements of plant growth. Depending on what is planted in your garden, you can try pairings of onions with tomatoes, radishes with snap beans, leeks with carrots, or Swiss chard with parsnips. Refer to the Characteristic Rooting Depth chart to come up with other good combinations for your garden.

In addition to rooting patterns and aboveground growing shapes, consider light and nutrient needs when planning an intercropped garden. A very important concern should be that sufficient light is available to low-growing plants. Ground-hugging leaf crops like lettuce and spinach are natural companions for tall plants

Light- and Shade-Tolerant Plants

These pairings combine plants with differing light needs that grow well together. The left half of the pairing prefers full sun, while the right half tolerates shade.

Bean, bush–celery	Corn–lettuce	Onion–carrot–lettuce
Bean, bush or pole–lettuce	Cucumber (trellised)–celery	Pea (trellised)–lettuce
Bean, bush or pole–spinach	Cucumber (trellised)–lettuce	Pea (trellised)–spinach
Cole crops–celery	Eggplant–celery	Tomato (staked)–lettuce
Cole crops–lettuce	Okra–cucumber	
Cole crops–spinach		

like beans and tomatoes, since they will grow well in the shade cast by their neighbors. Leeks, on the other hand, need full sun so they would not be good candidates for that interplanting scheme. The chart on Light- and Shade-Tolerant Plants will give you more interplanting suggestions.

In terms of soil nutrient needs, try to avoid interplanting crops that feed heavily on the same nutrient. This will all too quickly deplete soil reserves, and could cause problems for the remainder of the season. Become familiar with the nutrient needs of each of the plants you raise and practice succession planting relays and rotations that replenish nutrients as they are removed. Of course, if adequate space is left between plants, or if fertilizers are added throughout the season and crops are followed by others that replace the lost nutrients, then competition is lessened and interplanting of such crops as cabbages and cucumbers (medium to heavy nitrogen feeders), or cabbages and carrots (heavy potassium feeders), may be successful.

Companion Planting

Science is discovering what garden lore has long suggested: certain plants are healthiest when grown in close combination with others. This is not simply because shade and protection are provided by plant neighbors; in addition, such things as insect repellence, disease resistance, and insect poisoning properties are at work in certain combinations.

The technique of companion planting is actually interplanting with such plant-to-plant relationships in mind. While experimental work is only beginning to clarify the interrelationships of plants, scientists have isolated some definite plant substances that benefit other crops. Certain roots, leaves, and fruits have materials that poison or repel insects. Such plants not only protect themselves, but they often protect surrounding growth as well. Two of our most useful organic insecticides, pyrethrum and rotenone, are derived from plants. Pyrethrum comes from a species of chrysanthemum and rotenone from a common weed, devil's shoestring. Other plants repel bugs with their thorns, stickers, color, taste, or odor. Barberry, garlic, horseradish, and raspberry are examples of these. All of these special plants, weeds as well as cultivated crops, have a place in the interplanted garden.

Many of the vegetable crop combinations that seem good because of their complementary growth patterns or nutrient demands are also good for reasons of disease and insect repellence. Tomatoes, for example, secrete an alkaloid which repels certain cabbage pests, and marigold roots exude a powerful root substance that repels nematodes.

Certain brightly colored plants can serve as traps that lure potential pests away from the more valuable vegetables. Nasturtiums attract aphids and at times even cucumber beetles and cabbage worms. Pot marigold is said to work in a similar way for aphids, and nightshade for Colorado potato beetles.

A number of herbs are valuable companion crops, both for their ability to repel insects and for their alleged ability to improve the flavors of certain other crops. Chamomile, sage, tansy, thyme, and wormwood work against cabbage worms and cabbage butterflies. Savory repels tomato hornworms and Mexican bean beetles, and borage repels black flea beetles. Among the herbs that supposedly improve the flavors of other edibles are savory, which is supposed to enrich beans and make onions more pungent, and thyme, which enhances the aroma of most other herbs.

A Companion Planting Guide

Crop	Companions	Antagonists
Asparagus	Basil, parsley, pot marigold, tomatoes	Onions
Beans	Beets (to bush beans only), cabbage family, carrots, celery, corn, cucumbers, eggplant, marigold, nasturtium, peas, potatoes, radishes, strawberry, summer savory, Swiss chard	Garlic, onions, shallots
Beets	Bush beans, cabbage family, garlic, lettuce, onions	Pole beans
Cabbage family	Beets, catnip, celery, chamomile, cucumbers, dill, garlic, hyssop, lettuce, mint, nasturtium, onions, potatoes, rosemary, southernwood, spinach, Swiss chard, tansy	Tomatoes (stunt kohlrabi)
Carrots	Beans, chives, lettuce, onions, peas, peppers, radishes, rosemary, sage, tomatoes	Dill
Celery	Beans, cabbage family, chives, garlic, nasturtium, squash, tomatoes	Carrots, parsnips
Corn	Beans, cucumbers, melons, odorless marigold, parsley, peas, potatoes, pumpkins, squash, white geranium	Tomatoes
Cucumbers	Beans, cabbage family, corn, marigold, nasturtium, oregano, peas, radishes, tansy, tomatoes	Sage
Eggplant	Beans, marigold, peppers	None
Lettuce	Beets, cabbage family, carrots, chives, garlic, onions, radishes, strawberry	None
Parsley	Asparagus, corn, tomatoes	None
Peas	Beans, carrots, chives, corn, cucumbers, mint, radishes, turnips	Garlic, onions
Peppers	Carrots, eggplant, onions, tomatoes	None
Potatoes	Beans, cabbage family, corn, eggplant, horseradish, marigold, peas	Tomatoes
Pumpkins	Corn, marigold, melon, nasturtium, oregano, squash	Potatoes
Radishes	Beans, carrots, chervil, cucumbers, lettuce, melon, nasturtium, peas	Hyssop
Spinach	Borage, cabbage family, marigold, nasturtium, oregano, strawberry	Potatoes
Squash	Borage, corn, marigold, melon, nasturtium, oregano, pumpkins	Potatoes
Swiss chard	Beans, cabbage family, onions	None
Tomatoes	Asparagus, basil, bee balm, carrots, celery, chives, cucumbers, dill, marigold, mint, onion, parsley, peppers, pot marigold	Corn, dill, kohlrabi, potatoes
Turnips	Peas	Potatoes

In planning companion arrangements, also keep in mind the negative effects plants may have on one another. Just as certain secretions or odors may assist one plant, they may harm another. Sometimes this is because the plants are victims of the same pests. Corn and tomatoes are both attacked by the corn earworm. By growing the two crops side by side, you are increasing the amount of "earworm attractant" in the area and hence, the likelihood of infestation. It would be better to separate the plants, intercropping corn with one companion plant and tomato with another.

Other crops more directly harm the vegetables around them. Pumpkins, for example, tend to inhibit the growth of potatoes, and wormwood that of anise, celery, and sage. Pole beans do not do well with the cabbage family, and fennel harms beans and tomatoes. Sunflowers inhibit the growth of pole beans and potatoes. Consult the chart, A Companion Planting Guide, for a listing of various beneficial and hazardous planting combinations.

Extending the Garden Season

In spite of all the charts and maps you see, don't believe for a moment that gardening has to begin after the last spring frost and end with that first hard one in autumn. Starting seeds indoors is just one way to extend the gardening season. If you really want to get top yields from your vegetable patch, try constructing and using a cold frame, a solar growing frame, a hotbed, or any of the various row and plant protection devices discussed below. With these, a spring garden can be started months before outdoor conditions seem to permit, and autumn crops can be harvested into the winter.

Cold Frame

A cold frame is nothing more than a heavy box with a glass or plastic lid through which the sun shines. Because of the greenhouse effect, in which short waves of light enter through the glass and turn to longer heat waves which cannot escape, the soil and air in a cold frame stay much warmer than that of the surrounding area. Ventilation is achieved by partially opening the glass covering during the day. The venting is crucial to keep the interior from overheating and roasting your plants. Venting requires a special eye toward plant needs in order to assure that temperatures remain tolerable and the atmosphere moist, but not soggy. Poor ventilation quickly results in damping-off or other soilborne diseases, and crops suffer drastically. If, however, proper temperature and relative humidity are maintained within the cold frame, and good soil is used in its planting bed, then the device will prove to be a very useful garden tool. (See the box on Soil for the Cold Frame, Solar Growing Frame, and Hotbed.)

Spring plants, particularly hardy ones, may be started in the cold frame several weeks before outdoor temperatures permit. Transplants may be hardened-off, hardy fall plants overwintered, and certain salad crops like spinach and leaf lettuce grown from seed to harvest throughout the winter. During the summer,

Cold Frame: This modest-looking structure is a valuable and versatile season extender. The "greenhouse effect," created when light waves pass through glass and turn to heat waves, accounts for the warmer soil and air temperatures inside the frame. So even when it's still too cool to plant outdoors, hardy crops can get off to an early start in the frame. In addition, the cold frame can be used to harden-off transplants and winter over hardy crops.

the cold frame may be completely opened and used as a nursery area.

You can build a simple cold frame at almost no cost from recycled lumber and an old window sash. It is also possible to purchase more permanent, slightly fancier versions from nursery suppliers, or to build a more substantial model from masonry, concrete blocks, or brick. For most gardeners' needs, the simple wooden frame will prove more than adequate, particularly if the wood has been treated to prevent rot, the walls insulated on cold days, and seams well caulked. Any preservative that you use on the wood should be a nontoxic type, like copper naphthenate (available under the trade name Cuprinol).

The best site for the structure is a location that receives no more than one to two hours of shade per day. The slanted cold frame lid should face directly south to receive the sun, although a slight variation may be made without significantly affecting the absorption of solar radiation. In choosing a location, consider windbreaks and convenience as well. A cold, driving wind can lower temperatures considerably, so it may be worthwhile to choose a slightly less sunny

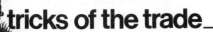

tricks of the trade

Soil for the Cold Frame, Solar Growing Frame, and Hotbed

Since drainage could be a problem inside these growing structures, the soil must be quite light and friable. It should be rich enough to provide nutrients and to generate carbon dioxide for growing plants. A good soil mix is one part topsoil, two parts fully decomposed compost or leaf mold, and one part well-rotted manure. Add sand or peat as needed to lighten very heavy topsoils.

area if it is well protected—along the side of a house or shed, for instance. Also, consider whether you plan to use the frame primarily for seedling production and hardening-off, or for winter salad crops. This will determine whether the frame should be placed near the garden, or closer to the house.

Sizes vary from a typical home-built cold frame of 3 by 6 feet to a nursery frame of 6 by 10 feet. Those much smaller than 3 by 6 are difficult to ventilate and heat, while those larger than 6 by 10 may be hard to handle.

The best sashes are ones made especially for cold frames. These have only vertical supports, no horizontal ones, and usually consist of many glass panes, overlapping one another like shingles. This allows water to run off before it freezes on the sash. Recycled window sashes or glass panes perform almost as well in all but the coldest weather, particularly if care is taken in preparing them for cold frame use. If double thickness glass (⅛ inch) is available, use that, for it will provide much-needed insulation. You can also line regular thickness window glass with plastic sheeting to achieve the same effect. Use polyethylene for the strongest, cheapest liner. Plastics may be used alone as a glazing, but they do not transmit light as efficiently as glass, nor do they seem to insulate as well. If, however, you are attracted by the durability of plastic, select clear fiberglass, polycarbonate sheeting, polyethylene, or a polyester film treated with ultraviolet absorbers.

In northern areas, you can make your cold frame more efficient by banking soil around the high back and sides. You can further warm the structure by laying an insulating 1- to 2-foot-thick layer of fresh manure beneath the planting soil in the frame's base. This will provide some warmth, but for truly successful winter gardening in very cold areas you should use solar or supplementary electric heat, making the cold frame into a solar growing frame or a hotbed.

Solar Growing Frame

A somewhat fancier, much more efficient version of the cold frame is the solar growing frame. With this structure, it is possible to grow many different green vegetables throughout the winter. Thickly insulated underneath and on all sides, with a close-fitting nighttime shutter and double-glazed sash, the solar growing frame needs no heating cables, fuel, or manure. Even in the dead of winter, air and soil temperatures stay well above freezing. Detailed information on constructing a growing frame is available in the book, *Solar Growing Frame*. (See the Bibliography.)

In order for a crop to grow with any measure of success in the growing frame, it must be able to tolerate fluctuating light levels and temperatures. And, to make the frame a steady source of fresh greens, this crop should do more than simply survive—it should also provide substantial harvests throughout the winter. Traditional cold-tolerant plants like broccoli, cabbage, endive, lettuce, and spinach are not the best choices because of their slow growth and insubstantial harvests in the frame. After several seasons' observation, researchers at the Organic Gardening and Farming Research Center in Maxatawny, Pennsylvania, have found a large group of oriental vegetables (mostly brassicas) that flourish

Solar Growing Frame: This structure is really an updated, insulated version of the basic cold frame. Design features like thick insulation on all sides, night shutter, and double-glazed sash help keep soil and air temperatures above freezing, enabling the gardener to grow and harvest hardy greens throughout the coldest part of the year.

under the light and temperature conditions in a growing frame, and keep you busy harvesting fresh greens through the coldest part of the year. See the box on A Taste of the Orient for a description of some of these vegetables.

Hotbed

A conventional-design cold frame probably won't be capable of maintaining high enough temperatures to force or raise vegetables in the dead of a northern winter. A hotbed is constructed in just the same way a cold frame is built, except that all walls penetrate 1 foot below the soil surface and some added heat is supplied through an electric cable, incandescent bulb, or other device. Traditionally, hotbeds were warmed by manure, with huge amounts laid beneath the soil surface and sometimes around the sides as well. Rotting animal waste will certainly provide heat, but it also contributes fungi and potential insect problems if the hotbed is not properly constructed and adequate ventilation is ignored. Manure-heated beds are tricky to manage and require lots of experimentation before they can be termed successful.

A much cleaner method of heating, but one which requires more money and energy, is the use of heating cables or incandescent bulbs. If a temporary hotbed is planned, then a simple hotplate can be used as the heat source. Construct a raised platform to rest over the hotplate, and set the seed flats on this platform.

For a more permanent setup, choose heating cables that are covered with vinyl or lead, and are intended specifically for hotbed use. Cables come in various

digging deeper

A Taste of the Orient

A solar growing frame is your key to an exotic category of vegetables, seldom grown by Western gardeners. In trials conducted over the course of several winters at the Organic Gardening and Farming Research Center (OGFRC), staff researchers have found a wide range of oriental vegetables that produce an abundance of succulent, tender growth under cool temperatures, damp conditions, and low light intensities. The fact that they do so well should come as no surprise, since for centuries oriental gardeners have been developing vegetables that will grow and be productive in a climate that is frequently damp and chilly with overcast skies.

Many of the oriental vegetables featured here will give you a prolonged harvest of fresh greens at a time of year when such vegetables command premium prices at the local market, if they are available at all. By using them raw in salads, incorporating them into stir-fry dishes, or adding them to soups, you are taking delicious advantage of all the vitamins A and C, iron, calcium, and other minerals they have to offer.

Here is a rundown of some of the oriental vegetable varieties that produce well in the OGFRC solar growing frames. By the way, they do just as well in solar greenhouses.

Yellow Bud Radish
Brassica rapa, Pekinensis Group
This Chinese celery cabbage develops a loose, thick head of crinkly, pale green leaves with a delicate, mustardy flavor. Pick the outer leaves when they are about 6 inches high for the best flavor and texture. (Seed source: Tsang and Ma International, 1556 Laurel St., San Carlos, CA 94078.)

Flowering White Cabbage
Brassica rapa, Chinensis Group
The fact that this Chinese mustard cabbage bolts to flower is no cause for concern, since the leaves, flower stalk, and buds are all edible and good-tasting. The tender, sweet heart is the relished portion of the plant, and its flavor is sweetest when the plant is in bloom. The best way to harvest this cabbage is to cut the whole plant, rather than pick outer leaves. (Seed source: Herbst Brothers Seedsman, 100 N. Main St., Brewster, NY 10509.)

Seppaku Taina
Brassica rapa, Chinensis Group
This Chinese mustard cabbage produces large, dark green leaves on the ends of white stalks. Both the leaves and stalks are used, and are sweet-flavored. Keep the outer leaves picked for an ongoing harvest. If the plant is allowed to mature, the stalks will thicken and develop into an edible celerylike bunch. (Seed source: Herbst Brothers.)

Tokyo Cross F–1 Turnip
Brassica rapa, Rapifera Group
This turnip is as attractive as it is good-tasting. The root is a smooth, pure white, semiglobe shape, with smooth green leaves that grow up to 13 inches tall. The root is very sweet, and the greens are equally tasty. (Seed source: Thompson and Morgan, P.O. Box 100, Farmingdale, NY 07727.)

Garland Chrysanthemum
Chrysanthemum coronarium
The gray-green, serrated leaves, yellow flowers, and fragrance will remind you of the common garden ornamental, but this particular plant is used as a potherb. The young, tender, leafy shoots are picked when 3 inches long, and lend a slight pungency to your cooking. Their aromatic flavor resembles the fragrance of chrysanthemum flowers. (Seed source: Redwood City Seed Co., P.O. Box 361, Redwood City, CA 94064.)

Kyo Mizuna
Brassica juncea var. *multisecta*
A quick glance, and this brassica may look like a feathery endive. But the taste tells you it's not, for Kyo Mizuna has a distinctive, delicate cabbage flavor. It is particularly pretty in salads. (Seed source: Herbst Brothers.)

Manure-Heated Hotbed: A layer of fresh manure is the heat source for this season-extending structure. A gardener with a good source of fresh horse manure will find this to be a relatively inexpensive way of providing up to three months of temperatures conducive to plant growth. Allow the manure to ferment in a flat pile for several days. Construct a bottomless frame over a 2- to 3-foot pit, then fill the pit with manure, tamping it down after every 6 inches have been added. When the manure is 8 inches from the soil surface, add several inches of straw, then 4 to 6 inches of good soil. Sow seeds directly in this soil, or in flats set in the hotbed.

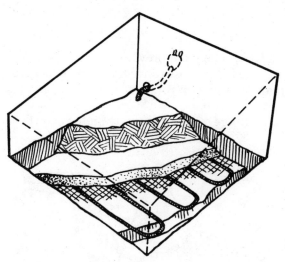

Cable-Heated Hotbed: This hotbed is more expensive to run, but is also longer lasting and more reliable than the manure-heated model. Add a layer of vermiculite to the bottom of the frame, then loop special heating cables across the surface so they do not touch. Add a 1-inch covering of soil and a piece of hardware cloth or other screening on top, then pour in the growing medium.

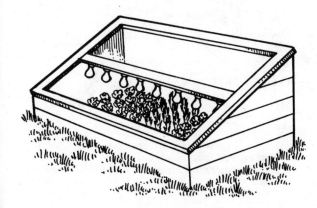

Incandescent-Bulb Hotbed: Convert a cold frame into a hotbed by attaching a wood strip fitted with 25-watt bulbs under the frame's sash. Allow a safety margin of at least 20 inches between the bulbs and the soil surface to keep plants from getting overheated.

lengths and wattages. For a typical 3-by-6-foot hotbed, you would want around 200 watts of power and about 40 feet of cable to distribute the heat adequately throughout the bed. Place a 2-inch layer of vermiculite in the bottom of the cold frame, about 1 foot beneath the soil surface. Lay lead heating cables in loops 7 inches apart, or vinyl ones 5 inches apart on top of this bed. Don't allow the cables to touch one another. Cover this with 1 inch of soil, and then a window screen or other protective material. Finally, add 5 to 8 inches of rich growing medium.

Incandescent bulbs may be used as a heat source, whether in conjunction with manure or cables, or alone. To heat a 3-by-6-foot frame entirely with bulbs, 8 25-watt incandescent light bulbs are needed. Mount these at equal spacings on a narrow, 6-foot strip of wood and screw or nail this in place just under the center of the cold frame's sash. Wire the bulbs to a thermostat, and wire this thermostat to the house or garage for easy regulation. The only danger in this setup is that any plant leaves that come too close to the bulbs could be singed. To avoid this problem, keep the soil surface at least 20 inches below the bulbs.

Plant Protectors

Various kinds of devices have been developed to provide frost protection for individual plants or groups of plants in the field. These range from paper "hotcaps" and glass bell jars for individual plants, to plastic row covers or portable glass enclosures for large groups.

Individual protectors have the advantage of being easy to handle, easy to set

Plant Protectors: Dropping temperatures don't have to put a damper on your gardening endeavors. Just cover vulnerable, tender plants with any of these protectors, and they should come through a cold spell unscathed. From left to right, the items shown here include a bottomless plastic milk jug, a perforated section of a milk carton, a commercial tent-shaped cloche made of wire and glass, a purchased heavy waxed-paper hotcap, and a slatted bushel basket.

Row and Bed Covers: These easy-to-assemble structures are very effective in providing frost protection. The frame can be made from wire or wood, and the clear polyethylene sheeting can be stapled or tacked in place. Free-hanging sides can be rolled up for ventilation, or the sides can be slitted so that ventilation is automatically supplied. Depending on the growing area to be covered, the basic design can be adapted to cover a single long row or a whole raised bed.

up just before a frost seems imminent, and easy to remove when the sun comes out the next morning. Yet, while they are perfect for nighttime protection, they are not terribly useful as long-term daytime plant protectors. Their small size does not trap adequate amounts of solar radiation to provide heat during very cold spells. Since they are small, they also tend to overheat during the day, offering plants little ventilation. Glass hotcaps may even burn plants on sunny days when the glass magnifies the sun's rays.

To avoid problems with hotcaps, use them sensibly. Newspaper "hats" or purchased waxed-paper hotcaps will provide excellent late afternoon and nighttime frost protection, but don't try using them to warm the plant during the day. Translucent plastic jugs, like the kind milk and cider come in, with the tops removed and bottoms cut away, can serve as daytime hotcaps. They allow just enough light to penetrate without causing overheating. Special glass or plastic bubbles, known as cloches, are specifically designed for longer-term protection and will extend the garden season considerably. Some of these are tent-shaped, covering several plants with glass panes fastened over wire A-frames. If you can find these, they are excellent for protecting warm-season transplants such as eggplants, peppers, and tomatoes.

Row and bed covers are helpful in large gardens where a number of plants must be given frost protection, or where warm-season vegetables are to be seeded early and raised under field "greenhouse" conditions. Like cold frames, you can use them to force endive, rhubarb, or other crops during late fall or early spring months. Used in conjunction with a black plastic mulch, these generally offer more nighttime warmth to plants and are easier to ventilate during the day. They actually rival the well-built cold frame in efficiency.

4

Culture through the Season

While good gardening does take time, it need not be an all-consuming hobby unless you wish to make it one. The best approach is a kind of sensible, "preventive" attitude toward garden care in which plants are given all the materials they need to grow and produce without constant attention from you. Crop rotation, interplanting, companion planting, thorough soil preparation, mulching, and other good gardening techniques actually produce crops that can withstand unfavorable conditions to some degree. If plants are off to a healthy start, you can take an occasional vacation without seriously endangering them.

Of course, some special care is needed during the course of the growing season, particularly for certain crops. Even where a heavy mulch has been laid down, some watering may be necessary in order to get plants through dry spells. Extra feeding may be necessary for a few crops, or for transplants set out later in the season, and weeds and insect pests need to be kept in check. There may be some crops that require pruning, staking, blanching, or other special care. Finally, there are crops to be harvested and new ones to be planted from week to week. A certain kind of perseverence is needed to keep up with these demands, but as long as the garden has been kept down to a reasonable size, the tasks are enjoyable, and by no means overwhelming.

What follows in this chapter is a discussion of the cultural practices which may be needed during the growing season. Emphasis has been placed on general descriptions and suggestions, with more specific plant-by-plant requirements outlined in the individual vegetable entries in A Guide to Vegetables for the Home Garden.

Watering

Water is the most misunderstood of all plant needs. Essential for growth and development, it carries minerals from the soil to the leaves, and acts as the raw material from which plants manufacture food. In order to benefit crops, it must

Droughtproofing Your Garden

There's no need to feel helpless when the rains don't come. There are effective measures you can take while preparing the soil, while planting, and then afterward during the hot, dry spell, that alleviate drought damage to your garden.

CHOOSE VEGETABLES WITH LOW WATER REQUIREMENTS

Droughtproofing your garden begins when you select vegetables that don't make heavy watering demands on you. Crops with deep, well-developed root systems (like squash and tomatoes) have access to more moisture in the soil than shallow-rooted crops (like cabbage and celery). Also, since the top layers of soil dry out first, shallow-rooted crops will be the first to suffer from a lack of moisture.

There are certain types of plants that can get by on less water. A small plant with few leaves needs less water than a large, leafy plant. A quick-maturing crop will need less water than one that matures over a long period. Fast-growing plants that can be grown early in the season take advantage of the naturally higher moisture levels in the soil. Plants with a low-lying growth habit need less water than plants that grow upward and are staked or trellised. The low-lying plants have less surface area exposed to wind and sun, so transpiration (water loss through the leaves) occurs more slowly. Vegetables that exhibit the characteristics described above include collards, cowpeas (Crowder type), Jerusalem artichokes, leaf lettuce, lima beans, okra, peas, spinach, summer and winter squash, and tomatoes. Check your seed catalogs for descriptions of specific varieties which are drought-tolerant or drought-resistant.

CHOOSE YOUR GARDEN LOCATION CAREFULLY

If you're laying out your first garden or if you have the luxury of enough space to relocate your garden, there are several things you can do at this stage to cut down on water loss in your garden and make it a better producing area under drought conditions.

- **A small garden** allows you to concentrate the available water on fewer plants.
- **Avoid large trees** at all costs—their expansive root systems act like sponges, absorbing water from the surrounding soil at an astonishing rate. One large oak tree is said to take up 3,000 gallons of water a day! Locating your garden outside the drip-line (the circular area extending from the trunk to the tip of the outermost branches) provides a safe margin.
- **A garden set on a slight slope** can be more efficiently irrigated.
- **Siting the garden near the house,** or better yet, the kitchen door, makes it easier to transfer recycled kitchen and household water to the vegetables.
- **Any rapid air movement** robs the soil of water by increasing the rate of evaporation. Take advantage of any natural windbreaks when you lay out your garden, such as buildings, fences, or hedges. By setting the rows or beds at right angles to the direction of the prevailing wind, water loss can also be cut down.

MAKE SURE YOUR SOIL IS IN GOOD CONDITION

Your best insurance against drought damage is a soil that is rich in humus. Humusy soil absorbs water readily and holds it right where the roots can reach it. This is especially critical when the amount of water available to your garden is limited, because that's when you want every drop to count.

TAKE PRECAUTIONARY MEASURES WHEN PLANTING

Whether you're sowing seed or setting out transplants, there are several steps you can take to ensure that your plants get off to a good start, despite the hot and dry conditions.

- **Start your garden early** in the season to take advantage of the naturally higher moisture levels in the soil. And the cooler temperatures of the season mean less surface evaporation will occur.
- **If you must sow seed later in the season** when the conditions are less than ideal, you should make sure that the sprouting seed has a steady supply of moisture. Plan to plant in the evening when it is cooler, and the morning prior to planting, soak the seeds in a shallow container of water.

• **When you are working with midseason transplants,** dig the hole a bit deeper than usual, and set a handful of peat moss, compost, shredded newspaper, or tea leaves into the bottom. Fill the hole with water and let it seep in. When all the water is gone, set the plant in place, and cover the roots with dry soil. Leave a slight basin around the plant that will collect rainfall and eliminate runoff of precious water. The organic material clustered below the plant's roots will retain water in the exact spot where it is needed.

MULCH TO CONSERVE WATER

Use any organic mulch, and apply it after the soil has been thoroughly watered. With this simple measure you lock in moisture and increase the time that plants can go between waterings by cutting down on surface evaporation; keeping the soil temperature cooler than the surrounding air temperature; protecting any shallow roots from heat damage and excessive drying; and discouraging weed growth that competes for available water.

WEED OUT ANY UNWANTED PLANTS

• **Thin out any excess seedlings** as soon as possible, to cut down on the competition for the water supply. Also remove all weeds to lessen the drain on available soil moisture.

• **One word of caution**—don't cultivate with a rotary tiller during a drought. The action of the blades can chew up plant roots that lie near the surface, and these roots alone account for 40 percent of the water the plant pulls in from the soil.

SUPPLEMENT YOUR GARDEN'S WATER SUPPLY

There are several relatively effortless things you can do to increase the amount of water available to your garden.

• **Use a rainbarrel** to catch the otherwise wasted runoff from your house. Just divert the water from your gutters through drain pipes into barrels or plastic tubs. Any algae that forms won't harm the plants at all. If mosquitoes take to breeding in your collected water, discourage them by adding several drops of linseed oil from time to time, or add several drops of hot paraffin to the water occasionally. Neither of these additives will harm your plants.

• **If you have a dehumidifier** running, use the water it collects in the garden.

• **Forty to 60 percent of all household water escapes** down the drain after bathing, dishwashing, and doing laundry. With a little effort, this wastewater (called graywater) can be rerouted from the drain to the garden. Wash dishes in a plastic basin rather than in the sink itself (but avoid using greasy, particle-laden water in the garden), and bring a bucket into the shower with you. Also, when you step out of the bathtub, instead of pulling the plug, get a bucket brigade going and transport the water to your garden. To divert the rinsewater from your washing machine, you'll have to do a little rearranging of the draining system, and have it empty into a collection area instead of losing it into your plumbing system. (If you garden in an area that faces chronic water shortages each season, it could be to your advantage to investigate installing a more permanent graywater system. See the Bibliography for some helpful books on this subject.)

• **If you have any doubts about what this sudsy water may do to your plants,** remember these general guidelines. Soap is preferable to detergent, but don't use any soaps that are perfumed or high in lanolin. The safest is biodegradable soap with less than 1 percent phosphate. If you do use laundry detergent, you can still use the wastewater, but be aware that these detergents are often high in sodium, which after prolonged use can raise your soil's pH level. Test your soil every year to keep tabs on the pH. Any product containing bleach or boron will harm your plants, as will those promising "extra softening power" and "enzyme action," so don't use water containing any of these in your garden. Softened water containing high levels of soluble salts is not a good addition to the garden either, for such minerals can build up to harmful levels in the soil.

• **When you water,** sprinkle it around the plants and avoid getting any directly on the foliage. It's best to use this graywater mainly on well-established plants which have a higher tolerance to the impurities in the water than seedlings. It is advisable to alternate the use of graywater with clean, nonrecycled water.

be supplied to the main roots—not just to the leaves and the top inch of soil. It must also be supplied in the right amounts and at the right times according to soil and plant requirements. Since rain does not always come when needed, gardeners often have to resort to artificial watering with hoses, cans, sprinklers, and other devices.

Successful artificial watering is a bit more complicated than just hosing down the garden every day or two. In fact, light daily waterings can do more harm than good by encouraging roots to grow along the wet soil surface, rather than reaching down to the lower levels where moisture and nutrients remain in fairly stable supply. For best results, you should water less frequently, and when you do, make sure it is for a long enough period so that moisture soaks deeply into the soil, reaching the main root masses of the plants. These intermittent, deep waterings stimulate deep root growth and, where the soil is alkaline, wash harmful salts downward, past the roots. With a thick organic or black plastic mulch covering the soil surface, little moisture is lost by evaporation when the water has been allowed to soak deeply into the ground.

The quality and temperature of water are also important in any type of garden irrigation. Warm water is much better for plants than cool water since it can be more readily absorbed and speeds growth, whereas cold water actually slows growth. Even on the hottest summer days, give drooping plants a draft of lukewarm water rather than the cold water you might think would refresh them.

When to Water

There are two simple ways you can determine whether the garden should be watered: by the feel of the soil, and by the look of the plants themselves. When the soil is holding as much water as it possibly can without any puddling or runoff, its particles stick together, forming a durable, pliable ball that will stick to your hands as you shape it. At this point, the soil is said to be at "field capacity." The more crumbly the soil, the less water it contains, and the further it is from field capacity. Generally, when the soil around a plant's roots is below 50 percent field capacity (when it is holding half the water it is capable of holding), it is time to water. To test this, don't judge by the surface soil. Just because it appears

Deep Watering for Deep Roots: A plant with a deep root system like the one on the right is better equipped to survive droughts than the shallow-rooted one on the left, since it can reach down to where the moisture level is more stable. A deeper root system also enables the plant to pull up nutrients from a greater area. Encourage deep root systems to form by giving good, thorough soakings at infrequent intervals, instead of dribbling a little water on the soil surface every day.

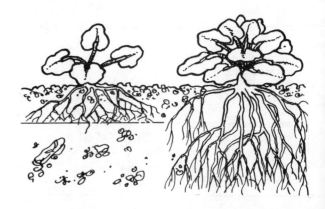

to be dry doesn't mean the root zone is dry. In a vacant spot in the garden, dig down to the approximate depth of the crop's root mass. You can judge how far down to dig to arrive at the root zone of your crops by consulting the chart in chapter 3 on Characteristic Rooting Depth. Press some of the soil you bring up between your fingers, and check its response against the accompanying chart, "Hands-On" Guide to Soil Moisture. If the soil barely holds together, then it's time to water.

A simpler check can be made with a hollow metal rod or a specially designed probe. Insert the probe deep into the soil, once again in an unoccupied space. If it penetrates easily to the root zone, chances are there is plenty of water available. If the probe does not penetrate easily, or if it comes out perfectly clean, then the soil is probably below field capacity and should be watered.

"Hands-On" Guide to Soil Moisture

	Sand	Sandy Loam	Clay Loam	Clay
Moisture Available for Plants	**Feel or Look of the Soil**			
Close to 0%. Little or no moisture available.	Dry, loose, single-grained. Flows through fingers.	Dry, loose, and flows through fingers.	Dry clods that break down into powdery condition.	Hard, baked, cracked surface. Hard clods difficult to break. Sometimes has loose crumbs on surface.
Up to 50%. Nearly time to irrigate.	Still appears to be dry. Will not form a ball with pressure.	Still appears to be dry. Will not form a ball.	Somewhat crumbly, but will hold together with pressure.	Somewhat pliable. Will ball under pressure.
50–75%. Enough available moisture.	Same as above.	Tends to ball under pressure, but seldom will hold together.	Forms a ball, somewhat plastic. Will sometimes stick slightly with pressure.	Forms a ball. Will ribbon out between thumb and forefinger.
75%. Plenty of available moisture.	Tends to stick together slightly. Sometimes forms a very weak ball under pressure.	Forms weak ball. Breaks easily. Will not become slick.	Forms a ball and is very pliable.	Easily ribbons out between fingers. Feels slick, like modeling clay.
Soil won't hold any more water.	After squeezing, no water appears, but moisture is left on hand.	Same as for sand.	Same as for sand.	Same as for sand.
Waterlogged soil.	Water appears when soil is bounced in hands.	Water will be released with kneading.	Can squeeze out water.	Puddles, and water forms on surface.

SOURCE: Adapted from "Saving Water in Landscape Irrigation" (Public Service Office, University of California, Davis, California).

Plant behavior is also an indication of the soil's moisture content. The most obvious plant response to low moisture is wilting, although this can be misleading. Some plants wilt in response to excessive heat, whether or not adequate moisture is available in the soil. Cucurbits, eggplants, lettuce, peppers, tomatoes, and others will wilt almost every day in the heat of the summer sun, but they quickly recover as the sun sets and temperatures drop. This temporary wilting does not necessarily indicate a need for additional water. If, however, a plant does not recover by evening or begins wilting early in the morning, then water immediately, for soil moisture reserves are certainly depleted. Any wilted plants that do not recover after they have been watered may be suffering from root damage or disease and you should watch them carefully for further signs.

Overwatering can also cause plants to wilt. Crops requiring high amounts of oxygen, such as corn, cannot be grown on poorly drained soils. Waterlogged ground usually has a high carbon dioxide content since the water in the soil pores keeps it from being released into the air. In this situation, plant roots use all the available soil oxygen, but none is replaced. This is called physiological drought, a kind of wilting which has nothing to do with lack of water, but with an excess of it. This can only be corrected by adding organic matter and by actually altering the soil structure.

Under normal soil conditions, plants' moisture needs change dramatically

Critical Times to Water Common Vegetables

Crop	Growth Stage When Water Is Needed Most
Asparagus	After harvesting is over, when ferny top growth is developing
Beans	Flowering, pollination, pod enlargement
Broccoli	Head development
Cabbage	Head development
Carrots	Root enlargement
Cauliflower	Head development, just before harvest
Corn	Silking, tasseling, ear development
Cucumbers	Flowering, fruit set
Eggplant	Through all stages
Leeks	Through all stages
Lettuce	Head development or through all stages for leaf types
Onions, garlic, shallots	Bulb enlargement
Peas	Flowering, pollination, pod enlargement
Peppers	Through all stages
Potatoes	Tuber enlargement
Radishes	Root enlargement
Soybeans	Pollination, pod development
Spinach	Through all stages
Squashes	Bud formation, flowering
Tomatoes	Through all stages, especially flowering and fruiting
Turnips	Root enlargement

according to their level of development. Generally, large amounts of water are needed during early growth, flowering, and fruit set. If they don't get the moisture when they require it, crops will be of poor quality. Blossom-end rot in tomatoes, splitting in cabbages, and blossom drop in peppers are just a few examples of water-related problems. Check the chart on Critical Times to Water Common Vegetables so that you can better anticipate crop moisture needs and make the best use of your water supply.

In all but emergency cases, watering should be carried out in late afternoon or early evening. Plants grow considerably at night, using the energy they've garnered from the sun during the day, and water is necessary for this growth. Watering at night also helps plants recover from the toll taken by the day's heat. Earlier waterings are mostly lost to evaporation. Therefore, water several hours before sunset, giving leaves a chance to dry before dark. However, if you water too late in the day and the garden is left wet during the night, fungi tend to grow, and their related diseases set in.

How Much Water?

Many factors influence the amount of water needed for a given garden, making any general rule misleading. One inch of water per week might be appropriate for one garden, while 1 inch every two weeks is better for another. Some summers, you may need to water every few days; other years watering may be all but unnecessary.

Sandy soils, which hold so much less water than loamy ones, need to be watered more frequently, yet less water is needed to achieve their field capacity. Where the subsoil is gravelly, only enough water should be applied to moisten the upper soil levels, since any excess could wash away needed nutrients.

Planting arrangements and the growth habits of individual plants also affect water requirements. Shallow-rooted crops such as cabbages and onions need more frequent waterings than pumpkins or tomatoes, which have roots that penetrate some 4 feet below the soil surface. Raised beds, particularly ones without structured sides, lose water through evaporation and usually require more waterings than level beds. Intensively planted beds generally require more water than conventional rows per square foot of garden space since more plants are competing for the moisture. However, since it is easier to direct moisture right to the planted areas and to avoid wasting any on unplanted ground (paths and borders), total moisture needs are probably less in the well-planned intensive garden. Finally, mulching always diminishes the need for watering and may even make any artificial watering unnecessary.

In deciding how much water to give plants, follow the guidelines for determining when to water. When the soil around the plants' root zones is near field capacity, and sticks to a probe, enough water has been applied. This may require ¼ inch of water, or 1 inch, depending on the amount already present and on the soil type. Use the chart on Characteristic Rooting Depth which appears in chapter 3 to assure that moisture is being supplied to the right level, and water evenly beneath each plant's canopy of leaves so that the entire root mass is moistened.

Watering Aids

Lots of special hoses, cans, and sprayers are available for watering the garden. Which one you use depends on the size and layout of your garden and on the proximity of the water supply. Probably the best watering device for any gardener, whether he or she has a water supply handy or not, is a bucket or watering can full of warm water. These containers are perfect for applying liquid fertilizers like manure or compost tea and dilute fish emulsion. With a watering can, you can direct the moisture right where it's needed without spraying leaves or garden paths. A Haws-type can, or any other with a fine-holed head, is excellent for tender plants, transplants, and seedlings. Mature crops can be watered directly, with just about any sort of watering can, although care should always be taken to avoid eroding soil away from the plant base. Pour the water slowly, letting it soak in before the full amount is applied. Also, if you pour it through a light mulch the soil will not be washed away as easily from plant roots.

If you wish to use equipment you have on hand for an efficient watering system, consider the garden hose, minus its sprinkler attachment. With a hose laid directly on the ground you can apply the water exactly where it is needed, without any being wasted on leaves or sidewalks or nearby weeds. When you stretch a piece of burlap over the hose end, the ground will not be washed away beneath the stream of water. A board or rock placed under the hose end will serve the same purpose. You can set the hose in the center of a raised bed, being careful not to damage surrounding plants, or in a slight furrow dug between the crop rows of a conventional row garden. If the garden is mulched, place the hose well under the material so that the water is not lost to evaporation. As puddles begin to form, move the hose, so that the entire area is evenly watered. Allow water to penetrate slowly, gradually soaking the furrow or surrounding area. Too strong a stream could result in erosion or runoff problems, particularly in an unmulched garden. Keep water pressure very low for best results.

The main drawback to hose watering is the simple problem of getting moisture to all the plants. Hoses are heavy, uncooperative items to move, and simply dragging them through the garden usually results in several mangled plants. In the intensively planted bed, hose watering is discouraging at the very least; sometimes it is downright impossible unless you can devise some sort of system-

Gentle Waterer: This Haws-type watering can releases a gentle sprinkling of water droplets through its multi-holed head, making it the perfect choice for watering seedlings.

atic approach. One method is to leave a center aisle in each bed where the hose can be laid. Begin watering at the far end of the bed, with the hose fully extended. As you continue the watering, just pull it down the aisle until the the entire bed has been watered. The same setup would work in an ordinary row garden, where the hose would be stretched beside a single row.

make your own

Homemade Drip Irrigators

With a little ingenuity, you can rig up some drip irrigators from used gallon jugs, tin cans, or spare clay pots. No matter which container you start with, the effect in the garden will be the same—water will be released slowly, right where it is needed, so it can seep deeply into the root zone with no loss through runoff or evaporation.

If you have a glass gallon jug on hand (like the kind cider and wine come in), take the lid and poke holes into it with a hammer and a finishing nail. Fill the bottle with water, screw on the lid, then set it on its side in the garden, with the dripping lid directed toward the base of the plant to be watered. Gardeners who use this technique report that one visit per plant a week from this portable irrigator supplies adequate moisture.

Plastic gallon jugs that commonly hold milk can also be adapted as drip irrigators. Heat a nail, and punch small holes near the base of the jug. In the garden, partially bury the upright jug between two plants, and refill it about once a week or as needed.

Individual plants like cucumbers and tomatoes that are big drinkers benefit from clay pots or tin cans sunk into the soil near their roots. You can easily replenish these containers with water from a watering can or garden hose, adding enough to equal a gallon per week. This way, the roots get deep, thorough watering, and the surface soil isn't displaced by a forceful gush of water.

Clay pots will already have drainage holes, but you must add them to the bottom of the tin can with a hammer and nail. Sink the pot or can into the ground before you plant the seeds, or bury the container just before you set a seedling in place. You should always allow at least a 3-inch margin between plants and the rim of the container. Don't bury the container so deeply that it

is level with the ground; let about 1 inch protrude. If you are caging your tomatoes, sink the pot or can into the middle of the cage.

When your garden needs an extra shot of nutrients, these clay pot or tin can irrigators can be pressed into action. If you add a scoopful of fresh manure or compost to the container, the water that seeps out into the soil will be transformed into a nourishing drink of manure or compost tea.

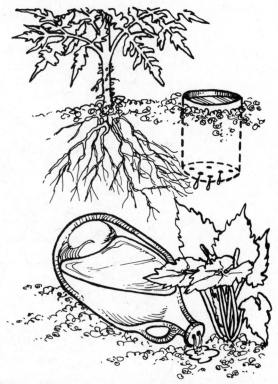

Home-Style Irrigators: The steady drip, drip, drip of water from these modified kitchen cast-offs will supply your plants with water right where they need it.

An even better setup is the drip or trickle method, one of the most efficient ways to water. For this system, a special hose is required—either a canvas soaker, a fabric hose with tiny pores through which the water passes; or a perforated plastic hose with a row of tiny holes along its entire length. Since moisture is released all along these there is no need to move them once they have been set in place. Either hose may be buried under a mulch, or set atop the soil surface. The plastic type, in particular, can be left buried under a mulch throughout the summer, provided you have enough hose length to cover the entire bed or patch. Since the canvas soaker type might weaken or clog, it should not be buried for long periods of time. Both may become clogged, and you should check·them periodically to be certain that water is being released from all holes.

Plastic perforated hose has one decided advantage over the older canvas soakers. Whereas the soakers can be used only for soil watering, plastic hoses can also serve as sprayers. This feature comes in handy on occasions when your crops' leaves are coated with dirt and need a rinsing, as well as when you want to coat the leaves and stems with water to serve as protection against frost. (See the section on Frostproofing Your Garden later in this chapter.) If the hose holes face upward and water pressure is strong, a large area may be soaked by the spray.

Both hoses are well worth the investment and make the job of watering very simple and efficient. The way they deliver water to the garden suits plant growth to a tee, for the water that trickles out soaks in slowly in a concentrated area. Their only real disadvantage seems to be a loss of water where the hose crosses unplanted areas. Since they emit water wherever they are, moisture is wasted

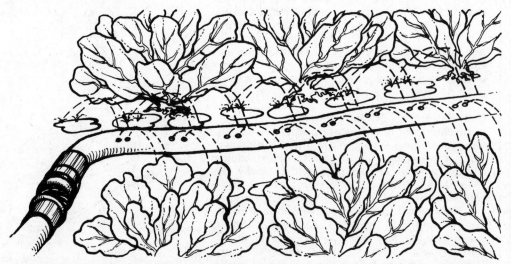

Slow and Steady Irrigation: This is one of the most efficient means of watering the garden, for the special plastic soaker hose delivers the water right where it is needed, and at a slow and steady rate so that it is absorbed by the soil rather than lost to the air. The hose is hooked up to a regular garden hose which connects to a spigot; this avoids wasting water, which would occur if the perforated hose had to cross areas other than the garden to reach the water source.

on paths, lawn, or other areas crossed to get to the vegetable garden. You can avoid this problem by purchasing one that attaches to ordinary garden hose.

If you have a fairly reliable source of water, and one that is relatively close to the garden area, you may want to consider installing a formal, permanent system of drip irrigation. Such a system has the same advantages of the portable soakers and perforated hoses, but may be left in place all year long. Usually, it consists of two soft, flexible plastic perforated pipes for each 5-foot-wide raised bed, or one pipe every 2 to 3 feet in the conventional row garden. A main pipe along one side of the beds or patch connects to these smaller feeder pipes. The feeder pipes may be installed on the soil surface or underground, although above-ground pipes have fewer problems with clogging. As water is pumped through the system, it drips through the tiny holes, evenly supplying the growing area. Again, as with the plastic and canvas hoses, water goes only where it is needed. No runoff occurs and no water is wasted outside the crop root zones. By reducing and increasing the pressure, you can regulate moisture flow to suit any soil type, gradient, or crop requirement. However, unlike the hoses which can be easily maneuvered and removed for cultivation, this system is to a large degree permanent. The main supply lines, often placed below ground, usually remain in place, with feeder lines possibly being more mobile. For this reason, wait to install a permanent system until the ground has been gardened for several years and is in near-optimum condition. Also, if you use a rotary tiller to work the soil, be careful not to disrupt the pipe system when you till.

When you are ready to set up a permanent watering system, research equipment and techniques by consulting your state or province agricultural extension service and various suppliers. For several good sources of further information, see the Bibliography, later in this book.

Supplemental Fertilizing

As long as the soil has been properly prepared, very little supplemental feeding is necessary in the organic vegetable garden. A soil rich in organic matter, with the proper pH and adequate moisture, will continue to supply a wide variety of plants with the necessary nutrients throughout the season. Where a well-planned system of interplanting, companion planting, rotation, and successions is being used, major nutrient deficiencies will only rarely occur. Deficiencies of iron, sulfur, and most trace elements will almost never occur. To fertilize for these nutrients may actually increase the risk of toxicity problems for the plants.

However, in order to keep levels of certain nutrients in reserve for succeeding crops, you should continue to work organic substances into the soil whenever the opportunity arises. This is especially important for potassium-rich substances which, because of leaching losses, are best applied in small doses throughout the season. Crops requiring medium to heavy amounts of potassium should be generously fertilized with wood ashes at least once during their growth. Compost and well-rotted manure should also be incorporated whenever you can work them in. Not only do these materials boost overall fertility, but they replenish trace elements as well. After an early crop is harvested, work in additional compost, well-rotted manure, or other materials. Keep in mind the nutrients the first crop used, and those the next will require. If your planning has been good, they will probably be different. Thus, you may want to apply blood meal to replace some of the nitrogen lost to an early cabbage crop, and add wood ashes for the upcoming carrots. Be wary of overfertilizing that could result in nutrient toxicity (harmful to plants, not to the gardener) or of applying a material that prevents the fruiting or development of the succeeding crop.

Dealing with Nutrient Deficiencies

Occasionally, when soil preparation has been inadequate or when drought or other conditions hinder nutrient availability, fertility problems occur. Depending on the nutrient lacking and the crop itself, symptoms will vary greatly. Diseases or insects may attack the weakened crop and disguise its deficiency signals. At other times, the deficiency is so slight as to be almost undetectable. Nevertheless, it is important to stay on the alert for signs of yellowing, stunted growth, or any of the other symptoms presented in the chart on Nutrient Deficiencies—Their Symptoms and Remedies. If the deficiency is noted early on and the missing nutrient supplied quickly, the deficiency may be correctable before harvest. However, by the time signs of deficiency appear in plants, it is often too late to remedy the matter organically since organic fertilizers take time to break down. Although the soil may, and should, be improved for subsequent plantings, the nutrient will not usually be available until several weeks or even months have passed.

There are a few organic fertilizers that break down more rapidly than others and, with an eye to the risk of overapplications, these can be applied to remedy certain nutrient deficiencies. These materials are also good choices for general midseason feedings of transplants, heavy feeders, and long-season crops. (For specific guidelines on midseason feedings, see individual crops featured in the Vegetable Guide.) When your soil is in good shape, light-feeding crops will do well without a midseason boost.

For nitrogen, use dried blood, fish emulsion, fresh chicken manure, compost, or cottonseed meal. For potassium, wood ashes act the fastest. Unfortunately, organic phosphorus fertilizers are slow-release and should be applied early in spring or during fall preparation in order to benefit summer crops.

Applying the Fertilizer

Midseason fertilizers may be applied in liquid form to the soil or sprayed on the leaves, or they can be side-dressed in dry form alongside established crops.

With solution feeding, you are pouring enriched water onto the soil, where it can soak down to the plants' roots. You may use either manure or compost tea (see the Introduction for directions), or a dilute solution of fish emulsion or seaweed extract. The latter two are available commercially in concentrated form, and directions are given on the package telling you how to dilute them. The usual solution is one tablespoon concentrate per gallon of water.

When you water with these enriched solutions, you want to apply them as close to the plants as possible, so the nutrients will seep directly down to where they are needed. Because these are dilute solutions, there is no concern about burning the plants.

Instead of applying nutrients to the roots, in the case of foliar feeding you are spraying them on the leaves in weak solutions. Because the leaves absorb the nutrients almost immediately, this method of fertilizing gives the most rapid

Nutrient Deficiencies—Their Symptoms and Remedies

Nutrient	Function	Deficiency Symptoms	Common Organic Sources	Deficiency Occurrence
Nitrogen (N)	Required for all phases of growth and development (roots, stems, leaves); excesses increase leaf and shoot growth, causing delay in maturity of certain crops.	Leaves are light green or yellowish (lower leaves first to show discoloration); plant is stunted; some nitrogen deficiency symptoms are normal during fruiting.	Blood meal, cottonseed meal, sewage sludge, animal tankage, farm manure, poultry manure, compost.	Mostly on very light soils where leaching occurs; may result wherever planting has been heavy and fertilization inadequate.
Phosphorus (P)	Constituent of plant's genetic material; found mostly in the growing points of plants (shoot tips and roots); increases rate of crop maturity; strengthens stems; helps in resistance to pests and diseases; necessary for proper fruiting, flowering, seed formation, and root branching.	Lower leaves and stem have reddish coloring; upper leaves are dull, pale; plant is stunted; failure to flower or produce fruit.	Bone meal, animal tankage, phosphate rock, fish meal.	On acid soils; temporary deficiency occurs on cold, wet soil.
Potassium (K)	Required for formation of sugars, starches, and proteins, and for action of certain enzymes; contributes to cold-hardiness; enhances flavor and color of some crops; needed for development of root crops; also aids in development of fruits and seeds.	Lower leaves spotted, mottled, or curled; leaves may appear scorched along edges or tips; corn leaves appear streaked; root system underdeveloped; yields low; fruit misshapen, small; grain is chaffy; stem tissue may appear weak.	Nonwoody plant residues, (particularly hulls, peelings, and rinds), manure, seaweed, wood ashes, greensand, granite dust.	Leaches from very light soils; most likely to be deficient in upper layers of soil since plants remove it from these levels.
Calcium	Required for cell growth and division; helps plant use nitrogen.	Blackheart in celery; brownheart in escarole; tipburn on lettuce or cabbage leaves; blossom-end rot in pepper, tomato, watermelon; cavities in carrot, parsnip.	Liming materials, bone meal, gypsum, plant residues.	Mostly on acid soils or on soils with high potassium levels; very dry soil may be deficient.

(continued)

Nutrient Deficiencies—Their Symptoms and Remedies—*continued*

Nutrient	Function	Deficiency Symptoms	Common Organic Sources	Deficiency Occurrence
Magnesium	Constituent of chlorophyll; required for enzyme action.	Whitish patches appear first on older leaves, between leaf veins.	Dolomite lime, talc, epsom salts.	On acid soils, light soils easily leached, and high-potassium soils.
Sulfur	Constituent of protein, certain vitamin complexes.	New leaves are yellowish.	Barnyard manure, plant residues, gypsum.	Rarely occurs in eroded, leached soils; toxicity a problem in coal areas.
Iron	Acts as catalyst in production of chlorophyll; essential to development of young growing parts of plants.	Yellow in leaf veins; pale growing points (not common in vegetable crops).		On soils with pH above 6.8.
Boron	Affects flowering, fruiting, hormone movement, and cell division; closely related to uptake of calcium.	Buds die; stems become shorter; leaves are thick, curled, brittle; fruit, tubers, and roots may be discolored, cracked, or misshapen; cracked stem in celery; browning of cauliflower; blackheart in beet.	Lime, manure	On soils with pH above 6.8.
Manganese	Required for production of chlorophyll; involved in enzyme systems.	Young leaves show dark veins against lighter areas; beet leaves become dark red; onion and corn develop yellow striping on the leaves.		On soils with pH above 6.7; toxicity may occur on acid soils.
Copper	Part of enzyme systems; possibly helps to transport and utilize proteins.	Shoot tips and terminal leaves die back from their tips; leaves appear pale or fail to form.		On muck or peat soils.
Molybdenum	Essential for nitrogen transformation; required by root nodule bacteria.	Nitrogen deficiency symptoms may appear; leaves pale with rolled margins; older leaves turn yellow; potato tubers fail to form; cauliflower head forms small, open curds; leaves of cabbage and related plants are narrow, "whip-tailed."		On very acid soils.
Zinc	Needed for formation of chloroplasts, starch, and certain hormones; legumes need it for seed formation.	Bean cotyledons develop red or brown spots; corn leaves develop green and yellow striping at base; iron deficiency symptoms may follow.		On wet, heavy soils in early spring; may be due to excess phosphorus fertilization.

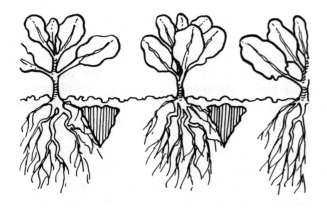

Side-Dressing: This simple technique is a good way to make midseason feedings of materials like rotted manure, compost, or bone meal. Dig a furrow alongside the plant or group of plants to be fed, add the material, then draw a layer of soil over the furrow with a hoe.

results. Foliar feeding is especially helpful during very wet or very dry spells when nutrient uptake through the soil is hindered. The fertilizers to use are seaweed or fish emulsion concentrates, diluted as directed on the package. Because the nutrient benefits are not long-lasting, you must spray your plants with these enriched solutions every two to three weeks throughout the season.

Side-dressing calls for applying the dry fertilizing material in a shallow furrow alongside the crop. It has been shown to increase the rate at which some materials become available to plants, especially bone meal and phosphate rock. Side-dressing is a good method to use with potent materials such as fresh chicken manure, which could burn plants if applied too close to the roots. The disadvantages of side-dressing are the relatively slow results and the chances for losses due to leaching. Blood meal or cottonseed meal applied in a side-dressing could take two weeks to reach a usable level for plants. Wood ashes, so susceptible to leaching, might never provide nearby plants with the potassium they require.

To side-dress plants, dig a 2- to 3-inch-deep furrow about 4 inches away from each plant, between rows, or around a block of bedded plants. Apply the material, then push back the soil with a hoe to cover the furrow. If you are side-dressing newly sown seeds, material may be placed slightly closer, but no nearer than 2 inches.

Timing of fertilization can be critical, particularly in dealing with nitrogen fertilizers. Plants just preparing to flower or fruit are winding down their development of leaves and shoots. If you boost the available nitrogen supply at this point, crops will revert back to an earlier stage of development and the harvest will be delayed. Similarly, since nitrogen tends to make crops succulent and tender, late plantings of salad crops and greens, or any perennials, should not be given nitrogen fertilizers in the fall. This would only promote top growth, making the plants an easy target for frost damage.

Mulching

A properly applied mulch can be the best friend a small-scale gardener has. In addition to the obvious advantages of water conservation and weed control, mulches provide physical protection for growing crops. Vining vegetables tend to stay cleaner and drier when they are surrounded by a mulch. Soil compaction is lessened so there is less opportunity for root damage. A mulch plays a different role in the garden as the seasons progress. During the winter, it protects perennials from freezing and heavage. In spring and summer, it forms an insulating blanket, reducing sharp temperature shifts which could shock exposed plants. A mulch also keeps cool-weather plants cooler in the spring and summer. And in the fall, a good mulch may extend the garden season several months beyond the first frost.

Organic and inorganic mulching materials are discussed in the Introduction. Refer to this information to help you decide which material (or materials) will be most beneficial to your garden. Whether or not the material is readily available, and its cost (if any) should figure in your final selection of mulching material.

Whether you are applying an organic or inorganic mulch, it is necessary to wait until the ground is prepared, and is neither soggy nor dry. A mulched wet soil stays wet; a dry one will remain dry. The same principle also applies to cold and warm soil.

Organic Mulches

For an organic mulch to be effective, it must be thick enough to provide a good soil covering. When loose material such as straw or leaves is used, make the mulch 8 to 10 inches thick. Once the material has been on for a while, it will compact down to about 4 inches. There's no need to apply finer materials as thickly. For example, just 2 to 3 inches of sawdust form a satisfactory weed barrier.

Where tiny seedlings are just getting established, or where plants have not yet emerged, pile mulching material in windrows alongside the rows or around the raised bed. This will protect the plants from excessive exposure to sun and wind until they become established. When they have reached thinning size, gently pull the mulch around each plant, allowing some room around plant stems. While some gardeners report success with mulching crops right after seeding, this could pose problems with seedling development. With heat-loving crops, mulching too soon before the soil has a chance to warm up can retard their development. If you choose to mulch immediately after seed has been sown, use only a very light, loose mulch, applying more as the plants grow stronger.

Transplanted stock should be mulched as soon as it is set out, but be wary of allowing organic matter to touch the plant stalks at this early stage. Leave an unmulched circle around the base of each plant, until plants are over their shock and have built up their resistance to diseases and insects. Contact with damp or rotting mulch as soon as they are set out in the field could cause tender transplants to fall victim to damping-off.

You must replenish organic mulches throughout the summer in order to replace material that has decomposed. As crops are harvested, remove plant debris, pull back the mulch from that section of the bed or row, and plant new seeds. Replace the mulch as crops become established. When weeds begin popping through the surface, it is time to pile on more mulch, maintaining a thick barrier over the entire garden surface. If your mulch supply is limited, try placing a heavy layer of newspapers beneath the main mulching material. This will diminish weed penetration and make a little straw or compost go a long way toward protecting and enriching your garden soil.

With the arrival of fall, organic mulches may be left in place, raked to the side, or incorporated into the soil. Gardeners disagree about the best procedure, and local conditions probably make some more practical than others. Most soils respond well to a good mulch that has been tilled under at the end of the season and allowed to break down over the course of the winter (chopping or shredding the material helps the breakdown process). As long as the soil's nitrogen level is sufficiently high to break down that amount of woody material, the soil will not only be structurally improved, but nutritionally enriched as well. On the other hand, soils with barely enough nitrogen to supply the needs of the current season's plants may be in poor shape for spring planting if a woody, high-carbon mulch is tilled under in fall. Combining the mulch with a green manure crop or a nitrogen-rich material such as blood meal or cottonseed meal would correct the problem and make decomposition more complete.

Inorganic Mulches

Plastic, foil, or "carpet" mulches are strictly for use during the growing season, and should not be left in the garden after harvest. Far from replacements for organic mulches, these should be viewed as supplements. They may be placed on top of layers of compost, straw, leaves, or manure, or used alone in specific sections of the vegetable beds. If a winter mulch seems desirable, forego the inorganic mulch and apply organic material after the ground has frozen.

Black and clear polyethylene are sold in rolls of several hundred feet, or in some hardware stores by the yard. Three or 4 feet is the most widely available

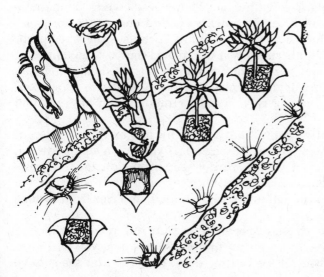

Planting in Plastic Mulch: Setting transplants in place is a snap as long as you've made some preparations. To anchor the plastic along the row, dig shallow ditches on both sides and hold the sheet down with rocks and soil. Cut slits in the plastic at the appropriate spacings, and slip seedlings into place.

width, and the easiest to handle in the garden. In a row garden, lengths of plastic may be laid between rows, with narrow spaces left open for planting, or the sheeting may be placed over rows with slits cut for planting. Since 3 feet is a bit wide for most between-row spacing, the latter method is usually preferred. By covering the entire area with plastic, you eliminate the places for weeds to emerge. However, it does become necessary to cut holes in the material and this may make it harder to use the following year.

Raised beds and band plantings are easily mulched with plastic since the entire area can usually be covered with one length of sheeting. If you plan on using plastic mulch, consider shaping your growing beds to fit the widths available. This will save lots of time and trouble.

Crops planted in a plastic-mulched garden will require no further mulching during the growing season. If the soil seems to become dry, a light watering beneath the mulch will quickly revive plants. Do not overwater plastic-mulched plants since there is little opportunity for excess moisture to escape. If fertilization is needed, use foliar sprays or solutions poured around the base of the plants where it can seep in through the slits or holes in the plastic.

Weeding and Cultivating

There is no trick to weeding: it's simply a matter of getting down on your knees and yanking up the weeds, one by one. That's simple enough, provided you can recognize a weed (not always an easy task), and you have a good supply of perseverence. The dream of every gardener is a virtually weed-free garden. While it is unrealistic to hope that you'll never see a single weed in your garden, there are certain preventive and control measures you can take to ensure that the weeds don't outnumber the vegetables.

Nothing helps eradicate weeds better than a clean, thick layer of organic material or a single sheet of black polyethylene. Those weeds which do manage to force their way through a mulch can be quickly spotted and easily uprooted. Occasionally, gardeners find that their mulch actually increases the weed problems in the vegetable garden. This occurs when unfinished compost, hay, uncomposted manure, or other material containing viable seeds is used. To avoid the problem, compost manures before using them as mulches. Use straw, which contains no weed seeds, instead of hay, or rely on grass clippings, salt hay, or wood chips.

Unmulched gardens usually require cultivation by hoe or rotary tiller in order to keep weeds under control and to loosen soil. If yours is a small garden, hand weeding will suffice. Mulched gardens rarely need hoeing during the growing season, unless it is to prepare soil for new plantings in certain small areas. For the most part, mulch keeps the soil loose, well aerated, and free from serious weed problems.

If for some reason, such as excessive moisture in your soil or a sheer dislike of the "mulched look," you have opted for an unmulched garden, you will need to begin cultivation for weed control some three days after the first seeds have been sown. It is necessary to begin this early so that weeds do not get a head start on the crops you are trying to raise. This preemergent cultivation is a job requiring painstaking care, for while you need to destroy the weeds, you must not disturb the yet-unsprouted vegetable seeds. When tiny weeds appear on the soil surface, use a steel rake to gently uproot them in the between-row areas. If you planted seeds fairly deep, go ahead and rake the entire area; otherwise be content with eliminating most, but not all, of the young weeds. In the raised bed, rake cultivation is possible, but a hand cultivator may be easier to manage. Where seeds have been broadcast or equidistantly spaced, the old-fashioned method of hand-pulling is best. Be careful not to yank too hard or to compact the soil where seeds have been planted.

When seedlings have emerged and begun to make good growth, you do not need to be quite so cautious in your cultivation. You should still be respectful of the young growth, and not work so deeply that you uproot the seedlings. The steel rake is still a fine tool for the job in a row garden since it does not disturb the seedling roots and allows you to weed quite close to the plants without harming them. You can also employ a pointed Warren hoe or a flat-bladed draw hoe, but use these gently; do not hoe any deeper than 1 inch, and avoid handling the tool as if it were a sledgehammer. A hoe is meant to push or pull the soil, not to chop it. A special scuffle hoe (or Dutch hoe), with a sort of stirrup-shaped blade, will even get rid of weeds without moving the soil at all. When you push it across the ground, it chops off the weeds at ground level, diminishing their chances for survival.

The best time for weeding, whether it be by hoe, rake, or hand, is midafternoon when the sun burns its brightest. Weeds come up most easily from damp soil, but you can't work in soggy ground or among crops when their leaves are damp for fear of spreading disease. Wait until the plants have been dried by the sun; then weeds may be uprooted and left in the path where their exposed roots will shrivel.

A wheel cultivator or rotary tiller is helpful in managing large areas, or in eliminating pernicious weeds that cannot be handled by manual hoeing. Do not use such tools as routine methods for cultivation, however, for they may tend to damage soil structure if used excessively. Eventually they will plow under rich topsoil and expose the less valuable subsoil.

No matter what type of equipment you use, be careful not to overcultivate in midseason. Cultivation exposes moist soil particles to the drying sun and air, causing significant loss of soil moisture. Very deep tillage, of more than 5 or 6 inches, is of little use unless you need to correct a special aeration problem or plow under diseased plant material.

Frostproofing Your Garden

One way to recognize a truly successful, seasoned gardener is to check his or her garden in the fall, after the first frosts have hit. Chances are there will still be many vegetables left for the picking. If you happen by there again in

make your own

Supporting Your Vegetables in Style

Lanky vegetables need something to cling to as they grow, something that will provide support for their tendrils and vines. Peas and pole beans come to mind first, but even space-hungry vines like cucumbers, melons, pumpkins, and squash can be trained vertically. Two lesser-known vegetables, luffa and Malabar spinach, also take well to vertical growing surfaces.

With this in mind, here are some basic approaches to providing support for your vegetables. The supports range from very simple to somewhat more complex, but there's sure to be a method that suits the type of vegetables you grow and the particular space you grow them in.

VEGETABLE FRAME

In this method, you set up a wooden frame that serves as an anchor and support for a vertical surface on which the vegetables can climb. This method and any variations are suitable for cucumbers, luffa, Malabar spinach, peas, and pole beans.

Begin by driving two sturdy 6- to 8-foot wooden poles at least 12 inches into the ground, one at each end of the row. You'll avoid possible repair work later in the season if you set the poles parallel to the prevailing wind. You can also increase the longevity of your poles by treating them with a nontoxic wood preservative like copper napthenate. Staple wire fencing or nylon trellis mesh to one pole, with the lower edge 6 inches from the ground. Use a large-sized mesh (5- to 6-inch squares) for cucumbers, pumpkins, and squash; beans and peas grow well on smaller mesh, with 1½-inch openings. Unroll it until it reaches the other pole, then pull it taut and staple it to the pole. If the row is very long, you may need to position another post in the middle to keep the fencing from sagging. A good rule of thumb to follow is to allow no more than an armspan between posts.

A-FRAME SUPPORT

Once you build this support, it is sure to become a perennial in your garden. This A-frame is a permanent support that is also portable, which means that you can move it around your garden, and use it season after season without having to go through the tedious work of taking it apart and putting it back together again. This A-frame is just the thing for your pole beans and peas (especially the Sugar Snaps).

From lightweight scrap wood, build an A-frame measuring 6 feet wide, 8 feet tall, and 2 feet deep. For extra support to keep the middle from sagging under the weight of the mature plants, attach an upright to the middle of the 6-foot peak of the frame. Take wire fencing or nylon mesh and staple it to both 6-by-8-foot sides of the frame. When the A-frame is set in place, you can use the mesh pattern as a guide for planting your seed.

OFF THE WALL

The methods presented in this section are variations on the general theme of eking a garden out of tight places, and taking advantage of surfaces that normally couldn't be used for gardening. What these methods do is to provide vertical surfaces or an alternative form of trellising that transforms sides of garages or storage sheds and areas under the eaves of a house into viable gardening spaces. Depending on which variation you use, you can harvest peas, pole beans, cucumbers, luffas, squash, and pumpkins from areas you may have overlooked as gardening sites.

A vertical support system located under the eaves or overhang of a house is good for peas and pole beans, and can be incorporated into the landscaping when you grow an especially attractive variety like scarlet runner beans. Start by drilling a hole in the overhang and inserting a screw eye. This procedure can be repeated, inserting a screw eye every 4 to 6 inches, depending on how much area you want to cover. Attach a piece of string to each screw eye and run it down to the ground, where you should secure it to a stake and then pound the stake into the ground. Plant your peas or pole bean seeds at the base of each string.

Vines bearing heavy fruit like cucumbers, pumpkins, and squashes need more than a single string for support. To support these vegetables in the proper manner and to make use of idle sunny space alongside a house, garage, or shed, you need to construct a wooden frame lean-to that will act as a sloping trellis. Using scrap wood, build a wooden frame intersected at regular intervals by crosspieces. If your frame is very wide, you may want to add a single vertical support to the middle of the frame. For extra stability, sink the posts into the ground and use extra pieces of wood and nails to brace the support against the wall. Plant your vine crops at the base of the trellis and as their vines lengthen, drape them up onto the trellis.

TEPEE OR TRIPOD

Simple yet functional is the charm of these vegetable supports. The basic idea calls for three or more poles to be arranged in a triangle or circle in the ground, and lashed

(continued)

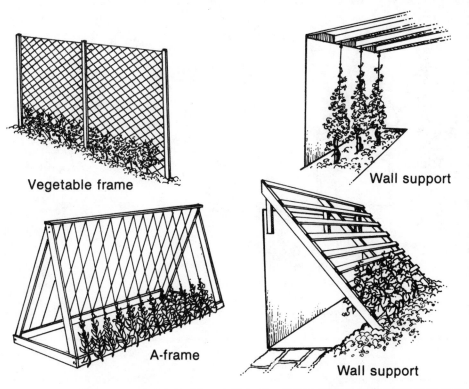

Vegetable frame

Wall support

A-frame

Wall support

Supporting Your Vegetables in Style—*continued*

together at the top to provide an upright surface for vegetables planted at the base of each pole. Pole beans, pumpkins, and squash respond well to this treatment, and you can take advantage of the cool, shady area inside the structure to grow lettuce or some other sun-shy leaf crop.

For a tripod, you'll need three 6- to 8-foot poles and strong cord. Take each pole and position it so that together with the others it forms the three points of a triangle. Push each pole firmly into the ground. Bring the tops of the poles in together and lash them securely to one another. Each pole can support three bean plants, but only one pumpkin or squash plant. Remember that the poles must be set in place before planting time.

A tepee is constructed on the same principle, only you use more than 3 poles (8 to 12 are common) and arrange them in a circle in the ground. This arrangement is especially recommended for pole beans, with one bean planted per pole.

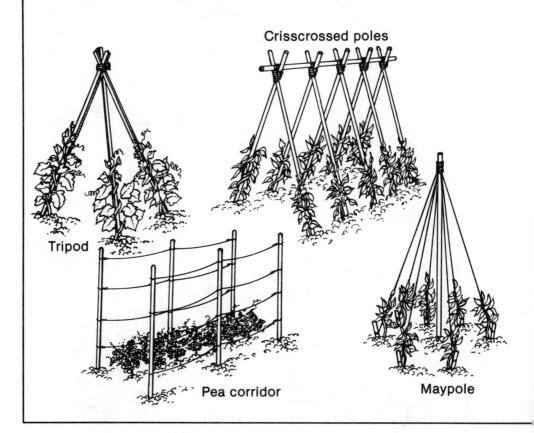

Crisscrossed poles

Tripod

Pea corridor

Maypole

CRISSCROSSED POLES

With this method you create a strong, self-supporting series of crossed and lashed poles that provide upright growing surfaces for climbing plants like peas and pole beans. An added feature is the shady and cool interior that's just right for raising a crop of lettuce or spinach.

You'll need to select pairs of canes or poles, ranging from 6 to 8 feet in height, plus extra poles to be used as horizontal supports. Bamboo is a good choice since it is strong, yet flexible and lightweight. How many pairs of canes you'll need depends on how long you want the structure to be. Plan to place each pair about 12 inches apart, and figure out how many pairs you'll need from there. The number of extra poles for horizontal support that you'll need depends on how long the series of crisscrossed poles is. For example, if the series extends for 8 feet, you'll need a support pole 8 feet long. And, if the crossed poles cover 16 feet, you'll need two 8-foot support poles.

Take each pair of poles and lash them together, the same distance from the top. Spread the free ends of the joined poles and insert them 2 to 3 inches into the ground, straddling the row. Repeat until all the pairs of lashed poles are used, and make sure that the ends pushed into the ground form two parallel lines, spanning the row by an equal distance on each side. Take the extra support pole and set it down the middle of the lashed tops, where it will nestle right into the row of V's formed by the crossed poles. Lash this horizontal support pole securely to each set of crossed poles. You can plant three beans per pole.

MAYPOLE

Although you may never catch your pole beans bobbing and weaving around it, this bean support does resemble a maypole with its tall central pole and individual strings that radiate outward in a circle.

To assemble it, you must find a 6- to 7-foot pole and notch it 4 inches from the top. Collect six wooden stakes and a ball of sturdy twine. Tie one length of twine to the center pole, in the notch, and extend it out to the ground. Then tie it to a notched stake and pound the stake into the ground about 2 feet out from the pole to anchor it. Repeat this procedure with the five other strings, evenly spacing them in a circle around the center pole. Plant three pole beans per pole.

PEA CORRIDOR

This method is especially well suited to peas, and allows you to contain and direct the growth of a single or double row in an airy corridor made of stakes or poles and string.

You'll need enough pairs of 4-foot-tall stakes or poles to extend along the row length. These poles can be spaced rather far apart (2 to 2½ feet), so you won't need a large number of them. Set them in place opposite each other, along a row of pea seedlings. Join the poles on one side of the row together by running a length of string between them. Starting with the first pole in the row, fasten the string securely, continue to the next pole, pull the string snug and loop it around the pole, then proceed down the row of poles in this fashion. Do this three times, spacing the string at three different levels along the height of the poles, at bottom, middle, and top. Repeat with the poles on the other side of the row.

A Guide to Training Tomatoes

Not all tomatoes need to be trained. Determinate types are stocky and bushy and stop growing at a certain point as the tomatoes set and ripen at the ends of the stems. These sedate plants require no training and should never be pruned, since that reduces the number of fruit clusters that develop. Indeterminate plants are a different matter. Their stems will grow until they are halted by frost. As they grow, each stem produces a flower cluster, three leaves, a flower cluster, and so on. By letting these plants sprawl as they please, you will end up with an unruly mass of stems and leaves before the season is through. And chances are, many of the tomatoes that are sitting on the ground will rot or be hollowed out by slugs by the time you get to them.

To control an indeterminate plant, you must prune it and train it to grow vertically. Pruning is as simple as pinching off the suckers (small shoots) that appear in the leaf axils. If allowed to grow, each sucker will develop into a full-fledged branch with leaves, flower clusters, and suckers of its own. You must be conscientious and check for suckers about twice a week. If you remove all the suckers, you will have a single-stemmed plant that is easy to manage. If you remove all but the one sucker immediately below the first flower cluster, you will create a double-stemmed plant that will have a little more foliage, lessening fruit loss due to sunscald and cracking.

You should prune the top of the main stem above the uppermost blossom cluster about three to four weeks before the first expected frost. This halts the plant's growth and channels energy into ripening the green fruit that has already developed.

The easiest way to train your plants is to support them with a single stake. Select stakes that are at least 5 feet tall, with rough or smooth surfaces. At transplanting time, pound them into the soil at least 6 inches deep, before you set the seedlings in place. A depth of 10 to 12 inches is recommended in windy areas. Leave a space of 3 to 5 inches between the plant and the stake. You will need to tie the tomato stem (or stems) to the stake and for this you should use soft material, such as old sheets, strips of nylon stockings, or thick woolly yarn. Avoid any fine string or wire that can cut into the stems and damage them. Make a "figure eight" loop that allows for some stem movement but still holds the plant to the stake. To do this, make a single loose loop around the stem, cross the ends and make a double loop around the stake, then tie tightly with a firm knot. There should be 1 to 2 inches of slack. Add more ties as the plant grows taller.

A variation on the single stake method is the "three for two" method that provides three stakes for every two plants. Center a stake between adjacent plants all along the row, and use strong cord to connect the poles, forming a truss that supports the plants. Drill holes in the stakes to keep the cord from slipping down. In this method, there is no need to tie the individual plant to a stake, but some pruning must still be done to keep the plants in line.

With tomato cages, no pruning or tying is necessary, because the plant grows up inside a wire-mesh cage which allows the developing branches to push through the spaces and rest on the mesh, which supports the whole plant. There is enough foliage to keep sunscald and cracking from becoming a concern, and the shaded soil under the plant stays moist longer, reducing the occurrence of blossom-end rot.

Different types of wire can be used for cages, ranging from hog fencing wire to concrete reinforcing wire. There is no hard and fast rule as to which type of wire is best—just make sure that whatever wire you purchase has a large enough mesh so that you can fit your hand through to pick the ripe tomatoes (4-by-4-inch or 6-by-6-inch meshes are large enough). The common height for tomato cages is 4 to 5 feet, and the generally recommended diameter is 18 inches. A rule of thumb to determine how

(continued)

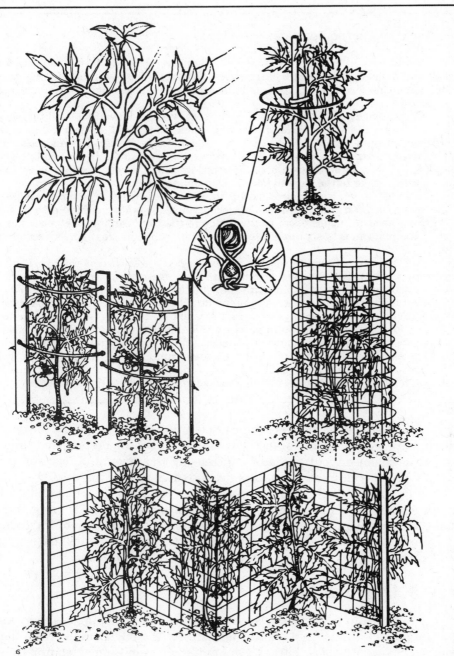

Tomato-Growing Tactics: Removing suckers (as shown, upper left) is an important part of training a plant along a single stake (upper right). Anytime you tie a plant to a support, use the "figure-eight" loop, shown in the detail. The "three-for-two" method of staking (center left) provides a secure support for lanky plants, as does the tomato plant cage (center right). The zigzag fence shown at bottom conveniently folds up into a manageable shape for storage at the end of the season.

A Guide to Training Tomatoes—*continued*

much wire you will need for each cage is to figure you'll need 3 feet of material for each foot of diameter, plus about 3 extra inches to be used for fastening the cage together. So, using this formula, an 18-inch-diameter cage requires roughly 57 inches of wire fencing.

Carefully cut the desired length of wire with wire cutters and bend the piece into a cylinder, so that the width of the wire becomes the height of the cage. Loop the cut wire on the ends together to lock the cylinder in place. To serve as an anchor for the cage once it is in place, clip out the crosswires that run along the bottom to leave wire spikes that can be pushed into the ground. In windy areas, you may need to add a supporting stake to the cage to keep it from flying away.

A variation on basic caging is called the "Japanese ring" or "compost ring." In this method, you build the cage as above, set it in place, and then add a thick layer of compost (about 6 inches deep) to the inside of the cage. Around the perimeter of the cage you plant four to six tomato seedlings, and prune and tie them as needed as they grow.

Another type of tomato support can be properly described as the hybrid offspring of caging and fencing. In this design, you use 13 feet of 5-foot-tall wire fencing, with 6-inch mesh. Cut the length of wire into smaller sections, 30 inches long. Allow the horizontal wire on the cut edges to protrude. These open end wires are used to hinge the individual pieces together to form a straight fence. When it comes time to place this in your garden, set it up in zigzag fashion, bending it at the hinges. Fasten the free ends to strong stakes that are pounded firmly into the ground. You can plant on both sides of this fence, and proceed with your pruning and tying as needed. The best feature of this fence is apparent at the end of the season, when storage becomes a snap as you fold the fence up into a bundle measuring 5 feet by 30 inches.

spring, while most gardeners are just beginning to set out plants, he or she will again have some crop to harvest. Extending the season on both ends allows you to get more out of your garden by increasing the amount of food you can grow and by giving you fresh vegetables for a greater part of the year.

A large part of this success depends on knowing varieties and on having good, fertile, well-cultivated soil. Plant hardy and half-hardy crops like beets, kale, and spinach in late summer and fall to take advantage of the cooler temperatures. Where the growing season is short, choose varieties that will mature quickly.

Protecting Plants

An important part of early spring and late fall gardening is simply knowing how to protect plants from frost. It is those occasional, sporadic frosts that keep you from planting out as early as you might, or even from extending the season beyond that fateful "first fall frost." Plenty of warm Indian summer weather remains after that first night freeze, so take advantage of those days. Use the tips presented below to help vegetable crops survive those frosty nights.

Hotcaps, cloches, and row covers: These frost guards are not only valuable in the spring garden as protectors for seedlings and tender transplants, but in the fall garden as well. Cover late-planted salad greens or root crops with paper hats, bottomless glass jugs, or plastic hotcaps. Ripening of late melons can be speeded under such a covering. For larger plants such as beans, eggplants, or peppers, invert a cardboard box or bushel basket over the plant and cover it with a sheet, burlap, or plastic. Use old feed or dog food bags to cover groups of corn plants or single tomato plants. Entire rows or raised beds may be protected with wooden or wire frames covered with polyethylene or cloth. Be sure to remove any cover you have laid down early the next morning so that humidity does not build up; this is particularly important if plastic or glass is used. See the section on Plant Protectors in chapter 3 for more hints on how to keep frost from nipping at your crops.

Mulches: Draw straw, hay, chopped leaves, or other dry material closely around the plant base and, if possible, lightly cover its crown to form an insulating blanket to ward off frost. The thicker such a mulch is, the more effective it will be, so don't skimp on materials. Celery, root crops, salad greens, and almost any other crop respond well to this sort of frost protection. Black plastic mulches will also help insulate crops, by protecting the roots from freezing. In fact, any dark-colored material will absorb more heat during the day than will lighter-colored mulches. The difference is minimal, but if you have a choice between two mulching materials, choose the darker one for best frost protection.

Cold frame: Move celery, lettuce, spinach, Swiss chard, and other cool-season crops from the garden after the first frost and transplant them into the cold frame. They will continue to grow there for at least another month's worth of harvest. Consider the cold frame an important extension of the garden, not just a separate structure for starting new plants in spring. During autumn, leave the frame open during the day, and close and cover it only when frost threatens.

Irrigation: Market gardeners regularly use sprinkler irrigation to prevent frost damage to strawberries and other crops. You can adapt this method to fit your home garden, and it will almost always be successful, provided the sprinkling is thorough and continuous and wets all the leaves and stems. The phenomenon that accounts for water's role as frost protector is this: the water being sprayed on the plants is warmer than the surrounding air, and as it gradually cools, it releases heat in the process. Temperatures on the plant surface have been recorded as high as 10 degrees above that of the surrounding air. Thus, even if air temperatures dip to 22°F, the sprinkling will prevent your crop from freezing. This warming effect of water may also be used under row covers or in cold frames. Shallow pans of water, set in the frame or under the row cover, will freeze, releasing warmth to the surrounding plants.

If, despite your best efforts, your plants have been touched by a quick frost, you can often save them by misting or spraying them early the following morning. Water them before the sun defrosts them, using cool, not warm water. This slowly relaxes frozen cells so that they do not burst or fall apart when the sun warms them. However, any vegetables damaged by frost should be harvested and prepared immediately.

Keep Those Varmints
Out of Your Garden

Oh, those sneaky creatures—they infiltrate your garden in a multitude of ways, to perpetrate their dastardly deeds. They hippety-hop in to nibble young green things; slip in on furry feet to savor ripe corn; swoop down from the sky to pluck just-germinated seed; prance in on cloven hooves to strip the garden bare; and sidle in on sneakered feet to do malicious things to tomatoes.

What can a gardener do to protect all those defenseless plants, short of taking shotgun in hand and keeping all-night vigils? Well, for a start you can read through the suggested deterrents presented here, which are claimed by some gardeners to work some of the time. But the problem with smelly and noisy artifices, at least as far as animal pests are concerned, is that they lose their effectiveness after a short time and must be changed to keep the unwanted animal diners on their guard. Very often, a good sturdy fence is the only thing that stands between your garden harvest and the local wildlife population.

Birds peck out newly planted seed and sprouted seed (especially corn); pick at young lettuce leaves.

- To protect germinating corn, plant garlic cloves or oats along with the corn. Birds don't like the taste of the earlier-sprouting garlic and oats, and won't be interested in coming back to peck at the sprouted corn. When the corn seedlings are established, thin out the garlic and oats.
- Plant seeds in a shallow trench and cover with chicken wire to keep out of the birds' reach.
- Push wooden stakes in a random pattern into the newly planted garden. Connect them with an irregular gridwork of heavy thread or string, about 2 inches from the ground.
- String tin can lids, strips of aluminum foil, or shredded plastic bags along a length of twine or wire and suspend between two stakes, to sparkle and make sporadic noise.
- Make low plastic tunnels to cover newly sown rows. Bend a series of wires to straddle the row, then drape plastic film over these supports, forming a long "Quonset hut" with open ends. Remove when seedlings are about 6 inches tall.

Deer have nondiscriminating taste and will eat any tender vegetable in the garden; active both day and night.

- Fences, unless they are at least 9 feet tall, do not daunt deer, which can easily leap tall objects in a single bound. Try laying a 4-foot-wide length of wire mesh on the ground all the way around your garden. Since the deer do not like to walk on wire, they may leave your vegetables alone.
- Hang fabric pouches full of human hair (available in abundance from beauty and barber shops) or dried blood on the fence or from nearby trees.

Groundhogs have a voracious appetite for any vegetable; active during the day.

- Soybeans are a groundhog delicacy, so plant several rows around your garden as a border decoy. The idea is to have the groundhog feast on soybeans and leave the rest of the garden alone.
- Erect a chicken wire fence. Take the bottom 10 inches and bend it out at a 90-degree angle, then bury this flap so that it faces out from the garden. This will act as a barrier to any burrowing the groundhog has in mind.
- Dig raised beds (at least 12 inches deep) and line the bottom with wire mesh.

Humans may occasionally vandalize and steal, usually under the cover of darkness.

- Make a fence into more than a physical barrier—turn it into a visual barrier by growing climbing vines like sweet peas, morning glories, and Malabar spinach. You want to make the bounties of the garden less tempting by making them less visible.
- Camouflage a healthy, almost-ripe-and-ready-to-eat vegetable by sprinkling talcum powder on the leaves and fruit. This disguise implies a diseased fruit to any marauders—while you know better.
- Grow off-color, eccentric vegetables that aren't commonly recognizable as edible. For example: purple bush beans, orange and yellow tomatoes, white eggplants, white and lemon-shaped cucumbers, and banana-shaped peppers.

Moles perform beneficial task of eating slugs, grubs, and other soil insect pests, but also eat helpful earthworms; uproot plants while tunneling.

- Tread along all mole tunnels and flatten. The ones that pop up again are the active ones, and you should channel your efforts into these.
- Drop castor beans (which are repulsive to moles) down the hole. Be careful with small chil-

dren around, since these beans are poisonous when eaten.

• Set pinwheels into the ground around a hole. The vibrations may be annoying enough to cause the moles to leave.

• Blend together two parts castor oil, one part liquid detergent and three parts water. Add 2 tablespoons of this mixture to a watering can full of water and pour over the garden areas that are bothered by moles.

Rabbits are vegetarian epicures with an appreciation of all that is green and luscious.

• Sprinkle any of the following on leaves of young plants: powdered aloe, phosphate rock, flour, talcum powder, cayenne, black pepper, wood ashes.

• Sprinkle cow manure or dried blood around seedlings. (Replace dried blood after rainfall.)

• Grow a crop of soybeans to divert the rabbits from other crops in the garden. (See Groundhogs.)

• The best protection is a sturdy chicken wire fence, 30 inches tall, that extends 4 to 6 inches into the ground.

Raccoons eat most anything, but relish ripe corn in particular.

• Periodically sprinkle ammonia around the garden.

• Ring your corn patch with a cluster of vining plants. Their tangled growth will interfere with raccoon dining habits, since the animal wants to have good visibility all around as he dines surreptitiously.

• Wait for the circus to come to town, or visit the local zoo or wildlife park and gather up some lion dung. It does wonders when scattered throughout the garden.

• Sprinkle red or black pepper on corn silks.

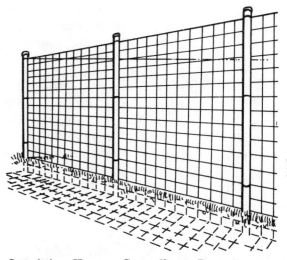

Outwitting Hungry Groundhogs: Protecting your garden against hungry wildlife calls for a sturdy fence. In the case of marauding groundhogs, turn the bottom 10 inches of fence outward at a right angle, and bury this lip under the soil to thwart underground attacks.

Dealing with Insects and Diseases

Insects and diseases will not be a serious problem if you practice sensible organic gardening techniques. Building a rich, well-structured soil should be first priority not only for high yields, but for insect and disease control as well. As long as plants are supplied with the nutrients, moisture, and air they require, they will be healthy enough to withstand damage caused by most pests. Equally important is the maintenance of a clean growing area; remove and dispose of garden debris, or periodically rake it under the soil surface where it will decompose. Where soil is wet and cold, avoid placing a heavy mulch around plants, for this would only encourage fungal diseases, molds, and other problems. Maintain a clean, moist, but light growing medium. Since many diseases are spread by contact, you should wash your hands after working around diseased plants, and sterilize any tools that you used by dipping them into a 10 percent bleach solution (rinse and dry these tools promptly to keep rust from forming). In fact, it is a good idea to wash your hands whenever you go out to work in the garden, for powerful chemicals and cigarette tars that they may carry can transmit some diseases. Furthermore, try to avoid ever touching a bean plant that is wet, for this spreads rust, anthracnose, and several other diseases. Most other vegetables can be handled safely when wet.

Rotation, interplanting, and companion planting are particularly effective ways of preventing serious pest problems. They not only limit insect and disease problems once they begin, but they also keep most from ever taking hold. Where plantings are diversified, pest populations will be relatively small, so that natural predators like the chalcid wasps, lady bugs, and praying mantids can control them.

Next in your line of defense should be the selection of resistant varieties and certified seed. Read catalog selections carefully and, where possible, select varieties that can withstand the disease or pests you know are present in your locale. Even if a given pest has not occurred in your garden, select varieties that are able to resist it and that are also appropriate for your climate. This will most likely prevent the pest from ever establishing itself in your soil, on seeds, or on plant debris. Choose disease-free seed and stock, and do not plant seeds or transplants that look suspiciously abnormal.

Insects

As an organic gardener, you have various alternatives to consider when combating insect pests, without having to unleash a flood of chemical poisons that taint your harvest and cause long-lasting damage to the garden environment. These alternatives are effective as long as you are a good observer and become familiar with the visual clues that tell you what's ailing your plants. To help you in this task, refer to the Common Insect Pests chart.

Potentially harmful insect populations can often be managed if their life cycle and living habits are known to the gardener. Altering planting times so that crops are not available when insects feed is probably one of the best, and least practiced, organic controls. Because the timing of planting depends on when the insects begin feeding and laying eggs in your locale, it is also the most difficult to explain. Begin by keeping garden records of insect "attacks." Write down when they occur, how long they seem to last, and any likely reasons for them such as too heavy a mulch, weakened plants, or overwatering. This, along with some information about life cycles from a reliable insect guide (see the Bibliography), should provide you with enough information to alter future planting times of the host plant. Thus, squash plants that are normally devastated by borers in early July might be planted a few weeks later so that they will miss the onslaught of the larvae. Such timing requires experience and a great deal of information on insect life cycles, feeding habits, and overwintering stages, as well as knowledge of your own range of planting dates. Consult your extension services, your own records, and an insect guidebook. When you finally begin to understand the

Common Insect Pests

Insect	Description	Feeding Habits	Vegetable Hosts	Natural Controls
Aphids	Come in a variety of colors; soft-bodied; pear-shaped; winged or wingless; less than $\frac{1}{10}$ in.	Suck leaves, vegetables, and stems, causing foliage to curl, pucker, and yellow; transmit viral disease.	Most vegetables	Foil mulch; soap-and-water spray with clear rinse; rotenone; predators will take care of most aphid infestations before serious damage occurs.
Beetles	Hard wing covers meet in straight line in middle of back.	Chew on leaves, fruit, roots.		
Asparagus beetle	Blue-black with 4 white spots or stripes and reddish margins; oblong shape; $\frac{1}{4}$ in. long.	Chews spears and leaves.	Asparagus	Rotenone dust for serious infestations; otherwise, handpick.
Blister beetle	Yellowish with black stripes or black with gray wing margins.	Chews foliage, fruit.	Most vegetables (although seldom a problem)	Handpick, wearing gloves for protection from insect's secretion.
Colorado potato beetle	Yellow with black stripes and orange head covering; convex shape; $\frac{1}{3}$ in. long; eggs bright yellow; larvae red, plump.	Chews foliage.	Eggplants, peppers, potatoes, tomatoes	Clean cultivation; heavy mulching; handpick and remove eggs; use rotenone as last resort.
Cucumber beetle	Yellow with black stripes or spots; oblong shape; $\frac{1}{4}$ in. long; eggs orange; larvae found near plant base.	Chews leaves, flowers; transmits mosaic and bacterial wilt.	Beans, corn, cucumbers, eggplants, peas, potatoes, pumpkins, squash, tomatoes	Handpick; cover plants with cheesecloth; use rotenone or pyrethrum as last resort.
Flea beetle	Shiny, black; may have yellow or white markings; very active; $\frac{1}{10}$ in. long; jumps like a flea when disturbed.	Chews tiny holes in foliage; transmits viral and bacterial disease.	Most vegetables, especially cole crops, eggplants, radishes, turnips	Lime; diatomaceous earth; or rotenone dusts.
Mexican bean beetle	Yellow to gold with 16 black dots; round; $\frac{1}{4}$ in. long; yellow eggs; orange larvae.	Chews holes in leaves.	Beans	Handpick; rotenone; pyrethrum dusts.
Bugs	Small triangular patch on back; overlapping heavy wings have thin membraneous tips.	Suck fluids from plant tissue; carry diseases.		
Harlequin bug	Patterned in shiny black and red; shield-shaped with large triangle on back; $\frac{1}{4}$ in. long.	Sucks leaves, causing them to wilt and die; white blotches may appear.	Brussels sprouts, cabbage, cauliflower, horseradish, kohlrabi, mustard, radishes, rutabaga, turnips	Handpick; control weeds; plant trap crops of turnips near main crop; pyrethrum for serious infestations.

(continued)

Common Insect Pests—*continued*

Insect	Description	Feeding Habits	Vegetable Hosts	Natural Controls
Bugs (continued)				
Squash bug	Brown to black with light-colored outline on abdomen; ½ in. long; brown shiny eggs; greenish gray nymphs.	Sucks leaves; plant wilts as vines are damaged.	Cucumbers, pumpkins, squash	Handpick; practice clean cultivation and rotation; select resistant varieties.
Tarnished plant bug	Yellow to brown with darker markings; ¼ in. long.	Sucks stem tips, buds, fruits, causing black spots and pitting.	Most vegetables	Practice clean cultivation.
Carrot weevil	Brownish with hard shell; ⅕ in. long; pale, brown-headed larvae, with no legs.	Larvae chew celery hearts and tunnel into the tops and roots of carrot, destroying most of the plant's tissue.	Carrots, celery, parsley	Practice crop rotation and clean cultivation.
Caterpillars	Larval stage of butterflies and moths.	Chews leaves, stems, fruits, or roots.		
Cabbage looper	Light green with yellowish stripes; loops as it walks; round white eggs; adult brown moth.	Chews leaves.	Beans, broccoli, cabbage, cauliflower, celery, kale, lettuce, parsley, peas, potatoes, radishes, squash, tomatoes	Handpick; *Bacillus thuringiensis* for serious infestations.
Corn earworm	White to greenish red with 4 prolegs; spined; 1½ in. long; adult brown moth.	Chews buds, leaves; plant may be stunted; ears are destroyed from tip down; tomato destroyed from stem end.	Beans, corn, peas, peppers, potatoes, squash, tomatoes	Apply half a medicine dropper of mineral oil to silk; remove pests after silk has browned; *Bacillus thuringiensis* for serious infestations of garden vegetables.
Cutworm	Grayish to black, possibly with markings; curls up when disturbed; hides during the day; 1 to 2 in. long; adult is mottled night-flying moth.	Chews stems at or below ground level.	Most vegetables, particularly when young	Protect seedlings and transplants with a collar; diatomaceous earth for serious infestations.
European corn borer	Grayish to pink with darker head and spots on each segment; white eggs in groups on foliage; adult yellowish moth.	Chews leaves and tassels of corn; bores into stalks and ears later in season; may chew stems or leaves of other crops.	Beans, corn, peppers, potatoes, spinach, Swiss chard, tomatoes	Make relay plantings; handpick.
Imported cabbage worm	Light green with 1 yellow stripe; leaves soft green excrement; 1¼ in. long; bullet-shaped white to yellow eggs; adult white moth.	Chews leaves.	Brussels sprouts, cabbage, cauliflower, kohlrabi, mustard, radishes, turnips	Cover plants with cheesecloth; handpick; garlic spray; diatomaceous earth; *Bacillus thuringiensis* for serious infestations.

Insect	Description	Feeding Habits	Vegetable Hosts	Natural Controls
Caterpillars *(continued)*				
Potato tuberworm	Pinkish to white with dark head; ½ in. long; adult grayish moth with mottled wings.	Tunnels into leaves, stems, and tubers.	Eggplants, potatoes, tomatoes	Remove infested vines or tubers; practice clean cultivation.
Squash vine borer	White with dark head; 1 in. long; adult orange and black clear-winged moth with black stripes around the abdomen.	Chews base of stems in early summer, then moves into other plant parts, causing plant to suddenly wilt.	Cucumbers, pumpkins, squash	Alter planting dates; practice clean cultivation; when signs of infestation occur, slit stem and remove borer, then cover damaged stalk with dirt; during the season, bury every fifth leaf node on trailing squash (this causes them to take root and keep the vine going).
Tomato hornworm	Green with white stripes and a horn projecting from rear; 3 in. long; adult grayish moth.	Chews leaves and fruit.	Eggplants, peppers, potatoes, tomatoes	Handpick; if larva has papery cocoons on its back, natural parasite has already doomed it, so do not kill.
Flies (maggots)	One pair of clear wings; maggots are small, white, legless worms.	Maggots feed within host plant; flies lay eggs in plant tissue.		
Cabbage maggot	Adult resembles housefly; maggot white, ¼ in. long.	Maggots tunnel into plant roots and stems; wilting, bacterial diseases may result.	Broccoli, Brussels sprouts, cabbage, cauliflower, turnips	Dust base of plant with phosphate rock or diatomaceous earth.
Carrot rust fly	Black fly with long yellow hairs and yellow head and legs; maggots yellow to white, ⅓ in. long.	Maggots chew roots, causing plants to be dwarfed; soft rot bacteria may become a problem; entire plant quickly decomposes.	Carrots, celery, parsley, parsnips	Alter planting dates; practice clean cultivation; prevent egg laying by sprinkling phosphate rock around plant base.
Leafminers	Small black flies usually with yellow stripes; tiny yellowish larvae.	Maggots feed between the upper and lower surfaces of leaves; white tunnels or blotches appear.	Beans, beets, cabbage, lettuce, peppers, potatoes, rutabaga, spinach, Swiss chard, turnips	Remove and destroy infested leaves before maggot matures; cover with wire screening.
Onion maggot	Humped-back fly; white maggots found near bulb or neck.	Maggots chew into neck and bulbs in spring and early summer.	Onions, radishes	Scatter onion plants throughout the garden, rather than planting them all together; dust with diatomaceous earth.
Pepper maggot	Yellow to orange fly with brown marks on	Maggots enter fruit from any end and feed	Eggplants, peppers, tomatoes	Remove and destroy infested plants; *(continued)*

Common Insect Pests—*continued*

Insect	Description	Feeding Habits	Vegetable Hosts	Natural Controls
Flies (maggots) *(continued)* Pepper maggot *(continued)*	the wings; maggots white, pointed, quite small.	within; infested fruit is decayed and falls prematurely.		sprinkle talc, diatomaceous earth or phosphate rock on fruit in midsummer during egg-laying season.
Leafhoppers	Green, wedge-shaped with wings held in a rooflike position above their bodies; very active; 1/4 to 1/3 in. long; move sideways.	Adults and nymphs of various species suck juices from leaves and transmit various diseases.	Beets, celery, eggplants, potatoes, rhubarb, tomatoes, and other vegetables	Dust susceptible plants with diatomaceous earth; cover potato plants with netting in early summer.
Whiteflies	Small, mothlike, dusty white-winged adults; yellowish nymphs are legless, resembling scales at certain stages.	Nymphs and adults suck juices from plant leaves, buds, and stems; plants weaken.	Most vegetables, particularly greenhouse-grown transplants	Spray with soapy water; predators will control when in the garden.
Wireworms	Dark brown to yellowish; hard-shelled; cylindrical; 1/3 to 1 1/2 in. long; adult black beetles.	Wireworms chew seed, roots, and tubers.	Most vegetables	Rotate crops, practice clean cultivation; trap wireworms in pieces of potato buried 1 inch below the ground for 1 or 2 days.

insects, you will also have begun to control them.

When it comes time to set out transplants, physical barriers will serve as protectors against many insects. Paper collars are the most common example. These are used around young broccoli, Brussels sprout, cabbage, cauliflower, and tomato seedlings to keep cutworms and cabbage maggots from attacking the stems. Use stiff roofing paper or triple-thick newspaper to make an upright collar that penetrates at least 2 inches below the soil surface and 1 or 2 above. There should be a 1/2-inch margin between the collar and seedling stem. Some gardeners place slitted asphalt shingles on the ground around the plant, or a thick layer of gritty sand or diatomaceous earth as a mulch. These materials work by abrading the insect's waxy outer coat, allowing its internal fluids to dry up. All such devices should be set in place as soon as seedlings are planted out, or if direct-seeded, when seedlings emerge.

Physical barriers also work in controlling certain beetles. Try covering cucumbers and other cucurbits with cheesecloth early in the season to prevent cucumber beetles from setting up house on the leaves. This technique is only effective when the entire plant is covered, for if cucumber beetles get a chance to chew on any portion of it, bacterial wilt infection most likely will result.

The most common insect problems that do arise in the garden can be managed with daily handpicking. Always try this method of control first—it costs nothing but your time, and may stop the problem before it ever really gets serious. Remove not only feeding adults, but the usually smaller and often hard-to-find nymphs (immature adults with undeveloped wings), larvae, and eggs. Check around the base of plants, under leaves, and in surrounding mulch to be sure you find them all. Drop captured pests into a can of turpentine, gasoline, or paint thinner, or simply drown them in soapy water. If you are thorough in your handpicking, and are able to distinguish the growth stages of potentially harmful insects from those of helpful predators, you may not need any other types of controls.

Insects too small for handpicking should be sprayed off with clear water. A harsh spray of water early in the day will often be sufficient to control aphids, mites, and whiteflies. If this does not work, try adding a little mild, nondetergent soap to the water. This type of mild insecticide not only does away with aphids and mites, but discourages leafhoppers, leafminers, and some caterpillars as well. Some gardeners suggest rinsing plants after such a dousing, while others claim that the soap residues should be left on the plant for a few days to discourage a return infestation. If you do decide to leave the residue on, watch your plants carefully. If they show signs of flagging, rinse the residue off immediately; certain plants are damaged by the presence of this film on their leaf surfaces.

Equally benign yet effective sprays can be made by dissolving or soaking any of the following in warm water: yogurt, buttermilk, garlic, and cedar chips. Red pepper "tea" sprayed on foliage is said to repel flea beetles and aphids, while a molasses solution discourages cabbage moths from laying eggs on the plants.

As a last resort for very serious infestations, organically derived insecticides and pathogens may be necessary. Although these are not as harmful as the so-called chemical insecticides, they are by no means "safe." Use them only as a last resort, and handle them as carefully as you would any harsh cleanser or other poisonous material.

Bacillus thuringiensis: Also called BT, this material is sold under the names Dipel, Thuricide, Biotrol, and others. A naturally occurring bacteria, it is dusted or sprayed on plant leaves, flowers, or fruits. When feeding insects ingest it, they become ill from the spores and toxin, stop feeding, and die soon after. BT is only effective against caterpillars such as cabbage loopers, canker-worms, corn earworms, European corn borers, gypsy moths, and imported cabbage worms.

Diatomaceous earth: This material is sold as Perma-Guard. It consists of the ground, dried skeletons of microscopic algae. The fine, sharp particles of this material abrade away the outer, waxy layer of soft-bodied insects that come in contact with it and they simply die by loss of body fluids. Dust it on infested plants just after a fine rain or light watering so that the material will not be blown away. Cover the entire plant thoroughly, particularly the undersides of leaves. It is effective in controlling beetle grubs, caterpillars, aphids, fly maggots, and other soft-bodied creatures. Earthworms will not, however, be affected.

Pyrethrum: This material is derived from the flower heads of several chry-santhemum species. It, too, is effective against soft-bodied insects, but also kills certain beetles, bugs, and leafhoppers in their adult stages. Because of its extreme potency, use pyrethrum only when absolutely necessary.

Rotenone: Also called derris, this is another of the plant-derived insecticides. It is very potent, but its effects last for only a short time. Apply it periodically to clear up any insects that have not been controlled by other, less drastic means. A 1 percent solution spray is usually strong enough to do away with any insects.

Diseases

Controlling diseases in the home garden is not as easy as coping with insect pests. For that reason, prevention is absolutely essential, and you should use resistant varieties wherever possible. Since most diseases occur when plants are otherwise weak or unhealthy, practice the organic gardening methods which are needed to maintain healthy plants. In the interplanted, intensive garden where plants are closely spaced, this is sometimes difficult. Overwatering or overcrowding may snuff out some of these plants and allow a disease to start before you realize the damage has been done. Do not plant so closely that lower leaves never receive sunlight. Constantly wet conditions, particularly where summers are humid, favor diseases. Be sure that air circulates through all levels of the garden—not only through the parts aboveground, but through the soil as well.

Some diseases are carried through seeds, so certified seed is essential to good gardening. Do not plant blackened, shriveled, or soft seeds; instead return them to the grower, or discard them if they are seeds you have saved yourself.

Other diseases are carried through plant matter or soil. When you find a diseased plant in the garden, remove it—roots, surrounding soil, top growth, and all. If your compost heap is very deep, you might risk burying diseased material there, but the best method is to burn it. If it is a disease such as clubroot, which remains in the soil for several years, you will have to forego growing host crops in that area until the disease disappears. Avoid infesting your soil with such diseases by carefully checking any transplants and seeds for signs of clubroot, stem rot, black rot, or similar fungal diseases.

Vegetable gardeners have one significant advantage over farmers concerning the spread of disease. While a farmer tends to plant in large blocks of a single crop, the vegetable gardener who is working on a smaller scale mixes groupings of different vegetables in his plot. Because the home gardener is not engaged in monoculture, if his peppers succumb to anthracnose, he will eat fewer peppers, but the garden as a whole will be unaffected. Disease problems in a home vegetable garden are usually minor, and if severe, are limited to one or two crops.

Aside from removing diseased plants, and practicing the usual organic gardening methods of crop rotation, clean cultivation and good soil management, there are few good disease control measures available to the environmentally conscious gardener. Mildews and fungi that arise on damp leaves or fruit may be somewhat controlled by dustings of flour, talc, agricultural lime, or sulfur. Flour, talc, and lime will not harm plants, but they have little effect on the disease-causing organisms. They do, however, dry the leaves and make the environment less attractive to the fungi. Sulfur is a stronger fungicide which kills

Vegetable Crops and Their Common Diseases

Crop	Symptoms	Disease	Organic Remedies
Asparagus	Reddish yellow spots on stem, branches; gradually entire plant yellows, weakens, and eventually dies.	Asparagus rust	Use rust-resistant varieties; do not plant in a damp or low-lying area.
	Wilted, stunted spears with brownish surface color.	Fusarium wilt	Select healthy stock; do not plant in infected soil.
Beans, lima	Reddish brown lesions on stem, leaves, and pods; young diseased pods may fall from plant.	Bacterial spot	If possible, keep bean plantings far from lilac or wild cherry which also harbor the disease; practice crop rotation and clean cultivation; dust leaves with lime.
	Pods are mottled, with white fuzzy fungus strands on them.	Downy mildew	Rotate crops; destroy diseased vines; use clean seed; dust affected plants with lime.
Beans, snap	Dark red, sunken spots on leaves and stems; pinkish red spots on pods; seeds are often black.	Anthracnose	Use disease-free, western-grown seed; do not work near plants when they are wet; rotate crops.
	Large brown blotches on leaves, possibly bordered with yellow or red; water-soaked spots on pods; seed may be discolored.	Bacterial blight	Use resistant varieties.
	Leaves crinkled with mottled areas; pods may be rough, misshapen.	Mosaics	Control aphids; use resistant varieties.
	Many small, reddish orange to brown spore masses on leaves and possibly stem; leaves rapidly yellow, dry up, and drop.	Rust	Use resistant varieties; remove diseased plant matter at the end of the season; use new stakes each year; dust leaves with lime if case is serious; avoid handling wet plants.
Beets	Small round tan to brown spots on leaves and stems; later leaves turn yellow and drop.	Leaf spot	Rotate crops; use resistant varieties; till deeply.
Cabbage (also broccoli, Brussels sprouts, cauliflower, turnips)	Leaves yellow, veins become black; plant becomes stunted and heads of cabbage, cauliflower, or Brussels sprouts are one-sided or nonexistent; stem cross section shows a brown, woody ring.	Black rot	Use hot-water-treated seed; practice clean cultivation; avoid wetting plant foliage.
	Yellowed leaves that wilt during the day; plants may be stunted; roots misshapen and enlarged with club-shaped knots that eventually rot.	Clubroot	Check seedlings before purchasing and transplanting; maintain pH above 7; sprinkle a mixture of wood ashes and whitewash lime around the plant base in spring; rotate crops.
	Seedlings develop purplish lesions on leaves and stems; white downy substance covers these areas; plants die very rapidly after contracting the disease.	Downy mildew	Dust with lime, flour, or sulfur.
	Lower leaves yellow, turn brown, and finally drop; heads may appear stunted and taste bitter; symptoms similar to black rot.	Yellows	Use resistant varieties.

(continued)

Vegetable Crops and Their Common Diseases—*continued*

Crop	Symptoms	Disease	Organic Remedies
Carrots	Yellow to whitish spots on leaves; girdling of roots; water-soaked spots or lesions on roots.	Leaf blight	Use hot-water-treated seeds; cultivate soil thoroughly; use 4-year rotation where infection has occurred.
	Small galls on lateral rootlets; pimple-sized swellings on main root; plants may be yellow and stunted.	Root knot nematode	Rotate carrots with grain, velvet bean, or cowpea crops, which are resistant to nematodes.
Celery	Greenish or water-soaked spots on leaves; sunken lesions possible on stalks; growth may be stunted; spore threads may be visible in wet weather.	Blights (early and late)	Transplant seedlings before they become overcrowded; use seed more than 2 years old; select resistant varieties.
	Reddish tissue on stalks and leaves; yellowing of foliage.	Fusarium yellows	Select resistant varieties; practice clean cultivation.
	Water-soaked spots on stalks; bitter-tasting, rotted stems; damping-off may occur in an infected seedbed.	Pink rot	Use resistant varieties; avoid planting cabbage, celery, or lettuce in the same soil; destroy sick plants.
Corn	Pale, streaked leaves; yellow, sticky substance exudes from a cut stem.	Bacterial wilt	Control flea beetles which carry the disease; use late-maturing varieties; plow under stubble in fall.
	Large galls develop on stalk, ears, and roots; later, grayish galls blacken and release spores; ripened spores appear oily or powdery.	Corn smut	Gather and destroy smutted plants before spores are released; use disease-resistant seed; practice clean cultivation.
Cucumbers (also squash)	Small, dark spots on leaves; eventually spots grow together and entire leaf is destroyed; fruits may blacken and drop; problem develops in warm, moist conditions.	Anthracnose	Three- to 4-year crop rotation with nonvining plants; use disease-free plants and seeds.
	Leaves wilt quickly, possibly while still green; white sticky material might be seen when a stem is cut.	Bacterial wilt	Remove affected plants and destroy; control spotted cucumber beetle; use resistant varieties.
	Yellow to purplish spots start on leaves, gradually cover entire plant.	Downy mildew	Use resistant varieties; remove infected plants.
	Leaves of cucumber and squash develop rough, mottled surface; cucumber fruit may be entirely white; plant may be stunted and yellow in several cases.	Mosaic	Use resistant varieties; keep area weed-free; do not grow host plants near catnip, ground cherry, or milkweed; control aphids and cucumber beetles that carry the disease.
	Round, white spots on undersides of leaves; eventually entire leaf is covered with powder; fruits ripen prematurely and have poor flavor and texture.	Powdery mildew	Use resistant varieties of squash and cucumber; dust squash with sulfur if infection is severe (cucumber will be harmed by sulfur).
	Dark spots on fruit of cucumber and pumpkin; leaves may have water spots and stems shallow lesions; sap oozes from fruits, then greenish mold develops.	Scab	Do not grow cucumbers in the same soil more than once every 3 years, particularly in the northern states; select resistant varieties.

Crop	Symptoms	Disease	Organic Remedies
Eggplant	Brownish spots on leaves; damage is particularly bad during wet weather when fruit may develop small tannish cankers which later rot.	Fruit rot	Use resistant varieties; practice rotation on a 4-year basis.
	Yellowing of foliage and gradual defoliation; plants may become stunted.	Verticillium wilt	Do not grow eggplant where potato or tomato have just been raised; use clean seed.
Onions (also garlic, leeks)	Early symptoms are sunken spots on leaves; later, a purplish mold develops over spots.	Downy mildew	Rotate crops; use resistant varieties; be sure that soil is well drained; do not overwater plants.
	Mature bulbs and sets develop sunken, dried areas around the neck, usually during storage; only attacks injured bulbs or sets.	Neck rot	Pungent varieties are less susceptible than mild-tasting ones; store sets and bulbs at correct temperatures (near 32°F) with good air circulation; do not plant diseased sets.
	Roots turn pinkish or red, eventually rot; plant is stunted, with wilted tops.	Pink rot	Once soil is infested, do not grow any bulb crops; select tolerant and resistant varieties; grow on well-drained soil.
	Black spots on leaves and between the sections of the bulbs; young plants may have twisted leaves; common in northern regions.	Smut	Use healthy sets and resistant varieties.
Peas	Leaves shrivel and die; roots and lower stems may blacken and rot; disease overwinters on plant debris.	Ascochyta blight	Use western-grown seeds; rotate crops on a 3-year basis; practice clean cultivation.
	Brownish or yellow blotches form on leaves and pods; stems may turn purplish; leaves eventually yellow.	Bacterial blight	Protect plants from physical injury that could allow bacteria to enter.
	Stems, leaves, and pods dusted with white powdery mold; black specks appear later in the season; plants are stunted and vines shriveled.	Powdery mildew	Do not wet foliage during the afternoon; dust infected plants with sulfur; practice clean cultivation.
	Yellowed, gangly plants with rotting roots and lower stems; plant may die before pods form.	Root rot	Plant early on well-drained soils; practice long rotation with nonlegumes.
Peppers	Dark, round spots on fruit; entire pepper may rot or dry up; serious problem particularly in southern and central regions.	Anthracnose	Use clean seed; do not touch wet plants; separate bean and pepper plantings.
	In dry areas, leaves develop yellowish spots with darker margins; older leaves eventually drop.	Bacterial spot	Practice clean cultivation; rotate crops; select resistant varieties.
	Blossom end of fruit becomes soft and spotted, eventually shrivels.	Blossom-end rot	Water continuously after flowering; avoid overfertilization with nitrogen-rich materials.
	Leaves yellow, curl, and become mottled; early fruits are stunted; later flowers fail to set fruit.	Mosaic	Keep garden area free of weeds, particularly nightshade and wild cucumber; control aphids; wash hands after handling infected plants; use resistant varieties. *(continued)*

Vegetable Crops and Their Common Diseases—*continued*

Crop	Symptoms	Disease	Natural Controls
Potatoes	In warm, moist climates plants become stunted and leaves yellow and roll; stem base develops brown rotted areas on the inside; inside of tubers shows darkened blotches and a soft rot that worsens during storage.	Black leg	Plant certified seed potatoes where disease is prevalent; plant only whole tubers; use well-drained soil.
	Spots develop in rings on leaves; eventually leaves may die; tubers develop puckered skin and shallow rough lesions; mold may result.	Early blight	Select clean, certified seed potatoes; use well-composted humus to prevent infection.
	Tissue just beneath the skin on tubers breaks down, eventually turning black; condition does not appear until after harvest and storage.	Internal black spot	Carefully handle tubers during harvest; do not overfertilize with nitrogen materials.
	Mottled, crinkled foliage; brown specks appear on tubers and plants may droop and die prematurely.	Mosaic	Plant certified tubers; select resistant varieties.
	Dark brown cankers appear on young sprouts; mature stalks may become brown; tubers are covered with hard black "scurfs"; tubers may also be roughened in a cross-patched pattern.	Rhizoctonia	Plant certified seed; rotate potatoes with cereal or corn crops; in wet, cold ground, plant either shallow or very deep with thick mulch covering to encourage rapid growth.
	Late in growing season plants begin to decay below ground; just under skin of tuber, ring of rotting tissue appears; eventually, entire inside rots, leaving a shell of firm tissue.	Ring rot	Use disease-free stock; disinfect tools that have come in contact with infected plants.
	Late in season, older leaves yellow; affected vines die prematurely; stem tissue discolors from base; tubers may be pinkish.	Verticillium wilt	Rotate crops on a 4-year basis; use resistant varieties.
Spinach (also Swiss chard)	Yellowish, curled leaves; stunted leaves and plants.	Blight	Control aphids; maintain weed-free growing areas; select resistant varieties.
	In moist areas, leaves develop yellow spots with fuzzy purplish growth beneath.	Downy mildew	Use clean seed; plant in well-drained soil; do not overcrowd plants; use resistant varieties.
Sweet potatoes	Small, round brown spots on potato tubers; stem may also show decay.	Black rot	Use certified seed potatoes.
	Soft, watery rot on stored tubers.	Soft rot	Select resistant varieties; store in a humid atmosphere at 80°–90°F for about 2 weeks before placing in permanent storage.
	Pits develop on potatoes; dark lesions may form on underground portions of stems.	Soil rot (scurf)	Maintain soil acidity below 5.5; use resistant varieties.
	Young infected plants may die after transplanting; survivors develop bright yellow leaves, and later stems rot; harvest is of poor quality.	Stem rot	Use only certified seed potatoes; practice clean cultivation; use resistant varieties.

Crop	Symptoms	Disease	Natural Controls
Tomatoes	Fruits develop small, round, water-soaked spots; later, fruits darken and rot.	Anthracnose	Rotate crops; use hot-water-treated seeds; practice clean cultivation; do not let ripe tomatoes remain on the vines.
	Seedlings wilt, become stunted; older plants may show dried leaves; cankers develop on stems; small, raised white spots show on fruits; these spots darken eventually.	Bacterial canker	Use clean seeds; rotate on a 3-year basis; sterilize infected tools; practice clean cultivation.
	Irregular, water-soaked spots may develop on leaves; plant becomes partly defoliated; seedlings may girdle; stem end of fruit becomes grayish green; blossoms or young fruits may drop.	Blights (early and late)	Rotate all solanaceous crops on a 3- or 4-year basis; practice clean cultivation; select resistant varieties.
	Blossom end of fruit darkens, eventually becomes sunken, black, and leathery.	Blossom-end rot	See Peppers.
	Leaves yellow and droop; cross section of stem shows brownish liquid within; fruit usually decays and drops.	Fusarium wilt	Do not grow in contaminated soils; practice crop rotation; select resistant varieties.
	Mottled leaves; young leaves are bunched or puckered; plants are stunted; yield is reduced; in some types of mosaic, fruit is also mottled.	Mosaics	Eradicate perennial weeds; keep tobacco oils away from plants; spray infected seedlings with milk once a week; control aphids.
	Older leaves thicken and roll upward; young leaves curl; plant is spindly; fruit is soft.	Psyllid yellows	Control psyllids with a garlic spray; keep area free of ground cherry and other weeds.
	In midsummer, old leaves develop small, dense spots with grayish centers; later spores appear in the centers of the spots; fruit is seldom affected.	Septoria leaf spot	Practice crop rotation; keep area weed-free; maintain fertile soil.

mildew and controls fungal diseases. Its only real drawback is its toxicity to most varieties of cucumbers and squash. While a few muskmelon varieties are sulfur-resistant, most other cucurbits are harmed by it. Certain bacteria may be killed by specially derived antibiotics such as streptomycin, but such materials are not always easy to find and high cost prevents their widespread use in the vegetable garden.

Use the chart on Vegetable Crops and Their Common Diseases not only to identify problems as they occur, but to troubleshoot other potential disease problems even before crops are planted. Use it in conjunction with a good handbook on garden diseases. (See the Bibliography.)

5

Natural Storage Techniques

Natural storage is a simple method of preserving food throughout the winter. It is appealing because it involves storing fresh, raw whole vegetables under easily attained natural conditions that halt the ripening and decay processes. When you can, dry, or freeze your harvest, you are altering the nature of the vegetables to increase their keeping quality. However, with natural storage, the keeping quality of vegetables is determined by how you combine the external conditions of temperature, humidity, and light within a storage area.

There are many advantages to natural storage. First, it involves less time, work, and effort than if you were to process the same amount of vegetables. Second, it is a very energy-efficient means of storage. Most vegetables require cool and moist conditions which can be provided inexpensively by taking advantage of either one or both of these very basic and accessible elements: soil and air. For example, in an outdoor storage area the soil lends its cool temperature, high moisture level, and insulating properties. In an indoor storage area, the season's chilly air can be employed (through the use of vents) to keep temperatures low without artificial cooling devices. The small group of vegetables that requires warmer storage temperatures can be kept in areas of the home where they take advantage of the heat already being provided for the comfort of your family—thus requiring no extra expenditure of energy.

The third and most important advantage of natural storage is that you will have a ready source of fresh vegetables to serve throughout the winter. Vegetables which are properly stored and prepared suffer little nutrient loss, and can go a long way in relieving the monotony of several months of canned or frozen foods.

Keep in mind that the storage methods described here are offered as guidelines. Because everyone's conditions will differ, what works for one gardener may not work for the next. As is so often the case in raising vegetables, trial and error will be your best guide in determining which storage spaces and methods fill your needs and fit your particular conditions.

146

Conditions for Natural Storage

The purpose of any natural storage area, whether it is incorporated into the home or dug into the ground, is to slow down enzyme activity which leads to overripening, to reduce the loss of moisture, and to prevent, as much as possible, the development of bacteria and fungi which cause decay. In order to do that, you must control the temperature, humidity, ventilation, and light levels in the storage area.

Temperature

Most vegetables keep best when stored in cool temperatures, between 32° and 40°F. If your stored vegetables begin to sprout and add new growth, that's a sign that the temperature is too high. However, there is a small group of vegetables that needs warmer temperatures (50° to 60°F). This group includes pumpkins, sweet potatoes, and winter squash. A thermometer kept in the storage area will let you monitor the temperature to be sure it remains within the appropriate range.

Humidity

A majority of vegetables, especially the root crops, need high humidity levels (80 to 95 percent) to store well. Crops in outdoor storage areas (such as mounds) have the proper humidity level supplied naturally by the moisture in the soil. It is the vegetables stored indoors that require your attention, for if you find that they are shriveling up, that's your cue that the humidity is too low. Invest in a standard wet and dry bulb-type hygrometer so that you can keep the air moisture within the prescribed range. You can raise the humidity by setting pans of water on the floor or by covering the floor with dampened sand or sawdust. To raise the moisture level around root crops, dampen the bedding material in which they are packed.

However, not all vegetables need moist conditions, and crops such as garlic, onions, sweet potatoes, and winter squash must be stored where it's dry (60 to 70 percent humidity) to avoid decay.

Ventilation

Air movement is important in any storage area, whether indoors or outdoors, to keep mold from developing and to remove any objectionable odors. In addition, some vegetables require more ventilation than others, and should be stored accordingly in slatted crates or open boxes, on newspaper-lined shelves, or hung in mesh bags, all of which allow the air to circulate freely. This category of vegetables includes Brussels sprouts, cabbage, cauliflower, celery, endive, garlic, leeks, onions, potatoes, pumpkins, squash, and sweet potatoes.

In an enclosed room used for cold storage, a ventilation system also helps to maintain a low temperature by drawing in cold air to replace any warm air which may have collected. You can set up this air movement easily by opening a door or window to the outside when the temperature there is lower than the temperature in the storage area. A slightly more involved, but more efficient, venting system can be created with the installation of two vents at different levels; the lower vent brings in cool air while the upper vent serves as an outlet for warm air.

Light

While the vegetables are growing, the gardener's concern is that they receive all the light they need. But once those vegetables are stored, you must keep them in the dark. Light can cause crops like potatoes and onions to sprout, can raise the temperature in a confined storage area, and may accelerate vitamin loss.

Natural Storage Areas

Storage areas range from a very basic straw-lined, earth-covered mound to the more elaborate construction of a root cellar room in the basement. This section outlines various storage area options available to you, both indoors and out. For additional sources covering storage areas, consult the Bibliography.

Four Basic Storage Environments*

	Moist (80–95% humidity)	Dry (60–70% humidity)
Cool (32°–40°F)	Acorn squash (1½ mos.) Beets (2–5 mos.) Broccoli (2 mos.) Brussels sprouts (3–5 wks.) Cabbage (5–6 mos.) Carrots (5–6 mos.) Cauliflower (2–4 wks.) Celeriac (5–6 mos.) Celery (3–4 mos.) Chinese cabbage (1–4 mos.) Collards (1–2 wks.) Endive (1–2 mos.) Escarole (1–2 mos.) Hamburg parsley (5–6 mos.) Horseradish (5–6 mos.) Jerusalem artichoke (1–2 mos.) Kohlrabi (5–6 mos.) Leeks (2–3 mos.) Lima beans (2 wks.) Parsnips (5–6 mos.)	Dried beans and peas (many yrs.) Garlic (6–7 mos.) Green soybeans (in pods, 2–4 wks.) Onions (6–7 mos.) Popcorn (many yrs.) Shallots (6–7 mos.)

	Moist (80–95% humidity)	Dry (60–70% humidity)
Cool (32°–40°F)	Rutabaga (5–6 mos.) Salsify (5–6 mos.) Turnips (4–5 mos.) White potatoes (5–6 mos.) Winter radishes (2–4 mos.)	
Warm (50°–60°F)	Eggplant (1 wk.) Green or snap beans (1 wk. at 45° to 50°F) Sweet peppers (1–2 wks. at 45° to 50°F)	Gourds (6–7 mos.) Pumpkins (5–6 mos.) Sweet potatoes (4–6 mos.) Tomatoes, mature green (1–2 mos.) Tomatoes, ripe (1–3 wks.) Winter squash (except acorn type, 5–6 mos.)

*The information in parentheses accompanying each vegetable is the time it keeps in good condition in the given environment.

Cool and Moist

Indoors, your basement is the most likely location to provide these conditions. If you have an older home with a stone-walled, dirt-floored cellar without a furnace—congratulations! You have the ideal storage location. In lieu of that, in a more modern home with central heating, consider building a root cellar room. Pick a corner of the basement with northeast or northwest exposure, free of heating pipes, and preferably with a window to allow for ventilation. You can build a simple air-duct box to fit the window that will take advantage of the natural air flow pattern and help keep the temperature down and the air circulating. You will need to build two walls and insulate the room against the furnace heat, but once you're done you'll have a perfectly acceptable counterpart to the traditional root cellar.

Another location to check in the basement is the window well. A well can be converted to a small cold-storage area by lining the bottom with hardware cloth to keep rodents from burrowing into your cache, then adding a 6-inch layer of straw or hay as insulation. Set your vegetables into the well, alternating a layer of vegetables with a layer of straw or hay. Lay a board over the top of the well, and protect the whole construction with a waterproof covering held down at the edges by rocks. The heat from the basement will prevent vegetables from freezing, and the outside air and soil temperatures will cool the stored produce. A window that opens into the well provides easy access.

Another convenient basement storage area can be obtained easily if you have a stairway leading into your basement from the outside, covered by a sloping door. If there's no inside door at the bottom of the cellar steps, install one and the closed-off stairs become a convenient storage area.

Outdoors, you can keep your vegetables cool and moist by using a mound or

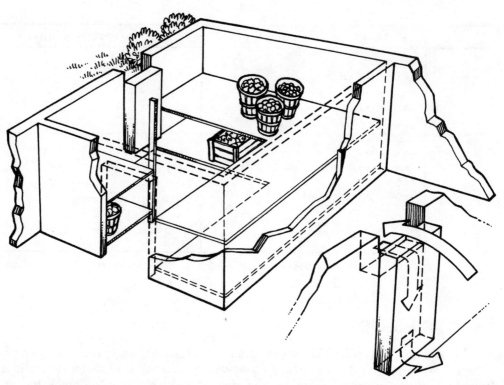

Root Cellar Room: Turn an idle corner of your basement into a handy cold-storage area like the one shown here. Insulated walls and an air-duct box built into the window help maintain the cool temperatures that enhance the longevity of many vegetables. Tiers of shelves provide ample room for stashing away crates and bushel baskets laden with carrots and beets. The detail of the air-duct box shows how the simple design allows the cool air from the outside to enter and any warm air that has collected to escape.

clamp. This method works most successfully in climates where the winter temperature averages about 30°F. An average temperature 10 to 20 degrees warmer can cause your vegetables to spoil, while an average temperature 10 degrees cooler might cause them to freeze. Once this storage area is opened, you must remove all the vegetables at the same time since it is almost impossible to reclose the area satisfactorily. Vegetables which store well in a mound include all root crops, Brussels sprouts, cabbage, kohlrabi, and potatoes. You may mix different vegetables within the same storage area, but do not mix vegetables with fruit, since the ethylene gas given off by some fruit (especially pears and apples) can alter the quality of the vegetables. A word of caution: Cabbage, rutabaga, and turnips are notorious for giving off a strong odor in storage, so to spare your home from a malodorous scent, always plan on storing these vegetables outdoors.

Cool and Dry

Seek out an attic, breezeway, shed, or unheated room to provide these conditions. If your home is heated by a woodstove, there should be plenty of places in the home suitable for vegetable storage, such as a closet on the north side of the house.

Warm and Dry

A cellar which contains a furnace is a suitable location for vegetables that need warmth and dryness. If your home doesn't have central heating, you can wrap vegetables in fireproof paper, set them in wire baskets and store near the woodstove or close to a warm chimney.

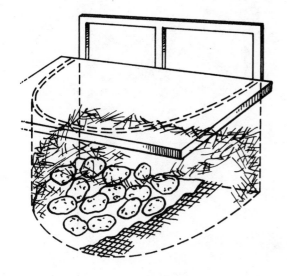

Window Well Storage: Don't overlook a window well as a possible cold-storage area in your home. Rodentproof it by laying a piece of hardware cloth on the bottom, and weatherproof it by setting a board across the top, followed by a waterproof covering.

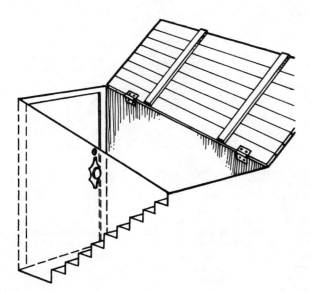

Stairwell Storage: Cellar stairs are a convenient cold-storage area that involves little work to set up.

Building a Vegetable Mound: Vegetables that need cool and moist storage conditions can be kept outdoors in a well-built mound. The first step, shown upper left, is to dig a hole about 1 foot deep and 3 feet square. Line the bottom with a piece of hardware cloth (to deter rodents), then add 2 to 4 inches of bedding material (straw, hay, dry leaves). Pile vegetables into a cone or pyramid shape, anywhere from 2 to 3 feet high (see upper right). Cover this pile with a 12-inch layer of bedding material. Mound up a layer of soil, 12 inches deep, over the straw- or leaf-encased pile (as shown lower left). Extend a handful of bedding material up through the soil at the peak to allow for ventilation. Or, set a tin can with both ends removed at the top so it extends from the straw layer through the soil to the outside. Pack the soil firm with the back of a shovel. A piece of screen set over the ventilation hole keeps out wildlife and a board set over the hole keeps out rain. The final step, shown lower right, is to dig a shallow channel around the perimeter of the mound to serve as a drainage ditch, and furnish a runoff from this ditch so excess surface water can drain away.

Underground Storage: Take advantage of the soil's ability to maintain cool and moist conditions by storing vegetables underground. Layer vegetables with bedding material in boxes, barrels, galvanized steel garbage cans, or drainage tiles, then set the containers in the soil. In very cold regions, protect the vegetable cache by building up layers of bedding material or soil over the buried container, as described for the vegetable mound. The drainage tile shown here has a layer of rocks in the bottom, and the vegetables are set into the tile in a bushel basket, then surrounded by bedding material. A board anchored with a rock protects against the elements and hungry animals.

Warm and Moist

The few vegetables which need these conditions (such as eggplants and sweet peppers) are not suitable for outside storage. You must scout around your house for the right setting which provides 45° to 60°F temperatures and high humidity, such as the top shelves in a damp basement storage room with a furnace.

Preparing Vegetables for Storage

No matter which natural storage area you use, there are certain ground rules to follow in preparing the vegetables for storage.

Harvesting

Vegetables intended for storage should be planted so that they mature as close as possible to the end of the growing season. Late varieties are especially well suited for storage. Delay the harvest for as long as possible, but make sure all the vegetables are out of the ground before the first killing frost. Vegetables differ as to their frost tolerance, with some tender crops like eggplants, squash, and tomatoes very susceptible to frost damage. Others, like Brussels sprouts, kale, parsnips, and salsify have their flavor enhanced by light frost.

Select only the pick of the crop for storage—those vegetables that are mature, and free of cuts, holes, and bruises. Damaged vegetables spoil readily, and have no place in your storage area; cut off any salvageable portions to be used immediately. The best time to harvest is when the air is cool and the ground is dry.

Cleaning

Washing the vegetables is not necessary, and in fact can be harmful if the skins are cut or nicked in the process. Any opening encourages rapid spoilage, and one rotting vegetable can quickly turn to many when they are stored in close proximity. Instead, gently shake or brush off any dirt. Trim the tops of root vegetables back to 1 inch, with the exception of beets, which should have 2 to 3 inches of top left on.

Curing

Certain crops must be specially treated before storage to toughen their skins and heal surface cuts so there is less chance that mold or rot will develop. This procedure, known as curing, also reduces moisture content which in turn increases the keeping quality of the vegetables, and converts their starches to sugar. (This use of the term "curing" should not be confused with the method of food preservation which goes by the same name and involves the use of heavy concentrations of pickling salt.) Here's how to cure those vegetables that need it:

- **Garlic and Shallots:** After the bulbs are lifted from the garden, dry for several days in an airy location away from direct sun.
- **Onions:** When the bulbs are dug, spread outdoors in a sunny, airy location for three to seven days to dry. Then, move indoors to a warm, dry, shady site and allow to finish drying for three to four more weeks.
- **Sweet Potatoes:** Provide warmth (80° to 90°F) and high humidity for 10 to 14 days. At lower temperatures (65° to 75°F) curing will take up to three weeks.
- **White Potatoes:** One to two weeks in a dry, dark spot at 60° to 75°F will cause skins to thicken adequately for storage.
- **Pumpkins and Winter Squash:** Always leave stems on the vegetables to be stored. Set in a warm (75° to 85°F), dry location for one to two weeks, so rinds can harden. Although acorn squash is a winter squash, it should not be cured.

Storage Materials

There are certain materials you will need to ensure that your vegetables remain in the best possible condition while in storage. If you keep your eyes open, you may be able to find slatted bushel baskets, wooden crates used for shipping

Impromptu Vegetable Shelves: These pumpkins and squashes will last longer when they've got plenty of air circulating around them. A board supported by cinder blocks is an easy way to provide an airy perch. Layer the board with straw or newspapers and arrange the vegetables so that they don't touch to discourage decay.

fruits and vegetables, barrels, pails, and tubs that can be had for the asking. Storage containers can be made of plastic, wood, or metal. Check wooden containers to make sure they are free of protruding nails, staples, or roughened areas which could damage vegetable skins. Metal containers should be galvanized or in some other way made rustproof.

For your pumpkins and squash, provide sturdy shelves or improvise by raising boards up from the floor on cinder blocks. Cushion these long-keepers with a layer of newspaper or straw underneath, and don't set them so close that they touch, otherwise you may find some decay developing where they come in contact with each other.

Brussels sprouts, Chinese cabbage, endive, escarole, and leeks will remain at their freshest if you take them from the garden, roots intact, and replant them in a sand- or soil-filled container. They should be set upright, densely packed together, and watered occasionally to keep their roots moist. The plants will not continue to grow in this arrangement, but their roots will continue to draw up water to keep the vegetables crisp.

All other vegetables will need to be packed in some type of storage containers. With the exception of onions and potatoes, the stored vegetables should never come in direct contact with each other, to prevent any possible decay from spreading and spoiling the whole containerful. As you pack them in the storage container, make sure each vegetable is completely surrounded by a layer of bedding material, and never put more than three layers in a single container. Suitable bedding materials include buckwheat hulls, leaves, peat or sphagnum moss, sand, sawdust, and wood shavings. To maintain high levels of humidity around root crops, moisten the bedding material in which they are packed. In addition, cover with moist sand or soil any heads of cabbage and cauliflower from which the roots have been removed.

Storage in the Garden Row

With the help of a thick layer of insulating mulch, you can store some of your crops right where they grew and continue to harvest them up until the time the ground freezes hard. This storage method is the easiest one of all, since you're letting the excellent insulating and moisture-holding properties of the soil do all the work for you. Crops which store well in the ground include: carrots, Hamburg parsley, horseradish, Jerusalem artichoke, kale, leeks, parsnips, rutabaga, and salsify. In areas where the winters are mild, a thick mulch is enough to protect beets, cabbage, celeriac, turnips, and winter radishes.

You will need enough mulch (leaves, straw, hay) to make a 1- to 2-foot layer over the root crops, and enough to pull around the stems of upright plants to form a snug blanket. Boards, cornstalks, or sunflower stalks make good anchors to hold down flyaway mulch. A layer of hardware cloth set over the root crops will help keep hungry rodents away. Mark with tall stakes the areas where vegetables are stored in-ground so you will be able to locate them even under snow. Also, planting the vegetables you wish to store in one area of the garden will make it easier to find them later.

You have two options with garden row storage. First, you can hold the vegetables in the garden until just before the ground freezes hard. Once the growing season ends and the weather cools, apply the mulch, which will keep the ground open so you can continue to harvest throughout the fall. Just before the ground freezes hard, take the remaining crops from the ground and place them in cold cellar storage or use them at once.

Garden Row Storage: The foresighted gardener who has put down a deep layer of mulch over rows of hardy vegetables at the end of the season will be able to harvest them all winter long. The mulch keeps the ground from freezing, and the soil's natural coolness and moisture keep the vegetables in good condition until they are needed.

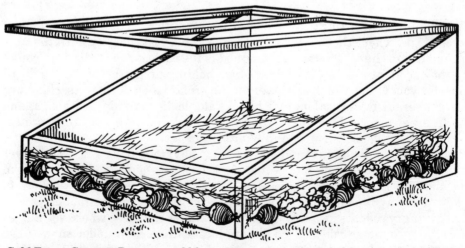

Cold Frame Storage: Press your cold frame into service at the end of the season by storing harvested root crops inside.

Your alternative is to use the frozen ground as a storage area through the winter, and harvest the vegetables in early spring, before they begin to sprout with new growth. To do this, mulch lightly at the end of the growing season. When the weather turns cold enough to freeze the ground, remove the mulch so that the soil will freeze hard. Then reapply the mulch to prevent the ground from thawing during any warm spells, since alternate freezing and thawing will damage the vegetables and make them unfit to eat.

Also, don't forget your cold frame as a handy resource to use for storing vegetables in the garden. After the first frost, transplant any celery, Chinese cabbage, endive, lettuce, mustard, spinach, and Swiss chard plants that remain in the garden into the frame. In this way, you extend their harvest season for a month or more after the first frost. The cold frame can also hold harvested root crops covered with a 6-inch layer of mulch. In this case, glass panels in the cold frame should be replaced with solid boards to afford better protection.

Forcing Roots
for Winter Salad Greens

You can lift the roots of certain vegetables from the garden, relocate them in a container of soil set in a warm place, and coax them into a second harvest of shoots and leaves for salads. The forcing process is an easy one, and it starts when you go out into your garden in the fall, shovel in hand, and dig up the roots before the ground freezes hard. Gather any old pails, dishpans, or wooden boxes you can find that are at least 6 to 8 inches deep and put a 2- to 4-inch layer of sand or soil in the bottom. Next, add the roots, making sure the tips are pointing down and the crowns are facing toward you. The spacing of the roots is not critical, and they can actually be set so close together that they touch. Cover the roots with another 2 inches of sand or soil and then water gently.

Set the container in a warm (50° to 65°F), dark place and keep the growing medium moist. Light is not necessary for these vegetables to make their growth, and although the greens and shoots may be paler than the summertime crop produced outdoors, they will be especially succulent and tender, and certainly welcome as a fresh vegetable in a season when garden produce is hard to come by. You may be able to make your first basement harvest in as short a time as three weeks, although a month is the average amount of time for greens and shoots to appear.

Both rhubarb and asparagus roots need a cold period to break their natural dormancy before they will sprout. Once their roots are in soil or sand, set them in a garage, shed, or unheated room for about six weeks before continuing with the forcing procedure. Keep the roots dry until you expose them to warmth, at which time you can begin watering to keep the growing medium moist.

Follow the basic forcing procedure as described above for the following roots to try your hand at growing winter salad greens:

• **Asparagus:** Forcing exhausts these roots so they cannot be replanted in the garden come spring. Use three-year-old roots that have been grown especially for forcing, or use the ones pulled out when thinning the patch. Harvest the light green spears by breaking them off at the soil level.

- **Beets:** Tuck in as many beet roots from your garden as a bucketful of soil can hold (push the beets in until their shoulders are covered with soil) and you can look foward to several pickings of tasty leaves for salads.

- **Witloof Chicory:** With relatively little effort and minimal expense you can force these roots for a gourmet treat. The roots you force are those of Witloof chicory, but the shoots that emerge are known as Belgian endive. Trim the leaves of roots lifted from your garden to 1 inch. In a slight variation on the basic forcing instructions, bury them in 10 inches of moist soil, then apply a 6- to 8-inch layer of dampened sand or sawdust. The creamy tips, or "chicons" are ready for harvest when you see them poking through the sand (in about three weeks). Brush away this top layer and snap the tips off where they join the root.

- **Dandelion:** Forced roots produce very tender and tasty leaves, without the bitterness of the outdoor-grown greens, since they are not exposed to light. Leaves are ready to harvest in five weeks.

- **Rhubarb:** Use two- to three-year-old roots with the dead leaves stripped away. Within six weeks you can expect to begin harvesting succulent, pink stalks.

tricks of the trade

Drying Your Bean Harvest for Storage

Shell beans, which include such well-known varieties as kidney, pinto, white marrowfat, and black turtle, are generally raised to be dried at the end of the growing season, for use in soups and a host of other hearty dishes. Lima beans may also be dried, and some people even dry snap beans, although these beans don't hold up in cooking as well as other shell beans.

The basic procedure is to leave the beans (still in their pods) on the plant in the garden until they have dried. You can tell the beans have reached this point when the pods become dry and papery, when you can hear the beans rattle when you shake the pods, and when the plant has lost nearly all its leaves. Pick the individual pods as they dry, or, if most of the pods dry at the same time, lift the whole plant by the roots. Snap beans are ready when the pods have withered and begun to brown, and the beans are swollen.

The next step, shelling the beans, doesn't have to be done immediately—the dry plants can wait in a dry, warm, and airy place until you find a convenient time. There are several ways you can go about extricating the beans from the pods. One method calls for grasping the plant stems and banging the pods against the inside of a clean garbage can. Or put the plants inside a large cloth bag and thrash it with a stick or other hard object. Never beat the pods on a hard surface without some buffer like a piece of burlap underneath. If you do so, you risk bruising the beans themselves. Shelling the beans by hand is a time-consuming task, but one that becomes more pleasant when you do it on a chilly fall or winter's eve, huddled around the fireplace or woodstove.

After the beans are shelled and the small plant particles are culled away, spread the beans on screens or a bedsheet in a dry, warm, airy place to ensure that nearly all the moisture has a chance to evaporate. This may take up to three weeks, and you can determine whether the beans have dried enough for storage by biting one. If your teeth make no indentation, the bean is sufficiently dried.

If the weather is cold and wet at the time you want your beans to be drying on the plants, the best way to remedy the situation is to bring them inside. Pull all the bean plants and hang them by the roots in a dry, airy place until they have dried. Then proceed with shelling as described above.

At this point, there is one more step you will need to take before storing your dried beans in airtight, lidded containers. In order to make sure all weevils and bugs are out of your beans and any of their eggs are destroyed, spread them on shallow trays and place these in a 180°F oven for one hour, or put jars or bags of the beans in the freezer for a few hours (freezing will not hurt the viability of the beans, while the heat treatment will). You can further protect your stored dried beans from bug infestation by including a dried hot pepper in each storage container. The pepper will keep out the bugs without affecting the flavor of the beans. Make sure to store your dried beans in a cool, dry place.

As a side note, both peas and corn can be dried in a similar fashion. Peas that have lingered too long on the vine to be of much use in their fresh state can simply be left to mature on the vine. When their pods start to wither and brown, treat them the same way you would beans. Corn kernels won't dry completely on the stalk because of the enveloping husks. Pick mature cobs, remove the husks, and dry the cobs in the sun or a slow oven until the kernels are hard and don't yield to fingernail pressure. You can store the cobs as is, or strip the kernels, and store them in containers under the same conditions as dried beans.

Winnowing: This time-honored, relatively effortless way to separate the good (shelled beans) from the bad (pieces of pod and other debris) is an outdoor activity that calls for a slight breeze. Shake the container so that the beans fly up in the air. The heavy beans will fall directly back into the container, while the light, papery debris will be carried off by the breeze.

A Guide to Vegetables for the Home Garden

AMARANTH

Chinese spinach, tampala
Amaranthus tricolor
Amaranthaceae

Many gardeners are familiar with the flowering amaranth that is grown strictly as an ornamental, not for use in the kitchen. Less familiar are two basic types of amaranth grown for food—the grain amaranth and the vegetable amaranth. Although young leaves of the grain type are suitable for culinary use, the tiny, protein-rich grain is the primary harvest. This type is not generally recommended for the home gardener, because cleaning the grain is too involved and expensive a process to pursue

160

on a small scale.

On the other hand, the vegetable type is eminently suited to the home garden, and is the type discussed in detail here. It is a quick-growing annual that produces an abundance of edible leaves in a relatively small amount of space. True to its tropical origins, the plant grows best when temperatures are high, making it a valuable potherb to fill the gap between the cool-season greens like lettuce and spinach. It may be especially useful in the Deep South to fill the gap between early and late harvests when it is too hot for continuous production of anything but okra and peppers. It can be harvested as a cut-and-come-again crop, spreading the harvest over a period of weeks.

The harvest of leaves, besides being bountiful, is nutritious. The greens are rich in calcium, magnesium, iron, and vitamins A and C. The young leaves may be used raw in a salad, but the larger, older leaves are best when lightly steamed. Amaranth greens can be used in any recipe calling for spinach, to which they will impart their own distinctive flavor.

A vegetable amaranth, commonly called tampala, has been on the home-garden market since 1944, but has never achieved widespread popularity. The Organic Gardening and Farming Research Center, located in Maxatawny, Pennsylvania, has been gathering amaranth seeds from around the world and experimenting with various types since 1974. Researchers there are developing varieties of both grain and vegetable types that can be grown successfully in temperate climates. Eventually, they hope to boost amaranth's popularity and see that the best varieties are made available to gardeners.

Growing Range: Vegetable amaranth is a warm-season crop that thrives in a warm, humid climate. It does well in temperate climates with average minimum temperatures of 68°F during the growing season. It is highly susceptible to frost damage, and does not grow well in periods of cloudy, wet weather. Amaranth is sensitive to daylength, and bolts to seed with the advent of short days in the fall.

Soil Preparation: Amaranth needs loose, fertile, well-drained soil. Soil which has been manured the previous fall forms a good base for growth. A good organic nitrogen fertilizer is necessary to promote rapid and full leaf development. Soil pH does not seem to be a critical factor in growing amaranth.

Propagation: Amaranth seed can be started indoors or sown directly in the garden. Start plants three weeks before setting out, which can be done after all danger of frost is past. The best transplants are 3 inches tall, with four to seven true leaves. Best quality greens are produced when plants are grown in beds. Allow 6-inch spacing in each direction between seedlings and direct-sown seeds. Sow seed ¼ inch deep when all danger of frost is past. To keep soil crusting from hampering germination, cover seeds with ½-inch layer of grass, hay, or sifted compost. Unused seed is good for seven years.

Culture: Keep soil evenly moist around the roots. Weed to keep down competition for moisture and nutrients. Put down a mulch if excessively dry conditions persist; otherwise, mulching is not necessary because the plants grow so rapidly they shade the ground with their own leaf growth.

Pests and Diseases: Caterpillars, stem borers, leaf curl, and stem rot may on occasion bother the crop.

Harvest and Storage: The entire plant can be cut off at ground level for harvest, but this is a wasteful method. For the best harvest in terms of quality and quantity, pinch off the leafy rosette at the top of the plant when the plant is 4 to 6 inches tall. This causes more stems with leaf rosettes to develop on the same plant. Pick these tender rosettes as they develop to usable size. This second cutting will be more tender than the first, and will prompt more stems with new leaf rosettes to form for an extended harvest. Vegetable amaranth can be frozen like spinach.

Varieties: Vegetable amaranth is available under a wide variety of common names, almost all of which are the species *A. tricolor* or cultivars of that species. Catalogs may list vegetable amaranth in the following ways: tampala, Chinese spinach, hin choy, edible amaranth, or edible amaranth spinach.

ASPARAGUS

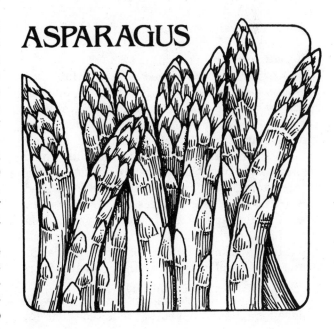

Asparagus officinalis
Liliaceae

Asparagus is a fernlike plant when fully developed, and people who are familiar with edible asparagus spears will walk by stands of mature plants without recognizing it. The thick, fleshy roots are invasive and go deeply into the soil (as much as 30 feet), allowing the plant to withstand harsh winters and high levels of salt in the soil. The tops, when mature, are stringy and tough and look like the feathery foliage of asparagus ferns, to which edible asparagus is related. The part that is eaten is 8 to 10 inches of the growing tip that pushes up through the soil in early spring. These edible spears are produced from small buds or "crowns" that are at the center of the root system. Each year, following dormancy, new crowns are produced that will form new spears.

White asparagus was in vogue years ago, but now nutrition-conscious consumers reject blanched spears for their lowered nutrient value. Commercial growers and home gardeners alike seldom blanch their crops anymore, since green spears are pleasantly flavored and tender, as well as being chock full of vitamins A and C, with lesser amounts of vitamin B_1, B_2, calcium, and trace minerals.

Asparagus is a long-lived plant that, once established, can produce for 15 to 25 years on the average. Home gardeners have traditionally started their beds with crowns purchased from nurseries, garden centers, or through mail-order catalogs. Recent studies have shown, however, that there are decided advantages to starting asparagus plants from seed. Starting from seed reduces the chances of fusarium disease and is a less costly proposition. Within a few years, the seed-started bed will produce a greater number of somewhat larger and more tender spears than a crown-planted bed.

Even small gardens can contain a few asparagus plants, but asparagus does tie up space, space that it cannot share with other plants. Asparagus is harvested for only a few weeks out of the year, even though it occupies a portion of the garden for the whole year. Another disadvantage is that there is an interim period of about three years between planting and harvesting. Furthermore, its roots can spread to nearby areas of the garden and become a nuisance.

Ideally, then, asparagus is best suited to the larger garden where it can be established in one location for a number of years. And once the bed is established, it is relatively maintenance-free.

Growing Range: Asparagus is a hardy plant that will grow well in any climate that provides several months of weather cold enough to freeze the soil and kill back the tops to induce dormancy.

Soil Preparation: Asparagus is extremely adaptable to soil types, but well-drained, sandy loam is the preferred type. No matter what the soil, drainage is very critical, for standing water will be fatal to asparagus. In heavy, clayey soils, work in coarse sand.

The trench method is the traditional way to establish a long-standing bed. After testing the soil, adjust the pH to within 6.5 to 6.8 by adding lime as needed. Work the lime deeply into the soil where the trench will be dug. Dig the trench 12 to 15 inches wide and about 18 inches deep. Remove the topsoil and set it aside. Remove the subsoil and discard. Fertilize the soil at the bottom of the trench by forking in compost, well-rotted manure, leaf mold, or peat moss. Fresh manure can be used, but the trench should be deeper than 18 inches and the manure separated from the roots of the asparagus by at least a 3-inch layer of earth. Add bone meal and some source of potassium, such as greensand, to the bottom of the trench.

Propagation: Asparagus can be started from purchased crowns or from seedlings started indoors and set into the garden. Buy the largest one-year-old crowns available; two- or three-year-old crowns are sometimes offered, but they do not adapt and grow as well as younger ones. Crowns can be planted about 2 to 4 weeks before the frost-free date; seedlings are set out 4 weeks after the frost-free date. Soak the seed for 24 hours to improve germination, and sow 12 to 14 weeks before the desired setting-out date. Seedlings are ready for setting out when

Trench Planting of Asparagus Crowns

12 inches tall. Unused seed is good for three years.

Crowns and seedlings are set in the garden using the same procedure. Space trenches 36 to 48 inches apart, and plant every 24 inches along each trench. Usual planting depth is 6 inches below the soil surface; 8 inches is used on very sandy or peat soils, and 10 inches for larger and more tender spears. However, the deeper the planting, the later the spears will emerge. (Some gardeners stage the trench at different levels to schedule the arrival of harvestable spears at different times.) Make a mound of soil or compost every 24 inches along the trench. Set crowns in place on the mounds so eyes are facing up and roots are fanned out. With seedlings, nestle one seedling into each mound, so that the roots are supported. Cover crowns with 2 inches of soil, and draw 2 inches of soil up around the seedlings' base.

Throughout the season, as crowns put forth shoots and seedlings grow taller, add 1 to 2 inches of soil at a time, until the trench is brought up to ground level around midseason. At this point, mulch around the fern growth with leaves, compost, rotted manure, or grass clippings.

Culture: The ferny tops produced throughout late spring and summer manufacture carbohydrates to be stored in the crowns over winter. These carbohydrates serve as an energy reserve for the next season's growth. Even though the tops turn brown and die back at some point in fall or winter, it is best not to cut them off. Rather, leave them on the plant over the winter, and remove them in spring before new growth begins. In this way, there is no chance of the tops being removed too soon, cutting short the plant's energy storage process.

Keep the asparagus bed free of weeds through the summer. An especially dry period in the summer may hamper the growth of ferns and limit next year's production of spears, so water deeply if there is an extended dry period. Although asparagus is resistant to salt in the soil, there is no truth to the tale that the plants want salt. Apparently this tale grew up around the practice of salting the soil to keep the weeds down.

Early in autumn, apply 6 to 8 inches of manure or compost over the bed to act as a winter blanket and to keep the soil rich in nutrients. Uncomposted manure may be used without danger to the plants; as it breaks down through the winter, nutrients will be leached out into the soil.

Pests and Diseases: Two asparagus beetles, the common and the 12-spotted, are frequent pests. Rust is the big problem, and can be dealt with by choosing varieties which are rust-resistant. Fusarium wilt is also a problem in some areas.

Harvest and Storage: Some gardeners start to harvest a few spears two seasons after crowns have been planted. Current research shows, however, that the plants (started from crowns or seedlings) should be grown untouched for two full seasons before harvesting begins. Even a very light harvest in the second growing season can cause dwarf plants the following season and reduce the lifetime yield of the bed. Make the first harvest three seasons after planting, and pick for two weeks. The next season's harvest can continue for four weeks, and in subsequent seasons, it can go on for six to eight weeks, depending on the vigor of the bed. Once the harvesting period is over, let the stalks that emerge develop into ferns and start their work of replenishing the crowns.

Spears are ready for harvest when they are 8 to 10 inches tall and less than 1 inch around. If the leaf bracts at the tip are open, that signals a tough, woody spear that is past its prime. Knives are used commercially to pick the spears, but in the hands of the inexperienced a knife can cause damage to the subterranean crown. The best way to harvest and the least damaging way is to break the spears off at their tenderest part, at or above ground level.

One of the best features of asparagus is the ease with which it is harvested, cleaned, and prepared. It can be steamed, stir-fried, or eaten raw. Be careful not to cook the spears too long or they will turn gray. Cooked asparagus can be frozen or canned.

Asparagus

Variety Name	General Description and Comments
California 500	The standard variety grown on the West Coast of the U.S. originated from Mary Washington variety; does not have the purplish cast of that variety; rust-resistant.
Mary Washington	The most widely grown; rust-resistant but not immune; green spears with a slight purplish cast.
Viking (also Mary Washington Improved)	Developed for the most northerly parts of the U.S. and Canada; paler green than Mary Washington; seed is available.
Waltham Washington	Developed for northeastern areas; rust-resistant but not immune; seed is available.

BEANS

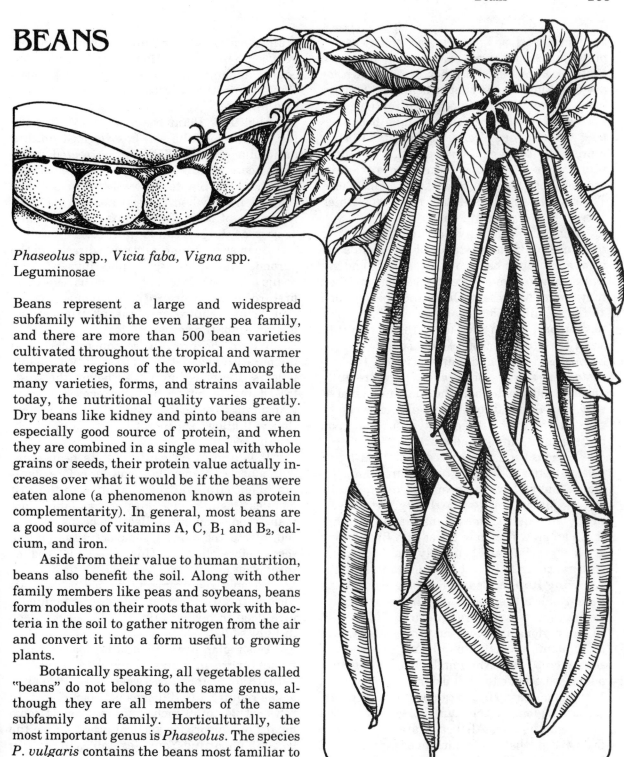

Phaseolus spp., *Vicia faba*, *Vigna* spp.
Leguminosae

Beans represent a large and widespread subfamily within the even larger pea family, and there are more than 500 bean varieties cultivated throughout the tropical and warmer temperate regions of the world. Among the many varieties, forms, and strains available today, the nutritional quality varies greatly. Dry beans like kidney and pinto beans are an especially good source of protein, and when they are combined in a single meal with whole grains or seeds, their protein value actually increases over what it would be if the beans were eaten alone (a phenomenon known as protein complementarity). In general, most beans are a good source of vitamins A, C, B_1 and B_2, calcium, and iron.

Aside from their value to human nutrition, beans also benefit the soil. Along with other family members like peas and soybeans, beans form nodules on their roots that work with bacteria in the soil to gather nitrogen from the air and convert it into a form useful to growing plants.

Botanically speaking, all vegetables called "beans" do not belong to the same genus, although they are all members of the same subfamily and family. Horticulturally, the most important genus is *Phaseolus*. The species *P. vulgaris* contains the beans most familiar to gardeners, such as French beans, kidney beans, pinto beans, Romano beans, snap or green beans, wax beans, and other beans grown for dry use. Lima beans, runner beans, and tepary beans are all different species within the genus *Phaseolus*. Adzuki beans and mung beans belong to the genus *Vigna,* and the fava beans represent a third genus, *Vicia*. And, as a final illustration of the scope of the bean subfamily, the garbanzo bean represents the genus *Cicer*. The soybean is an additional bean type which is treated in a separate entry.

Beans are generally classified according to their use in different stages of the plant's development. Snap beans are eaten, pods and all, while they are immature and tender, or when they "snap" when bent. Green shell beans, such as the familiar lima bean, are used for their seeds alone, which are eaten fresh when full-sized but still immature. Dry beans, such as kidney, garbanzo, and pinto varieties, are harvested for storage only when they are fully mature and used when the moisture level is very low (about 10 percent). Some beans can be used in any of the three stages, such as fava, horticultural, mung, and scarlet runner.

Various beans are offered in both bush and pole varieties, such as green snap, lima, Romano, and yellow wax beans. Pole beans take up less garden space (since their growth is vertical), but require some means of support, since they can grow from 5 to 8 feet tall. Bush beans are low-growing and generally require no support, reaching only 15 to 20 inches in height.

Growing Range: Beans may be grown in any region offering a warm growing season with average temperatures ranging from 70° to 80°F. In cool regions, use early-maturing varieties or start plants indoors. Snap beans are a short-season crop, while shell and dry beans require a long season due to their drying requirements. Many long-season beans can be grown in short-season regions if they are harvested at the green shell stage. All beans are sensitive to frost except the fava, which needs a long, cool growing season and can stand light frosts.

Soil Preparation: Beans do best in a well-drained soil, rich in organic matter, with a pH between 6.0 and 7.5. Make sure there are adequate amounts of potassium and phosphorus worked into the soil; beans will supply their own nitrogen.

Propagation: Plant beans anytime after the last frost, when the soil has warmed up to a minimum of 60°F (65°F for untreated seed). Lima beans are the most cold-sensitive variety, and should be planted at least two weeks after the last frost, when the soil has warmed to a minimum of 65°F. Fava beans can be planted as soon as the soil can be worked.

Bean seed is generally sown directly in the garden. Make successive plantings of bush beans once a week up to two months before the first frost date, to ensure a continuous harvest. Pole beans require only one planting at the beginning of the season.

Where the growing season is short, and temperatures cool, it's best to start bean plants indoors, three to four weeks before the frost-free date. Beans are not the easiest crop to transplant; use peat pots or a similar system that will allow transplanting without disturbing the roots.

It is a good idea to inoculate bean seeds with a bacterial inoculant powder before planting to encourage nitrogen fixation in the root nodules (legume inoculant is available from many seed companies). Because beans are susceptible to rot, do not soak or presprout the seeds before planting. Unused seed is good for three years.

Spacing requirements for beans vary according to growth habit. All seed is planted 1 inch deep in heavy soils, and 1½ inches deep in light soils.

Bush snap beans should be spaced 3 to 4 inches apart in conventional row plantings, with 18 to 30 inches between rows. Pole snap beans require 4 to 6 inches between plants, in rows set 24 to 36 inches apart. Provide some means of support for vertical growth. (See the box on Supporting Your Vegetables in Style in chapter 4 for some ideas.) Pole varieties may also be planted in hills. Plant 6 to 8 seeds per hill (thin later to 3 to 4 plants), setting the hills 36 inches apart. Growing bed spacing for snap beans is 6 inches.

Bush lima beans should be planted 3 to 6 inches apart, in rows set 24 to 30 inches apart for conventional row spacing. Pole limas need 8 to 10 inches between plants, 30 to 36 inches between rows, and vertical support. Pole limas may also be planted in hills as described for pole snap beans. Growing bed spacing for lima beans is 8 inches.

Other green shell and dry bean varieties may be planted following the spacing guideline for bush snap beans. Any bush bean variety is suitable for wide-row culture.

Culture: Supports for pole beans should be set in place when two seedling leaves have appeared. Bush beans generally do not need staking, but in windy areas support can keep plants upright. A simple method of supporting bush plants is to run a strong cord around stakes set at the row ends, or around stakes set in each corner of a growing bed.

A midseason feeding of potassium is necessary only for beans growing in sandy soils, or in areas where repeated rains may have leached away nutrients. In these cases, sidedress the plants with wood ashes, or apply a seaweed extract solution. Keep the soil evenly moist, especially while the seeds are germinating, and from the time flowers have opened until the pods have set. Cultivate carefully to avoid damaging shallow roots, and do not cultivate or work around the plants while the foliage is wet to prevent any spread of disease.

Pests and Diseases: Insect pests include aphids, cabbage loopers, corn earworms, cucumber beetles, European corn borers, leafminers, and Mexican bean beetles. Seeds are subject to seed rot, and damping-off may affect emerging seedlings. Lima beans are susceptible to downy mildew and bacterial spot. Snap beans are susceptible to anthracnose, bacterial blight, mosaics, and rust.

Harvest and Storage: Snap beans may be harvested as soon as the pods are large enough to make picking worthwhile, but before the seeds have begun to fill out the pods. By regularly picking young pods on bush beans, the plants will continue to flower and produce for at least three weeks. Snap beans that aren't eaten fresh may be canned, although they are better frozen. Green shell beans should be picked when the seeds have reached full size, but before pods have begun to deteriorate.

Dry beans are left on the vine to dry, and are harvested when the pods are dry and papery and the foliage has yellowed and withered. Refer to the box on Drying Your Bean Harvest for Storage in chapter 5 for complete instructions. Store dried beans in an airtight, lidded container set in a cool, dry place.

Beans

Out of the more than 500 cultivated bean varieties in the world, the listings in the accompanying chart are limited to the most popular and valuable species and strains cultivated in Western temperate regions. The letters that appear under the heading "Use" indicate the use for which the bean is suited. S = snap bean, to be eaten pods and all; G = green shell bean, to be shelled and eaten at the immature green stage; and D = dry bean, to be harvested when dry for storage and later use. Many of the beans may serve two or all three uses.

Bean	Average Days to Maturity	Use	General Description and Comments
Adzuki	90	S–G–D	This small plant from Japan produces long, thin pods, each containing 7 to 10 small, maroon seeds, nutty in flavor and extremely high in protein; excellent as a snap bean, but also good at shell and dry stages; suitable for both long- and short-season areas. *(continued)*

Beans—*continued*

Bean	Average Days to Maturity	Use	General Description and Comments
Black Turtle Soup	85–115	S–G–D	A good, standard bean, long popular in the southern United States where it is used in soups and stews; bush-type plant with jet-black seeds.
Fava (also English broad bean, horse bean)	85–90	S–G–D	This bushy plant produces long pods, each containing 5 to 7 large, flat seeds; fragile stalks need support once they reach 24 in.; one of the few cool-climate beans that will do well when planted early in spring and cultivated like peas; ready for use as a snap bean when young and tender, before the inside of pod turns cottony; ready for use as green shell bean in about 2 months; dry beans can be popped like corn; ingesting a large amount of these beans can cause sickness or an allergic reaction in some people; soaking or cooking beans in hot water and moderation in the amount eaten can lessen the chances of any problems.
Garbanzo (also chick pea)	65–100	G–D	A very popular bean, used for baking, as a salad ingredient when cooked and chilled; has a distinctively nutty flavor; harvest for shell beans at about 65 days; bushy plant is not recommended for cool-climate areas.
Great Northern White	85	G–D	Long a standard for baking; bushy plant is high-yielding and good for short-season areas; harvest for use as green shell bean at around 65 days.
Horticultural (also shell bean, wren's egg bean)	65–70	S–G–D	Most commonly used as a green shell bean, with a rich, nutty flavor; can also be eaten as a snap bean while immature, or as a dry bean at about 90 days; pole or dwarf plants bear colorful, mottled pods containing red-speckled seeds; produces a very high yield in a small area and is popular in home gardens; especially good for canning and freezing; most popular variety is the French Horticultural bean.
Lima (also butter bean)	60–75	G–D	This popular shell bean takes its name from the capital city of Peru, where it is thought to have originated; a warm-weather plant, highly sensitive to even the slightest chill; green shell beans freeze very well; dried limas can be used in any recipe calling for dried beans; choose between thick- or flat-seeded varieties, and large- or small-seeded (baby) varieties; bush and pole varieties are available; popular pole varieties are Florida Speckled Butter Bean (also Speckled Butter Bean), King of the Garden, and Prizetaker; popular bush beans are Henderson Baby Bush, Fordhook Bush Lima, and Fordhook 242.
Pinto	85–90	D	Closely related to the red kidney bean; a favorite for baking and use in Mexican cuisine; the strong vines need more garden space than bush snap beans, and can be grown in the same manner as pole beans.
Red Kidney	100	D	The most popular and easiest of all dry beans to grow; the hearty flavor and red color enhances soups, stews, chili, and other Mexican dishes.
Scarlet Runner (also multiflora bean, painted lady bean, Dutch caseknife bean)	70	S–G–D	A very versatile bean that can be eaten in all three stages of development and used as a spectacular ornamental; grows 10 to 12 ft. tall along walls or trellises and produces beautiful scarlet flower clusters; a perennial usually grown as an annual in cooler climates; black and scarlet speckled beans are encased by rough-looking green pods.

Bean	Average Days to Maturity	Use	General Description and Comments
Snap (also green bean, string bean, stringless bean, wax bean)	40–55	S–D	The most popular garden bean, with many different strains available of both bush and pole types; pole beans mature more slowly than bush beans, but will produce more heavily throughout the entire season; bush beans are quick to mature, but they bear for a shorter period, so succession plantings are necessary for a steady supply; pods may be green, purple, or yellow; most often used in a tender immature state as a snap bean, but can also be used as dried bean once the pods have turned brown and shriveled; dependable bush strains include Tendercrop, Tendergreen, and Topcrop; standard pole strains are Kentucky Wonder and Blue Lake.
Soldier	85	D	A white, oval-shaped bean, good for baking; does well in cool climates and withstands drought better than most; viney plant needs plenty of growing room.

BEETS

Beetroot
Beta vulgaris
Chenopodiaceae

Both parts of the beet are edible—the leaves as well as the roots. The roots have a high natural sugar content, ranging from 8 to 21 percent, depending on the variety grown and the growing conditions. They may be steamed or baked, and eaten hot or cold. They are often pickled in vinegar, and are commonly associated with the Russian soup, borscht. The leaves are nutritious greens, packed with vitamins A and C. They may be steamed and served as you would spinach.

Beets are one of the easiest crops to grow in the home garden. These attractive plants with red-veined, dark green leaves aren't fussy about the soil they grow in, and they produce a high yield in a small space—a boon for cramped gardens.

Beets are classed according to their color, shape, and intended use. Red to purple roots are the most common, but there are also gold and white varieties that won't bleed when sliced. Beets vary in shape from round to oval to long and cylindrical (easier for slicing). Baby beets, generally about 1½ inches in diameter, were developed especially for canning and pickling. There are bunching varieties, grown mainly for their greens, and canning varieties, grown specifically for their roots.

Growing Range: Beets are a cool-season crop that is well adapted to all regions and climates. They are fairly heat-tolerant, but in areas with extremely hot summers, plant them as an early spring, fall, or winter crop, so maturity does not coincide with the hottest temperatures. They make the best growth with temperatures averaging from 60° to 65°F. These half-hardy plants are resistant to cold, but are unable to withstand severe freezing. Beets will tolerate partial shade.

Soil Preparation: Beets do reasonably well in any soil. A sandy, well-drained soil with plenty of organic matter such as compost or well-rotted manure promotes speedy growth and high-quality roots. Never grow beets in soil to which fresh manure has been added. Work in ample amounts of potassium-rich material like wood ashes. Remove all rocks and debris from the top 4 inches of soil to allow roots to develop fully. Beet growth is stunted when soil is too acidic; the recommended pH is 6.5.

Propagation: Beets can be started indoors or seeded directly in the garden. Start seeds in individual containers four weeks before setting out, which can be done four weeks before the frost-free date. Sow seed outdoors two to four weeks before the frost-free date, when the soil has warmed to at least 40°F. Make successive plantings every three weeks until midsummer. Begin a second planting phase for a fall crop about ten weeks before the first expected frost.

Each large beet seed is actually a cluster of tiny seeds which can produce from four to six seedlings. Some fragmented seed (also known as monogerm) is available, which produces only one seedling as opposed to a cluster, thus eliminating the need to thin. Soak seeds for at least 12 hours before planting to promote germination. Since beet seed is slow to germinate, sow radish seed at the same time to mark planting areas. Unused seed is good for four years.

For conventional rows, sow seed every 2 to 6 inches in rows spaced 8 to 12 inches apart. Plant fragmented seed 2 inches apart with the same spacing between rows. Raised bed spacing is 6 inches. Beet seed may also be planted in wide rows. Sow all seed ½ to 1 inch deep. During hot and dry spells, prevent crust from forming over germinating seed by covering the seed

with organic material such as leaf mold, a mix of sand and soil, or peat moss mixed with sand.

Set transplants every 3 inches along the rows, using between-row spacing given above. To set transplants into a raised bed, use spacings given above.

Culture: Beets sown directly in the garden (except those grown from fragmented seed) should be thinned twice. Make the first thinning when the first true leaves appear, by clearing out the seedling clusters. When the plants are about 6 inches tall and tiny roots have begun to form, make the second thinning, leaving 3 to 4 inches between plants (6 inches for fragmented seeds). These thinnings are a treat for the table with their tasty greens and small, tender roots.

An adequate supply of water promotes rapid growth, which in turn ensures good flavor. Lack of water during a warm spell causes plants to bolt or roots to crack and become tough. Beets are light feeders and need no supplemental feedings. Remove weeds by hand since a hoe may easily damage roots and cause bleeding. After thinning, tuck mulch close to the plants to help keep soil moist.

Pests and Diseases: Beets are generally not bothered. Possible pests are aphids, leafhoppers, leafminers, slugs, and snails. The only disease that may be a problem is leaf spot. Black, bitter-tasting spots indicate a boron deficiency; top-dress soil with granite dust.

Harvest and Storage: Beet greens can be harvested at any time throughout the season. Roots should be harvested when fairly small, before they turn tough and woody; 1½ to 3 inches is the best size range. Pull them out by hand rather than dig them out with a tool to avoid damaging the roots.

Plan to store the late summer crop rather than the early-season crop. Before storing, carefully twist off the tops, leaving 2 inches of greens extending. Handle gently to avoid bruising the roots. Mishandling the roots may cause bleeding, which means juice is being lost and the quality of the root is declining. Store roots, layered in sand or peat moss, in a cool (32° to 40°F), moist place. Beets will keep for two to five months.

In mild winter areas, beets can be stored right in the garden, protected by a thick mulch.

Take them as needed until the ground freezes hard, and dig them all up in the spring as soon as the ground has thawed.

Refrigerated beets remain good for several weeks. Beets are easy to can, pickle, or freeze.

Beets

Variety Name	Average Days to Maturity	General Description and Comments
Standard-Sized Roots		
Detroit Dark Red	55–60	Dark red round root; especially adapted to all regions; good early variety; stores well; good for canning and freezing; AAS.
Ruby Queen	52–55	Deep red round root; short greens; an extra-early variety; excellent for pickling; the best canning variety; AAS.
Early Wonder	48–55	Deep red oval roots; especially good greens; good early variety; excellent as a transplant; stores well; good for canning.
Burpee's Golden Beet	50–55	Distinctive orange skin and yellow flesh; fine-tasting greens, used fresh or cooked; oval roots develop rapidly, but do not lose tenderness or sweetness as they become large.
Long Season	78–80	Dark red cylindrical roots; rough-looking exterior belies tenderness and sweetness; very good greens; remains tender as it grows larger; excellent for storage.
Formanova (also Cylindra Improved)	55–58	Very sweet and tender; roots are cylindrical; excellent for pickling, freezing, canning.
Mono King Explorer	59	Oval, dark red roots are very sweet; good for pickling; fragmented seed.
Greens		
Lutz Green Leaf	80	Roots shaped like toy tops; deep purple-red and very sweet; glossy green leaves with pink midribs are very sweet and tender.
Baby Beets		
Baby Canning	54	Roots are cylindrical.
Little Ball	56	Round roots stay small even as they age.
Little Mini Ball	54	Round roots; short tops good for greens.

BROCCOLI

Calabrese
Brassica oleracea, Botrytis Group
Cruciferae

Although there are heading types of broccoli, the vegetable discussed here is the sprouting kind that produces many thickened flowering branches rather than a solid head. The blue-green variety is the most familiar, but there are also purple sprouting varieties that can liven up the garden's color scheme.

Most broccoli grows about 2 feet tall, and the plants require a good amount of growing space between them, a demand that does not make broccoli a space-saving vegetable for the small garden. During its early growth, fill the in-between spaces with short-term vegetables like lettuce and radishes to make better use of the garden area. Many gardeners overlook the fact that broccoli is a type of cut-and-come-again crop. Instead of cutting the whole plant off at ground level, only the main head should be cut. When the main heads are removed, the plants grow more side sprouts, which appear at the leaf joints over a period of weeks. Growing broccoli is not a once-and-done affair—both a spring and fall crop can be grown.

Sometimes gardeners find broccoli a vexing crop to grow, seeing their efforts rewarded by nothing more than inferior little buttons instead of full flower heads. The trick to successful broccoli is quick, steady growth—which means a rich soil, plenty of water and nutrients, and cool temperatures.

Many people feel that broccoli has a better smell and few of the digestive complications associated with cabbage. Besides being relatively benign, broccoli is also very nutritious. It has large amounts of vitamins A and C, plus lesser amounts of B vitamins, calcium, and iron. Both the florets and the stalks (with any pithiness peeled away) can be eaten raw, steamed, or stir-fried until tender-crisp. Broccoli stands by itself as a tasty side dish with a dash of lemon juice or a topping of melted cheese. It can also be incorporated into casseroles and creamed into soups.

Growing Range: Broccoli can be grown in almost any area of the temperate zone as long as its requirements of a cool and moist long grow-

Broccoli

Variety Name	Average Days to Maturity	General Description and Comments
DiCicco	70–80	Flat, dark green heads measure 4 in. across; produces many side-shoots; an old standard.
Green Comet	55	Blue-green heads are 6–7 in. across; AAS.
Premium Crop	58–65	Large blue-green heads are 7–9 in. across; heads hold tight bud for a long period; produces few side-shoots; AAS with disease resistance.
Spartan Early	58	Dark green heads reach 7 in. across; a short, stocky plant; good production of lateral shoots after central heads are cut
Waltham 29	74–85	Blue-green heads are 5–6 in. across; produces few side-shoots; not suited for spring planting; the best variety for a fall crop.

ing season are met. The best growth is made when temperatures average between 40° and 65°F. In areas of hot, dry summers, plant in early fall for a late fall and winter crop. Seedlings are damaged by frost, while mature plants can withstand light frosts.

Soil Preparation: Broccoli needs a soil rich in nitrogen. Furnish this by digging 3 to 4 inches of well-rotted manure into the soil two weeks before planting. When preparing a bed in the fall for planting the subsequent spring, fresh manure can be applied 6 to 8 inches deep and dug in before the onset of winter. Soil pH should range from 6.7 to 7.2. Lime to achieve the higher pH if clubroot is a known problem. This inactivates the clubroot organism.

Propagation: Broccoli can be direct-seeded in the garden or started indoors for a jump on the season. Sow seed outdoors 4 to 6 weeks before the frost-free date. Seeds will germinate if soil is at least 40°F. Start a spring crop indoors, 6 to 8 weeks before setting out, which is done 4 weeks before and up to 2 to 3 weeks after the frost-free date. Wait until the soil has warmed to 60°F before setting out young plants. Start a fall crop 18 weeks before the first expected frost. Unused seed is good for five years.

Space conventional rows 20 to 36 inches apart and set seedlings every 18 inches; when sowing seeds, plant three at the same interval. Cover seed with ½ inch of fine soil. Growing bed spacing is 18 inches.

Culture: When they are 1 inch tall, thin those plants seeded directly by pinching them off. Leave only the most vigorous plants. Place cutworm collars around young plants.

Give the plants a nitrogen boost after three weeks of growth by side-dressing with rotted manure or compost or by applying manure tea. Keep the plants moist, and make sure roots stay cool by applying 4 to 6 inches of mulch. Successful commercial growers use 1 to 1½ inches of water weekly to produce prime heads for market. It is important to keep the area free of weeds, since weeds are very competitive with this crop and most of the other cabbage family members.

Pests and Diseases: See Cabbage. Buttoning or lack of head development is not a disease. It is a result of inadequate water, inadequate fertilizer, or both.

Harvest and Storage: Do not cut the flower heads off and throw the plant away after one harvest. Extend the harvest period by first cutting the largest head that develops at the end of the main stem. Cut the stem close to the base of the head to stimulate many more small broccoli heads to develop. These can be nipped off and used, stimulating yet a third and fourth head development. Of course, the size of the heads will gradually decrease, but they will be useful nonetheless. Any heads on which the yellow florets are visible are past their prime. Broccoli can be canned, frozen, and pickled. It can be kept fresh in the refrigerator for up to two weeks.

BRUSSELS SPROUTS

Brassica oleracea, Gemmifera Group
Cruciferae

Brussels sprouts are distinctive-looking plants in the garden. The stem, up to 3 feet tall in some varieties, is covered along its length with miniature cabbage heads that appear to be so many green balls stuck on a stick. These sprouts develop at the points where the leaves join the stalk. Each plant produces somewhere between 60 and 100 sprouts, which are 1 to 2 inches in diameter. The cluster of leaves at the top of the stem looks like a bunch of collard leaves, and can be prepared and eaten as a cabbage substitute.

Brussels sprouts are a long-season crop that ties up garden space for a large chunk of the season. However, they are suitable for small gardens because they produce a lot in return for the space they take up. While the Brussels sprout plants are still small, quick-maturing vegetables like lettuce and radishes can be grown in between them. Once the sprouts at the bottom of the stalk begin maturing, they may be harvested over a period of six to eight weeks. This prolonged harvest can even continue well after the first killing frost, when the sprouts will hold up well and taste better for the nip in the air.

The sprouts are very nutritious: they have high amounts of vitamins A, C, B_1, and B_2, and they are rich in calcium, potassium, and iron. They are often steamed and served with a cheese sauce, and can even be added to stir-fries. Be careful not to overcook the sprouts.

Growing Range: Brussels sprouts can be grown anywhere there is a cool season in which to mature them. They can withstand frost very well, but are averse to extreme heat. They are not suited for areas that have long, hot, dry summers, unless they are grown as a fall and winter crop. The best average temperature range for growth is 60° to 65°F.

Soil Preparation: Brussels sprouts need rich, well-drained soil with lots of organic matter to hold in moisture. They prefer heavy soil to light, sandy soil. Lay down 6 to 10 inches of compost or well-rotted manure and work it into the soil as deeply as 12 inches. Put in ample amounts of potassium- and phosphorus-rich materials, such as wood ashes and phosphate rock. Adjust the pH to between 6.0 and 6.8; lime toward the higher pH if clubroot disease is known to be a problem.

Propagation: The common practice is to sow seeds directly in an outdoor seedbed 10 to 12 weeks before the first killing frost. In areas with extremely short growing periods, the seed can be started indoors to gain time. Plants need 5 to 6 weeks to reach transplant size, and can be set out at the same time recommended above for seed sowing. Unused seed is good for five years.

In the outdoor seedbed, sow ½ inch deep and cover seeds with fine, friable soil. Space seeds about 2 inches apart. When the plants are 5 to 7 inches tall, transplant to their permanent place in the garden.

Plant seedlings deeply, so that the lower leaves are just above the soil. Place the transplants 18 inches apart in the growing bed and 18 to 24 inches apart in the conventional row. Space rows 30 to 36 inches apart. Firm the soil around the roots, otherwise the sprouts will be loose and leafy instead of firm and overlapped.

Culture: All transplants need cutworm collars. Brussels sprouts need even moisture and good fertility. Keep moist during hot weather, and feed with a high-potassium fertilizer such as wood ashes or seaweed extract. If setting out plants in warm weather, mulch as soon as they are transplanted and provide shade to prevent transplant shock. Keep area free of weeds, but be careful of shallow roots as you cultivate. In windy areas, these top-heavy plants benefit from supporting stakes.

Sprouts begin to form at the lower leaf axils first and then develop up toward the crown of the plant. When the sprouts have begun developing, the leaves turn yellow. Break or cut these yellow leaves off, gradually working up toward the crown. Leave about 2 inches of leaf stem on the stalk. This gives the sprouts more room to grow, resulting in rounder, neater sprouts. Trimming off the leaves also seems to stimulate growth in the sprouts.

Pests and Diseases: See Cabbage.

Harvest and Storage: Warm weather will cause the sprouts to become loose-leaved and strong-flavored, but these same sprouts will firm up and improve in flavor as soon as the weather cools and they are touched by light frost. The first sprouts of the season are usually not the best-tasting.

Harvest by cutting 1- to 1½-inch sprouts from the bottom of the plant and gradually work up as the sprouts develop. The harvesting can go on for several weeks until the sprouts are finished.

In areas where winters bring severe cold that would freeze and destroy the sprouts which have yet to be harvested, lift the plants with root ball intact, and bring them into a protected place where they will stay fresh and edible until all the sprouts are harvested. The protected area can be a pit, a cold frame, a root cellar, or an unheated greenhouse. Pack earth around the roots so that they will not dry out.

Fresh sprouts plucked from the stem can be stored in a cool (30° to 42°F), moist place for three to five weeks. Sprouts are easily frozen after having been blanched.

CABBAGE

Brassica oleracea, Capitata Group
Cruciferae

Cabbage is very well suited to small gardens. There is a great deal of nutrition present in this compact vegetable. Besides being high in vitamin C, it has good amounts of vitamins B_1, B_2, and A, plus calcium. The gardener of small spaces, therefore, gets a lot of nutritious food for the area that cabbage occupies, especially since the entire aboveground part of the plant is eaten.

Cabbage in its later stages of growth has large leaves which take up a lot of space, but it can be successfully interplanted with beets, lettuce, or radishes during its early growth, thereby gaining better use of the ground.

Cabbage is a versatile vegetable, used in both its raw and cooked form. Uncooked cabbage is, of course, higher in nutrients than cooked cabbage. Grated, raw cabbage is a well-known ingredient in cole slaw. Slivers of cabbage can be added to stir-fries, soups, or stews.

There are literally hundreds of different cabbages, but the easiest way to group them all

Brussels Sprouts

Variety Name	Average Days to Maturity	General Description and Comments
Catskill	85–95	18 in. tall with green leaves; sprouts are 1¼ in. around; compact growth good for small gardens; best as fall crop.
Jade Cross Hybrid	90	26 in. tall with blue-green sprouts up to 1¾ in. in diameter; a popular early, heavy yielder; adapts to a variety of climates; popular in the home garden; AAS.
Long Island Improved	95–115	20 in. tall with medium green leaves; sprouts to 1½ in. in diameter; best for fall harvest; sprouts freeze well.

is to classify them as early, midseason, and late. Beyond that, some have special uses. Some varieties are good for long storage, while others are better eaten fresh. Most have smooth green leaves, but there are red-leaved, and green, crinkly-leaved Savoy types, too (which, incidentally, have a higher iron content than the smooth-leaved green types). Savoy cabbages are hardy and make good winter and early spring crops. In addition to the basic edible cabbage, ornamental cabbages are also on the market. These "flowering" cabbages have loose heads of ruffled leaves that are red, white, or pink, with an outside border of green leaves. These colors are seen in full splendor in fall. Ornamental cabbages are edible as well as eye-pleasing, and are good additions to salads.

Growing Range: Cabbage is a hardy crop that is easy to grow in spring and fall in temperate regions. It can withstand temperatures as low as 20°F. To grow cabbage in hot, dry zones in summer is to court failure, but if these areas have cool winters, cabbage makes a very good winter crop. For a successful crop, it should mature in short days with cool temperatures. The wide range of variations among the types—early to late—makes it easy to fit the right cabbage to the particular climate.

Soil Preparation: Cabbages will grow on most soils, but they prefer rich garden loams that are well drained. Muck soils yield very good, fast-growing crops. Good crops can even be taken from sandy loam and heavy clay if the critical requirement of moisture is met. Adequate moisture will help get cabbage through periods of heat, periods which would otherwise cause it to flower. Spread rotted manure or compost as much as 6 to 8 inches deep and dig in thoroughly, down to 12 inches, before setting out cabbage. Add ample amounts of a potassium-rich material such as greensand, and a phosphorus-rich material like phosphate rock. The recommended pH is 6.0 to 6.8, but in areas where clubroot is a problem, lime the soil to reach a pH of 7.2.

Propagation: Early varieties are generally sown indoors for a two- to three-week head start on the season. Mid- and late-season crops are generally direct-seeded in the garden.

Start seeds indoors six to eight weeks before transplanting, which can be done from five weeks before to three weeks after the frost-free date. Use seedlings that are 4 to 5 inches tall, and set them in holes up to the bottom of the first pair of leaves, making sure the crown is not too close to the soil surface. In conventional rows, allow 14 inches between early varieties, 16 inches between midseason varieties, and 24 inches between late varieties. Space rows 28 to 36 inches apart. Growing bed spacing is 12 to 15 inches. Provide cutworm collars.

Outdoors, sow midseason varieties on the frost-free date, and late-season varieties one month later. Sow seed ½ inch deep, one per inch, using distance between rows given above. Unused seed is good for five years.

Culture: When direct-sown seedlings are 1 inch tall, thin in rows according to spacings given for transplants. Throughout their growth, cabbage plants need even moisture at their roots to prevent cracking of heads. Overhead sprinkling which dampens heads can be counterproductive, especially in periods of high humidity or cool temperatures. Insect and disease problems occur if dense cabbage leaves do not dry out. Weed carefully to avoid damaging shallow roots. Weeds and moisture can be taken care of in one stroke if a mulch of straw or compost is used. Cabbage benefits from a mid-season nitrogen boost if leaves are beginning to yellow. Three weeks after transplanting, side-dress with rotted manure, or apply manure tea every three weeks until harvest.

Pests and Diseases: Cutworms and flea beetles attack young plants. Aphids, cabbage loopers, cabbage maggots, harlequin bugs, imported cabbage worms, and leafminers are all pests to cabbage. Diseases are black rot, clubroot, downy mildew, and yellows.

Harvest and Storage: The heads are ready for

harvest any time after they have formed, and are hard and solid to the touch. Splitting heads are a sign of irregular watering or of cabbages past their prime. An old gardener's trick to hold maturing cabbage in the ground longer is to pull or twist the heads to break off some of the feeder roots. This shock seems to keep them from bolting or splitting for a period.

To harvest, cut the heads off the root system with a sharp knife. Discard the inferior outer leaves and inspect for insects along the leaf stems if long storage is planned. A second harvest can be coaxed from early varieties once the initial heads have been harvested. Cut off the heads, leaving stalks and roots in place.

These stalks will resprout with little buds; remove all but one or two of these new sprouts, and let them develop into small, tasty heads by winter.

Cabbage tastes the best when eaten soon after harvest, but it does store well when kept in a cool (32° to 40°F), moist place. (This is especially true of late-season varieties.) Under proper conditions, cabbage can keep for five to six months. In mild-winter areas, cabbage can be stored outdoors in the garden row, or in pits and trenches. A thick mulch is needed for protection. These long storage methods require cabbages with hard, dense heads and good reputations for storage quality.

Cabbage

Variety Name	Average Days to Maturity	General Description and Comments
Early		
Copenhagen Market	70	Ball-shaped 6-in. heads on short stalks; not yellows-resistant; a good keeper; long-standing.
Golden Acre	60	Over 5-in. heads on short stems; uniform maturity; yellows-resistant; does not stand long in hot weather.
Morden Dwarf	60	Small plant with 4-in. heads; good for small gardens; sweet and tender; resistant to cracking.
Stonehead	60	Round 6-in. heads; compact growth; good for close spacing in small gardens; dense, hard heads; yellows-resistant; heat-resistant.
Midseason		
Glory (also Enkhuizen)	75	Round, blue-green, 7½-in. heads; dense and solid; an old Dutch variety that is popular in North America.
Red Acre	75	Blood red, round, 6-in. heads; yellows-tolerant.
Savoy Ace	70–85	Round heads weigh 4 lb.; crinkly leaves are very sweet, flavorful; AAS.
Late Season		
Danish Ballhead	110	Round, blue-green, 8-in. heads; an excellent keeper; somewhat tolerant to heat.
Drumhead	90	Large, round but flattened, 9-in. heads; extra hard; one of the best keepers.
Savoy King	80–120	Semiflat heads with crinkly, flavorful leaves; 4 to 6 lb. each; AAS.
Chieftain Savoy	80–90	Flat heads weigh up to 5 lb.; leaves are crinkly and sweeter than regular cabbage; AAS.

CARROTS

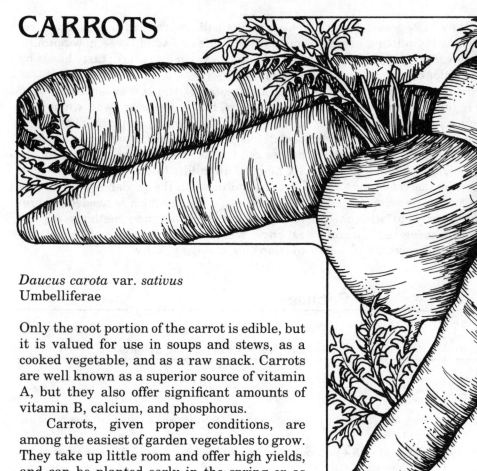

Daucus carota var. *sativus*
Umbelliferae

Only the root portion of the carrot is edible, but it is valued for use in soups and stews, as a cooked vegetable, and as a raw snack. Carrots are well known as a superior source of vitamin A, but they also offer significant amounts of vitamin B, calcium, and phosphorus.

Carrots, given proper conditions, are among the easiest of garden vegetables to grow. They take up little room and offer high yields, and can be planted early in the spring or as late as 12 weeks before the first fall frosts. They are suitable for gardens of all sizes, including container gardens. They are also good succession crops and are often chosen to follow peas, since the strong root system of the peas opens up the soil for the long carrot roots.

Classification of carrots is based on the length and shape of the roots. They can be taper-rooted (the root tapering gradually from crown to tip of the root), cylindrical (the root beginning to taper more than two-thirds of the way down), or stump-rooted (in which almost no tapering occurs at all). Cylindrical carrots are further classified according to length: long, half-long, or short. There are also a few varieties that are ball-shaped and perfect for container gardening. Stump-rooted, short, and half-long varieties are generally recommended for heavy loam and clay soils, while the long varieties require light, deeply prepared soils. Planting long varieties in shallow soils will cause misshapen and branched roots.

Growing Range: Carrots are suitable for growing nearly everywhere because they tolerate light frost, yet can withstand midsummer heat. In northern areas, they are grown throughout the summer; in southern regions, they are commonly grown in the fall, winter, and spring. Carrots grow best at an average temperature of 60° to 65°F.

Soil Preparation: Carrots do best in a light, deeply tilled, sandy loam soil that provides adequate moisture, yet drains well. Work in phosphate rock and wood ashes to ensure good fertility. Remove any rocks, clods, and other solid objects to prevent undesirable branching of the roots. Very good results can be achieved by preparing special raised beds for long varieties, offering at least 10 inches of a special mixture of two parts aged compost or manure and one part garden loam. Any manure added to the soil at planting time must be well aged, otherwise the excess nitrogen will cause misshapen roots. Carrots do best at a pH of 6.5, but can tolerate any pH between 5.5 and 6.8.

Propagation: Carrots are commonly started by direct-seeding. Be careful not to sow too thickly, otherwise overplanting results, calling for extensive thinning. Soak the seed for several hours or overnight, then sow it directly into well-prepared garden rows, four to six weeks before the frost-free date. Soil temperature for best germination ranges from 45° to 85°F. Unused seed is good for three years.

For conventional row planting, scatter seed thinly in rows spaced 12 inches apart. Spacing for growing beds is 3 inches. Carrots are also suitable for wide-row planting. Once the tiny seed is sown, cover it with ¼ to ½ inch of soil. The seed is slow to germinate and soil crusting may hamper germination. To prevent crusting, cover seed with sand, vermiculite, peat moss, or sawdust, instead of garden soil. Keep the rows moist but not soggy until all seed has germinated. Successive sowings, spaced 2 to 3 weeks apart, will ensure a year-long supply, since the late crop can be stored through the winter in a root cellar. Sow seed 12 weeks before the first expected frost for a fall harvest.

Culture: Thinning is an important step which can be done at two stages of growth. When the seedlings are nearly 2 inches tall, thin them to stand about 2 inches apart in rows. Snip off the unwanted plants at the crown rather than pull them up to avoid disturbing the plants that remain in the ground. At midseason, if the carrots are crowding each other, begin to thin the plants further, gently pulling some of the carrots to use in the kitchen. Keep the bed or rows free of weeds, especially in the early stages when the young seedlings cannot compete with quick-growing weeds. Mulch can be applied just after the first thinning.

Throughout the season, supply plenty of moisture for lush and quick root growth. Be careful when watering at the later stages of growth; too much water can cause roots of mature size to split. Keep root shoulders covered with soil to prevent them from turning green.

Pests and Diseases: Insects are seldom a problem in the home garden, but occasionally aphids, carrot rust flies, carrot weevils, and cutworms may become nuisances. Possible diseases are leaf blight and root knot nematode.

Harvest and Storage: The first harvest can be made as soon as roots are large enough to be of use. (Usually, this harvest also serves as a midseason thinning for the remaining plants.) After that, pull roots as they are needed. In cold-weather areas, the last harvest can be delayed until the ground has begun to freeze. At that time, dig up the crop for storage, or apply a thick mulch to prolong the last harvest for a month or more. In areas where winter temperatures rarely drop below 20°F, carrots may be left in the ground over the winter, if they are mulched heavily. In light soils, pull the carrots by grasping the green stems at the crown of the plant. In heavier soils, loosen the ground gently before pulling the roots. In either case, avoid disturbing roots of the plants that are not to be removed. In large plantings of short and half-long varieties, carrots may be harvested with a potato picker. Carrots keep well in a root cellar, under cool (32° to 40°F), moist conditions. They may also be canned or frozen for use in stews and as a cooked vegetable, although these methods are not popular, considering the ease of fresh storage.

Carrots

There are more than 50 carrot varieties available to the gardener. Most can be placed in one of the categories given in the chart, and the appropriate category for nearly any variety can easily be identified by the variety name or catalog description.

Category	Average Days to Maturity	General Description and Comments
Chantenay	70–78	This type has 4–6-in. roots of exceptionally good quality; shape tapers gradually from crown to root tip; it is well suited to shallow soils.
Danvers Half-Long	75–80	The root is thinner and longer than that of the Chantenay, growing to about 7 in. and tapering to a sharp point.
French Forcing (also Earliest Short Horn)	60–68	The smallest-sized root of any category; the root is nearly as thick as it is long, almost plum-shaped; very easily grown and especially suited to heavy soils and shallow containers.
Imperator	85–95	These are the long, slender, tapering types usually grown for commercial use and seen in grocery stores; roots grow 8–11 in. in length and require very deep, light soils for proper development.
Nantes	65–70	A half-long type, similar in character to the Danvers Half-Long, with a more cylindrical and slightly longer root; it has a very high sugar content and an inconspicuous core; varieties of this type are generally considered to be best for the home garden, because they are of medium length, of good quality, and quick to mature.
Oxheart	70–80	Blunt and short-shaped root suited to heavy soils, growing to about 3 in. in length; this type is often used for canning, since the roots pack well into jars without first being cut.

CAULIFLOWER

Brassica oleracea, Botrytis Group
Cruciferae

Cauliflower does not like hot, dry weather, which is usually the cause of the most common failure—buttoning. The much enlarged flower head (called the "curd") is the edible portion, and when stressed, the plant develops a small, inferior head—the button. Prolonged heat or stress from lack of water also makes the plant bolt. Cauliflower is often considered to be one of the most challenging vegetables to grow, but any gardener who provides rich soil and constant moisture for quick, vigorous growth will reap a successful harvest.

In the later stages of growth, cauliflower has large, sprawling, cabbagelike leaves that take up a lot of space. For this reason it may not be the first choice of a gardener with only limited space. Only the gardener who appreciates the fine and delicate taste found in homegrown cauliflower can be the judge of whether or not the garden space is well used. The long growing period helps to offset the space it occupies by allowing the gardener to intercrop short-term vegetables in intervals between the young plants.

Besides the white-curd type of cauliflower that is best known, there are also purple-headed and green-headed cauliflowers. These colorful types are treated the same as the white-curd plants, except that no blanching is needed. One advantage to growing them is that they stay in good condition in the garden longer than the white-curd type.

Cooked cauliflower is universally appreciated but raw cauliflower is too often overlooked. Not only is uncooked cauliflower more nutritious, but it also has a great deal more flavor. White cauliflower is not as nutritious as the colored cauliflower. The colored cauliflowers are equal to broccoli in amounts of vitamins C, B_1, and B_2, as well as calcium and iron. Nevertheless, even one serving of the more popular white-curd type has more vitamin C than the recommended daily allowance.

Growing Range: Cauliflower does not do well in extremes of either heat or cold, and makes its best growth in average temperatures of between 60° and 65°F. It must be planted so that it matures in cool weather. Early-maturing varieties can be transplanted in early spring to mature before summer temperatures rise. Seeds sown in early to midsummer make up the main crop that matures in fall. In mild-winter areas, seeds sown in late summer produce a winter harvest. For beginning gardeners, or those with limited space, it is advisable to plant only a fall crop, since spring crops aren't as successful and may be a waste of space.

Soil Preparation: Cauliflower needs a rich, moist, well-draining soil with lots of humus. If growth is checked by lack of fertility or moisture, the crop will be either lost or inferior. Add large amounts of compost or rotted manure to the soil prior to planting. Also work in adequate amounts of phosphorus and potassium, using materials like phosphate rock and wood ashes. The custom of adding fresh manure to the soil in late summer, planting with a green manure crop in fall, and tilling under the crop in spring is an excellent one. The same program can be followed in spring and summer for a fall crop if the soil is not to be otherwise occupied. Heavy applications of compost in mid or late summer would allow another crop to be grown in spring on the same spot.

Lime the soil to bring the pH to a range of 6.0 to 6.8. Liming the soil is especially important in acid soils where clubroot is a known problem, and if such is the case, bring the soil to a pH of 7 or higher. Cauliflower is especially sensitive to boron deficiencies in the soil, a condition which causes discolored and deformed curds. Have a soil test done and follow the recommended rates for applying a dilute solution of borax to the garden.

Propagation: Spring crops are best when started from transplants; fall and winter crops can be direct-seeded in the garden or transplanted.

Start transplants six to eight weeks before setting out, which can be done anywhere from four weeks before to two weeks after the frost-free date. Before setting out, inspect seedlings. Use only those that have developed at least three true leaves in addition to the first two seed-leaves. Look for a tiny bud in the center of the seedling; if no bud is present, no head will form. Set out in the spacing given below.

Direct-seed the fall crop about 12 weeks before the first expected frost. Plant two or three seeds every 24 inches along conventional rows spaced 36 inches apart. Raised bed spacing is 18 inches. Sow seed ½ inch deep. For fall crop transplants, start seed 12 weeks before the first expected frost and set out about 6 weeks later. Unused seed is good for five years.

Culture: Thin clusters of direct-sown seedlings when they are 1 inch tall, leaving the sturdiest one to grow. Keep the soil moist at all times during growth. If the soil tends to dry out, provide a thick mulch of straw or compost. Culti-

Cauliflower

Variety Name	Average Days to Maturity (from transplants)	General Description and Comments
Chartreuse (also Green Ball)	115	Bright green heads to 8 in.; taste is superior to white cauliflower; large plants that take up a lot of space; use only for a fall crop; freezes well.
Danish Giant (also Dry Weather)	70	Round white heads to 8 in.; tolerant of soils and weather that would cause other cauliflower to fail; a sure header when grown under good conditions in the fall.
Early Snowball (also Snow Drift)	55–80	Compact, white heads to 6 in.; very short plants with pale green leaves; good for the small garden.
Purple Head	110	Dark purple heads to 8 in.; head color turns green when cooked; heat- and cold-resistant; suitable for spring and fall planting; large plants take up a lot of space; freezes well.
Self-Blanche	70	Round white heads to 7 in.; wrapper leaves curl naturally around the smaller heads when night temperatures go below 55°F; in hot weather, plant stops growing; more mature and larger heads may need tying up; recommended as a fall crop only.
Snow Crown	50	Round white heads to 8 in.; heat-resistant but its chief advantage is that it matures before hot weather sets in; also good for fall harvest; AAS.

vate lightly to avoid damaging the shallow roots. Treat plants gently, for leaf damage in young cauliflower has also been found to be a cause of buttoning.

The colored-head and self-blanching varieties do not need to be blanched, but the standard, open-leaf varieties do. Sunlight causes browning on the exposed white curd, a condition that sometimes impairs the flavor. (Frost can also discolor the white heads.) To produce the best-looking white curd, begin the blanching process as soon as the developing head begins to push back the inner leaves and exposes itself. Make sure the head is dry. Blanch by gathering up the longest leaves around the head and tying them in place with a strip of cloth or soft twine.

Pests and Diseases: See Cabbage.

Harvest and Storage: Weather will be the variable in determining harvest time after blanching. Warm weather can make the heads ready a few days after blanching. In cooler weather the heads may take two weeks. Check the heads periodically in both blanched and self-blanched varieties to determine when to harvest. The best heads are uniform, compact and clear white. Cauliflower that is overblown and "ricey" (a term used by growers to indicate that the curds have begun to break apart into individual flowers) has little market value, but it is certainly edible and can taste equally as good as the picture-perfect, compact heads. However, there is a point beyond which the head starts to lose flavor, too; harvesting too early is better than harvesting too late. To harvest, use a large knife to cut the head well below the innermost leaves.

If long-term storage is desired, cut as much stem from below the head as possible and leave some of the large, protective leaves on. Storage of cut heads longer than three weeks is not recommended. A better method is to lift cauliflower with the rootball intact and hang it upside down in a cool (32° to 40°F), moist place. Spray from time to time with water.

CELERIAC

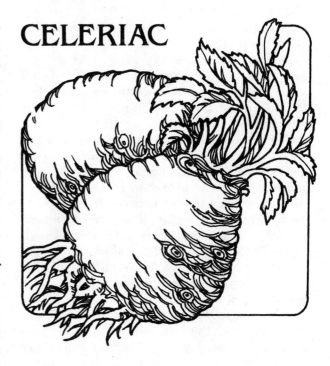

Celery root, knob celery, turnip-rooted celery
Apium graveolens var. *repaceum*
Umbelliferae

Celeriac, a close relative of the more popular celery, is grown not for its leaf stalks, as is celery, but for its crisp, bulbous root crown, which grows half underground and half aboveground. The edible crown, which has the texture of a potato or turnip, has a sweet and mild celery taste and is highly valued—more in Europe than in America—for use in soups and stews. The crown, thinly sliced, is also used raw in salads or boiled and mashed with potatoes. Celeriac can be used in any recipe calling for celery or turnips. The leaves, unfortunately, are too bitter to be of use in the kitchen.

Growing Range: Celeriac is suited to all temperate climates. The ideal climate offers temperatures averaging 60° to 65°F, but this plant's climatic tolerance is quite broad. It will grow well both in mild-winter regions, where it is planted as a fall and winter crop, and in northern areas that can offer a minimum of 110 frost-free days. Hot and windy weather as well as drought will interfere with successful growing, since celeriac requires constant moisture. The tough-skinned plant is half-hardy and is not injured by a few light frosts.

Soil Preparation: Celeriac does well in a fertile, well-limed, and rather heavy loam, rich in organic matter. A few stones or clods will not hinder growth. An overly acid soil causes poor growth, so keep the pH between 6.0 and 6.5.

Propagation: Celeriac is generally direct-seeded in long-season areas, but in short-season areas it should be started indoors. Start the slow-to-germinate seeds about eight weeks before the setting-out date, which can be anytime all danger of heavy frost has passed.

Scatter seed in conventional rows set 2 feet apart, or across the surface of raised beds. Space seedlings according to thinning guidelines given below. Unused seed is good for five years.

Culture: To thin, pull seedlings when they reach 3 to 4 inches tall, allowing 6 to 8 inches between plants in rows, and 12 inches between plants in growing beds. Keep young plants well watered and apply a good mulch. Avoid using cultivating tools that can damage feeder roots which often lie close to the soil surface. Removing the fine roots that emerge laterally from the top of the crown results in a larger and smoother edible portion.

Pests and Diseases: Celeriac is seldom bothered. Check for slugs and snails on young plants, and for aphids on mature plants. Septoria leaf spot can occasionally be troublesome.

Harvest and Storage: Plants may be used anytime the root crowns have reached 2 inches in diameter, but generally are harvested when they are double that size. After the first sharp frosts in autumn, plants that remain in the garden can be removed and stored under cool (32° to 40°F) and moist conditions. Or, if mulched well, the plants can be left in the ground all winter, even in cold climates.

Celeriac

Variety Name	Average Days to Maturity	General Description and Comments
Alabaster	120	A popular variety with very large, thick roots and white flesh.
Large (or Giant) Smooth Prague	110	A large, smooth root; the choice for short-season gardens.

CELERY

Apium graveolens var. *dulce*
Umbelliferae

Celery is a plant with thick, well-developed roots, on which there is a compact crown stem. From this short, fleshy crown the leaf stalks emerge. It is for this bunch of stalks that celery is grown. Celery has a strong flavor which blends well with other vegetables in a host of dishes. Homegrown celery has a fuller flavor than the type usually encountered in grocery stores and produce markets. The usual practice is to eat only the stalks with the leaves trimmed off. This is a waste of the leaves, which are as flavorful and more nutritious than the stalks.

Celery acts as a stimulant to the appetite, and it furnishes a good amount of food fiber. The stalks are not highly nutritious, but the leaves contain significant amounts of vitamin A. Its low calorie count is a boon to the weight-conscious. Use the stalks raw with dips or slice into salads for a crunchy texture. Steamed or braised celery makes a delicious side dish, diagonal slices are at home in stir-fries, and both stalks and leaf tips are tasty additions to soups and stews.

Celery is a challenging, but not impossible, vegetable for the home gardener to raise. Although the beginning gardener is usually discouraged from attempting celery as a crop, attention to cultural details should overcome any difficulties.

Years ago, celery was always blanched by covering the stalks with paper or boards to keep the sunlight from greening them. Blanching is no longer widely practiced, for green celery stalks have now become accepted as people realize that green plants have a great deal more nutritional value than those grown in darkness. The distinctive taste of celery is only a little stronger in green, unblanched stalks.

The home gardener has the option to blanch or not to blanch. Certainly, from a nutritional standpoint, blanching is not recommended. Deciding against blanching also means less attention needs to be directed to the plant during the growing season. However, for gardeners who just plain like the milder taste of blanched stalks, there are golden or self-blanching varieties available. The growing conditions of green and self-blanching types are the same.

Growing Range: Celery needs a relatively stable climate where it can mature over a long growing season. It is tolerant of heat after it is established and intolerant of sudden drops in temperature near maturity. In northern areas, freezing temperatures can damage the crop just as it approaches harvest. Exposure to temperatures as low as 40° to 55°F for about two weeks while the plants are young will cause mature plants to bolt. The average temperature range for best growth is 60° to 65°F.

Soil Preparation: Celery favors muckland gardening, since it is a heavy feeder and demands abundant moisture. In the absence of muckland soil, the available soil should be worked deeply—about 18 inches. Get as much organic material such as compost, rotted manures, and peat moss into the soil as possible. Organic matter in the soil will help the ground hold its moisture evenly over the growing period. Celery also favors soils rich in potassium, so if needed, work wood ashes, greensand, or granite dust into the soil at the same time that the organic matter is mixed in. Celery can be grown well in pure compost alone should enough of it be available. However, good drainage is essential. Adjust the pH to a range of 5.8 to 6.7.

Propagation: Celery can be seeded directly in the garden or started indoors for a considerable head start on the season. Seed should be sown directly only in mild climate areas with a long growing season. Soak seed for several hours before planting.

Start seeds six to eight weeks before setting out, which can be done anywhere from three weeks before to four weeks after the frost-free date. Set out when there is no danger of temperatures falling below 50°F. (Such drops in temperature may cause the celery to bolt prematurely.) Set out seedlings that are 4 to 5 inches tall. Have the root crown level with the soil or set plants a little deeper than they were in the flat.

Sow seeds outdoors two to four weeks before the frost-free date, when the soil is at least 60°F. Place two or three seeds every 6 inches apart in rows spaced 24 inches apart. Growing bed spacing is 9 inches. Cover seeds with ¼ inch of fine soil, peat moss, or sifted compost. Keep the soil around the seeds moist for as long as it takes to germinate the seeds. With the variable temperatures that can be expected outdoors, the seed may take as long as 20 days to germinate. Make sure that the seeds remain moist and that the soil does not crust over. Unused seed is good for five years.

Culture: When the plants grown by direct-seeding are 2 to 3 inches tall, thin back to allow only one plant per 6 inches in the row. Mulch when plants are 6 inches tall. Celery is shallow-rooted and frequent irrigations are needed to establish the plants and to produce prime stalks. After plants have become established, water should be given every 10 to 14 days. About three weeks before harvesting, water every 3 or 4 days. Avoid overhead watering, which may cause moisture to collect inside the bunch of stalks, an invitation to pest and disease problems.

Celery is a heavy feeder and benefits from supplemental nitrogen. Side-dress with rotted manure or apply manure tea every three weeks during the growing season. When cultivating, be careful not to go into the soil too deeply with gardening tools and cause damage to the shallow roots. It is important to keep the area free of weeds that compete with this slow-growing plant.

If blanched celery is desired, the safest way to proceed is to lay 12-inch-wide boards up against the sides of the plant. Hold the boards in place with stakes. Another method calls for tying the stalks together with twine or strips of soft cloth, and wrapping the trussed plant with brown paper. Secure this wrapper with twine. Allow the top several inches of leafy growth to protrude. Pulling the soil up onto the plants will also blanch them, but this method is not recommended because there is a danger that soil will fall into the interior of the plant, making the stalks difficult to clean and susceptible to rot. Start to blanch when plants are 12 to 15 inches tall; they should be ready in about two weeks.

Pests and Diseases: The moisture needed to keep celery growing well encourages slugs and snails. Aphids, cabbage loopers, carrot rust flies, carrot weevils, leafhoppers, whiteflies and, when the plants are immature, cutworms, all attack celery. Early and late blights, fusarium yellows, and pink rot are diseases that afflict celery. Brown-checking (a boron deficiency) and blackheart (excessive soil salinity in combination with high nitrogen and lack of water) may appear where growing conditions are unsatisfactory.

Harvest and Storage: The whole plant can be taken at once, or individual stalks can be removed as needed before the plant has matured. To harvest the entire plant, pull it up and cut off roots below the base of the crown. When cutting individual stalks, take from the outside and work in toward the middle. If not for immediate use, store the stalks in plastic bags in the refrigerator. Experience shows that celery chilled quickly after picking with a cold-water bath will last longer in storage than celery which is not rapidly cooled.

Celery

Variety Name	Average Days to Maturity	General Description and Comments
Fordhook	130	Compact, dark green stalks are tender and relatively stringless; lasts well in storage; 18 in. tall.
Giant Pascal	120–140	Dark green stalks are medium length, thick, and overlapping; blight-resistant; 18 in. tall.
Summer Pascal	120	Compact, bright green stalks; vigorous and blight-resistant; heavy heads with a well-developed heart; 26 in. tall.
Golden Self-Blanching	90	A self-blanching type; stocky, compact yellow stalks are relatively stringless; blight-resistant; a good keeper; 24 in. high.

CELTUCE

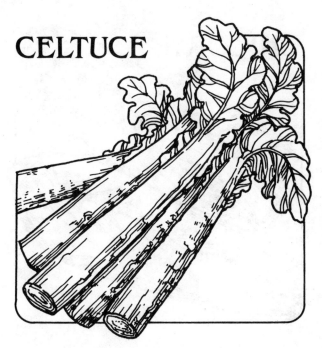

Asparagus lettuce, stem lettuce
Lactuca sativa var. *angustata*
Compositae

Celtuce is a variation of leaf lettuce which is grown mainly for the central seed stalk, with the leaves providing a secondary harvest. The combination name conveys the idea that it can be eaten like **cel**ery and let**tuce**.

Like other kinds of lettuce, celtuce favors cool weather, but will produce stalks good enough to make it worth growing in warmer climates where ordinary lettuce does not do well. The usual problem with ordinary lettuce in hot weather is that it bolts to seed. What is a problem with most lettuce becomes a special feature of celtuce: the seed stem which develops is in fact relished as an edible part. However, the longer the plant can be grown without having the seed stem actually produce seed heads, the thicker and more desirable this central seed stalk will be. So, even though this member of the lettuce family will perform in warmer weather, the cooler climates favor development by retarding bolting.

Use the crisp leaves from thinnings and those of younger plants rather than the more mature leaves, which are not of good eating quality. Celtuce leaves resemble cos or romaine-type lettuce in flavor and texture, and may be used in salads and stir-fried dishes. These leaves contain four times the vitamin C found in all other forms of lettuce. Any leaves with an objectionably bitter taste indicate that the plant was grown in too high a temperature, on poor ground, or was deprived of moisture. The stalks can be eaten raw for texture in salads or steamed or stir-fried.

Growing Range: Celtuce will grow well in temperate climates. It is heat-tolerant, and can withstand mild fall frosts which enhance the production of stalks.

Soil Preparation: Celtuce will grow in any soil, but a fertile, loose, well-drained soil rich in humus promotes the best growth. Additions of well-rotted manure or compost result in larger plants and thicker stalks. Only slightly tolerant of acid soils, celtuce does best in soils with a pH range of 6.0 to 6.8; a level of 6.5 is best.

Propagation: Start celtuce by direct-seeding four to six weeks before the frost-free date, or by setting transplants in the garden about two weeks before the frost-free date. The best soil temperature for germination is 68°F. Sow at two-week intervals until midsummer; a second planting phase begins about eight weeks before the first expected frost, when seeds can be direct-sown every two weeks for a fall crop. Sow to a depth of ½ inch. For conventional rows, scatter seed in rows set 18 inches apart; broadcast seed in raised beds and thin as described below. Start transplants four weeks before planting out, and set 2-inch-tall transplants 18 inches apart. Unused seed is good for five years.

Culture: Thin seedlings when they are 2 inches high, to stand 18 inches apart. Provide constant moisture and keep area free of weeds; a layer of mulch applied when the plants are established does both. When plants are one month old, side-dress with well-rotted manure or water with manure tea; repeat feedings when plants are about 50 days old.

Pests and Diseases: Celtuce is relatively free of problems, but occasionally may be bothered by aphids, flea beetles, and slugs. In areas where downy mildew and mold afflict other forms of lettuce, they can appear on celtuce as well.

Harvest and Storage: Harvesting takes place in two stages, beginning with the leaves. These must be picked from the base of the plant while young; once they are around four weeks old a bitter sap develops and harvesting ends. As leaves are harvested, avoid damaging the plant's growing tips. The second harvest occurs when the stalks are thick and succulent (about 1 inch in diameter at the base), and before the seed heads appear. Slice off stalks at the ground and pull off leaves. A bitter, milky sap is carried by plant tissues on the stalk surface; peel away the outer skin to remove the bitter flavor. If wrapped in plastic to preserve their moisture, celtuce stalks will last many days under refrigeration; the leaves remain in good shape under refrigeration for only several days.

Varieties: There is no variation in seed and all seed is available under the name "Celtuce."

CHICORY

Succory, Witloof chicory
Cichorium intybus
Compositae

There are three types of chicory which are cultivated today for different uses. The most widely grown type is the forcing chicory known as Witloof chicory. This plant is grown mainly for its roots, which are forced indoors to yield creamy white heads known as chicons, or Belgian or French endive. As a secondary harvest, a few leaves can be plucked from this type of plant, for use as a piquant salad green.

It is the leafy chicory, however, that is grown expressly for its greens. It produces compact heads of broad leaves, and is sometimes confused with endive and escarole, which are members of a related species. The leaves must be blanched to tone down their bitter flavor, but there are now self-blanching varieties on the market which do not require special treatment.

The third type of chicory is cultivated for its roots alone, which are not forced, but rather dried, ground, and used as an addition to, or substitute for, coffee. This root chicory is a perennial and should be given a permanent bed in the garden. All types of chicory are cultivated in the same manner.

Chicory is extremely easy to grow and is relatively free of diseases and pests. It is not a large-growing plant, but it does tie up the ground for a whole growing season, so space-conscious gardeners should carefully consider whether they want to devote space to it.

Eaten green, chicory leaves have an extremely high vitamin A, B complex, and C content. The mineral and trace element content is very high, also. Unfortunately, there is a drawback to this nutritive value—the minerals and vitamin A in green chicory are so pronounced that it is considered inedible by many people. The same bitter leaf when blanched is transformed, as if by magic, into a very delightful salad plant, though one without high vitamin and mineral content. Gardeners who wish to preserve as much of the nutrient value as possible can blanch it for only a short period of time and then prepare it by stir-frying or boiling with a change of cooking water to reduce the bitterness.

The creamy chicons of Witloof chicory, long considered gourmet fare, have a mild, tangy flavor that perks up midwinter salads. The chicons can also be steamed and served with a sauce, or sliced into soups to add a crunchy texture.

Growing Range: This cool-season plant can be successfully grown throughout the temperate zone, and prefers average temperatures between 55° and 75°F. Chicory is very cold-hardy and tolerates light frost.

Soil Preparation: Chicory is extremely tolerant of soil variations, but grows best in a friable soil with good organic matter present to keep the roots moist. Add ample amounts of compost for the Witloof type, to promote formation of large roots. Also, remove rocks and any debris to a depth of 24 inches, so roots will not fork. Provide for good drainage whatever the soil type, and add lime to achieve a pH of 5.0 to 6.8.

Chicory

Variety Name	Average Days to Maturity	General Description and Comments
Forcing Chicory		
Witloof	110	Broad, dark green leaves grow upright, 16 in. tall and 14 in. wide; forced shoots are 6–10 in. high.
Leaf Chicory		
Sugarhat	85	Self-blanching type; outer leaves are light green and inner leaves are yellow-white, blanched by the tight heads; very hardy; tastes like fine endive; 12 in. tall and 12 in. wide.
Rouge de Verone (also Red Verone)	75	Long, thin, dark green leaves have heavy midribs and indentations along the frilled leaf margins; the stalk midribs become red, pink, and yellow when blanched; grows 14 in. tall, 12 in. wide.
Root Chicory		
Magdeburgh (also Coffee Chicory)	100	Broad, smooth-edged, dark green leaves form loose, upright heads; 14–16-in. roots used as coffee enhancer or substitute; a perennial.

Propagation: All types of chicory are best sown directly into the garden. Transplanting increases the likelihood that many plants will bolt to seed, and that misshapen roots will be produced. Sow seeds of leaf types in midsummer; sowing too early will cause plants to go to seed in the heat. Sow seed of forcing and root types in early spring in northern areas, and in midsummer in warm, long-season areas. Space rows 18 inches apart and set seed every 4 inches. Spacing for growing beds is 8 inches. Sow seed ¼ to ½ inch deep.

Culture: Thin plants when they have four or five true leaves and allow 8 inches between plants in the row. As a further guide to thinning, remove all plants that have narrow, drooping leaves. Keep the most vigorous, upright plants that have a tendency to hold their leaves tightly together in the center.

Keep the plants moist. Add a mulch if the soil has a tendency to dry out in hot weather. Make one midseason feeding with a side-dressing of rotted manure or a watering of manure tea. Keep the weeds down by frequent shallow cultivations or by use of a loose mulch.

Blanch the leafy varieties in late summer or autumn, about three weeks before the desired harvest. Before blanching, the crowns of the plants should be thoroughly dry, otherwise they will rot. Wait for dry weather if the plants are wet. Then cover the plant with a pot in which the hole is plugged, or simply tie up outer leaves to blanch the inner leaves.

Forcing of Witloof chicory requires more effort and planning. The usual method is to dig the roots from the soil three weeks to a month before the chicons are needed. The procedure is described in detail in chapter 5, in the section on Forcing Roots for Winter Salad Greens.

Pests and Diseases: For the most part, there are few problems with these plants.

Harvest and Storage: Harvest the leaf types as needed, by cutting the heads from the root crown. They can be stored for up to several weeks in the refrigerator, but are best when eaten soon after harvest.

Harvest chicons from Witloof chicory by twisting or breaking them off when they stick 6 inches above the soil surface. Be careful not to injure the delicate heads. A second and even third crop can be gotten if the chicons are cut around their bases, separating them from the crowns but leaving the core, a 1-inch spike, intact. Press the sand or soil back over these spikes, and wait to see if another harvest appears.

To harvest the root chicory for use as an additive to, or substitute for, coffee, dig the roots when needed. After cleaning them thoroughly with a brush to remove all the sand and soil, lay them out to dry in an airy place, shel-

tered from the sun. Let them dry for several weeks. Finish off the drying in an oven set to low heat if necessary. When thoroughly dry, chop the roots into fine pieces, roast them until crisp and dark, then grind them as for coffee. Stored in a sealed container, they keep for months. To get the strongest-flavored roots, wait one season after planting and harvest the second year after the flowering season has ended.

CHINESE CABBAGE

Chinese celery cabbage, nappa, wong bok
Brassica rapa, Pekinensis Group
and
Bok choy, Chinese mustard cabbage, pak choi
Brassica rapa, Chinensis Group
Cruciferae

The name Chinese cabbage is a catch-all term for a number of plants which have distinctive appearances. Basically, there are two types—heading and nonheading. The Pekinensis Group contains the heading plants, which are the most familiar and are known as Chinese celery cabbage. Certain varieties (michihli for one) form torpedo-shaped, cylindrical heads that are self-blanching, while other varieties (the wong bok types) form slightly squat, rounded heads. The nonheading plants of the Chinensis Group slightly resemble Swiss chard. They produce loose bunches of green, spoon-shaped leaves with a thick, white midrib. These plants go by the common names of bok choy, pak choi, or Chinese mustard cabbage.

The term "cabbage" is something of a misnomer for all these plants, for they are botanically more closely related to mustard than to cabbage. However, they all thrive under the same growing conditions as cabbage.

Home gardeners who have tried to grow these oriental brassicas and have not had good results have usually broken one of the rules for growing them successfully. They need a superior soil, rich in moisture-holding organic material; they must never suffer stress from lack of water; they need a fertilizer boost to speed their growth; and they are highly sensitive to daylength. Long days in combination with fluctuating temperatures (especially during the four weeks following germination) cause stalks of insignificant yellow flowers to develop before a good head of leaves has formed. This is particularly true for spring-grown crops. Crops planted in midsummer for fall harvest are less prone to bolt. The gardener who has the knowledge to provide for these needs will find that Chinese mustard cabbage and Chinese celery cabbage are easy to grow.

Anyone who has grown standard cabbage would do well to consider adding one or all of these oriental brassicas to the garden plot. They are quicker to mature than most cabbages, and some varieties mature as quickly as eight weeks after seed is sown. They are generally more delicate and mild than cabbage, with a slight mustardy flavor; they can be used before they have reached maturity; they are more digestible than cabbage; and they do best in late fall when many traditional occidental vegetables have long been harvested. In terms of nutrition, they furnish potassium and vitamins A and C to the diet. These advantages more than offset the extra effort their culture requires. Moreover, they are admirably suited to the small garden.

Chinese celery cabbage can be prepared like traditional Western cabbage and Chinese mustard cabbage like mustard greens, but many choose to use them as the Chinese and Japanese do. The Asian tradition is to stir-fry or add them to soups. They are also delicious when used fresh in salads.

Growing Range: Chinese cabbage is a cool-season crop that makes the best growth when average temperatures are between 60° and 65°F and days are becoming shorter. In northern areas, it is generally grown as a fall crop. In mild-winter areas, it grows well as a winter and spring crop. Plants withstand heavy frost (down to 20°F) with little damage. Hybrids have been developed to tolerate long days and heat without bolting, which opens up a wider range of growing conditions.

Soil Preparation: Chinese cabbage will grow on a wide range of soil types, and will do well as long as adequate moisture is present. It prefers a moderately rich soil but will still grow fairly well on less fertile soils, although growth may be somewhat slower and the plants smaller at maturity. To prepare for spring planting, lay down fresh manure in the fall. Work this manure deeply into the soil right away if weather permits, or in the spring as soon as the soil can be safely worked. If planting in spring or summer without having previously manured the ground in fall, apply 3 to 4 inches of well-rotted manure or compost and dig in before seeding. Soil pH is acceptable in a range from 6.0 to 6.8.

Propagation: Chinese cabbage can be started indoors or in the garden, depending on the season it is grown in. For spring planting, unless the variety is bred to tolerate lengthening days, start plants indoors 4 weeks before setting out, which can be done about 4 to 6 weeks before the frost-free date. To further ensure that these plants don't bolt, protect them in the garden by covering them in the late afternoon and making sure they aren't exposed to cool temperatures.

Direct-seed the fall crop about 12 weeks before the first expected frost.

Sow the seed about 2 inches apart in raised beds and in conventional rows. Space rows 18 to 24 inches apart. Cover seeds with ½ inch of fine soil. Unused seed is good for five years.

Culture: Thin both rows and beds when the plants are four weeks old and have four to five true leaves. Use these tender thinnings in the kitchen. Thin nonheading varieties (Chinese mustard) to 9 inches apart. Thin heading varieties (Chinese celery cabbage) to 16 inches apart.

Keep the ground moist. Add a mulch during dry periods. Avoid the mulch in autumn when the sun's power is waning, in order to give the soil as much heat as possible. Watering from below is preferable to overhead watering. In areas of high humidity overhead watering may promote pests and diseases in the interior of the plant. On soil that is not adequately enriched, plants may need a midseason nitrogen boost. Side-dress with well-rotted manure after thinning, or water with manure tea every two weeks once plants are four weeks old.

Pests and Diseases: See Cabbage. Pests may be common, while diseases are occasional problems.

Harvest and Storage: The harvest can begin as soon as plants reach a stage which the gardener finds usable. Plants sown at the same time tend to mature at the same rate, so start taking some early to stagger the harvest period.

To harvest, pull out the whole plant and cut the leaf growth from the root crown. Discard the outer leaves. The nonheading types can be also treated as a cut-and-come-again crop by harvesting a few outer leaves at a time from each plant. Make sure at least five leaves remain on the plant to promote continuous production.

Heading and nonheading cabbages store for one to four months under cool (32° to 40°F), moist conditions. The tall, cylindrical heading types should be placed upright to prevent them from growing into an L-shape during storage.

Chinese Cabbage

Certain varieties are being developed that are adaptable to longer daylengths and may be grown successfully as a spring crop. Check catalogs and seed packet descriptions for mention of this before purchasing seed for spring growing.

Variety Name	Average Days to Maturity	General Description and Comments
Heading Types		
Michihli	75	Tall cylindrical heads of tightly folded, bright green leaves; sow for fall harvest; 18 in. tall by 4 in. wide.
Spring A-1 (also Early Hybrid G)	60	Wong bok type with short, round, thick heads of light green leaves; good for spring and summer sowing; relatively resistant to bolting; 10 in. tall by 4 in. wide.
Treasure Island	85	Suited for mild-winter growing areas; cylindrical heads are 12 in. tall, 8 in. wide.
Nonheading Types		
Pak choi or Bok choy	50	Dark green leaves fold outward from thick, prominent, white midribs; 10–12 in. tall by 5 in. thick.
Crispy Choy	45	White midribs have slight greenish tinge; ribs have crunchy texture and slightly pungent flavor.

COLLARDS

Tree cabbage
Brassica oleracea, Acephala Group
Cruciferae

In the United Shates, collards are so often associated with southern gardens that they have become thought of as a warm-weather vegetable. It is true that collards are more heat-resistant than kale and especially more tolerant of heat than other members of the cabbage family, but in spite of all that, collards definitely favor cooler weather. Their usefulness is often overlooked by gardeners in cooler regions, and in northern areas that have short but hot summers, collards make a good crop. Planted in late spring or early summer, the plants will develop satisfactorily during the hot, humid days of summer, and will reach their prime as the cool fall weather arrives. Warm region gardeners start collards in late summer or early fall to provide winter and early spring greens. Light frost mellows the flavor of the leaves.

Collards are a stronger-flavored vegetable than many plants in the cabbage family. They are rich in vitamins and minerals, especially vitamins A and C, and calcium.

Growing Range: Collards will grow in an exceptionally wide range of climates. Although tolerant of, and slow to bolt in heat, they really grow and taste the best where they can mature in cool weather, with an average temperature ranging from 60° to 65°F. Collards can withstand moderate frosts (25° to 26°F) if exposed to them gradually.

Soil Preparation: Well-drained, sandy silt or clay loams are preferred, but collards will grow well in a variety of soils. Collards tolerate a pH range from 5.5 to 6.8, but they do best at a pH of 6.0. The plants are heavy feeders with shallow roots, so dig in lots of nitrogen-rich organic fertilizers when preparing the soil.

Propagation: Collard seed can be sown directly in the garden, or started indoors and transplanted. Start transplants 6 to 8 weeks before they are to be set out, which can be done from 4 weeks before to 2 weeks after the frost-free date. Use seedlings that are 3 inches tall. Start a fall crop about 10 to 13 weeks before the first expected frost.

Direct-sow seed about three to four weeks before the frost-free date. Sow seed ½ inch deep. The minimum soil temperature for germination is 40°F, and the best germination occurs at about 65°F. For conventional rows, set two or three seeds or a single transplant every 15 inches in rows spaced 36 inches apart. Growing bed spacing is 15 inches. Unused seed is good for five years.

Culture: When seedlings are 1 inch tall, pinch out all but the strongest from each grouping. When they reach 6 inches tall, side-dress with well-rotted manure, or give liberal doses of manure tea, and repeat the tea application every three weeks throughout the season. The roots are shallow, so don't dig deeper than 1 inch to cultivate. During hot weather and on extremely well-drained soil, keep the roots from drying out by mulching. In cold climates, a thick mulch in fall insulates the roots and

prolongs the harvest for several extra weeks.
Pests and Diseases: See Cabbage.

Harvest and Storage: Leaves should be harvested when they are young, tender, and mild-flavored, around their 40th day of maturity. For a once-and-done harvest, the entire plant can be cut off at the stalk. The tender leaf rosette at the top is especially succulent. To extend the harvest period, pick clusters of lower leaves from the stalk before they are full-sized, tough, and woody. This allows the top growing bud to continue to produce more leaves. As the harvest progresses, the bare stalk may require support. Collards are used in any way that cabbage is used. Collards can be stored for several weeks under cool (32° to 40°F) and moist conditions.

Collards

Variety Name	Average Days to Maturity	General Description and Comments
Georgia Green (also Southern or Creole)	70–80	The standard variety; has a reputation for doing well in hot weather and tolerating poor soils; a nonheading variety with blue-green leaves; grows to 36 in. tall and 40 in. wide.
Vates Nonheading	75	Good cold tolerance; grows 28 in. tall, 30 in. wide.

CORN

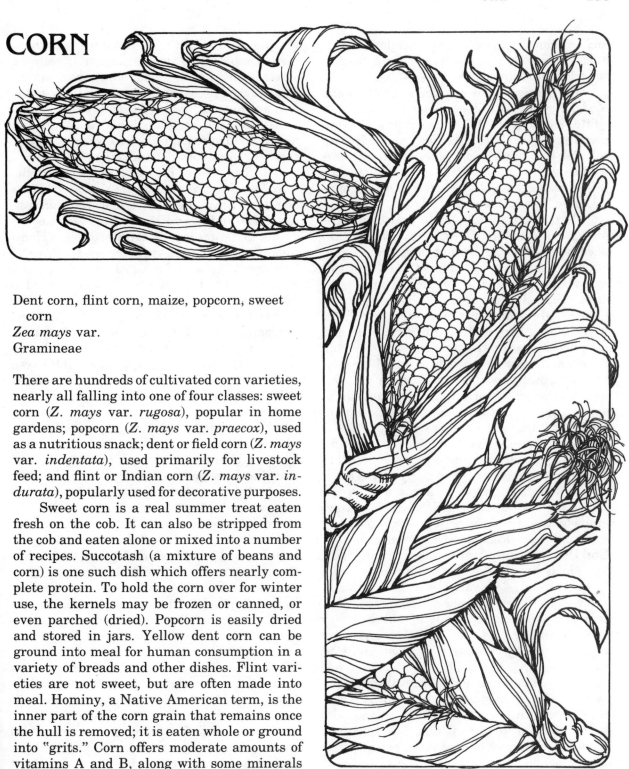

Dent corn, flint corn, maize, popcorn, sweet
  corn
Zea mays var.
Gramineae

There are hundreds of cultivated corn varieties,
nearly all falling into one of four classes: sweet
corn (*Z. mays* var. *rugosa*), popular in home
gardens; popcorn (*Z. mays* var. *praecox*), used
as a nutritious snack; dent or field corn (*Z. mays*
var. *indentata*), used primarily for livestock
feed; and flint or Indian corn (*Z. mays* var. *in-
durata*), popularly used for decorative purposes.

    Sweet corn is a real summer treat eaten
fresh on the cob. It can also be stripped from
the cob and eaten alone or mixed into a number
of recipes. Succotash (a mixture of beans and
corn) is one such dish which offers nearly complete protein. To hold the corn over for winter
use, the kernels may be frozen or canned, or
even parched (dried). Popcorn is easily dried
and stored in jars. Yellow dent corn can be
ground into meal for human consumption in a
variety of breads and other dishes. Flint varieties are not sweet, but are often made into
meal. Hominy, a Native American term, is the
inner part of the corn grain that remains once
the hull is removed; it is eaten whole or ground
into "grits." Corn offers moderate amounts of
vitamins A and B, along with some minerals

and protein. The less highly developed varieties—especially the flint types—are generally superior nutritionally.

The kernels span a wide range of colors. Modern sweet corn appears golden yellow to white, and some of the white varieties have a greenish tinge. Older varieties are much more colorful, and have black, blue, red, orange, as well as white and yellow kernels. Indian corn is purposely cross-pollinated to achieve its multicolored, decorative effect.

Corn is an annual easily grown in most areas. The standard varieties (5 to 7 feet tall) need a considerable amount of growing room, but there are dwarf varieties (3 to 4 feet tall with 4- to 5-inch ears) for limited-space gardens. The tall-growing stalks may be interplanted with pumpkins or winter squash, or may follow a very early spring crop. They can also be enlisted as vertical supports for pole beans. Gardeners with only a small area at their disposal may find that corn is not productive enough to warrant the large amount of space it takes up, since only a small portion of the entire plant is actually eaten.

Growing Range: Most corn may be grown in any area that offers a frost-free season of 70 to 100 days. (Flint corn needs a fairly long season, 100 to 120 days, but it performs well in the cooler regions.) Best growth occurs where average temperatures range from 60° to 75°F. Any exposure to frost damages this tender crop.

Soil Preparation: Corn does well in most soils, but yields best in a loose, well-drained loam. In heavier soils, late varieties do best, while in sandy soils the early types are preferred. Corn is a heavy feeder, especially of nitrogen. For this reason, it does well where beans were planted the previous season, or when preceded by a cover crop of alfalfa, clover, or another legume crop that will add to the soil's nitrogen supply. The recommended pH range is 6.0 to 6.8. At planting time work the rows and beds to a depth of 6 inches, and add generous amounts of compost or aged manure, as well as bone meal and wood ashes.

Propagation: Corn is almost always sown directly into the garden, although it may be started indoors in individual containers in very short-season areas. Start seeds four weeks before setting out, which is done two to three weeks after the frost-free date. Take extra care not to disturb roots, otherwise growth will be checked. Corn does not transplant easily.

Early varieties may be direct-sown on the frost-free date; mid- and late-season varieties about ten days later. For a dispersed harvest, use early-, mid-, and late-season varieties together in the garden. Or make successive plantings of early-season varieties every three to four weeks, up to three months before the first expected frost. The soil should have warmed to 50° to 60°F for best germination. (Use the higher temperature as the guide for planting untreated seed.) If the soil is too cool for planting, warm it up for a week prior to planting by covering the rows with black plastic. If the seed is planted too early before the soil has warmed sufficiently, it will rot. Unused seed is good for up to two years.

To aid in pollination, plant corn in concentrated blocks of three to four rows, rather than long single or double rows. All open-pollinated varieties cross-pollinate easily, which can alter the quality of the kernels. Also, sweet corn will cross with field corn, with the result that the sweet corn won't taste nearly as sweet. Grow any varieties with the potential for crossing no closer than 40 feet from each other, and to further guard against unwanted crossing, plan to have some barrier between the two varieties such as a row of sunflowers or a hedge. You can also stagger the planting dates so that the two varieties won't tassel (produce pollen) at the same time.

Standard varieties are spaced 3 inches apart in conventional rows set 30 inches apart. Dwarf or early varieties which are smaller will grow in rows spaced 24 inches apart. Spacing for growing beds is 18 inches. Corn may also be planted in hills, six seeds to a hill, the hills spaced 6 feet apart in each direction. Plant

Corn

Variety Name	Average Days to Maturity	Pollination Habit	General Description and Comments
Early Varieties			
Golden Midget	58	Hybrid	Stalks grow 2½ ft. tall; 4-in.-long ears average 8 rows; good for limited-space gardens; freezes well.
Seneca	60–65	Hybrid	Stalks 4½–6 ft. tall; ears 7½ in. long with 12 to 14 rows of yellow kernels; several strains now available, including Seneca Chief, Seneca Sunbeam, Seneca 60, and Seneca Explorer; a highly popular variety in cold-weather areas.
Early Sunglow	63	Hybrid	Stalks 4–4½ ft. tall; 2 ears per plant, each 7 in. long with 12 rows of medium-yellow kernels; grows well in cool temperatures.
Midseason Varieties (mature about 1 week later than early varieties)			
Golden Beauty	73	Hybrid	Stalks 4–6 ft. tall; ears 6–8 in. long with 12–14 rows of yellow kernels; dependable in short-season areas; AAS.
Early Xtra Sweet 77	73	Hybrid	5–6-ft. stalks bear 7–9-in. ears, each having 12–16 rows; germination rate may be lower than other varieties with a greater amount of starch; stays sweet for a long time; AAS.
Early Golden Bantam	73	Open-pollinated	Earliest strain of the very popular Golden Bantam; stalks 5 ft. tall; ears 6½ in. long with 8 rows of yellow kernels.
Kandy Korn EH	76	Hybrid	Tender and sweet kernels retain their quality for up to 2 weeks on the stalk.
Gold Rush	66–74	Hybrid	Stalks 6 ft. tall; 2 ears per stalk, each 8½ in. long with 12–14 rows of yellow kernels; adapts to most climates; very tender and sweet.
Main Crop or Late Varieties			
Golden Bantam	80	Open-pollinated	Slender ears, 5½–6½ in. long; 8 rows of yellow kernels; this variety introduced in 1902 and long the standard used to judge sweetness; good for all purposes and for freezing whole.
Illini Xtra Sweet	85	Hybrid	Medium-tall stalks; two 8-in. ears per stalk with 14–18 rows of yellow kernels; germination rate may be lower than other varieties with a greater amount of starch; a good freezer; stays sweeter longer than other varieties.
Golden Cross Bantam	85	Hybrid	Stalks 6–7 ft. tall; ears 7½–8 in. long with 14 rows of light golden yellow kernels; very popular all-purpose hybrid for home growing.
Illinichief	87	Hybrid	Ears are 11 in. long with 18 rows of yellow kernels; recommended for cool-season areas.
Country Gentleman	85–100	Open-pollinated	Tall stalks grow to 7 ft.; 1 or 2 ears per stalk; ears 7–8 in. long; sweet white kernels can and freeze well.
Silver Queen	92	Hybrid	Tall stalks produce ears 8–9 in. long with 14–16 rows of pure white kernels; a very popular late white variety.
Stowell's Evergreen	96	Open-pollinated	Ears 8 in. long with 14–18 rows of white kernels; long a favorite in many areas. *(continued)*

Corn—*continued*

Variety	Average Days to Maturity	Pollination Habit	General Description and Comments
Popcorn Varieties			
Burpee Peppy	90	Hybrid	Stalks 5–6 ft. high with 2 or 3 ears per plant; ears 4 in. long.
Strawberry	100	Hybrid	An ornamental used both for popping and decoration; ears 2 in. long; kernels mahogany-colored; husks straw-colored.
Flint varieties (most local varieties of flint, not available commercially, are traded back and forth among growers)			
Rainbow Flint	110	Open-pollinated	Tall stalks with long ears; kernels are blue, black, yellow, orange, white, maroon; sold for decorative use.
Garland Flint	105	Open-pollinated	Stalks are 7–8 ft. tall; one of the earliest to mature; kernels are bright yellow to bright red.

seeds 1 to 2 inches deep (shallower in heavy soil, deeper in sandy soil), and side-dress with dried blood.

An alternative planting method results in quick initial growth and maturation up to two weeks earlier than by conventional methods. Dig a 6-inch furrow and set seeds along the bottom of the furrow; cover with 2 inches of soil. Stretch a sheet of clear plastic over the top of the furrow and secure the edges. Cut slits for rainwater drainage. This will create a miniature greenhouse along the furrow. When the corn presses up against the plastic, or when the inside air temperature reaches 105°F, remove the plastic. After plants are 8 inches high, fill in the furrows with soil and add a hay mulch.

Culture: When plants are 2 to 4 inches tall, start thinning. Thin plants of standard varieties to stand 12 inches apart in the rows; dwarf varieties to 8 inches. Thin hills to the four strongest seedlings. Close planting reduces yields, so be sure to allow enough room. Feed with manure or compost tea when the plants have grown 5 to 6 inches tall, and again when 18 inches tall. Cultivate very shallowly early in the season to keep weeds down, until a mulch can be applied when the plants are 6 to 8 inches tall.

Adequate moisture is critical to ear development, especially from the time tassels appear until harvest. Conditions that can cause stunted or partially filled ears are disturbance of the roots during cultivation, too-close spacing, earworm damage, overly acid soil, lack of sufficient nutrients or moisture, or heavy rains during pollination. Do not remove any suckers that may appear along the main stalk, as removal may reduce yield.

Pests and Diseases: Corn may be affected by bacterial wilt and corn smut. The most serious insect pest is the corn earworm, although cucumber beetles, European corn borers, and Japanese beetles may present problems in some areas.

Harvest and Storage: Sweet corn is picked at the peak of perfection, when the kernels are fully plump and full of a milky liquid. To test, strip one of the leaves partially down the ear and press a fingernail into a kernel; if the milk spurts out, the ear is ripe. Kernels that have no liquid are past their prime. The silky tassels are another indicator of ripeness; the silk will be deep brown and damp when the kernels are ripe. Also, the top of the cob in the husk will be round and blunt, not pointed, when the ear is ready.

Give the cob a sharp twist downward to remove it from the stalk. As soon as the ear is picked, the sugars in the kernels begin to convert to starch and their quality begins to deteriorate. For this reason, corn should be cooked and served, or processed for canning or freezing, as quickly as possible after harvesting. (However, breeding advances have led to varieties listed as "Xtra sweet," which do not convert their sugar to starch as quickly as other varieties; these can keep in the refrigerator for several days with little loss in flavor.)

Leave flint, dent, and popcorn to dry on the stalks in the garden until hard frost, as long as the weather is not cool and rainy for long periods. (If the weather is poor, cut the stalks and pile them in an airy, sheltered spot to dry.) Continue the drying and storing process as described in chapter 5. Keep popcorn in a cool location—not in a warm kitchen—to preserve its inner moisture and popping ability.

COWPEAS

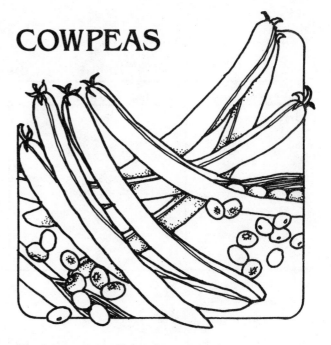

Blackeye peas, China beans, protopeas, southernpeas
Vigna unguiculata
Leguminosae

The cowpea is actually a bean, both botanically and according to its use. The most popular cowpeas generally fall into one of three groups: blackeye, crowder, or cream.

Cowpeas are high in protein (up to 20 percent), low in fat, and provide a large amount of vitamin B_1. They can be used in any of their three stages of growth: as a green snap bean, picked while immature and tender; as a fresh shell bean; and as a dry bean for storage. They are a popular soup ingredient and are often simmered with salt pork or a ham hock. Cowpeas are also grown as livestock feed or as a green manure crop. Since they are legumes, they enrich the soil's nitrogen supply, and they act as good soil conditioners, making sandy soil more compact and loosening heavy soils.

Cowpeas are now available as bush or semivining varieties, in addition to the standard vining varieties. All cowpeas produce slender pods varying in size from 3 to 12 inches.

Cowpeas

Variety Name	Average Days to Maturity	General Description and Comments
Brown Crowder	74–85	A crowder variety with buff-colored seed that changes to brown upon cooking; high yield of long pods with good-quality seed.
California Blackeye	75	Vines are high-yielding and resistant to disease; blackeye variety with long pods.
Mississippi Silver	64–70	A crowder variety that is multiple disease-resistant; pods have silverish tint; bushy plants are high-yielding; easiest of all varieties to shell.
Pink Eye Purple Hull	50–85	Classified as a table field pea, this semivining plant has purple pods that produce abundant white seeds with pink spots; grows to 24 in. tall; very good for freezing.

The seeds are small but of good quality, and there are many different flavors among the varieties.

Growing Range: Cowpeas will do well in any region that offers long, hot summers with temperatures averaging between 60° and 75°F. These tender plants are very sensitive to frost.

Soil Preparation: Cowpeas are not particular about soil, as long as it is well drained. Slow-draining, waterlogged soil will damage the plants, as will flooding, so avoid low-lying areas that collect runoff. Phosphorus and potassium are important nutrients, but excess nitrogen will encourage foliage growth to the detriment of pod and seed formation. They tolerate a pH of 6.5 to 7.0.

Propagation: Cowpeas are sown directly in the garden at least one week after the frost-free date. Wait until the soil is at least 60°F. They can be grown through the summer, even in very warm areas with successive plantings made three weeks apart. Plant the seeds 1 inch deep.

For conventional rows, space seeds 2 to 3 inches apart in the row, with rows set 24 to 42 inches apart, depending on the variety (refer to the seed packet). Pole types may be planted in rows or hills like pole beans (see Beans). Bush varieties are suited to planting in wide rows. Unused seed is good for three years.

Culture: Treat cowpeas the same as other beans (see Beans). They need no supplemental feeding during the growing season, and they withstand drought even better than soybeans, which are noted for that quality.

Pests and Diseases: Both insects and diseases have always plagued cowpeas, especially in very warm regions, although breeders are continually working on new disease-resistant varieties. The plants attract cornworms, Southern green stinkbugs, and weevils. The cowpea curculio is especially attracted to the developing pods. Diseases include root knot, wilt, and others caused by viruses.

Harvest and Storage: For use as a green snap

bean, pick cowpeas while they are young and succulent. As a green shell bean, wait until the seeds are nearly mature in size and harvest before the pods have yellowed and begun to deteriorate. Green shell beans can be canned or frozen. For dry use, cowpeas may be treated like dry beans (see Drying Your Bean Harvest for Storage in chapter 5). Because of their small size, cowpeas dry fairly rapidly.

CRESSES

Garden cress, mustard cress,
   pepper grass
Lepidium sativum
and
American cress, upland cress
Barbarea verna
and
Watercress
Nasturtium officinale
Cruciferae

All cresses are grown in soil with the exception of watercress, which is an aquatic plant that grows best in cool, running water. The other cresses are referred to as land cresses.

Of the land cresses, garden cress is the one most often planted. An annual and one of the fastest seeds to germinate, it is a small, upright plant with feathery leaves that are sometimes curled. It has a sharp, tangy flavor very similar to that of watercress, with the advantage that it is easy to grow indoors. All that is needed are moisture and sunlight to produce hundreds of edible, delicate little seedlings. Seeds can be sprouted successively for greens all winter.

Upland cress is not as commonly grown as garden cress. This annual produces compact rosettes with parsleylike leaves, and small yellow flowers when temperatures climb too high. It shares the peppery, pungent taste characteristic of the cresses.

Watercress has fleshy stems covered with white root hairs that establish themselves in the soil along the banks of streams, allowing the stems to trail in the water. If grown in clean, cool running water it needs very little attention. (However, if left unchecked it can almost restrict the flow of water in shallow streams.) It can be grown for short periods in garden soil, but this type of culture is not easy and the plant requires a lot of attention. Watercress makes a good winter crop in mild-winter areas where it can be harvested throughout the cooler part of the year.

Cresses are the perfect crop to tuck into shady areas not suitable for more light-hungry crops. These prolific plants will yield bountiful harvests of tangy greens to add zip to a wide variety of salads, soups, sandwiches, and other dishes.

Growing Range: Land cresses and watercress will grow in any temperate zone, where they make a good fall crop. They all like cool weather and can tolerate mild frosts.

Soil Preparation: Land cresses do well on a wide range of soils, and can be grown on any ground which is prepared for lettuce or mustard. The recommended soil pH for land cresses is 6.0 to 6.8.

Propagation: Land cresses germinate and grow so quickly they are always seeded directly in the ground. They will germinate in soils of at least 65°F. Sow in early spring and make succession plantings every two weeks as long as the weather remains cool. Begin sowing again in late summer and early fall. All unused cress seed is good for three to five years.

Sow all land cress seed ¼ inch deep. For conventional rows, place seed 2 inches apart and rows 12 inches apart. Growing bed spacing is 4 inches.

Garden cress is an even more successful crop when sprouted indoors. Sprouts can be grown in soil, on a dish of damp cotton, or in sprouting devices. Sprouted near a window, seedlings will absorb enough light to provide rich greens even during the winter months.

Watercress can be seeded by casting seeds along the banks of an unpolluted stream with cool water, about 6 inches above the water level. Where the seeds touch damp soil, they will sprout. The most successful and fastest way to propagate watercress is to root branches from an established plant or from a cluster purchased from the store. These cuttings can be grown in the soil of a stream bank as suggested above, but a container setup with running water, or simply a container in which the water is frequently changed, will probably develop a better crop.

Culture: Thin land cress seedlings to 4 inches apart when they are 10 days old. Use the thinnings in the kitchen. Land cresses grow naturally in damp areas, so try to provide the moisture these plants need by mulching or watering frequently. Even before harvest time, pinch out the growing tips of watercress to produce denser plants.

Pests and Diseases: Cresses are extremely free of problems.

Harvest and Storage: Land cresses are ready to cut after ten days of growth. Cutting out the growing centers of land cresses will encourage branching. In cool weather the harvest may continue for two months. Land cresses can be used in salads, soups, and sandwich fillings, as a substitute for parsley, and as a garnish for

any number of dishes. Garden cress grown indoors for sprouts can be cut with scissors as soon as the third leaf appears.

Watercress is ready for harvest about two weeks after seed is sown, sooner if cuttings were used to propagate. It should be harvested from the tips where the flavor is sweetest and the plant is most tender. When the flowers bud on watercress, the flavor becomes unpleasantly sharp, so remove flowers as soon as they appear.

Varieties: Cresses are available under a confusing variety of common names. To differentiate among the types on the market, and to ensure that the cress being purchased is the exact one that's wanted, use the botanical name as a reference.

CUCUMBERS

Cucumis sativus
Cucurbitaceae

The cucumber is an annual plant, bearing large leaves, trailing vines, and fruits growing from 2 to 36 inches, depending on the variety. The common phrase "cool as a cucumber" is an apt one, for not only are the fruits a cool and crisp treat, but, growing in a field on a hot summer day, the interior flesh is 20 degrees cooler than the outside air temperature.

Cucumbers traditionally were among the most difficult crops to raise because of their great susceptibility to disease and insect attack. In the past several decades, however, breeders have developed scores of new hybrids that are resistant (in some cases highly resistant) to the common diseases. These varieties are strongly recommended for organic gardens.

Most cucumbers are classified as "green short pickling" or "green long slicing" types. Although all slicing types may be pickled while they are very young, pickling varieties seldom are suitable for slicing if left to grow on the plant. If only one variety is grown, then, it should be a versatile slicing type.

Standard cucumber vines take up lots of garden space, sprawling to as much as 8 to 10 feet in diameter. Space-conscious gardeners should either grow the standard plants vertically, or use the bush varieties, which need only about 3 feet of space but produce full-sized fruits.

Some gardeners plant cucumbers in corn rows as a companion crop. This is a good idea with the slicing types, which will grow vigorously after the corn has been harvested and the stalks knocked down in midsummer.

Growing Range: Cucumbers may be grown in any region that offers warm and sunny summers, with average temperatures between 65° and 85°F. Since the fruits are always harvested while immature, the number of growing days in a region is not critical. The plants are extremely frost-sensitive, however, and may be harmed by long periods of cool, damp weather.

Soil Preparation: Any well-drained, well-limed, humus-rich loam will support good cucumber crops. They do well on sandy loams, too, but must be assured of adequate moisture for proper development. The pickling types can be grown in slightly poorer soils, since the fruits are harvested while very immature.

To provide an especially fertile growing base, dig holes 12 inches deep and 12 inches square wherever seeds are to be planted (this is especially suited for hill plantings). Fill each hole with compost or well-rotted manure and a phosphorus-rich material like phosphate rock, then cover with soil and tamp down. Make sure there are 4 inches of soil between seeds and organic matter. Cucumbers may also be planted in a compost heap, where the vines will trail down the sides of the heap.

Propagation: Cucumbers are commonly started from seed in the garden, at least one week after the frost-free date, when the soil has warmed up to at least 60°F and the daytime air temperatures are also above 60°F. Unused seed is good for five years.

Seeds are traditionally sown in hills, six to seven seeds to each hill, and the seedlings are later thinned to the best three in each hill. In medium loams, plant seeds 1 inch deep, and in sandy loams, 2 inches deep. For standard-sized varieties, the hills are spaced 4 feet apart in rows set 6 feet apart. Dwarf and bush varieties may be planted more closely, in rows, according to directions on the seed package. Growing bed spacing for standard varieties is 18 inches; more compact varieties can be spaced more closely.

Cucumbers may also be trained to climb on a trellis, a method which conserves garden space, and results in cleaner, straighter fruit. Plant seeds 4 inches apart along the trellis, and later thin seedlings to 8 inches apart. As soon as the plants begin vining, train them vertically. Use nylon stockings or soft yarn rather than wire to hold tender vines on the trellis.

In very short season areas, seeds may be started indoors two to three weeks before planting out, which should be done one week before the frost-free date. Raise seedlings in individual pots, and make sure seedlings are not disturbed in the transplanting process. If cloches are used to protect the transplanted seedlings, and the soil is warmed up first with a black plastic mulch, planting time may be advanced three weeks.

Culture: The roots of cucumbers are very shallow and sensitive to disturbance. Therefore, cultivate shallowly and as infrequently as possible. Apply a mulch as soon as the soil has warmed up, about three weeks after the seedlings emerge. Watch soil moisture carefully throughout the season, and water plants when necessary to keep the soil constantly moist. It is common for leaves to wilt at midday in hot weather, but no permanent damage is done as long as plants are kept well watered. Generally, cucumbers recover nicely from short-term droughts, but lack of water when fruits are developing can cut down on production.

Successful pollination is critical for good yields. Most cucumber varieties are monoecious, bearing both male and female blossoms. The activity of flying insects, particularly honeybees, is necessary for pollination to take place. The male blossom lives for only one or two days, then withers and drops from the plant. The female blossom, which can be recognized by the swelling just behind the blossom (the ovary), lives for about three days, but it must be fertilized on the first day for perfect fruit to develop. If it is pollinated after the first day, fruit will be small and thin. Further, pollination must take place early in the morning, because pollen will not germinate after noon. Often, male flowers are more profuse early in the season while female flowers become more abundant as the season progresses.

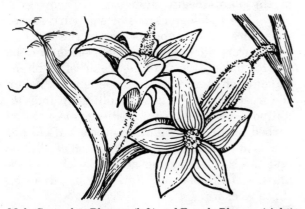

Male Cucumber Blossom (left) and Female Blossom (right)

Pollination and fruit development of these monoecious varieties is almost impossible if they are grown in a greenhouse or other place devoid of honeybees and flying insects (such as on a high-rise apartment terrace, or in an open garden where pesticides have decimated the insect population). In these circumstances they must be hand-pollinated.

There are gynoecious varieties (those that produce all female blossoms) that are largely self-pollinating. Sometimes, a few male seeds will be included in the seed packet of a gynoecious variety, and these are stained with color for identification. If so, be sure to label the male seedlings when they emerge, and include a few in each row to ensure pollination of female plants. With some gynoecious varieties, no male seeds are included. These will bear fruit, but they should not be planted near other cucumbers, since cross-pollination will result in imperfect fruit. Generally, gynoecious varieties produce earlier and heavier yields, since all the blossoms are capable of bearing fruit.

Pests and Diseases: Common pests are aphids, cucumber beetles, squash bugs, and squash vine borers. Anthracnose, bacterial wilt, downy mildew, mosaic, powdery mildew, and scab can attack cucumbers.

Harvest and Storage: "Green short pickling" types should be harvested every day, since they can quickly grow too large for use. "Green long slicing" varieties should be harvested as needed, whenever they are large enough to be of use, but should not be left to turn yellow or orange on the vine. Remove misshapen fruits promptly, as they will not improve with age. If a single fruit (of both pickling and slicing types) is left to ripen on the vine, the vine will stop producing altogether. Aside from pickling, there is no practical way to store cucumbers. However, there are literally hundreds—perhaps thousands—of pickle recipes from which to choose, using tiny gherkins all the way up to large fruits which are cut into chunks.

Cucumbers

The larger seed companies offer up to 40 cucumber varieties, and new ones are being introduced each year. Here, the listing is limited to those disease-resistant varieties that have proven popular over the years, and to some unusual types that offer special advantages.

Variety Name	Average Days to Maturity	General Description and Comments
Green Short Pickling Type		
Pioneer	51	A high yielder recommended for northern gardens; bears uniform, dark green fruit; gynoecious.
Wisconsin SMR 18	56–64	Produces excellent yields of uniform, dark green fruit.
Spartan Dawn	50	Very high yielder early in the season; compact vines; gynoecious.
Green Long Slicing Type		
Marketmore 70	55–67	Produces 8-in.-long, medium green fruit; high yielding throughout the summer; highly recommended for northern gardens.
Gemini	60	Highly resistant to at least 5 different diseases; dark green fruits measure 7–8 in. long; gynoecious.
Victory	50	Very early yielder; produces heavy crops of deep green fruits, 8 in. long; gynoecious; AAS.
Marketer (also Early Green Market)	60	Long a favorite, particularly in southern gardens; very attractive 9-in. fruit; not high in disease resistance; AAS.
Special Types		
Patio Pik	48–57	Hybrid good for pickling or slicing; compact growth does well in containers, spreads about 2 ft. in all directions; good disease resistance.
Cucumber Bush Whopper	55	Dwarf plants produce no runners; vines are short; cucumbers measure 6–8 in. long.
Sweet Slice	62	Hybrid producing long, slender fruits, 10 in. long; named for its unusually sweet flavor; very good disease resistance; burpless type.
Lemon	58	Yellow-skinned and almost round; resembles a lemon but with an extra-sweet cucumber taste; can be used while green and immature as well as when yellow and fully ripened.
China Long (also Kyoto, Japanese Climbing)	75	Light green fruits are 15–20 in. long and 2–3 in. wide; burpless; highly disease-resistant; should be trellised to prevent curling of fruit; harvest only when fruit attains yellow tinge for best taste.
West Indian Gherkin	60	Botanically known as *C. anguria;* the true gherkin; 2–3-in.-long oblong fruits are superior for sweet pickles; very productive.

EGGPLANT

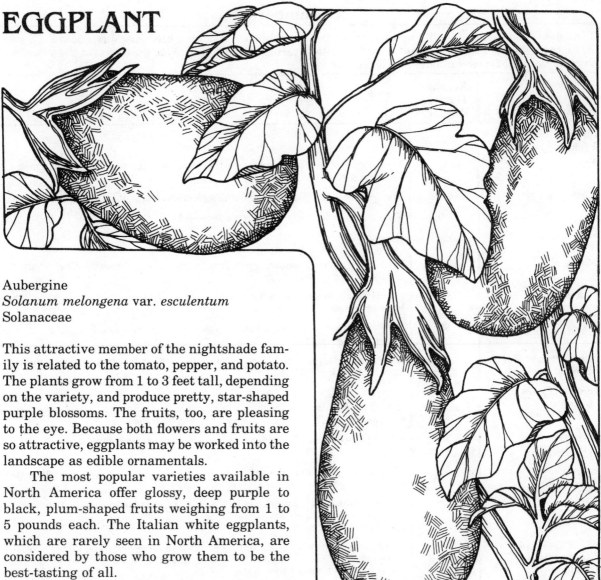

Aubergine
Solanum melongena var. *esculentum*
Solanaceae

This attractive member of the nightshade family is related to the tomato, pepper, and potato. The plants grow from 1 to 3 feet tall, depending on the variety, and produce pretty, star-shaped purple blossoms. The fruits, too, are pleasing to the eye. Because both flowers and fruits are so attractive, eggplants may be worked into the landscape as edible ornamentals.

The most popular varieties available in North America offer glossy, deep purple to black, plum-shaped fruits weighing from 1 to 5 pounds each. The Italian white eggplants, which are rarely seen in North America, are considered by those who grow them to be the best-tasting of all.

Eggplant is a warm-weather crop and produces the best harvest in a long, hot summer. Although early-maturing varieties have been developed for short-season gardens, even these will bear poorly during an extended cool and damp period. Ideally, each plant of the common varieties should yield from four to eight fruits. More often, however, the home gardener will harvest two or three.

Most eggplants are classified according to the shape of the fruit, either oval or elongated.

Many gardeners, having always grown the large, oval varieties, are surprised to find that the smaller slices of the elongated fruits are more convenient to use in recipes. The fruits may be peeled, sliced and broiled, or dipped in batter, then fried.

Growing Range: Eggplant is a very tender crop which grows best in average temperatures

Eggplant

Variety Name	Average Days to Maturity	General Description and Comments
Black Beauty	73–83	A very popular variety bearing plump, oval, dark purple fruit; tolerates drought and is a dependable producer.
Burpee Hybrid	70–75	Dark purple fruit is oval and medium-sized; plant is drought- and disease-resistant and spreads slightly.
Burpee's Jersey King Hybrid	73–75	One of the longest-fruited varieties; elongated, dark purple fruit can grow to 10 in. long, but should be harvested no longer than 7 in.
Dusky	55–62	Extra-early variety suited for short-season areas; slender oval fruit is black; plants are compact.
Ichiban	65	An early variety bearing elongated purple fruit; yields are very high; fruit is especially suited to oriental recipes.
White Italian	75	White, medium-sized fruit is milder in flavor than purple varieties.

between 70° and 85°F. Long-season varieties are best grown in regions that offer a hot summer and a mild fall. Early-maturing varieties may be grown in all temperate regions, although it must be realized that all eggplants are harmed by chill (extended temperatures below 50°F) and destroyed by frost. Also, the fruit won't set when temperatures dip below 60° to 65°F.

Soil Preparation: Eggplant will do well in an average loam that is well drained, deeply prepared, and well supplied with organic matter. Avoid low-lying areas and heavy soils. The pH should be in the range of 5.5 to 6.8.

Propagation: Eggplant is usually started in the garden from transplants, although it can be direct-seeded in very warm climates with a long growing season. (Sow seed according to spacings given below for transplants.) Start plants eight to ten weeks before transplanting time. Seedlings can be set out two to three weeks after the frost-free date when the soil is warm. Set plants 2 feet apart in conventional rows spaced 2 to 3 feet apart. Growing bed spacing is 24 inches. Unused seed is good for five years.

Culture: Eggplant requires plenty of moisture for best growth. Apply a mulch as soon as the soil has warmed up thoroughly and the plants are established. Keep the area free of weeds. On less than fertile soil, eggplant may benefit from a nitrogen and potassium boost one month after planting. Side-dress with well-rotted manure or compost and wood ashes, or water with solution of manure tea and seaweed extract.

Pests and Diseases: Eggplant may be bothered by a wide range of common insects, including aphids, Colorado potato beetles, cucumber beetles, cutworms, flea beetles, leafhoppers, potato tuber worms, and tomato hornworms. Diseases include fruit rot and verticillium wilt (the latter in cool-climate areas especially).

Harvest and Storage: The common practice has been to delay the harvest until the fruits are of nearly mature size, which means the entire crop is picked during a short period of only a few weeks. To extend the harvest period, begin picking whenever the eggplants are large enough to use, around 3 to 5 inches, depending on the variety. These immature fruits are more tender and generally of much better quality than those left to grow to full size. Young fruit has glossy skin, while older fruit past its prime has a dull sheen. When eggplant slices reveal seeds that have turned brown, that fruit has passed its peak of quality. Since the fruits are difficult to remove from the plant, use a sharp knife or pruning shears. The fruits may be kept for about one week in any location that offers high humidity and a warm temperature. Eggplant does not can or freeze well.

ENDIVE

Curly endive, also escarole or broad-leaved
  endive
Cichorium endivia
Compositae

Some confusion has arisen over the common
names of these particular leafy salad plants.
Gardeners in Britain use the species name, endive, and consider escarole to be a broad-leaved
variety of endive. Gardeners in the United
States and Europe have tended to use the genus
name in referring to these plants as chicory. In
this book, the British usage is being adopted,
and the term chicory is being applied to plants
classified as *Cichorium intybus,* which are
grown mainly for their roots, which can be
forced indoors for tender shoots (see Chicory).

These leafy greens are more flavorful than
lettuce, with a coarser texture. They are cultivated in the same way as lettuce, but they
require a longer growing season, and are much
hardier. Endive and escarole are good sources
of roughage, and provide a good amount of vitamin A and as much vitamin C as lettuce.
They have a reputed bitter taste, but this reputation is the result of an unfair comparison
with lettuce. The gardener who grows endive

and escarole should bear in mind that just as
lettuce develops a bitterness in hot weather, so
will these greens. A common way to avoid this
bitterness is to blanch the inner leaves.

Endive and escarole are distinguished from
one another by their leaves: the frilly, narrow
type is called endive and the broad, smooth type
is called escarole. Both are cultivated alike in
the garden and both can be prepared similarly
in the kitchen.

Growing Range: Endive and escarole will
grow in a wide range of climates, and are
strongly recommended for cooler regions. In
regions with mild winters they can be grown
as a winter crop. They grow better than many
kinds of lettuce in warm weather, but their
taste will be greatly improved if they are grown
in cool weather (especially in the fall), with
temperatures averaging between 60° and 65°F.
Long days cause plants to bolt. These half-
hardy plants can tolerate a few light frosts,
which will improve their flavor.

Soil Preparation: Any soil that will produce
good lettuce and cabbage crops will support
good crops of endive and escarole. They are very
tolerant of acid soils, growing well with a soil
pH between 5.0 and 6.8. Soils with a lot of humus are ideal, for a high humus content prevents the soil from drying out quickly, and
moisture keeps endive and escarole from bolting. The best soil is prepared by working a great
deal of manure and organic material into the
plot in late autumn.

Propagation: Endive and escarole are usually
direct-seeded 2 to 4 weeks before the frost-free
date, as soon as the soil can be worked. They
are also easily transplanted. Start seeds 4 to 5
weeks before desired setting-out date, which is
anywhere from 4 weeks before to 2 weeks after
the frost-free date. Start transplants for a fall
crop about 15 weeks before the first expected
frost. Use row and bed spacings given below,
and make sure seedlings are not planted too
deeply. Keep the crown slightly above the soil
surface, to prevent rot from setting in.

Seed will germinate at soil temperatures
as low as 60°F. Sow seeds ¼ inch deep, and

Endive

Variety Name	Average Days to Maturity	General Description and Comments
Endive (curly-leaf)		
Green Curled (also French Green Curled, Green Curled Ruffec, Giant Fringed Oyster)	80–90	Very frilly, crisp leaves have white midribs; grows 9 in. tall, 18 in. wide; the most popular variety.
Salad King	80–100	Finely curled leaves have light green midribs; slow to bolt; grows 9 in. tall, 24 in. wide; a widely grown variety.
Escarole (broad-leaf)		
Broad-leaved Batavian	90	Almost forms a solid head of large lettucelike leaves; grows 7 in. tall, 16 in. wide.
Batavian Full Hearted (also Deep Heart, Florida Deep Heart)	85–90	Leaves are slightly crinkled with a white midrib; grows to 12 in. wide.

Blanching Endive with an Inverted Pot

plant three seeds in a group. For conventional rows, space seeds 18 inches apart in rows set 24 inches apart. Spacing for growing beds is 18 inches. Make succession plantings three weeks apart until temperatures start to rise. Unused seed is good for five years.

Culture: When seedlings are 1 inch tall, pinch out all but the strongest from the group. They will eventually leaf out to fill up the 18-inch spacings, but until the plants grow big enough, mulch to keep the soil moist. Any plant exposed to high temperatures or lack of water will become bitter and bolt. Side-dress after the first

month with rotted manure or apply manure tea every three weeks for the balance of the season.

To blanch, tie up the healthy outer leaves with string or a rubber band two to three weeks before the desired harvest. Don't let the blanching hearts become wet. Tie them up when they are dry, and untie them if it rains. Should water stand within the bound plants, they will rot. Another method for blanching is to invert a large clay pot, with the drainage hole covered, over the endive or escarole head.

Pests and Diseases: Endive and escarole are subject to the same ills as lettuce, but less so.

Harvest and Storage: When endive and escarole have developed full, leafy heads, cut them off at the base of the leaves. Or, treat them as a cut-and-come-again crop, and take only a few outer leaves at a time. You can also cut out the tender leaves in the center of the plant, and new center shoots will appear for another harvest.

In northern areas, the plants can be lifted in fall and grown in hotbeds through the winter. Or they can be moved indoors, packed closely together with their roots in soil, and blanched in a cool, dark basement.

FLORENCE FENNEL

Finocchio, sweet fennel
Foeniculum vulgare var. *azoricum*
Umbelliferae

Florence fennel is popular in several European countries as a vegetable, but only around the Mediterranean is it commercially important. In America, Florence fennel shows up in fall in markets that cater to the tastes of people of Italian ancestry. Practically every part of the plant is edible, although it is the bulb formed at the plant base by the overlapping leaf stalks that is especially relished. When blanched and grown in cool weather, this bulb has just a hint of anise flavor and can be eaten raw or cooked, prepared in the same manner as celery. The seeds are used as flavoring in baked goods and are valued for the licorice-flavored oil that is extracted from them. The dense, feathery leaves can be used fresh or dry as an herb or dried and brewed as a tea.

Fennel has very few calories, and the vitamin and mineral content is also minimal. Florence fennel does add a good amount of fiber to the diet, however, and its fresh taste and distinctive flavor stimulate the appetite when it is served as an antipasto.

There is another type of fennel which is distinct from Florence fennel. An herb called common fennel (*F. vulgare*), will not develop the bulbous base found in Florence fennel, though it shares the characteristic anise taste in its seeds and leaves.

Growing Range: Florence fennel requires a long, cool season and is suitable for regions where there are over 100 days of frost-free weather from the time of planting. Fennel tolerates cold, but is killed by frosts. Conversely, temperatures that are too high cause the plant to bolt.

Soil Preparation: Florence fennel will grow on poor soil, but to encourage quick growth and thick, tender stalks, prepare the soil richly as for celery. Fennel is tolerant of acid soils but does better with soil at a pH of 6.8. A heavily manured soil will assure the gardener of large bulbous stems and healthy plants; make sure to add lime as needed to bring such heavily manured ground to a more neutral pH.

Propagation: Florence fennel can be direct-seeded or transplanted in the garden. In a short growing season, set transplants in place as soon as the ground warms to 68°F. Start transplants four to six weeks before setting out, and use 3-inch seedlings set 8 inches apart in rows. In a long growing season, sow seed in late summer for an autumn or winter harvest. Sow seed at a depth of ½ inch, 4 inches apart, in rows set 18 inches apart. Unused seed is good for four years.

Culture: When seedlings are 3 inches tall, thin to stand 8 inches apart in rows. Monthly side-dressings of well-rotted manure or waterings with manure tea will greatly assist these plants in producing tender, thick-fleshed stems. Mulch to keep plants moist and cool, which prevents bolting to seed and encourages the tenderest bulbs. When the bulbs reach 2 inches in diameter, blanch them by raking up mulch to cover completely or by mounding earth around and over them, leaving the upper stems and leaves free.

Pests and Diseases: Florence fennel is extremely free of problems.

Harvest and Storage: As soon as the plants are 18 inches tall, the leaves and tenderest branches can be used for garnishes, soups, salads, and flavorings. The best harvest comes in 90 to 120 days when the bulbous stems are fully grown, usually measuring 2½ to 3 inches in diameter. Delaying the harvest past this point may yield only tough and stringy bulbs. Dig up the whole plant, remove the roots, and cut back the upper branches. The white, fleshy bulb comes apart in sections, which are ready for use in a wide variety of recipes.

Varieties: There is no variation in the seed.

GARLIC

Allium sativum
Amaryllidaceae

This relative of the onion is a perennial that is grown as an annual in temperate climates. The plant produces a compound bulb made up of as many as 12 individual sections (called cloves), and a leaf stalk, 8 to 24 inches high, which produces both seeds and bulblets (which may be planted). Although garlic may be grown from seed, most gardeners find it simpler to plant the cloves, each of which will grow into a whole new bulb.

Garlic is an essential ingredient in many recipes, especially those of southern European and central Asian origin. It is also reputed to have medicinal value, particularly in fighting the common cold and in preventing high blood pressure. It is also used in the garden as an insect repellent, either when interplanted among other crops or ground up and made into a spray.

Growing garlic is not difficult, although the plants are somewhat more sensitive to soil and climatic conditions than most onions. Since they take up so little room, the plants are often used in interplanting, to make best use of garden space.

In addition to the common garlic, the gardener may come across references to elephant garlic. This is an entirely different species (*A. scorodoprasum*), producing large bulbs with a milder flavor than the more well known *A. sativum*. Elephant garlic is so mild, in fact, that it can be diced and used raw in salads. In all but extreme northern areas, this plant can be grown as a perennial, and any corms left at the end of the season can remain in the ground.

Growing Range: Garlic may be grown in all regions, as long as it receives cool temperatures during the early stages of growth when the leaves are developing. Later in the growing season, warm temperatures and long days are needed for best bulb development. Garlic is among the hardiest of garden crops, and is not damaged by frost or light freezing. Elephant garlic is extremely hardy and can withstand lower temperatures than regular garlic.

Soil Preparation: Garlic needs a fertile, well-drained soil that will supply ample nutrients and moisture during the growing season. A good soil is more important to garlic than to most alliums, and a sandy loam with lots of organic matter promotes vigorous, healthy growth. Till and rake the soil finely before planting. The recommended pH range is 5.5 to 6.8.

Propagation: Garlic may be grown from seed, in the same way as onions (see Onion), but the home gardener who needs relatively few plants will find it more convenient to start from cloves. One-half pound of cloves will plant 100 feet of row, and will produce up to 5 pounds of mature bulbs, more than enough for the annual needs of most families.

Cloves can be planted directly in the garden, or sprouted indoors, then set outside. Start cloves indoors four to six weeks before setting out, which can be done from two to four weeks before to one week after the frost-free date. Plant cloves directly outdoors four to six weeks before the frost-free date, as soon as the soil can be worked. In warm climates, plant in the fall. In climates with severe winter temperatures, cloves also may be planted in fall and mulched over winter for early spring growing.

Set cloves 1 inch deep with the pointed end up and the blunt end down. Space them 3 to 4 inches apart in conventional rows set 12 to 16 inches apart. Spacing in growing beds is 6 inches. Garlic may also be grown in wide rows. Gardeners usually plant only small areas with garlic, since only a few cloves yield up a bumper harvest. Many gardeners simply work garlic in among other crops.

Culture: The greatest threats to good production are dry soil and weeds. Water the ground thoroughly after planting, and mulch between rows. Hand weeding is essential, especially early in the season when plants are becoming established. Remove any flower heads that appear; this produces the largest bulbs.

Pests and Diseases: See Onion.

Harvest and Storage: Leaves can be snipped like chives and used wherever a mild garlic flavor is desired, although this practice slows down bulb formation. Garlic is ready for harvest when the tops begin to yellow and droop. At that time (approximately 90 to 110 days from planting), stop watering and knock down all the tops to hasten bulb curing. Three to five days later, loosen the soil around the bulbs before pulling, or use a fork to lift them. Leave them outdoors in a dry, shady location for several days until the tops are completely dry and the skin has become papery. If the weather is rainy, bring them indoors and spread on screens in a cool, dry spot. Once bulbs are completely dry, trim off the leaf stalks and trim the roots close to the base. Hang them in mesh bags in a cool and dry storage area. Garlic can also be braided into decorative strands for storage; if this method is preferred, don't trim the leaf stalks. (See Onion for instructions on how to braid.) Garlic will keep for up to a year under proper storage conditions. Even braids hung in the kitchen will keep for several months. If garlic is desired in next year's garden, set aside the largest bulbs for planting.

Garlic

Variety Name	Average Days to Maturity	General Description and Comments
White or Mexican cultivars	90	Early-maturing garlic; high yield of bulbs that don't store as well as the Pink or Italian cultivars.
Pink or Italian cultivars	110	A late-maturing garlic; stores very well; bulbs are of better quality than White or Mexican cultivars.
Elephant Garlic (also Jumbo Garlic)	100	A different species than common garlic; produces bulbs 6 times the size of common garlic; each clove weighs about 1 oz.; a mild garlic flavor.

GLOBE ARTICHOKE

Cynara scolymus
Compositae

The globe artichoke is the original and only true artichoke; all other plants called "artichoke," such as the Chinese artichoke or Jerusalem artichoke, derive their names from the globe artichoke.

Artichokes are perennials that produce rosettes of tender, fleshy leaves. From the center of these rosettes the terminal flower buds grow. The immature flower heads are the parts that are harvested, and the thickened base of the bud bracts and the fleshy base of the stems which bear the flowers (the "heart") are the parts that are eaten. (The only part of the flower head that is not edible is the hairy center.) If the bud is not removed from the plant, it forms a purple to violet thistlelike flower. Properly prepared, these flowers can be used in dried floral arrangements.

Several misconceptions about growing artichokes are widespread. It is believed that artichokes have to be grown as a perennial; that artichokes must be grown in cool coastal areas; and that artichokes cannot tolerate heat.

French plant breeders have developed varieties to be used solely as annuals in those areas where the ground freezes and makes growing artichokes as perennials difficult, if not impossible. Despite the difficulties present in areas of extreme cold, growers of artichokes as perennials have been successful as far north as New York and Massachusetts. Artichokes can take periodic temperatures down to 20°F as long as the freeze does not penetrate the soil and kill off the tender roots. To make sure the roots survive, winter protection is absolutely necessary. As for heat being fatal to artichokes, they can take prolonged temperatures over 100°F as long as adequate water is provided.

Artichokes are large and sprawling plants. They are not well suited for the small garden because they take up so much room for such a long time. Nevertheless, they can be planted successfully in areas not ordinarily given over to vegetables, areas near alleys, along fences, in the unused soil strips between boundaries, and in borders where flowers are usually planted. Some gardeners have successfully grown their artichokes at the edge of a compost pile.

Globe artichokes are relished as a gourmet treat. The gardener who grows his or her own will have an ample supply, for each plant produces from 12 to 16 buds. A plant can produce edible buds for four to seven years before its vigor declines. The common procedure for preparing artichokes is to boil them in salt water. For those on a salt-free diet, add vinegar and herbs to the boiling water in place of salt. Don't overcook—the artichoke should be tender, not mushy. Avoid using carbon steel knives and pots made of rolled steel or cast iron, for these materials will impart a metallic taste to the artichokes. The cooked buds can be eaten hot accompanied by a sauce, cold with a vinaigrette, or even stuffed.

Growing Range: Artichokes grown as perennials can be cultivated successfully wherever the ground does not freeze. They prefer a moist climate with average temperatures between 60° and 65°F. They can be grown with a relative degree of success in areas where deep ground freezes are common, as long as they are adequately protected in winter. In areas with an unfavorable climate, a wise choice may be to use the varieties grown as annuals.

Soil Preparation: A light, sandy, well-drained loam is best. If heavy soil is all that is available, work in coarse sand or use ditches to ensure good drainage. A heavy soil with standing water interferes with good growth. Artichokes need fertile soil. Work rotted manure and compost deeply into the soil before planting. When digging in the organic materials, add phosphate rock and wood ashes to make sure plenty of phosphorus and potassium are present. Lime, if necessary, to bring the soil to a pH of 6.0. Soil pH, however, is less important in producing good artichokes than good drainage and soil fertility.

Propagation: Artichokes grow readily from seed, but this is not the preferred method, for the seedlings are highly variable and may grow into plants with inferior qualities. The best method for the home gardener is to start with suckers that are purchased or taken from established plants.

Suckers are offshoots that appear around the base or crown of the parent plant in spring (in cool climates) or fall (in warm climates). When these suckers are about 10 inches tall, cut them from the base of the parent so that each new section has a piece of root attached. Plant in rows spaced 3 feet apart, with 2 feet between plants. Set each sucker into a hole 4 inches deep, and firm the soil around it.

Culture: Mulch heavily in dry weather, and water frequently. Good bud production is dependent upon liberal amounts of moisture and fertilizer. Side-dress with rotted manure or feed every two weeks with plenty of manure tea. Stalks and buds appear in late summer or early fall. Water becomes critical as the buds form; water weekly to encourage large buds. In areas of mild winters, bud growth will continue through the cold season.

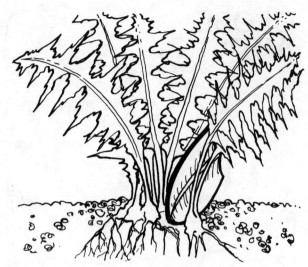

Dividing a Globe Artichoke Plant

When mature plants show signs of declining vigor, take young suckers from their base and replace the older plants. In areas of extreme cold, suckers can be removed in late fall, potted up with their roots and soil intact, and carried over the winter in a protected place. These will be next year's bearing stock.

In areas of light ground freezes, steps must be taken to protect the roots. In the fall, when the leaves die, cut the stalks back to within 12 inches of the ground. Use wood ashes to cover the trimmed stalks. Next, construct a protective cover of wood or plastic over the artichokes.

Globe Artichoke

Variety Name	General Description and Comments
Artichaut Gros Vert de Laon	Grown as an annual; matures in 160 days; very thorny, but sweet; grows 4 ft. tall and spreads 5 ft.
Green Globe	Bracts are thick and fleshy; hearts are solid; prefers long-season, mild-winter, and moist climates; not recommended for cold-winter areas; grows to 4 ft. tall and spreads to 6 ft.
Grande Beurre	Grown as an annual; matures in 150 days; buds similar to Green Globe; grows to 3 ft. tall and spreads to 3 ft.

Another method involves drawing soil up around the trimmed stalks to form a thick hill. Then the plant is covered with a fresh manure and straw mulch. Should a mat of wet straw or manure be formed over the roots without the hill of earth, rot will certainly set in and destroy the plants. In areas of light frosts, artichokes are hardy enough to be held in the ground without protection.

Pests and Diseases: Curly dwarf is a virus that stunts and eventually kills artichokes. Botrytis is a fungal disease that is a problem in areas of high humidity and moderate temperature. The principal insect pest is the artichoke plume moth. Aphids, caterpillars, slugs, and snails can also be problems. Generally, however, the homegrown artichoke is free of most diseases and pests.

Harvest and Storage: The first spring after planting suckers, there will probably be no large heads on perennial varieties. (Annual varieties will, of course, produce heads.) The small buds that do appear should be nipped off to direct the plant's energy into building up vigor for the following season. The harvestable crop will appear the second season.

Harvest when the buds are plump and the bracts are still closed. When the bracts extend outward the flower head is daily becoming tougher and stringier. When the bracts turn purple and the flowers are visible, the bud is no longer edible. The large, central globe is usually the first to reach harvestable stage. Once it has been cut, harvest the side-shoot globes. Size is not a sure way to judge readiness; some of the smaller buds will be ready at the same time as larger ones. More of the stem is edible than commercially cut heads would indicate. Cut the flower heads as far down on the stem as experience warrants (as much as 5 to 6 inches). Frost damage will cause brown spots on the bracts. This damage, however, is merely cosmetic. No decline in taste will be noticeable. Buds can be kept up to one month in the refrigerator. Cooked artichoke hearts can be pickled, frozen, and canned.

HAMBURG PARSLEY

Parsnip-rooted parsley, turnip-rooted parsley
Petroselinum crispum var. *tuberosum*
Umbelliferae

Hamburg parsley is parsley with a bonus. The green tops are used (and taste like) ordinary garden parsley, but the roots may be used much like turnips or parsnips.

These roots are crisp and white-fleshed, carrot-shaped, and have a mild flavor similar to celeriac. They are an excellent flavoring for soups and stews, and are often roasted with beef. Raw strips can be served with dips as a healthful snack. The broad, flat greens are similar to Italian parsley, and may be used for garnish and flavoring.

Hamburg parsley is a long-season crop, yet may be grown even in short-season areas, since the roots may be harvested and used long before maturity. This is not a difficult crop to grow, even in poorer soils, if adequate moisture is provided. It is often used to plant borders that are partially shaded by large trees, although it will not grow in dense shade.

Growing Range: Hamburg parsley is a hardy, long-season crop that may be grown in all areas, although best texture and flavor of the roots are reached if they are exposed to a few sharp autumn frosts, which improve their sugar content. In short-season areas, it is planted as early in spring as possible. In regions where winters are mild, seed may be sown in late autumn and the plants then carried over winter to produce spring crops.

Soil Preparation: Hamburg parsley will produce adequate crops even in poor soil but very light soils will not provide the moisture needed for good root development. It should not follow legume crops, since excess nitrogen will force top growth and slow root development. Never add fresh manure the same season planting takes place, otherwise roots will fork unattractively. The soil should be worked well to a depth of 8 inches and all clods of soil and rocks removed to give the roots easy progress in growing. Incorporate lots of compost into the rows. The pH should be between 6 and 7.

Propagation: Hamburg parsley may be direct-seeded into the garden on the frost-free date. The soil temperature for best germination is 70°F. Since the seed is slow to germinate, it should be presprouted or at least soaked overnight and sown in premoistened rows. In short-season areas, sow seeds in peat pots or other individual containers that will allow transplanting without disturbing the roots. Sow seed indoors no more than six weeks before transplanting time (on the frost-free date) so that the roots do not become cramped in the pots. Unused seed is good for one to two years.

In conventional rows, sow seeds three to the inch and cover with ¼ inch of soil. Rows should be spaced 12 to 18 inches apart. Since seed germination is slow, many gardeners sow one radish seed after each ten parsley seeds, to provide row markers. The radishes are harvested as the parsley seedlings need room to expand. Growing bed spacing is 4 inches.

Culture: When seedlings are up, thin them to stand 1 inch apart; then, in two or three weeks, thin them again to stand 4 to 6 inches apart. Keep the rows well supplied with moisture until the plants are well established, after which no water need be added except in severe drought. Mulch the rows at the time watering is discontinued. Keep after weeds in the early season, until the mulch is applied. After that, the plants will require little or no care.

Pests and Diseases: Hamburg parsley is seldom bothered by anything. Celery worms may occasionally eat the young foliage.

Harvest and Storage: Although Hamburg parsley may be harvested at any time the roots are large enough to be used, most people wait until they have reached their full size, 6 to 8 inches. Unlike other root vegetables, Hamburg parsley tastes better the larger the root.

In areas where winters are severe, all roots should be dug before the ground freezes hard, and they may be stored in a cool (32° to 40°F), moist environment for five to six months. In mild-winter areas, roots may be mulched heavily and left in the ground, to be harvested as needed. These roots will retain better texture than those stored indoors.

The green tops may be clipped during the season for use as ordinary leaf parsley, although no more than one or two stems should be removed from any one plant, since root development depends on top growth. When taking the major harvest in fall, the greens may be dried and stored.

Varieties: Most seed houses offer no choice of varieties.

HORSERADISH

Armoracia rusticana
Cruciferae

Horseradish is valued as a pungent condiment to be used with meat and fish. Although some people clip a few of the young leaves to use in springtime salads, it is primarily the thick taproot with its crisp, white, extremely piquant flesh that is used for culinary purposes. The plant spreads by the vigorous action of its many lateral roots that grow from the main taproot. This perennial herb belonging to the mustard family is most often grown as an annual crop. Although it can be left in the ground over winter, gardeners usually lift the roots in fall and replant in spring. This practice keeps the plant from spreading all over the garden, and also promotes thicker taproot growth.

Growing Range: Horseradish grows best in cool climates, with average temperatures around 60° to 65°F. A few moderate frosts improve the quality of this hardy root.

Soil Preparation: Although horseradish will grow in nearly any soil capable of holding sufficient moisture, prize roots are grown in deeply prepared, well-drained loam of medium texture

and moderate richness. Potassium is critical for root development, while excess nitrogen encourages foliage growth at the expense of root development. Prepare the soil as deeply as possible, and incorporate a moderate amount of well-aged compost or manure, concentrating most of it 8 to 10 inches below the surface. This concentration will discourage excessive growth of lateral roots at the surface, while encouraging long and fleshy taproots. Also work in a potassium-rich material like wood ashes or greensand. Horseradish can tolerate a pH range of 6 to 8; a pH of 7 yields the best results.

Propagation: Horseradish is started by root cuttings, particularly from lateral roots growing from the upper portion of the main taproot. Cut the laterals straight-sided at the point where they meet the main root, and cut the tip end at a slant. (The straight-cut end will be thicker than the slant-cut end.) These roots, harvested in fall, are stored over winter for planting the following spring. Till and rake the planting area in the early spring, as soon as the ground can be worked. Save room by establishing beds, set 2 to 3 feet apart, each containing two rows. Dig furrows about 6 inches deep, spacing rows 12 inches apart. Space root cuttings 10 to 12 inches apart in the row, placing them in the soil at a 45-degree angle, with the straight-cut end at the top (3 inches below the surface), and the slant-cut end at the bottom. Pack the soil firmly around all the roots and level the soil.

Culture: The main requirements are a clean bed and ample moisture. Provide both by applying a mulch once the plants are well established and the ground has warmed up in the spring. A midseason side-dressing of high-potassium fertilizer such as wood ashes will promote vigorous root development.

To encourage growth of a straight taproot, try a technique used by commercial growers. When a plant has grown to about 9 to 12 inches tall, carefully brush aside the top 4 inches of soil surrounding the root and strip away the fine lateral roots from the main root, then re-

place the soil carefully around the main root.
Pests and Diseases: Cultivated horseradish
is seldom bothered by anything, although white
rust may be spread by wild horseradish growing nearby.

Harvest and Storage: Horseradish matures
with the onset of cool fall weather, and for the
best flavor should not be harvested until after
several frosts have hit. Loosen the soil with a
spade or fork, then lift the roots by hand. While
you are harvesting you can save root cuttings
for next year's crop by cutting the best-looking
lateral roots, tying them in bunches, and packing them in moist sand. They will keep well in
a cool (32° to 40°F) and moist root cellar until
spring planting time. Roots intended for culinary use can also be stored in a root cellar, or
layered in sand and buried in outdoor pits. The
roots may also be mulched heavily and left in
the ground for use over the winter.

Horseradish

Variety Name	Average Days to Maturity	General Description and Comments
Bohemian	120	The standard variety; very hardy; produces large white roots of good quality.
Maliner Kren	120	A vigorous plant with good-sized white roots.

JERUSALEM ARTICHOKE

Girasole, sunchoke
Helianthus tuberosus
Compositae

The Jerusalem artichoke is not from Jerusalem, and it is not an artichoke. It is a native
North American perennial sunflower with
knobby stem-tubers that are eaten raw, added
to salads, or used like potatoes. The crisp tubers, white with brown or reddish brown skins,
have a sweet and nutty taste, although they
will be bland-tasting if harvested before the
ground has started to freeze in autumn.

The Jerusalem artichoke is unique among
vegetable crops in that it has no starch content,
storing its carbohydrate in the form of inulin.
For this reason, it is often used by diabetics as
a potato substitute. The tubers offer significant
amounts of several vitamins and minerals and
are especially rich in vitamin B_1 and potassium. They are also very low in calories, having
only one-tenth the number found in an equal
serving of potatoes.

The Jerusalem artichoke is perhaps the
easiest of all vegetables to grow—certainly the

easiest of the perennials. A single tuber planted in a corner of the garden will soon expand to supply the needs of any family. In fact, the major problem with Jerusalem artichokes often is attempting to keep them from taking over the entire garden.

The tubers are delicious raw, and they can be used as crudités with dips, or sliced thinly into salads. Jerusalem artichokes can also be cooked—but just steam or sauté them lightly.

Growing Range: Jerusalem artichokes are extremely hardy and will grow in all regions. They are a long-season crop, requiring 120 days to mature. In frost-free areas the texture and taste of the tubers will be inferior.

Soil Preparation: Any warm, well-drained soil will support good stands of Jerusalem artichokes. It's a good idea to set aside a separate bed for this crop so their rampant growth doesn't interfere with other garden crops. Till soil to a depth of 10 inches. Add some compost to poorer soils to give the plants a good start. The pH level should be close to 5.8.

Propagation: Jerusalem artichokes may be planted four to six weeks before the frost-free date, as soon as the soil can be worked. In warm climates, plant them in fall to provide a spring crop. They are planted like potatoes, using either an entire tuber or one that is cut up so that each piece contains an "eye." Plants have even grown from peelings placed in a compost heap. Many gardeners plant this crop in a row along the back of the garden, where the tall-growing plants will not shade other vegetables. Set the tubers 6 inches deep every 12 inches along rows spaced 36 to 48 inches apart. The tubers may also be planted in hills, one per hill, with hills set 12 inches apart. Jerusalem artichokes can be planted in "mulch pockets," described under Propagation in the Potato entry.

Culture: Once planted, Jerusalem artichokes need little further care. They should be given moderate moisture until they have become established. A mulch—applied when the soil has warmed up thoroughly—will help to keep weeds down. However, since each tuber sends up from 1 to 12 stalks, the Jerusalem artichokes will most likely outrace the weeds and smother them. In windy areas, plants may need supports. If the top 12 to 18 inches of stem is cut off as flowers form, the size of the developing tubers will be increased. Do not cut the stems off completely—otherwise the yield of tubers will be decreased.

Pests and Diseases: None are serious.

Harvest and Storage: For best taste and texture, tubers should not be dug until the foliage has died down and the ground has just begun to freeze, in late autumn or early winter. Then, the easiest harvesting method is to loosen the soil slightly with a garden fork, grasp the thick stem of the plant, and pull it out of the ground. Some tubers will adhere to the roots, and the others may be exposed easily with a hoe or garden fork. Rarely will all the tubers be recovered, and those that remain behind will ensure the following year's crop.

To clean the tuber surface of all dirt, soak it in water for five minutes, and scrub with a brush. Rinse and use at once, or store in a plastic bag in the refrigerator for three to four days.

Because of their thin skins, Jerusalem artichokes are difficult to store successfully indoors unless they are kept in a cool (32° to 40°F) location. In addition, stored tubers are less flavorful than ones that are freshly dug. It is better to store them in the garden itself, and dig them as needed. In most temperate regions, a heavy mulch will keep the ground from freezing hard, enabling tubers to be harvested throughout the winter. In severe-winter regions, pack them in moist sand and store them in a box, barrel, or garbage can placed under the ground. Hard freezing will not damage the tubers.

Varieties: The best variety is American (formerly called Improved Mammoth French), although many catalogs do not bother to mention a variety. Tubers are sold by the pound. A fraction of that will be enough to establish a lifetime planting.

KALE

Borecole
Brassica oleracea var. *acephala*
Cruciferae

The edible leaves of this nonheading plant are available in curled or smooth varieties. Kale can be used as an eye-catching edible in an ornamental garden, due to its blue-green to gray-green, textured leaves. In the kitchen, young leaves can be used raw in salads or as a garnish. The larger leaves can be cooked and treated in the same manner as spinach and cabbage. Leaves of any size can be used in soups.

The easy-to-grow kale is an exception among the difficult members of the cabbage family. Extremely hardy by nature, its true merit lies in providing a welcome crop of vitamin- and mineral-rich greens in fall and winter—a time when fresh greens are scarce. Kale is a particularly good source of vitamins A and C, as well as being rich in calcium. It contains two times the amount of vitamin C found in an equal amount of orange juice, and contains more calcium than milk. Its cold resistance allows for successive planting in both early spring and late fall, and a light frost even improves the flavor by making the leaves sweeter and more tender. This trait makes kale a perfect crop for a fall garden. Where winters are not too severe, a well-protected plant can keep producing through spring.

There are three basic types: Scotch kale (called borecole), which has tightly curled leaves; Siberian kale, which has smoother leaves with frilled edges; and attractive bicolored ornamental types which are also edible.

Growing Range: Kale will grow in any region where there are frosts. It is very cold-hardy and is averse to long periods of intense summer heat. Best growth occurs when average temperatures range between 60° and 65°F.

Soil Preparation: Kale grows best in a loamy soil, to which a moderate amount of well-rotted manure or compost has been added. The taste and texture of the leaves decline slightly when plants are grown on light, sandy soils or heavy, clayey soils. However, too rich a soil (with an excess of nitrogen) will cause extra-succulent growth which attracts pests. Recommended pH is 6.5 to 6.8.

Propagation: Kale seed may be started indoors or sown directly in the garden. Start transplants six to eight weeks before the desired setting-out date, which can range from five weeks before to two weeks after the frost-free date. Set seedlings 12 to 15 inches apart in conventional rows spaced 18 to 24 inches apart. In growing beds, set plants 15 to 18 inches apart.

Sow seed in the garden four to six weeks before the frost-free date for an early crop. Sow again about ten weeks before the first expected frost for a late crop. Soil temperature must be at least 40°F for good germination. Scatter seed ½ inch deep along conventional rows, using between-row spacing given above. Sow seed ½ inch deep in intensive beds, using spacing given above. Unused seed is good for five years.

Culture: Thin seedlings in conventional rows to stand 12 to 15 inches apart. Kale prefers damp, not soggy soil; keep well watered in dry weather. When plants are 4 or 5 inches tall,

Kale

Variety Name	Average Days to Maturity	General Description and Comments
Scotch Type		
Blue Curled Scotch	65	Compact, low-growing plant, 12 in. tall; blue-green color; finely curled leaves.
Dwarf Green Curled	50–65	Extremely hardy, can withstand severe frost; white ribs in yellow-green leaves; 15 in. tall, with 30-in. spread.
Vates (also Dwarf Blue Curled)	55	The standard dwarf curled variety; compact, low-growing, 12 in. tall; withstands below-freezing temperature; blue-green, curled leaves.
Siberian Type		
Blue Siberian	65	Hardy and vigorous grower; a favorite in warm climate areas; coarse, frilled leaves; up to 16 in. tall with 36-in. spread.
Dwarf Siberian	65	Thick head of frilled gray-green leaves; withstands cold temperatures well; 12–16 in. tall.
Hungry Gap		Very hardy; withstands drought, wet periods, and frost very well.
Ornamental Flowering Kale	55–75	Variegated types feature crinkly leaves in combinations of purple and green or white and green; color disappears when cooked; 12–15 in. tall.

side-dress with nitrogen-rich fertilizer such as rotted manure or blood meal, or water with manure tea. Apply mulch once plants are well established. Kale is a very low-maintenance crop, requiring scant attention after sowing or transplanting.

Pests and Diseases: See Cabbage. Kale has a degree of built-in resistance to clubroot.

Harvest and Storage: Two methods of harvest are possible; you can pick individual leaf rosettes for a cut-and-come-again crop, or cut the entire plant. Peak harvest is when leaves are firm, crisp, and bright green. If allowed to get too old, leaves appear dark green and heavy and become tough and bitter. The tenderest leaves are those in the unfolding rosette at the top of the plant. In general, the leaves on the uppermost portion of the plant are tenderer than those on the bottom. Delaying harvest until after a frost will greatly enhance the flavor.

Kale can be held in the garden with a protective mulch for an extended harvest. In the fall, pull earth up around the stem to the level of the basal leaves and mulch thickly when frost is expected. If the plant is covered well, it will survive through the winter and even produce an early spring crop of new leaves. In areas with mild winters, kale will remain green and available for harvesting.

KOHLRABI

Brassica oleracea, Gongylodes Group
Cruciferae

Kohlrabi has been described as a "turnip grow-ing on a cabbage root." Indeed, the edible bulb (actually a swollen stem) of this unusual-look-ing plant does resemble a turnip, but it has a delicate cabbagelike taste. True kohlrabi affi-cionados swear that it is the best-tasting mem-ber of the cabbage family.

Although the young tops of the plant are sometimes eaten as a steamed green, it is the white, green, or purple bulb that is the main attraction. It is often steamed with the skin on and eaten as a hot vegetable, or cooled for use in salads. Older bulbs should be peeled to re-move the fibrous skin before eating. Sliced thinly or grated, the bulbs may also be used raw in salads. Kohlrabi is a good source of vi-tamins A, C, and some of the B complex, plus calcium, phosphorus, and iron.

Although kohlrabi is not difficult to grow, many gardeners fail, either because they do not give the plants sufficient nutrients and mois-ture to make quick, tender growth, or because

they harvest the bulbs too late, after they have become woody and bitter.

Growing Range: Kohlrabi may be grown in gardens in any region that can offer a growing season of at least 80 days. It is a hardy cool-season crop which grows best in early spring or fall when the mild days and cool nights en-hance its development. The average tempera-tures for best growth are 60° to 65°F. In warm regions, kohlrabi should be grown as a fall and winter crop. In an area where the growing days number between 120 and 140, two or three suc-cessive plantings may be made during the sea-son.

Soil Preparation: Kohlrabi grows well in any medium- to light-textured soil with an ample supply of organic matter and good water-hold-ing capacity. Remove any rocks and other ob-structions that may stunt the plants' growth and work plenty of aged compost into the soil, to a depth of 8 inches, before sowing seeds. Also work in potassium-rich material like wood ashes or greensand. Kohlrabi tolerates soils with a pH from 6 to 7.

Propagation: Seeds of this crop can be sown directly into the garden, four to six weeks be-fore the frost-free date. In very short-season areas, they may be started indoors six to eight weeks before being transplanted into the gar-den, which can be done from five weeks before to two weeks after the frost-free date. In con-ventional rows spaced 18 inches apart, set seed-lings every 9 inches. In raised beds, space seed-lings 9 inches apart.

For conventional row plantings, sow ten seeds to each foot of row, burying them ¼ inch deep, spacing the rows as directed for trans-plants. Use the raised bed spacing given above. For an especially fine-flavored and tender har-vest, sow seeds about ten weeks before the first expected frost so that the bulb reaches edible size during the first cool days of autumn and experiences a few light frosts. Unused seed is good for five years.

Culture: Once seedlings have reached 4 to 5 inches tall, thin to stand 9 inches apart in the row. Keep kohlrabi well watered and mulch to conserve soil moisture. Tender, good-quality kohlrabi must be grown quickly, which calls for constant moisture and adequate nutrients. Deep cultivation is very likely to injure the shallow lateral roots. Avoid disturbing roots of young plants in any way, as they are very sensitive.

Pests and Diseases: Kohlrabi is susceptible to the same pests and diseases that affect cabbage (see Cabbage). Harlequin bugs and imported cabbage worms can be especially bothersome.

Harvest and Storage: Kohlrabi must be harvested while the bulbs are young and immature, as small as 1½ inches in diameter and no larger than 2 inches. To harvest, slice through the stem an inch below the bulb. With the leaves removed, they will keep for several weeks in a refrigerator, and they may be stored for longer periods in a cool (32° to 40°F) and moist root cellar. Kohlrabi may also be diced, blanched, and frozen for later use, and can be substituted wherever turnips are called for.

Kohlrabi

Variety Name	Average Days to Maturity	General Description and Comments
Early Purple Vienna	60–70	The purple skin of the bulb hides greenish white flesh inside; the best variety for late summer and fall crops.
Early White Vienna	60–65	Smooth green bulb covers creamy white flesh; good for freezing.

LEEKS

Allium ampeloprasum, Porrum Group
Amaryllidaceae

The leek, a relative of the onion, has been a staple in European gardens and kitchens since ancient times. Thick, white stems with a sweet, subtle onion flavor are relished by gourmets, and are eaten raw in salads, added to soups or stews, or sautéed as a vegetable side dish. The elegant vegetable's most famous use is in potato and leek soup (which when chilled is known as vichyssoise). Unquestionably, the stalks are the main crop, but the leaves can be used in soups and stews also. Leeks are milder and sweeter than most onions, very low in calories (about 20 per 1-ounce serving), and supply ample amounts of vitamins A, C, and E.

In addition to the fact that leeks are absolutely delicious, gardeners appreciate their insect-repellent quality. Traditionally, leeks have been grown near carrots to dispel carrot flies, and in gardens where clubroot is a problem.

Growing Range: Leeks are extremely hardy and may be grown in all temperate regions, provided the climate is on the cool side. They grow best in temperatures between 55° and 75°F. Growth may be slowed by long periods of hot weather.

Soil Preparation: Most soils will support leeks, although they do best in well-drained and well-limed soils that can offer good moisture supplies throughout the season. To ensure plenty of good stalks, work well-rotted manure and compost into the soil. It is also a good practice to plant them where a legume crop grew before. The recommended pH range is 6 to 7.

One of two soil preparation systems may be used. In the first, a trench is dug 6 to 8 inches deep and 4 inches wide. Manure or compost is worked into the soil at the bottom of the trench. The seedlings are then planted in the trench, which is gradually filled in as the plants grow, thus producing the desired, long white stems. In the other method, seedlings or seeds are planted in level soil, which is then hilled up around the plants as they grow.

Propagation: Leeks may be grown in the garden from seed or transplants, depending on the climate of the area. In warm climates, seed is usually sown in the garden in summer, for harvest in late fall or early winter, or in fall for late winter harvest. Seed will germinate in soils at least 65°F, but the best germination results between 70° and 75°F. Unused seed is good for one to three years.

In cooler areas, seed is usually started indoors four to six weeks before the frost-free date, hardened-off, and then transplanted into the garden from five weeks before to two weeks after the frost-free date. The best seedlings to use are those at least 4 inches tall. Although the days to maturity may be as long as 190, good-sized leeks may be harvested in a much shorter time. Nevertheless, short-season gardeners should take advantage of the early start indoors since it takes roughly 80 days for transplants to mature.

If conventional rows are used, space them 20 inches apart. Sow seeds ½ inch deep in the garden, and later thin plants to 3 to 4 inches apart in the rows and trenches, and 6 inches apart in growing beds. When starting seeds indoors, keep the tops trimmed to 1½ inches until a week before transplanting time. Then set the seedlings 3 to 4 inches apart in rows or trenches, or 6 inches apart in raised beds.

Culture: Mulch between rows, and weed regularly within rows and beds, especially early in the season when the young plants cannot compete with quick-growing weeds. Never let the soil dry out around the plants.

If the trench method is used, begin to fill in the trench only after the plants are as thick as a finger, gradually filling in around the bottom of the plants. Never fill in more than an inch at a time; filling in too quickly or too early

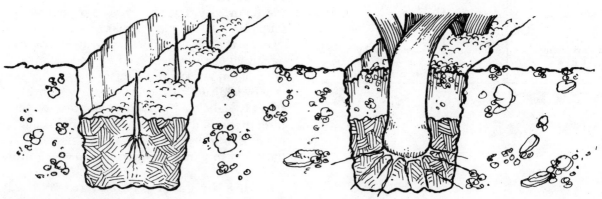

Trench Planting of Leeks

in the season may cause the plants to rot. Only when they have grown to 8 inches tall should the trench be filled in completely. If trenches are not used, simply hill soil around the plants as they grow, never hilling it over the point where the leaves begin to branch out from the stems. Careful hilling or trench filling will enable the plant to develop the treasured, long white stems.

Pests and Diseases: The onion maggot or onion thrip may occasionally bother plants.

Harvest and Storage: Leeks may be harvested whenever they reach a usable size, about 1 inch in diameter. At full maturity, their stems will be as large as 2½ inches around. They may be pulled by hand in loose soils, or dug with a fork or spade in hard soils.

With the advent of freezing weather, leeks can be dug from the garden and stored under cool (32° to 40°F) and moist conditions. They can also be packed upright into boxes with their roots set in moistened sand or soil, and then stored in a cool cellar. Most gardeners keep

Leeks

Variety Name	Average Days to Maturity	General Description and Comments
Broad London (also Large American Flag, London Flag, Broad Scotch)	130–150·	The most popular variety, with 1½-in.-thick, sweet-flavored stems.
American Flag	120–150	Stems grow from 9½–15 in. tall; suited for fall and winter harvest.
Elephant Leek	85–150	A widely grown variety noted for its vigor and large stems.

them in the garden over the winter, mulched heavily, and harvest them as needed. Leeks are biennials, and if left in the garden until spring they are likely to develop seed heads, at which point their flavor changes and they are no longer fit to eat.

LETTUCE

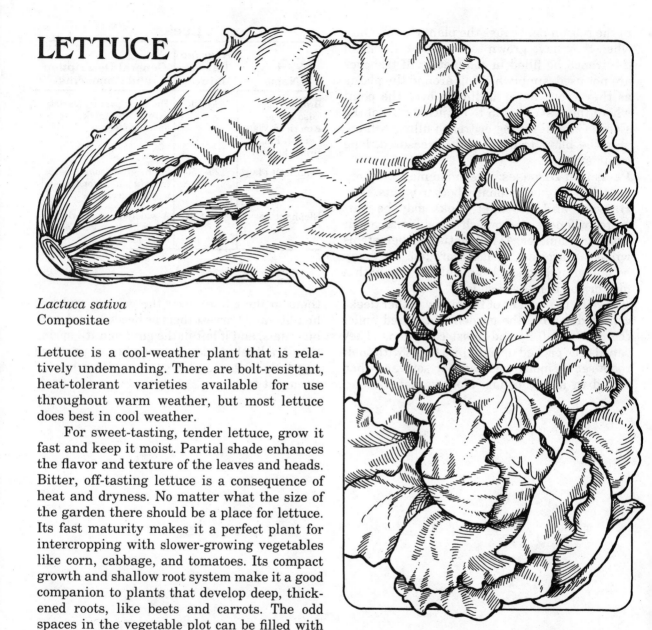

Lactuca sativa
Compositae

Lettuce is a cool-weather plant that is relatively undemanding. There are bolt-resistant, heat-tolerant varieties available for use throughout warm weather, but most lettuce does best in cool weather.

For sweet-tasting, tender lettuce, grow it fast and keep it moist. Partial shade enhances the flavor and texture of the leaves and heads. Bitter, off-tasting lettuce is a consequence of heat and dryness. No matter what the size of the garden there should be a place for lettuce. Its fast maturity makes it a perfect plant for intercropping with slower-growing vegetables like corn, cabbage, and tomatoes. Its compact growth and shallow root system make it a good companion to plants that develop deep, thickened roots, like beets and carrots. The odd spaces in the vegetable plot can be filled with lettuce, and even a head or two can be slipped into unoccupied spaces in the flower garden.

Lettuce is generally grouped in four types which can all be grown the same way. Crisphead lettuce (also known as iceberg) is the kind commercial growers have more success with than home gardeners. Crisphead lettuce demands good soil, ample fertilizer, and specific climatic conditions which occur in a limited number of areas. The large cabbagelike heads have the least nutrition of all the lettuce types, yet it is the type most often found in markets, largely because it stores for long periods and will ship long distances.

Romaine or cos lettuce is also crispy, but its upright growth of loosely overlapping leaves allows the light to penetrate, boosting the nutritional value of the plant. The leaves are coarse and grow into an almost cylindrical shape. Romaine varieties are easy to grow.

Leaf lettuce has the greatest number of varieties, and is the most popular type in the home garden. Some varieties form loose, compact heads and others have neatly arranged rosettes of loose leaves. The leaves themselves can be frilly or smooth, light green, dark green, or red to brown. Leaf lettuce is generally a good source of nutrients.

Butterhead lettuce (also called Boston lettuce) stands apart from the other types in that its leaves have a soft and buttery texture and a very delicate flavor. The outer leaves are dark green and loosely folded, forming a white inner head. Butterhead types require excellent soil and are extremely sensitive to high and low temperatures. They rate highest among the four in taste and texture, and they are also very nutritious.

Lettuce, with the exception of the crisphead types, has high amounts of vitamin A, more vitamins in the B groups than most vegetables, and some vitamin C. Lettuce is best known for its contribution to salads, but it can be cooked as a side dish known as wilted lettuce, and it is the basis of a very good soup.

Growing Range: Basically favoring cool, moist climates, lettuce can be grown as a winter crop in areas that have hot, dry summers. Elsewhere it makes excellent spring and fall crops. The average temperature for best growth is 60° to 65°F. Lettuce can tolerate light frost, with minimum night temperatures down to 25°F, but doesn't take hard frost well.

Soil Preparation: Lettuce grows best in a moist, rich, well-drained soil. Any soil type will do, as long as plenty of organic matter is worked in. A standard practice among experienced gardeners is to manure heavily (with fresh manure) in the fall prior to spring planting. When the soil can be worked in the spring, the manure should be fully rotted and ready to be dug in thoroughly. Fall manuring is not critical to producing good lettuce, but it is an economical practice that assures a better-than-average crop. If no organic matter was added prior to the planting season, work in a 4-inch layer of well-rotted manure or compost before planting. Poor soils will produce edible lettuce, but top quality demands the extra effort of improving the soil. Soil pH should be 6.0 to 6.8.

Propagation: Too often gardeners practice a feast-or-famine program, which leaves gaps in the season when lettuce could be growing, but isn't. For a continuous harvest throughout the growing season, adapt the following planting schedule to meet your needs and climate.

Start lettuce indoors four to six weeks before the setting-out date, which is anywhere from six weeks before to three weeks after the frost-free date. Set out only when night temperatures remain above 25°F. In conventional rows and growing beds, space leaf lettuce 9 inches apart and head lettuce (cos, crisphead, and butterhead) 12 inches apart. Space conventional rows 14 inches apart.

At the same time that transplants are put out in the garden, make a fresh sowing of seed directly in the soil. (The soil must be at least 35°F for seed to germinate.) Sow ¼ inch deep and distribute the seeds thinly—about one every 2 inches in rows and beds. Wide-row plantings may also be used.

Every three weeks sow another short row (4 feet or less) or section of a bed. As temperatures increase, switch to bolt-resistant lettuce and plant ½ inch deep in fine soil. Shade the seedbed in hot weather to prevent the soil from crusting. For soil that has a tendency to crust over, put ¼ inch of finely sifted compost over seeds sown at a depth of ¼ inch—making the total depth ½ inch. Row and bed spacings remain the same as given above.

About eight weeks before the first expected frost, go back to using cool-weather lettuce types for fall harvests. Stick to short rows or small sections of bed planted every three weeks in preference to larger areas planted less frequently. This method gives a steady supply of lettuce without sudden gluts of produce.

In mild-winter areas, start succession planting in early fall, and continue planting and harvesting through late fall, winter, and

Lettuce

Variety Name	Average Days to Maturity	General Description and Comments
Crisphead		
Great Lakes	95–100	Fringed, medium green, glistening leaves; large, shiny heads up to 6 in.; resists warm weather better than others of its type; good for early summer sowings; AAS.
Ithaca	72–85	Medium green heads about 5 in. in diameter; leaves are glossy and frilled; disease- and heat-resistant; slow to bolt.
Romaine		
Parris Island	75	Dark green, upright leaves; uniform and vigorous; 10 in. tall; mild flavor.
Paris White Cos (also Valmain)	85	Medium green leaves with prominent crisp midribs; does not do well in hot weather; 10 in. tall; sweet flavor.
Loose-Leaf		
Black-Seeded Simpson	45	Light green, frilly leaves; quick-growing and dependable; 9 in. tall, 9 in. wide; good for spring sowings.
Grand Rapids	45	Leaves bright green with deeply cut margins, wavy and frilled; long-standing; disease- and heat-resistant; 9 in. tall, 9 in. wide; good for spring sowings.
Oakleaf	50	Light green, oak-leaf-shaped leaves; small, compact plants resist summer heat and tip burn; suited for early summer sowings; 8 in. tall, 7 in. wide; long-standing.
Salad Bowl	45	Light green, deeply lobed leaves; slow to bolt; 7 in. tall, 9 in. wide; good for early summer sowings; AAS.
Slobolt	45	Bright green leaves are crumpled; resists bolting in summer better than any other lettuce in this group, and especially recommended for early summer sowings; 8 in. tall, 9 in. wide.
Ruby	53	Green leaves shaded with dark red; heat-resistant; 8 in. tall, 7 in. wide; AAS.
Butterhead		
Big Boston	75	Medium green leaves with rippled edges; needs cool conditions to head up well; the largest of this type; 10 in. tall, 11 in. wide.
Buttercrunch	75	Dark green, soft leaves, heads are denser and heavier than other butterhead types; larger than Bibb and somewhat more heat-resistant; 8 in. tall, 9 in. wide; AAS.
Summer Bibb	62	Medium green, soft leaves; extremely heat-resistant for this type; 6 in. tall, 7 in. wide.

in spring. Unused seed is good for five years.

Culture: When lettuce seedlings become 3 to 4 inches tall, thin back the rows and beds to the spacing recommended above for transplants. Remove the lettuce thinnings, root and all, for transplanting to another small area. The transplants will be two weeks behind the ones allowed to remain in the row or bed. Thinnings are also good for the table and make the most delicate of salads. Keep rows and beds moist but not soggy. As the ground becomes warm and the temperature rises, use a mulch to help conserve moisture and give fertility to the soil. In place of this fortifying mulch, on soils which may be deficient in nutrients, apply manure tea about three weeks before harvest to gain good leaf development. If the plants are overcrowded and the soil is very wet, lower leaves may start to rot. To counteract this, spread a layer of sand or a thick layer of straw around the plant base.

Pests and Diseases: Cutworms and flea beetles are the bane of young plants. Aphids, cabbage loopers, leafminers, slugs, and snails all attack lettuce.

Harvest and Storage: Crisphead, cos, and butterhead lettuce are harvested when heads are firm and mature. Cut off the whole top at the root crown. For loose-leaf varieties, cut the outer leaves one by one when large enough to be of use, and allow the inner leaves to develop. All lettuces are at their best when picked as needed and used at once. If the harvest is more than can be used immediately, refrigerate it. Crisphead lettuce can be stored up to three weeks; romaine and loose-leaf lettuces can be stored up to two weeks without losing quality; butterhead lettuce, which is the most fragile, shows signs of deterioration after only a few days of refrigeration.

LUFFA

Dishcloth gourd, loofa, towel gourd, vegetable sponge
Luffa aegyptiaca and *L. acutangula*
Cucurbitaceae

The unusual luffa must be the most versatile of all vegetables. The young fruits are delicious and may be used as zucchini, either cooked or sliced raw for salads. Slices are also delicious when sun-dried. The leaves make a lovely addition to salads as well, and the yellow blossoms can be batter-fried for an unusual delicacy. Left to mature on the vine, the fruits reach a length of 1 to 2 feet and then can be used as bath sponges or pot scrubbers. The sponges do not hold water well, but are valued for their scrubbing ability as they remove loose tissue and bring a healthy glow to the skin, abrade food particles from cooking pots, or scour vegetables.

The luffa is no more difficult to grow than summer squash or cucumbers, although it must be given sufficient time to develop for sponge use. Since the vines are natural climbers and can grow from 10 to 15 feet long, luffa is a natural for a vertical garden. Its lush, viny growth and large yellow flowers make it a particularly attractive, as well as useful, natural screen. The yield from plants grown with support can be two or three times the yield from plants allowed to sprawl along the ground.

Growing Range: Luffa requires a long, hot summer for best development, with average temperatures between 65° and 75°F. The minimum length of growing season is 100 frost-free days, and the progress of the plant will be helped by long, sunny periods. However, even in short-season areas, the plants can be grown for culinary use (since the fruits can be picked while quite immature) and for use as small bath sponges. Luffa is very sensitive to cold and highly susceptible to frost damage.

Soil Preparation: Luffa will do well in any soil that supports cucumbers or summer squash. It should be light, moist, and rich in humus for large and quick-developing fruit. Do not add extra nitrogen, since an excess will promote leaf development and result in fewer and smaller fruits. The pH range is 6 to 8.

Propagation: Gardeners in long-season areas may sow seeds directly into the garden, at least one week after the frost-free date. In northern, short-season areas, start seeds indoors, four to six weeks before transplanting time. Seedlings may be set out one week after the frost-free date, and should be at least 3 inches tall when transplanted. The seeds are slow to germinate and should be soaked or presprouted. Indoors or out, germination time is about two weeks. The optimum soil temperature for germination is 70° to 95°F.

Like squash, luffa can be planted in hills. Sow seed ½ inch deep, with three to six seeds per hill, the hills spaced 6 feet apart. Set two seedlings in every hill. The seeds and seedlings may also be planted in rows along fences, trellises, or other supports, where the plants are spaced a foot apart.

Culture: Thin hills to the two sturdiest seedlings. The soil must never be allowed to dry out. A mulch helps conserve soil moisture and is especially recommended when the vines are allowed to trail on the ground, since it offers a clean bed for the developing fruit. Side-dress plants with aged compost or water with manure tea when the first blossoms have appeared. If the vines are to be grown vertically, start to train them as soon as possible. Young vines may need some help clinging to the support, so attach them gently with soft cloth or twine. As the plants mature, the vines develop tendrils and need no further assistance.

To encourage branching which promotes a bigger crop of fruit, pinch off the growing tips of the vines when they reach 10 feet long.

Pests and Diseases: Neither are a great problem with garden-grown luffas, although the plants are sometimes subject to the same insects and diseases that attack cucumbers and summer squash (see Cucumber and Squash).

Harvest and Storage: The young fruits may be used for culinary purposes when they have reached 4 to 5 inches in length. Fruits that grow much longer become stringy and inedible. Don't delay your harvest, for the fruit can grow as much as 1½ inches a day. Leaves may be picked anytime for use in salads, although the young leaves are more tender. Blossoms may be picked at full size. Seeds of mature fruit may be eaten, too, when they are roasted like pumpkin seeds (see Pumpkin).

When grown for sponges, the time to harvest depends on how the sponges will be used. The inside of the fruit is composed of fine strands of cellulose. Like the cellulose in a tree, it becomes tougher as the fruit grows larger. Therefore, for a soft sponge—such as one used for facials—the fruits should be picked while young, 7 to 8 inches long. Luffas of slightly larger size make good back scrubbers, and fully mature fruits (around 18 to 24 inches long) make the toughest sponges, suitable for heavy jobs such as pot scrubbing. The fruit has reached full maturity when the stem and skin have yellowed. Once it has reached the desired length, cut the fruit from the vine and let it dry in a sunny window for two weeks, turning it occasionally. Then cut off both ends and shake out the seeds (which can be roasted or saved for next year's crop). Soak the fruit in water overnight before peeling the outer skin away. The skin of older fruit is the easiest to remove. For younger fruit, a ten-minute bath in boiling water will aid in loosening the skin, and will also make the sponge softer and more pliable. After the fruit is peeled, wash out the sponge thoroughly, removing any remaining seeds and loose tissue, cut it into conveniently sized pieces, and let them dry slowly in a shady place. The sponge color can be lightened by soaking it in a weak solution of household bleach for half an hour.

Luffa

Variety Name	Average Days to Maturity	General Description and Comments
Sing-kwa (*L. acutangula*)	120	Ridged fruit grows to 1 ft. long; is cucumber-shaped and dark green in color.
Sze-kwa (*L. aegyptiaca*)	120	Large, smooth-skinned, light green fruit measures up to 2 ft. long; the more popular variety, for it makes better sponges.

MALABAR SPINACH

Basella, Ceylon spinach, climbing spinach,
  Malabar nightshade
Basella alba and *B. alba* 'Rubra'
Basellaceae

Malabar spinach is a vining plant with thick, succulent, edible leaves, and it can grow to 3 feet when given support to climb on.

Malabar spinach is extremely nutritious, with significant amounts of protein, calcium, and iron. It has large amounts of vitamin A, some vitamin C, and a good dose of vitamin B_1.

The advantage of growing Malabar spinach, besides for its high nutritional value, is that it can tolerate extremes of heat and thus can grow in areas too warm for spinach. The disadvantage is that it cannot tolerate cold. In northern climates some gardeners have successfully raised it indoors as a potted plant kept near a stove or a heater.

One characteristic of Malabar spinach to note is that it is sensitive to the photoperiod, or amount of daylight and darkness it receives. It requires short days to promote good leaf growth, and should it receive too much daylight, it will begin to flower and leaf production will decline. This problem can be avoided by having the plant mature before or after the long days of midsummer when it will go to seed.

Malabar spinach may be compared to spinach, but it does not taste like spinach. Malabar spinach has a raw, succulent taste, and its consistency tends to be mucilaginous like okra.

Malabar spinach makes a nice addition to a tossed salad and can also be combined with other greens for a steamed vegetable dish. Prepare Malabar spinach in the same way spinach and Swiss chard are prepared.

Growing Range: Malabar spinach is a distinctly tropical perennial plant which is successfully grown in the temperate zones as an annual. It is a short-season plant that is extremely sensitive to cold and does not tolerate frosts. Gardeners in northern latitudes can grow it successfully in containers, bringing the plant into a protected place when cold sets in. In warmer regions, Malabar spinach responds well to heat and humidity.

Soil Preparation: Malabar spinach requires highly fertile soil that retains moisture. To provide the richest soil possible, manure the ground heavily in the fall. At the same time, add ½ cup of a phosphorus fertilizer like phosphate rock per plant and an equal amount of a potassium fertilizer like greensand. Adjust the soil to a pH of 6.0 to 6.7.

In a container, mix equal parts rich compost, well-rotted manure, and friable garden soil. Add a bit of blood meal and phosphate rock and provide good drainage.

Propagation: Malabar spinach can be direct-seeded in the garden at least one week after the frost-free date, when the soil is thoroughly warm. Sow seeds 1 inch deep in conventional rows with 4-inch spacings between seeds, and 24 to 36 inches between rows. Keep growing medium moist for as long as three weeks before giving up on germination.

In northern climates the seed may take a

Malabar Spinach

Variety Name	Average Days to Maturity	General Description and Comments
Red Malabar Spinach	70	A loose vine or, with pinching out, a compact bush; grows to 3 ft. tall and 2 ft. in circumference; round leaves are a glossy dark green; leaves and stems are tinted with dark red.
White Malabar Spinach	70	Growth and size is similar to the white variety; leaves are oval-shaped instead of round; considered to be the superior type.

very long time to germinate, and cool night temperatures below an average of 60°F will keep the seeds from germinating. Presoaking the seeds should speed up germination. In these areas, better luck can be had by starting seed indoors, eight to ten weeks before the frost-free date, and then transplanting when all danger of frost is past and the soil has warmed up thoroughly. Set seedlings every 12 inches in rows, using between-row spacing given above.

Rooted stem cuttings are the most rapid means of reproducing the plants.

Culture: When the seedlings have developed several sets of leaves, thin to 12 inches apart. Provide a vertical support for each plant to climb on. Malabar spinach commonly grows as high as 3 feet, and in rich soil with adequate warmth and moisture it may exceed that. Mulching is the most effective way to keep the plant's roots moist.

Pests and Diseases: Malabar spinach is free of problems in the temperate zones. A fungus (*Cercospora beticola*) sometimes causes red spots and holes on the leaves. Remove and destroy all spotted leaves at once to keep disease from spreading.

Harvest and Storage: Begin to harvest when the plant has developed many leaves and has begun to branch. Avoid the older, tougher leaves and harvest only the tender, young ones by cutting the leaves from the vines. Cutting from the growing tips will result in bushier plants. After the Malabar spinach is three months old, it should have a few leaves cropped every week even if they are not going to be used for the table, since a certain amount of cropping stimulates the plant to produce new leaves.

MUSHROOM

Agaricus bisporus, Lentinus edodes
Agaricaceae

Mushrooms are the only form of fungi commonly used as human food. *Agaricus bisporus*, the common button mushroom, is popular both in Europe and in North America, where it is ubiquitous in supermarkets and grocery stores. *Lentinus edodes*, the shiitake or Black Forest mushroom, is virtually a food staple in Japan, but at the present time is little more than a novelty in the Western countries.

Mushrooms have long been regarded as a delicacy. They are sautéed in butter and served as a complement to many dinners, added to soups and stews, or eaten raw in salads. The shiitake is a popular ingredient of many oriental recipes, and has a hearty flavor all its own. Mushrooms are good sources of phosphorus, iron, vitamins B_1, B_2, and B_3. Button mushrooms are a good source of vitamin C, and shiitake is high in vitamin D. Button mushrooms have approximately 43 percent more protein than shiitake.

Because mushrooms grow without light, they are in a class by themselves as a garden crop. They may be grown anywhere, so long as they are given proper humidity, temperature, and light, and a suitable growing medium. They are not as easy to grow as most garden vegetables; even when conditions are met, there are sometimes inexplicable crop failures. Nevertheless, an increasing number of gardeners—even those without gardens—find mushroom raising a challenging and rewarding endeavor, especially during winter when outdoor gardening comes to a halt.

Growing Range: Mushrooms may be grown anywhere, indoors or out, where temperatures may be maintained between 55° and 70°F and the humidity is controlled at 80 to 85 percent. Mushrooms cannot be raised successfully in dry air.

Growing Medium: The cultivation methods for button mushrooms and shiitake are completely different. Buttons are raised by implanting spawn, usually in a mixture of compost and manure and shredded straw or hay. Shiitake, a native of oriental mountain forests, are raised on logs of oak, maple, cherry, poplar, or persimmon trees to which the mushroom spores have been added.

The easiest method of raising either type—and the one recommended for first-time growers—is to purchase a preinoculated kit. The kits are offered only during the cooler times of the year.

All mushrooms, since they cannot manufacture their own food in the presence of light, depend on the stored energy of partially decayed organic matter. Most commercial and amateur growers depend on a carefully prepared compost based on manure as the key to successful button mushroom production.

Horse manure is considered the ideal manure, and poultry or pig manure are also suitable, but cow manure should not be used, since it is too low in nitrogen and produces a slimy compost not suited to mushroom raising. (Those who gather manure should avoid veterinarians' stables, where the manure might be sprayed with disinfectants which can retard biological activity in the heap.) If the compost is being made especially for mushroom raising, it should be started five weeks before it is to be used, which is enough time for it to compost thoroughly, but not completely. (It should still have some biological activity and warmth when inoculated with the spawn.) The compost heap should be constructed on a concrete floor, to prevent insects from invading it from the bottom and laying eggs, and under cover to prevent rains from soaking the heap and washing away nutrients. A covered shed is an ideal location, if it can be screened to keep out insects.

If the manure has been mixed in the stable with a good amount of straw bedding, then no extra straw is required. If not, then plan to use equal parts of hay (or straw) and manure. Shred the hay and soak it before mixing it with the manure for composting.

Gypsum is an essential ingredient, for it makes the growing medium alkaline and ensures a crumbly texture to the final compost. Sprinkle the gypsum over each layer of manure as it is added to the heap. The recommended amount is 2 pounds of gypsum to 100 pounds of compost. In order to kill all disease organisms and insect eggs, be sure that the temperature in the center of the heap reaches 160°F. Turn the compost every five or six days so that every portion takes its turn in the hot inner part of the heap. Watch moisture carefully, keeping the heap moist but not soggy. When the compost is brown, loose, and crumbly, and still warm but no longer hot, it is ready to be used for button mushroom raising.

Propagation: This step is called spawning, which is simply the mixing of the spawn (available from commercial suppliers) with the growing medium. Wooden trays should be constructed, 10 to 12 inches deep and any width and length desired. They should be held together with screws, to resist warping, and placed in a dim or dark location where the temperature is between 55° and 65°F. The trays may be stacked, allowing enough space between them to enable working with the mushrooms. Drill small holes in the bottoms of the trays for aeration, and raise the lowest tray of each stack off the floor to allow for air circulation. Each square foot of growing area should produce 2 pounds of mushrooms.

Fill each tray with the growing medium, packing it fairly firmly so that it comes to within 2 inches of the top. Then mix in dry, flake spawn, using 1 quart of spawn for each 15 square feet of growing space, or according to the supplier's directions. If possible, increase the temperature to 65°F at this point.

Culture: Mist the surface of the growing medium daily to keep it moist but never soggy. Within three weeks, a cottony web will appear over the surface. This is the mycelium of the mushroom, which is the parent of the fruits that will appear later. When it has fairly well covered the surface, add a 1-inch layer of moist topsoil or peat. This covering is called the casing, and no mushrooms will be produced without it. If possible, lower the temperature at this stage to 55° to 50°F. Higher temperatures will produce quicker crops but increase chances of disease and spoilage; lower temperatures prolong the harvest period.

The next stage is a critical one, since the casing must be kept constantly moist, but not so wet that water drips down to the mycelium and drowns it. Immediately after casing, put several layers of newspaper over the surface, then mist the newspaper daily to keep it moist.

After ten days, remove the newspaper and mist the casing every day, again just keeping it from drying out. Within a week, white pinheads will appear which will grow into mushrooms.

Pests and Diseases: Insect larvae and competing molds are the major problems. Most can be eliminated by careful composting and clean cultivation. If mushrooms are raised in a barn or outbuilding, be sure that all windows and doors are tightly screened to keep out insects. Slugs are voracious consumers of mushrooms. In the home, serious diseases may be avoided by growing the crop not all in one place, but in several places around the basement, so that a disease that might occur in one location does not spread to the others.

Harvest and Storage: Mushrooms are produced in flushes, which are sudden appearances of substantial numbers of heads. Flushes appear once every 10 to 12 days, for as long as the nutrients in the growing medium can support them, usually three to six months. After flushes stop appearing, the growing medium is exhausted and it may be added to the outdoor compost pile. This compost is "spent" only for purposes of mushroom growing; it is a very high-quality soil addition for outdoor crops.

Button mushrooms may be picked while small for use in salads, and are sometimes pickled at this stage. If allowed to grow larger so that their caps open and their light purple gills are exposed, they attain a full and rich flavor that enhances soups, stews, and sauces.

Pick mushrooms by grasping the stem near the growing medium surface and gently twisting it. After harvesting a flush, cut away any remaining stumps to a point slightly below the surface to prevent disease. Mushroom growers call this "trashing."

Mushrooms are easily frozen, canned, pickled, or dried.

Varieties: There is no choice of varieties among shiitake or button mushrooms.

MUSTARD

Mustard greens
Brassica juncea
Cruciferae

Mustard deserves to be more popular than it is, for besides being quick to mature, it is rich in vitamins and minerals. A 100-gram serving supplies 91 percent of the vitamin A and 74 percent of the vitamin C recommended as the minimum daily requirement for an average adult. Mustard is also rich in calcium, and contains lesser amounts of iron, phosphorus, and B vitamins.

There are basically three types of mustard, grouped by leaf appearance: curly-leaf, smooth-leaf, and broad-leaf with prominent white stems. The first two types come from India and the white-stemmed type comes from China and Japan. This oriental type is also referred to as Chinese mustard cabbage, bok choy, or pak choi. Although botanically it is more a mustard than a cabbage, it is discussed under Chinese cabbage along with other oriental brassicas which share the same culture.

All mustard greens can be used in the many, varied ways that lettuce, Swiss chard, spinach and beet greens are used. The curly-leaf mustard dresses up salads nicely with its crisp-looking leaves, and it can also be used as a potherb. The smooth-leaf mustard is easier to clean since its leaves do not trap dirt and sand as the curly-leaf varieties do. It can be eaten raw but is usually cooked by steaming or sautéing.

Growing Range: Mustard is a cool-season crop that will bolt and develop fiery, peppery-flavored leaves in warm weather. It will grow in any region that provides a cool growing season, with average temperatures around 60° to 65°F. Mustard is a half-hardy crop that can resist drops in temperature, especially if they occur over a period of time. Its flavor is improved by mild frosts.

Soil Preparation: Mustard will grow on a wide range of soils, and will even tolerate heavy clay soils. But for the best-quality leaves, provide a moist, rich soil. Prepare and fertilize the soil in the same way as for lettuce crops. Mustard will tolerate a moderately acid soil, with a pH range of 5.5 to 6.8.

Propagation: Mustard can be started from seed sown directly in the garden or from transplants. In northern gardens, seed can be sown in early spring, two to four weeks before the frost-free date, with successive sowings made every 10 to 14 days until temperatures get too warm. Sow again about eight weeks before the first expected frost for a fall crop. Although mustard can be grown at both ends of the season, it is far better as a fall crop. In areas where the ground does not freeze mustard can be planted successively as a winter crop, every 10 to 14 days. Minimum soil temperature for germination is 45°F. Sow seed ¼ inch deep. Scatter seed thickly in raised beds and in conventional rows spaced 18 inches apart. Unused seed is good for four years.

Start seeds indoors four to six weeks before setting out, which can be done from five weeks before to two weeks after the frost-free date. Space seedlings every 9 inches along rows, and use 9-inch spacings in raised beds.

Culture: After the direct-sown mustard seedlings reach 6 inches tall, thin to allow 9 inches between plants in rows and in growing beds. Use the thinnings in salads, sandwiches, and as garnishes. No additional fertilizer should be necessary if they are growing in rich soil. If grown on poor soil, fertilize midseason with a high-nitrogen side-dressing of manure, or water with manure or compost tea every three weeks. Mulching will keep the roots cool and moist and keep the plants from bolting to seed. Mustard plants which have been allowed to dry out or suffer from a lack of nutrients will be very hot to the taste. Remove any flowers as they appear, since flowering causes the leaves to taste bitter and become tough. Also, if the seed heads are allowed to develop and the seeds scatter, mustard plants can spread throughout the garden area and become a pest.

Pests and Diseases: Flea beetles may cause holes in young leaves. Aphids, cabbage maggots, imported cabbage worms, and whiteflies can also be problems.

Harvest and Storage: The whole plant can be cut at once or individual outer leaves can be picked over a period of time for a cut-and-come-again harvest. The best-flavored leaves are those that are 4 to 5 inches long. The older leaves taste better when prepared as cooked greens, rather than used fresh in salads. Mustard can be frozen and canned in the same manner as spinach.

Mustard

Variety Name	Average Days to Maturity	General Description and Comments
Fordhook Fancy	40	A curly-leaf type; feathery, bright green leaves have milder flavor than other mustards; plant is slow to bolt; grows 18 in. tall, 12 in. wide.
Green Wave	40–50	A curly-leaf type; bolt-resistant; bright green leaves are finely curled and ruffled; grows 12 in. tall, 10 in. wide; AAS.
Florida Broadleaf	40–50	A smooth-leaf type; broad, succulent leaves have a tender rib; large vigorous plants grow to 3 ft. tall, 20 in. wide.
Tender Green (also Mustard Spinach)	30–40	Botanically classified as *B. rapa*, Pervidis Group; a smooth-leaved plant that resists bolting, it is more heat-resistant than other mustards; distinctive flavor is a cross between spinach and mustard; light green leaves have a prominent white midrib; grows to 30 in. tall and 6 in. wide.

NEW ZEALAND SPINACH

Tetragonia expansa
Aizoaceae

New Zealand spinach is not related to spinach, although the leaves are slightly similar in appearance and some people find the taste of cooked leaves to be slightly reminiscent of spinach. Whether that opinion is shared or not, it is fair to say that New Zealand spinach is at least as good as spinach, with a clean, rich, green taste all its own.

New Zealand spinach is nutritious, supplying substantial amounts of iron, and vitamins A and C. Although not as nutritious as spinach, New Zealand spinach remains among those vegetables that have excellent food value.

New Zealand spinach is offered by seedsmen as a hot-weather spinach, because unlike true spinach and many other greens, it develops best in warm weather and declines when cool weather comes. Also, it produces over a longer season than spinach and other greens. It is a low and spreading plant that can measure to 4 feet across unless pinched back to make it more compact.

Growing Range: New Zealand spinach should be planted in a region that has at least three months of frost-free weather. The average temperature range for best growth is 60° to 75°F. It does not do well in extreme heat, and this tender plant is damaged by frost.

Soil Preparation: New Zealand spinach is not fussy about soil, but a well-manured, humus-rich growing medium will promote the healthiest plants, the quickest growth, and the best taste. New Zealand spinach is only slightly tolerant of acid soils, preferring a pH of 6.5 to 7.0.

Propagation: New Zealand spinach can be started by seed or by transplant in late spring or summer. Rub each seed with a file or sandpaper to weaken a spot on the seed so that it will germinate more easily. Or pour boiling water over seeds and let them soak for 24 hours. Gardeners in cool regions should start seed indoors four to six weeks before the frost-free date. Put three seeds down in each spot in which a plant is to grow, and cover with 1 inch of soil. For conventional rows, leave 12 inches between seeds or seedlings and 3 feet between rows. Spacing in raised beds is 12 inches. The sprawling habit of New Zealand spinach makes it suitable for planting in hills, like those in which melons and squash are cultivated. Plant five seeds per hill, and space hills 4 feet apart. Unused seed is good for five years.

Culture: Pinch out the weaker seedlings when they are 2 inches tall, and leave a 12-inch space between the sturdiest seedlings in the rows. Thin hills to leave the three strongest seedlings. Keep weeds cleared from around seedlings until they are established and have formed their own living mulch with branches and leaves. To help this mulch develop, pinch out the growing tips to promote bushy growth, as soon as the plants are 1 foot tall. Later in the season, even when leaves are not needed for the kitchen, nip out the ends of the sprawling plants. The roots must stay cool and moist, so water adequately in warm weather.

Pests and Diseases: New Zealand spinach is seldom bothered.

Harvest and Storage: Cut 3- to 4-inch lengths from the tender growing tips, and use only the young, succulent leaves. New Zealand spinach is a welcome cut-and-come-again plant during the warmer months when most other greens are flagging. It must be pinched back constantly to keep the leaves from getting too old and inedible. New Zealand spinach will produce large amounts of harvestable leaves until the first cold weather. With frost the plants will die back and seeds can be taken from the hard pods that developed after the flowers faded for next year's planting. New Zealand spinach can be used raw in salads or cooked, either alone or with other greens. For those who are unused to the taste, mix them at first with other salad or cooked greens. The leaves may be frozen.

Varieties: There is no variation among seed offered by seedsmen.

OKRA

Lady's finger
Abelmoschus esculentus
Malvaceae

Okra is one of the oldest of cultivated food crops. The edible portion of the plant is the long, pointed seed pod, which is best picked when green and used as a vegetable dish, often rolled in cornmeal and fried, or added to soups, stews, casseroles, and curries. Okra is also a major ingredient of gumbo, a very popular Creole dish. The mucilaginous texture of the pods often comes as a surprise to first-time okra eaters, but it is valued as a thickener for gumbos, soups, stews, and catsup. An easy way to avoid releasing the mucilaginous material from the pods is to cook them with their caps on. This crop is a good source of calcium and fiber, and also offers some vitamin A.

Okra is not difficult to grow, given the proper conditions. It is a good succession plant, following early spring crops. It is a good yielder in the garden, producing pods over a long period of time. Standard-sized plants grow to a height of 4 to 7 feet, and dwarf strains measure 2 to 4 feet tall. The red and yellow blossoms are very attractive, resembling ornamental hibiscus, and they add a bright spot of color to punctuate the predominant green of the garden.

Growing Range: Okra is a warm-weather crop, growing best when average temperatures are between 70° and 85°F. However, since it matures so quickly (first harvest is two months from seeding), it may be grown in any area that offers ten weeks of warm and sunny weather. The plants do poorly in cool, damp, or cloudy regions. Okra is very susceptible to frost damage.

Soil Preparation: Any soil that is well drained and rich in nutrients will support okra. The recommended pH range is 6 to 8. In spring, after the last frost, till the soil to a depth of 8 inches and incorporate copious amounts of well-aged compost or well-rotted manure. If okra follows early peas, it will make good use of the nitrogen stored in the soil by the pea nodules.

Propagation: Okra is direct-seeded on the frost-free date only after the soil temperature has reached 60°F. In very short-season regions, plants may be started indoors six to eight weeks before transplanting time, which is three to four weeks after the frost-free date. Use individual containers for transplants so roots are not disturbed. Set seedlings every 14 inches in

Okra

Variety Name	Average Days to Maturity	General Description and Comments
Dwarf Green Long Pod	50	Dwarf plants grow 2–2½ ft. tall; pods are 7 in. long; an early, high yielder.
Clemson Spineless	55–60	The most popular of all okra varieties; plants are 4–5 ft. tall; pods measure 7–9 in. long; recommended for short-season gardens as well as hot-summer areas; AAS.
Emerald Green Velvet	55	A popular variety and a prolific yielder; plants grow 6–7 ft. tall; pods are 7–9 in. long; recommended for short-season gardens, but also suitable for other areas.

rows for tall varieties, and every 10 inches for dwarf varieties. For between-row and raised bed spacings, see below.

Soak seed overnight to hasten germination, both indoors and out. Space conventional rows 48 to 72 inches apart for large varieties, 24 to 48 inches for dwarf varieties. Sow seed every 3 inches in rows. Growing bed spacing is 18 inches. Set seed ½ inch deep in heavy soils, 1 inch deep in lighter soils. Unused seed is good for five years.

Culture: After the seedlings are 3 inches high, thin tall varieties to stand 14 inches apart in rows, or 10 inches for dwarf varieties. Okra is a heavy feeder and a quick grower, so give it nitrogen-rich supplementary feedings. Side-dress with manure or compost, or water with solutions of fish emulsion or manure tea every three weeks.

Plants should be mulched to a depth of 4 inches; if compost is put on top of a hay mulch, the compost will act as a long-lasting top-dressing, and no nutrient-rich watering or side-dressing is needed. If no mulch is used, keep the soil loose by frequent cultivation. Water plants only if the soil becomes very dry. To contain rampant growth, prune a few branches and leaves below each pod you have harvested.

Pests and Diseases: Okra may be attacked by corn earworms, green stinkbugs, and imported cabbage worms. In hot-summer regions, Southern blight may be a problem.

Harvest and Storage: Pods begin to form in about two months. For use as a green vegetable, pick them when they are no more than 2 to 3 inches long and still soft. They will reach this stage in only five days after the flowers fade. If pods are allowed to grow much longer, they become fibrous and unfit for green use, and if they are allowed to mature on the plant, no more young pods will be produced. For a continuous harvest up until frost, pick pods at least every third day. Cut the pods from the branches rather than tug at them to avoid disturbing the roots.

Some people are quite sensitive to contact with okra plants. To avoid the burning itch, wear a long-sleeved shirt and gloves. Waiting until the dew has dried completely can also make picking painless.

Okra is best when used immediately after harvesting. If fresh pods will be held for more than a day before being used, sprinkle them lightly with water and spread in a single layer in a cool place. When stored in a closed container, fresh pods tend to generate heat.

ONIONS AND SCALLIONS

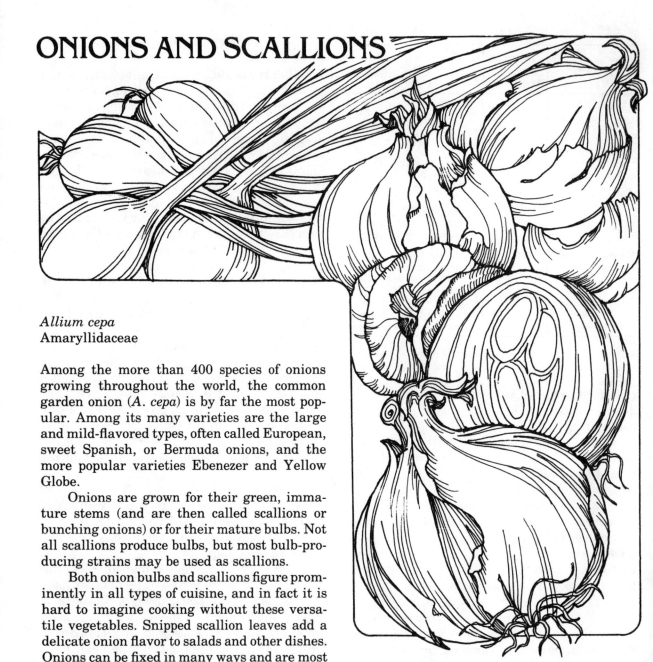

Allium cepa
Amaryllidaceae

Among the more than 400 species of onions growing throughout the world, the common garden onion (*A. cepa*) is by far the most popular. Among its many varieties are the large and mild-flavored types, often called European, sweet Spanish, or Bermuda onions, and the more popular varieties Ebenezer and Yellow Globe.

Onions are grown for their green, immature stems (and are then called scallions or bunching onions) or for their mature bulbs. Not all scallions produce bulbs, but most bulb-producing strains may be used as scallions.

Both onion bulbs and scallions figure prominently in all types of cuisine, and in fact it is hard to imagine cooking without these versatile vegetables. Snipped scallion leaves add a delicate onion flavor to salads and other dishes. Onions can be fixed in many ways and are most commonly fried, sautéed, or boiled.

The small, pungent varieties will easily keep through the winter if stored in a cool and dry location, but the large sweet Spanish types are not good keepers and are usually eaten fresh throughout the growing season. Many gardeners plant several different varieties for use as spring scallions, mid- and late-season fresh onions, and for winter storage. Generally, the strongest-tasting onions are the best keepers, because they usually have the toughest skins.

A common sight in springtime are onion sets for sale. These sets are small, dormant bulbs that have been grown from seed, harvested, and then stored over the winter. They are planted out the following spring, and can be grown for bunching onions or for mature bulbs. Onion sets mature sooner than onions sown from seed, which gives the gardener in a short-season area a head start, ensuring that the crop will have adequate time to mature and ripen. Many gardeners feel that onions are easier to grow from sets than from seed, and plants grown from sets seem to be bothered less by onion maggots and weed growth.

Onions are suitable both for succession planting (in which they may be used as either an early or midseason crop) and for interplanting. Because their top growth is so slender, they can be worked in among most other plantings, in otherwise unused corners of the garden, or interplanted with ornamentals. They are good container-garden crops, and may even be used in windowboxes.

Growing Range: Onions are easy to grow in all regions. They generally prefer cool weather (55° to 75°F), especially in the early stages when they are making top growth. Warmer temperatures at the end of the season are beneficial for bulb development. The large Bermuda and sweet Spanish types are best suited to warm climates, although they may be grown to good size in northern areas where the summers are warm. The small, pungent types grow better in cool climates.

When selecting varieties, note the day-length requirement. Short-day varieties form bulbs when they receive at least 12 hours of light each day, and are suited for mild-winter areas where they will grow through fall and winter. Long-day onions require 13 to 16 hours of light per day in order to form bulbs, and are generally grown in northern gardens where summer days are long.

Onions grown from seed sown outdoors need 90 to 130 days to mature. In short-season areas, the time may be reduced by using sets or transplants started indoors. Onions are not sensitive to mild frost, in either spring or fall.

Soil Preparation: Any soil that is well drained, well limed, and rich in organic matter can support good onion crops. Sandy loams will produce good early onions planted from sets. Average loams (neither clayey nor sandy) will produce good onions of any kind, and muck soils have traditionally been used for the commercial production of sets and seedlings. Very heavy soils will impede the bulb's expansion and should have large amounts of organic matter worked in for good yields of well-developed bulbs. In soils with questionable drainage, use raised beds. For an especially fertile growing base, work in a mixture of five parts compost or well-rotted manure, one part wood ashes, and one part bone meal. The recommended pH range is 6.0 to 6.5. Prepare the planting bed finely so that no soil clods or rocks remain.

Propagation: Onions are started in the garden from seed, seedlings, or sets, depending on the variety and the climate in which they are grown. All onions may be grown from seed if there are enough growing days in the season. They may be sown directly in the garden four to six weeks before the frost-free date, as soon as the soil is workable. In mild climates, sow seed in fall to yield early spring scallions. Onion seed can be sown as closely as ¼ inch apart in conventional rows and wide rows, to be thinned later. Space the conventional rows 12 to 18 inches apart. In raised beds, allow 3 to 4 inches between seeds. Cover seeds with ½ inch of soil or screened compost and tamp it down firmly. Some gardeners include a little radish seed with the onion seed. The early-germinating radishes serve as markers for the slower onion seed, and are harvested before the onion plants need room to expand. They also act as a trap crop for onion root maggots. Unused seed is good for one to two years.

To get a head start on the season, start seeds indoors four to six weeks before setting out. Bermuda and sweet Spanish types in particular are started in the garden as seedlings,

Onions and Scallions

The following listings are only representative of the dozens of varieties to be found in seed catalogs. The gardener who grows onions from seed will have the widest choice, since only a few common varieties are offered as sets or seedlings.

Variety Name	Average Days to Maturity	General Description and Comments
Crystal Wax (also Eclipse)	95	An old favorite with a mild flavor; a Bermuda type which seldom bolts; short-day variety that does well in warm-climate areas.
Excel 986	180	Yellow Bermuda type with mild, firm flesh; early-maturing and very popular; keeps longer than most of this type; a short-day variety suited for warm-climate areas.
Red Bermuda	93	Large, flat bulbs have red skins and appear early; a good slicing onion; mild flavor and crisp texture; a short-day variety well suited for warm-climate areas.
Yellow Globe	98–112	Several strains have been developed from this variety; medium-sized bulbs with good flavor; good keepers and an all-purpose kitchen onion; long-day variety suited for cool-climate areas.
Autumn Spice	92	Hybrid with pungent, firm flesh; a good keeper; suitable for deep muck soils; bulbs are medium-sized and globe-shaped; long-day variety recommended for cool-climate areas.
White Portugal (also Silverskin)	100	A versatile onion, suitable for both scallions and mature bulbs, which are flat-shaped; stores well; short-day variety.
Ebenezer	105	One of the most popular varieties, a favorite for planting from sets; fairly large, flat bulbs at maturity; both white and yellow varieties available; a good keeper; grows well in cool climates.
Beltsville Bunching	65–120	Recommended for use as scallions; grows well even in hot, dry weather; good texture; crisp and mild.
White Lisbon (also Improved Green Bunching)	60	Favorite bunching onion; hardy plant can withstand both extremes of cold and heat; mild taste; stays crisp long after harvesting.
Egyptian Onion (also Garden Rocambole, Walking Onion, Tree Onion, Top Onion, Salad Onion, Winter Onion, Pickle Onion)	Perennial	This North American native (*A. canadense*) is an unusual sight in fall when clusters of small onionlike bulbs appear on the tops of stalks; these small bulbs are very potent and can be used sparingly in cooking; plant is self-propagating by means of these bulb clusters which weigh down the stalks and root where they come in contact with the soil; plant also divides at the bottom; these new young stalks can be used as scallions until bulbs form, which causes the stalks to toughen; these hardy onions winter over and produce new crops of stalks and bulbs each year.

especially in cool climates. Keep seedling tops trimmed to a length of ½ to 1 inch until a week before setting out. The trimming process will not harm the seedlings and these young tops may be added to salads or used like chives. Set bunching onions out anywhere from four to five weeks before to two weeks after the frost-free date. Bulbing onions can be set out from six weeks before to two weeks after the frost-free date. Use the same spacing given below for sets.

Onion sets may be planted soon after the frost-free date. When selecting sets to plant, choose bulbs between ½ and ¾ inch in diameter. Larger ones tend to bolt to seed, while smaller ones take longer to produce onions of good size. Space these bulbs 3 to 4 inches apart in rows and beds, or 2 inches apart if young onions will be harvested as scallions. Allow 14 to 16 inches between conventional rows. Always place bulbs with their pointed ends up. On ordinary soils, sets are planted so that just the tip is exposed. On heavy soils, one-third of the bulb should be exposed. If the onions are to be harvested early for scallions, the entire bulb may be covered with ½ inch of soil so it will produce a longer white portion of stem. Onions grown from sets will mature in about 100 days.

Culture: Thin throughout the growing season to make sure that the plants grown for mature bulbs are given 3 to 4 inches of space on all sides. Plants can be thinned as soon as they reach a usable scallion size. Seedlings grown to be used as sets for next year's crop require little thinning, or just enough to allow ¼ to ½ inch between plants.

Keep the soil loose and open by frequent cultivation, and keep down weeds, which offer strong competition to the slow-growing onions. Mulching between rows is highly recommended, and can be done as soon as seedlings are 2 to 3 inches tall. As bulbing onions expand, they sometimes appear to be popping out of the ground. Do not hill up these bulbs, but throw some very light mulch over them to prevent sunscald. They will make good progress even if only one-third of the bulb remains underground.

Onions need a steady supply of moisture, and the soil should never be allowed to become extremely dry, otherwise the onion flavor will become strong and unpleasant. Seed heads that form on onions grown from sets should be removed as soon as they appear, to direct the plants' energy to bulb formation.

Pests and Diseases: Neither are major problems in cool-climate gardens. Occasional insect pests include onion maggots and thrips. Growing plants may be affected by downy mildew, pink rot, and smut. Neck rot sometimes attacks stored bulbs.

Harvest and Storage: During the season, onions may be harvested as they are needed and such harvesting serves as a thinning process.

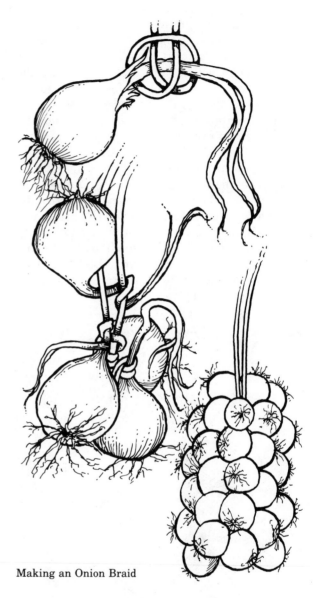

Making an Onion Braid

Scallions are ready for harvest in a matter of weeks when they are planted as sets or seedlings, and somewhat later when planted from seeds. They are at their best flavor when less than 10 inches tall. "Pickling onions" are those harvested early, when they have formed small bulbs, and pickled and used as a condiment.

Seedlings grown for sets should be harvested when their bulbs are ½ to ¾ inch in diameter and cured as for larger, mature bulbs. To lessen the chance that these sets will bloom when planted the next year, store them over the winter in a cool (30° to 32°F) and dry location. Two to three weeks before the planting date, expose these bulbs to warmth (80°F).

For winter storage, allow the onions to grow until their tops fall over naturally. If some do not fall with the others, they should be knocked down. After the tops have died down, keep the bulbs in the ground for a week or two, where they will begin to develop the tough skin necessary for good storage. When the leaves are shriveled and brown they are ready to be dug up with a spade or fork. See chapter 5 for directions on curing and storing the bulbs. Onions can be braided by their stems for a decorative means of storage.

PARSNIPS

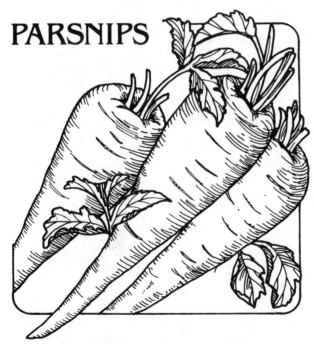

Pastinaca sativa
Umbelliferae

Although it is not one of the more popular vegetables today, devotees of parsnips insist that few dishes are better than parsnips, sliced and steamed, served with butter. The sweet, nutty flavor can also enhance soups and stews. Parsnips can be prepared in the same manner as carrots, and besides being quite tasty, they are also quite nutritious, providing vitamins B_1, B_2, and C, as well as potassium.

The parsnip is a biennial, but is treated as an annual like most root crops. It is grown for its long, slender, white roots. The most frost-resistant of all vegetables, parsnips can be left in the garden over winter, even in the coldest climates. The parsnip requires a long growing season, and any inconvenience this may present to the gardener in terms of tying up garden space is offset by the fact that it stores so well in the ground and is available throughout the winter for fresh, tasty eating—a time when fresh, crispy vegetables are rare. It is indeed a winter vegetable and its flavor is enhanced by light frosts that change its starches to sugars.

Growing Range: Parsnips may be grown in all regions. They require a growing season of 80 to 120 days, and are generally grown in regions with autumn or winter frosts, which promote the sweetest taste and crispiest texture.

Soil Preparation: Like other long-rooted crops, parsnips need a deep, rich, well-drained and well-aerated soil. Sandy loams are ideal, but parsnips may be grown in any average loam if the soil is loosened before planting. Heavy clays will not produce good crops. Prepare the soil to a depth of 12 to 18 inches before planting, removing any rocks or other debris. Incorporate plenty of compost or well-aged manure, but avoid using fresh manure before planting, since it will cause roots to fork. Also work in a potassium-rich fertilizer like wood ashes or greensand. Recommended pH is 6.0 to 6.8.

Propagation: Parsnips can be started using seeds or transplants. In mild-winter areas with temperatures that seldom dip below freezing, sow seed in late fall and winter for a spring crop. In areas with cold winters and freezing temperatures, sow seed as soon as the ground can be worked in spring, two to four weeks before the last frost, or get a head start with transplants. Start seeds indoors in individual containers four to six weeks before setting out, which can be done from four weeks before to four weeks after the frost-free date. Set seedlings every 4 to 6 inches in conventional rows, and use spacing given below for raised beds.

For direct-sown seed, the soil temperature for best germination is 50° to 70°F. Seed is very slow to germinate, and should be soaked in water for several hours or overnight. Sow seed thickly, ½ inch deep, and cover the furrows with vermiculite or a mix of leaf mold and sand, since the seed has trouble coming up through crusted soil. Mix in radish seed to act as a planting marker. Keep the furrows moist to hasten germination. Conventional rows should be spaced 18 inches apart. Wide-row planting is suitable. Spacing for growing beds is 6 inches. Unused seed is good for one to two years.

Culture: When the radishes have been harvested and the parsnip seedlings are about 1 inch tall, thin them to stand 4 to 6 inches apart in the conventional rows and wide rows. Keep weeds down during this period, and mulch between the rows when the radishes are harvested. Although parsnips are not particularly heavy feeders, a midseason side-dressing of wood ashes or compost will hasten roots along to maturity. Keep parsnips well watered.

Pests and Diseases: Parsnips are seldom bothered.

Harvest and Storage: The parsnip's flavor is greatly improved by a few hard frosts and it should not be harvested before being touched by frost. Parsnips may be left in the ground over winter and dug up as needed. The only requirement is a thick hay mulch to facilitate digging in areas where the ground freezes hard. The roots may be harvested in early spring, as the ground begins to thaw, even if no protection was given over the winter, but make sure to harvest before new growth begins in spring, since they will become woody, limp and tasteless after that. They may also be dug just before the ground freezes hard in fall and stored over the winter in a cool (32° to 40°F) and moist storage area.

Parsnips

Variety Name	Average Days to Maturity	General Description and Comments
Hollow Crown (also Gurnsey Long Smooth)	95–105	The standard parsnip; an old favorite and not much improved upon; roots taper sharply, grow 12 in. long and are about 2½ in. in diameter at the shoulder; heavy yielder.
All American	120	Good texture and small core; 12-in. roots; dependable producer.
Harris Model	100–120	A popular variety with smooth, white flesh; 10–12-in. roots; does not discolor quickly after harvest.
Premium	80–110	A short-rooted variety for shallow soils; dependable, good producer; recommended for short-season areas.

PEAS

English pea, garden pea, green pea
Pisum sativum
and
Edible-podded pea, Oriental pea, snow pea
Pisum sativum var. *macrocarpon*
Leguminosae

The green pea is one of the oldest of cultivated vegetables. The quick-growing vines of this annual legume produce four to ten seeds in each pod. There are wrinkled and smooth-seeded varieties. Wrinkled peas are sweeter, are usually planted in spring, and account for most peas grown in the garden. Smooth-seeded varieties have more starch and less sugar, and they are hardier, so they are used generally for fall plantings.

Peas are prized as the earliest vegetable to come out of the garden. Garden peas are always shelled before use (in green or dry state), since their pods are fibrous and not particularly tasty. The shelled peas are savored as a steamed vegetable, as well as enjoyed in soups, casseroles, stews, and in salads, cooked or raw. Snow peas (often called edible-podded peas) are savored for their crisp, succulent pods and not for their peas. In fact, if the peas are allowed to develop in the pods, the edible quality of the pods declines. These peas are popular in oriental stir-fry recipes. Sugar Snap peas blend the best of both worlds, for they are relished for both their juicy pods and sweet-tasting peas. Pods and peas should be allowed to mature fully for the finest flavor and texture. Although Sugar Snaps can be lightly steamed or stir-fried, they are in their glory when popped fresh from vine to mouth.

Peas offer significant amounts of vitamins A and C, and are a good source of protein.

In suitable climates, peas are not a difficult crop to grow. They are quick to mature, and can be followed by a warm-weather succession crop. There are both tall and low-growing varieties available. The tall ones reach to 6 feet in height and need a means of support. Although this means a little extra work, vertical growing takes advantage of space usually overlooked and underused in the garden. The low growers require no staking, and are spaced more closely together to form a kind of self-supporting network of branches.

Growing Range: Peas are a definite cool-weather crop, growing best when average temperatures range between 60° and 65°F. Excessive heat prevents blossoms from setting fruit and retards development of pods that have formed. In cool climates they are grown as an early spring to midsummer crop. In warm climates they are a fall, winter, or very early spring crop. Light freezes will not hurt seedlings; only blossoms are seriously damaged by frost.

Soil Preparation: A sandy loam is best, but good crops may be produced on heavier soil if it is well prepared and kept as loose as possible. The soil should be well drained and fertile, well supplied with potassium and phosphorus (for example, in the form of bone meal and wood ashes), but not overly rich in nitrogen. Peas, a legume, draw their own nitrogen from the air and fix it in their root nodules. If too much nitrogen is already present in the soil, leaf growth will be stimulated at the expense of pods. The recommended pH range is 6.0 to 7.5.

The best time for preparing the soil in cool climates is the fall prior to spring planting. Till the soil, work in fertilizers, and mulch with straw or compost. Pull the mulch back about one week before planting to allow the soil to warm up a bit. Seeds can be planted directly with no need to dig or till beforehand.

Propagation: Peas can be sown directly into the garden four to six weeks before the frost-free date, when the soil temperature has reached at least 40°F. If you are using untreated seed, and find that the germination rate is low, wait until the soil has warmed to 55°F before planting. Gardeners in warm-season areas may wish to start seeds indoors for an extra-early spring crop. Peas are temperamental, however, and must be seeded in individual containers to avoid disturbing roots. Start seed four weeks before setting out, which can be done four weeks before to three weeks after the frost-free date. For a long-term harvest, plant several varieties that mature at different times, but do not stagger plantings of a single variety, since doing so will push the last harvests into the hot months. Presoak seeds for 24 hours, then inoculate them just before sowing with special legume inoculant. Unused seed is good for three years.

There are several ways to arrange the rows, depending on the growing habit of the variety. Tall or short crops can be planted in single conventional rows; allow 30 to 36 inches between rows for tall crops, 24 inches for low ones. Tall varieties do well in double rows, 8 inches apart, with a vertical support run between the rows. Allow 30 inches between the sets of double rows. (In all row plantings, space seed 1 to 2 inches apart within the row.) Low-growing varieties can be broadcast in wide rows 18 inches across; space wide rows 36 inches apart. Tall or low varieties can be planted in raised beds, spaced 6 inches apart. Plant seeds 1 inch deep in heavy soils, 2 inches deep in sandy soils.

Make late plantings in midsummer, about 12 weeks before the first expected frost, to mature in the cool days of autumn. To keep the roots cool and allow for proper blossom and fruit

Peas

Variety Name	Average Days to Maturity	General Description and Comments
Garden Pea Varieties		
Alderman (also Tall Telephone)	70–75	A tall variety; oval, curved pods are 4½–5 in. long with 8 to 10 peas per pod; needs good support; retains color when cooked.
Alaska	55	Earliest of all; the commonly grown garden pea; vines are short; smooth-seeded type recommended for green shell use or for drying for split pea soup; resistant to fusarium wilt.
Freezonian	63	Popular freezing pea with short vines; pods are 3½ in. long, holding 7–8 seeds per pod; vines are wilt-resistant; AAS.
Little Marvel	63	Long a popular and dependable variety; vines are short; pods grow 3 in. long with 7–8 peas per pod; equally suited for fresh use and freezing.
Thomas Laxton	62	An old standard; a heavy yielder and good freezer with short vines; pods grow 5 in. long with 8–10 peas per pod; Laxton's Progress, a successor variety, is very similar with vines that are only 18 in. long.
Wando (also Main Crop)	68	A heavy producer; withstands hot, dry spells; vines are short; pods grow 3½ in. long with 6–8 peas per pod.
Snow Pea-type Varieties		
Dwarf Grey Sugar	65	Vines reach 2–2½ ft. long; pods grow 2½–3 in. long; needs no staking.
Mammoth Melting Sugar	75	Vigorous-growing vines reach 5 ft. long; pods are 4–4½ in. long; yields heavily over a long harvest period; needs support.
Sugar Snap	70	Pods and peas are edible at all stages of maturity; unlike standard snow peas, the peas are at their sweetest and tastiest when mature; vining type reaches 6 ft. or more and needs sturdy, tall support; dwarf types need no support; pods are 2½–3 in. long.

formation, dig trenches 6 inches wide and 6 inches deep. Scatter seed or plant two rows along the edges of the trench. Cover with 2 inches of soil. As seedlings emerge, cover them with soil until the trench is filled.

Culture: Thin seedlings to 3 to 4 inches apart in the conventional and wide rows. Tall varieties need support when they are 3 inches tall; without support, the vines will form dense mats, air circulation will be impeded, and production will be reduced greatly. Use fences, trellises, or any vertical surface that is at least 5 feet tall, to which the tendrils can cling. Apply a thick mulch right after sowing, but leave the growing space immediately above the seed open. The mulch will keep the soil cool and, if

a killing frost should come, seedlings can be protected by pushing the mulch over them. When plants grow taller than the mulch, gather the mulch around the plants. Peas rarely need extra moisture if the mulch is thick enough. Peas are not heavy feeders, and when grown on well-prepared, fertile soil there is no need for midseason feedings.

Pests and Diseases: Bothersome pests include aphids, cabbage loopers, corn earworms and cucumber beetles. Peas may be affected by ascochyta blight, bacterial blight, damping-off, powdery mildew, root rot, and seed rot.

Harvest and Storage: Garden peas for green shell use should be harvested at the peak of ripeness, when they have filled out the pods but before the pods have begun to deteriorate, evidenced by yellowing and shriveling. Peas are usually close to ripeness about three weeks after the blossoms appear. It is best to harvest daily, or at least every other day, during the harvest season. Once this "peak of perfection" is reached, the plant begins to convert the seeds' sugar into starch, and both flavor and texture begin to deteriorate. The starch conversion also begins as soon as peas are removed from the vine, which is why peas should be either served or processed as quickly as possible after being harvested.

Garden peas that have matured past their prime for fresh use aren't a total loss. You can dry the peas and use them to make a hearty, warming soup that helps take the chill off winter evenings. Let the peas hang on the vine until the pods wither and turn brown, then harvest. Shell the peas and spread them out in a single layer in a dry, warm, airy place. Within three weeks nearly all of the moisture will have evaporated, and the peas will be ready to store in an airtight, lidded container.

Sugar Snap peas are best when picked when pods are full-sized and peas are large and completely mature. Snow peas are harvested when the pods are flat, and before the seeds have begun to form bumps. Both these peas should also be served or processed quickly.

Pea pods should not be jerked roughly from the vines, since the plants are quite sensitive to this treatment and may stop producing pods. Rather, cut them with a pair of small scissors or pruners.

PEANUTS

Earth nut, goober, goober pea, ground nut
Arachis hypogaea
Leguminosae

Although the peanut is an important food and livestock crop in many tropical and semitropical areas of the world, this plant is more often grown as a novelty in the home garden.

The "nut," actually a seed, is both a tasty snack and a solid nutritional package offering good amounts of vitamins B and E, healthful oils (3:1 ratio of unsaturated to saturated fatty acids), and up to 30 percent protein.

The plants grow from 1 to 2 feet tall, and are either of erect or creeping habit. Limited-space gardeners should look for erect-growing or bush varieties.

Growing Range: Peanuts are a very tender, long-season crop. They can be grown successfully in any area that offers 120 frost-free days, as long as the climate is warm and sunny. Peanuts need a long period of warm nights to develop properly.

Soil Preparation: Peanuts will grow and yield on poor soil, but yields will be improved by adding compost rich in phosphorus and potassium, or by adding bone meal and wood ashes. Peanuts, a legume, take their own nitrogen from the air and store it in the soil. Thus there is no need to add nitrogen to the soil, since an excess will result in too much top growth and poor seed development. The soil should be well drained and light (a sandy loam is ideal), and on the acid side (a pH of 5 to 6). Work through the soil to make sure all rocks and other debris are out of the growing area. Short-season gardeners should try to provide a south-facing slope in a sheltered area for this warmth-loving crop.

Propagation: Seeds are most often sown directly into the garden on the frost-free date. In short-season areas, gardeners sometimes gamble on earlier outdoor planting dates or start plants indoors. Sow seeds in individual containers that will allow transplanting without disturbing the roots. Peanuts do not transplant easily, and any damage to the roots will set back growth. Start seeds four to six weeks before the frost-free date, at which time they can be set out in the garden.

Seed may be planted either in or out of the pod. If the pod shell is thin, it is best to plant pods without shelling them. If not, then the seeds should be removed very carefully; if the red skin of the seed is torn, germination will not occur. Seeds are subject to rot, especially on heavy, cool, or damp soils. Soil temperature should be at least 60°F before planting. Although peanuts are a legume, it is generally not recommended to treat them with bacterial inoculant before planting. Unused seed is good for five years.

Space conventional rows 2½ to 3 feet apart, and plant the seeds every 4 to 6 inches along the rows. The spacing in growing beds is 18 inches. Peanuts may also be planted in hills, like squash, four seeds or pods to the hill, the hills spaced 18 inches apart. In cool weather or in heavier soils, seeds are planted 1½ inches deep; in long-season areas and in very light soils, seeds are planted at least 4 inches deep.

Culture: After seedlings have been up for two

Peanuts

Although many catalogs do not specify varieties and simply refer to "Virginia" or "Spanish" types, these are the recommended varieties for both warm and cool areas. All mature in 110 to 120 days.

Variety Name	General Description and Comments
Warm-Season Varieties	
Virginia Bunch	1–2 large nuts per pod.
Mammoth Virginia	A favorite commercial variety.
Jumbo Runner	A vigorous grower.
Cool-Season Varieties	
Red Tennessee	A Spanish type; peanuts form close to center of plant for easy harvesting.
Early Spanish	Perhaps the most dependable for short-season areas.

weeks, thin them to stand 10 to 12 inches apart in rows. Thin the hills so the sturdiest three seedlings remain. Supply only enough moisture to keep the soil from drying out until a mulch is applied. Cultivate shallowly to eliminate weeds, being careful not to disturb the peanut roots.

The plant will produce two kinds of flowers—relatively large and showy blossoms on the upper portions, and inconspicuous ones growing at the base of the plant at the ends of runners (called pegs). It is the inconspicuous flowers that are important, for they contain ovaries that will develop into peanuts. The runners will grow laterally for a short distance, then dip down and bury themselves in the soil, each to produce an underground seed pod. To hasten the burying process, hill up loose-textured soil around the base of the plant, once it reaches 2 inches in height, so that the runners may make soil contact in a shorter time. It is important to keep the soil surface loose, so the runners can work their way into the soil.

After the runners have implanted themselves, add a thick mulch on top of them, and around plants. The mulch, in addition to serving the usual purposes, will encourage the peanuts to develop close to the soil surface, which makes harvesting easier. After the mulch has been applied, the crop will need no more care for the rest of the season.

Pests and Diseases: There are no serious pests or diseases of peanuts when they are grown in the home garden.

Harvest and Storage: In longer-season gardens, peanuts are traditionally harvested before the first autumn frosts arrive, when the seeds have filled out the pods, the pods' veins have begun to darken, and the foliage has yellowed. In shorter-season areas, the crop may be left in the ground past the first light frosts if the pods have not fully matured. Even after the tops have died down, the nuts will continue to mature for several weeks. Keep testing to see when peanuts have matured.

If the plants have been properly mulched, they may be pulled up by hand with ease. Most of the peanuts will adhere to the roots, and the others may be recovered by probing in the ground. If the peanuts have formed more deeply in the ground, use a spade to dig them up.

There are two ways to cure peanuts. The traditional practice calls for the entire plant, containing the peanuts, to be hung in a warm, dry location with good ventilation. The other, perhaps more convenient, practice is to remove the pods and dry them on screens or trays, also in a warm, dry place. Whichever method is used, the curing period is at least one month or longer, if conditions are not ideal.

After curing, the peanuts may be eaten raw or roasted. To roast, place the pods in a 350°F oven for 20 minutes. Be careful not to scorch them. Save some of the largest pods for planting the following season's crop.

PEPPERS

Capsicum annuum var. *annuum*
Grossum Group (bell or sweet pepper)
Longum Group (cayenne, chili, hot or red pepper)
Solanaceae

There are several types of hot pepper that are edible, but the one most commonly grown in the home garden is the chili or cayenne pepper, which has a slender and tapering fruit, up to 12 inches long. This pepper may be used fresh, or dried and ground up to add fieriness to chili, goulash, and assorted hot sauces.

In addition to the spicy hot pepper, gardeners often grow the mild-flavored sweet or bell pepper that is large and chunky in shape. It is a common ingredient in many recipes, and often appears raw in salads or as a crudité accompanied by dip. This bell type can also be stuffed and baked with various fillings.

Peppers offer good supplies of vitamin A and of several important minerals, but are especially noted for their high vitamin C content.

Peppers are not difficult to grow, although their yield is easily reduced by very cool (55°F or less) or very hot (90°F and up) weather, or by low humidity, any of which may cause blossom drop. Both sweet and hot peppers are green in their immature state, later turning yellow, orange, then red as they ripen. They are handsome, bushy plants (about 30 inches tall) with bright or dark green foliage, filling the roles of both edible and ornamental crop. Peppers may be grown in any sunny area of the garden. They are also ideal for containers and limited-space gardens, producing high yields for the amount of space they consume.

Growing Range: This is a warm-weather crop that stops growing and drops blossoms when the temperature dips below 55°F. The ideal growing temperature is 70° to 75°F during the day and 60° to 70°F at night. All peppers are very sensitive to frost and cool winds. In very hot-summer areas, they are often grown in fall and winter.

Soil Preparation: Peppers do best on a sandy or sandy loam soil that is well drained and well supplied with organic matter such as compost or well-rotted manure. Choose a location sheltered from strong winds. Magnesium is a key nutrient, since a deficiency will cause leaf drop, poor production, and sunscald of fruits. If such a deficiency exists, add dolomite lime, talc, or epsom salts. The ideal pH range is 6 to 7.

Propagation: Peppers are seeded in the open garden only in very long-season areas, one week after the frost-free date. Usually, they are started indoors six to eight weeks before transplanting time, which is two to three weeks after the frost-free date. Seedlings can be set out when the average night temperature is 55°F and the soil temperature has reached 60°F or above.

For conventional rows, set seedlings every 18 to 24 inches in rows spaced 36 inches apart. Spacing for growing beds is 15 inches. Close planting increases humidity in the area of the developing fruits, which decreases the chances of blossom drop. Unused seed is good for four years.

Culture: Immediately after setting out seedlings, water the rows. Keep the rows free of weeds (but be careful not to injure the plants' roots) until plants are established and a mulch can be applied. Peppers need constant and even moisture throughout the season; adequate soil moisture is especially important when the blossoms open and as fruits are forming. In areas with very hot summers, offer the plants partial shade with lath frames to prevent leaf scald.

Pests and Diseases: Insect pests include aphids, Colorado potato beetles, corn earworms, European corn borers, leafminers, pepper maggots, and tomato hornworms. Diseases include anthracnose, bacterial spot, blossom-end rot, and mosaic. Despite the impressive list of potential enemies, however, garden peppers are not greatly subject to injury by insects and diseases.

Harvest and Storage: Sweet peppers may be picked when immature or full size, in the green or red state, although the vitamin C content is higher when the fruit is red. Hot peppers may be picked at any time for fresh use, and when they have become fully ripe for drying or pickling. Cut the pods rather than pull them from the vines to keep from disturbing the plant's roots. When even light frost is predicted, pick all pods. They will keep for about one to two weeks at 50° to 60°F in a moist place.

Both hot and sweet peppers may be frozen without preliminary blanching. Thin-walled hot peppers are easy to dry and can be ground and stored in jars. Cut the whole plant and hang it in an airy place to dry, or harvest the individual pods and string them to hang in the kitchen for both ornamental and culinary purposes. Hot peppers may also be pickled for use as condiments.

Peppers

Variety Name	Average Days to Maturity	General Description and Comments
Sweet Type		
Calwonder	60–70	Large, bell-type fruits with sweet flavor; an old favorite, perhaps the most popular garden pepper in North America; production may be uneven in hot summers; plants are compact.
Bell Boy	70	Bell type; widely adaptable to both cool and hot climates; tolerates tobacco mosaic; AAS.
Early Prolific Hybrid	60	Extra-early bell type; good production of small fruits even in areas with cool and somewhat cloudy summers.
Early Set	68	Fruit sets well in cool weather; high yields of small, blocky fruits on compact plants; recommended for cool-summer areas.
Gypsy Hybrid	65	High yields of 4½-in. fruits; color begins yellow, turning to red; compact plants are well suited to containers, limited-space gardens, and ornamental beds.
Hot Type		
Jalapeno	70–80	Deep green fruit matures to red; perhaps the hottest of all commonly grown North American varieties; tapering 3-in. fruits; can be pickled.
Hungarian Yellow Wax	60–65	Yellow fruit turns red as it matures, measures 6–8 in. long; moderately hot; bushy plant; fruit very good for pickling; also good canned or fresh.
Long Red Cayenne	70–75	Yellow fruits turn flaming red when mature; fruit is 5 in. long and slender; very hot flavor; may easily be dried, ground, and stored in jars.
Red Chili	70–80	A fiery hot pepper; fruits 2 in. long; green fruit matures to red; good for drying and braiding.

POTATOES

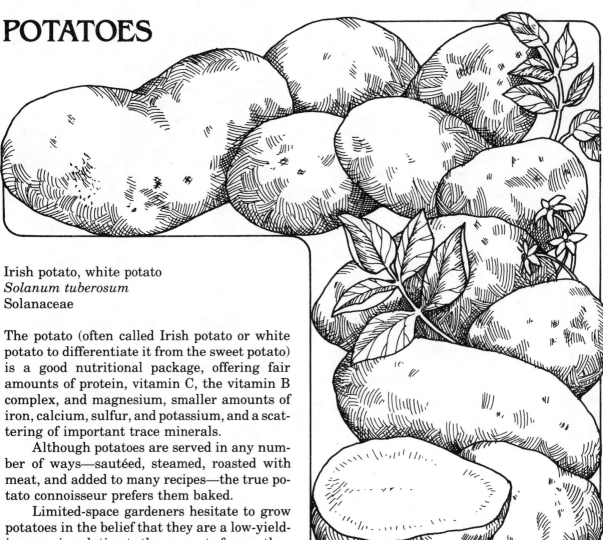

Irish potato, white potato
Solanum tuberosum
Solanaceae

The potato (often called Irish potato or white potato to differentiate it from the sweet potato) is a good nutritional package, offering fair amounts of protein, vitamin C, the vitamin B complex, and magnesium, smaller amounts of iron, calcium, sulfur, and potassium, and a scattering of important trace minerals.

Although potatoes are served in any number of ways—sautéed, steamed, roasted with meat, and added to many recipes—the true potato connoisseur prefers them baked.

Limited-space gardeners hesitate to grow potatoes in the belief that they are a low-yielding crop in relation to the amount of space they consume. However, as many as 20 pounds of the tubers may be grown in a square yard of space—a figure that should raise the potato's status in the eyes of many gardeners.

Potatoes are classified by their shape, skin color, and maturation time. There are early (summer), midseason (late summer), and late (fall) varieties, which are further classified according to their skin color (red or white), and then according to any number of shapes—long, round, elliptical, oval, thick, oblong, and so on. "New" potatoes are those (red or white) used immediately after harvesting. Contrary to common belief, there is no "Idaho" variety of potato. Idahos are simply potatoes grown in Idaho, and they are usually long, round white varieties, such as the popular Russet Burbank, prized for baking.

Growing Range: Potatoes may be grown in all temperate regions, although the selection of appropriate varieties is important to success in any area.

Potatoes develop best in cooler areas where they are planted in early spring. The best tuber formation occurs when the daytime air temperature is 60° to 65°F and night temperatures are about 10 degrees lower. There are some varieties developed especially for growing in warm regions, and these are usually planted as a late-winter, spring, or fall crop.

Soil Preparation: Although potatoes do better than most other food crops on poor soils, yields will be significantly higher in a well-drained and loose soil which is high in organic matter such as compost or well-rotted manure. Gravelly or sandy loams are well suited, and peat or muck soils will produce well if they are well drained. Both phosphorus and potassium are essential to good tuber development, which materials such as phosphate rock and greensand will supply. Nitrogen is needed for good foliage development, although an excess will reduce yields and the quality of the tubers. Yields are often reduced because the heavy-feeding potatoes exhaust the soil of its potassium reserves before the tubers have developed fully. Many serious home growers prepare the potato area in fall, grow a green manure crop, and turn it under before the spring planting.

Much has been made of the proper pH range. Commercial growers often maintain a very acid soil (4.8 to 5.4) to keep potato scab from afflicting the crop. Recent research, however, indicates that the best range for the highest yield is 5.2 to 5.7. Anything above 5.7 encourages scab, while a pH below 5.2 begins to reduce yields. In any case, the pH range is not a critical factor in obtaining good yields in the home garden. Best yields will be achieved at a pH of 5.2 to 5.7, but good results may be had if potatoes are planted in a soil suitable for other crops, at a pH range of 6.0 to 6.5. Never put lime on the plot at the same time potatoes are growing there; wait at least a year between heavily liming the soil and planting potatoes. An easy way to lower the pH and keep the soil

Hilled-Up Potato Plants

in good shape is to mulch the bed with oak leaves in the fall prior to spring planting.

Propagation: Since potatoes are subject to a number of diseases, it is safest to buy certified seed. Catalogs usually offer seed "eyes" or pieces, while garden centers usually sell whole seed potatoes. If plans are made to save seed for next year's garden, begin with the most disease-resistant varieties available. (Don't use potatoes purchased at the grocery store for seeding. These are often treated with chemicals to inhibit sprouting.) Cut each whole seed potato into pieces so that each piece has one or two eyes (dormant buds, from which vines will grow), and as much fleshy tuber as possible (to feed the vines in their early growth). Let the pieces dry overnight before planting them. This allows a corky layer to form which reduces the possibility of rot.

Sow two to four weeks before the frost-free date. If space allows, plant early-, mid-, and late-season crops for a continuous harvest. Rows should be spaced 20 inches apart for the smaller, early varieties, and 30 inches apart for the mid- and late-season varieties that make more root and top growth. Dig a 4-inch-deep furrow in heavy soil and a 6-inch furrow in light soil. Set the potato pieces, cut side down, 12 inches apart for small varieties, and 15 inches apart for larger varieties. When pieces are in place, cover with soil. Spacing in growing

Potatoes

Variety Name	Average Days to Maturity	General Description and Comments
Early Varieties, White		
Irish Cobbler	100	An old favorite, now losing popularity because of its limited disease resistance (although it is resistant to mosaic); round to oval tubers of medium size have deep-set eyes.
Superior	115	Oval-shaped with shallow eyes; all-purpose use, doesn't gray or discolor after cooking; scab-resistant; bears through midseason.
Late Varieties, White		
Katahdin	110	Oval-shaped; not a heavy yielder, so may be planted closer together than most (6–8 in.); resistant to mosaic, and very resistant to blight.
Kennebec	115	Tubers are large and elliptical with fine flavor; a very high yielder; resistant to mosaic and late blight.
Chippewa	110	Long, oval shape; resistant to mosaic; good for peat and muck soils; well suited to northern areas.
Early Varieties, Red		
Norland	115	Thick, oblong-shaped tubers with smooth skin; resistant to scab, but susceptible to blight and viral diseases; very good yields.
Red Pontiac	115	Oblong-shaped tubers with thin skins and shallow eyes; does well in heavier soils; heavy yielder well into midseason; a good winter keeper.
Viking	115	New potatoes can be harvested as early as 70 days after planting; will develop into larger roots; very drought-resistant.

beds is 12 inches. Planting too close will result in small-sized potatoes.

An alternate planting method has the tubers developing in a pocket of mulch. Press the seed pieces into a shallow trench of very loose soil. Then add an 18-inch layer of rich organic mulch on top of them. This method is especially effective with red-skinned varieties. Since the tubers always grow above the seed piece, harvesting is simply a matter of reaching down through the mulch and removing as many potatoes as needed. The potatoes are much cleaner at harvest time than if they had been grown in soil.

Culture: Keep the planted area well supplied with moisture (but not soggy) until the plants have emerged from the soil. Throughout the remainder of the season, slightly less water is needed, but the soil should be kept evenly moist

for good tuber development. When plants are 6 to 8 inches tall, pull soil from the row to snug around the stems. Leave the tops free. As the stems grow taller, repeat this earthing up to cover the stems, always leaving the top leaves free. The hilling process adds loose soil to the area where tubers will grow (allowing free expansion), offers good drainage in the growth area, eliminates weeds somewhat, facilitates easy harvesting, and protects plants from freezing in the event of a late frost. Add mulch after the last hilling. If any growing potatoes poke through the soil surface, hill them up immediately, before their skins turn green. The green color signifies the production of solanine, which is moderately toxic. The flesh of green-skinned potatoes may be eaten safely, but not the skins themselves.

Pests and Diseases: Potential insect pests include aphids, Colorado potato beetles, cabbage loopers, corn earworms, cucumber beetles, European corn borers, leafhoppers, leafminers, potato tuber worms, and tomato hornworms. Diseases include black leg, early blight, internal blackspot, late blight, mosaic, rhizoctonia, ring rot, scab, verticillium wilt, and several other fungal and viral diseases.

Harvest and Storage: New potatoes may be harvested anytime they have grown to usable size. The early varieties, of course, are best suited for "new" potato use. Begin to test tuber size a week or two after flowering. Harvesting may continue until the foliage has died down. If the hills were properly constructed with loose soil, you may simply reach into the soil, feel for a good-sized tuber, and gently separate it from the mother plant.

Late varieties should be harvested for storage around the time of the first autumn frost, as the foliage dies down. As long as the ground does not freeze, potatoes may be left in the ground, to sap every bit of energy they can from the vines. But do test the tubers every few days for signs of rot or blight. (If the tops die down well before the first frost, suspect late blight.) Don't gamble on the weather and leave them in the ground for too long; once the tubers freeze, they turn watery and unusable. Use a garden fork—or, in very loose soils, a pitchfork—to lift up the entire root system. It will take some practice to avoid spearing any prize potatoes. Blackening problems in storage are often caused by rough handling during the harvest. Treat potatoes gently at all times. Break off any loose, moist soil clinging to the potatoes, then take them indoors and let them dry for a few hours. Brush most of the dry soil from them, and store them for one to two weeks in a dark, cool (60°F), and dry location to prepare for storage. Then transfer them to a dark storage area, where they will keep for five to six months at 32° to 40°F, with high humidity and good ventilation.

PUMPKINS

Cucurbita pepo var. *pepo, C. maxima,*
 C. mixta, C. moschata
Cucurbitaceae

Botanically, the classification pumpkin includes many vegetables that gardeners commonly call squash (see Squash). Here, we will treat only the yellow-to-orange pumpkins grown for use in pies, for jack-o'-lanterns at Halloween, and for their seeds.

Although some pumpkins can be used for both pies and holiday carving, most varieties are carefully bred for one purpose or the other. Pumpkins come in various sizes, ranging from the small, sweet, 5-pound pie types to giant varieties weighing 100 pounds or more. The shapes vary, too, from the standard round variety to the cushaw pumpkins, which develop long curving necks. It is the sweet flesh within the neck that is put to culinary use.

Pumpkins are easy to grow but have high water and nutrient requirements. Most vining varieties take up considerable garden space, from 10 to 20 feet, although there are now some bush types for limited-space gardens which require only 6 square feet of growing room. Pump-

Pumpkins

Variety Name	Average Days to Maturity	General Description and Comments
Jack O'Lantern (also Halloween)	100–115	Weighs 10 lb., measures 8–9 in. around; smooth shell is easy to carve.
Funny Face	90	A hybrid good for short-season areas; weighs 10–17 lb.; ideal carving shape; also good for pies.
Small Sugar (also Boston Pie, New England Pie)	100	The standard pie pumpkin; 8-by-10-in. fruit weighs about 7 lb.; high sugar content; excellent taste.
Cinderella	95–102	A bush type with compact growth habit for small gardens; 7- to 10-lb. fruit; used for pies and baking.
Spirit	90–100	A compact hybrid that takes up less space than standard-sized varieties; 10- to 15-lb. fruit; good for short-season areas; good for pies and carving; AAS.
Triple Treat	110	Bears 6- to 8-lb. fruit with sweet flesh that is excellent for pies; seeds are hull-less and can be roasted for snacks.
Lady Godiva (also Streaker)	110	Grown for the hull-less seeds and not for the flesh; seeds are exceptionally high in protein; skin is striped with green and yellow; vines grow from 8 to 10 ft. long.
Green-Striped Cushaw	110–115	Attractive fruits are pale green with deeper green stripes; fruits weigh 10 to 15 lb.; thick flesh is suitable for baking and pie making; does well in warm climates.

kins tolerate more shade than most other squashes, and this trait can be used to good advantage by planting the pumpkins in every third row of corn, allowing 8 to 10 feet between pumpkin plants along the row. In summer, when the corn is harvested, knock down the stalks to allow full sun to reach the pumpkins. Yields may not be as high as for pumpkins planted in their own patch, but a great amount of space is saved.

In terms of cuisine, most people associate pumpkin with pie. But the delicious flesh can also be used for breads, soups, and casseroles. The seeds are good roasted or dried, and even the blossoms can be eaten.

Growing Range: Pumpkins may be grown in any area that offers more than 90 growing days. Some varieties require as many as 120 days, and they may not be harvested before they have fully matured. Thus, gardeners in short-season areas should be careful in choosing varieties. Pumpkin plants are very tender and are highly susceptible to frost damage. The best average temperature range for growth is 65° to 75°F.

Soil Preparation: A loam or sandy loam is best for pumpkins. It should be rich in organic material, well drained, well aerated, and capable of holding ample amounts of moisture. For top yields, incorporate generous amounts of compost or aged manure 18 inches deep into the soil before planting. The recommended pH range is 6 to 7.

Propagation: Seeds are generally sown directly into the garden one week or more after the frost-free date when all danger of frost is past. Short-season gardeners may warm up the soil more quickly by laying black plastic over it two weeks before planting. This plastic is removed for planting and replaced later with an organic mulch. If cloches are used, the planting dates may be advanced two to three weeks. Cold-climate gardeners may start seeds indoors three weeks before planting out, which is done at the same time seed is sown outdoors.

Pumpkins are usually planted in hills. For vining types, plant six seeds per hill, allowing 10 to 12 feet between hills. For bush types, plant six seeds per hill, spacing hills 4 to 6 feet apart. Pumpkins may also be planted in conventional rows. Vining types should be spaced 3 to 4 feet apart in rows set 8 to 12 feet apart. Bush types require 2 to 3 feet between plants, in rows set 4 to 6 feet apart. All seed is planted 1 inch deep. Unused seed is good for five years.
Culture: When the seedlings are established, remove all but the two sturdiest ones. Keep the growing areas free from weeds early in the season, and mulch between hills before the plants start to vine. Side-dress the plants midseason with well-rotted manure or compost, or water with fish emulsion or manure tea. Keep the plants well watered. Pumpkins, like squash, must be insect-pollinated. Pollination problems are discussed under Squash (see Culture).

For champion-sized pumpkins, allow only one plant per hill, and one or two pumpkins per plant; do not trim back the vines, but remove new flowers as they appear. If garden space is tight, pumpkin vines may be trained to grow upward along a trellis. As fruit develops, it will require some form of support to remain on the vine.

Three to five weeks before frost is expected, nip off the growing tips of the vines and remove any small fruit to concentrate the plant's energy on maturing the more developed fruits.
Pests and Diseases: See Squash.
Harvest and Storage: Pumpkins can be used as soon as their skin loses its sheen. Pumpkins intended for storage should not be harvested until they are fully mature and yellow, just before the first fall frosts, when the shells have become tough and cannot be dented easily by a thumbnail. Cut the fruit from the vine, leaving 4 to 6 inches of stem attached.

Pumpkins should be cured in preparation for winter storage as described in chapter 5. Store them on shelves in a warm (50° to 60°F) and dry storage area. Bruised fruit will not store well and should be used first.

Pumpkin seeds can be enjoyed raw or roasted as a nutritious snack. Rinse the fibers from the seeds, and place in a baking pan, toss with butter or oil, and brown for 1 to 1½ hours in a 250°F oven. Hull-less seeds can be dried easily by spreading the rinsed seeds in a warm, airy place.

RADISHES

Raphanus sativus
Cruciferae

The Latin name of the radish comes from the word *raphanos* which means "easily reared." Radishes are indeed easily reared, which is one reason why they are grown in most vegetable gardens. The common spring radish is a favorite companion crop, since it grows so quickly, takes up so little room, and is reported to repel some insects. It is often planted to mark rows of slower-germinating crops, and is harvested before the other crops need the growing room. It serves as an early succession crop in many gardens, and even as a trap crop to attract root maggots away from onions and other root vegetables. Many gardeners give radishes no block

Radishes

Variety Name	Average Days to Maturity	General Description and Comments
Cherry Bell	22	A very quick-maturing globe type; roots have bright red skin and short tops; early-season; AAS.
Scarlet Globe	23	An old favorite with uniform globe-type roots; often grown for market; does well indoors; early-season.
Comet	25	Flesh retains crispness in heat better than most varieties; globe type with short tops; early-season; AAS.
White Icicle (also Short Top)	27–30	The standard long white type, never excelled; white roots grow 5–8 in. long; young roots are sweet and tender and become stronger-flavored as they age; midseason.
Summer Cross	45	A hybrid that shows resistance to heat and drought; roots are white, crisp and sweet; roots measure 12–15 in. long and 2 in. in diameter; midseason.
Round Black Spanish	60	A winter variety with dark brown, nearly black skin and white flesh; roots measure 3–4 in. in diameter.
China Rose (also Scarlet China)	52–55	A winter variety with bright pink flesh; roots grow 5–6 in. long; stores in good condition for a long time.
White Chinese (also Celestial, California Mammoth White)	60	Delicately flavored; roots measure 6 to 8 in. long, 2–3 in. in diameter; a winter variety.

of garden space at all, finding that they can interplant this undemanding crop in among others, in nearly any part of the garden. In winter, they are easily grown indoors, on a south-facing windowsill where the temperature is 60°F or below.

Radishes are classified in several ways. The first is according to their planting time. There are early or spring varieties, midseason or summer varieties, and late or winter varieties. Radishes also are classed according to the shape of their roots—oblong, flat, round, half-long, and long. Among these, their size varies tremendously, from the small, early, round radishes commonly found in supermarkets all the way up to some oriental late varieties that are bigger than a soccer ball and weigh 50 pounds or more.

Early and midseason radishes, with their crisp white flesh and sharp flavor, are generally used while immature as a condiment or in salads. The late varieties, which grow much larger, are generally cooked, and are used in soups and stews, or as a vegetable side dish, much like turnips. These late varieties are called winter radishes because they store well over the winter without developing hollow cores. All radishes are good sources of vitamin C.

Growing Range: Radishes may be grown in all regions, although most require cool weather (averaging 60° to 65°F) for best development. Midseason varieties can withstand more heat, and are recommended for warm climates. All radishes are half-hardy and resistant to light frosts.

Soil Preparation: Give this crop a loose, light, well-drained soil that is moist and contains large amounts of compost or well-rotted manure. Avoid an excess of nitrogen, for that will promote top growth at the expense of quick root development. A heavy, compacted soil will result in slow-growing and misshapen roots. The soil pH should be between 5.5 and 6.8.

Propagation: Radish seeds are always sown directly into the garden. For all varieties, the minimum temperature for germination is 40°F. Unused seed is good for five years. Early varieties should be sown as early in spring as the soil can be worked, four to six weeks before the frost-free date. In warm climates, grow them as a winter crop. Succession plantings can be made every 10 days until the weather becomes too warm. They can be planted again in the fall. Plant seeds ½ inch deep, in conventional rows 10 to 12 inches apart, or use the wide-row method. Growing bed spacing is 3 inches. Avoid sowing too thickly. Since germination is quick, bare spots may easily be filled in later.

Midseason varieties are planted in mid to late spring, and require more growing room. Plant them ¾ inch deep in rows set 10 to 15 inches apart. Successive plantings can be made until midsummer.

Late varieties (winter radishes) should be planted ¾ inch deep in rows spaced 18 to 20 inches apart. In northern gardens, plant about 10 weeks before the first expected frost for a fall harvest. In southern gardens, seed can be sown two months before the frost-free date for an early spring harvest or in fall for a winter crop.

Culture: When seedlings are 1 inch tall, thin in rows as follows: 2 inches apart for early varieties, 3 to 5 inches apart for midseason varieties, and 6 inches for late varieties.

The key to good radish production is loose soil, and sufficient moisture for quick and tender growth. Radishes need little care after they have been planted. A good mulch, applied when seedlings are 3 inches tall, will help to keep the soil cool and conserve moisture. Do not cultivate close to the plants, since the roots are easily disturbed. Bolting to seed is common when early varieties meet midsummer weather. The cause of bolting is not primarily the heat, but the longer daylength. Early varieties planted in early fall in northern areas, for example, will not bolt even if hot weather persists. (But they still will not be equal in quality to spring-grown crops.)

Pests and Diseases: Cabbage loopers, flea beetles, harlequin bugs, imported cabbage worms, and onion maggots may present problems.

Harvest and Storage: For best texture and mildest flavor, pull up early radishes while they are under 1 inch in diameter. Midseason varieties may be harvested anytime they are large enough to be of use. Late varieties should be left in the ground to mature, since they are greatly improved by the first autumn frosts. In warm climates, they may be left in the ground for a few weeks after they have matured, but will gradually become woody after that. Winter radishes may be stored in a cool (32° to 40°F) and moist storage area.

RHUBARB

Pieplant
Rheum rhaponticum
Polygonaceae

Rhubarb's leaf stem, properly called a petiole, is the only edible portion of the plant. Both roots and leaves are toxic to humans and should never be eaten. The petiole which supports the large round leaf is pink, red, or reddish green and thick and fleshy. The taste is slightly acid and serves as an interesting foil to the palate when sweetened and added to other cooked fruits. It is commonly prepared in sauces, pies, and jams. The stems are also pulverized and fermented with sweetener to make an interesting homemade wine. Rhubarb stems are a good source of vitamin A and potassium, and provide some vitamin C as well.

Rhubarb is not a suitable plant for a small garden. It is a long-lived perennial that grows large and rangy. It needs a well-prepared site where it will remain for many years. Although it occupies the garden all season long, its useful harvest period is eight to ten weeks at most. But in larger gardens, rhubarb certainly deserves a spot, for it produces its delicious leaf stems with little attention from the gardener, once it is established.

Growing Range: Rhubarb favors cool weather. The upper half of North America is more favorable than the lower half. Areas where the mean temperature in summer is above 75°F and in winter is above 40°F are not suitable. Areas where winter dormancy is brought on by temperatures that freeze the crown are most desirable. In some areas with mild winters the plant will remain dormant in the summer and leaf out in winter.

Soil Preparation: Rhubarb will do well in a wide range of soil types, although well-drained sandy loams are preferable. Whatever the soil type, good drainage is critical. Dig a trench, and lay aside the good topsoil. Make it 18 inches wide and 2 to 3 feet deep—the deeper the better. Discard the subsoil and fill in the trench with well-rotted manure and rich compost. At this point, add a shovelful of bone meal and two shovels of granite dust per plant. Mix these thoroughly into the organic material. Other long-term phosphorus and potassium fertilizers such as phosphate rock and greensand can be substituted for the bone meal and granite dust. Pack down the organic material to within 12 inches of the top and fill in with topsoil. Shortcuts can be made, of course, but these directions

Rhubarb

Variety Name	General Description and Comments
Cherry Red	Cherry red color on outside of stalk, greenish shade inside cut stalk; very tart and juicy; good producer; suited for mild-winter areas.
Chipman's Canada Red	Heavy stalks, bright red outside and inside; very sweet and juicy; keeps color when cooked; seldom goes to seed.
Flare	Stalks vary in color from red to green; good producer; pleasant balance of tart and sweet taste.
McDonald's Canadian Red	Dark red outside and inside the stalk; reputed to be the sweetest; peeling the stalk is unnecessary; lends deep pink hue to sauces and pies.

are predicated on a rhubarb bed constructed for use over a long period of time. Soil pH can range from 5.0 to 6.8.

Propagation: Rhubarb is best started in the home garden from crowns that are purchased or donated by a fellow gardener. Crowns can be planted as early as possible in spring, before their dormancy has broken, or in fall before the ground freezes hard.

The plants in an established bed should be divided and replanted every five years to keep them from crowding each other and producing slender, inferior stalks. Divide plants that are at least three years old and dormant, either in early spring or fall. Dig the crowns and split them to leave at least two large buds or "eyes" on each piece; leave as much root on each piece as possible. Roughly four to six pieces can be split from each crown. Do not allow these divisions to dry out before planting.

In the prepared bed plant crown divisions 3 feet apart in rows set 4 feet apart. Bury the crowns 2 to 3 inches deep, then firm the soil.

Culture: Keep the bed free of weeds, moist, and in good, workable condition. Rhubarb leaf and stem production will fall off sharply when the roots become dry. Mulch with straw or hay when plants are 4 inches tall, and side-dress with manure through the summer and fall months. Allow the leaves and stems to mature without cutting the first year; from the strength stored in the roots more growth will be produced the following year. Remove seed heads as they appear in order to redirect energy into the roots and leaves. After the leaves die down and the ground has frozen, cover the bed with a deep layer of manure, leaf mold, or compost.

Pests and Diseases: Only the rhubarb curculio causes serious damage. Eliminating wild dock growing in the nearby area helps to prevent infestation of this pest because wild dock is, along with rhubarb, a host to the larvae.

Harvest and Storage: Do not harvest any stalks the first year. The second year, take only a few. Full harvesting begins in spring of the third year, when the stalks are 12 to 24 inches long and the leaves are fully developed, but before the stems become tough. Pull the stems from the crown with a sidewise, twisting motion. Harvesting can continue for eight to ten weeks, but always leave at least half the plant intact. Too heavy a harvest one year will undercut the next season's production.

After harvest, rhubarb cuttings can be stored in the refrigerator for two to three weeks without losing quality. Cooked rhubarb can be frozen and stored for up to a year. Rhubarb is also candied and preserved by canning.

To extend the harvest, rhubarb roots can be forced to produce shoots over the winter. Check chapter 5 for complete instructions.

RUTABAGA

Canadian turnip, swede, Swedish turnip, turnip-rooted cabbage
Brassica napus, Napobrassica Group
Cruciferae

The biennial rutabaga, thought to be a cross between a turnip and a cabbage, is relished for the dense flesh of its bulbous root, which may grow to weigh as much as 6 or 7 pounds. There are both white and yellow-fleshed varieties.

Although the taste of the rutabaga is similar to that of the related turnip, the rutabaga takes about a month longer to mature and is primarily a fall crop with much better storage characteristics. The smooth, waxy, blue-green tops are a rich source of vitamins A, C, and E, and the roots themselves contain plenty of vitamin A and calcium. In the kitchen, rutabaga roots are used much like turnips, usually steamed and mashed or served whole as a vegetable dish, or added to soups and stews. The roots can also be cut raw into slivers and served with a dip. The strong-flavored greens may be used as a potherb.

Rutabagas are not difficult to grow, provided they are given ample moisture and cool

Rutabaga

Variety Name	Average Days to Maturity	General Description and Comments
Laurentian	90	Roots are globe-shaped with purple tops; perhaps the most dependable of all rutabagas.
American Purple Top Yellow	85–90	A standard variety; yellow, globe-shaped roots have purple tops; flesh is sweet and smooth-textured.

nights as they approach maturity. A hot autumn may destroy the quality of the root, as may a deficiency of potassium or boron. Only one planting is usually made in a season.

Growing Range: Rutabagas do best in medium- and short-season areas where they are planted in late spring or summer so that the roots may mature in cool autumn weather. Best root development is made in temperatures averaging from 60° to 65°F. Planted in spring or in hot climates, the tops will grow rankly, producing small and pithy roots. This hardy crop tolerates frost well, but when roots freeze, taste and texture are altered.

Soil Preparation: Rutabaga does best in medium-heavy soils, including the heavier sandy loams, although it may be grown in lighter soils if ample nutrients and moisture are provided. The soil should be well limed (the ideal pH is 6.5 to 7.2), rich in organic matter and nutrients, but not overly rich in nitrogen, which will force top growth to the detriment of the root. Prepare the soil to a depth of 10 inches and incorporate plenty of aged compost and some wood ashes for extra potassium.

Propagation: Sow seeds directly in the garden 15 weeks before the first expected frost. Space seed ½ inch apart in conventional rows set 18 inches apart. Growing bed spacing is 9 inches. Rutabagas may also be grown in wide rows.

Cover the seed with ½ inch of soil and do not tamp the soil too firmly after planting. Unused seed is good for four years.

Culture: As soon as seeds have germinated, thin the seedlings to stand 1 inch apart in rows. In two weeks, thin again to 8 inches apart. Mulch the rows deeply after the second thinning, to keep the soil cool and moist through the growing season. Rutabagas need no further attention until harvest time.

Pests and Diseases: See Cabbage. Rutabaga is bothered far less than cabbage.

Harvest and Storage: Rutabagas may be harvested anytime they are large enough to be of use. They are at their best when 3 to 5 inches around and no longer than 5 to 7 inches. Most gardeners wait to harvest until after the first sharp autumn frost, which improves both the taste and texture of the roots. At the same time, do not let the roots freeze, for this will shorten their storage life and alter their flavor unpleasantly. They keep for five to six months in good shape, provided they are stored under cool (32° to 40°F) and moist conditions. They can also be stored right in the garden, covered with a deep mulch to keep the ground from freezing, and harvested as needed. If any roots remain in place until spring, they will sprout forth with new growth which can be used as a potherb.

SALSIFY

Oyster plant, vegetable oyster
Tragopogon porrifolius
Compositae

This biennial root crop has been grown for centuries in Europe, and in North America since early colonial days. Its fleshy white root grows to a length of 8 inches and is more slender than a parsnip. Similar plants, sometimes called salsify, are *Scolymus hispanicus* (Spanish oyster plant), which has higher yields but a milder flavor, and *Scorzonera hispanica* (black salsify or black oyster plant), which has black-skinned white flesh and a flavor considered by some to be superior to that of common salsify.

The common name of "oyster plant" is derived from the delicate flavor of the sautéed or steamed root, which is akin to that of the oyster. Salsify is used in all the ways that parsnips and rutabagas are used, as a side dish or in soups and stews. Thin slices of raw salsify make a nice accompaniment to dips. The roots may also be used to make mock oyster stew. Although it is not the most popular of root crops, its adherents are loyal, planting it each year.

Growing Range: Salsify is a long-season crop that may be grown in all areas where the season is at least 100 days long. Plantings in shorter-season areas may yield good, but smaller, crops. It grows best when temperatures are 55° to 75°F, and withstands frost quite well. In very warm climates, the texture and taste will be inferior, since both are improved by freezing weather.

Soil Preparation: Salsify needs rich, loose, well-drained soil. Till the soil to a depth of 10 inches and remove any stones or clods, which will cause misshapen roots. Work compost into the soil along with extra wood ashes or other potassium-rich material, but do not add extra nitrogen. The presence of fresh manure in the soil will cause roots to fork. On the pH scale, soil should be as close to neutral (7) as possible, even leaning slightly to the alkaline side (greater than 7). Add ground limestone if needed.

Propagation: Direct-seed into the garden two to four weeks before the frost-free date. Soil temperature must reach at least 40°F for germination. Sow seed thinly, 1 inch deep, in conventional rows spaced 12 to 15 inches apart. Growing bed spacing is 6 inches. Unused seed is good for one to three years.

Culture: When seedlings are 3 inches tall, thin them to stand 4 inches apart in the rows. Keep the plants well supplied with moisture until they have become well established, then add mulch. Side-dress monthly with wood ashes, or water every three weeks with seaweed extract solution.

Pests and Diseases: There are no serious problems.

Harvest and Storage: Salsify roots may be dug with a spade or fork as soon as they have grown to usable size; however, their taste and texture are greatly improved by the first sharp freezes of late autumn or early winter.

They may be stored in a root cellar for five to six months, if given cold (32° to 40°F) and moist conditions. They do not keep as well as parsnips, however, since they tend to shrivel and lose both taste and texture if the proper conditions are not maintained. A better storage method involves cutting the tops and keeping the roots in the garden rows over the winter. In most areas, a heavy mulch will enable them to be harvested throughout the winter. In very cold areas, store the crop in a box, barrel, or garbage can sunk in the ground. Roots left in the ground too long after the soil warms may produce shoots, which become another harvest. Cut them when they are 5 to 6 inches tall, and prepare them like asparagus for an early spring treat.

Varieties: The only variety commonly found in catalogs is Mammoth Sandwich Island (around 120 days to maturity), which has been the standard for generations.

SHALLOTS

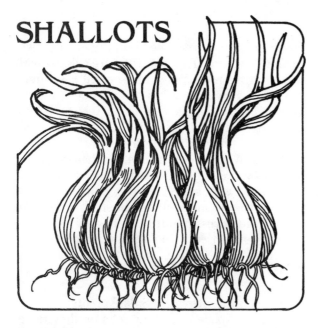

Allium cepa, Aggregatum Group
Amaryllidaceae

Mild-flavored shallot bulbs are highly prized for use in soups and stews, in salads and salad dressings, and are an important ingredient in many French recipes. The young plants may be harvested for use as green onions. But most gardeners prefer to wait until the bulbs have developed and matured. The small bulbs grow in clusters, like garlic, but instead of being held together by an enveloping membrane, they are attached at the base. Shallots rarely produce seed, so they are generally propagated by planting individual bulbs which proceed to multiply into a cluster of 8 to 12 bulbs.

The planting bulbs or "sets" are very expensive to purchase since many are imported from Europe. But they are worth the initial investment since they are easy to grow and are very productive—1 pound of sets will grow 5 to 7 pounds of shallots. Once the sets have been purchased, the gardener can save a portion of each crop to replant the following season. And for gourmet cooks, growing shallots can be economical, since these tasty bulbs are very high-priced items in the store.

Shallots are perennials that can be left in the ground in mild-winter areas from season to season. But for the best quality and the largest-sized bulbs, they should be lifted and replanted each year, no matter which region they are grown in.

Growing Range: Shallots may be grown in all regions. They prefer average temperatures between 55° and 75°F, but they are hardy plants and a few light frosts will not hurt them.

Soil Preparation: Shallots need a well-drained soil, rich in nutrients (especially phosphorus and potassium), that has good water-retaining capacity. Prepare the soil to a medium fineness. Raised beds are a good way to compensate for heavy soils. The recommended pH range is 6 to 7.

Propagation: In warm climates, start shallots in the fall. In cool climates, plant them two to four weeks before the frost-free date, when the soil is workable. Plant the sets 4 to 6 inches apart in conventional rows spaced 9 inches apart. Shallots are also well suited to wide-row planting. Spacing for raised beds is 6 inches. Plant the sets with pointed ends up and blunt ends down, so that just the tip of the bulb shows above the ground. Replant any bulbs that have pushed their way out of the soil or have been dislodged by birds.

Culture: Mulch around the plants once five or six shoots have appeared, three to four weeks after planting. Mulch lightly, using straw, leaves, or peat moss, and avoid covering the shoots. Cultivate very shallowly to eliminate weeds during the growing season. Do not let the soil dry out, but avoid soggy soil which may rot young plants. As frost approaches, withhold water to hasten the withering of the tops which in turn promotes the curing of the bulb clusters.

Pests and Diseases: Shallots are not affected to any great extent by either. Pink rot may be a problem in warm climates.

Harvest and Storage: For use as a green onion, dig or pull clusters at any time. For dry bulbs, wait until the tops have browned, withered, and dropped off, then harvest and treat exactly like garlic (see Garlic). Shallots are very good keepers in cool (32° to 40°F) and dry storage areas. Save some of the healthy, small-to-medium-sized bulbs for next season's crop.

Shallots

Variety Name	Average Days to Maturity	General Description and Comments
Giant Red	100	Sprouts earlier than yellow types; excellent for salads and cooking; stores well through winter and spring.
French Epicurean	100	Delicately onion-flavored bulbs can be planted in spring or fall; may be left in the ground over winter.
Yellow Multiplier	100	The most commonly planted type; good keeper.

SORREL

French sorrel, garden sorrel
Rumex acetosa, R. scutatus
Polygonaceae

The sorrel that is cultivated today is not much different from the sorrel which was grown during Roman times. Sorrel's standing among the ancients as a medicinal herb is understandable when the food value of the plant is studied. Sorrel contains a number of minerals and is extremely high in vitamin C, and it is this vitamin and mineral content that is responsible for the unique tart flavor of the leaves. Although sorrel is often recommended as a spinach substitute, those familiar with sorrel will know that a liking for its tartness is an acquired taste that cannot always be transferred from spinach. There is very little similarity between the two, aside from a shared acidic nature.

French cuisine makes wonderful use of sorrel, but old English recipes for sorrel are equally good. Whatever the language of the recipe, cream of sorrel soup is a delightful way to prepare this herb. It is a tasty ingredient in omelets, sauces, and stuffings, and its piquant flavor combines well with steamed greens such as kale, mustard, and Swiss chard. In addition, raw sorrel can be tossed with other salad greens, especially those greens that are a bit bland.

Garden sorrel and French sorrel produce fleshy green leaves in a rosette at the base of the plant. Garden sorrel grows a little taller and has larger leaves than its French cousin. Many people prefer the tangier flavor of French sorrel to the milder flavor of garden sorrel. Both of these species are perennials, and when grown in a well-tended bed they will yield a crop of tasty greens for three to four years.

Growing Range: Sorrel can be raised successfully in any temperate region.

Soil Preparation: Sorrel will adapt to a wide variety of soils, but it prefers a moderately acid soil (pH of 5.0 to 6.8), and a moist location. Best growth results from a soil that is rich in nitrogen. Since sorrel is a perennial, prepare the soil well at the outset to provide a good rich bed for many years' growth. Mix in plenty of compost and well-rotted manure.

Propagation: A sorrel bed can be started from seed or from root divisions of established plants. Sow seed directly in the garden in spring or fall, when the soil temperature is above 60°F. Scatter seeds in rows spaced 18 inches apart, and cover with ¼ inch of soil. Unused seed is good for four years.

Sorrel

Variety Name	Average Days to Maturity	General Description and Comments
Large Belleville	70	The standard garden sorrel variety; grows quickly to 2 ft. tall and will eventually spread laterally to cover an area of 2 ft.
Narrow Leaf	70	The standard French sorrel variety; low-growing, compact plant has darker, coarser leaves and tangier flavor than garden sorrel.

Roots of established plants can be divided in spring or fall. This is especially helpful when the beds have become overcrowded. Select the healthiest clumps that are sending out vigorous shoots. Remove them from the ground and divide so that each piece has some new shoots and roots. Replant these pieces no deeper than they were before, in newly tilled and fertilized soil.

Culture: When the seedlings are 1 inch tall, thin to stand 18 inches apart in the rows. Once the plants are established, pick off a few outer leaves from each rosette to encourage good branching. Each spring, side-dress the plants with well-aged manure or compost. Supplemental feedings of fish emulsion once a month are necessary only on poor soil. Apply a mulch during the hot part of the year to keep the plants from drying out and bolting to seed. Within a year or two the sorrel will have spread out to fill the growing space, and the plants will form their own living mulch. After their second year in the ground, the plants usually attempt to go to seed. Pinch or cut back the fibrous seed stalks sent up by the plants in midseason to channel more energy into leaf production. Also, if the seed forms and scatters on the ground, there may be a critical case of overpopulation in the bed. If the bed becomes overcrowded, in addition to lifting and dividing the roots, a sprinkling of lime will discourage further growth.

Pests and Diseases: Sorrel is relatively free of insect damage and disease, although whiteflies can be a minor problem.

Harvest and Storage: Leaves can be harvested anytime throughout the growing season. Young, tender leaves are preferred over older leaves which are tough and fibrous. Harvest from the outer leaves in, cutting or pinching off as many as needed, always leaving a rosette of young growth intact for continuous leaf production. The leaves wilt soon after harvest, so plan on cutting them right before they will be used.

SOYBEANS

Glycine max
Leguminosae

Traditionally used as a green manure crop or livestock feed, it has not been until the last several decades that Westerners have discovered the soybean's great value in human nutrition.

The plants grow from 12 inches to more than 24 inches tall and most are bushy, although some have an indeterminate habit. These legumes produce pods usually containing three to four seeds, in shades of yellow, brown, black, or in various combinations of these colors. The seeds are about the size of navy beans.

Soybeans have a rich nutty flavor all their own. The home gardener can fully appreciate their versatility and good taste by using them as a fresh vegetable or as dried beans. The green shell beans can be steamed as a vegetable dish, chilled for use in salads, roasted like peanuts, or added to soups, stews, and chili. The dry beans are also used for soups and stews, and in addition can be ground into flour, or processed into soy milk, tofu, or tempeh. Nutritionally speaking, soybeans are protein powerhouses, containing 40 percent protein. They are a favorite meat substitute among vegetarians.

Growing Range: Most soybeans require a long and hot growing season, with temperatures averaging between 70° and 80°F. There are some varieties, however, that mature in as little as 70 days, affording gardeners in all areas the opportunity to grow this crop. Soybeans are slightly more cold-tolerant than other beans, but are still susceptible to frost damage.

Soil Preparation: The soil should be light, well drained, well limed, and not too rich in nutrients—especially nitrogen, which will impede the production of pods and seeds. Even clay soils will support good crops, as long as they are not waterlogged for long periods. Choose the sunniest area of the garden. Prepare the soil to average fineness, and do not add compost unless the soil is very deficient in nutrients. Soybeans, which are legumes, will add nitrogen to the soil for crops that follow. The recommended pH is 6.5 to 7.0.

Propagation: Soybeans are generally direct-seeded. Soak the seeds overnight to hasten germination, and inoculate them before planting. There are inoculants specifically suited for soybeans but these may not be readily obtainable; in lieu of soybean inoculant, one suited for peas and beans can be used. Plant the seeds only when the soil has warmed up thoroughly to an optimum germinating temperature of 65° to 70°F, about a week after the frost-free date. The planting area can be warmed up by covering it with black plastic for two weeks before planting. Remove the plastic when planting. Plant the beans 1½ inches deep in moist soils, or 3 to 4 inches deep in dry, warm soils (generally in hot climates). Space seeds 1½ inches apart in conventional rows set 30 inches apart. Soybeans are suitable for planting in wide rows. Raised bed spacing is 9 inches. Unused seed is good for three years.

Culture: After the plants are 2 to 3 inches tall, thin them to 4 inches apart in rows and apply

Soybeans

There are two groups, the field soybeans (used for soil improvement and livestock feed) and the sweet or edible soybeans which are covered here. The variety chosen will depend largely on the number of frost-free days in the growing season. Soybeans are sensitive to daylength, with long days hastening maturity. Most varieties will mature only within a certain geographical area that offers the proper daylength. The home gardener should check with the local extension agent for the varieties recommended for that particular area.

Variety Name	Average Days to Maturity	General Description and Comments
Kanrich	100–115	A long-season variety; heavy yields of low-starch beans appear on 24-in. plants; suitable for canning and freezing; can be enjoyed green or dried; recommended for warm climates only.
Extra Early Green	70	A short-season variety; produces many tender, delicious beans.
Early Green Bush	85	A midseason variety; bushy plants grow to 16 in. tall.
Altona	90–100	A reliable producer, even in northern gardens; beans are bright yellow when mature.
Frostbeater	75	A reliable, heavy producer; bright green beans have a robust flavor; does well in northern gardens.
Fiskeby V	91	An especially high-protein variety; 18-in., bushy plants will bear even in northern gardens.

a mulch. Avoid working among plants when the leaves are wet, since leaves are easily broken then, and disease can be spread. Keep the soil evenly moist, especially after flowers have opened, until pods have set.

Pests and Diseases: Soybeans are subject to attack from both, although none is usually serious. Potential insect pests include cutworms, grasshoppers, Japanese beetles, leafhoppers, Mexican bean beetles, and white grubs. The fuzzy leaves of the plant seem to drive insects to more succulent garden plants. Diseases include bacterial blight (in cool, rainy weather), bacterial pustule, and downy mildew.

Harvest and Storage: For use as a green shell bean, pick when the seeds are mature, or nearly mature, but before the pods and foliage have begun to wither. To make hulling easier, steam the pods for ten minutes, drain them, break them in half crosswise and squeeze out the beans. At this stage, soybeans may be eaten fresh, or they may be canned or frozen.

For storage as dry beans, harvest when the pods are dry but the plant stems are still green. Waiting longer than this may give the pods time to shatter, thus losing the seeds. Follow the directions given for shelling and drying beans. (See Drying Your Bean Harvest for Storage in chapter 5.) Store soybeans in airtight containers in a cool (32° to 40°F), dry location.

SPINACH

Spinacia oleracea
Chenopodiaceae

Spinach, a member of the same family as beets and Swiss chard, is a cool-weather annual that is very sensitive to changes in daylength. Long days cause it to bolt, and this tendency to flower is encouraged by the onset of warm temperatures. Once spinach changes to its flower-producing stage, it is no longer desirable as a good plant. The leaves that grow in compact rosettes from the root crown are the edible parts. Spinach needs to be grown quickly to provide the best-tasting and largest-sized leaves. It grows well in partial shade.

Because of the ease with which it grows, its compact size, and the rapidity with which it matures, spinach deserves a place in every garden. A few plants tucked into the smallest garden will produce a lot of leaves in return for the space they occupy. These low growers do well when placed between tall shade-throwing crops like peas. Homegrown spinach is superior to the taste of even the freshest market produce. At the end of summer, spinach makes an ideal succession plant to put in after other vegetables

have been harvested, since it matures quickly and tolerates frost.

Spinach's nutritional value is another convincing reason for including it in the garden. Besides having only 20 calories in the average serving, it provides an adult with 100 percent of the vitamin A, 56 percent of the vitamin C and 28 percent of the iron recommended as average daily requirements. The leaves can be enjoyed raw, and make an especially tasty salad when combined with mushrooms and tossed with a mustardy dressing. The leaves can also be steamed as a vegetable dish, or added to soups.

There are basically two types of spinach, the smooth-leaf and the savoyed (wrinkled and curly) leaf. The savoyed spinach tends to trap grit in its leaf crevices, and is somewhat harder to clean. Varieties have been developed that are resistant to bolting in warm weather, and will stand in the garden in good condition for some time. These heat-tolerant varieties should be used for spring planting. When temperatures climb too high for successful spinach growing, try New Zealand spinach, which thrives in the heat (see New Zealand Spinach).

Growing Range: Spinach can be grown in a wide range of areas, as long as short days and cool temperatures are present. It is a hardy plant that can undergo light frosts without damage. The average temperature range for best growth is 60° to 65°F. In mild-winter areas where temperatures rarely dip below 25°F, it is successfully raised as a winter crop.

Soil Preparation: Spinach will tolerate a wide variety of soils, but it prefers a well-drained, sandy loam with ample organic matter. The best preparation is to apply fresh manure in the fall, then till it under in early spring. In lieu of that, well-rotted manure or compost can be worked in in spring, along with organic sources of potassium and phosphorus.

Propagation: Spinach can be direct-seeded in the garden or started indoors to get a head start on the season. Spinach tolerates transplanting only if seed is sown in individual containers.

Spinach

Variety Name	Average Days to Maturity	General Description and Comments
Savoyed-Leaf		
America	50	Dark green leaves; good for spring planting; slow to bolt; heavy yielder; AAS.
Longstanding Bloomsdale	48	Dark green, thick leaves; erect plant; slow to bolt; good for spring planting.
Melody	45	Semisavoyed leaves; semierect plant; adapted to spring and fall planting; resistant to downy mildew and yellows; a heavy yielder and fast grower; AAS.
Winter Bloomsdale	45	Dark green leaves are especially crinkled; good for spring and winter culture, but especially suited for cold-weather growing because of its hardiness; slow to bolt.
Smooth-Leaf		
Hybrid 424	45	Light green, arrow-shaped leaves; resistant to downy mildew.
Monnopa	40	Light green, arrow-shaped leaves; low oxalic acid content makes it suitable for baby foods; very mild; cold-hardy.
Viking	45	Relatively smooth, light green leaves; a fast grower; long-standing; suited for spring or fall planting.

Start four to six weeks before setting out, which is done three to six weeks before the frost-free date. Set transplants every 6 inches along conventional rows spaced 14 inches apart. The spacing for raised beds is 6 inches.

Sow seed in the garden four to six weeks before the frost-free date, when soil temperature is a minimum of 35°F. Sow ½ inch deep every 6 inches in growing beds. Spinach can also be planted in wide rows. Plant every two to three weeks for small, nonstop harvests. Sow seeds up to six weeks before daytime temperatures can be expected to stay above 75°F. Sow the fall crop about nine weeks before the first expected frost. Unused seed is good for one to two years.

Culture: When seedlings in conventional and wide rows are 4 to 5 inches tall, thin to 6 inches apart. Use the thinnings for salads or add them to dishes with other mixed greens.

Keep the growing area free of weeds. The shallow fibrous roots through which spinach takes up nutrients are easily dominated by more vigorous weeds, and easily damaged by deep cultivation. Apply a mulch when plants are established. Keep soil evenly moist to promote quick growth and to forestall bolting.

Pests and Diseases: Aphids, European corn borers, leafminers, and whiteflies are frequently the agents of damage on spinach leaves. Blight and downy mildew are frequent diseases.

Harvest and Storage: For a prolonged harvest, treat spinach as a cut-and-come-again crop. When outside leaves are large enough to be useful, pinch or cut them individually from the plant. Don't strip the plant bare; at no time should more than half the plant be taken. Inner leaves will keep developing until either the seed stalk appears or extreme cold weather sets in. To harvest the entire plant, cut it from the root crown and discard the older leaves. Spinach can be refrigerated for a short time. Cooked spinach can be canned or frozen.

SQUASH

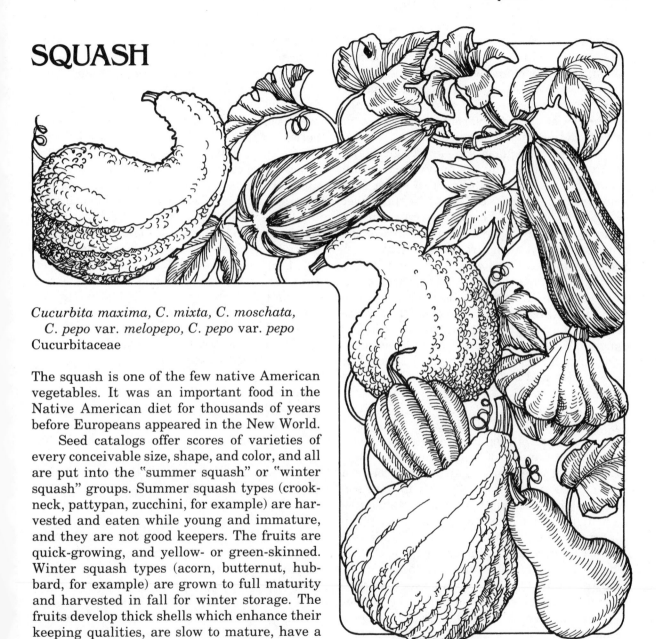

Cucurbita maxima, C. mixta, C. moschata,
  C. pepo var. *melopepo, C. pepo* var. *pepo*
Cucurbitaceae

The squash is one of the few native American vegetables. It was an important food in the Native American diet for thousands of years before Europeans appeared in the New World.

Seed catalogs offer scores of varieties of every conceivable size, shape, and color, and all are put into the "summer squash" or "winter squash" groups. Summer squash types (crookneck, pattypan, zucchini, for example) are harvested and eaten while young and immature, and they are not good keepers. The fruits are quick-growing, and yellow- or green-skinned. Winter squash types (acorn, butternut, hubbard, for example) are grown to full maturity and harvested in fall for winter storage. The fruits develop thick shells which enhance their keeping qualities, are slow to mature, have a pronounced seed cavity, and are usually heartier in flavor.

Just what is a squash and what is a pumpkin has long bothered botanists and confused gardeners. Botanically, a true pumpkin (*C. pepo* or *C. moschata*) has a hard stem leading to the fruit, while a true squash (*C. maxima*) has a soft or spongy stem. This places most summer squash, as well as the acorn squash, in the botanical category of pumpkins. In this book botanical distinctions will be set aside for the moment, and those vegetables commonly grown and used as squash will be listed as "squash." Those varieties commonly thought of as pumpkins will be listed under that name regardless of the softness of their stems.

Summer squash is delicious when baked, boiled, or steamed, and when used in a variety of recipes. Winter squash is traditionally baked. Both types are good sources of vitamin A. The flowers of some varieties can be eaten, as well as the dried or roasted seeds.

All types of squash are easy to grow and high-yielding, but they are heavy feeders and generally take up a lot of garden space. The standard vining types need about 10 square feet of growing room if allowed to sprawl on the ground. One way to save space is to train the vines vertically along trellises or tripods. A practical alternative for space saving in the garden is the use of bush varieties, which are available in both summer and winter types.

Growing Range: Squash is a warm-climate crop and may be grown in any area that offers warm and sunny summers. The best temperature range for growth is 65° to 75°F. Squash is very tender, and is very susceptible to damage by frost.

Soil Preparation: The ideal soil is a rich, sandy loam. But squash will grow in any soil that is adequately fertile, well drained, well aerated, and capable of holding moisture. They produce best when copious amounts of compost or aged manure are worked deeply into the soil before planting, along with some phosphorus-rich material such as phosphate rock. When planting in hills, concentrate the organic material to a depth of 12 inches under each hill. The recommended pH range is 6 to 7.

Propagation: In long-season areas (120 days or more), seeds of both summer and winter types are sown directly in the garden one week or more after the frost-free date. In short-season areas, summer squash can be direct-seeded at the same time, but gardeners who wish to get a jump on the season, and especially those who are raising winter types, should start seeds indoors (see below). The minimum soil temperature for germination is 60°F. A black plastic mulch applied two weeks before planting will help warm the soil more quickly. Remove the mulch when planting, and replace later with an organic mulch. If cloches are used, the planting date may be advanced two to three weeks.

Squash is often planted in hills. Plant vining types in hills spaced 6 to 8 feet apart, six seeds per hill. Bush types require 4 to 5 feet between hills, with six seeds to a hill. Conventional rows may also be used. Space vining types 3 to 4 feet apart in rows set 8 to 12 feet apart. Bush types are set 2 to 3 feet apart in rows spaced 4 to 6 feet apart. Growing bed spacing for summer squash is 24 inches; spacing for winter squash is 36 inches. Plant all seed 1 inch deep. Unused seed is good for five years.

Start seed indoors four weeks before setting out. Use individual pots so that there is minimal disturbance to the roots during the transplanting process. Set summer types out four weeks after the frost-free date. Winter squash can be set out sooner, three to four weeks after the frost-free date. Use the spacings given above as a guide.

Culture: Thin seedlings in hills, leaving the sturdiest two or three to continue growing. Cultivate frequently and destroy all weeds early in the season. Apply a heavy hay mulch around all plants before the vines spread out. Keep the soil evenly moist throughout the season. If your soil is not in good shape, side-dress the plants monthly with aged manure or compost, or water with fish emulsion every three weeks.

Squash is not self-fertilizing so pollination by bees or other insects is essential. Male and female flowers are distinct, and sometimes appear on separate plants. Male blossoms appear first, about a week before female flowers, and will drop off without producing fruit. Immature fruit that refuses to grow probably has not been fertilized, usually because of adverse weather or a scarcity of insects. Pollination may be carried out easily by using a camel hair brush to transfer pollen from the male stamen to the female pistil. Female flowers have an enlarged swelling (the ovary) just behind the blossom, and a four-part curved pistil in the center of the blossom; the male flower has no swollen

Squash

Variety Name	Average Days to Maturity	General Description and Comments
Summer Squash		
Aristocrat	48–53	A hybrid zucchini of good quality; very widely grown; bears fruit upright for easy harvesting; AAS.
Gold Rush	50	Yellow-fruited zucchini type; a vigorous grower and good producer; AAS.
Scallopini	50	A hybrid that is actually a cross between scallop and zucchini types; bright green shell is scallop-shaped; compact growth habit; AAS.
Butterbar	50	A hybrid straightneck type bearing long, cylindrical, yellow fruits; bushy growth.
Early Prolific Straightneck	51	Very productive straightneck type; cylindrical fruit are 6 in. long; bushy plant; AAS.
St. Pat Scallop	75	A hybrid bearing greenish white scallop-shaped fruit; heavy yields; AAS.
Winter Squash		
Hercules Butternut	95–110	Larger fruit than standard butternut types; small seed cavity; delicious-flavored flesh; AAS.
Waltham Butternut	82–85	A high yielder; fruits are 9–12 in. long; necks are slightly crooked; small seed cavity; AAS.
Blue Hubbard	110–120	Large fruit with blue-gray shell; average weight is 15 lb.; a good keeper, excellent for baking and freezing.
Golden Hubbard (also Red Hubbard)	90–100	Orange-red shells have reddish stripes; flesh is suitable for canning and freezing; good keeper.
Turk's Turban	100	Brilliant orange, red, cream, white, and dark green shell; fruit measures 8–10 in. in diameter; a turban-shaped fruit grown for novelty as well as table use.
Royal Acorn (also Mammoth Table Queen)	80–90	Acorn type with dark green shell that changes to orange when stored; fruits measure 7 by 6 in.
Table King (also Bush Acorn)	70–80	A compact, bushy acorn type; fruits weigh 1½ lb.; a plant usually bears 6–8 fruits; very good for small gardens.
Vegetable Spaghetti	95–100	Introduced from Japan; white-skinned fruits grow 10–12 in. long; to prepare, boil the fully ripe fruit for 30 minutes, then open and remove the "spaghetti strings"; serve with tomato sauce as a spaghetti substitute, or with butter.

portion behind it, and a single, fat stamen in the center of the blossom.

Pests and Diseases: Potential insect pests are cabbage loopers, corn earworms, cucumber beetles, squash bugs, and squash vine borers. Squash are affected by the same diseases that strike cucumbers (see Cucumber). Blossom-end rot may affect fruit development.

Harvest and Storage: Summer squash is ready for use less than two months after planting. They should be harvested while they are young and tender, when the skin yields to thumb pressure or can be penetrated easily by the thumbnail. Zucchini are best when they are about 7 inches long and 1½ inches thick. Pattypan are at their peak when 3 to 4 inches across, crookneck and straightneck when 4 inches long. Summer squash allowed to grow too big lose flavor. Keep picking throughout the season to promote continuous fruit production.

Winter squash take longer to mature (80 to 120 days) and should not be harvested until as late as possible in the fall, before the first hard frost. They can withstand a few light frosts, which will help change their starch to sugar and enhance their flavor. If picked too early, they will be watery and bland. The shells should be hard enough to resist denting by a thumbnail. Cut the fruits from the vine, leaving 3 to 4 inches of stem on the fruit. Be careful not to bruise the fruit at any time during curing and storage. Cure all types except acorn squash as described in chapter 5. They should be stored in a warm (50° to 60°F), dry location. Acorn squash should be kept in a cool (32° to 40°F) and moist storage area.

Saving seeds of *C. maxima* (which includes Hubbard, Banana, Turban, and Mammoth types) is not recommended because of the high possibility of cross-pollination.

SWEET POTATOES

Ipomoea batatas
Convolvulaceae

The sweet potato, despite its humble appearance, is a nutritional powerhouse. Its fleshy tuber-roots offer good amounts of carbohydrate and vitamins A and C, and adequate amounts of protein, calcium, iron, and other minerals. It is probably the only vegetable capable of supporting the full nutritional needs of human beings. The sweet potato can be baked, boiled, eaten whole or mashed, made into casseroles, puddings or soups, and even sweet batter-fried as tempura.

The most commonly homegrown tubers have moist, sweet, and tender flesh, and are sometimes referred to as yams. The true yam (*Dioscorea alata*), however, is a vegetable of a completely different genus, grown only in true tropical regions.

Sweet potatoes are not the easiest of vegetables to grow—in northern areas because of climatic limitations, and in warm regions because of problems with diseases. Still, many gardeners plant them each year, with a success rate high enough to continue the practice. In the garden, sweet potatoes are generally large space consumers, with spreading vines that form a dense, low groundcover. However, there are several vineless or bush varieties for space-conscious gardeners.

Growing Range: Sweet potatoes grow the best in long-season areas (150 to 160 days) where summers are hot and not excessively rainy. But northern gardeners can grow them, too, in areas where summers are warm. (The temperature range for best growth is 70° to 85°F.) The longer days of northern latitudes help to offset the shorter season. Although the true maturation time for sweet potatoes is as high as 170 days, ample crops may be harvested in as few as 90 to 100 days. Sweet potatoes are most difficult to grow in very short-season areas (under 100 days) or in regions frequently overcast in summer. This very tender crop is easily damaged by frost.

Soil Preparation: Adequate crops may be raised on soils too poor to support most other vegetables, although better yields will result from well-prepared soils. The soil should be on the light side; a sandy loam is ideal. Too heavy a soil will yield inferior roots that are long and stringy. Most important, the subsoil must be open, so that the long roots of the tubers may search out water at lower depths. For sweet potato success, a rich topsoil cannot compensate for a hard subsoil.

Prepare the soil to a depth of 8 inches around the time of the last average spring frost. Incorporate average amounts of compost and some wood ashes or other potassium-rich material, but do not add excessive nitrogen, which will spur vine growth and stunt tuber development. A combination of excessive nitrogen and excessive rainfall will delay the maturation of the tuber-roots and produce long and slender potatoes instead of the full and chunky shapes desired. Further, a deficiency of potassium will prevent the potatoes from filling out properly. The soil should be acid (pH 5.5 to 6.5) in order to discourage some of the soilborne diseases that mar the surface of the tubers.

Propagation: Start with sweet potato plants purchased at garden centers or by mail order or with plants sprouted at home.

Set young plants out when night temperatures remain above 60°F and the soil temperature is at least 65°F. Short-season gardeners often plant earlier, out of necessity, but offer protection from possible late frosts.

Set 1 to 2 inches of well-rotted compost or manure in a furrow 12 inches wide. Ridge soil 10 inches high over this furrow, and insert plants into soil, 4 to 5 inches deep, every 15 inches along the ridge. If more than one ridge is planted, space them 36 to 48 inches apart. Growing bed spacing is 12 inches; plant each slip in a hill of its own, ridged up to 10 inches tall over a pocket of compost or manure.

Culture: A mulch may be applied after the soil has warmed up thoroughly, but generally the vines grow quickly enough to smother most weeds. In any case, weeds are serious competitors for water and nutrients and should be held in check, especially early in the season as the plants are becoming established.

No supplemental feeding is needed in well-prepared soils. In poorer soils, apply compost

tricks of the trade

Homegrown Slips

To start your own young plants (called slips), set whole tubers lengthwise in a moist rooting medium. Begin the sprouting process six to eight weeks before the setting-out date, which is two to three weeks after the frost-free date. Keep the tubers warm (70° to 80°F). When sprouts have rooted and are 4 to 8 inches tall, gently pull them off the tubers. Each tuber produces a large number of slips. Set these sprouts in individual pots if it is too early to plant outside, or move them directly outdoors if it is warm enough.

Rooted Sweet Potato Slips

Slips can also be started from tubers set in a pan of water. Detach sprouts when they are 4 to 8 inches tall, with four to five leaves and roots, and treat as above.

tea, or a side-dressing of wood ashes about two weeks after planting, and again four weeks after the first application.

Once the plants are established, they need very little additional water. Sweet potatoes tolerate hot, dry conditions very well, and can even survive droughts in good shape.

Pests and Diseases: In cool regions, flea beetles may cause some problems. In warm areas, pests include nematodes, sweet potato beetles, sweet potato weevils, and wireworms. Sweet potatoes may be affected by black rot, soft rot, soil rot, and stem rot.

Harvest and Storage: In a five-month growing season, the tuber-roots often double in bulk during the final month. Thus, although tubers of good quality may be dug while they are immature (called "baby bakers"), the main crop should not be harvested until the first autumn frost. Do not delay, however, since frost-killed vines can quickly lead to rot in the tubers.

Use a spade or fork, and dig the tubers carefully; any bruising of the skin will cause disease problems in storage. Let them sit out on the ground for several hours before bringing them in, provided it is not raining. Cure under conditions described in chapter 5. They are then ready to be stored for the winter at 50° to 60°F in a dry location. If they are harvested while the ground is wet, considerable shrinkage of the roots may occur in storage.

Sweet Potatoes

Variety Name	Average Days to Maturity	General Description and Comments
Centennial	90–100	Sweet, moist, yellow-orange flesh; vining-type plant; recommended for short-season areas; stores well; the most widely grown variety.
Bush Porto Rico	150	High yield of tubers with moist, red-orange flesh; compact growth habit for limited-space garden; very sweet flavor.
New Jewell	100	Vining type with sweet, moist tubers; quick to mature; good storage quality; recommended for short-season areas.

SWISS CHARD

Leaf beet, perpetual spinach, spinach chard
Beta vulgaris var. *cicla*
Chenopodiaceae

Swiss chard and beets share a common plant ancestor, both being derived from the same wild European plant. Swiss chard, however, develops without the thickened, fleshy roots characteristic of beets. Where Swiss chard is short on root development, it compensates by being long on leaf production. The prolific leaf development over the life of a single plant has made it a garden favorite of long standing.

The main advantage of growing Swiss chard is that it can stay in the ground a long time, even during hot weather, yet faithfully keep producing succulent leaves. Swiss chard does well in a wide variety of soils, tolerates some shade, takes a great deal of heat without bolting, and will allow the gardener to strip leaves from it, sometimes for as long as two years, before it becomes unusable. Certain varieties of Swiss chard are very attractive, worthy of a place in an ornamental garden, with deep green leaves and snowy white midribs, or crimson midribs with red or green leaves.

On soils and in climates where spinach has difficulties, Swiss chard will thrive. It is an excellent culinary substitute for spinach and is especially high in vitamin C, calcium, and iron. The red-leaved varieties of Swiss chard are also extremely rich in vitamin A.

Growing Range: Swiss chard can be grown in a wide range of climates. It will tolerate a good deal of frost and will even keep growing during the warmest part of the season. It can be cropped from late spring to late fall, an unusual growing period for any vegetable. In areas of mild winters, it can winter over in the ground and will sometimes produce a second crop.

Soil Preparation: For the best Swiss chard, provide a well-drained, fertile soil rich in humus. Fertilize before planting by digging in liberal amounts of well-rotted manure or compost. Swiss chard will tolerate a soil that is slightly acid, with a pH of 6.0 to 6.8.

Propagation: Direct-seeding is the most common way to start Swiss chard, but transplants can be used for an extra-early crop. Sow seed two to four weeks before the frost-free date. In mild climate areas, make a late summer planting about ten weeks before the first expected frost for a winter and spring harvest. Sow seed ½ inch deep. The optimum soil temperature for germination is 50° to 85°F. For conventional rows, space seed 3 inches apart in rows set 18 inches apart. The spacing for raised beds is 9 inches. Swiss chard is also suitable for wide-row planting.

Start transplants in individual pots four weeks before planting out, which can be done three to four weeks before the frost-free date. Be careful not to disturb roots while transplanting. Use between-row spacings given above and set seedlings every 9 inches. Use the raised bed spacing above.

Swiss chard, like beets, will sprout more than one plant from a seed. These extra sprouts will have to be pinched out later, while thinning. Unused seed is good for four years.

Culture: When the seedlings are 5 to 8 inches tall, thin back to 9-inch spacings in the rows.

Swiss Chard

Variety Name	Average Days to Maturity	General Description and Comments
Fordhook Giant (also Dark Green Lucullus)	50–60	Dark green crumpled leaves have very thick white stalks; a reliable producer; grows 30 in. tall and 36 in. wide.
Lucullus	50–60	The most commonly planted variety; large, crumpled, dark green leaves have broad white stalks; grows 20 in. tall, 30 in. wide.
Rhubarb Chard	55–60	Dark green, crumpled leaves have deep red stalks which darken in cooking; especially sweet and tender leaves; grows 30 in. tall, 30 in. wide.
Ruby Red	60	Stalks are red to white; leaves are red and crumpled in texture; grows to 24 in. tall.

These thinnings can be transplanted if carefully lifted or, if cut, they can be used in the kitchen as tender greens. Swiss chard likes to have moist roots. If the plant undergoes stress from lack of water, it tends to produce seed stalks instead of leaves. In dry climates and exceptionally well-drained soils, mulch in warm weather to prevent bolting. If the seed stalk does appear, cut it off quickly to prolong leaf development. Swiss chard normally requires no feeding, but plants grown on poor soils will benefit from a midseason boost of high-nitrogen fertilizer like manure tea or fish emulsion.

Pests and Diseases: Swiss chard is relatively trouble-free. When plants are small, holes in the leaves may be caused by flea beetles. Aphids, European corn borers, and leafminers sometimes attack the plants. In areas where slugs and snails frequent the garden, they may bother the chard. Possible diseases include blight and downy mildew.

Harvest and Storage: Within 40 days from the time of sowing, some leaves will be usable. The most toothsome leaves are those from 6 to 10 inches long. Take a few leaves from the outside of each plant and do not damage the inner leaves. This allows the plant to continue producing. Break off the leaves rather than use a knife, as cutting sometimes causes the plants to bleed. Harvest through the summer and fall as needed, keeping in mind that the older, larger leaves are not as tasty as the young leaves.

TOMATOES

Lycopersicon lycopersicum
Solanaceae

The tomato, native to tropical America, was long thought by Europeans to be poisonous, probably because of its association with the deadly nightshade family. Overcoming centuries of abuse and adversity, the tomato is now the most popular vegetable crop in North America, grown in 98 percent of all home vegetable gardens. It is a warmth-loving annual, easy to grow in both long- and short-season areas, and remarkably versatile, suited to containers as well as garden plots.

Tomatoes are versatile in their kitchen use, as well, appearing in a wide variety of recipes, salads, any number of sauces, catsup, and juice. Although the fruit may not be kept in its fresh, ripe state for more than 3 weeks, it is easily preserved by canning or freezing. However, breeders are developing new varieties which can be stored ripe (or partially ripe) for 12 weeks or more. Tomatoes are a rich source of vitamins A and C, and offer some B_1 as well.

Tomatoes are classified by several criteria, based on characteristics of the fruit or of the plant itself. The fruit may be large or small; red, pink, yellow, orange, or white in color; and round, cherry-, or plum-shaped. It is further classed by intended use: for salads, for slicing, for paste, and so on. The plants may be classified by their maturation time—early-, mid- or late-season. The growth habit is an important distinction: plants are either determinate, semideterminate, or indeterminate. Determinate varieties are compact, generally measuring 12 to 18 inches tall, and once they reach a certain point in their growth, production comes to a halt. Since they bear their crop all at once, they are suited for short-season areas, and for gardeners who plan on processing the harvest. Semideterminate plants stop growing and producing when they reach 18 to 24 inches in height. Indeterminate varieties continue to grow and bear all season long, curtailed only by the onset of frost in northern areas, and by late blight in southern areas. Because of this growth habit, they are often staked and pruned to control the vines.

There are scores of varieties from which to choose—whether open-pollinated or hybrid. Some gardeners grow nothing but hybrid tomatoes, citing increased vigor, disease resistance, and high yield as their reasons. But others stand faithfully by the older, open-pollinated types, feeling they have the finest flavor, color, and size. However, the emphasis in the home-garden market is on hybrids, which are being continually developed to conquer specific growing problems such as limited space and a short, cool season, and to meet specific kitchen needs, including high vitamin content, good storage life, and low acid content. (These so-called "low-acid" tomatoes, incidentally, are not appreciably lower in acid than other tomatoes; however, their very high sugar content masks the acid they do contain.)

Growing Range: Tomatoes are a warm- and long-season crop by nature, but they may be grown in all areas with some measure of success. Short-season and cool-climate gardeners should be careful in their selection of varieties. Gardeners in areas where summers are very hot should offer partial shading of plants to prevent blossom drop during the very hottest weather. Tomatoes develop the best when average temperatures are between 70° and 75°F. This tender crop is injured by the least light frost unless protected.

Soil Preparation: The ideal soil is a sandy loam or loam, rich in organic matter and well drained. Tomatoes will not do well in heavy, slow-draining soils. In heavier soils, use the raised bed system. The recommended pH range is 6 to 7.

Prepare the soil one week before transplanting or sowing by incorporating good amounts of well-rotted manure or compost. To encourage the soil in warming up, cover the rows with black plastic, which will be removed at transplanting or sowing time.

Propagation: In long-season areas (2½ months of warm, sunny weather) seed may be sown directly in the garden on the frost-free date, or when soil temperature reaches 60°F. Sow seed ½ inch deep every 2 inches in rows set 36 inches apart for determinate or staked indeterminate plants, or 48 inches apart for unstaked indeterminate plants. When seedlings are 2 inches tall, thin to 3 inches apart; when 12 inches tall, thin to in-row spacing given below for transplants. Although direct-seeding is not a popular method, it will lead to fruit production at the same time as, or only a few days after, crops grown from small transplants. Direct-seeding requires considerably less work, and often leads to healthier plants, and should be practiced in areas of suitable climate. Unused seed is good for three years.

Most often, however (and always in short-season areas), transplants are used. Start seeds six to ten weeks before setting out, which can be done four weeks after the frost-free date,

Tomatoes

The varieties designated "V" are highly resistant to verticillium wilt; those designated "F" are resistant to fusarium wilt; and those marked "N" are resistant to root nematodes. A "VFN" variety offers widest disease resistance.

Variety Name	Average Days to Maturity (from transplants)	Disease Resistance	Growth Habit	General Description and Comments
Early Varieties				
Burpee's Big Early Hybrid	62	—	Indeterminate	Dependable, early, large-fruited variety that continues to bear well into the season; fruits are meaty, red-skinned, weigh about 7 oz.
Early Girl Hybrid	54–62	V	Indeterminate	Red-skinned fruits average 5 oz.; a dependable producer, both early and late in the season; resists cracking.
Spring Giant Hybrid	65–70	VF	Determinate	Large, red-skinned fruits weigh 8–10 oz.; heavy yielder when staked and planted closely; AAS.
Springset	65	VF	Determinate	Recommended for cool-weather gardens where blossom drop is common; short harvest season; fruits weigh 5–6 oz.; resistant to cracking.
Sub-Arctic Midi	56	—	Determinate	Bred specifically for northern gardens; matures extra early; sets fruit almost all at once; 2½-in. fruit weighs about 1¼ oz.
Midseason Varieties				
Better Boy	72	VFN	Indeterminate	Large fruits are somewhat susceptible to blossom-end rot; adaptable to all climates.
Floramerica F-1 Hybrid	75–80	VF	Determinate	A dependable yielder; good resistance to most diseases; produces well in warm-region areas where disease decimates most other varieties; AAS.
Marglobe	73	F	Determinate	An old and dependable open-pollinated favorite; vigorous vines; large red-skinned fruits weigh 6 oz.
Rutgers	74	F	Determinate	One of the most popular of all main-crop varieties; open-pollinated type; heavy yields of large, globe-shaped fruit.
Yellow Plum	70	—		Popular for making preserves; yellow-skinned, plum-shaped fruits, 2 in. long; can also be eaten fresh.

Variety Name	Average Days to Maturity (from transplants)	Disease Resistance	Growth Habit	General Description and Comments
Late-Season Varieties				
Beefmaster	80	VFN	Indeterminate	Very large red-skinned fruits often weigh 2 lb. or more; tolerates cracking.
Beefsteak (also Crimson Cushion)	80–90	—	Indeterminate	Open-pollinated variety; large red fruits average 10–12 oz.; solid, fleshy meat has few seeds; similar to Ponderosa, except for color; fruits sometimes irregularly shaped; somewhat subject to blossom drop.
Burpee's Big Boy	78	—	Indeterminate	Large red fruit weighs up to 2 lb.; very popular and dependable variety; long-term yielder; somewhat susceptible to diseases.
Burpee's Big Girl	78	VF	Indeterminate	Similar to Big Boy, but with good disease resistance; ample leaf cover prevents sunscald.
Roma	75	VF	Determinate	A favorite paste tomato; pear-shaped, red-skinned fruit averages 1½–2 in. in diameter; very heavy yields; good foliage cover to prevent sunscald.
White Beauty	78–85	—	Indeterminate	Skin creamy white, flesh almost snow white; a very low acid variety of good quality; can be used for juice, sliced, or canned.
Container Varieties				
Sweet 100	65	—		Very sweet red cherry tomato, less than 1 in. in diameter; recommended for very dry, vt30hot areas.
Pixie	60	—	Determinate	Early-season; plants are under 2 ft. high; cherry-type fruits 1¾ in. in diameter; good variety for both containers and the open garden.
Presto	55–60	—	Determinate	An early-season, dwarf bush with small leaves; small red fruits average 1–3 oz; recommended for cool-weather areas.
Small Fry Hybrid	60–65	VF	Determinate	A very early cherry type with fruit measuring 1 in. in diameter; AAS.

tricks of the trade

Trench Planting

For straggly, long-stemmed plants, use the trench-planting method. Pinch away all but the top few leaves, then lay the bare stem into the soil horizontally, and cover with 2 to 3 inches of soil. Leave the top cluster of leaves uncovered. In a few days, the top growth will straighten up and the buried stem will send out roots to serve as a good base for strong growth.

Trench Planting for a Leggy Tomato

when night temperatures remain above 55°F. Young plants will need the protection of cloches or other coverings if nights are chilly.

Transplant determinate varieties into conventional rows spaced 36 inches apart; set a plant every 24 inches. Indeterminate varieties which will be staked are set 18 to 24 inches apart in rows set 36 inches apart. Indeterminate varieties left to sprawl should be given 48 inches in each direction. Raised bed spacing (for staked plants) is 24 inches.

At transplanting time, set plants into the soil 2 inches deeper than they were in pots, to encourage strong root development. To provide a nutrient boost just when the plants will need it for fruit production, dig the holes about 8 inches deeper than necessary. Add some well-rotted manure and bone meal to the bottom, then cover with 3 to 4 inches of soil before setting the transplant in place.

Culture: If stakes are to be used, insert them at the same time the plants are set in the garden, or when direct-sown seedlings are thinned for the second time. Cages should be set in place while the plants are still young. Protect young plants from cutworms.

Keep weeds down and keep the soil evenly moist until the plants have become established, then apply 2 to 4 inches of mulch. This is especially important with unstaked plants to keep the fruit clean and free of disease and insect damage. Good tomato production depends on even moisture. Both blossom-end rot and fruit cracking are brought on by moisture imbalances in the soil. A good mulch will encourage moisture balance.

Determinate varieties need no training or pruning. Indeterminate varieties can be trained and pruned at the gardener's discretion. Plants that are staked produce more fruit per square foot of garden space, but less per plant. The fruit of staked plants is more susceptible to blossom-end rot and sunscald. Further, staking involves a good amount of work both initially and—since season-long pruning is then required—for the entire growing period. Unstaked plants require less work, but do consume more garden space, and are more susceptible to disease.

Plants can be trained to grow along stakes, trellises, or inside wire cages (where they need not be pruned). The techniques of pruning and training are described in detail in chapter 4.

Tomatoes are heavy feeders, but the timing of the feeding is critical. Water plants with fish emulsion or weak manure tea only after they have set fruit, and once again a month after the first feeding. If plants are fed too soon, they will direct their energy into producing leaves and will never set fruit.

Blossom drop may occur when night temperatures are below 55°F early in the season, or when they are above 75°F in midsummer. Cover plants when night temperatures threaten to dip too low; use open-lath screens to shield plants from extreme heat. Sunscald is caused by long and direct exposure of the fruit to hot sun; arrange leaves so they provide protection for all fruits.

Pests and Diseases: Insect pests include aphids, cabbage loopers, Colorado potato beetles, corn earworms, cucumber beetles, European corn borers, leafhoppers, nematodes, pepper maggots, potato tuberworms, and tomato hornworms. Tomatoes are subject to anthracnose, bacterial canker, damping-off, early blight, fusarium wilt, late blight, mosaics, psyllid yellows, septoria leaf spot, and verticillium wilt.

Harvest and Storage: Tomatoes ripen from the center of the fruit to the outside. There is no mistaking an absolutely ripe tomato. However, the natural red color of the skin will not develop in temperatures above 86°F so gardeners in hot-summer regions should pick fruit when it is pink, then let it ripen fully indoors, in cooler temperatures. A mixture of early, midseason, and late varieties will provide fresh tomatoes for several months in most areas.

Gardeners in the South will find that the tomato season is not cut short by frost, but by late blight that sets in and wipes out the crop.

In the North, when the first light frost is forecast, protect plants in the evening with coverings of sheets, blankets, plastic bags, and such, which should be removed during the day. Often, an early light frost will be followed by two to three weeks of warmer weather. When a killing frost is forecast, pick all tomatoes, ripe and unripe. The green tomatoes can be ripened indoors, in a warm spot (60° to 70°F). To delay ripening, store them at 55° to 60°F.

Most gardeners favor canning tomatoes, although freezing is a time-saving alternative, provided that room in the freezer can be found. Tomatoes may also be dried or made into a wide array of sauces, pastes, catsup, or juice.

TURNIPS

Brassica rapa, Rapifera Group
Cruciferae

Turnips are enjoyed both for their roots, which are steamed or baked, and for their zesty green tops, which are used as potherbs or raw in salads. Some varieties are grown primarily for their greens.

Gardeners who do not use turnip greens are missing a powerful nutritional package, for these tops are among the highest of all vegetables in vitamins A, B_2, C, and E, as well as some important minerals. The roots, although a good nutritional source, cannot compare. Turnip greens, for example, offer six times the vitamin C content that is found in an equal amount of turnip roots.

Turnips are closely related to rutabagas, and are similar in taste and texture, although turnip roots are smaller and their leaves have a rough surface. Since turnips are a short-season crop while rutabagas take several months to mature, many gardeners plant both during the season (but not in the same soil) for a continuous supply of both roots and tops.

Turnips are classified according to the

Turnips

Variety Name	Average Days to Maturity	General Description and Comments
Early Purple-Top Milan	45	Flattened roots have white flesh and purple tops; one of the earliest to mature.
Purple-Top White Globe	55	Round roots are purple-red on upper part extending aboveground, creamy white below; flesh is tender and firm; a high yielder that stores well.
Tokyo Cross Hybrid	35	Very early maturer; resistant to viral diseases; white roots measure up to 6 in. across; gets woody in warm weather; AAS.
Shogoin	30	Grown mainly for the tops, which quickly reach 16–18 in.; roots are ready for harvest in 70 days; white roots are globe-shaped and of good quality; AAS.

shape of their roots—flat, round, or cylindrical. Regardless of the shape, there is little or no difference in taste among the several varieties.

Growing Range: Turnips may be grown in any climate that offers 35 to 50 days of cool weather. In short- and medium-season areas, they are planted with the earliest spring crops; less often, they are planted in midsummer for fall harvesting. In warmer regions, they are often planted in fall and carried over winter, in which case they will be among the first crops ready in the spring. Turnips will attain the best taste and texture only when grown quickly under cool conditions (60° to 65°F). Hot weather will force rank top growth and woody roots. This crop does not withstand heavy frost well.

Soil Preparation: Turnips need a rich, loose soil, well supplied with compost and phosphate rock. The best pH is slightly acid, 6.5 to 7.0.

Propagation: Seed is commonly sown directly into the garden four to six weeks before the frost-free date. The soil must be at least 40°F for germination. Make successive plantings every three weeks until midsummer. For a fall harvest, sow seeds about nine weeks before the first expected frost. Space conventional rows 12 to 15 inches apart and sow three seeds to the row inch. Seed can also be broadcast in wide rows. Raised bed spacing is 6 inches. Bury seed lightly with no more than 1/4 inch of soil. Unused seed is good for five years.

Turnips can also be transplanted, although they must be handled gently to avoid disturbing the roots. Start seeds in individual containers three to four weeks before setting out. This can be done four weeks before the frost-free date. Set seedlings every 4 to 6 inches in rows, and use raised bed spacing given above.

Culture: When the first true leaves have appeared, thin plants in the rows to one per inch. After these plants have begun to touch each other, thin again to 4 to 6 inches. Use these tender greens in salads. Mulch to preserve moisture and to keep the soil cool once the plants are established. Supply moisture when needed during the short growing season. No supplemental fertilizer is needed in good soil.

Pests and Diseases: See Cabbage. Turnips are largely resistant to pest and disease attack.

Harvest and Storage: Harvest turnips while young and succulent. The ideal root diameter is about 2 inches, never more than 3 inches.

If an early hot spell arrives in spring, taste-test the roots every day; if you notice any deterioration of quality, harvest the entire crop. They will keep well in a refrigerator for several weeks, or they may be diced, blanched, and frozen. The tops are best frozen, which will preserve much of their nutritional value.

The fall crop should be stored under cool (32° to 40°F) and moist conditions. In mild-winter areas the roots can be left in the garden with a mulch covering for an extended harvest. They are not as long-lasting as rutabagas.

FRUITS

6

Planning the Fruit Garden

Due to extensive commercial shipping, we can purchase fruits from all over the world at the local supermarket. But there are special rewards in growing our own, and savoring the juicy sweetness of tree-ripened fruit. Although they are not all native to North America, an astonishing variety of fruits will grow within the confines of the United States and Canada. Fruits that are grown for commercial use—picked when immature and shipped long distances—cannot compare in flavor to homegrown varieties picked at the peak of ripeness. And many lesser-known fruits (like pawpaw, for example) can offer a whole new range of taste treats to the gardener.

There are lots of fruit varieties that are not grown commercially, because their fruit is perhaps not as large or attractive-looking as that of the commercial varieties, or because they do not store and ship as well. But the flavor and quality of these fruits is often superior to what's sold on supermarket shelves. And some have other desirable features, too, such as greater resistance to cold or hot temperatures or other extreme weather conditions.

Along with their edible qualities, fruits are a welcome addition to the backyard landscape, too. Fruit trees provide welcome shade on hot summer days, and a sturdy place for children to climb (especially apple trees, with their strong branches and wide crotches). When positioned properly, groups of trees can serve as a windbreak. And trees decorate the yard with their fragrant flowers in spring and colorful foliage in fall. Fruiting shrubs and vines are useful, too. They can be trained on trellises or along fences to serve as privacy screens, or to hide a shed, garage, or compost pile from view.

Deciding What to Grow

Chances are that no matter where you live, the combination of sunshine, temperature, soil, moisture level, and wind that make up the growing environment will support several kinds of delicious fruit. The key to success is understanding the environmental conditions you have to offer, and choosing the fruits that will grow best under those conditions. If you want to be successful at growing fruit, you will have to do a little research and experimentation to determine what fruits you will be able to grow in your geographical area and what conditions you need to provide for their best growth. You will also need to assess carefully your family's preferences, your storage capacity, and the amount and kind of growing space you have available. In this chapter we will be giving you some general guidelines to follow. More specific information on conditions in your area can be had from your local extension agent of the U.S. Department of Agriculture (USDA). (In Canada, contact local extension personnel of the Provincial Department of Agriculture, listed in the phone directory under "Provincial" government, Department of Agriculture.) Other good sources of information include local nurserymen, garden editors, growers, amateur orchardists, and members of orcharding societies. It's a good idea to talk to more than one person and get a variety of opinions. Let's go on, then, and examine the factors that you will need to investigate when determining what kinds of fruits you can grow.

Climate

The first and most important consideration in deciding what to grow has to do with climate. You will be able to accommodate only those fruit species and varieties that can stand the most extreme temperatures of the year in your geographical area. For example, warm-climate plants like pomegranate can grow only in sunny, warm regions that are frost-free. Warm-climate fruits are usually divided into two categories: subtropical and tropical. Subtropical fruits are usually evergreen and grow in areas that experience only light frosts in the winter. Tropical fruits are also evergreen, but they grow only in frost-free regions since their tissues cannot withstand freezing temperatures. Although the culture of these fruits is limited to warm growing areas outdoors, or to containers in greenhouses or sunny living rooms farther north, they provide unique challenges and rewards to adventurous gardeners.

Tropical fruits enormously increase the range of texture, taste, and color that we can experience. Some tropical fruits, such as papaya and ceriman, are considered among the most delicious in the world. Some, like acerola with its high vitamin C content, are very nutritious. They make superb and unusual juices and preserves. Tropical fruit trees, vines, and shrubs are often highly ornamental, with flamboyant flowers (pomegranate, passion fruit), and large, glossy leaves. They make excellent shade.

The more familiar temperate-zone fruits, which are all deciduous, are fewer in number but are more widely grown and have been more highly developed horticulturally. Many of these fruits have been extensively bred, and many varieties have been developed that are adapted to a range of growing conditions; there are varieties with increased tolerance of heat and cold, and others with greater resistance to insects and disease. Dwarf varieties are available which yield sooner and produce greater yields per acre than standard-sized fruit trees. There are well over 600 varieties of apple alone grown in the United States. The adaptability of temperate fruit trees (at least of trees that have been grafted, as most available varieties are) to climate is determined primarily by the rootstock, although the climatic preference of the scion wood must also be considered.

Plants from temperate areas can grow within a range of temperatures, but all of them require a cold period each year (the chilling factor) in order to bloom and set fruit. Generally speaking, temperatures of 45°F or lower over a period of at least 45 days will be a sufficient cold period. If temperatures are too cold for a prolonged period, blossom buds can be damaged or destroyed. Apples are generally the hardiest of fruits—their buds can withstand temperatures down to −25°F. Least hardy of the temperate fruits are peaches and nectarines, which can sustain damage if temperatures fall below −12° to −15°F. Between these two extremes are (in order of decreasing hardiness) pears, European plums, sour cherries, sweet cherries, Japanese plums, and apricots.

When climatic requirements have been assessed, there remains the challenge of choosing not just kinds of fruits but specific cultivars that are suited to the winter climate in your area, and to the spring and summer growing conditions as well. Besides average winter temperatures, other characteristics to be mindful of in the case of temperate fruits include whether there are sudden swings from

digging deeper

Chilling Factors

People who live in areas with mild winters—especially places where no snow settles on the ground—should be aware that a primary limit to the kinds of temperate fruits they can grow is the "chilling factor." That is, the total number of hours at or below 45°F which each variety needs during winter in order for the tree to break dormancy and reliably set fruit.

Any reputable nursery should be able to tell you the chilling requirement for particular varieties you wish to grow. If these are not listed in the nursery's catalog, you should inquire about any particular variety's requirement before purchase. Normally, the chilling requirement is a major determinant in the "zone" or "range" listings which some nurseries publish in their fruit-growing recommendations.

Some apple and pear varieties require as many as 1,500 hours of winter chilling in order to properly break dormancy. Peaches can vary widely in their chilling requirements. For example, Flordawon, a Florida variety, needs only 50 hours of chilling while the Polly peach requires 1,100 hours.

Additionally, recent studies have indicated that winter day temperatures above 60°F may actually subtract from the total chilling effect on a variety. So, in a home landscape, particular types that require longer chilling terms should not be planted in areas exposed to sudden winter warmth, such as patios and blacktopped areas facing the southern sun.

Without an adequate chilling period, trees may grow weak and spindly, flower or leaf-out erratically, or eventually become unfruitful altogether.

Areas with very cold winters (−20°F and lower) or with broad fluctuations between cold and warm winter weather will prove difficult, if not impossible, places for growing most types of deciduous fruits.

—Jamie Jobb

warm to cold weather or strong winds that make damage from cold more likely even at usually acceptable temperatures, and whether summers are too long, hot, or dry for good results. Finally, you must determine whether the fruit's bloom date is so early as to risk damage from late spring frosts. This is one of the greatest risks faced by fruit growers, who must take into account not just wood hardiness but that of the flower buds as well.

Family Likes and Dislikes

Given the range of fruits it is possible to grow in your part of the country, the next step in planning the orchard or garden is to take a good look at what fruits your family likes, and how you will use the harvest. Along with the number of people in your family, how you are going to use the fruit will guide you in determining how much of each type to plant. If your family likes apples, of course, you'll want to eat some of the fruit fresh. But will you also want to bake pies or make cider or applesauce? You need to be familiar with which apple varieties are best suited to your purpose, and how much of a yield to expect from your plants, bushes, or trees.

The variety charts in the Guide to Fruits for the Home Garden, later in the book, will give you information on the characteristics and best uses for popular and traditional fruit varieties. You can also talk with your county extension agent about recommended varieties and look at nursery catalogs (but read between the lines—nurserymen are in the business of selling trees, and do not always mention undesirable characteristics of the varieties they sell).

Choosing the Site

Environmental Conditions on Your Property

Gardeners with little space and no choice of sites need to choose a kind of fruit that will tolerate the environmental conditions they have to offer. But for gardeners with a large property, enough emphasis cannot be placed on the importance of careful site selection for the fruit garden, orchard, or berry patch. After you have become familiar with the general environmental conditions of your area, you will need to carefully assess your property in order to determine which will be the best fruits for your location and the best location for your fruits.

First, keep in mind that growing fruits means a long-term commitment of space. Annual vegetables like snap beans complete their life cycle in a single growing season. The gardener growing such plants must be concerned with meeting their environmental needs for only that one season, and if some aspect of planting or culture goes awry, the mistake will be ended with the first frost and can be mended the following spring. Most fruit trees and small fruit plants, however, are perennials which live anywhere from three to several score years. Programmed for a long life, such perennial fruits direct much of their strength and energy to survive toward building a durable root system that will sustain them through extremely cold or dry seasons. Because of their extensive roots and considerable size at maturity, most fruits are difficult to successfully move once they're established (although with care, certain trees can be grown in containers for several seasons before being planted in the ground). Certainly the decision as to which ones to plant and where to plant them requires both thought and foresight. It is important to be aware of the conditions described in the following paragraphs, but don't let them scare you away from growing fruit. If you choose your crops and varieties carefully, you can grow fruit just about anywhere.

In general, fruits will grow best where there is full sun and good (but not excessive) air movement to foil frost damage and the spread of fungal diseases. In warm, humid areas exposure to full sun is extremely important; a southern and eastern exposure will let the sun dry morning dew quickly, making the environment less favorable for bacteria and disease-causing organisms. The soil should be deep and well drained, so that no surface water remains in puddles after a prolonged rainy spell. At the same time, the soil must retain moisture long enough for roots to absorb it, and must be of moderate fertility. Excessively rich soils, especially those abundant in nitrogen, will produce lots of weak, succulent shoot growth at the expense of fruit quality and quantity.

Most fruits need an even supply of moisture in order to grow well. If your soil tends to dry out, mulching can help to hold in moisture. Another technique, especially useful with young trees, is to leave the soil around the trunk slightly depressed, to catch every bit of rainfall and prevent runoff.

Conserving Water: If your soil tends to dry out, leave a small depression around newly planted trees to serve as a reservoir for rainwater and to catch runoff moisture.

If your soil is a heavy, slow-draining clay, or has hardpan or bedrock less than 3 feet below the surface, you will have to install drainage tiles before you can plant the trees or bushes. Those soils with a higher percentage of sand and organic matter will have better drainage to begin with and should not need any modification below the surface.

The soil pH must also be considered, and it can be modified somewhat. Overly acid soil can be limed, and alkaline soils can be conditioned with peat moss, oak leaves, or cottonseed meal. But you will never be able to make drastic or permanent changes in pH. Most fruits grow comfortably within a slightly acid range of pH values, although some are quite specific in their requirements. Watermelons and blueberries, for example, need a very acid soil with a pH between 4 and 6 to do well. See the Guide to Fruits for information on the pH needs of individual fruits.

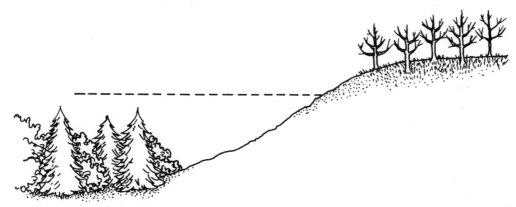

Analyzing Air Drainage: Generally an orchard site should have good air drainage to reduce the possibility of spring frost damage. Cold air, like water, settles in low spots. When eyeing-up your land prior to setting an orchard, any area that would fill with cold air should be avoided. This includes hillsides above dense woods where the trees and undergrowth may prevent the cold air from "draining."

It is important to think about air drainage, too, when determining what types of fruits your property can support and where you will put them. It is vital to keep most common fruits out of low-lying areas like valleys and riverbottoms where cold air will settle and form frost pockets (although same native fruits do grow in low areas). Cold air, like water, settles in low spots, and you may lose crops if you plant in a cold pocket. Instead, plant your trees and bushes on a rise where cold air can drain away. If you have a hilly piece of property, do not plant your fruits closer than 50 feet to the floor of a low-lying area. Conversely, keep them away from the crest of the rise where the trees could be exposed to temperature extremes and drying winds. The ideal setting would be on the slopes of high, rolling hills, perpendicular to prevailing winds and away from cold areas. If you must plant in a low-lying spot, you can lessen the danger of a cold pocket by aligning the rows of trees in the same direction as the air flows.

You must also consider the direction of the slopes. There are advantages and disadvantages to both the north and south sides of hills. South-facing slopes receive more sunshine than the north and are generally warmer—good conditions for plant growth. Plants grown on southern slopes, however, tend to flower earlier, which makes them susceptible to damage from late spring frosts. Less hardy fruits like apricots, peaches, and sweet cherries should be planted on the north-facing sides of hills so that they will flower later and avoid the frosts. On the other hand, north-facing slopes are cooler and will delay the spring bud break and bloom. Trees planted in cool places may exhibit a tendency for the bark to crack in the winter unless painted white.

Another consideration in locating fruit plantings, for gardeners who live in windy areas, is the presence of a suitable windbreak to protect the fruit trees from prevailing winds in spring and summer. A windbreak will protect an area on the downwind side that is five times the height of the windbreak. Fruit trees should not be planted closer than one windbreak-height away from the windbreak. In urban areas, shade trees and nearby buildings may give enough wind protection.

A final climatic factor to keep in mind is that large bodies of water, such as lakes, will help to moderate the climate of nearby areas. This effect is most pronounced downwind of the water, where humidity will be increased and winter temperatures not as severe. The humid air will stay cooler longer in spring, meaning that trees will tend to bloom a bit later than normal and will not be likely to be damaged by late spring frosts. Areas which experience frequent foggy conditions will also experience delayed bloom. However, during the summer the presence of fog may encourage mildew and other disease problems in fruits, and can reduce yields.

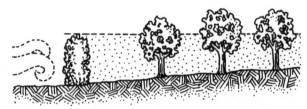

Protecting Trees with Windbreaks: Planting a windbreak helps to protect fruit trees from prevailing winds in spring and summer. Plant the fruit trees no closer to the windbreak than one windbreak-height. The windbreak, which can be a high hedge or a wooden fence, will protect an area downwind that is five times the height of the windbreak.

Size and Space Needs

The size and shape of your property directly affect the number and kind of fruits that you grow. Obviously, a large piece of property will accommodate a number of types of fruits, but a small property will limit your choice. Keeping in mind that some of the fruits will need cross-pollination, which makes it necessary to plant more than one fruit of that type, your next consideration after climate, family preferences, and soil and site would be the amount of space needed for each bush or tree to grow to maturity.

Dwarf vs. Standard Varieties

In recent years, dwarf and semidwarf trees of the most popular temperate tree fruits have been on the market in increasing numbers. Dwarf varieties are a boon to commercial growers and home gardeners with limited space—they

Comparing Tree Sizes: The dwarf tree on the left matures to a height less than half the size of the standard tree on the far right, while the semidwarf tree in the center attains a height 50 to 85 percent that of the standard tree.

produce full-sized fruit on a tree that is much smaller than the normal size. They are often more productive per unit of space, too. Dwarf trees are generally more expensive to purchase than those of standard size, but they begin to bear at an earlier age and are easier to prune and harvest. A tree is considered to be a dwarf when it is less than half the size of the standard tree at maturity. A semidwarf tree is one that reaches 50 to 85 percent of the size of a standard tree.

Smaller trees can be created in a number of ways: by budding or grafting standard varieties onto dwarfing rootstocks, by tree-training practices such as espalier or bonsai, and by breeding and selection. Some of the popular dwarf varieties, such as the North Star cherry, are genetic dwarfs, which are kept small throughout their lifetimes by their own genetic makeup.

Another kind of tree dwarfed by mutation is the "spur-type" tree which has been selected from a mutant or "sport" branch growing on a standard tree. These sport branches are full of short, fruit-bearing spurs rather than long and leafy branches. Generally, spur-type trees are smaller, grow more slowly, and produce larger crops sooner in their lives than standard varieties. The spur trees are also sometimes grafted or budded onto dwarfing rootstocks, in which case they are referred to as "double-dwarf." In nursery catalogs, spur-type trees are listed as such, and many of them have the word spur included in their names.

Most of the fruit trees sold by nurseries are actually parts of two different trees: a rootstock which is selected to give the tree a firm, strong anchor in the ground, and a scion, the top part, which is selected for the type of fruit it bears. The most commonly employed method of producing dwarf or semidwarf trees is by grafting scions onto rootstocks that reduce their growth. For example, quince rootstocks are used for dwarfing scions of standard-sized pears. Scions are chosen for characteristics like the quality of their fruit, market availability, and resistance to disease. A dwarfing rootstock creates a smaller tree by impeding the flow of nutrients between the scion and the roots. The leaves of the scion produce more food than the rootstock can absorb and transport. As a result, carbohydrates build up in the scion and encourage earlier production of flowers and fruit.

Apples are by far the most-dwarfed fruit, and there are a number of rootstocks that are used, which vary in the degree of the dwarfing effect they produce on the scion. The natural vigor of the scion also has an effect on the size of the tree. The McIntosh, for example, is a very vigorous scion that produces a larger tree than would a Golden Delicious scion grafted to the same rootstock.

Spur-Type Trees: A spur-type tree (left) has fewer lateral branches and more fruit-bearing spurs than a standard tree (right). They also bear fruit more heavily while being somewhat smaller than standard trees.

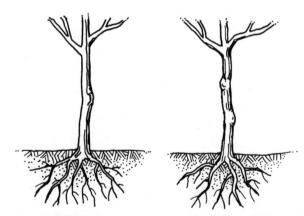

Scions, Rootstocks, and Interstocks: Many fruit varieties have inferior root systems despite their excellent fruit characteristics. To overcome this problem, a scion of a good fruiting variety is grafted onto a rootstock of a strong-rooted variety, as shown on the left. Often the rootstock has size-controlling qualities. Sometimes an interstock is grafted between the scion and the rootstock (shown on right) to avoid incompatibility between the stock and the scion or to make use of its growth-controlling properties. Graft-unions are recognized by bulges on the trunk.

digging deeper

Malling Stocks

More than any other fruit, apples have been bred, selected, and scrutinized for their adaptability to a wide range of soils and growing conditions. More than 50 rootstocks especially suited for apples have been studied and cataloged since 1913 at England's East Malling Research Station. These are known, collectively, as the "Malling stocks."

Most of the original Malling stocks were selected from old European seedling apples grown around the turn of the century. But in the 1920s, breeding and selection began on another series of stocks meant to extend the range of apples. This series, developed jointly by East Malling and the John Innes Horticultural Institute of Merton, England, is known as the "Malling–Merton series" and was developed especially for growers in Australia and other dry regions.

East Malling rootstocks usually are given Roman numerals (EM IX for "East Malling nine") while the Malling–Merton stocks use arabic numerals (MM 106). All these stocks are propagated clonally so they remain "true to type." Some of them are particularly useful in creating dwarf trees.

American nurseries that list a diversity of dwarf and semidwarf apple varieties commonly offer trees budded or grafted onto these Malling rootstocks:

EM VII: Semidwarf trees up to 60 percent of standard size. Produces open, spreading trees which come into bearing early in life, are widely adapted and cold-hardy. Prefers rich soils, but must be planted deeply or staked. Tends to produce suckers and is subject to crown gall.

EM IX: Truly dwarfed trees, no taller than 40 percent of standard. Promotes early bearing, sometimes in first or second year of planting out. Requires fertile soils and consistent moisture. Well suited to espalier shapes, but must be supported. Often used as interstock for dwarfing varieties on stocks better suited to particular soils. Brittle roots subject to breakage. Also susceptible to woolly aphids and fireblight.

EM XIII: Semidwarf to semistandard. Especially suited for heavy clay soils and shy-bearing varieties. Shallow-rooted and will not tolerate drought. Recommended for areas with soggy conditions or high water table. Well-anchored, does not need support.

EM XXVI: Dwarf, up to 50 percent of standard. Newest EM stock, developed in 1959 and still undergoing trials. Better anchored than EM IX, but still requires support. Needs well-drained soils, not suited to areas of drought. Some susceptibility to fireblight, woolly aphids, and collar rot.

MM 106: Semidwarf trees up to 70 percent of standard. Early-bearing and very fruitful. Tolerates hot and dry conditions. Well-anchored, does not sucker. Susceptible to mildew and early winter freeze damage. Not recommended for wet soil conditions.

MM 111: Semidwarf, up to 75 percent of standard. One of the hardiest Malling stocks. Produces vigorous, upright trees. Heat- and drought-tolerant. Best anchored roots of Malling series, but slower to reach bearing age than MM 106 or EM VII. Resists collar rot.

—Jamie Jobb

Another means of grafting to produce dwarf trees involves a two-stage process. In the first year, a dwarfing "interstock" is budded or grafted onto a rootstock that suits the particular soil and climate. Then the selected scion is budded or grafted onto the interstock the following year. This is done to improve the compatibility between scion and rootstock, or to create a truly dwarfed tree on roots that do not have true dwarfing capability. For example, Hardy or Old Home pear varieties are often used as interstocks which make most other pear scions compatible with quince rootstocks; while a true dwarfing interstock, such as EM IX (see the box on Malling Stocks) is used to create smaller apple trees on semidwarf rootstocks, such as MM 111, which are chosen to combat particular soil problems. In all cases, the interstock should be at least 6 inches long. Such three-part trees are called "double-worked." Double-working is viewed by some nurserymen as the direction of the future for fruit trees, because it allows more opportunity to combine dwarfing, hardiness, and disease-resistant characteristics to produce trees ideally suited for the conditions provided in North American gardens.

The right cultural practices can also help to keep trees small. It is important not to overfeed trees, particularly with nitrogen, which would produce weak, rapid shoot growth that is susceptible to pests, diseases, and injury. Regular, moderate pruning also helps keep growth in check, and careful tip pinching and pruning in summer can help, too.

Although dwarf trees have come a long way in recent years, there are still problems, and work continues. One problem is incompatibility—between scions and rootstocks, and between rootstocks and American growing conditions. This is particularly a problem with pears grafted directly onto quince stocks. Not all pear varieties are compatible with quince, and the trees may live only five or six years. Also, the quince rootstock is weak and susceptible to fireblight and damage from cold winter temperatures, and it has little tolerance for slowly draining soil.

When planning your orchard, whether you will grow dwarf or standard-sized trees, it is important to choose varieties and rootstocks that are well suited to conditions in your area and your particular site. The trees must be able to tolerate the climate, of course, but they should also be resistant to the diseases that are common in your area. Some mail-order nurseries graft their varieties onto a number of different rootstocks matched to various geographic regions. A reputable local nurseryman or your local extension agent should be able to advise you about the best fruit varieties and rootstocks for your area.

Planning the Plot

When placing fruits relative to each other on your site, keep in mind the ultimate size of fruit trees and bushes, situating them where they will receive the full sun that most of them need. Be sure to locate them far enough from the house and other structures so they will not eventually block the light or the view or become difficult to maintain. Trees close to the house can clog drains, crack foundations, or become damaged by eventual digging by plumbers or utility crews. If you plan to plant fruit trees or bushes along property lines shared with neighbors, discuss your plans with them. They may not mind having the plants right on the line and contending with occasional dropped fruit on their side if you offer to share some of the fruit with them. On the other hand, if they are not pleased at the prospect of cleaning up dropped fruit from your plants, it will be better to plant somewhere else rather than risk arguments later.

You will probably want to locate standard-sized trees farther away from the house than your vegetable garden, for they won't need tending as often in one season, and the distance will be conducive to a better view of blossoms and ripening fruit. Dwarf trees can be managed around the fringes of vegetable gardens, and genetic dwarfs, especially peaches and nectarines, were developed with patios, front yards, and other landscaping situations in mind.

If you live where winters are cold, keep in mind the degree of hardiness of various species. The more tender fruits should be given comfortable settings—perhaps espaliered along a wall—and may need to be positioned so they can be sheltered from prevailing winds. (Likely sites might be where snow tends to melt first. Often this is a south-facing location backed on the north by a structure or hedge.) In very sunny but cold areas, a northeastern exposure can be advisable to prevent fruits from flowering too early, and lessen the possibility of damage from sunscald.

Fruits must be spaced according to their size when mature, but that can vary considerably depending upon the cultivar, the soil, the care given, and the climate of the growing region. For guidelines on spacing distances for individual fruits, consult the Guide to Fruits. Where temperate tree fruits are concerned, dwarf forms often make the most sense for home gardens. A standard-sized tree may require as much as 20 to 40 feet, thus dwarf trees can convert the space needed

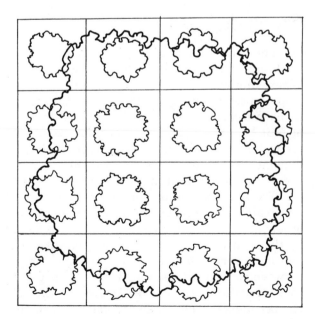

Space Savers:
16 dwarf trees can be grown on the same amount of ground that a single standard tree would normally occupy.

for one standard tree into an orchard of several kinds or of varieties chosen to ripen in succession to assure a minimal waste of fruit. Don't make your trees compete with one another for soil moisture and nutrients, though. Never plant a tree so that its drip-line will overlap the drip-line of another tree. This is especially easy to overlook when you are planting a whip or small tree (you must base planting distance on its mature size), and when planting in spring before neighboring trees are in full leaf (it is easy to misjudge their actual size).

Besides size at maturity, another variable also will influence the number (and perhaps the kind) of fruits you can grow and the layout you choose. That factor is whether a given fruit is self-fertile or whether two or more plants of different varieties are required for cross-pollination. If several varieties are indicated, position them in the same area—perhaps in alternate rows—to make visits by pollinators more likely.

To get the most from the space available, you might consider interplanting vegetables or small fruit around and among fruit trees for the first several years. This is particularly feasible if you are growing dwarf fruits, which have shallow root systems and cast little shade. Just be sure the interplanted crops are not planted inside the drip-line of any of the young trees. This would hinder the tree's development due to competition for nutrients and especially moisture.

It is sometimes recommended that raspberries or other brambles be interplanted in this way. However, brambles can grow tenaciously and if not trained and arranged carefully they will be very difficult to eliminate from the orchard when the time comes. It's better to plant brambles in their own patch.

Traditional Approaches

Orchards

The arrangement of fruits in orchards is determined by the lay of the land, the kinds and varieties of plants to be grown, and by soil management practices. Where annual rainfall is over 35 inches, permanent sod can be laid or a cover crop planted between the trees to add organic matter to the soil and help hold in moisture. However, the soil inside the drip-line of each tree should be cultivated or mulched. Sod and cover crops planted close to trees will compete with them for water and nutrients. Some orchardists plant "filler" trees among the permanent trees to boost yields until the regular trees reach full size. Filler trees are usually varieties that begin to bear sooner in life than the main varieties.

Trees can be laid out in a number of ways. In the often-used square system, which allows for easy access to standard-sized trees, a tree is placed in each corner of a square, the dimensions of which are determined by the spacing demanded by the fruit being planted when it matures. Sometimes filler trees are planted between every two trees in the row and a row of the temporary trees is placed between rows of the regular trees and spaced at one-half the distance from each other that the regular trees are. When the fillers begin to crowd each other or the permanent trees, they are removed. In the quincunx, or diagonal, setup, a

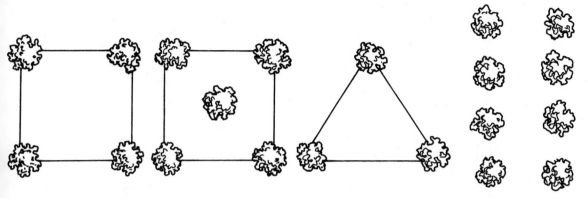

Four Systems of Laying Out Trees: From left to right; trees planted at each corner of an imaginary square in the square system; a fifth tree is added to the center of a square in the quincunx system; trees are placed equidistant on a triangle in the triangular system; and compact trees or bushes are planted side by side in the hedgerow system.

fifth, filler tree that may be removed later if necessary is placed in the center of a square; this system yields more fruit per acre than the square and works well when different varieties are in alternate rows. Under triangular, or hexagonal, placement, all trees are equidistant on a triangle, making possible the planting of more trees per acre than does the square system using the same spacing. In the hedgerow system, compact trees are planted side by side, and enough space is left between the double rows to allow for maintenance and harvest.

Orchardists working with sloping land practice contour planting, which allows the trees in any one row to be at the same elevation and height. In conjunction they use either level terraces, or terraces with outlets between contour lines (where rainfall is over 35 inches per year), or permanent sod and mulch (where the land slopes more than 10 percent). With contour planting one first determines the minimum distance that must be kept between the trees to be planted. The next step is to lay out the first line along the highest elevation to the limits of the site, using an engineer's level and rod, or simply by estimating the line by sight. If you are planning a large orchard on a slope, you might find it helpful to obtain a U.S. Geologic Survey topographic map. (These are available from the U.S. Government Printing Office in Washington, D.C., for most areas of the United States.) The line can be marked with lath stakes at 25- or 50-foot intervals. Then the orchardist finds the highest elevation below the first contour line and marks a point at the minimum spacing between rows. A second contour line is then established just as the first one was. This procedure is repeated down the hill and if the distance between the two lines ever becomes twice the minimum space allowed, an additional short or long line of filler trees can be planted. If a planting is large enough, the local office of the Soil Conservation Service (of the USDA) will sometimes assist, at no charge, with contour layout. At the very least, they can provide valuable information on doing it yourself.

Plots

Low-lying vining or bush fruits which don't require support may be grown in prepared plots either by themselves or in proximity to vegetables. Annual

Training Strawberries: The matted row system (left) popular in home gardens allows the runners to fill in open areas between the plants and form a mat. The hill system (right) requires more work as all the runners are removed from the parent plant, but the result is larger fruit and higher yields.

fruits such as melons thrive when two or three healthy plants grow in hills mounded about 4 inches above the surrounding soil. These mounds are spaced from 4 to 10 feet apart, depending on the varieties being grown. Permanent beds can be established for pineapples or berry perennials.

Strawberries are sometimes grown in 8- to 10-inch-high hillrows, spaced 1 to 1½ feet apart—a planting arrangement often used for everbearing types. Unlike the matted row system, in which runners originating from the mother plants are left to fill in open spaces around the plants, strawberries grown in the hill system have all their runners removed, leaving only the mother plant at maturity. With the hill system, all the plant's energy goes into the mother plant, resulting in larger fruit and higher yields. Strawberries are grown more efficiently in the matted row setup, where rows are 3½ to 4 feet apart and plants 1½ to 3 feet apart with runners allowed to fill in or mat the space between. The hill system also can be used for upright raspberries and the bush forms of blackberries. Arching types are planted in rows in patches, as are blueberries, currants, and gooseberries, while trailing berry plants are trained to grow up or along trellises. Berries do well when mulched to keep weeds and annual plants from crowding them.

Espalier and Cordon

Fruit growers are increasingly coming to appreciate the advantages of growing tree, bush, and vine fruits on trellises, trained as cordons or various types of espalier. These training methods are detailed in chapter 10. Trellising demands a lot of attention, but it is a great space-saver, and provides a way to grow fruits in places that would otherwise be too small to accommodate them. Yields can be higher, too. Some sort of trellis growing is mandatory for vine fruits such as grapes, and is recommended for plants with trailing canes, such as boysenberries and loganberries.

The profusion of flowers and fruits of superior quality which trellis growing produces in a greatly limited growing space is due to several factors which foster the growth of fruit-bearing spurs. These include generous feeding coupled with repeated pruning; the bending of branches toward the horizontal to slow growth (which is best done early in the growing season when new growth is limber); the optimal exposure of the center of the plant to sunlight, and the symmetrical shape of many espaliered forms, which facilitates an even flow of sap.

Although apples and pears are said to make the best espaliers, virtually all fruit trees and vining types of fruits are amenable to some form of trellising. Supremely elegant and often very practical, espaliered fruits are enjoying renewed popularity, and are a good choice for a narrow plot hemmed in by a pavement or driveway; for a trellis or fence marking property lines; or for a stunning specimen plant grown in a container on the patio.

Espaliered Fruit Tree:
In areas where space is limited, fruit trees can be espaliered against the wall of a garage or other outbuilding, or along a fence.

In planning where to locate espaliered fruits, remember that white brick or concrete walls—especially if they are south-facing—may cause plants to flower too early in spring or to become subject to overheating in summer. Painting tree trunks white will help keep them cooler and reduce the chance of sunscald. But in general, except in areas where winters are very severe and the heat radiated by a white wall would be helpful, dark brick or stone and a wall facing east or west make the best site for espaliered fruits. In placing these trained plants, also keep in mind any future necessity to move them in order to paint or maintain a wall.

Container Tactics

Genetic dwarf varieties are the best choices for container fruit cultivation. Next best are trees grown on dwarfing rootstocks.

After choosing trees for container cultivation, you should pay careful attention to the size and portability of each container, soil mixes and tree placement, plus water and pruning requirements.

Some people may feel that container cultivation of fruit trees is more trouble than it's worth. So if you choose to try trees in containers, it may help to think like a nursery proprietor, who understands that nothing requires a container tree to spend its entire life confined to the same container in the same spot. Indeed, the main reason for growing fruit trees in containers is so they can be moved when the need arises.

CONTAINER SIZES AND PORTABILITY

Almost anything—bathtub, bucket, barrel—may be used to contain a fruit tree, as long as it has enough holes for adequate drainage and enough room for tree roots. Holes can be drilled in wood, plastic, or metal with a brace and bit.

Here's a rule of thumb: the smaller the container, the shorter term a tree is able to remain in its captivity; while the larger the container, the harder it is to move.

One-gallon containers are useful for starting and sheltering a number of recently budded or grafted varieties. However, these trees will eventually need to be "potted up" to larger containers, normally after the first season.

Two-gallon pots, if you can find them, can be useful for keeping trees beyond the whip stage. But again, the trees eventually will need to be potted up to a bigger size before they reach bearing age.

Two big reasons to use these smaller containers are, first, to give yourself more room to experiment with different varieties, and second, to have extra trees to give away as gifts on special occasions or on the spur of the moment.

Trees can remain in 4- and 5-gallon buckets for several seasons, including the early years of maturity. Some sources for suitable plastic buckets this size are restaurants, delicatessens, or markets which make bulk purchases of mustard,

pickles, or dessert toppings shipped in them. Solvents and other harsh chemicals are sometimes moved in 5-gallon buckets, but these must be thoroughly cleaned, if used at all for living soils and roots of fruit trees.

Ideal for patio and balcony cultivation are large (25- to 50-gallon) oak barrels or other similar-sized wooden boxes built of cedar, cypress, redwood, and other hardwoods. These containers can be very attractive, but unless you add casters or wheels before planting, these will be very difficult to move. Without this consideration, care should be taken to determine a somewhat permanent placement of larger containers.

To prolong the life of a wooden planter, it can be coated with plastic film, or a nontoxic wood preservative such as copper naphthenate, which will not harm roots or other soil life forms. Do not use creosote for this purpose.

THE GROWING MEDIUM

The most important aspect of fruit tree container culture is the soil structure—which should mirror, as closely as possible, conditions the tree would find in the ground.

Most deciduous fruit trees require a healthy soil that is well drained. Container soils, however, should not be so well drained that they need to be watered every day in dry weather. The entire container bottom should have enough holes so that nowhere does the soil remain soggy for a prolonged period. Exactly how well the container drains should depend on the particular rootstock, variety, and type of fruit intended for it. Trees that demand the driest conditions may need holes along the lower portion of the container sides, as well as holes in the container bottom.

To assist drainage and prevent pooling, it's a good idea to first put a 1-to 2-inch layer of crushed rock, charcoal (*not* the kind used for barbecues), or another chunky material in the bottom of the container.

The soil mix itself should be much richer than for trees planted in the ground. A combination of 1/3 compost and 2/3 garden loam is fine. However, if the garden soil is heavy clay, it's advisable to add coarse sand to the mix.

For trees intended to spend several seasons in containers, the soil mix should be periodically changed and enriched with compost during dormant seasons. Root pruning is also a good practice at this time, for it will help keep the tree small.

As with other garden plants, a thick mulch can prove invaluable for reducing the amount of summer evaporation. In larger containers, a 6-inch mulch is suitable. Lime, bone meal, and other soil amendments can be added under the mulch layer.

In areas with very hot summer sunshine, it helps to place thin-walled containers (especially dark-colored ones) in positions where the sun does not strike them directly and cause baking of roots which touch the container's sunny side. Some growers in these areas plant annual flowers and vegetables in the ground or in smaller containers around the base of contained trees in order to reduce this problem of overheated roots. Of course, with trees held in dense wood or clay containers, the sun is less of a problem.

WATERING

Because trees in planters are cut off from groundwater flows, irrigation becomes a crucial factor in their successful cultivation. Even in stormy weather, a container tree may need water, because the leaf canopy may prevent rainwater from penetrating thoroughly into the container soil.

The quickest way to tell if a tree needs moisture is to poke a finger into the soil and feel if it's moist below the surface. Slow and deep watering is best and you should be certain that you've watered each tree long enough for the entire soil profile to be moistened. Usually this happens when a pool begins to form on top of the soil. Of course, this puddle should drain through quickly after watering has ceased.

Some soil mixes, especially those with lots of organic matter, may have a tendency to shrink when dry. This often forms gaps around the edges of the planter, thus reducing the effectiveness of irrigation. A thick mulch will help reduce this problem, and new soil can be added to fill any gaps that do form.

During the active growing season, an occasional spray of seaweed or fish fertilizer is beneficial, especially with older trees. Seaweed as a leaf spray is highly recommended for trees suffering from loss of vigor due to trace element deficiencies.

RESTRICTING GROWTH

Another requirement for contained fruit trees is the careful management of their growth into shapes that suit each particular tree's location. (See chapter 10 for information on pruning.)

In general, container trees should be pruned back harder than normal trees, so they don't become too top-heavy for their containers. Genetic dwarfs, which have a naturally bushy habit, are an exception to this general rule because they seldom require much pruning to restrict their growth.

The ultimate height of trees in containers should be no taller than you can reach. Trees with upright growth habits can be opened up by tying down branches early in their lives and early in the growing season, before new growth begins to turn woody. This will help trees attain more of a vase shape in later years.

In addition, the tree's growing tips can be pinched, buds aimed in the wrong directions can be rubbed out, and unwanted branches can be pruned away to assure that a container fruit tree stays within the bounds you set for it.

—Jamie Jobb

Container Culture

Whether pruned to a natural shape or trained flat in espalier or sculptured into a three-dimensional form such as a pyramid, fruits can be raised in containers. Since such plants—even when mature—can be grown in deep containers as small as 9 to 12 inches in diameter, a delightful variety of fruits can be enjoyed even in a small garden, yard, patio, terrace, or whatever. Fruit trees planted in containers will require more time and attention than trees grown in the ground. But for many people container cultivation may be the only way to obtain fresh fruit. For others who want to experiment with a large number of dwarf varieties, containers are a necessary tool of the craft.

The mobility of container fruits makes them a decorator's dream, and certainly containers are invaluable if you are renting or expecting to move to a new home. A great advantage in this situation is that young trees can gain a head start toward maturity before you eventually put them into the ground in their permanent location. Indeed, many serious home orchardists have several con-

digging deeper

Fruit Varieties for Container Cultivation

Apples: Almost any variety grafted or budded onto EM IX or EM XXVI dwarfing rootstocks or interstocks. EM XXVII, a very dwarfing rootstock with mature trees reaching 4 feet, is the best rootstock to use, but it is hard to find. Spur-type varieties are best for containers; try to avoid tip-bearing varieties.

Apricots: Garden Annie, Aprigold (both are genetic dwarfs developed by Floyd Zaiger).

Cherries: Recommended container varieties include Garden Bing, Stella, which is self-fruitful, and Montmorency.

Citrus: Suitable varieties include Marsh seedless grapefuit, Ruby pink grapefruit, Lisbon lemon, Bearss (Persian) seedless lime, Minneola tangelo, Washington dwarf navel orange, Robertson navel orange, Valencia orange (which is seedless), and the Owari satsuma mandarin orange.

Figs: Try Brown Turkey or any other variety which will fruit without caprification.

Grapes: Use any self-fruitful variety. In containers, grapes can be trained in a spiral form around four stakes which are inserted in the container. The lateral shoots on which the fruit is borne should be pruned back to the base after fruiting.

Nectarines: Three Zaiger varieties have been bred especially for containers and small spaces—Garden Beauty, Garden Delight, and Garden King.

Peaches: Try Bonanza, Gold Treasure, Starlet, Garden Gold, and Garden Sun.

Pears: Most varieties grafted onto Quince A rootstocks (may need interstem if variety is incompatible with quince). Two good ones are Seckel, which is not compatible with Bartlett for cross-pollination, and Duchess, which is self-fruitful. All self-unfruitful varieties will need a pollinator such as Bartlett or Magness.

Plums: Try Damson dwarfs, Green Gage, or Stanley.

tained trees tucked away in odd corners, waiting to fill in for a grounded tree lost to pests or diseases. Containers are also useful if you are growing a type of fruit or a particular variety not commonly grown in your area, because you can observe its progress before committing it to a spot in the orchard.

In addition, containers make it possible to grow certain fruits beyond their normal geographic range. Northern gardeners with greenhouses or other suitable winter quarters can grow citrus, figs, or other subtropical or tropical fruits outdoors in summer and under cover in winter. Under such conditions it is possible to eke out several harvests a year of some fruits like the fig and to avoid the need for laying on winter protection. Containers also make it possible to save your bounty from unseasonal frosts, damaging winds or hail, and hungry birds.

Of course, there is inevitably a certain price to be paid for such flexibility, for as British horticultural writer Alan F. Simmons has observed, "The more limited the space in which your fruit grows, the more work you will have to do." Potted fruits must have good drainage, top-dressings of composted manure and other soil amendments as needed, more frequent watering than ground-planted fruits, periodic soil changes during dormant seasons, and either periodic root pruning or transplanting to a larger container. Container-grown fruits are also notoriously subject to dropping off the trees before they are ripe, possibly because of fluctuating moisture levels.

However, for adventurous gardeners or those with very little space, container culture is worth a try. It is currently an area of much experimentation, and new dwarf varieties that are better suited to container growing are being developed.

Landscaping with Berry Bushes: Line your driveway with berry bushes to provide eye appeal as well as a profusion of juicy berries during the summer months.

Landscaping with Fruits

The changing aspect of fruit plants and trees makes them decorative specimen plants in all seasons. In spring their fragile blossoms stir winter-dulled emotions; in summer their brightly colored bounty delights the eye and hand. In autumn the fiery foliage of deciduous trees warms the cooling air; and in winter their angled silhouettes offer beauty of a starker kind. This range of aesthetic effects can be enjoyed on every property, no matter how modest in size.

Potted dwarf fruits adorn patios or bright porches as little else can, while espaliered forms can glorify the otherwise uninteresting and unused wall of house, garage, or outbuilding. Small bush fruits such as currants can be used instead of more conventional flowering shrubs to frame a doorway or line a driveway or walkway. (Such borders also can be enhanced by strawberry plants or rows of dwarf fruits.)

Low-growing fruits are particularly handsome in front of stone walls. (The heat stored and gradually released by the masonry causes fruits to ripen faster and may even permit the successful culture of fruits usually raised farther south.) If the terrain slopes sharply, the effort of mowing grass and monotony of the usual groundcovers can be avoided by making terraces with bricks or railroad ties and creating a festive tiered strawberry patch.

Uninteresting fences take on a positive appeal when used as the backdrop for sculptured grapevines or neatly trained trailing bramble fruits. Another visually agreeable way to mark a property line is with a line of dwarf apples and/

Creating a Privacy Screen with Fruit Trees: Fruit trees can be incorporated into any home landscape to serve a variety of purposes both functional and ornamental. One option is to place fruit trees along the edge of your property to serve as a privacy screen between you and the neighboring property.

make your own

A Strawberry Pyramid

Gardener Melvin Thacher developed a simple design for a five-tier strawberry pyramid, and each tier can be added as you plant. The pyramid holds about 40 plants.

Start with 34 feet of 1 × 4 lumber. Unfinished redwood is a good type to use because it is reputed to stand the weather better than most other woods. The bottom frame is made of four 30-inch lengths of wood, the next tier is made of 27-inch-long wood, and so on, each tier being 6 inches smaller than the last. After cutting all of the pieces, scribe lines for the screws ½ inch from the one end of the bottom frame pieces, and 3½ inches from the one end of all the other pieces. Attach the frame pieces with two brass screws, 2 inches long, at each corner. There is a 2-inch planting bed on all tiers.

The five frames of the pyramid are not permanently fastened together, so when you are ready to plant, start with the bottom frame, fill it with soil, and build on up with each frame, setting the plants in around the edges as you go.

Strawberry Pyramid: Designed to accommodate 40 strawberry plants, this space-saving pyramid will lend itself to small places with limited growing area. The easy-to-build frames are stacked, not fastened, and each tier is 6 inches shorter than the one below. There is a 2-inch-wide growing bed on each tier.

or pears planted 10 to 12 feet apart and trimmed in pyramid shapes or trained to four strands of wire on posts set 12 feet apart. Or instead of planting a privet hedge, how about one of blueberries, which will yield its sweet fruit in summer and flame scarlet in autumn; or a richly fruiting barrier of blackberries or upright raspberries.

Unattractive, idle corners of a yard can be brightened into color and productivity with a group of quinces, gooseberries, or brambles. Double rows of red raspberries, currants, elderberries—or perhaps grapes on a good-looking wooden arbor or raspberries trained on wires—also can form an attractive living screen to block a poor view or partition a yard. Information on training techniques for fruits can be found in chapter 10.

For splendid ornamental effects based on contrasting forms and foliage, fruits can be interplanted. Drooping black or purple raspberries, for example, make a graceful spreading mound that will do well in partial shade near dwarf fruit trees and complement their uprightness pleasantly. For other studies in contrast, bush fruits can be interplanted with other flowering shrubs—blueberries, for example, make handsome, culturally compatible companions for evergreens, since both favor an acid soil. Plantscapes in which fruits and flowers are combined can be especially picturesque, as when berries along a wooden fence form the background for a border of flowers, or some daffodils or other early-flowering bulbs are planted in circular beds beneath dwarf fruits. Nearby flowers will also enhance pollination of fruits. A few blooming flowers tolerant of filtered light can be tucked under deep-rooted fruit trees pruned to an open center. (Be careful of planting too many flowers under your trees, though, lest they compete for the nutrients and moisture.) As space-conscious Europeans know, even vegetables lend themselves to colorful geometrical arrangements featuring fruits. Hedgerow plantings of cucumbers, squash, tomatoes, broccoli, and so on can be intercropped with young berry bushes or dwarf trees. Where just one accent plant is wanted, consider a lush elderberry with ornamental foliage or a delicately beautiful Japanese plum.

There are many ways to integrate fruits into your landscape. Your own sense of proportion and design will serve to guide you, and you'll also be able to pick up valuable tips from a good book on landscaping, or, if you can afford it, get help from a landscape architect.

7

Planting

The preferred seasons for planting fruits are determined by the winter hardiness of the plants or trees and the temperature extremes of the planting locale. Basically, the goal in planting is to allow as much time as possible for the young trees or bushes to establish themselves before the most stressful conditions of the year occur. In northern areas where extended periods of temperatures at −10°F pose the greatest danger to trees and flower buds, early spring is generally the best time for planting deciduous fruit trees—especially for dwarfs and for the tender stone fruits. Spring planting also is recommended in colder climes for bare-rooted persimmons, raspberries, blueberries, and for blackberries and their relatives. For such fruits early spring planting makes severe winter injury less likely by offering the advantage of a long, mild growing season that allows them to mature and harden-off before experiencing extreme temperatures. Strawberries also benefit from early spring planting in all but the mildest climates, for they thrive in moderate to cool weather, which stimulates runner production. In the northern United States, spring-planted fruits also profit from the higher level of soil moisture present then.

In warmer areas where the long, hot summers are the most stressful time for plants, most fruit trees do better if planted in fall or early winter. Fall planting allows the young stock to regain its strength lost in transplanting before its energies are called upon to produce new spring growth. The soil at that time of year is warm enough to allow good root growth before strong top growth gets under way in spring.

The soil in fall is often more workable. Fall planting avoids competition with heavy spring rains that often make the soil difficult to manage. Many fruit trees also benefit from the winter's alternate freezing and thawing, which helps to settle their roots. Furthermore, the roothold gained over the winter affords almost a year's head start toward bearing and allows fruit trees to withstand midsummer droughts more successfully. Plants settling in over the winter also get growing earlier the following spring than do just-planted fruits.

tricks of the trade

Some Tips on Buying Nursery Trees

- Buy from a reliable nursery with a good reputation.
- Don't go bargain-hunting. Cheap trees are almost never as healthy, and your best chance for success is with a healthy, sturdy specimen.
- Most trees are grown in the ground and then dug up and sold bare-rooted. Watch for broken and dried-out roots, and always carefully inspect roots as well as branches of any bare-rooted tree you buy.
- Buy the biggest, oldest tree you can afford, preferably one that is two to three years old and has a well-developed root system. If the tree has branches (many are just unbranched whips), be sure they are spaced evenly around the trunk.

Preparing the Plant

Ideally, fruits should be planted as soon as possible after they arrive by mail or are brought home from the nursery. If the plant is bare-rooted and planting must be delayed, dig a shallow, foot-deep trench for trees (6 inches deep for small fruits) in a shady location and lay the exposed roots in it so the top of the plant emerges at a sharp angle. Then cover the roots with soil, which should be kept moist. This interim treatment is called "heeling-in" and can be used for up to several weeks if necessary.

Another approach is to keep the plant in a humid cellar or shed, soaking its bare roots, then covering them with moist soil, straw, or burlap. If planting is to be postponed for only a day or two, soak the plant's roots as described below and keep it in a cool, shady spot. If the plant has a rootball wrapped in burlap, simply keep the covered roots moist until planting time.

Whether you do or do not plant right away, it is essential to keep bare roots from drying out, and it is best to unpack and unwrap such plants immediately, then soak the roots for anywhere from several hours to overnight before planting. You can use a slurry of 1 cup of compost per gallon of water. If you are planting a group of new fruit plants at one time in the garden, keep the roots of the vines, trees, or shrubs in plastic or under the wet burlap to keep them from being dried out by exposure to the air, wind, or direct sun before you can set them in the ground. Dipping the roots in a slurry of clay and manure in water right at planting time will help to seal in the moisture.

Preparing the Site

Either before or after you have attended to matters of root moisture, you must prepare a suitable site for your fruit planting. Advance planning can be helpful, especially if the soil at the intended location is not of high quality or has been used to grow corn or other demanding crops. If a sizable spring or fall planting of fruits there is anticipated 1 or 1½ years ahead, you can plant and till under a green manure cover crop of winter rye, oats, or clover or other legumes to add nitrogen to the soil. Another option is to dig the hole for spring planting the preceding fall and make compost in it. If this is done the hole should be at least twice as wide and deep as the root spread of the plant that will go in it. If you plan to plant in spring in an area formerly covered by sod, till the area in autumn, digging in lots of fresh or dried manure (this is especially important if you will be putting in heavy feeders such as berries, grapes, or melons). You can also add lime at this time if a soil test indicates acidity and you do not intend to grow blueberries or other fruits favoring a soil with a low pH. In any case, work this area well before planting fruits the next spring. For fall planting where the soil is good enough to grow grass or vegetables, you can simply dig the hole a month ahead.

Whether you plant in spring or fall, it is imperative that the hole be deep and wide enough so that roots can be fully extended without crowding or bending. Indeed, for best results the hole should be half again as wide and deep as the roots reach when extended to their full length. A good rule of thumb for a bare-rooted tree would be a hole 3 feet deep by 3 feet wide; if there is a rootball instead of bare roots, the hole should be at least 6 inches wider in all directions. In digging the hole, be sure to shovel the topsoil and the subsoil on different heaps, so you can later place the richer topsoil, either alone or amended, at the bottom of the hole, where it can do the best job of feeding the roots.

If you are growing an apple tree on a very dwarfing rootstock or another tree or bush that either is weak at the graft-union or has brittle roots, you should next drive a 1½- or 2-inch-square wooden stake (treated with copper naphthenate,

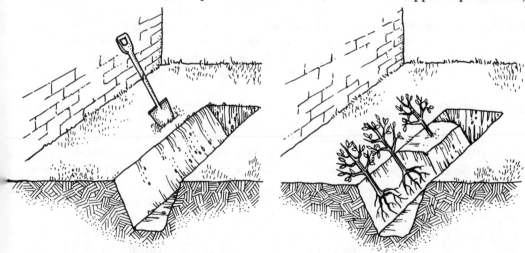

Trenching and Heeling-In: If the planting of bare-rooted nursery stock is delayed, the new plants should be "heeled-in" immediately upon arrival. Dig a temporary trench deep enough to hold the roots, in an area protected from direct sun and wind. Place the young stock at an angle in the trench (preferably with their tops pointing to the south to prevent sunburning of the trunks) and cover with soil. Water thoroughly and keep moist until they are transferred to a permanent site.

Preparing the Site: First, dig the hole deeper and wider than you think is really necessary. Most bare-rooted trees will fit comfortably into a 3-by-3-foot hole. Make three separate piles; sod, topsoil, and the lighter-colored subsoil. Discard any large rocks present in the soil.

Second, add a cup of bone meal to the bottom of the hole; then if you want, you can put the sod back in, upside down. Gently tread on the sod to remove any air pockets.

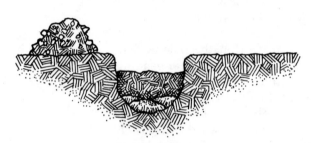

The topsoil is put in next, because you want the best soil near the roots. Lime or cottonseed meal can be added if the pH needs adjusting.

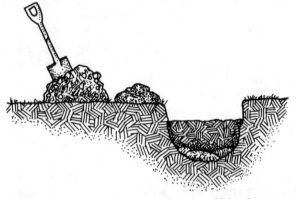

Supplement the subsoil with a few shovelfuls of compost, rock powders, peat moss, and whatever else will help improve its quality, trying to make it as close to good topsoil as you can. Mix together well. This enriched soil will be used to fill in around the tree when you plant.

a wood preservative nontoxic to plants) several inches into the bottom of the hole. The stake can be 6 feet long for a fruit tree, shorter for a short-stemmed bush fruit. To allow more movement, which helps a staked tree increase in girth, consider double-staking—that is, driving in a stake on both sides of the plant.

Before You Plant

Before the tree or plant is actually set in the hole, matters of drainage must be attended to. If the substratum is clay, it may be necessary to use drainage tiles or, before digging the hole, to raise the planting area by about 2 feet using a mound of topsoil and humus with the sides sloped. If the drainage is fairly good, however, it is sufficient to put down 2 inches of gravel or a layer of rocks in the bottom of the hole or container.

The next step prior to setting in the fruit is to put down a layer of topsoil. Often it is desirable to improve the drainage and nutrient content of that soil by mixing it with amendments such as sand, fibrous peat, leaf mold, and compost. Generally speaking, manure should not be mixed directly in the planting soil of temperate-zone fruits, for the single growth cycle they experience each year limits the amount of fertilizer they can use and any excess can promote vegetative growth that can delay fruiting, and make the plant more vulnerable to insects and disease—or, if it is planted in fall, to cold-weather injury. Shape the soil into a mound or pyramid, so the roots can be gently arranged downward over the sides of the mound and into the bottom of the hole.

Pruning at Planting Time

When planting bare-rooted stock, before placing your fruit tree or bush in the hole, use a sharp knife or pruning shears (which actually make a cleaner cut than a knife) to cut back any broken tips by ½ inch so that healthy, vital tissue is next to the soil and more fine roots are stimulated to grow. Since about half of the plant's root structure was left behind when it was dug up at the nursery, it will also be necessary to remove an equivalent amount of top growth just before or after planting. Otherwise, the disproportionately greater amount of evaporative surface aboveground will slow or stop growth, or may even cause branches to die.

If the tree you are planting is simply a whip with no branches, cut off roughly the top third. If you are working with branched stock, a good rule of thumb is to remove any branches that emerge from the main trunk (or leader) at an angle of less than 45 degrees. At this time in the tree's life, you want to encourage the development of a strong system of scaffold branches to support the fruit later on. Branches growing more or less vertically (at less than 45 degrees) will compete with the central leader, and also form narrow, weak crotches that tend to split under a heavy fruit load. Choose three to five branches that will become scaffolds and remove, completely, all others except the main stem or leader. The scaffold branches that remain should be radially distributed as evenly as possible around the tree. Head back the leader to a total length of 3 feet or so, except in the case of peaches, nectarines and apricots, and spreading, low-growing plums, which do better with an open center. For open-center trees, cut out the entire leader.

It is not a good idea to merely tip-prune all the branches, because this encourages the growth of lateral branches, which is undesirable at this stage of the tree's growth.

Pruning should be done down to buds on the outside of branches so that new growth will be outward rather than toward the center of the tree. Bush fruits should be trimmed of dead or damaged wood and short twigs, and any fruit buds removed so growth of roots and branches is encouraged. All pruning cuts should be made close to the trunk or limb, with no stubs left (these can be a ready site for disease entry).

If you plant a bare-rooted bush, take the same care that you would with any other plant to ensure that the top and the roots are in balance with each other. Remove any damaged roots and cut the top back about half. In order to encourage the development of a bush plant, pinch any blooms that appear the first year, and for the next few years, the only pruning necessary is the removal of damaged or dead branches.

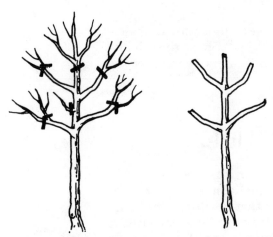

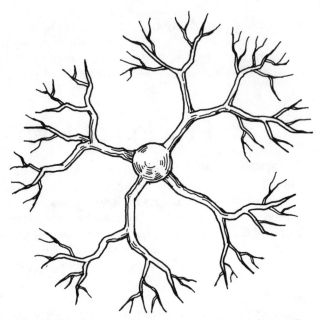

Pruning Young Trees: Most nursery stock will be un-branched (a whip), so the question of pruning anything other than the leader does not apply. If you are working with branched stock, it is unwise to "head" (remove the tips of) the branches. This process only promotes growth of lateral shoots on the scaffold or main branches at a time in the tree's life when development of a strong foundation (scaffold system) is the goal. The best approach is to remove the less than 45-degree branches, since they will tend to break under heavy fruit loads. Choose three to five branches that will become scaffolds and remove, completely, all others. The leader should be headed to a total length of at least 3 feet.

Scaffold Arrangement: As shown in this aerial view, the three to five scaffolds maintained in the initial pruning should be radially distributed evenly around the trunk of the tree. This arrangement will be the foundation for a sturdy scaffold system that will endure through many abundant fruit-bearing years.

Positioning the Plant

After topsoil has been placed in the bottom of the planting hole in the shape of a pyramid, the bush or tree should be lowered on top of it in as straight a position as possible. If the plant is bare-rooted, gently extend the roots outward and downward over the hill of soil. Cut off any broken or dead roots. Any large root that is inextricably wrapped around another should be pruned back, so that in growing it does not choke off the other root's supply of moisture and nutrients.

If you are planting a tree with a burlapped rootball, first cut the burlap in several places—it takes longer to decompose than you might imagine, and can confine roots to their detriment.

The depth at which fruits are properly positioned varies. Bear in mind that fruits should not be planted too deep, for it's important that feeder roots grow near the soil surface to anchor the bush or tree firmly. (Mulching also encourages feeder roots.) Bush fruits or ungrafted trees are usually put in at the same depth they were at the nursery or 1 or 2 inches deeper. (To ascertain the original planting level, look for differences of color on the bark or stem.) Where grafted trees are concerned, standard sizes are always planted with the union 2 inches or so below ground for protection from severe weather and for anchorage. Dwarfs, though, must be placed so that the graft site is an inch or two above the ground so the scion cannot send forth roots and turn the diminutive tree back into a large specimen. Fruit specialist Norman Childers recommends placing fruit trees so the bulk of their roots, the bud or graft-union, and, if possible, the lowest scaffold limb are pointed toward the prevailing wind. If a stake is being used, the roots should be fitted around it.

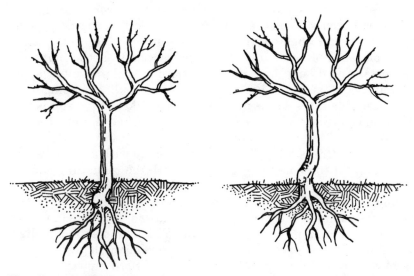

How Deep to Plant: When planting a dwarf tree (right), *do not* bury the graft-union where the dwarfing rootstock joins the scion. The graft-union is easily identifiable as a discolored bump on the trunk. If the union is underground the scion will root and you will lose the effect of the dwarfing stock. When planting a standard-sized tree (left), the graft-union should be planted below ground level. Otherwise the rootstock will send up shoots that will compete with and eventually crowd out the main tree. Instead of picking big, juicy Red Delicious apples, you will end up with little crab-apples, or whatever the rootstock produces.

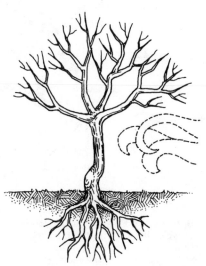

Direction of Unions: The position of the graft-union is also important when planting a tree. You can provide greater stability for the tree by pointing the bud or graft-union toward the prevailing winds to reduce the possibility of union failure in high winds. If the lowest limb and bud-union are on different sides of the tree, the union should receive precedence over the limb.

Settling In the Plant

When the fruit plant is positioned, an assistant will be needed to move it gently up and down and sideways while you carefully spade in more of the improved soil around the roots. This movement will help soil particles to sift snugly around all the roots. As you spade in the soil you can help this process by pushing some of it into root hollows to make sure all the cracks and crevices are filled. When several inches of soil are covering and protecting the roots, begin to stamp down on it now and then between additions of soil while your partner holds the tree in place. Tread carefully, however, especially if the plant has shallow, fragile roots. And do not press down too hard on soil above burlapped roots, although you should pack soil firmly around the rootball. Stamping down firmly also is not desirable if the soil is moist enough to cake. (If the soil is that wet, you would actually do best to delay planting for a few days, until the soil is more workable.)

When the hole is two-thirds filled, follow some treading with a pail of water. After it has soaked in, fill the hole to ground level with the remaining subsoil. Then stamp the soil one last time, which will leave a bowl-shaped hollow a few inches deep around the plant. This depression will help the young plant or tree trap moisture over the summer. If a harsh winter lies ahead, very late in the fall mound the surface soil 6 to 12 inches up the trunk or stem and extend a slight mound to beyond the perimeter of the roots. If you're working with grafted trees, remember to remove any soil covering the graft-union before growth starts in spring, or scion rooting may occur.

At this time, if you have not already done so, remove the wire tag put on the plant at the nursery so it does not cut into the plant later as it grows.

Settling the Plant: Proper settling of a new plant is best accomplished with two people. While one shovels the soil into the planting hole, the other gently moves the plant in different directions so that the soil can settle in around the roots. This process prevents the formation of any air pockets, which can dry out the roots.

Caring for Newly Planted Fruits

The basic planting completed, plants being staked should be fastened to the support(s) at three places if they are trees and at one place if they are bushes. The tie should not abrade the wood of the new plant and create a weak place that could snap in high wind. A handy choice is an old nylon stocking or strip of cloth which can be looped three times around the stake and once around the stem or trunk. Or the plant may be secured with sturdy wire that is passed through pieces of old garden hose.

Newly planted trees and bushes must compete with surrounding weeds and even grass or sod for water and nutrients, and eliminating the competition will help the young trees along. To keep down weeds and grass, mulch or keep cultivated an area extending outward to the drip-line or 3 feet in all directions from the trunk of the young tree. Another way to keep down weeds in areas where several trees are planted is to mow the orchard several times during the growing season, or let a few sheep or cows in to graze. Do not allow horses or goats into the orchard, however—both like to eat bark, twigs, and leaves. And keep all animals out when the ground is wet—the trampling of their hooves will compact the soil.

If you opt for mulching, the mulch should be 6 inches deep to be effective and can consist of a layer of compost, straw, or well-rotted manure. Acid-loving plants like blueberries should be mulched with acidic materials such as pine needles, peat moss, or oak or pine bark. Mulch of some kind is also important for espaliered trees, and to protect shallow-rooted plants such as blueberries, melons,

Double-Staking: Double-staking offers good support and is especially important for dwarf trees due to their shallow root systems. Fasten the tree to stakes with wire that's been covered with pieces of rubber hose.

digging deeper

Painting Whips White

Some nurseries recommend that year-old trees, technically called "whips," be painted with whitewash, white interior latex paint, or a combination of both. (Oil-base paints are not recommended.) Trees should be painted in early spring as the weather begins to warm, but before buds begin to swell. In cooler areas, the trunk is coated from 1 inch below the new soil line to a point beyond the graft- or bud-union. In warmer areas, the entire tree may be covered, as long as buds are still closed. The paint should eventually wear off as the trees grow and bark expands during the season.

Nurseries that recommend painting cite several reasons for the practice. Whitewash or white paint protects young bark from sunscald by reflecting unseasonally hot sunlight, discourages borers from digging into tender trunks and shoots, and delays the premature opening of buds, especially in areas where early spring warmth may cause trees to begin growth before roots are capable of supporting it, or where late spring frosts may pose problems.

In addition, the white coating keeps trees cooler (temperatures above 60°F during dormancy

Winter Damage of Tree Bark: Fluctuating winter temperatures, frigid weather, and spring frosts damage the inner bark and adjacent tissues of trees, causing the bark to split and come off.

may actually subtract from the total amount of "chilling" hours each tree requires to perform well in a particular climate). The coating also can disrupt life cycles of emerging pests whose eggs were laid upon the bark last season, and it makes small trees more conspicuous in their dormant state so they won't be damaged by careless movement around the home landscape.

Some home orchardists continue the practice of early spring painting until trees become large and woody enough for the bark to begin protecting itself.

—Jamie Jobb

and quince from heat and dryness. A small circle immediately around the stem or trunk should be left mulch-free since mulch can encourage crown rot in some perennials like strawberries, and it also encourages mice to take up residence. In fall, pull the mulch away from the trunk and install mouse guards.

The stem or trunk can be protected by encircling it with a 2-foot-high piece of ¼-inch hardware cloth that extends 2 inches below the soil surface. If the wire circle is too much larger than the trunk, mice will climb right inside it and spend a cozy winter munching on the bark. Other acceptable tree guards include a commercially available heavy plastic sleeve, light-colored building paper, tree wrap, tape, or even a magazine, but avoid black materials which can cause harmful heat buildup during cold weather when trees are dormant.

Young fruit trees also need to be guarded against the effects of the sun in winter when they have no foliage. A coat of white paint on the trunk makes an effective, inexpensive sunburn preventive. Using the cheapest white exterior latex you can find (do not use an oil-base paint), paint the entire trunk up to and including a bit of the lowest scaffold branches. You may need to repeat the procedure every two or three years, but it's well worth the time and effort involved.

digging deeper

Winter Protection for Fruits

Extreme winter cold can profoundly affect fruit trees, especially young ones. Assuming that you have planted fruits whose chilling requirements and hardiness are compatible with your climate, there are a number of cultural techniques that can be employed to help thwart damage during dormancy.

Three or 4 inches of mulch applied after freezing in late fall and removed after the spring thaw will help moderate below-ground temperature swings and offer some protection to exposed roots while fighting loss of soil moisture. Another helpful practice during dormancy is to regularly and gently brush snow from tree branches before it turns to ice that can weigh down limbs and cause breakage.

Another approach is to wrap the trunks and branches of trees less than six years old from the top down in stretchable, weatherproof paper called treewrap, or in heavy burlap or fiberglass blankets much like those used to insulate hot water heaters. Especially tender fruits like the fig can be wrapped, then bent over to spend the winter under mulch held in place by soil.

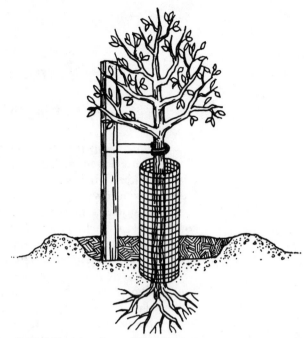

Tree Guard: A hardware cloth tree guard acts as a good barrier between tender tree bark and nibbling rodents.

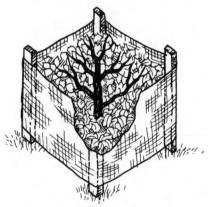

Winter Protection: Tender young trees can be protected from winter's chilling blasts of wind by enclosing them in a burlap box. Drive four stakes into the ground around the tree and run burlap from stake to stake, creating a rectangular enclosure. Add further protection by filling the box with dried leaves.

Threatening sudden temperature changes caused by sun or wind also can be foiled by placing four stakes or dowels around a plant, then creating a rectangular enclosure by wrapping burlap around the supports. For small, less hardy plants or recent transplants, the burlap windbreak—or for that matter, a cylinder of chicken wire or hardware cloth—can be filled loosely with hay, evergreen needles, wood shavings, or dried leaves (oak leaves are ideal because they will not compact and impede vital air circulation). The arrangement can be topped with any kind of waterproof, wind-secure cover. Fruits in containers also can be buffered by bales or chunks of hay or straw or fiberglass blanketing placed around the plant base.

Covering the ground around a fruit by mounding up additional soil or putting down mulch also supports hardiness by promoting a deep root system and moderating temperature changes in the root zone. Protective covers of all kinds should be left in place until midspring when the special risk posed by warm days succeeded by bitter nights is minimal.

Bringing Young
Trees into Bearing

To ensure optimum cropping and fruit quality when the tree is mature, it is important not to let the tree bear fruit too heavily early in its life. Remove the fruit produced during the first two growing seasons at home. The third year the tree can be allowed to bear a light to moderate crop. Always thin heavy crops so that limbs do not break under the weight or distort the shape of the tree. With some trees, dwarf apples in particular, you must pay special attention to the leader; if it is bent by a heavy load of fruit it may turn into a lateral fruiting branch, and the tree will be left without its central growing branch.

Trees will usually come into bearing with no assistance needed from you, the gardener. The start of bearing is sometimes delayed when a tree grows vigorously (varieties known for their vigorous growth, like the McIntosh apple, are especially prone to this). In such cases, slowing the growth will encourage fruit production, so do not fertilize the tree. Some trees may need special treatment to encourage fruiting.

Getting Reluctant Trees to Bear

When a tree is of bearing age and does not produce fruit, there are some steps you can take to encourage fruiting. The first step would be to get a soil and leaf test done by your local agricultural extension office. If the analysis turns up

Reluctant Bearers: Encourage your reluctant-bearing fruit trees to set fruit by tying down their branches into a less vertical position. Increasing the angle of the scaffold branches to 45 degrees reduces vegetative growth and promotes the formation of fruit buds.

no nutrient deficiencies, other measures can be taken. One is to try and spread the branches into a more horizontal position—this slows growth and promotes the development of buds. You can purchase branch-spreaders from a nursery supplier, or tie the branches at a 45-degree angle with sturdy rope or wire covered with a piece of rubber hose to prevent damage to the tree. Keep the branches in this position until a crop is set; it may take more than one season because the buds are initiated in summer to bloom and bear fruit the following year. Branches can be spread and tied at any time, although the ideal time is immediately following the early spring pruning.

If spreading the branches fails to produce a crop, there is one further treatment that can be used on trees that are at least five years old. This is scoring the bark, and it should be attempted only as a last resort because it can easily injure the tree. Three to five weeks after the tree has bloomed, cut through both the outer and inner bark with a sharp knife, inscribing a circle on the trunk just below the lowest branch. The only time this method should be attempted is when you would otherwise get rid of the tree.

8

Pollination and Fruit Set

In order for fruiting trees, bushes, and vines to produce a crop, the flowers must be pollinated at just the right moment during bloom. An awareness of the pollination needs of the fruit plants in your garden will enable you when laying out and maintaining the orchard or berry patch to increase the chances for pollination to occur naturally, or to help it along when conditions are unfavorable.

How Pollination Occurs

The production of fruits and seeds (of which pollination is the first step) is for the plant a sexual process of reproduction involving both male and female flower parts. In some plants, each flower contains both the male and female parts (such flowers are called perfect); in others, some of the flowers on a single plant contain only male organs, and others are only female; in a third type of plant, all the flowers on a given plant will be either male or female (unisexual flowers are called imperfect).

The female flower part (see illustration), the pistil, is composed of a long tube called the style, which is topped by the sticky stigma that receives the pollen; the swollen basal part of the style is the ovary that contains the ovules or seeds. The male organs, the stamens, have small pollen sacs called anthers positioned on top of thin stalks known as filaments. In the flowers of our common deciduous tree fruits, the stamens grow in a ring around the pistil, although there are many different arrangements in other types of plants.

When it's time for fertilization to occur, the stigma becomes sticky and the ripe pollen grains are taken from the anthers by wind or pollinating insects, and fall or are dropped into the stigma, where they adhere. In order for fertilization to occur, the pollen grain must germinate and send forth a tubular "root" which grows downward through the style from the pollen grain to the ovary. Two sperm cells are channeled through this tube into the ovary where one of them joins with and fertilizes the egg and the other fuses with the polar nuclei. This "double fertilization" is necessary for the formation of seeds (and therefore fruit) and must take place. Without fertilization, that particular fruit will drop.

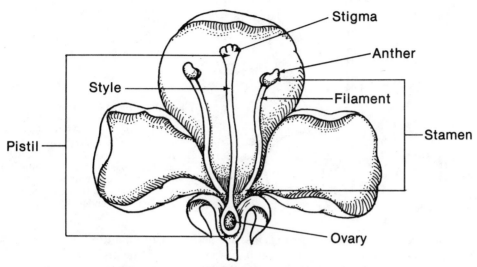

Reproductive Parts of an Apple Flower: The apple flower is a good example of a perfect flower, in which both female and male reproductive structures are present. The flower contains several female organs called pistils, each of which consists of three distinct parts: an enlarged basal ovary where seeds are formed, an elongated style, and a stigma positioned at the top of the style which serves as a receptacle for pollen grains. In addition to the pistils, there are many male organs called stamens. These consist of a thin stalk, the filament, which supports an anther that produces pollen grains.

In multiple-ovary fruits like strawberries and raspberries, the fertilization process is more complex. These flowers possess more than one stigma, and each one must be pollinated and fertilized successfully for the fruit to flesh out to its full capacity. Otherwise, the fruit will develop abnormally and be misshapen.

A plant that is self-pollinating will produce fruit successfully if the stigma receives pollen from the stamens of the same flower, from other flowers on the same plant or tree, or from flowers on plants of the same horticultural variety. Plants that successfully set fruit by self-pollination are said to be self-fruitful. Blueberries, grapes, peaches, raspberries, sour cherries and strawberries are all self-fruitful, and can be planted alone or in blocks of a single variety.

Plants requiring cross-pollination, the transfer of pollen between flowers of two different varieties or species, in order to set fruit are called self-unfruitful. In order to get a crop from a self-unfruitful tree, you must plant close to it another variety that can pollinate it (called a pollinator variety). To ensure successful pollination, plant the trees no more than 300 feet apart. Not all varieties can cross-pollinate one another, however, and you must plant varieties that will (this is called cross-compatibility). For example, the Emperor Francis cherry is cross-compatible with Windsor, but not Bing. In addition to sweet cherries, fruits considered to be self-unfruitful include apples, elderberries, pears, and plums.

To make matters more confusing, there are varying degrees of self-fruitfulness and self-unfruitfulness. Some plants can set fruit with either self- or cross-pollination. Generally speaking, apricots, nectarines, peaches, and sour cherries,

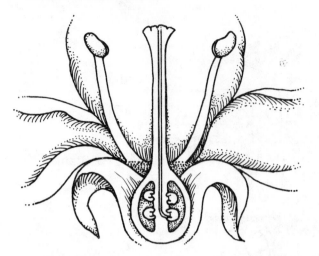

Fertilization of the Flower: After pollination has occurred, the pollen grain forms a pollen tube which grows down the style till it reaches the ovary, where fertilization takes place. In fertilization, male gametes from the pollen tube unite with female gametes in the embryo sac, resulting in the production of an embryo and endosperm.

and small fruits except for elderberries, are self-fruitful enough to set crops with self-pollination, and that most other fruits will have to be cross-pollinated. But varieties must be carefully chosen, because cross-unfruitfulness can also occur between varieties that belong to the same species. For example, not all sweet cherry varieties will cross-pollinate each other. Other fruit varieties, like the Winesap apple, have sterile pollen and cannot pollinate themselves or any other variety.

Choosing Pollinator Varieties

In addition to cross-compatibility of the pollen, there are a number of other factors to consider when selecting varieties to serve as pollinators for self-unfruitful trees. First, the blooming times of the two varieties should coincide—a

Cross-Pollination of Fruit Trees: A self-unfruitful plant is not capable of self-pollination that produces fruit; it must be planted near another compatible variety that can provide it with fertile pollen which results in fruit set. Even self-fruitful plants will produce more fruit if planted close to a different variety. To ensure adequate cross-pollination and optimum fruit production, plant trees within 300 feet or less of a pollinator variety (the closer the better).

tree that blooms in June obviously won't be able to pollinate one that blooms in April. The plant selected as the pollinator variety should produce lots of viable pollen, with a good rate of germination. To get the most value from the space, the pollinator variety should bear edible fruit. It should also bloom annually and at a young age, and should be relatively resistant to disease.

Information on the pollination needs of fruit varieties and recommended pollinator varieties for your area is available from your local USDA county extension agent. And any good nursery catalog will contain this information for the varieties that company sells.

digging deeper

A Guide to Pollination for Some Popular Tree Fruits

Apples: Some apple varieties are self-fruitful, but it is always best to plant two varieties to get a full crop. Cortland, Jonathan, Golden Delicious, Red Delicious, and Rome Beauty are all good pollinator varieties. Baldwin, Greening, Northern Spy, and Winesap produce sterile pollen.

Cherries: Stella is the only self-fruitful sweet cherry variety; Black Tartarian is often recommended as a pollinator for other varieties. Bing is cross-incompatible with Napoleon and Emperor Francis. Sour cherries are self-fruitful.

Peaches, Apricots, and Nectarines: All peach and nectarine varieties are considered self-fruitful except for the J.H. Hale peach, which must be planted with another variety. Most apricots are self-fruitful except for Riland and Perfection.

Pears: Most of the pear varieties grown by home gardeners need cross-pollination, and all varieties will pollinate each other except Bartlett and Seckel. If you plant these two, you'll need to grow a third variety for pollination.

Plums: Plums vary in their need for cross-pollination. Japanese and European varieties do not cross-pollinate readily because their bloom periods do not overlap, so plant either two Japanese varieties or two European varieties to ensure a good crop.

Hindrances to Pollination

Gravity and wind are the vectors which carry the pollen from one flower to another in some fruits, such as grapes, peaches, raspberries, and strawberries. Other fruits require the help of insects to transfer pollen; these include apples, blueberries, plums, and sweet cherries. The wrong sort of environmental conditions during blooming time make it difficult or impossible for successful pollination to occur. One important factor is rain; heavy rain hampers the activity of pollinating insects, and also seriously affects the distribution of pollen by wind.

Cold temperatures also pose a problem. When temperatures fall below 65°F, honeybees are not very active. And in subfreezing weather, the flowers themselves can be injured. Cold tolerance varies among fruits, but cold hardiness of all fruits decreases near bloom time. Sometimes cold damage is readily apparent—in strawberries, frost turns the flower centers black. Other times it's not so noticeable.

Helping Pollination Along

There's not much a gardener can do to protect fruit plants, especially large trees, from cold weather. But there are some measures you can take to encourage better pollination generally in your orchard or berry patch. Growing more than one variety of a given fruit is good insurance that your flowers will be pollinated. As a temporary measure each year, you can suspend bouquets of pollinator flowers in cans of water up among the branches, and hope that the bees will spread the pollen. This approach can be very successful.

Pollination Aids: If the bees are inefficient at transferring pollen from nearby trees, you can lend them a hand by taking flowers containing fertile pollen and placing them in buckets of water hanging from tree limbs. It is best to do this in the early morning when temperatures are low and the bees are most active.

To be absolutely sure pollination is accomplished when conditions are unfavorable, you can pollinate the flowers yourself. This is feasible, of course, only on a very small scale, with a few trees, because you will spend hours tediously dusting your flowers. One method of hand-pollination is to knock ripe pollen into a container (pollen is ripe when it drops from the anthers), then with a soft brush dust it onto open, receptive stigmas of other flowers. Another technique is to clip a twig containing open flowers of a compatible variety and use this as your pollen source, carrying it around with you and dipping the brush into a flower to pollinate three or four flowers on the tree. Since you don't want to overburden your trees and bushes with too many fruits, pollinate only one or two flowers within each cluster on any given branch.

If your property is small, and there is room for only a few trees and bushes, you might want to consider top-working your trees for better pollination. This method entails grafting a branch of a pollen source onto a tree that needs the pollen, creating an all-in-one effect. This is reported to be one of the big advantages of the "five-in-one" apple trees offered by some nurseries. See chapter 9 for more information on grafting.

Fertilization and Fruit Set

After pollination has occurred, each developing fruit follows an inherited sequence of events that will eventually give it the characteristic size, shape, color, and flavor of that variety. The success of each one of these events depends on a number of outside factors—temperature, rainfall, amount of sunlight, activity of insects, diseases, and nutrition of the plants are five of the most important.

On apples, cherries, and other temperate plants, the flower buds form the summer before they will bloom and bear fruit. If the fruit crop during a particular year is a heavy one, you can expect fewer flower buds to form for the following season, and the next year's crop will usually be smaller. Conversely, a light crop with be followed by more buds and a larger crop the next year. The alternate bearing that is evident in many apple trees is a direct expression of this effect of crop size on subsequent bud set.

After the flower buds have formed, it is wise to make sure that your fruit trees and bushes are adequately fed and watered. This is the time of primary growth for the new buds, and if they have been well nourished they will grow strong and have a better chance of surviving the winter to develop into healthy fruit the next season. It's important not to overfeed the trees, however, and to stop all fertilization by midsummer so that growth stops in time for the new buds and shoots to harden for the winter.

Low temperatures and moisture loss during the winter can damage or kill the flower buds, but the biggest threat at that time of the year is a winter thaw. Orchardists dread it because there is a chance that the flowers will open during the warm spell only to be frozen when the cold weather returns. The same sort of cold damage will be caused by a cold spell during the normal blooming season.

Once the flower bud has bloomed and been pollinated in spring, environmental conditions again greatly affect the fertilization and fruit-setting process. Warm days aggravate the race between the growth of the pollen tube down the style and the deterioration of the ovary, a delicate process that can cause fertilization and fruit set to succeed or fail. The ovary is killed by hot weather, and may die before fertilization takes place. Cool temperatures and bright sunshine are the optimal conditions for fertilization.

If the flowers have been fortunate enough to withstand the obstacles set in the way of fertilization, you should eventually have a quantity of plump fruit ripening on your trees and bushes. However, if there are too many fruits on one plant, there may be a spontaneous drop or self-thinning four to six weeks after bloom to lessen the competition for hormones, nutrients, and moisture. The largest, most luscious fruits come from plants with a low percentage of fruit set, so in this case, quantity directly affects quality. Keep in mind that even if only a small percentage of the fruits mature, you'll still have a good crop. A 5 percent rate of fruit set is considered adequate for apples; for peaches the rate is even less. In fact, if your trees don't drop enough immature fruit, you should thin the crop to improve its quality. Thinning is discussed in chapter 10.

9

Propagation

While annual and biennial vegetables are usually started from seed, often where they are to grow, perennial fruits may be multiplied either from seed or from vegetative parts, and often a new fruit tree, vine, or bush is transplanted several times before reaching its ultimate location. Hardier deciduous fruits are often sown or rooted outdoors, sometimes with cold frame or other protection during early growth. Slightly more tender fruits are propagated in flats or pots in a greenhouse, hotbed, or cold frame over the winter and can be started directly outside only in spring—in sheltered beds if it is very early. Tender, tropical, or subtropical fruits may be started year-round if ample artificial warmth, light, and moisture are given.

Fruits are propagated from seed by breeders, but sexual propagation is not a very practical method for home fruit growers. Seedlings take much longer to come into bearing than do vegetatively propagated specimens, and they are highly unlikely to yield fruit as good as that produced by the parent plant. Moreover, plants raised from seed also show a usually unwelcome variability in yield, hardiness, and vigor. However, many worthwhile fruit varieties first occurred as natural mutations observed in seedlings, and there are some instances when propagation from seed may be desirable. This method is preferred sometimes when viral diseases are a problem, since most viruses are not transmitted from parent plants to seeds. Sexual propagation is also tempting for those tropical fruits which grow readily and speedily to bearing age from seed, and for fruits which have not yet been greatly improved by breeders. However, for the most part, especially in the case of temperate fruits, the home growing of fruit from seed is of interest primarily to amateur breeders or backyard hobbyists.

Multiplying plants by asexual means offers advantages that are particularly important to fruit growers. By creating new plants from stems or roots rather than from seeds, propagators eliminate the delays and difficulties linked to seed dormancy and capitalize on the substantial food stores in vegetative parts, which make it possible to shorten the juvenile stage of fruits and assure earlier bearing. Even more wonderfully, asexual propagation almost always guarantees fruit

330

plants with the exact same valuable traits as the outstanding specimens "parenting" them. It also permits the duplication of cultivars that produce delectable fruit but no viable seeds or no seeds at all. On the other hand, diseases causing slow degeneration—especially viruses—are more readily passed on by plant materials than by seeds. Asexual reproduction is accomplished through cuttings, division, grafting, budding, and layering.

Cuttings

Propagation from cuttings involves the removal and nurturing of a vegetative part that sooner or later regenerates into a complete plant. The missing part(s) to be grown may be a root or a shoot or both. For successful results, cuttings in general should be propagated in a medium that can hold moisture long enough for plant tissues to absorb it, but that allows excess water to drain off quickly so root rot is not encouraged. Perlite alone or mixed with peat moss meets that requirement especially well. Placing the cuttings in a mist chamber or otherwise humid environment can help make possible rapid and vigorous rooting of fruit cuttings with foliage any time of the year under full sun.

Cuttings are categorized by the plant part used. Stem cuttings in general should be taken from moderately vigorous, healthy plants and stems that are rich in the carbohydrates needed to power regenerative growth. To test the carbohydrate content of plant material, dip sample cuttings in a 0.2 percent solution of iodine and water for one minute. Cuttings having the highest carbohydrates will color least. The plants selected should also be in the juvenile stage of growth if possible, and the shoots used should preferably be lateral and vegetative rather than terminal or flowering. Choose shoots that are firm and stiff rather than flexible. The handling of stem cuttings depends on the age and condition of the material used—that is, on whether it is softwood or hardwood.

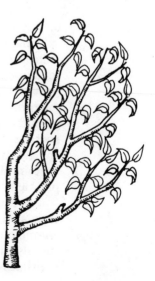

Choosing Stem Cuttings: To produce a surge of healthy new vegetative growth with a high potential for producing roots, vigorously prune the plant or stems from which you plan to take cuttings. Select cuttings with moderate vigor from lateral and vegetative shoots after rapid growth has ceased (and carbohydrates within the stems have accumulated). These cuttings should be firm and stiff. Avoid taking cuttings from terminal (at the tip) and flowering shoots. The illustration on the left is an example of a mature shoot which has produced many flowers. The shoots on the right have been severely pruned, inhibiting flowering but producing many vegetative shoots ideal for stem cuttings.

Softwood and Herbaceous Stem Cuttings

Softwood stem cuttings are taken from the new, unripened vegetation of woody plants having seasonal growth, whereas herbaceous propagation material comes from the soft, juicy tissues of nonwoody perennials. This kind of propagation is done when the plant is in leaf and at an intermediate stage of growth, usually in early spring in a greenhouse or bedding situation or from June to August for plants outdoors. The best time is when the stem snaps when bent double. Propagation of softwood cuttings is a difficult way to propagate fruits at home. Timing is critical. The shoot must be cut when it is at just the right stage of development; if it is too old, even by a few weeks, it will not root.

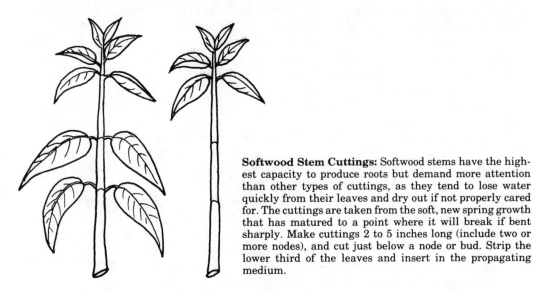

Softwood Stem Cuttings: Softwood stems have the highest capacity to produce roots but demand more attention than other types of cuttings, as they tend to lose water quickly from their leaves and dry out if not properly cared for. The cuttings are taken from the soft, new spring growth that has matured to a point where it will break if bent sharply. Make cuttings 2 to 5 inches long (include two or more nodes), and cut just below a node or bud. Strip the lower third of the leaves and insert in the propagating medium.

A sharp knife should be used to take a 2- to 5-inch-long cutting with a bud or node near the top. The bottom of the cutting should be at the base of an intermediately long side-shoot, or immediately below a bud. Remove the leaves from the bottom one or two nodes of the cuttings, then insert the cuttings immediately into a moist, firmly packed propagation medium. A mix of equal parts pasteurized soil, fine vermiculite, and fine sphagnum moss makes a good rooting medium; another good mix is two parts potting soil, one part peat moss, and one part sharp (builder's) sand. The undersides of the leaves should be as near the rooting medium as possible without touching it. Soak the medium to settle it in snugly around the cuttings. (If there is an unavoidable delay in planting, the bottom of the cuttings may be wrapped in moist towelling or newspaper and plastic.)

Softwood cuttings should never be allowed to wilt, and unless under mist they should be shaded from direct sun. The high humidity provided by a mist chamber or by a setup in which the cuttings are partly covered by glass or enclosed in polyethylene or polypropylene plastic is essential to successful rooting. Good ventilation is vital, too, to fend off the threat of disease. Bottom heat that keeps soil temperatures at 70° to 80°F is helpful, but even without it softwood material usually roots in from two to six weeks. You can supply bottom heat by installing a heating cable in the bottom of the flat or bed where the cuttings will be placed to root.

Hardwood and Semihardwood Stem Cuttings

Most temperate tree fruits and some tropical fruits can be propagated by means of hardwood or semihardwood stem cuttings. This is probably the most difficult way to propagate fruits at home; budding, grafting, or air layering are preferable methods if you have a choice. The techniques for propagating hardwood and semihardwood cuttings are the same; the chief difference is in when the cuttings are taken. Hardwood cuttings are taken in late fall to early spring from dormant, leafless plants. The cuts are preferably made in the current year's wood, which is fully ripened, but for some fruits (such as currants, figs, gooseberries, and olives) wood two or even three years old is acceptable.

Semihardwood cuttings are taken before the onset of dormancy, from early July to late September or when plant growth has stopped and the new wood is "half-ripe" (that is, still young but no longer soft).

Cuttings should be made early in the morning with a sharp knife or other tool. For some fruits, better results are obtained if a small piece of the larger stem (a heel) is taken along with the cutting. Traditionally, hardwood cuttings are 6 to 10 inches long and contain three or more nodes (where buds are); semihardwood cuttings should be 4 to 6 inches long. Roots tend to develop most readily from plant tissue that is "young" in the sense that it is still actively growing and has not yet differentiated into a leaf, some bark, or a vascular bundle inside the trunk. This kind of young tissue is most abundant near leaf axils and at the base of nodes. Thus, it is a good idea to make sure each cutting you take has a node at its base to encourage rooting, and one or two nodes farther up to form leaves. When you take a hardwood cutting, cut the bottom end square and the top end obliquely so you'll be able to tell readily which end to stick in the rooting medium. This will save you a lot of time at planting instead of trying to differentiate the top and bottom of a 6- or 8-inch piece of wood that varies only slightly in thickness along its length.

Hardwood Stem Cuttings: Prepare 6- to 10-inch cuttings with three or more nodes from wood of moderate size and vigor (found near the base of the stem). Cut the basal end square and slant the top so you will always be able to identify which end (the end cut square) is inserted in the rooting medium.

After gathering, hardwood cuttings need to be stored to break the shoot's rest period and form callus tissue at the root ends. They can be bundled, their thicker ends pointing in the same direction, and laid horizontally or stood upside down and covered with moist sawdust, sand, peat, sphagnum moss, or soil. The storage site should be a cool cellar, garage, trench, or cold frame where the air temperature is from 35° to 45°F. Easier yet, the base of the bundle of cuttings may be wrapped in moist sphagnum and the entire bundle put into a plastic bag, sealed tightly, and kept at 50° to 60°F for ten days, then refrigerated until spring. This method is supposed to work especially well for pear cuttings.

In spring the callused cuttings can be planted vertically, butt ends down and 4 to 6 inches apart, in trenches in a sheltered spot. They should be covered to three-fourths of their length or to just below the uppermost bud, and may be expected to root in a minimum of two months. This long rooting time may be shortened if the cuttings are given bottom heat.

Where the winters are relatively mild and a warm, well-drained outdoor site is available, hardwood cuttings may be planted in outdoor trenches right after they are taken. In regions where winters are more severe, root the cuttings in a cold frame or even indoors. Newly rooted semihardwood cuttings can be wintered over by plunging them in sand in a cold frame and covering them with leaves, or by keeping them on a bright but unheated sun porch or in a cool greenhouse at 45° to 50°F.

Root Cuttings

Used for both woody and herbaceous plants, root cuttings are a good choice for brambles and other fruits that sucker from their roots and for those that don't root well from stem cuttings. The method should not be used for grafted fruits, however, unless your goal is to produce new rootstocks for grafting, since the bearing characteristics of the stock are very likely to be inferior to those of the scion.

Root cuttings should be taken after the plant has entered dormancy, and for best results should be fleshy rather than fine and small. Cuts made at the "upper" end of the root (that closest to the stem) should be angled and those made at the "lower" end run straight across. This makes it easier to bundle the cuttings in the same direction and to propagate them right side up after the ends have

Planting Root Cuttings: Root cuttings from thin, delicate roots (left) should be planted horizontally in fine soil, whereas cuttings from thick, fleshy roots (right) are planted vertically with the top of the cutting level with or just below the soil surface.

callused. Root cuttings should be 3 to 4 inches long for berries, and 4 to 6 inches long for fruit trees. Store the root pieces in bundles over the winter, just like hardwood cuttings. In spring, cuttings from fine, thin roots can be planted horizontally 2 inches deep in fine soil. When the cuttings are fleshy rather than fine and thin, they should be planted vertically with their tops level with or just beneath the soil surface. Where trees are concerned, remove all but the most vigorous shoot before planting.

Division

When vegetative structures producing adventitious roots and shoots are removed from plants and rooted, the process is called division. One such specialized structure important in fruit propagation is the stolon or runner, an aerial stem that develops from leaf axils at the crown or base of plants with rosette stems and grows horizontally along the surface of the ground. In many species of strawberry the second node of these runners gives rise to leaf clusters which root easily. These may in turn create new runners, with up to 20 or 30 new plants routinely growing from the original one. Black raspberry is another fruit that sends out runners. Runner-plants may be pegged down to encourage rapid rooting, then the new little plants can be severed and transplanted as wished. Another option is to establish the plants in pots in the ground in order to later force growth in a greenhouse or cold frame.

Rooting Strawberry Runners: Strawberry plants are capable of producing new plants on specialized stem structures called runners. The daughter plants will eventually root and in turn produce new runners. To hasten the rooting process of the daughter plants, insert a wire staple near the new plant in the middle of a pot submerged in the soil. After the plant is fully established, sever the connecting stem and transplant.

Propagation by division also can be undertaken with various other lateral shoots, which are collectively known as offshoots or offsets. Suckers, for example, originate from root systems, or underground stems, or from below a graft-union, and can occur on such diverse fruits as apples, bananas, blackberries, elderberries, juneberries, nectarines, peaches, pears, plums, pomegranates, Japanese quince, and raspberries. Although these often-unwanted shoots tend to pass on the suckering habit if propagated, they are sometimes used to grow rootstocks or continue a good seedling. In temperate climates they can be pulled or cut off or dug up and separated and replanted either in fall or spring. Virus-free suckers from

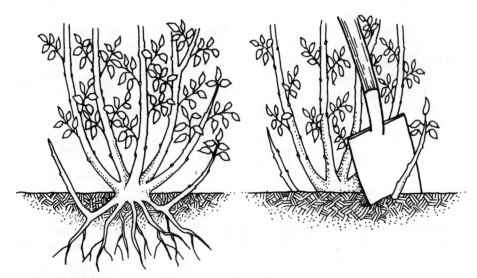

Division of Raspberry: Raspberry plants produce natural suckers which develop their own root systems. Late in the growing season, separate the roots of the sucker from the parent plant with the sharp edge of a spade. After the sucker is established, dig out the rooted sucker and transplant.

cane-forming plants should be transplanted in fall or winter and cut back to 9 inches. To encourage the plant to produce suckers for propagation, prune back the canes before they flower.

In so-called crown division, clumping herbaceous perennials or shrubs are lifted, and sections containing top growth and roots are pulled, cut, or forked apart, often along natural lines. Spring-flowering plants are generally divided in fall, and when replanted should be watered well, given shade if they seem to wilt, and mulched for winter protection. Crown division is done with blueberries and also with large strawberries with few runners. New blueberry plants should be mulched very lightly and planted near other acid lovers.

Grafting

In the various methods of grafting, parts of two or even three plants are brought together to create one new one. This vegetative approach is favored for many deciduous fruit trees and for other fruit plants and cultivars that either do not breed true from seed, do not produce seeds, or do not root easily from cuttings. Grafting is a particularly advantageous kind of propagation, for it shortens the time to bearing, allows the most desirable qualities of different plants to be united in one, and makes possible the growing of numerous varieties ripening at various times on a single tree. Grafting a new top onto a rootstock enables the grower to completely change a tree's fruit variety to a different one (called top-working). Damage to trees from storms or other causes can be repaired by grafting.

Grafts are usually made in spring before fruits come to full flower, but the year-old wood to be used for the top of the new plant should be cut off earlier, when it is unfrozen but still completely dormant, and wrapped in slightly moist peat moss. The entire bundle should be sealed in a plastic bag and kept in the refrigerator or a cold frame at from 32° to 40°F until grafting time. Another method, one that is useful only for new planting stock, is to perform the actual graft in winter and store the grafted stock in moist sand or moss in a cool cellar until spring, when it can be planted.

Cutting the Scion: When top-working an established tree, the top three or four buds on the shoot to be the scion should be discarded, since they are immature or may be flower buds. Also discard the bottom three or four buds to ensure a good graft-union.

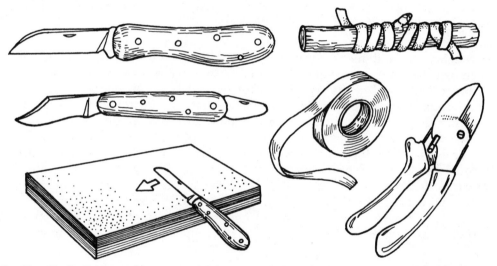

Grafting Tools: Proper tools are essential for any grafting (or budding) job. A good propagator will need materials to tie and wrap the union, knives and shears to prepare the stock and scion, and a stone to keep the tools razor sharp since close, clean cuts are essential. Clockwise from the upper right: rubber strips, pruning shears, tape, a sharpening stone, budding knife (the blunt part on the right is for opening the flaps for T-budding), and a grafting knife.

Whip or Tongue Graft

A graft quite commonly used for fruits, this is an easy way to top-work a young tree—that is, to change its variety or sometimes species by attaching a new top part (scion) to the rootstock (stock). Top-working is also done to add more varieties to the tree. This method can also be used in any other situation when two branches that are ½ inch in diameter or smaller are being joined, such as in interstem grafting, where one or even two intermediate stocks are fitted between the rootstock and the scion variety.

In the whip graft, the stock is cut back to within a few inches of the ground or trunk and complementary long, diagonal cuts are made on a stock and scion

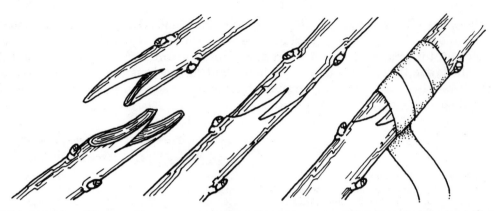

Whip Grafting: When grafting, no matter what technique you use, it is extremely important that there is good contact between the actively growing cambium tissue of the stock and scion. For a whip graft (shown above) cut the stock and scion, matching the cuts as closely as possible so the cut surfaces will have maximum contact. The union is held together tightly by wrapping it in adhesive nursery tape or rubber strips.

of roughly equal diameter so that about 1½ inches of cut surface are created on each. On the stock, a second cut parallel to the first is then made about an inch below it downward to the center so a tongue is formed. An identical second cut is then made on the bottom of the scion so that when the two pieces are fitted together they form a tongue and groove joint, with the cambiums (rings of generative tissue just under the bark) lined up on at least one side of the graft and preferably on both. If one part being joined is larger than the other, the overhang created can be cut so scion and rootstock line up exactly at the graft site. The union is then held together tightly by rubber bands or adhesive latex nursery tape, and asphalt emulsion paint or grafting wax is used to coat any exposed surfaces, in order to keep the wound from drying. Another useful wrapping material is narrow strips of cloth that have been dipped in warm grafting wax and

tricks of the trade

Homemade Grafting Wax

Although commercial grafting wax is available, many growers prefer to make their own. A simple formula you may want to use contains four parts finely broken resin, two parts beeswax, and one part tallow. Melt the tallow and then add beeswax. When this is melted, add the resin. Boil slowly for 30 minutes, stirring occasionally, and then pour the mixture into cold water. Grease your hands, remove the cooled wax and work it by pulling and twisting until it becomes smooth-grained and straw-colored. Twist the wax into skeins and wrap it in waxed paper. It will keep almost indefinitely and should be applied with greased hands. The wax hardens in storage but will soften again with heat—usually with just the heat from your hands.

drawn over the edge of a pane of glass or piece of metal to remove the excess wax. Wrap the cloth strips tightly around the graft; when the wax hardens they produce a tight but yielding wrap. As with all grafts, the wrapping should be removed in several months lest it choke the growing branch.

Cleft Grafting

Cleft grafting is often used to fashion multi-variety trees or to repair young trees that have been girdled by disease or by a wire nursery tag that was never removed. The best time of the year to do it is late in the dormant period before the buds open. In this method, two scions the width of pencils are inserted in a cleft made in a fairly upright branch having a diameter of 1 to 2 inches. The scions should be short, with two or three plump buds, and their end portions cut

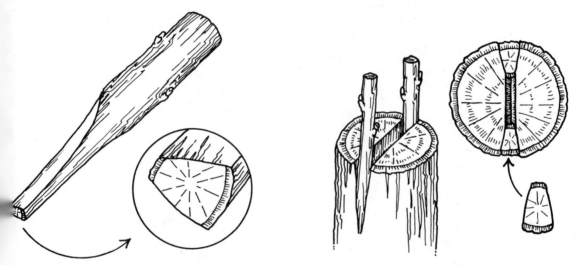

Cleft Grafting: Shave the edge of the scion that will be inside the stock thinner than the outside edge. The inside edge should be blunt, not tapered to a fine point. Place the scion slightly inside the stock so the cambium layers will match up.

off just above a bud. Two smooth downward diagonal cuts meeting in the middle are made in each scion, starting below the lowest buds. The stock is first cut straight across with a fine-toothed saw, then split down its center to 4 to 6 inches with a hammer and chisel. The depth of the cleft should be predicated on having the top of the scion cuts correspond as closely as possible with the top of the stock.

While the cleft is kept wedged open with a screwdriver or other wedge a scion is inserted on each side. At least at the top of the graft and if possible, farther down as well, the cambium tissue of the scion should be in full contact with that of the stock. Good contact can be ensured by shaving the side of the scion that will be placed inside the cleft slightly thinner than the outside edge. Since the stock is much larger in diameter than the scion and the cambium of the stock will be under a thicker bark, it is necessary to place the scion slightly within the outer edge of the stock in order to match the cambium layers.

When the wedge is removed the closing cleft ideally should trap the scion snugly in place. If it does not, pressure can be exerted by wrapping string-reinforced tape around the union. All exposed wood should be sealed with asphalt emulsion paint or grafting wax (which is somewhat harder to handle).

Bark Grafts

Bark grafting is becoming popular with amateur orchardists doing top-working, for it can be used when scion and stock vary in width. Bark grafting is not very desirable because it produces a weak graft. However, bark grafts are more likely to "take" than other types of grafts, making this a rewarding method for amateurs.

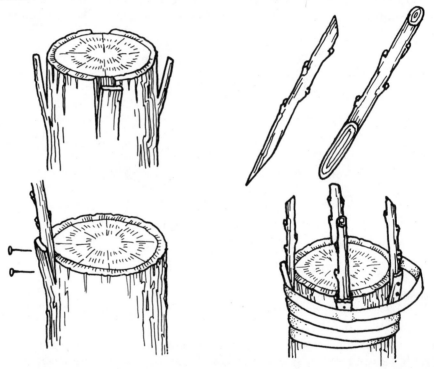

Bark Grafting: First make four equidistant vertical cuts in the stock and separate the bark from the wood on both sides (top left). Cut the scion with a sloping edge, pointed at the end (top right). Place the scion between the flaps of bark with the cut surface touching the wood of the stock (bottom left). Nail each scion in place and wrap with waterproof plastic or grafting wax (bottom right).

The first step in a bark graft is to make a horizontal cut across the stock. Next make equally spaced vertical cuts through the bark and pull back four 1½-inch-long strips of bark. The scion is cut with one end pointed. Pull back a flap of bark and insert the pointed end of the scion between the bark and the wood. Tack down the bark with small brads. Wrap the graft with waterproof plastic or grafting wax. Keep the graft covered for 12 weeks. After the wrappings are removed, it is a good idea to stake or otherwise support the newly grafted tree.

Budding

A form of grafting done with younger and smaller plant parts, budding involves the use of a bud rather than a stem as a scion and is often accomplished by novices more easily than other types of grafting, although the wait for fruit will be a year or so longer. The stock used in budding is a pencil-thin seedling or shoot of an older tree, and the budstick (containing the bud to be used as the scion) is taken from the middle portion of some thriving disease-free growth of the current season. The budstick is cut after the buds mature in summer, and the budding operation itself is done in late summer or early fall.

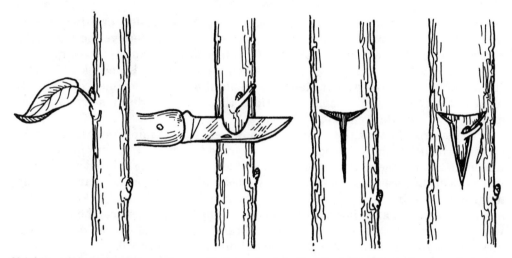

Shield- or T-budding: Choose the small, flat and pointed leaf buds found in leaf axils on branches. Using a sharp knife, cut the bud in a shield shape and remove the leaf while leaving the petiole intact to serve as a handle. Make a T-shaped cut in the stock and pull the bark away from the wood. Insert the bud into the cut and tie with rubber bands above and below the bud-union.

The most frequently used form of budding on fruit tree rootstocks is shield- or T-budding, which derives its two names from, respectively, the shape of the cut bud and the cut made on the stock. To prepare the bud, first remove the leaves from the budstick, leaving ¼ inch of each petiole (leaf stem) to use as a handle when positioning the adjacent bud. Trying to work with just a shield-cut bud with no stem to hold onto is very frustrating. Next cut upward with a sharp knife from ½ inch below the chosen bud to ½ inch above it, finishing with a horizontal cut that detaches the bud. The cut should be done shallowly so much wood is not taken along, but be deep enough to include all of the vital cambium layer just under the bark. If a small piece of wood adheres to the cut bud, it may be carefully removed. To receive this shield-shaped bud, make a T-shaped cut 1½ inches long, lengthwise on the stock. The top of the T should be about the width of the bud shield. Very carefully pull apart the two flaps that are produced, being careful not to damage or tear any of the wood or bark. To accomplish the actual budding, slip the scion/bud downward between the two flaps on the stock until it is in place, with cambium tissue coming together exactly on each side with that of the stock. Wrap a rubber band or strip of polyethylene plastic above and below the flap-enclosed bud to hold it in place. In a successful budding, in three weeks the scion should grow to the stock and the bud will look fat and healthy. (If the graft does not "take," the bud will usually appear shriveled and can be easily removed.) Before growth begins the following spring, cut off the stock about 6 inches above the bud-union. Also, latent buds in the stock may sucker and should be removed.

Layering

When propagation by cuttings or grafting proves too slow or otherwise unsatisfactory, fruit growers often rely on the simple but effective method called layering. Used frequently for bush fruits, sometimes for vining types, and only occasionally on fruit trees, layering involves the rooting of branches while they remain attached to the parent plant. When plant parts are flexible, this can take place in the ground; when the stem is rigid, the rooting medium is firmly packed around it in a method called air layering.

To perform the traditional method known as true or simple layering, in early spring a healthy one-year-old shoot is wounded or ringed at one place on its underside. Bend the shoot as flat as possible and bury the injured part 3 to 6 inches deep in loose, humus-rich soil. Remove all leaves on the part to be underground and, if you wish, wedge a pebble or twig in the wound to keep it open, and apply some rooting hormone. If necessary the buried shoot can be held down with a good-sized stone or with a forked branch or piece of curved wire. Stamp down the soil firmly but carefully to avoid breaking the shoot.

Anywhere from 3 to 6 or more inches at the end of the shoot should emerge from the ground so the tip is upright. The layered branch should be mulched and, if necessary, watered. By late fall new roots usually have formed where the stem was injured. When they have, the new plant can be severed from the old and transplanted. (This is usually done the following spring.)

In an even simpler variation known as tip layering, the shoot tips of bramble fruits—which tend to self-root anyway—are simply inserted in a dibble-made hole (either in the ground or in a pot) to a depth of 6 inches. The shoots should be pegged to the ground.

Mound or stool layering is a method appropriate for low, bushy fruits such as currants, gooseberries, and quince but is also done with clonal apple rootstocks. It involves heaping 8 to 10 inches of humusy soil around the stump of a plant which has been cut back to about 1 to 2 inches in late fall or winter (this is the stool). The mounding is done very early in spring before growth begins. If you will use shoots from the previous year as layers, they should be ringed or girdled at the base to promote the forming of callus and, ultimately, roots. To layer new shoots, no girdling is needed. Rather, add several inches of soil at intervals as growth proceeds. Don't add so much soil that you cover the tops of the shoots, though. Where blueberries are concerned, the parent plant can be pruned back to the ground, then covered with about 4 inches of a mixture of peat and sand, which should be kept moist. New shoots-with-roots created by any kind of mound

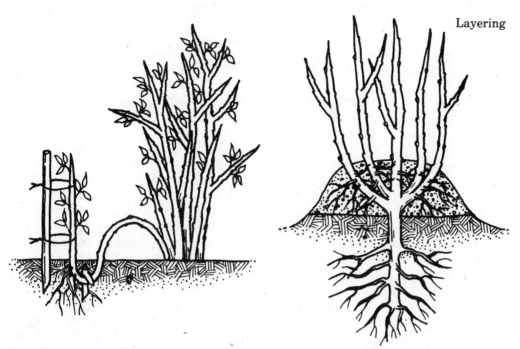

Methods of Layering: Simple layering (upper left) can be performed in early spring or fall. Bend a desirable shoot over to the ground, wound it at this point, and hold in place with a small wooden peg. Make a second bend a short distance from the tip and cover with soil. To give the shoot extra support, wire it to a wooden stake driven into the ground adjacent to the shoot. Plants used for mound layering (upper right) are cut back to about 1 to 2 inches in fall and then mounded with 8 to 10 inches of rich, humusy soil in early spring before growth begins. By the end of the season, each mounded plant will produce several new shoots with roots attached. You can form roots on the aerial

part of the plant by air layering (lower right). Make a notch on the stem and insert a matchstick in the cut. Place damp sphagnum moss around the notched area. Wrap the sphagnum moss with polyethylene and tie at each end. Trench layering (lower left) is effective on fruit trees that are hard to propagate, or plants with long, flexible stems. Before spring growth begins, the parent plant (which was planted at a 30- to 45-degree angle the previous season) is laid flat on the bottom of a shallow trench. The plant is then covered with soil, leaving the tips of the branches exposed. The parent plant will send up shoots that will root on the plant. The soil is removed at the end of the season and the rooted layers are separated from the parent plant and transplanted.

layering are separated from the stool and treated like the products of true layering.

Trench layering is employed to propagate difficult fruit trees, or vines or other plants with long, flexible stems. If you are trench layering an entire young tree, plant it at an angle of 30 to 45 degrees; then cut it back and let it grow for a year and over a winter. The following spring push it down and bury it in a trench 2 inches deep (a low, branching tree limb or branches of a bush also can be buried this way). Peg it down if necessary, and cover either with soil, sawdust, peat moss, wood shavings, or a mixture of these. Be sure to leave the tips of the branches uncovered. As new shoots emerge, cover them periodically to half their height until 7 or 8 additional inches of soil have been added. After growth ceases in fall or the next spring, the new shoots and their root systems can be cut free of the branches from which they sprang.

Air layering is the method used for larger and more rigid trees and is practiced ideally in bright indirect light on pencil-thick young growth on semihard wood in late summer or early fall. The shoot used should be either notched, ringed, or girdled with wire several inches below its tip. Some growers apply rooting hormone before the wound is wrapped in moist peat or sphagnum moss. The moss in turn is covered with polyethylene or polypropylene plastic that is tied with twine above and below the moss. (To protect the site on outdoor plants, the plastic should be tucked in on the bottom rather than the top and waterproof tape used.) If the moss needs to be wetted again during the following weeks the top tie can be loosened and enough water added to keep the moss moist but not soaked. In a month—or whenever the moss contains plenty of roots—the new growth is cut from the old, and its roots—still in the moss if they are very fine—are soaked in tepid water. Next they are placed in a very airy medium such as vermiculite and peat that has been moistened in compost tea, to which soil is added gradually.

10

Pruning and Training

There are essentially four main reasons for pruning fruit-producing plants: (1) to direct and control a plant's growth, (2) to encourage the production of flowers and, ultimately, fruits, (3) to maintain a plant's health, and (4) to rejuvenate a neglected plant. The old adage that an ounce of prevention is worth a pound of cure surely applies to pruning. In general, careful pruning during the first few years of a plant's life can encourage it to grow to a pleasing shape and stay healthy and strong and capable of producing a quality crop for many years. But always take into consideration the needs and habits of each particular tree: dwarfs should not be pruned much when young, and genetic dwarfs should not be pruned at all except to remove dead wood.

Except in the case of heading back, the pruning cuts you make on a plant or tree should stop the plant from growing in one direction and encourage it to grow in another, meaning that you can control both the size and shape of the plant. This control can be as extreme as espaliering, training a tree to grow flat along a wall, fence, or trellis, or it can be as simple as pruning to keep a tree at a reasonable height and make it easier to pick the fruit.

The ongoing process of controlling and directing a plant's growth usually begins when it is planted. As explained in chapter 7, when a fruit tree is planted, both the roots and top may be pruned so that they are in balance with each other. As the tree grows and matures, pruning ensures that the limbs are evenly distributed around the trunk and that they branch out at wide angles from the trunk. When the tree begins to bear, further pruning creates ideal conditions for fruiting. Fruit production is increased by thinning out branches so that more sunlight and air can get to the center of the tree, promoting the development of fruit buds, and as fruits begin to develop early in the season they can be thinned so that the remaining ones grow larger.

As a plant grows, pruning to maintain its health involves removing dead, diseased, or injured stems or branches as well as unwanted growth. Dead wood in trees not only looks bad, but it also can harbor diseases and insects that can ultimately destroy a tree. Branches cracked or broken by snow accumulation and

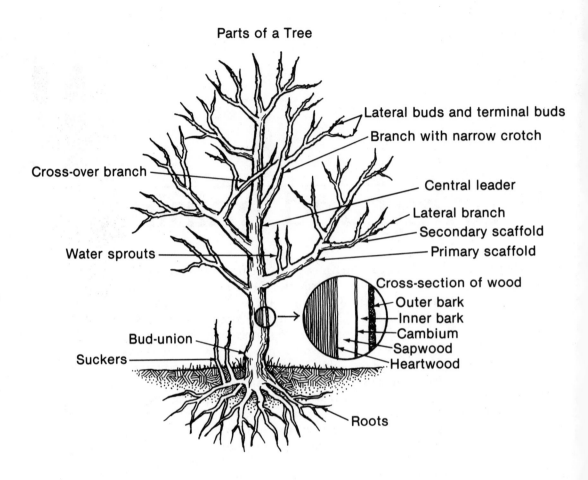

Parts of a Tree

Lateral buds and terminal buds
Branch with narrow crotch
Cross-over branch
Central leader
Lateral branch
Secondary scaffold
Primary scaffold
Water sprouts
Cross-section of wood
Outer bark
Inner bark
Cambium
Sapwood
Heartwood
Bud-union
Suckers
Roots

wind storms should also be pruned away. Various forms of unwanted growth can also injure trees. Branches growing into the center of the tree can rub against others and injure the bark, and since any type of damage to a plant or tree is an open invitation for disease or insects to enter, the growth of skewed branches should be kept to a minimum. Vertical-growing suckers and water sprouts, other types of unwanted growth on trees and bushes, rarely develop into healthy, fruit-producing branches and should be removed because they demand a lion's share of water and nutrients.

Each fruit has different growth habits and requires different training and pruning techniques, and the general information that follows will serve as a primer on basic pruning practices. See the Guide to Fruits for the Home Garden for details on pruning specific fruits. Remember too that practice makes perfect and that you can learn a lot about pruning just by keeping your eyes open. Watch your plants grow, and observe what happens to them after pruning. You'll be amazed at how much they can teach you over the years.

What to Prune

Water sprouts and suckers can form on deciduous trees, and because they weaken the parent tree, they're obvious candidates for pruning. Water sprouts grow vertically from a branch or trunk, often after heavy pruning. They seldom produce flowers or fruit and should be removed unless one is needed to replace a branch that has been injured or removed. Suckers sprout from the roots of a tree, or the base of a trunk, below the graft-union, and if they are not removed, they can eventually crowd out the main tree. Since the suckers come from the rootstock, they defeat the purpose of the grafting if they are not removed. Like water sprouts, suckers sometimes are not removed if they are needed to start a new grafted limb, or for repairing a trunk wound by grafting. Usually, though, it's best to remove both suckers and water sprouts because they steal water and nutrients that would otherwise go to productive branches.

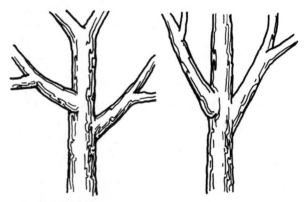

Looking for the Right Angle:
A strong scaffold system should have branches with wide angles (greater than 45 degrees) as shown on the left. Primary scaffold branches with narrow V-shaped angles (right) are undesirable as they will break under heavy fruit loads.

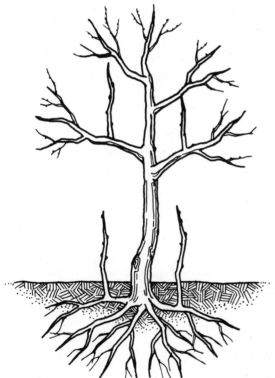

Getting Rid of Unwanted Suckers and Water Sprouts:
Remove all suckers and water sprouts soon after they appear on your fruit tree. Suckers on trees arise from roots and sometimes the base of trunks below the graft. Water sprouts usually appear following extensive pruning and grow from older stems and branches. Cut off the suckers from roots at ground level and cut back all other suckers and water sprouts to the trunk, stem, or branch with a clean cut leaving no stubs to rot.

Branches can be undesirable simply because they grow in the wrong directions. The ideal is to have primary scaffold branches that grow out at wide angles from a trunk. Branches with narrow, V-shaped crotches are weak and always in danger of splitting off during storms or under a heavy crop, leaving the bark of the trunk badly torn. Any rough tear is an invitation for disease, rot, or insects to set up housekeeping. Branches that grow straight up or straight down and those that grow inward are usually weak and unproductive and should be removed.

Buds are probably the most important part of a plant when it comes to pruning because a gardener can direct and control the growth of a plant by removing selected buds. Buds, which contain a bit of cambium at their tips, are defined by their location as terminal, lateral, or latent (dormant), and by their function as either flower or leaf buds. Flower buds are generally fatter than leaf buds.

Hormones control the growth of buds, but not all buds grow. If a bud is removed some of these hormones are lost, and this loss is a growth signal to buds lower on a branch. For example, every branch has a bud at its end called the terminal bud, from which the branch grows in length. Remove a terminal bud, and the closest lateral bud begins to grow in an effort to compensate for this loss. Lateral buds are arranged in clusters, pairs, or alternately along a branch depending on the species. Latent buds are usually invisible and grow only when other buds above them are removed. Adventitious buds are very rudimentary buds that develop only in an emergency if the buds above them are removed or destroyed.

It's easy to see how to shape a plant by removing certain buds. If you want to stimulate side growth on a plant, to make it bushy, remove the terminal buds and new branches will grow on the sides of the original branches. If a lateral bud comes out of the right side of a branch, cutting the branch off just above this bud will direct a new branch to grow out to the right. If you want an open-centered plant, prune so that all the topmost buds point outward.

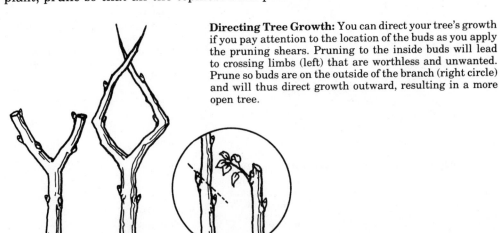

Directing Tree Growth: You can direct your tree's growth if you pay attention to the location of the buds as you apply the pruning shears. Pruning to the inside buds will lead to crossing limbs (left) that are worthless and unwanted. Prune so buds are on the outside of the branch (right circle) and will thus direct growth outward, resulting in a more open tree.

tricks of the trade

Selection and Care of Pruning Equipment

Manufacturers of pruning equipment offer a great variety of tools, most very useful, but a few of questionable value. Since many tools of different design may perform equally well, the choice is often based on personal preference rather than the performance of the tool itself. This guide presents the advantages and shortcomings of the major types of pruning equipment.

Hand Pruners: These are used for most pruning of wood less than ½ inch in diameter on trees, and for all pruning on bushes and brambles. They should be comfortable (cushioned handles are nice), durable, and leave a clean cut surface.

Shears cut with a shearing action like a scissors and are often considered the finest type of hand pruner. If kept sharp and adjusted (proper blade alignment is maintained by keeping the pivot nut snug), a shear will always give a smooth cut. Thinning or grape shears are a variation of the standard shear suitable for vine trimming and light tree pruning. Their thin blades allow for very detailed work.

In an anvil-type pruner, the shoot to be cut is pressed against the flat anvil while a blade slices it. When the blade is sharp, excellent results are possible. Anvils and, on some models, blades are replaceable. A good anvil-type pruner will be about half the price of a quality shear. On some fruits, especially grapes and stone fruits, this cutting action tends to crush the wood on the anvil side and may lead to problems; shears would be recommended in these cases.

Loppers: These are basically long-handled, heavy-duty versions of hand pruners for cutting wood up to an inch in diameter. They are available as both shears and anvil-type cutters, but because of the larger wood and greater force applied, the latter will crush the wood and should be avoided. As with any shear, the blade must be kept sharp and the action tight.

Saws: If you're serious about removing a limb (1 inch in diameter or larger) use a saw. The cardinal rule in pruning is that the cut be "close and clean," with no stubs or "shirt hooks" and no ragged edges. A good, sharp saw will meet these requirements and won't give you a hernia in the process. Teeth on rip or crosscut saws from the workshop will quickly fill with the damp sawdust from cutting green wood. If you don't mind the extra time spent cleaning them, they'll do an adequate job.

A bow saw is probably the handiest saw available to the pruner or outdoor builder. For some reason the finest blades and often the entire saw are Scandinavian. Blades come in a variety of tooth patterns, though the simple spike tooth works as well as the fancier raker and chisel setup. A new blade is sharp to the point of being dangerous and usually comes with a plastic sheath. Use it, for your fingers' sake and to protect the teeth—being made of a hardened steel, their tips can be chipped or broken. The blade is fairly thin and the tooth set is narrow so the kerf (width of the sawcut) is small.

The only advantage to a folding saw over the bow saw is its ability to get into tight corners like a keyhole saw. The teeth are usually large, as is the kerf. This makes for slow cutting, since you're going to convert a lot of wood into sawdust before you're done. Folding saws cut on the pull stroke, so keep the wingnut tight while sawing or it can fold on your fingers with painful results. To protect the teeth, keep folded when not in use.

Pole Pruners: Available with cord or chain pull, lever or pump gun action; the choice is largely personal. The latter may have a slight advantage in close quarters since the action is up and down the pole and may be more stable than the others since both hands are always on the pole. Possibly one of the most useful of the pruning tools; a good pole pruner will allow you to easily make cuts that would otherwise be next to

(continued)

Selection and Care of Pruning Equipment—*continued*

impossible. They are usually faster than working from and constantly moving a ladder, and are obviously safer. The general rule is "if you can get it into the cutting head, you can cut it," although the inclination to remove a shoot by cutting it in steps should be avoided. If one clean cut can't be made, use a saw to remove the shoot. Aluminum and wood poles are offered in lengths from 6 to 12 feet, with wood usually being cheaper, slightly heavier, and prone to splinters, which can be prevented by a light coating of linseed oil once a year.

Pole Saws: These are another matter entirely. If ever a tool was designed to torment its user, longer models of the pole saw could be used as design prototypes. Essentially a folding saw blade on a 6- to 12-foot pole, they are awkward to use and seldom produce a "clean and close" cut. If you really must remove a limb that's out of reach, you're better off on a ladder or climbing the tree with your bow or folding saw.

Ladders: Working from a ladder may be slower than using a pole pruner but more detailed pruning is possible. Be careful when setting the ladder to avoid breaking the fruiting spurs. Damage from a haphazardly placed ladder can be severe, though not evident until bloom time. Your present household step ladder may be sufficient, though with four points on the ground, they can be unnervingly wobbly on the generally uneven ground in an orchard. Orchardists long ago solved this problem by eliminating one leg and flaring the bottom of the side rails, resulting in the common tripod orchard step ladder that is remarkably steady. Available in wood (cheaper and heavier) and aluminum from 6 to 16 feet, one of these would be the wisest purchase if you need a ladder. The slender third leg fits neatly into areas between scaffold limbs with a minimum of tree damage. They are especially useful for harvesting, since the tree supports none of the ladder's or your weight.

The other basic ladder to consider is known as a stub, walk-up, or just orchard ladder. Straight, of either wood or aluminum in lengths from 12 to 22 feet, they are available with an open or pointed top. At the bottom, the side rails are flared a bit to improve stability. Open-top models can be awkward to place in a dense tree and damaging to spurs, and should be avoided. Pointed-top models are extremely useful in reaching the outer portion of the top of large, old trees. The point is placed in the crotch of a limb husky enough to support the weight of you and the ladder. As with all ladders and more so with walk-ups, the feet must be on solid ground and, when working, you must keep your weight over the ladder. If you reach too far out to the side, they have a tendency to pivot around the pointed end, leaving the chagrined pruner hanging like a monkey from what had been the upper side of the ladder. If you're contemplating using an extension ladder in your orchard, don't. All the drawbacks of the open-top walk-up are exaggerated.

Now that you've got all the necessary tools, they'll require some care to keep them working well. If there is one rule, paramount over all others, it is: *keep the cutting edges sharp!* A small $2 pocketstone is plenty adequate to touch up an edge that isn't quite what it used to be. For extensive pruning, a few swipes with the stone each day wouldn't be excessive. You'll know when the edge is dulling when it leaves a feather of thin bark on the back side of a cut.

Dull saws are great for exercise, but useless for pruning. Bow saw blades, when dull, should be replaced. They're cheap, but more important, the factory-sharpened edge is something remarkable. To call them sharp is an understatement. Folding saws should be sent to your nearest reputable sharpening shop.

A squirt of 20W oil on the moving parts occasionally keeps everything moving smoothly. The only special attention needed with lubrication would be when pruning

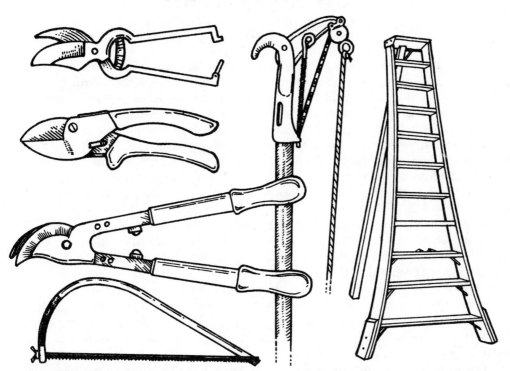

Pruning Tools: The proper tools make any pruning chore easier. From the left, top to bottom; hand shears and anvil-type hand pruners are good for wood less than ½ inch in diameter and for brambles and bushes; loppers with longer handles for better leverage are effective on wood up to 1 inch in diameter; and a bow saw is needed for limbs which are 1 inch or more in diameter. Pole pruners (center) are used for pruning high branches from the ground, eliminating the need for a cumbersome ladder. The tripod orchard step ladder, right, is designed for easy maneuverability and increased stability for safety.

pears or apples that may have fireblight. After each cut, to sterilize the cutting head and prevent spreading the bacterium, the tool should be dipped in a solution of five parts water to one part liquid chlorine bleach. A superior disinfectant, it is also extremely corrosive. Tools left overnight without rinsing in water and oiling may have rigor mortis by morning. Always rinse in clean water, dry, and oil to prevent rusting at the end of each day.

If any of your equipment has unfinished wooden parts, such as pole pruners or ladders, an annual application of boiled linseed oil will reduce drying, cracking, and the accompanying splinters. To speed drying and increase penetration, a one-to-one mixture of linseed oil and turpentine may be used. Simply brush it on liberally and, if any remains on the surface after a few hours, wipe it off.

Keep all nuts, bolts, and screws tight. A loose cutting head will never cut well and a swaying ladder may dump you, ingloriously, on your head.

With minimal care and some common sense during use, a good piece of equipment may last longer than your orchard.

—Tim White

How and Where
to Make Pruning Cuts

The pruning requirements of plants and trees vary, but in general, you won't go wrong if you always cut just above a healthy bud or back to a main branch, and leave a clean wound so that healing is rapid. Never leave a stub by cutting far away from a growing point. The stub will rot and invite diseases and insects. Remember always to make neat, clean cuts so the cambium tissue is damaged as little as possible and the wound will heal rapidly. Also, be careful when making the cuts that no outer bark is peeled off to expose the inner bark. Nutrients traveling from roots to other parts of the tree flow through this layer of wood; if the inner bark is damaged the transportation network is damaged, to the tree's detriment.

When you cut back to a lateral bud, select one that is growing outward and cut about ¼ inch above the bud in the direction in which it grows. When removing an entire branch with pruners or loppers, place the cutting blade next to the branch that will remain so that the result is a clean cut and the shortest possible stub. When possible, cut from the bottom up. Smooth any ragged edges with a pruning knife. If you use a pruning saw to remove limbs, first make a shallow cut on the underside of the branch. This prevents the limb from stripping away the bark on the larger branch to which it is attached if it falls before it is completely cut.

The ultimate goal in removing a large branch is the same as for removing a smaller branch: make a neat cut and don't leave a stub that will rot and encourage disease. If the branch is relatively light, you can support it with one hand while you operate a pruning saw with the other. If the branch is heavy, it will have to be removed in sections, and you might also have to use ropes and slings to support and lower sections of the branch to the ground.

The first step in removing a large branch is to cut off any side branches, and then saw off the branch to within about 2 feet of the parent branch or trunk. Remove the branch in sections if it is heavy. The final three cuts are the crucial ones. First, make a shallow cut on the underside of the branch about 6 inches from the trunk. This will prevent any tearing or ripping of the bark when the next cut is made. Make the second cut a few inches from the undercut, and farther out on the limb, sawing from the top of the branch. Finally, make the third cut from the top to the bottom and close to the trunk to prevent leaving a stub.

Any cut exposes the heartwood of a tree to the weather, diseases, and insects, so it is important to leave a neat and clean wound so that exposure to these is minimal. The healing process begins as the cambium layer produces callus tissue to grow over the wound.

After making a cut on a large (1 inch or more) limb, the cut end should be coated with a material to prevent disease entry and encourage healing. Usually some sort of asphalt-based compound, wound dressings, or pruning paints come in aerosols and bulk cans. A word of caution: some pruning paints now contain

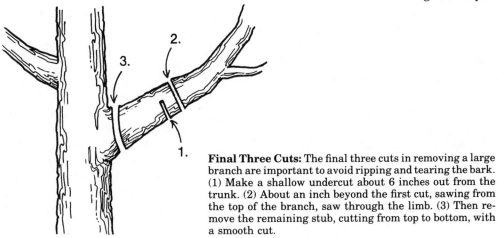

Final Three Cuts: The final three cuts in removing a large branch are important to avoid ripping and tearing the bark. (1) Make a shallow undercut about 6 inches out from the trunk. (2) About an inch beyond the first cut, sawing from the top of the branch, saw through the limb. (3) Then remove the remaining stub, cutting from top to bottom, with a smooth cut.

a plant growth regulator designed to reduce sucker growth from around cut areas. These growth regulators work, but they are quite strong, and for home gardeners they are probably unnecessary. If you wish to avoid them, check the label before buying any wound dressings.

Pruning Techniques

Now that you know how and where to make cuts, the next consideration is which method to use. There are a variety of pruning techniques: pinching, top cutting, thinning out, root pruning, and rejuvenation pruning. Many gardeners are always on the lookout for unwanted growth they can pinch off, and therefore save themselves from more involved pruning at a later time. During the summer when trees are in active growth, you can pinch off any new green growth that will break easily between your thumb and index finger. Pinching during the growing season removes unwanted growth or it can redirect growth. Pinching the tip of a main branch stimulates growth on lateral branches, and pinching the tips of lateral branches encourages the laterals to branch and the main branch to grow in length.

Top cutting, or heading back, means removing a branch back to a bud or back to a lateral branch and is done to stimulate new growth so that a plant becomes thicker and bushier. If you want a plant to grow outward, cut back to outward-facing buds so that the new shoots branch out. If you want a bushy plant, cut back to inward-facing buds. Keep in mind that haphazard top cutting early in the growing season when saps are flowing will result in a tangle of unwanted new growth and that cutting back is not the same as shearing, which is clipping the ends of branches without regard to cutting back to buds.

If a tree has been neglected, thinning is often the only way to invigorate it. Thinning is the removal of an entire branch back to the ground, the trunk, or the main branch. Fruit trees are often thinned so that more sunlight and air can reach the interior of the tree. New shoots and leaves are then freer to develop and fruit ripens quicker. Thinning is preventive medicine when branches that are weak and in danger of breaking are removed. Thinning in a time of drought can reduce the water needs of a plant because if there is less foliage, there is less need for water.

Fruits as well as branches benefit from thinnings. Thinning not only produces bigger fruit of better quality, it also encourages a tree to bear fruit each year. Early in the summer when the green fruit is the size of marbles, pinch off excess fruit so that there are a few inches between the remaining ones. This is usually done just after some of the small fruits have begun to drop naturally. Allow about 6 to 8 inches between apples, 3 to 4 inches between apricots, 4 to 5 inches between nectarines or peaches, 6 to 8 inches between pears, and 3 to 4 inches between large plums. Berries and other small fruits usually do not need thinning.

Rejuvenation Pruning

Throughout their lifetimes, fruit trees require care and adequate nourishment; if they are neglected they can either turn into a tangled mass of unproductive growth or they can become stunted and unfruitful. It is possible to rejuvenate a neglected tree by pruning, but the first step is to determine if it really can be saved. No amount of pruning will restore trees with rotten trunks or those that are extensively diseased or pest-ridden. But if a tree appears to be sound, and if there is some potential for fruit production, then pruning might save it.

The first step in rejuvenating an overgrown tree is to remove all of the competition for water and nutrients by removing the brush and weeds that surround it. Provide adequate nourishment by top-dressing with well-rotted manure and compost, and perhaps mulching. The first year's pruning will be to remove all dead, diseased, and broken branches. It's best to burn these branches since they are likely to house insects and disease. Don't remove an excessive number of limbs in the first pruning because this would upset the balance between the roots and the top of the tree. This initial pruning will stimulate new growth, and you will be able to see the following year which branches are the most vigorous and worthy of being saved. Summer pruning tends to limit growth while pruning in winter stimulates growth, so late summer might be a good time to remove unwanted lateral branches. A neglected tree might have a lot of vertical limbs (which tend to be unfruitful), so you might want to train some of them to grow more horizontally by using branch spreaders or tying them down as described in chapter 7.

In the second year, light thinning at the top will allow more sunlight to get into the interior of the tree. Take care not to remove too much, or the remaining branches and fruit may sunburn on hot days. Any older branches that are weak and unproductive can also be removed at this time. In the third and fourth years, remove any undesirable larger branches and continue to gradually thin out other unwanted limbs. In subsequent years, if the tree is in good condition and bearing fruit, prune it as you would any other tree.

Pruning can stimulate stunted trees to grow, too. Again, the first step is to eliminate weeds and brush that compete for water and nutrients, and provide adequate nourishment in the form of mulches and fertilizers. Since a stunted tree has grown slowly there should be fewer branches to remove, but the cutting back of any new growth should stimulate the tree to grow. Thinning spurs and removing all or most of the fruit for a few years can relieve the tree of the burden of reproduction while it is growing. But thinning spurs is a delicate operation—removing too many could set back the tree too much. When the tree begins to grow and produce, follow regular pruning procedures.

Pruning Shapes for Fruit Trees

Commercial fruit growers have developed three training methods for fruit trees that home gardeners can successfully adopt for their trees: the central leader, the modified central leader, and the open-center methods. In the central leader method (the best shape for most apple varieties), the central branch, which appears to be an extension of the trunk, dominates, and the tree takes on the shape of a pyramid. The advantage of this shape is that it creates a very strong tree, but the disadvantage is that the center is shaded and fruit production suffers if the scaffolds are not spread out sufficiently.

To establish a tree with a central leader, prune back a whip to about 3 feet at planting time. This stimulates the buds at the top of the whip to begin growing. In the second year, select one vertical branch to be the central leader and about four other branches to form the scaffold branches. Select scaffolds at slightly

Forms of Fruit Trees: The three forms in which fruit trees are usually trained are from left to right; central leader, open-center, and modified leader. For heavy-bearing trees of large fruit such as apples or pears, the pyramidal shape of the central leader is usually preferred. The strong branches which radiate out from the main trunk at wide angles can easily support the load of heavy fruits. The vase-shaped open-center form has a weaker branch structure than the central leader but it is excellent for growing the lightweight fruits of cherry, plum, and quince. A more natural way to grow apples and pears is by developing a modified leader. The tree is initially trained as a central leader but later the central trunk is allowed to form several tops so the fruit load at the top of the tree is never as heavy as it is on the larger limbs at the bottom.

different heights on the trunk and be sure they branch out at wide angles and are evenly spaced around the trunk. Wooden or metal branch spreaders may be used to ensure a wide crotch angle. Remove other branches that are likely to compete with these. In the following years, prune to direct the tree to grow into a pyramid shape, but prune sparingly until it begins to bear. Eventually you will have to cut back the central leader because it will become top-heavy with fruit and tip over.

The open-center method is used for peaches, Japanese plums and some apricots, and other trees that don't normally reach great heights. Three to five main branches form the framework of this type of tree, which has no central leader. The branches emerge from the trunk at wide angles to allow plenty of sunshine and air into the center of the tree, which encourages the development of fruit. Care should be taken when training a tree in this method to avoid having scaffold branches that emerge from the trunk at the same height. This greatly weakens a tree and creates the possibility of heavy damage from breakage. Also, water pockets can develop between the branches and make rot more likely.

To train a one-year-old tree in the open-center method, the first step is to cut it back to 2 to 3 feet above the ground. This cut stimulates the topmost buds to start forming lateral branches. The branches should be 6 to 8 inches apart, and come out from the trunk at wide angles. They should also be evenly spaced around the tree. Remove branches that do not meet these criteria. In the second year, remove all but the three or five main branches.

The modified central leader is a compromise between the central leader and open-center methods. It is widely used for fruit trees and puts equal importance on the central leader and the scaffold branches. The central leader is allowed to grow to a height of about 5 or 6 feet, and then it is cut back. Four to six well-spaced scaffold branches are distributed evenly along the modified leader.

With all three of these methods, after the shape of the tree is established and it begins to bear, pruning to maintain the health of the tree and encourage fruit production, as described earlier, is necessary.

During the first three years of life, most fruit trees—whether they are stone fruits such as peaches or plums, temperate fruits such as apples or pears, tropical fruits such as avocados or olives, or citrus fruits such as oranges—are pruned in essentially the same ways. But after a tree begins to bear, pruning requirements vary according to the species. Avocado trees, for example, are usually trained to the modified central leader form, and when mature they require little pruning. In fact, too much pruning in tropical climates opens an avocado tree up too much and it can literally get sunburned. So can apples. Olive trees, in the other extreme, require somewhat extensive pruning to keep them bearing. See the Guide to Fruits for details on best pruning methods for specific fruits.

How to Prune Bush Fruits

Bush fruits such as blueberries, cranberries, currants, and gooseberries are deciduous shrubs, and their growth patterns and pruning requirements are similar to those of fruit trees. Keep in mind, though, that bush fruits are trained to send up several stems, or canes, instead of developing a single trunk. Bush fruits, in general, require less pruning than other fruits, although pruning after a bush begins to bear encourages the production of quality fruit.

When the plant begins to bear, remove weak laterals, and cut back old canes to the ground to force new canes to grow. Never prune an entire bush back to the ground because the shock will be too great, and the plant will die. Knowing something about the fruiting habits of each type of bush fruit will help you determine which branches to cut back. A red currant bush, for example, should have one-, two-, and three-year-old wood because the fruit is borne at the base of year-old wood and on spurs of two- or three-year-old wood. It's a good idea to remove a few canes each year to keep this balance. On the other hand, black currant bushes bear most of their fruit on one-year-old canes so any weak canes and those over a year old should be removed. Cut back the remaining canes by about one-fourth. Blueberries, to give another example of a bush fruit, bear on old wood. At planting time, cut back the young bush by half, and allow it to grow for a few years. As the plant matures, thin some lateral branches, and when the bush begins to bear, thin out old, unproductive branches so that new canes will grow.

Pruning Bramble Fruits

Bramble fruits, such as blackberries and raspberries, must be pruned regularly or the plants will deteriorate. Almost all bramble fruits have roots that are perennial and woody stems, or canes, that are biennial. The canes develop into their full height in one year, and the following year they bloom, produce berries, and die or become barren. While some canes are bearing, others are growing in preparation for bearing the following year.

The primary pruning requirement for brambles is to cut back the canes to the ground promptly after fruiting, and then to train the new canes that grow up from the base of the plant. Frequently, brambles are trained on wire trellises

Pruning Brambles:
The biennial canes of bramble fruits grow vegetatively the first season and then flower, fruit, and die the second year. On this principle, cut off to the ground all the second-year canes after they have fruited. Keep five to six healthy canes of the current year (shown in black), cutting their tips off to encourage abundant lateral growth which will produce fruit the following year.

or poles, and depending on the variety, they can be trained in numerous ways. Canes that have produced fruit will become dry and brittle, and unless they are pruned down to the ground, insects and diseases are likely to set in. Burn these canes or haul them to a landfill.

Most bramble fruits are trained and pruned similarly. Cut back newly planted bushes to stubs a few inches from the ground. At the end of the first growing season, cut back to the ground all but the five or six most vigorous canes from each plant. Brambles have large root systems, so remove any suckers that appear. Remember, there will be no fruit produced this first year, so in order to encourage fruit production in the following year, cut back the tips of the canes to encourage fruit-bearing laterals to grow. The laterals that form can then be cut back also. As fruit develops on the previous year's growth, new shoots appear at the base of the plant. Usually about five of the most vigorous new growths are encouraged to grow and all of the others are cut back to the ground. In the fall, after the canes have fruited, cut them back to the ground, and if you are training your brambles on a trellis, tie up the new canes in preparation for bearing the following year.

Pruning Vines

Brambles are similar to grapevines because pruning is essential to both in order for quality fruit in sufficient quantity to be produced. But unlike brambles, grapevines produce fruit on canes that grow in the current season. Pruning, therefore, must always ensure an adequate supply of year-old wood in order for the vines to produce.

There are many methods for training and pruning grapevines, but most home gardeners opt for either a long-cane system or the arbor system. The former, also called the Kniffen System, involves the training of four laterals, two on each side of the trunk, to two horizontal wires secured to posts. One wire is about 3 feet from the ground, and the other is about 5 feet from the ground. In training a grapevine to follow a trellis or arbor, the trunk is allowed to grow very tall by cutting back the laterals. When the main stem reaches the desired height, laterals are encouraged to grow. Fruit production is encouraged by thinning the grape clusters and by pruning the laterals. See the entry on Grapes, in the Guide to Fruits, for details on the training and pruning of grapevines. Vine fruits are a diverse group, including fruits as different as kiwi, melons, and passion fruit. In general, these vines benefit from pruning, usually in the form of cutting back or thinning out to keep them from becoming a tangled, unproductive mass.

Decorative Pruning

Espalier is a way of training and directing the growth of a plant so that its stem and branches grow flat along a wall, fence, or trellis. Apples and pears, especially dwarf varieties, are excellent candidates for espaliering, but many different fruit trees and perennial vining fruits can be trained into some form of espalier. Training determines the pattern, which can be elaborate or simple, and pruning maintains the desired shape. The advantages of this training method, in addition to its obvious ornamental qualities, are that fruits can be grown in limited space and that the fruit is easier to reach. Also, the quality and quantity of fruit increases because the branches are exposed to more air and sunlight. Bending limbs away from the vertical means that carbohydrates manufactured by the leaves are more readily available to produce more flower buds and thus more fruit.

In cooler climates, espaliers are ideal for south-facing walls where sunlight is plentiful and the heat reflected from the walls can help in the production of flowers and the ripening of fruit. In areas with very warm summers, it is best to use a free-standing trellis because reflected heat from a wall can sunburn bark and fruit or otherwise damage a plant. You can support espaliers from pipe or wooden posts strung with horizontal, vertical, or diagonal strands of 14-gauge wire. Horizontal wires should be about 12 to 16 inches apart and the lowest one should be about 16 to 20 inches from the ground. Some gardeners use plastic-covered wires so that the branches are not injured when they rub against them. Any structure you devise should be strong enough to support the weight of the fruit, and be sure that the trunk, or stem, of the plant is 8 to 10 inches from a wall so that there is adequate air circulation, and so that you will be able to paint or maintain the wall. Use twine, rawhide, plant ties, cloth strips, or any material that will not girdle the branches, to secure them to the support structure.

For gardeners intimidated by espaliers, nurseries sell plants that have already been trained. It is a good idea to start out with a bare-rooted whip, which

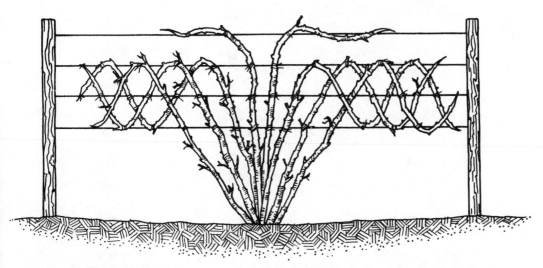

Making an Espalier Trellis: To construct a free-standing trellis, run horizontal strands of 14-gauge wire between two pipes or wooden posts. The wire should be 12 to 16 inches apart with the lowest wire 16 to 20 inches from the ground. Make sure the trellis is sturdy enough to support the weight of the fruit.

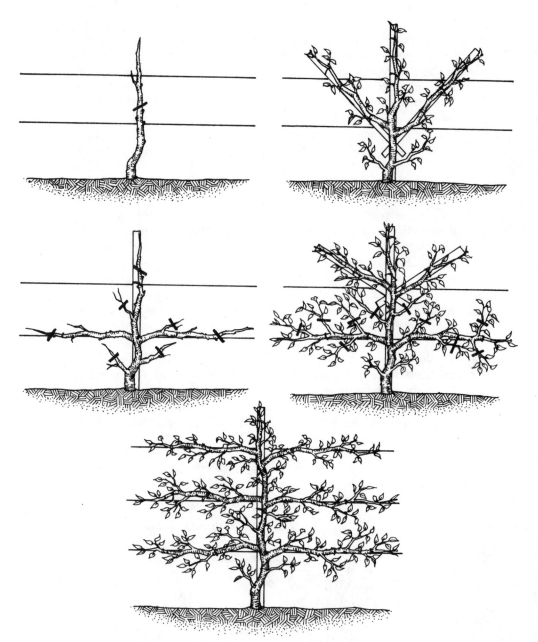

Training a Horizontal Cordon: From left to right, (1) If you start with a bare-rooted whip, after planting cut it back to the height of the lowest wire or about 15 inches from the ground. Cut it back so that there are three vigorous buds left at the top with the two lower buds pointing in opposite directions. (2) Train the top shoot to grow vertically and allow the other two buds to grow into branches that form a V-shape at a 45-degree angle from the central stem. Secure all three branches to the support structure. (3) At the end of the growing season, when the plant is dormant, lower the two side branches and tie them to the horizontal wire supports. Cut back any growth on the trunk below the second wire, leaving three vigorous buds which will form the extension of the central leader and the new side branches for the second tier. Cut back the horizontal branches on the first tier by about one-third. (4) Training the second tier is a repetition of the training for the first tier, and in the years that follow, continue to train the plant to the number of tiers you wish. (5) When the tree reaches its final shape, prune to remove lateral branches that grow from the horizontal branches.

tricks of the trade

Training Espalier Fruits

In Europe, where planting spaces have traditionally been limited, people have had time and tenure upon land to espalier their trees into special shapes and plant them along walls, promenades, garden borders, roadways, park paths, or anywhere else they'll be appreciated not only for their productivity but also for their beauty.

Here are some typical shapes into which young trees may be trained, based primarily on European espalier experience. These trees fall into two broad categories: flat-planed or three-dimensional.

FLAT-PLANED TREES

True Espalier: Virtually any two-dimensional tree, usually trained and pruned to grow along walls, up sides of houses, or parallel to any flat surface. May be shaped like any letter of the alphabet, although U, V, and Y are most easily attained. Useful in stretching northern limits of trees that wouldn't otherwise adapt to the climate without the wall's radiant heat. Attempt with caution in warmer areas.

Cordon: Single-stemmed tree with fruits growing on dense spurs up trunk. Can be trained to grow vertically, horizontally, or any angle between; supported and unsupported. Useful for apples, cherries, pears, and other plants producing fruit on spurs. Especially good method for keeping track of several individual varieties in a collection of uncommon specimens.

Palmette or Fan: Very graceful, usually symmetrical trees shaped like a fan or palm of a hand. May consist of from three to seven "fingers" spread from a single trunk. Very useful shape for nectarines, peaches, and others which grow fruit on new growth. Best supported along walls or in hedgerow plantings.

Belgian Fence: Artfully entwined row of cordon or palmette trees, usually all of same type and variety for ease of management. This living fence may enclose garden, yard, field, court, or other area. Started by training trees onto wires stretched from posts, which are later removed after branches have been inarch grafted or otherwise woven and grown together to form one self-supporting tree wall.

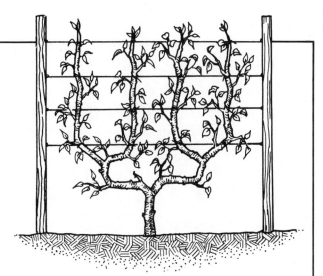

Double-U

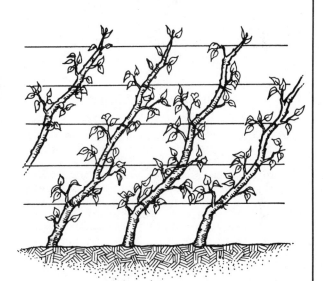

Single cordon

THREE-DIMENSIONAL TREES

Spindle Bush: Wildly graceful method of dwarfing trees producing on spurs. Fruit grows on short branches, dense with fruit. Originally limbs are trained horizontally, then pruned back in dormant season to eight buds from trunk. Technique developed in Rhineland Germany and Holland to bring trees into early fruitfulness, often two or three years after planting.

(continued)

Training Espalier Fruits—*continued*

Goblet or Urn: More orderly version of standard vase-type pruning practiced for backyard nectarine, peach, and other trees not producing fruit on spurs. Goblet or urn shape is formed first of wood or metal rods that will hold shape while tree limbs are trained upon it for several years. Can be trained two ways: with vertical branches arising from low point on trunk, or with branches bent down from high point at top of trunk. Usually trees remain on framework throughout life.

Winged Pyramid: Perhaps the most meticulously crafted tree shape, meant to create very productive trees. Louis Lorette, famed French espalier master, took more than seven years of attentive shaping and summer pruning to create a single winged-pyramid tree. He trained four main limbs along a pyramid-shaped framework of iron rods and wire until they met at apex and were united there. A single Lorette pyramid pear tree could produce hundreds of pounds of top-quality fruit.

TWISTING AND TYING DOWN BRANCHES

Perhaps you've noticed this habit of fruit tree growth: juvenile or unfruitful growth wants to charge on, straight for the sky; while fruitful wood, partly due to the weight of fruit, grows more toward the horizon. An observant tree trainer can use this tendency of tree growth to create trees that not only assume a graceful posture, but also become more productive sooner in life.

Two simple techniques have been developed through the years by patient tree trainers who understood this geometric fact of fruit tree growth. In both cases, it's best to start with whips or very young trees, as older trees have become too set in their ways.

The first technique involves tying down a flexible new shoot early in the growing season, before it begins to lignify, or turn to wood. Branches can be tied to a frame with raffia, coated wire, or anything else that can be untied and adjusted later, as long as it holds the limb firmly in the desired position. This must be done carefully because the shoot can easily be broken or otherwise damaged. Usually branches are aimed in directions which are horizontal or oblique, from 0 to 45 degrees of the horizon.

After the branch lignifies, it will hold its

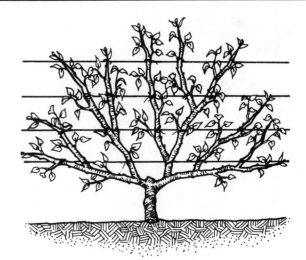

Fan

Belgian fence

shape indefinitely, although subsequent terminal growth will need to be tied down if the limb is to continue at the same angle. Otherwise, any new tip growth will invariably point itself straight up, toward the sky. Branches should be smoothly arched and tied, not bulged. Otherwise the bulge will remain once the shoot hardens up.

The other technique, which requires a bit more care and dexterity, is to slightly twist the new shoot while bending it into the chosen direction. This twisting and bending causes a new bud

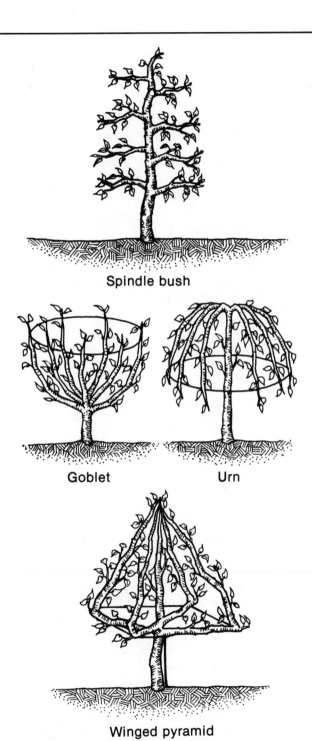

Spindle bush

Goblet

Urn

Winged pyramid

to develop below the point of the twist and this bud will produce a new shoot that can be steered in the opposite direction. This is one way to force a branch or lateral limb to balance out a horizontal cordon, palmette, or other symmetrical espalier shape.

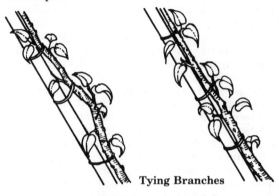

Tying Branches

NOTCHING BUDS

Notching or removing small pieces of the cambium layer around buds in year-old bark is an Old World tactic that helps tree trainers mold young trees into desired shapes.

However, the technique is used primarily on trees which produce fruit on spurs. This includes most apple and pear varieties, and to a lesser extent, many apricot, cherry, plum, and prune types. The technique is not practical, however, for trees like nectarines and peaches or terminal-bearing varieties which do not produce fruit on spurs.

A crescent-shaped notch through the cambium layer (greenwood) at a point just below a bud usually produces growth that develops into

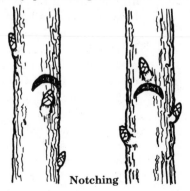

Notching

(continued)

Training Espalier Fruits—*continued*

a spur, where flowers will grow and produce fruit for several seasons. The technique takes advantage of the fact that fruiting hormones and carbohydrates which travel from the tree's growing tips and leaves downward cannot pass beyond the notch. Thus they get diverted through the bud at that point and usually produce a spur there.

A similarly shaped notch through the cambium at a point just above a bud most often produces a branch there—because the saps, which produce new growth, flow upward from the root and get diverted through the bud at that point, thus forming a new vegetative shoot.

As with most horticultural endeavors, timing is crucial for those who would notch buds. The technique is most effective in early spring just as buds are beginning to break, or shortly thereafter. Notching can be time-consuming when so many other springtime garden activities need attention. However, the practice will pay off later by greatly reducing the amount of time you must spend pruning out unwanted and misdirected growth.

PRUNING, PINCHING, AND RUBBING OFF BUDS

The ultimate control a tree trainer has in espaliering fruit trees is with pruning shears, knife, or thumb and forefinger, each of which can be used at any time during the growing season.

Buds which obviously will produce a branch aimed in the wrong direction, for example toward a wall or pathway, can be rubbed off the tree very early in spring. Or, after the bud opens, the new misdirected shoot can be pinched off with thumb and forefinger. Care should be taken so the young bark is not damaged to a point where borers or other pests can enter.

Later, when new growth becomes too solid for rubbing or pinching off, it can be cleanly cut with a knife or shears. However, midseason pruning is less demanding in late summer, when the tree's sap has begun to recede and the tree is less inclined to send out new growth at points where it has been pruned. The exact timing will vary with particular varieties and tree types, but generally summer pruning of espaliers is premature if done before mid-July.

To encourage fruitfulness with midseason pruning, the unwanted shoot should not be cut back all the way to the base of the limb where it arises. Instead, at least three buds should be left at the base of the branch being cut. It is more likely that these buds are developing into fruitful buds, while the part of the limb you remove is likely to produce vegetative growth next year. Always remember that the key to success with any trained tree is persistence.

—Jamie Jobb

will be easier to train than a more established tree. An easy and popular style is a single or double cordon in which the horizontal branches grow out at right angles from a cut-back trunk. Grapes and many varieties of apples and pears lend themselves beautifully to this style.

Apples and pears are frequently grown in oblique, single-stemmed cordons. In this form of espalier, trees are often planted and trained at 45-degree angles and secured to a support structure—although they can also be trained vertically or horizontally. In general, cordon espaliers are not well suited to the growing habits of stone fruits.

Growing plants on trellises is similar to espalier and is mandatory for grapes and recommended for other fruits such as blackberries and raspberries and for bush fruits such as currants. Trellises can be in the form of arbors, or they can simply be strands of wire strung horizontally between posts. The trailing canes of blackberries, for example, may be fanned out and tied to wires or they can be woven in and out among three horizontal wires of a trellis. Raspberries are usually allowed to grow vertically and then are secured to a wire trellis for support. In addition to supporting plants, trellises offer the same advantages of espalier in that plants can be grown in limited space and fruit production can be increased. The beauty and intricacy of both trellises and espaliers is limited only by the imagination and knowledge of the person making them.

When to Prune

After a tree or bush is planted and the initial pruning completed, regular pruning does not usually begin until a plant starts to bear. Of course, maintenance pruning to remove dead, dying, or diseased branches should occur when you spot the problem. Other pruning depends on the type of plant, when it blooms, its health, and whether it bears fruit on older wood or new growth.

Most gardeners, especially those in northern areas, do their regular pruning in late winter or early spring when plants are still dormant and there is no new growth. Pruning at this time removes some buds so that the remaining ones are stimulated to grow vigorously in spring. Gardeners living in warmer climates can prune any time in winter. Pruning in late winter is more convenient because there are no leaves on a plant, so it's easier to see what you are doing. If you don't neglect your plants, but prune them regularly, winter pruning should not result in excessive growth of wood in the spring.

In general, routine pruning in spring involves mostly maintenance-type pruning to repair damage from storms or pests, or to remove suckers or water sprouts. It's a good time, too, to pinch off unwanted buds. Since spring is a time of vigorous growth and a period of great sap movement in trees, it is not an ideal time for heavy pruning.

Pruning in summer usually involves maintenance pruning, but it's also a time to thin fruit for greater yields. Usually heavy pruning of fruit trees is not recommended for summer because it results in the loss of leaves whose function is to manufacture food. The growth of a standard-sized tree will be stunted because this reduction in the number of leaves causes a decrease in root growth, which in turn decreases the amount of food that can be stored in preparation for growth in the following spring. Sometimes pruning in late summer, especially in the north, can result in winter damage because the plant does not have enough time to recover from the pruning before the arrival of cold weather. For the same reason, fall is not an ideal time to prune fruit-producing plants because they might not have time to recover before winter sets in, and any damage as a result of this will just have to be corrected in the spring.

11

Pest and Disease Control

Safeguarding fruit plants and crops is a challenge, for the succulence and sweetness that make these luscious foods more alluring than vegetables to human taste buds are also a magnet for other forms of animal life. The fact that fruits are mostly perennials rather than annuals also makes pest control more difficult. Unlike the annual vegetable crops, fruits must endure the rigors of winter, when dramatic swings of temperature or prolonged cold spells can crack and loosen bark and in other ways weaken their defenses against infection and insect infestation.

The longevity of fruit plants also rules out or limits certain protective cultural practices such as regular rotation of crops, planting early or late to avoid certain pests, and destroying plants after harvest to prevent continuing reproduction of pests. And soil that is occupied by a sizable root system obviously can't be deeply tilled to combat soilborne organisms. Because fruits are reproduced vegetatively they are also vulnerable to subtle long-term deterioration caused by viruses passed on in propagation material.

All this aside, however, there are a plethora of ways to fight fruit pests organically. Gardeners who use them on fruits started locally (or in a similar climate), and who work with carefully inspected propagation material can reasonably hope for fruit that is good to eat although it may not be completely unmarked.

Preventive Measures as a Control

Good Soil Practices

For many reasons, healthy, organically grown fruits are less likely to fall prey to insects and diseases than weak, malnourished crops. The quantity of nutrients available plays a critical role in a fruit plant's well-being, with un-

366

balanced intake a direct cause of physical disorders such as little leaf, a zinc deficiency which affects various fruit trees, and Jonathan spot in apples, which is caused by calcium deficiency. Malnourishment also lowers immunity by creating weakened plants that are especially attractive to certain insects. For example, many species of bark beetles and wood borers thrive on improperly fed trees while avoiding or succumbing on vigorous ones.

Pests such as aphids and certain diseases like fireblight are particularly likely to take hold on "unbalanced" plants whose tissues are too high in carbohydrates—a condition characterized by overly lush growth of stems and foliage. One cause of this condition is overfeeding with nitrogen. A good, healthy soil and periodic applications of compost, manure, or other organic fertilizers make such unbalanced overfeeding unlikely. Organic matter breaks down slowly, making nutrients available gradually.

Cultural practices emphasizing large quantities of organic matter also help fight pests in some other ways. Plenty of humus in the soil works to moderate soil moisture—a fact important in pest control since too much or too little moisture can render plants vulnerable to insect damage, particularly from sucking insects which respond to changes in capillary pressure within plant parts.

Certain organic fertilizers such as seaweed meal or liquid kelp can also have pest-deterring effects. In tests done by agronomists at the University of Maryland (reprinted in *Acres,* vol. 7, no. 9), seaweed meal applied yearly to turf at the rate of 250 pounds per acre was found to be 50 percent more effective than toxic nematicides at reducing populations of pin and lesion nematodes. Another benefit that has been linked to seaweed is increased plant resistance to fungal and insect attack.

Another form of cultural control is a shallow spring tilling, which helps control grape berry moth and brown rot of stone fruits by exposing soil pathogens to weather and predators. Crop rotation of shorter-lived fruits such as strawberries and brambles to limit the buildup of insects is also helpful, as is cultivation around fruits so they do not have to compete with sod or weeds for nutrients and moisture. (Planting on sod can also pose problems with organisms such as white grubs.)

Pruning and Sanitation

Proper pruning is another cultural practice that contributes to optimum plant health and makes pest or disease infestation less likely. Ideally, fruit trees should be pruned so that every leaf receives sun. In actual practice, thinning out branches will serve to open the tree, fostering the ample air circulation that will allow the tree to dry quickly after a wet period, and help foil diseases such as sooty blotch and fly speck on apples. It's been said that sunlight is the best fungicide. By opening and lowering trees by pruning, the gardener also makes it easier to reach all parts of every plant with organic sprays. Thinning of top growth and root pruning at transplanting time to keep roots and shoots in balance can also provide a preventive measure against some kinds of borers. The prompt removal of raspberry and blackberry canes after they fruit is another good prophylactic measure that helps to inhibit the spread of pests; in fact, pruning is the only way to get rid of certain borers.

When the wood taken off is dead or broken (conditions conducive to rots) or afflicted with canker or other bacterial complaints, pruning becomes even more urgent and a matter of sanitation. All such pruned material should be picked up and burned promptly. Where there is evidence of systemic disease—examples are fireblight on apples and pears, and mosaic disease of brambles and peaches—it is necessary to remove and burn the affected parts or, in extreme cases, the entire affected plant so the sickness is not carried to other fruits by insects or wind. Called roguing, this radical preventive step is also sometimes used on infected host plants in the area (on cedar trees with cedar-apple rust, for example). Less drastic preventive sanitation practices include scraping off loose bark so insects can't winter over underneath it, and disinfecting garden tools and pruning wounds to limit the spread of bacteria. Wounds to the tree can be covered with asphalt pruning paint to keep out insects and disease.

It is also important to clear fallen leaves and fruit away from plants since such debris can harbor diseases like brown rot of peaches and black rot of apples,

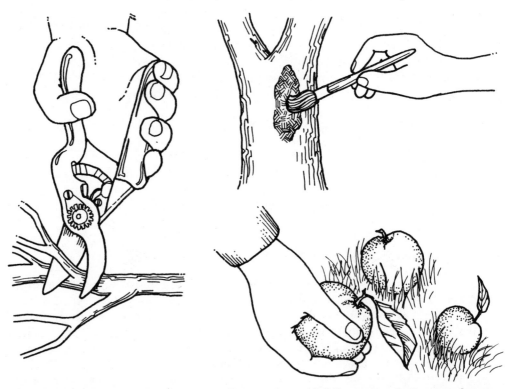

Sanitation Procedures: Most disease problems can be avoided if proper sanitation procedures are followed. Clockwise from the left, prune all damaged, dead, or diseased wood and burn any infected wood immediately. Paint all wounds and cuts with asphalt pruning paint to prevent infection, and clear away fallen leaves, dropped fruit, and any other debris. If any of the debris is diseased, burn it promptly.

and also attracts rabbits and mice. Fruits that never developed normally should be picked from trees, as should those that begin to rot while still on the plant, for they are likely to be harboring fruit rots or insects. Healthy leaves and fruits may be composted or buried in the garden, but all pest-infected orchard trash should be burned promptly. In areas where winters are mild it is a good idea to remove not only debris but to take up mulch during the coldest month or two of the year—a practice that will help control soil insects as well as weeds.

Resistant Varieties

Circumventing pests by planting varieties bred for their ability to repel, withstand, or even damage them is a valuable preventive approach. The development of resistant varieties of fruits has proved effective against certain insects (such as the grape phylloxera and the root knot nematode afflicting peach rootstocks). But resistant varieties are most important in controlling fungal, bacterial, and viral diseases. An outbreak of disease can destroy entire trees amazingly rapidly. For example, fireblight is a bacterial disease which, given the right conditions, can kill a tree in weeks. Outbreaks begin on blossoms and spread to leaves and twigs. Within days, leaves turn brown, wilt, and shrivel. Droplets of sticky ooze appear on the leaf stems. Twigs turn a dark, purplish brown, take on a sunken appearance and droop, sometimes with an upturned tip. Infection can travel rapidly down the stem, and even into the trunk, where it kills the tree. Trees are most susceptible when they are making vigorous growth—one reason to avoid overfertilizing them. As the weather warms and growth slows, the disease may become dormant, leaving black-rimmed patches of shrunken dead bark. The

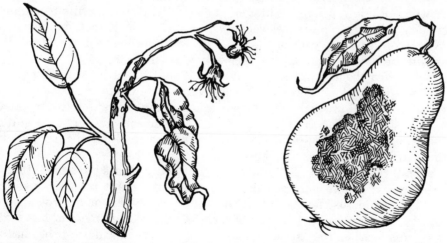

Fireblight Damage: Fireblight is a destructive disease of apples, pears, and quince; it can kill a tree in weeks, and can winter over to return the following year. The first symptoms appear on the flowers, which shrivel rapidly and turn brown. Nearby leaves are then infected and develop brown-black blotches, curl and shrivel, and hang downward as they cling to the blighted twig. Tiny droplets of bacterial ooze emerge from infected parts and infected fruit will turn brown, shrivel, mummify, and finally turn black.

digging deeper

Disease-Resistant Varieties

Planting resistant tree varieties can curtail or eliminate many disease problems that arise in the home orchard. Many years of research and breeding have resulted in the development of desirable fruit varieties which exhibit varying degrees of resistance to diseases that plague fruit trees. Listed below is just a sampling of resistant varieties that are commercially available. These varieties, along with other varieties mentioned in the Guide to Fruits, are noted for their resistance to various diseases.

Apple: Liberty, very resistant to apple scab and cedar apple rust; resistant to fireblight and powdery mildew; Prima, very resistant to apple scab; resistant to fireblight and powdery mildew; Priscilla, very resistant to apple scab and cedar apple rust; resistant to fireblight; Sir Prize, very resistant to apple scab; resistant to powdery mildew.

Cherry: Windsor, resistant to brown rot; Windsor, Van, and Vista, all resistant to Cytospora canker.

Peach: Loring, resistant to leaf curl and bacterial spot; Ranger, very resistant to bacterial spot; Raritan Rose, resistant to leaf curl.

Pear: Maxine, Seckel, Moonglow, and Magness, all resistant to fireblight.

Strawberry: Darrow, resistant to five races of red stele and to verticillium wilt; Guardian, very resistant to five races of red stele and to verticillium wilt, leaves resistant to leaf scorch and mildew; Sunrise, very resistant to red stele and to verticillium wilt, leaves resistant to leaf scorch and mildew.

next season it may revive, sometimes producing ooze from the cankers, which insects pick up, spreading the infection to new sites.

Powdery mildew, a fungus, first spreads a felty, grayish white bloom on the undersides of leaves. The leaves soon curl, crinkle, or fold, become brittle, and die. When it infects one-year-old twigs, it overwinters there, and will infect the tree again the next season. It, too, seriously weakens a tree,

The one drawback to resistant varieties is that all such painstakingly bred varieties eventually lose their resistance as the target insects and diseases mutate to get around it. However, this process takes many years; for example, some disease-resistant apple varieties are 75 to 100 years old and are still quite resistant. Along with biological control, resistant varieties may be our best hope of combating pest and disease problems in coming years.

Varietal resistance takes three forms, and many plants have more than one kind. In the type of resistance called antibiosis the plant releases substances (such as phytoalexins, for example) that prevent, injure, or destroy insect or fungal life. All plants tend to synthesize chemicals that are more or less toxic to other organisms when they are under attack, but plants considered to be antibiotic do this more vigorously, and may even kill their own injured tissue as well as the pest. Unfortunately not much is known of any potentially harmful effects that plants bred for toxicity may have upon beneficial insects. Nevertheless, antibiosis is a factor in the resistance of certain fruit cultivars—for example, in the ability of the Northern Spy apple and its hybrids and Lloyd George red raspberries to shrug off aphids. Antibiotic qualities also may explain the relative freedom from disease and insects exhibited by fruits such as oriental persimmons and wild American persimmons and pawpaws.

A second kind of varietal resistance is shown by so-called tolerant plants, which prevail over pests not by repelling or injuring them but by enduring their worst damage. Often besieged by insects, tolerant plants are able to generate ample amounts of growth hormone and to create new leaf or root tissue rapidly. Thanks to this exceptional vitality and to their ability to heal their wounds quickly and resist diseases invading the affected area, these survivors remain healthy and productive.

In the third form of varietal resistance, plants exhibit characteristics that make them unattractive to pests. These traits may be as diverse as hairiness, foliage color, widely separated leaves, the presence of a disagreeable odor or taste, or the disguising of an odor that ordinarily would summon insects to lay their eggs.

Just a few of the fruits resistant to one or more common pests are Concord grapes, which are more resistant to black rot than some others, and the scab-resistant apples Grimes Golden, Liberty, Prima, Priscilla, and Sir Prize. A host of other resistant varieties are described in nursery catalogs of fruit specialists and in publications coming out of agricultural experiment stations, which sometimes provide free scion wood on request.

Biological Control

The use of living organisms to control pest animals or plants is steadily increasing in importance and holds great promise for the future. Home fruit growers are increasingly coming to rely upon natural predators or parasites to keep pests at acceptable levels. Among insect predators, those most valued at present are the ladybug, which destroys aphids, mealybugs, red spider mites, and scale insects (and is now being viewed as the best hope of saving the northwestern United States' pear industry from the pear psylla); the larva of the *Trichogramma* wasp, which consumes moth and butterfly eggs; and the green lacewing larva, which demolishes aphids, leafhoppers, mites, thrips, and some caterpillars. All of these beneficial insects can be encouraged by organic methods of fruit culture and if desired they can be purchased by mail from biological control firms. (The most completely stocked source is Rincon Vitova Insectaries, Inc., P.O. Box 95, Oak View, CA 93022.)

Larger predators, such as most birds, are also valuable in controlling fruit pests—even the much-maligned blue jay, which in fact eats mostly nuts and acorns (rather than the eggs of other birds) along with unwelcome insects and even mice. You can invite bird predators to take up residence in the fruit garden by providing winter feeding, water, materials and sites for nesting, and landscaping that appeals to them either as food or nesting material. Plants attracting the greatest number of bird species in both the eastern and midwestern United States include autumn olive, cherry, crabapple, firethorn, hawthorn, highbush cranberry, holly, red cedar, and tatarian honeysuckle. Gardeners in the East can

Hedgerows to Attract Birds: Birds can be a help in the orchard as they eat many harmful insects that feed on trees and carry disease. Planting a hedgerow with many different types of trees and bushes that provide food, shelter and protection can attract a wide variety of birds. This hedgerow contains two cherry trees in the middle rear, flanked by crabapples. In the foreground, from left to right, are elderberry, blueberry, highbush cranberry, and blueberry.

also plant flowering dogwood, highbush blueberry, and Virginia creeper to attract birds. Midwesterners can grow elderberry and sunflower. Perhaps the single most important step you can take to lure bird predators is to create a hedgerow effect with shrubs and/or trees. A hedgerow area can boost your bird population by as much as five to ten times.

Other helpful, harmless animals that can mop up pests are toads (just one can devour as many as 15,000 insects from March to November), garter snakes, various lizards, and box turtles. If zoning permits, poultry allowed to roam and scratch among fruit trees make excellent predators.

Parasites also play a major role in biological control and are considered more valuable than predators against some pests because they attack that specific pest in preference to others, developing either internally or externally on it. Often, parasites lay their eggs in the grubs of pests, then after hatching consume their hosts. Insect parasites include many flies and wasps. In Australia such hymenopterous parasites have successfully conquered red scale on orange trees. Beneficial wasps can be attracted to your orchard area by nearby plantings of umbelliferous plants that are allowed to flower. Because the insects have short mouthparts, they can extract nectar easily from plants such as anise, carrots, coriander, dill, fennel, parsley, and parsnips.

Microbial parasites are pathogens used either to kill pests or to make them more vulnerable to other controls. The six groups of such organisms are bacteria, viruses, fungi, nematodes, protozoans, and rickettsias. Although research in this mode of pest control is only now starting to gain widespread acceptance, the environmental problems posed by pesticides have spurred the USDA into sponsoring more scientific investigation and exploring incentives for industry involvement. In 1978, a study group of the American Institute of Biological Studies concluded that certain spore-forming bacteria and baculoviruses make ideal biological insect control agents because they are host-selective; so far have not proved hazardous to man, other mammals, and plants; are suited to integrated pest management programs; and may contribute to long-term control by persisting through several generations of the target species or through several seasons. Thus far, however, only several microbial agents are being marketed—notably the bacterial insecticides milky spore disease (*Bacillus popilliae*)—sold as Doom—which wipes out Japanese beetle grubs, and *Bacillus thuringiensis*—sold as Dipel, Thuricide, and Biotrol—which targets moth and butterfly larvae.

Another emerging form of biological control is the development of biological insecticides consisting of chemicals that mimic the natural hormones regulating insect growth and development. The goal is to disrupt the cycle of pests and to keep them from reproducing without affecting other organisms. Like ultrasonic transmitters, which in effect they are, these substances can either destroy pests or lure them to traps or predators or parasites.

Mechanical Controls

Various traps baited with insect sex attractants (pheromones) are now on the market. These can be used to monitor oriental fruit moth, codling moth, and various leafrollers in order to determine the best time to use organic sprays or forms of biological control. Other commercially available bug traps use light as the lure. (Blue light works well on grape leafhoppers while black light is highly effective with night fliers such as codling moth and oriental fruit moth. And if a pheromone setup is used in combination with black light, nightly harvests of moths are increased from six to ten times.) Some light traps also feature an electric grid or electrified revolving wires, but these sizzle insects indiscriminately and keep the user from evaluating whether pests or harmless, perhaps beneficial insects are being caught.

There are many kinds of insect traps that you can make at home. A simple light trap may be built by hanging a light bulb with a reflector over a shallow pan of water topped with a thin film of kerosene. Another visual trap may be directed against apple maggots, which are irresistibly drawn to croquet balls painted red (or other red balls of similar size). These spherical traps should be coated with a sticky substance such as Tanglefoot or Stikem and hung six to a tree, where they can reduce maggot damage by up to 90 percent.

Fruitflies can also be caught in glass gallon jars containing a pint of vinegar, while a nine-to-one mixture of water and molasses placed in the bottom of paper cups will trap codling moths. The cups should be suspended in trees at blossom time, for the moths emerge as the petals fall (although they are present all season). Geranium oil can be used to trap Japanese beetles.

Larger pests such as porcupines, rabbits, and raccoons not chased off by an

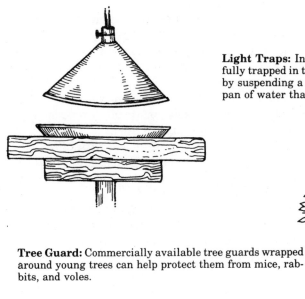

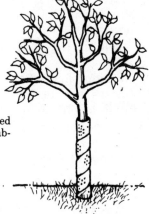

Light Traps: Insects that move by night can be successfully trapped in this homemade light trap. Build it yourself by suspending a light bulb with a reflector over a shallow pan of water that has a thin layer of kerosene on top.

Tree Guard: Commercially available tree guards wrapped around young trees can help protect them from mice, rabbits, and voles.

active dog can be captured in homemade box traps or the Havahart commercial kinds. A greater problem might be where to release these garden nuisances.

Where traps are inappropriate, fruit gardeners can safeguard their harvest and plants by setting up physical barriers or repellents. Tree guards made of ½-inch hardware cloth work very well against mice, moles, and rabbits. Deer can be kept away by woven-wire fences 6 feet high (with an outrigger) or 8 feet high. A simpler remedy found to give complete protection from deer was reported at the 1980 meeting of the American Society for Horticultural Science: suspend a bag containing 20 grams of human hair in each tree or at 20-foot intervals in perimeter trees. Hair may also serve to repel rabbits. An even better way to keep away rabbits is to soak a piece of liver in hot water for 30 minutes and spray trees with the resultant solution. Squirrels are discouraged by red pepper and moles by plantings of the mole plant *(Euphorbia lathyris)* or of crown imperial *(Fritillaria imperialis)*.

Where bird pests are the problem scare devices sometimes do the trick. Wind-animated scarecrows, inflatable or otherwise, suspended in the tops of the trees will confound the birds for a few days, when you should switch your defense to foil strips, shiny aluminum pie pans, or artificial snakes made of old garden hose, coiled and tacked to a 24-by-24-inch piece of plywood. Place this in the treetop so it is visible from a bird's-eye view. If your neighbors are a distance away and/or very understanding, noisemakers are good bird repellents in some areas, with tape-recorded avian distress calls; explosions of acetylene, propane, or gunpowder; or cackling Av-Alarms available. Looping black thread back and forth over the tree creates a barrier that, unseen but felt by the birds, frightens them away, or

Tree Nets: Some fruits, such as blueberries and cherries, are irresistible to birds, who can devour up to 90 percent of the fruit before the gardener has a chance to pick it. One way to prevent this is to cover the entire tree or bush with ¾-inch nylon netting, tying it together below the branches. This keeps the birds away while not restricting light, water, and air.

so the experts claim. Whatever you do, don't expect to keep all the birds out all of the time. Try several approaches simultaneously and change methods every few days as the birds become used to each previous method.

For trees and bushes bearing fruit that is especially attractive to birds, such as blueberry bushes and cherry trees, a more painstaking type of protection may be necessary. In such cases, the only surefire protection is to erect a barrier in the form of screen houses or cages that cover the entire tree. Or cheesecloth or tobacco shade cloth can be draped over bushes and fastened with clothespins several weeks before the fruit ripens. To protect trees, a better material to use is ¾-inch nylon netting which lets in light, water, and air readily. Tie the netting together below the branches. These covers are difficult to use on large trees, but they are 100 percent effective.

The stems of young trees vulnerable to borers and climbing pests can be wrapped in burlap, then painted over with whitewash. To deter slugs, scatter wood ashes around the base of plants or young trees.

Developing fruit can be protected from birds, molds, and insects by covering it. Self-fertile fruits like grapes can be stapled inside a waterproof paper bag with one bottom corner snipped off to allow drainage of condensate. Pears and apples can be inserted when small in pleated plastic sleeves that come to fit the growing fruit snugly, admitting air at both ends. (One source of such covers is Keystone Company, 555 Warren Street, Phillipsburg, NJ 08865.) Even strawberries may be covered a couple of weeks before harvest. One grower uses plastic food bags, removing them briefly to empty them if condensation forms.

tricks of the trade

Creative Controls

When deciding which method to use to combat fruit pests, it is essential to consider the nature and habits of the pest to be fought. Sometimes a simple control method can be devised specifically for the pest.

For example, curculio beetles will go into a sort of shock if they are disturbed while feeding. When an infested tree is shaken, they will simply drop off. To get rid of curculios, then, you can cover the ground beneath the tree with a piece of light-colored plastic, shake off the bugs, wrap up the plastic, and burn it or submerge it in a can of oil right away.

If borers are your problem, putting mothballs around the bases of trees will discourage the female borers from laying their eggs there. An alternate method is to surround the bases of the trees with a sticky material like Tanglefoot right before the time the borers normally lay their eggs.

Organic Sprays

Sprays of the organic kind work either by repelling pests or killing them on contact. The best-known contact type of spray is the dormant oil spray, which is applied to trunks and branches during the tree's dormant period. Dormant oil is a highly refined, light oil; apply it on a windless, frostless day (with a temperature of 40°F or above) when buds are just beginning to swell but have not yet turned green. Dormant oil sprays can be used against aphid eggs, aphids, mealybugs, overwintering red mite eggs, pear psylla, scale, thrips, and whiteflies. Dormant oil preparations may be purchased in an emulsified (miscible) form to be mixed with water, or they can be concocted at home. The formula recommended by Vermont orchardist Lewis Hill is a mixture of 2 quarts light motor oil and 1 pound of fish oil soap. (Used with water, fish oil soap is itself an effective scalecide and also kills mealybugs. In the dormant oil blend, however, ½ cup of liquid detergent may be substituted for it.) One part of the oil/soap mixture should be mixed with 20 parts of water as needed and used immediately (that is, before it separates, as undiluted oil can damage plants). A dormant oil spray must cover all parts of the tree to be really effective. The oil must coat the overwintering insects or eggs to be destroyed, because it kills by asphyxiation.

Other organic contact sprays are derived from plants. Remember though, that these botanical insecticides kill beneficial insects along with the pests, so they are best used only as a last resort. If you have only a couple of trees, it might be better to use botanical insecticides by dipping heavily infested branches into the solution, instead of spraying. Sprays of pyrethrum, rotenone, and ryania are relatively effective against a wide variety of soft-bodied insects such as aphids if they are applied frequently. Ryania also works against codling moth and rotenone is fatal to pear psylla. Nicotine solutions will also poison aphids. These botanical insecticides and other plant-derived sprays doubtless are effective because of highly potent insecticidal compounds in the plants used. When a volatile oil from a plant containing the antipest substance is used directly, the results can be striking. For example, garlic oil was found by Indian researchers to kill the fungus *Sphaceloma ampelinum,* which causes anthracnose disease (reported in the *Journal of the British Mycological Society,* vol. 73, no. 2). Similarly, the volatile oils of various evergreens—especially of certain pines and balsam firs—destroy various pests (including codling moths and apple moths). And a garliclike extract from the neem tree of India is anathema to Japanese beetles—they choose to starve rather than to eat vegetation treated with it.

Until such oil-based sprays are available commercially, fruit growers can devise their own by steeping or blending pest-resistant plants in water. To invent your own plant juice spray, find a nonpoisonous weed or other plant that is seldom bothered by pests (examples: clover, lilacs, marigold, wild cherry). Blend several handfuls of its leaves with a quart of water in a blender, and steep for a day. Dilute no more than five times with additional water and spray on the plants being damaged. A few hints for the adventurous: choose smooth-leaved plants rather than those with hairy leaves that repel insects mechanically, and look for plants with volatile oils—that is, those with a powerful smell or taste. Also, the more plants used in each spray, the more pests it is likely to counter.

A sulfur spray can provide effective control of fungal diseases like brown rot of cherries and peaches. When the weather during blooming and just before harvest is warm and wet—conditions favorable for the fungus—a spray made from ½ pound of powdered sulfur to 10 gallons of water when applied to the trees will retard the growth of the fungus. Sulfur will not affect bees, beneficial insects, or people.

Some Common Insect Pests of Fruits

Pest (Fruit Affected)	Damage	Description	Controls
Aphid Apple (apple, pear, wild crab) Black Citrus Currant (currant, gooseberry) Green Citrus Green Peach (apricot, cherry, peach, plum) Melon (melon, citrus, strawberry) Plum Rose Strawberry Strawberry Root	Nymph and adult suck sap from cells, usually of foliage, causing withering and reduction of plant vigor. Also excretes excess sugars and sap (known as honeydew), which will support growth of black, sooty mold. Aphids very injurious to young trees, curling leaves and checking growth. In large numbers sometimes also attack young fruits, stopping development and giving knotty, stunted appearance.	Pear-shaped soft body with long antennae and 2 tubelike projections from rear of abdomen. Color usually green or black but may be violet, red, yellow or brown. Wings present on some adults are held erect.	Vigorous early morning spraying with water; spraying with strong lime and water mixture, tobacco tea, other plant sprays, or with 1 or 2 tbsp. of nondetergent soap per gal. of tepid water. Use repellent companion plants. For large populations, well entrenched and hard to reach, predatory lacewing larvae or ladybugs may be released. Eggs of apple aphid laid on bark can be crushed in late fall or winter. *(continued)*

Some Common Insect Pests of Fruits—*continued*

Pest (Fruit Affected)	Damage	Description	Controls
Cankerworm Fall Spring (apple, apricot, other fruit trees)	Larva of fall type emerges in spring from gray eggs laid in fall on trunks, branches, or twigs and feeds on new foliage. In spring species, eggs are laid from February to end of April, hatching in about a month into larvae that feed for 3–4 weeks on new leaves. Skeletonizing of leaves causes tree to weaken each year, maturing little fruit and sometimes dying.	Also called inchworm. Inch-long striped worms; both species colored brown and green, with stripes running along their bodies. May drop from trees on fine silk threads when branch is jarred. Some attempt to mimic a twig, remaining stiff and motionless when jarred.	Sticky bands around trunks in February and from mid-October to December help foil wingless females crawling up to lay eggs. A good control is *Bacillus thuringiensis* sprayed in April or May. Natural enemies include chickadees and other birds, the mite *Nothrus ovivorus*, a minute parasitic chalcid fly, a Tachina fly, various ground beetles.
Cicada, Periodical (many fruit trees)	Nymph chews roots. Greatest injury comes from slits adult makes for egg laying, which may cause twig tips to die.	Also called 17-year locust. Nymph: stout, up to 1½ in. long, with large front legs, initially resembling very large, light brown ant. Adult: 1–1½ in. long, brown to black with orange legs and clear brittle wings held over body. Bright red eyes.	In years when large broods expected, do not set out transplants until after eggs laid. Protect young trees with mosquito netting. Use sticky bands on trunks when broods emerging. Cut off injured twigs promptly.
Curculio Grape (grapes; widely distributed east of Rockies) Plum (plum, apple, peach, cherry, apricot, nectarine, less on pear, prune, quince, other fruits) Quince Rose (wild and garden roses, wild brambles; common in northern regions)	Grape curculio: adults eat upper leaf surface, leaving whitish feeding marks, then lay eggs in young berries where larva feed on seeds. In some places destroys 50–75% of crop, which drops as larvae feed. Plum curculio: adult eats young leaves, buds, and blossoms, then lays eggs under skin of young fruit (leaving crescent-shaped scar). Young grub hatches and feeds on it; adult also eats pulp of fruit. Quince curculio: adult cuts small opening in fruit, eating cavity in pulp which becomes filled with hard knotty tissue; larva develops from eggs in cavities, burrowing through flesh of fruit, but seldom reaching core. Larvae infest up to 90% of crop in some areas. Rose curculio: adult eats holes in buds, stems, leaves; larvae hatch in buds, rose hips, devour seeds and flowers.	Grape curculio: adult is 1/10-in.-long brownish beetle with snout; larva is legless, white with brownish head, 2/7 in. long. Plum curculio: adult is 1/5 in. long, brown, gray-mottled beetle with snout. Has 4 humps on back; grub is white or yellowish, staying near pit of stone fruits. Quince curculio: adult is brownish gray, broad-shouldered snout beetle ¼ in. long—no humps; larva is footless, flesh-colored, maggotlike. Rose curculio: adult is red with long black snout; larva is white, legless.	Remove all trash and overgrown weeds used for hibernation; prune trees to admit sun. Handpick beetles. In early morning knock or shake beetles onto sheets or where poultry are. For quince curculio, pick off and destroy affected fruit a month before harvest. For other curculios clean up and bury dropped fruit often. For plum curculio, disk under trees in July and August to destroy pupae in ground; for quince curculio, use shallow repeated cultivation in spring.

Pest (Fruit Affected)	Damage	Description	Controls
Grape Phylloxera	Nymph drains sap from leaves or roots, forming pealike galls where young produced. In eastern U.S., heavily infested leaves become distorted and may die; roots may grow knobby. In western U.S., root types a serious pest of viniferas; weaken or kill plants, causing major damage.	Minuscule, wingless oval- or pear-shaped yellow-green or yellow-brown aphid.	Plant less susceptible varieties; European grapes are vulnerable, American (labrusca) varieties unaffected. Select only those vinifera types that have been grafted on resistant rootstock. Rotenone may work against leaf infestation.
Green June Beetle	Adult is night-feeder that devours foliage and also fruit beginning to ripen. (Larva is a white grub.) A general feeder that seriously damages ripening fruits in southern U.S. north to southern Illinois and Long Island.	Almost 1 in. long; broad, rather flattish, dull green beetle with bronze to yellow margin.	Handpick. Keep orchard free of debris such as grass clippings and manure piles. Catch larva in sunken flowerpots. (See also White Grub.)
Imported Currantworm (currant, gooseberry)	Larva devours edges of leaves, occasionally fruit. Can defoliate entire bush in days, starting with center foliage.	Young larva has black head, many spots. When mature, ⅘ in. long and all green.	Use hillebore or pyrethrum spray or dust with rotenone or pyrethrum.
Japanese Beetle (apple, cherry, grape, nectarine, peach, plum, quince, berries)	Adult eats foliage and fruit, flying only in daytime. Larva does lesser damage by feeding on roots. Often skeletonizes leaves, attacks foliage, flowers, fruit en masse. Highly destructive.	Adult: shiny metallic green beetle with copper brown wings; ½ in. long. Larva: grayish white grub, dark brown head, 2 rows of spines in V-shape on underside of last abdominal segment.	Handpick or shake off daily in early morning onto sheet. Repel with geraniums or attract, poison with larkspur. Milky spore disease (*Bacillus popilliae*) kills grubs, though may take several years to be effective. Imported parasites *Tiphia vernalis* and *T. popilliavora* also attack larvae. Odor traps effective for small area.
Leafhopper (apple, cherry, citrus, currant, gooseberry, grape, melon, peach, plum, quince, raspberry, rose, strawberry)	Nymphs and adults pierce tissue on undersides of leaves, sucking sap and removing chlorophyll from cells. Foliage becomes finely mottled with white and may drop. Large amounts of honeydew excreted, gives plant glazed appearance. Black sooty mold may grow. May spread virus diseases.	Small slender insects hold wings tentlike above body when resting; run rapidly sidewise. Colors variable, often greenish with nymphs paler. Grape leafhopper is white or pale yellow with red or yellow markings.	Pyrethrum and weed control often effective. For grape types, plant blackberries nearby to boost numbers of a beneficial wasp; avoid thin-leaved varieties.
Leafroller Fruit Tree Oblique-banded	Larvae hatch from egg clusters laid on leaves, attacking buds, leaves, and	Caterpillars of different colors—often yellowish, white, or greenish, head	Spray larvae with *Bacillus thuringiensis* or rotenone. Foliage must be thoroughly *(continued)*

Some Common Insect Pests of Fruits—*continued*

Pest (Fruit Affected)	Damage	Description	Controls
Leafroller *(continued)* Omnivorous Red-banded Strawberry Tufted (various types attack nearly all kinds of deciduous fruits, tropicals and subtropicals also)	eating large holes in fruit. Spin webs binding leaves or leaves and fruits together, forming sheltered feeding site. May weaken very young trees; can cause extensive fruit damage.	reddish brown or yellowish. From ½–1 in. long.	covered with spray.
Lesser Appleworm (apples, prune plums)	Larva bores into fruit, usually from side, remaining near surface to eat pulp and creating disfiguring area beneath whitened skin. Can continue to feed on fruit in storage.	⅜ in. long, pinkish or nearly white caterpillar.	Same as for codling moth.
Maggot Apple (apple, crabapple, blueberry, European plum, pear; cherry in northeastern U.S., southeastern Canada) Blueberry	Apple: Adult lays eggs through puncture in fruit skin. Larva rasps and tunnels through fruit pulp. Sometimes evidenced only by dark lines under skin. Also known as railroad worm because of its winding feeding paths. Blueberry: Larva of any of several different insects develops inside berry; evidenced by sunken spot on fruit, uneven or premature coloring. Spoils fruit and causes it to drop.	Both are ⅓ in. long; legless, white or yellowish maggots.	Apple: take up and destroy dropped fruit promptly. Plant later maturing varieties (sweet and subacid types are most vulnerable). Homemade sticky traps can be very effective. Blueberry: remove affected fruits promptly.
Mealybug (all citrus, avocado, currant, fig, grape, guava, mango, strawberry, many other fruits)	Nymph and adult pierce, suck soft-stemmed or succulent plants, removing sap from leaves, bark, buds, or roots and secreting honeydew that encourages sooty mold. Also attracts ants. In addition to stunting plant growth by causing bud drop and sticky foliage, can cause premature fruit drop.	Soft-bodied oval, flattened scale insect resembling cotton tuft. Has puffy waxy coat and leglike wavy filaments along sides or serving as tail. Various species ⅒–⅕ in. long.	Spray undersides of leaves forcefully with water to dislodge, or apply spray of soapy water or kerosene and water. For large populations, use predators such as ladybugs or green lacewing larve. Citrus mealybugs may be controlled with the Brazilian parasite *Leptomastix dactylopii* or with rotenone or pyrethrum.
Moth Codling Moth (apple, cherry, peach, pear, plum, quince) Grape Berry Moth (grapes)	Codling moth: overwinters as cocoon on bark. Larvae hatch from eggs laid on fruit and tunnel into core. Damaged fruit drops earlier than normal.	Codling moth larva is 1 in. long, white tinged with pink, with brown head. Grape berry moth larva is white or cream, gradually turning to green or purple.	Codling moth: keep corrugated cardboard band on trunk from spring to September, then burn along with cocoons on it. Or scrape bark in spring and spray

Pest (Fruit Affected)	Damage	Description	Controls
Moth *(continued)* Oriental Fruit Moth (peach, quince; also apple, apricot, papaya, pear, plum)	Grape berry moth: feeds on developing flower buds and maturing fruit. Tunnels into berries, leaving red spot at entry point; spins webbing in grape cluster. May cause berries to split or stick together. Oriental fruit moth: first brood feeds on young shoot tips (especially peach and nectarine), wilting them. Later generations burrow into fruit. Brown rot usually develops in peaches and nectarines.	Oriental fruit moth larva is pinkish with brown head.	forcefully with water to dislodge larvae. Try soapy water or fish-oil sprays or planting of nasturtium against caterpillars. Woodpeckers consume caterpillars and young larvae. Molasses-filled cans hung 2 per tree will catch adults. Grape berry moth: cultivate in early spring to bury pupae; remove all plant debris in autumn. Oriental fruit moth: plant early-season varieties; cultivate soil to depth of 4 inches 1 to 3 weeks before blooming; use parasitic wasps such as *Trichogramma minutum* and *Macrocentus ancylivorus*. *Bacillus thuringiensis* is moderately effective against all 3 moths.
Pear Psylla (pear, occasionally quince)	Adult and nymph suck sap of leaf petioles and undersides of leaves. Excrete honeydew promoting growth of black sooty fungus on leaves and fruit and drawing ants. Cause blackening and browning of leaves which fall prematurely; may stunt buds and scar fruits. Heavy infestation may reduce crop following year.	Tiny, broad, yellowish, wingless insect maturing in 1 month. Looks like a miniature cicada. Adults jump like fleas.	Prevent through early spring dormant oil spray applied thoroughly when buds first show green and again 5–7 days later. Natural enemies effective when there is a sizable infestation include pirate bug, ladybug larvae and adults, lacewing larvae (aphid lions), snake fly larvae and adults, and parasitic wasp *Trechnites insidiosus*. Rotenone also said to be effective.
Pear Slug (cherry, pear, plum, quince, juneberry)	Larva uses rasping mouth to skeletonize upper leaf surfaces. Can entirely defoliate tree by midsummer, stunting fruit, which fails to mature, and weakening tree so no fruit buds form following year. Usually not rampant for series of years.	A sawfly larva; ½ in. long, olive green to orange, slimy, legless tadpolelike creature with wide front end, tapered back.	Handpick, sprinkle with salt, or dust leaves with freshly slaked lime. Or spray with 1 oz. white hellebore to 3 gal. water.

(continued)

Some Common Insect Pests of Fruits—*continued*

Pest (Fruit Affected)	Damage	Description	Controls
Rose Chafer (rose; also grape, apple, peach, cherry, pear, plum, berries)	Adult appears in force in June, early July, devouring flowers, leaves, fruit. Skeletonizes leaves and eats and soils flower petals. Damage done in 4- to 6-week period, then pest disappears. More severe damage done in sandy areas.	Long-legged, ½-in.-long, slender fawn-colored or grayish beetle with black underside and dense yellow hairs on forewings.	Handpick; use barriers of cheesecloth or mosquito netting as canopy or fence. Cultivate soil in early spring and get rid of egg-sheltering refuse. Do not use poultry against the rose chafer—it contains a toxic agent poisonous to young chickens.
Tarnished Plant Bug (many plants from strawberry to fruit trees)	Adult injects poison into young shoots, flower buds, fruits when puncturing cells to suck juices. Causes serious damage—dying back of leaves and shoots on trees. On strawberry, pear, and peach, dwarfs fruit and creates sunken areas (called cat-facing).	¼-in.-long, oval, flattened bug, dull to yellowish brown with variable colored splotches and other markings. Often has reddish stripes on head and black spots on thorax and abdomen.	Handpicking or organic sprays applied early in morning when bugs are relatively inactive may help somewhat. Sabadilla dust for bad infestations.
Tent Caterpillar Eastern (apple, peach, plum, rose) Forest (apple, plum, prune plum, cherry, peach, pear, rose; common in western U.S.)	Larva feeds on foliage in spring. Can defoliate entire tree, weakening but not killing it. Tends to do great damage several years in a row.	Eastern species: dull yellow or reddish brown with white stripe down back and 2 parallel yellow lines and a row of bluish spots on sides. Forest tent caterpillar has row of creamy white spots on back instead of stripe and does not spin tentlike web in tree crotch like Eastern kind.	Scrape off or pick off egg masses, which are grayish, foamlike material encircling young twigs. (Masses are glossy in winter but duller in spring.) Or as worms hatch in spring tear out each nest and destroy. Tent caterpillar moths can be captured in blacklight traps or controlled with *Bacillus thuringiensis* or by Baltimore orioles or certain parasitic wasps and flies. Clean up wood piles, boxes, baskets, etc., which are favored sites for pupation; remove wild cherry trees nearby if possible. Hard-to-reach nests can be burned out (carefully!) with rag soaked in kerosene tied to a long pole.
Thrip Citrus (citrus, date, grape) Pear (pear, prune plum, apple, apricot, cherry, grape, peach, plum) Other types prey on avocado, banana, date palm, fig, guava, mango, strawberry.	Nymph and adult rasp flower buds, leaves, stems; suck sap. Bleach or silver leaves, which wither, and/or scar flowers and fruits. Where heavy infestation, foliage appears scorched and blossoms destroyed.	Minute to small, with wings—when present—narrow and having marginal fringe of long bristles, folded flat on back. Citrus: yellowish to orange with bright red eyes. Pear: pale whitish, needle-thin insects almost invisible.	Heavy mulch can keep adults from emerging from ground in early spring. Make sure plants are adequately watered. Employ strict weed control; also oil-and-water or rotenone sprays. Natural enemies include ladybugs, aphid lions.

Pest (Fruit Affected)	Damage	Description	Controls
Weevil Strawberry (strawberry, raspberry, dewberry) Strawberry Root (strawberry, raspberry, apple, grape, peach)	Larva of strawberry weevil feeds inside bud where eggs have been laid. Adult girdles stems, almost severing unopened buds, and eats pollen and blossoms for brief time. Can damage 50–60% of crop, but disappears after several years. Adult of strawberry root weevil devours leaves, berries at night; worst damage done by larva, which devours fine roots and eats off crown close to ground.	Strawberry weevil larva is 1/10 in. long, white or yellowish and strongly curved; adult is 1/4 in. long, black with white markings and turned-under snout half as long as body. Strawberry root weevil adult, 1/6 in. long, shiny, wingless and black with reddish brown antennae and legs; larva fat and curved, to 3/8 in. long, legless and white with light brown head.	Destroy damaged buds, which contain eggs; eliminate trash and nearby foliage affording hibernation sites for adult weevils. Handpick adults. If necessary, dust with diatomaceous earth. For strawberry weevil, consider planting very early, profusely blooming varieties with perfect flowers as trap crop, planting heavy-flowering varieties which can better sustain some bud loss, or planting 4 rows of variety with imperfect flowers and 50 rows of perfect-flowered variety to assure pollination. (Adult beetle is attracted mostly to staminate varieties.) Strawberry root weevil: destroy old plants after harvest and plant new ones where no strawberries planted for 1 year or longer.
White Grub (strawberry, blackberry; young apple trees and other nursery stock)	White grubs are the larvae of scarab beetles (such as May or June beetles). Most feed on roots and seldom cause noticeable damage unless they get very numerous. May cause sudden wilt of plants, usually in early summer.	Fat, whitish grub 1–1½ in. long.	Dig out and destroy. Milky spore disease (*Bacillus popilliae*) also effective. Problem worst if strawberries planted where grass or pasture was. Limit by rotating fruits with sweet potatoes or deep-rooted legumes such as sweet clover, alfalfa, which are unfavorable to white grubs. Also cultivate land deeply and frequently the winter before planting and regularly in late spring or early summer, when grubs near surface.
Whitefly (citrus, avocado, blackberry, grape, melon, Japanese persimmon, strawberry, others)	Nymph and adult pierce leaves and stems, sucking sap and excreting sticky honeydew conducive to black sooty fungus. Plants are weakened; leaves yellow and die; fruits affected by droppings of honeydew and fungus are undersized and poorly colored.	Nymph flattish, oval, losing legs after first molt. Often fringe or whitish filaments. Adult 1/16–1/12 in. long, 2 pairs membranous wings covered with white powdery wax.	Tobacco dust and tea; ryania; oil sprays. Use of parasitic wasp *Encarsia formosa* in greenhouse; also lacewings and ladybugs. Remove water sprouts.

A Guide to Fruits for the Home Garden

ACEROLA

Barbados cherry
Malpighia glabra
Malpighiaceae

The acerola is a shrub or small tree growing anywhere from 5 to 20 feet high. It has shiny, dark green, oval leaves and flowers which range in color from pale pink to rose, depending upon the variety. The small flowers develop after three to four weeks into bright red, juicy fruits that are similar to cherries in shape, size, and color. The shrubs bloom throughout the summer, producing two or three crops of fruit. While they are often too acid to eat raw, acerola cherries can be made into a juice that is very rich in vitamin C.

The plants begin to bear heavily in the third or fourth year; a seven-year-old Florida

Sweet variety can yield up to 170 pounds of fruit in a year.

Soil Requirements: The acerola needs full sun, but adapts readily to poor soil, growing well in clay or sand. The soil must be moist but well drained, since flooding may quickly destroy the roots.

Propagation: Acerola is usually propagated by means of hardwood cuttings, air layering, or grafting.

Cuttings may be up to 10 inches long and ½ inch thick, bearing two or three leaves. Root them in sand, peat moss or vermiculite. Keep the soil moist and the plot shaded. Within two months enough roots should develop to allow transplanting into containers.

To propagate by layering, remove a ring of bark from a mature stem, then cover the cut surface with damp sphagnum moss, wrap in plastic and secure with a rubber band. Within six weeks, roots will form. Sever the top part of the shoot from the tree and pot it in a large container. Set it out when well established.

Malpighia glabra is susceptible to root knot nematodes, and is sometimes grafted to *M. suberosa,* a resistant species. Use a cleft graft or side-veneer graft.

Ordering Stock: Unless you want to create a hedge, one or two plants are usually enough for a home garden, since the acerola is almost overbearing through the summer months.

Planting and Culture: In Florida, plants that are between 6 and 12 months old can be set out anytime in April, May, or June. Each one should be given 12 to 15 square feet of space for expansion on a lawn. For ornamental and fruiting hedges, space acerola 2 to 4 feet apart to make a hedge that requires only a small amount of trimming to keep in shape.

Mulch heavily with grass, hay, straw, or leaves to preserve soil moisture. Watering is important in early spring, but less so from November to April.

Acerola will also thrive and bear fruit in a greenhouse. Temperatures should not drop below 55°F in winter or rise above 75°F in summer for best results. Water freely in spring and summer, and moderately in the colder months. Repot only in spring or fall.

Pruning: Prune well-established, dense varieties every fall to open them up to sun and air.

Upright varieties can be headed back to prevent their branches from growing out of reach. Pruning in early spring will diminish the next year's crop.

Pests and Diseases: Root knot nematodes and scales are the worst enemies of acerola.

Harvest and Storage: Vitamin C content is highest when the fruit is half ripe or still slightly green. Since the ascorbic acid level diminishes quickly as the fruit ripens, pick every other day. Freeze the juice or pulp, or use the fruit soon after harvest.

Uses: Acerola juice and pulp is good in preserves and jellies.

APPLE

Malus pumila
Rosaceae

There are hundreds of apple varieties available, offering a wide choice of color, flavor, and season of maturity. To make maximum use of this diversity, the home gardener might plant green, yellow, and red apples, some early, some midseason, some late. Grow some for eating, some for cooking or processing in other ways. Diversity mitigates the risk from frost and disease and gives a longer season of fresh fruit.

Pollination: Most apple varieties are self-fruitful, except for Red Delicious, the Winesaps, Red Gravenstein, Rhode Island Greening, and the newer triploid crosses like Mutsu and Spigold. When planting any of the Stayman group (Stayman, Turley, Arkansas Black Twig, Winesap), a third variety should be planted or the

Apple

Variety	Area of Best Growth	Fruit	Tree
Baldwin	All except southernmost areas and coldest regions	Red over yellow, sweet apple.	Moderately hardy. Somewhat resistant to scab.
Duchess	North; avoid extreme southern areas	Red, good cooking apple. Poor keeper.	Susceptible to cedar rust.
Golden Delicious (many strains and sports)	All except southernmost areas and coldest regions	Yellow, moderately acid eating apple. Good for cooking. Fall apple.	Moderately hardy. Most strains somewhat self-fruitful. Good pollinator. Moderately resistant to scab; susceptible to fireblight, rust. Tends to biennial cropping.
Granny Smith	South to mid-north. A more-or-less subtropical apple with minimal chilling requirements. Grows in North but needs long growing season (170–175 days) to ripen fruit. Northeastern U.S.	Green to yellow apple. Eating or cooking.	Moderately hardy.
Gravenstein	Northern areas, all others except warm regions	Red summer apple; good eating, excellent for cooking. Rather poor keeper.	Only moderately hardy. Sometimes biennial bearing.
Grimes Golden	All except southernmost areas and coldest regions	Old variety again available. Yellow, fall apple. Bears when young. Excellent for cooking and eating.	Somewhat resistant to fireblight; susceptible to collar rot.
Haralson	North; avoid extreme southern areas	Red, fair cooking and eating apple. Good keeper.	Very hardy.
Jonathan (Jonagold, Jonared, Honnee, Jonamac, Double Red, etc.)	All except southernmost areas and coldest regions. In humid areas, powdery mildew a serious problem.	Reddish, high acid. Good eating and cooking. Moderately good keeper.	Moderately hardy. Very susceptible to fireblight, especially on EM III and MM 106 dwarfing rootstock.
Liberty	All except southernmost areas and coldest regions	Red over yellow. Fair quality.	One of the newest scab-immune varieties; resistant to cedar rust and powdery mildew.
Lodi	All but Deep South	Early summer apple. Green to yellow. Fair for cooking, poor eating. Supposed to be improvement of Yellow Transparent but is not, except in yield.	Hardy. Similar to Yellow Transparent, though fruit is larger.
McIntosh (Cortland, Macoun, Spartan, Empire, Jersey Mac, etc.)	Northern areas; all other areas except warm regions	Red, moderately acid. Good eating or cooking. Does not keep well. Early fall apple.	Very hardy. Very susceptible to scab.

Variety	Area of Best Growth	Fruit	Tree
Mutsu, called Crispin in England	All except southernmost areas and coldest regions	Yellow (a Golden Delicious cross). Excellent dessert and processing apple.	Moderately hardy.
Northern Spy	All except southernmost areas and coldest regions	Reddish, tart apple. Good cooking, good eating.	Self-sterile. Very hardy. Blooms late, avoiding frost. 7–12 years before begins to bear.
Paulared	All central to northern areas	Red, late-summer apple. Good processing apple.	Moderately hardy. Scab-susceptible.
Prima	All except southernmost areas and coldest regions	Red over yellow; fair eating and cooking. Fruit may hang until overripe.	Scab-resistant.
Priscilla	All except southernmost areas and coldest regions	Red over yellow. Fair dessert quality.	Very resistant to most strains of scab; susceptible to mildew.
Red Delicious (many strains and sports)	All except southernmost areas and coldest regions	Red, subacid, eating apple. Moderately good keeper. A fall apple.	Moderately hardy. Self-sterile. Fairly resistant to mildew, rust, fireblight, sooty blotch, and fly speck; susceptible to rust.
Rhode Island Greening	All except southernmost areas and coldest regions	Green-yellow apple. Excellent cooking apple. Late midseason.	Moderately hardy. Bears biennially. Poor pollinator.
Rome, Rome Beauty (many strains)	All except southernmost areas and coldest regions	Red, tart apple. Good for cooking; some good for eating. Keeps well. Late fall.	Moderately hardy. Susceptible to scab and powdery mildew.
Sir Prize	All except southernmost areas and coldest regions	Yellow, fall apple. Good dessert quality.	Scab-immune; resistant to rust, mildew, and fireblight.
Wealthy	North and central areas	Red-striped; good cooking apple, fair eating.	Very hardy, bears when young. Susceptible to fireblight.
Winesap (Stayman, and others)	All except southernmost areas and coldest regions	Red, medium-acid apple. Excellent for cooking or eating. Excellent keeper. Late fall apple.	Hardy. Somewhat self-sterile. Susceptible to scab.
Yellow Newtown (Newtown Pippin)	All central to northern areas	Green with red blush. Excellent keeper. Excellent for all uses.	Very hardy.
Yellow Transparent	All but Deep South	Yellow, high-acid cooking apple. Very early summer apple. Does not keep.	Very hardy. Moderately resistant to diseases.
York, York Imperial	All except southernmost areas and coldest regions	Red over yellow. Moderate acidity. Good keeper. Late fall.	Moderately hardy. Susceptible to cedar rust. Somewhat scab-resistant.

pollinator for the Stayman will not set fruit. The others listed all require at least two varieties for cross-fertilization. One of the best pollination choices is Golden Delicious, which is somewhat self-fruitful and pollinates almost every other variety. Winter Banana is another good pollinator, especially of Red Delicious. Even self-fruitful trees will profit from being planted with a companion tree.

Soil Requirements: Any good garden soil is suitable for apple trees. They tolerate a wide range of soil types, from sandy to clay, as long as the ground is well drained. A pH of 6 to 7 is best. A sloping site is better than a level one because the slope allows cold air to move or drain downward past the trees, and not pocket around them, possibly freezing the developing blossoms.

Ordering Stock: Apples are available in standard and dwarf sizes. The most popular dwarfing rootstocks for apples are the Malling or Malling–Merton Series from the East Malling Research Station in Kent, England. See the box on the Malling Stocks in chapter 6 for information on these rootstocks.

Root weakness is always a part of the dwarfing process. Some roots are weak and do not anchor a tree well, or the roots may sucker excessively. Trees on some dwarfing rootstocks (EM XXVI or EM VII) need to be staked in their early years, and EM IX trees always require staking or trellising. Dwarf trees tend to grow more upright than standards and therefore often need more training to spread the branches.

Propagation: Most backyard growers buy grafted trees to set out. Dwarf varieties begin to bear in one to three years. Standard varieties begin to bear in five to ten years.

Grafting your own apples is comparatively easy. Graft in spring just as the tree is beginning to leaf out. The scion to be grafted on, however, must be dormant for good results. Cut scion wood during the dormant season and store in a plastic bag in a cold place so it will not dry out. The simple splice graft or tongue and groove splice are the two easiest for apples. Use freezer tape to bind and seal the graft. Cleft grafting also works well for apples.

Planting and Culture: Trees can be planted in spring or fall, during dormancy. Growers in regions of colder winters usually plant in the spring. Growers farther south plant in the fall.

The planting hole should be large enough to accommodate the roots when they are spread out. Depth of planting depends to some extent on the rootstock. Most trees on dwarf rootstocks (MM 106, EM XXVI, EM IX, EM VII) are budded high to allow planting much deeper than they grew in the nursery. This encourages more rooting (better anchorage) while maintaining the dwarfing characteristics.

Do not put soluble fertilizers, even of an organic nature, in the planting hole because they could burn the roots. Cover the roots with the topsoil from the site and compost, and put the subsoil dug from the hole on top. Mulch around the tree with 2 to 4 inches of organic material, but don't pile it against the tree. Water well, to settle the soil around the tree roots. Mulch in a normal year will hold in enough moisture after that initial watering to keep the tree growing between rains, but if dry weather occurs, keep watering through the mulch. Once a week, give the tree a good soaking. Don't dribble a little on every day because this will encourage root development in the upper soil layer. In winter, pull the mulch away from the immediate area of the trunk and wrap a hardware cloth mouse guard around the tree to discourage mice from hiding under the mulch.

On any soil other than old orchard sites or those with a light, sandy structure potassium deficiency should be no problem. Keep potash and nitrogen in balance in the apple tree's soil. If excess nitrogen is available, the tree will become too lush in its growth, more prone to fireblight attack, and fail to "harden" before subfreezing temperatures begin. To make sure that potash and nitrogen are present in about the right amounts, mulch in summer with barn manure into or over which you sprinkle 8 to 10 cups of unleached wood ashes per year. Don't overdo it, or the pH will rise. In midsummer, add to the mulch several inches of clover clippings from the lawn, or some other legume. An apple tree's phosphorus requirements are much smaller. An annual application of 3 cups of bone meal per tree, which will become available for plant food only slowly, is adequate.

Pruning: No hard and fast pruning rules apply to apples beyond the general instructions in chapter 10. An apple tree's growth habit depends on its variety, the rootstock to which it is grafted, and sometimes to the peculiarities of the individual tree. A tree may be pruned to a central leader, modified leader, open-center, or urn shape. Most apples are trained to the central leader shape.

When planting the tree (usually a whip with a few scraggly side branches), cut it back by about half, or even more severely if the roots are not full and vigorous. In the second and third years, choose four to six strong side branches with wide crotch angles, the branches evenly spaced around the trunk and from each other, and prune out the others. Any side branches that threaten to outgrow the leader should be removed when the scaffold branches are selected. Remove all shoots competing with the leader. You can prune apples at any time, but beginners should stick with the late dormant season, a few weeks before the buds break.

Pests and Diseases: Most common insect pests are various aphids, apple fruitworm, apple maggot, codling moth, European apple sawfly, European red mites and other mites, flatheaded borer, leafrollers, plum curculio, roundheaded borer, and white apple leafhop-per. Most common apple diseases are bitter pit, black rot, cedar-apple rust, fireblight, fly speck, powdery mildew, scab, and sooty blotch.

Winter Protection: Only minimal winter protection is necessary for hardy apple trees. Young tree trunks should be wrapped to discourage mice and rabbits. To prevent sunscald, paint the trunks with a cheap exterior white latex paint. Keep deep snow trampled down around trees or shoveled back.

Harvest and Storage: Experience is the best teacher in learning when to pick an apple at its peak of quality. For storage, apples are usually picked before they are dead ripe. Many apples like Macoun taste better when not fully ripe. In general, an apple that will come from the tree with a slight upward lift and twist, the thumb of the picking hand flicking loose the stem at the same time, is ripe enough. If it won't come off then, it is most likely still too green, and if you force the apple off, it may tear loose a bit of branchlet containing next year's fruit buds.

Another indication of an apple nearing ripeness is the darkening of its seeds. This is a useful test when the variety and harvest date are not known.

Apples (depending on variety; see chart) will store in any cool place where humidity is high enough to keep them from shriveling later in the winter. A deep underground cellar with a spring in it is ideal. A barrel buried in the ground works well. In cellars where apples tend to shrivel, keep a bucket or two of water in the apple storage chamber.

Uses: Apples can be easily sliced and dried. They make excellent juice and fermented brews, butters, sauces, leathers, and, of course, pie.

APRICOT

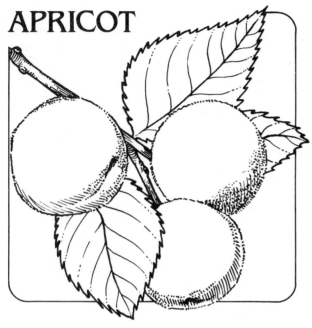

Prunus spp.
Rosaceae

A nutritional bonanza, fresh and dried apricots contain large quantities of vitamin A, vitamin C, iron, traces of B vitamins, and minerals. Apricots ripen in early June to early August.

Give very careful consideration to the apricot's site. Though its blossoms are no less hardy than those of other stone fruits, they are the first to bloom in the spring and are very subject to frost damage. In climates prone to spring warming trends followed by freezes, plant apricots in an area that warms slowly in order to retard bloom as long as possible. A north hillside is ideal if it's not subjected to frigid, drying winds all winter, which could kill buds. It's not uncommon for even a well-tended apricot to freeze out two years out of three, but the reward in that third year is worth the wait. In addition, the tree itself is attractive and eventually grows into a fine shade tree.

Apricots tend to be quite deep-rooted (up to 16 feet) so areas with a heavy hardpan should be avoided. Russian types are somewhat more bud-hardy than peaches or nectarines. Winter

chilling requirements are similar to those of peaches, so barring problems with spring frosts apricots will thrive in peach regions. See Peach for additional site selection guidelines.

Pollination: Most varieties are self-fruitful, except Riland and Perfection, but will not set full crops in single-tree plantings.

Propagation: Available rootstocks include American plum, apricot, myrobalan plum, and several peaches. On its own root or grafted to a selected apricot rootstock, the tree will do best on sandy soils and have a high degree of nematode resistance. Trees grafted to myrobalan plum, since it will tolerate more poorly drained soils than other rootstocks, will remain healthy on heavier, clayey soils, though bacterial canker may be more troublesome. The graft-union is occasionally weak with this combination and can break under heavy crops and/or high winds. On peach rootstock, the fruit will ripen a few days earlier than on other roots, but some tree vigor will be sacrificed.

A 3- to 5-foot seedling, ½ inch in diameter a few inches above the graft, is ideal planting size and should have no dead shoots or other areas of damaged bark.

Planting and Culture: Apricots should be treated exactly as peaches at planting time although, since they will be larger trees, apricots should be spaced 30 feet apart.

Fertilize an apricot tree like a peach, but be aware that an apricot's nitrogen needs are barely half as much. Overfertilization with nitrogen causes fruit to drop while still green, as well as causing a condition known as pit burn in which the flesh around the pit turns brown and soft. A dusting of lime, wood ashes, phosphate rock or other mineral dust and an inch or two of barnyard manure spread under the drip-line each winter will supply needed nutrients.

Thin varieties that overset badly, leaving one fruit every 3 to 4 inches. This system will yield the best crop and not overtax the tree's capacity, which could reduce hardiness for the following winter.

Lack of water will cause small, mealy apricots that are best suited for the compost heap. If the weeds near the tree wilt shortly after sunrise the soil may be reaching dry levels and will need watering two or three times weekly at a rate of 25 gallons each time until rains return. A prolonged drought can delay hardening of the wood in the fall, leaving the tree more susceptible to winter injury. Mulching heavily will help conserve moisture and hold back weeds.

Pruning: Follow the guidelines listed for Peach if the variety is a spreading type and to be trained to the open-center shape.

For more upright-growing varieties (and in light of the apricot's tendency to form heavier limbs than the peach), use the modified central leader form. To achieve this, follow the instructions for open-center training in chapter 10, but don't remove the leader. Allow it to remain dominant, and do not head it. Remove any vertical shoot competing with it. Heading the leader several feet above the main scaffolds in the third year after planting will encourage growth of secondary scaffolds. Prune lightly or fruiting will be delayed several years and the yield will be reduced.

On the main and secondary scaffolds, the fruit will be borne on short one-year spurs and the tips of last year's growth. They need plenty of sunlight to grow and remain healthy. After three or four years these spurs and branches will stop producing fruit, making it necessary to train new shoots to develop into fruiting limbs. If the center of the tree receives inadequate sunlight, the new spurs will be weak or nonfruiting. It is important therefore, once bearing begins, to prevent the foliage from be-

Apricot

Variety	Fruit	Tree
Blenheim	Large, excellent for cooking and drying. Midseason.	Vigorous, productive, upright growth.
Early Golden	Very large, golden yellow. Excellent quality.	Medium vigor, very seldom loses a crop.
Goldcot	Medium, orange freestone. Good for canning, drying, or fresh use. Late.	Vigorous, strong, tends to overset so thinning is a must if large fruit desired. Some bacterial spot tolerance.
Harcot	Medium-sized. Sweet, fine-grained, oblong. Good dessert quality. Very early.	Productive, vigorous, very cold-hardy; thinning required. Some bacterial spot resistance.
Moorpark	One of the best for eating fresh. Excellent flavor, soft yellow freestone. Very large.	Healthy, but may bear erratically.
Perfection	Very large, oval, orange-yellow, good quality. The favored variety in Washington State.	Very hardy, productive. Requires a pollinating variety.
Riland	Large, fleshy, flavorful. Excellent fresh. May crack. Early.	Vigorous, needs a pollinator. Will pollinate other varieties.
Stella (Russian type)	Medium, gold-yellow, freestone. Sweet. Midseason.	Very cold-tolerant, does well in most peach areas.
Tilton	Large, freestone. Superb canned or dried. Some strains produce 2½-in. fruit. Midseason.	Vigorous, hardy, productive.
Veecot	Medium-large, round freestone; deep orange. Cans well. Early.	Productive and hardy.
Wilson Delicious	Large, pinkish orange freestone. Excellent dessert quality, very sweet.	Strong, vigorous, very long-lived.

coming too dense by thinning out old wood. Decreased fruiting in the inside of the tree indicates that pruning has not been vigorous enough to allow sufficient sunlight to penetrate. On the other hand, too-vigorous pruning severely reduces the crop. Gauge your pruning by the health of the buds in the tree's center.

A mature tree may yield 200 pounds of fruit. Major varieties tend to bear only every second or third year. Thinning and careful pruning may reduce this tendency, but there will still be noticeable differences in the size of the crop from one year to another.

Pests and Diseases: See Peach.

Harvest and Storage: When apricots are fully ripe they will drop from the tree. If you can't wait that long at least allow them to turn from green to orange—the first sign of ripening—and let the flesh soften to light thumb pressure. At this firm-ripe stage, fruit will keep a week or so in the refrigerator in a moisture-tight container. Fruit can complete ripening at room temperature, but will not attain tree-ripened sweetness.

For canning or drying pick a few days past firm ripe to catch the highest sugar level. To dry apricots, split them in half, remove the pits (freestones are highly recommended) and lay the halves on racks cut side up for several days in full sun. When the cut dries they can be placed in a dryer or left outdoors to finish their dehydration. Outdoor drying is not practical in humid areas, where you'll usually wind up with trays of orange, rotted yellow-jacket food. Fruit leather made from dried apricots will store indefinitely.

AVOCADO

Alligator pear, avocado pear
Persea americana
Lauraceae

Avocado trees are divided into three horticultural races, based on differences in their climatic needs and variations in the fruit. The West Indian race is native to the moist lowlands and seacoasts of tropical America. The Guatemalan race comes from the highlands of southern Mexico and Guatemala and the Mexican race comes from central and northern Mexico.

Cultivars of the Mexican race are the most cold-hardy, sustaining temperatures of 18° to 23°F with little damage. Mexican cultivars are the most appropriate for north and north-central Florida. Fruits are the smallest and most thin-skinned of the three races, and purple-black or green in color. The leaves and twigs of the Mexican race have a strong anise odor. Fruits ripen five to eight months after blossoming in spring and weigh from 6 to 8 ounces. These fruits bear little resemblance to supermarket avocados, since their thin skin renders them prone to cracking and makes them unshippable.

Fruits of the Guatemalan race weigh 1 to 5 pounds and have thicker, tougher skin. The green or purple fruits ripen in winter and spring, 14 to 17 months after blossoming. They will tolerate temperatures between 24° and 29°F. Varieties of this race grow mainly in California.

The West Indian race is similar to the Guatemalan, but the fruit is lower in oil content and ripens six to nine months after blossoming. It is the most tender race, unable to withstand temperatures below 28°F. The fruits mature in summer and fall, range in size from medium to very large, and have thin, smooth skin that is green to purple in color. This race is planted mostly in southern Florida.

The avocado is evergreen but it sometimes behaves like a deciduous tree, losing all its leaves and beginning anew with fresh growth. A beautiful shade tree, it is usually held to 30 feet under cultivation, but can grow as tall as 60 feet.

The avocado is richer in fat than any other fruit except the olive, containing as much as 20 to 30% fat, of which 93% is unsaturated.

Pollination: In 1927, Dr. A. B. Stout, Director of Laboratories at the New York Botanical Garden, reported his discovery of an unusual characteristic of avocado flowers. He found that while plants produce flowers with both stamens and pistils, these would only function in alternating stages. For example, in one type of plant (now known as A type), all the flowers opened in the morning but only their stigmas were receptive—the flowers were functioning as females. Then, the following day in the afternoon, the flowers would again open, but only to expose pistils and release pollen.

In the other type of plant (B type), flowers which opened in the morning shed their pollen; these same flowers then opened the next day in the afternoon, with receptive stigmas only. As cross-pollination seemed the best way to promote maximum fruit set, Dr. Stout recommended interplanting A-type and B-type trees. Different varieties are classified as A or B

types, and are mixed in commercial cultivation for optimum yields. Plants can be self-pollinated successfully but they will not produce maximum yields.

Soil Requirements: Avocado trees like soil with plenty of humus to retain the large quantity of moisture they require. All three races will grow well in a pH range from 4 to 10. Good drainage is very important, because "wet feet" can easily lead to root rot. Although the trees will grow in a wide range of soil types, lime deposits will reduce growth.

Ordering Stock: There are many varieties and hybrids of the three races to choose among. Be sure when buying a tree that it is appropriate to the area where it will grow, and that it has been budded to a seedling grown from a disease-free seed.

Propagation: The best methods of propagating are side and veneer grafting, and chip and shield budding. Gardeners in the western United States should use Mexican rootstocks, preferably from a single parent variety. In Florida, use seedlings of West Indian and Guatemalan varieties. Avoid using seed from fruit that has lain on the ground and may be infected with a fungal disease.

A mature tree can be top-worked using a bark graft as described in chapter 10. Cover scions thoroughly with grafting wax and a paper bag to protect against heat and drying out.

Planting and Culture: Choose a site in full sun. Plant young trees out once danger of frost is past. When planting container-grown or field-grown stock, dig a hole only as deep as the rootball and about 6 to 8 inches wider. The top of the ball should be level with the soil surface. Fill the sides with topsoil and tamp it down firmly. Water immediately after planting, then as often as necessary to supply moisture to the roots. Though tolerant of brief dry spells, avocados require water year-round, and should not be allowed to dry out in winter.

Mature trees may require some supplemental nitrogen a year, but other elements are not usually necessary. Trees less than a year

Avocado

Variety	Area of Best Growth	Race	Fruit	Hardiness
Bacon	California	Mexican	Smooth, ovoid, dark green; produces few fruits per year.	Tolerates temps. 2°–3°F lower than Zutano.
Brogden	North and north-central Florida	Mexican	Purple; excellent quality; rarely cracks.	Withstands 24°–26°F.
Fuerte	California, Florida	Mexican × Guatemalan	Leading commercial variety; nearly smooth; medium-sized. Ripens from Nov. to May. Medium to high oil content.	
Hass	Southern California	Guatemalan	Purple-black, medium-sized, excellent flavor.	Hardy to 29°F.
Mexicola	Florida, California	Mexican	Purple; high quality.	Withstands 18°–20°F with little injury.
Puebla	California	Mexican × Guatemalan	Smooth, purple, high oil content; good quality.	Hardy to frost.
Winter Mexican	North and north-central Florida	Hybrid of Guatemalan × Mexican cross	Fruit 12–16 oz. each; very little cracking; high quality.	Withstands 24°–26°F.
Zutano	California	Mexican	Light green, smooth, pear-shaped. Ripens early Oct.; good quality.	Cannot withstand 25°F or below.

old do not require nitrogen, and young trees may suffer leaf "burn" or defoliation and die back if too much nitrogen is applied.

Container Culture: With luck, the avocado will bear fruit in a greenhouse. Summer temperatures should be 75° to 85°F, and the atmosphere made humid from abundant waterings. Winter temperatures should be 55° to 65°F with moderate waterings.

Propagate container trees by seeds, grafting, or budding. Seed will germinate best if the seed coats are removed. Wet the seed, dry, then cut thin sections from the apex and the base of the seed. Plant the seed with the broad end down and cover it with not more than an inch of soil. A good growing medium is equal parts of loam, peat moss, and sand. Pinch the plant to keep it bushy.

Pruning: Little pruning is necessary since new growth tends to come from the ends of the branches rather than from lateral buds. In young trees, all the leaves are necessary to shade the trunk and branches from sunburn. (Painting the trunk with white latex paint or wrapping with burlap also helps to prevent sunburn.) Do not prune away frost damage until midsummer in order to make certain which branches have put forth no new growth.

Pests and Diseases: Root rot is a serious and widespread disease; sun-blotch and verticillium wilt are less prevalent. Pest problems are minimal and include greenhouse thrips, mites, and scales.

Winter Protection: Mound up the soil around West Indian and Guatemalan rootstocks, particularly, to prevent freezing. Young trees of every race require frost protection during the first two winters after planting, however. Wrap the tree trunks in burlap or fiberglass. Mulch with coarse sand or chipped bark inside a 6- to 8-inch diameter ring around the trunk. Even if branches are killed by frost, sucker growth will appear from a main stem that has been protected.

Harvest and Storage: Clip or cut the fruit from the tree; pulling them off leaves a wound where rot might start. It is difficult to tell when to harvest because avocados do not soften until they are picked. Colored varieties are ready to pick when their color change is complete, but in the case of varieties that remain green the decision is less certain. Fruit that ripens within five to seven days after picking is of the best quality. It will keep for several weeks when stored where the temperature is above 42°F.

Uses: In Florida and southern California, avocados make handsome backyard trees, useful for both shade and fruit. The fruit is widely enjoyed in this country for its buttery consistency and rich, nutty flavor. It is eaten raw in salads, dips, and sandwiches.

BANANA AND PLANTAIN

Musa acuminata
Musaceae

The banana and plantain are closely related ancient fruits native to tropical Asia.

They grow from 5 to 25 feet tall. Despite their size they are botanically classified as herbs because they lack woody tissue in the stem. They consist of a basal corm that supports a pseudostem composed of upright concentric layers of leaf sheaths. The plants have huge leaves.

Plantains, otherwise known as "cooking bananas," are slightly richer in vitamins and blander in taste than bananas. They have greenish or reddish skins.

A banana stem produces only one fruit branch. After fruiting, it should be cut back to the underground rhizome until the next season when new suckers rise and produce a flower bud 6 to 8 months after their emergence from the soil. The time from planting to maturity can take from 12 months to three years, depending on the propagule used.

Soil Requirements: Plants will grow in any moist, fertile soil except sand or limestone, with a pH range from 5.5 to 6.5. Liming an acid soil to raise pH to 6 will increase yields. The soil should be deep and well aerated since bananas are very vulnerable to damage from flooding on soil with inadequate drainage.

Planting and Culture: Plant either large, healthy suckers or, less preferably, 7- to 10-pound pieces of the corm containing one or more buds, in March, April, or May in southern Florida if irrigation is available. Otherwise, wait for the start of June rains.

Site plants away from ocean spray or persistent winds that can easily shred leaves and impair growth. Make planting holes 3 feet wide by 2 feet deep and fill with compost or a sand/peat mixture. It is essential to mulch the soil surface around the suckers immediately after planting in order to conserve moisture and keep down weeds. Maintain the mulch at all times. Rotted manure and compost are the recommended materials to use.

Bananas and plantains are hungry feeders and need to be kept well supplied with potash and nitrogen. The soil for young plants should be especially fertile, and very rich in potash. The ultimate yield is contingent on the care

Banana and Plantain

Variety	Area of Best Growth	Fruit	Plant
Dwarf Cavendish (Dwarf Chinese)	Hawaii, South Florida	Fruit 6–8 in. long, 4–5 oz. apiece. Similar to Gros Michel.	Variety best suited to subtropics and container culture. Hardy and wind-resistant. 5–6 ft. tall.
Gros Michel or Bluefields	Hawaii	Common commercial banana.	25 ft. tall. Tender.
Lady Finger	Hawaii, South Florida	Fruit 4–6 in. long, 2 oz. apiece.	20 ft. tall. Fairly tender.
Red (Red Fig, Red Cuban)	Hawaii	Small branches of fat, colored fruits; mediocre flavor.	Tender.
Horse Plantain	Hawaii, South Florida		Tolerant to drought. Requires little attention. Use for cooking.

given the plant in its first four months.

Plant Dwarf Cavendish 8 to 10 feet apart, and other varieties 15 to 20 feet apart. After the plants are established they need relatively little attention although irrigation is necessary during dry months.

M. acuminata 'Dwarf Cavendish', the Cavendish or Canary banana, is a dwarf banana that will grow in a large greenhouse. The plant may grow as tall as 8 feet. It needs a minimum temperature of 65°F, and a pot 2 feet or more in diameter. Full sunshine, ample water, and warm temperatures with fresh air on hot days are essential.

When there is steady growth, prune frequently to remove surplus suckers and prevent crowding.

Harvest the bananas while still green and ripen them in a warm room. When fruiting is over and trunk dies off, cut it out. Another should already be growing in its place.

Pruning: Too many stalks lead to competition for water, light, and nutrients, with subsequent low-quality fruit. To ensure ample space between plants: leave only a single stem, cutting the less vigorous suckers off at ground level. Gouge out as much as possible of the remains, and continue to prune as additional suckers arise.

With young plants, remove all but one sucker. Let it bear and die back. Then allow three to five suckers to grow at one time from the stool, cutting out all others as soon as they appear, and allowing new ones to develop only every three months. By selecting and pruning suckers carefully, cultivation should be continuous for four to six years. After that, new stock can be planted.

Pests and Diseases: Pests include nematodes and the banana weevil. Neither pests nor diseases constitute a real problem in subtropical areas.

Harvest and Storage: Fruit is ready to cut when it is about four months old. Harvest when the fingers are plump but not yet yellow. Bunches of bananas and plantains are never allowed to ripen on the stalk, but are removed one to two weeks before ripening, then hung in a cool, shady spot to develop their flavor.

In commercial harvesting, the bunch is cut down with a knife in such a way that it settles right on the shoulder of the worker who will carry it away. Once the bunch is cut down, cut off the stalk, chop it into small pieces, and leave the pieces on the ground to incorporate into the mulch. You can hasten ripening by covering the bunch with a polyethylene bag.

Bananas, more than plantains, are highly

perishable once they ripen. When very ripe, peel and freeze them in chunks spread out on cookie sheets, then store them frozen in plastic bags, and use in cooking.

Varieties: There are many varieties grown in the tropics. Gros Michel is the variety most widely eaten in the United States, but it is imported because it is too tender to grow in any part of the country except for Hawaii, where it grows easily. Because of its susceptibility to Panama disease, caused by a soilborne fungus not prevalent in Florida, but widespread in the tropics, it is now being replaced by clones of the Cavendish group. Of these clones, Dwarf Cavendish is best adapted to the cooler climate of the subtropics and to greenhouse culture farther north (see chart).

BLACKBERRY

Boysenberry, dewberry, loganberry, youngberry
Rubus spp.
Rosaceae

There are two main types of blackberry, the erect and the trailing. The erect type has canes which may reach 5 feet in height, are four-sided, and can stand without support. The trail-

ing type has canes which may reach 15 feet in length and which trail over the ground unless supported. It is grown mainly on the West Coast and, except for the dewberry, which grows in the Southeast and as far north as Pennsylvania, it is less hardy than the erect type.

The blackberry is a bramble fruit, and produces new canes by suckering freely from its roots. The flowers are white. Without bees, which help pollination, the crop may be half or less of the normal quantity. The fruit, a drupe, ranges in size from ½ inch on small wild plants to 1¼ inch on the boysenberry, grown in California. The drupelets and the green core to which they are attached come away together when the berry is picked, and the eating quality of the berry partly depends on the core being small, soft, and insipid.

Soil Requirements: Blackberries grow well on most soils, except those that are poorly drained or acid, and the southern blackberry, or dewberry, will grow on dry, rocky soil not tolerated by other blackberry varieties.

Propagation: Blackberries are easily propagated from root cuttings, which can be as short as 3 inches. Plant the segments of roots in potting medium and keep moist until they send up canes. The tips of dewberry canes, if allowed to touch ground, will strike root and can then be pruned free of the mother plant.

Planting and Culture: Nursery plants are started from root cuttings and sold at one year of age. They should be planted in the spring 1 to 3 feet apart in the row. Within two years the row will fill in as the roots spread and send up new canes. Whether the plants are trained in a row or in hills, the canes which come up where they are not wanted must be rogued, that is, pruned away underground. Roguing is also used to keep the canes from growing too thickly together, which invites disease. A mulch can increase the yield of the blackberry by three to five times.

Pruning: In spring and early summer, blackberries send up suckers from the roots, which grow into canes and then go dormant during the winter. The next season they bear fruit and die. Blackberry pruning extends over both seasons. When the first-year cane of erect varieties reaches 3 to 5 feet in height, it should be topped—prune back the tip 3 to 4 inches. Topping stimulates the cane to branch, and the more branches, the more fruit will be produced next season. The next season, as soon as the cane bears fruit, prune it at ground level, remove and destroy it to prevent disease.

Trailing blackberries are usually allowed to run along the ground the first season. The canes, which can reach 15 feet in length, should be pruned to 10 feet in late winter, and then arranged on a 1- or 2-wire trellis in loops and curves to expose as many leaves to the sun as possible. As with the erect types, canes which have borne fruit must be pruned off at the ground and destroyed immediately after harvest. The dewberry is sometimes pruned off completely after harvest—first- and second-year canes alike—because the long season in the South affords enough time for regrowth, and the plants seem less subject to disease when forced in this way to start fresh in late summer. **Pests and Diseases:** Red spider mites can reach damaging numbers in hot, dry weather. A forceful spray of water under the leaves will

Blackberry

Variety	Growing Area	Fruit	Bush
Boysen (Boysenberry)	Milder regions of the West Coast	Large berries with a purplish black cast. Excellent flavor. Large seeds.	Western trailing type. Vigorous, excellent yielder.
Brainerd	Milder regions of the West Coast	Large, black, firm berries.	Western trailing type. Very vigorous, productive. Needs support. Drought-resistant, semihardy.
Cascade	Pacific coastal areas	Dark red berries. Soft, early.	Western trailing type.
Darrow	Northern regions, northeastern U.S.	Glossy black, firm berries. Excellent quality.	Erect, heavy producer over a long period. Very hardy, vigorous.
Evergreen	Milder regions of the West Coast	Large, firm, sweet berries. Good quality. Large seeds, late.	Trailing, vigorous, semihardy. Drought-resistant, productive.
Logan (Loganberry)	Milder regions of the West Coast	Long, reddish purple berries. Highly flavored. More tart than Young. Late.	Western trailing type. Vigorous, not hardy in eastern U.S.
Lucretia	Eastern U.S.	Large, long, firm berries. Good quality.	Trailing, vigorous, productive.
Marion	Milder regions of the West Coast	Large black berries. Early, good quality.	Western trailing type. Vigorous. Few canes make it easy to train.
Mayes	Eastern U.S.	Large berries. Good quality.	Trailing, vigorous, productive.
McDonald	Northern regions, northeastern U.S.	Large, firm berries. Very good quality. Early.	Erect. Vigorous, drought-resistant, very productive.
Thornless	Georgia, Florida and the Gulf states	Very large, purplish maroon berries. Nearly seedless.	Thornless. Not as hardy as the erect types. Semierect.
Young (Youngberry)	Milder regions of the West Coast	Large berries, excellent flavor. Outstanding for freezing, jams. Excellent dessert quality.	Western trailing type. Vigorous, easy to pick.

dislodge many of them. The several kinds of borer that attack the blackberry can be kept in check by removing canes that wilt or topple over near their tips.

Blackberries are subject to several virus diseases. When symptoms appear, such as stunted new canes, or withered yellow stunted leaves on second-year canes, the diseased plant must be uprooted and destroyed, or aphids will carry the virus to the other plants. Buy stock that is certified virus-free.

Avoid planting blackberries in plots that were used to grow eggplants, peppers, potatoes, and tomatoes within the previous four years.

These plants carry verticillium wilt. If the leaves on a blackberry wilt, starting from the ground up, the cause is usually verticillium, and the plant must be uprooted and destroyed.

Orange rust is the chief blackberry disease. It causes orange blisters on the undersides of leaves. Infected plants must be uprooted and destroyed. The best prevention for this and other blackberry diseases is to keep the canes from growing too thickly together.

Storage: Fresh blackberries keep only a short time under refrigeration, but they may be frozen for long-term storage. The frozen berries, however, lose much of their quality.

BLUEBERRY

Vaccinium spp.
Ericaceae

Although now a familiar fruit, the blueberry was first brought from the wild and domesticated only in this century. In spite of the late start, it is now grown widely and its cultivation is spreading rapidly into new areas, mainly because the two most important species, the highbush (*V. corymbosum, V. australe*) and the rabbiteye (*V. ashei*), have different natural ranges and soil requirements that, between

them, cover a large part of the U.S. Both are vigorous and productive plants, and many fine varieties are available, with new varieties ap-

Blueberry

Variety	Fruit	Bush
Highbush		
Angola	Early. Large berries, somewhat soft.	Canker-resistant. Very sensitive to soil and water variations.
Berkeley	Midseason. Very large, light blue color, sweet.	Medium hardy. Open, spreading habit, very productive.
Bluecrop	Midseason. Large clusters, very light blue, firm, somewhat tart. Excellent shipper and keeper.	Medium hardy. Upright bush, vigorous.
Blueray	Midseason. Large berries, light blue color, firm, sweet.	Medium hardy. Upright spreading, very productive.
Collins	Midseason. Large berries, light blue color, firm, sweet.	Medium hardy.
Covill	Midseason. Large berries, blue color, tart until fully ripe, good quality.	Medium hardy. Inconsistent.
Croatan	Midseason. Medium berries, medium firm. Ripens quickly in warm weather.	Canker-resistant. Erect, grows best on light soil.
Darrow	Late. Large, light blue color, firm. Tart to mildly tart flavor.	Erect, vigorous.
Earliblue	Early. Medium fruit, light blue color, firm, loose cluster.	Hardy, upright growth habit, well shaped, vigorous.
Herbert	Midseason. Large berries, excellent flavor.	Dwarfish bush, good grower, consistent.
Ivanhoe	Midseason. Large, firm berries.	Open and spreading bush. Vigorous, productive. Subject to canker.
Jersey	Late. Very large berries, light color.	Spreading bush. Vigorous. Somewhat canker-resistant.
Morrow	Early. Large berries borne on upright clusters.	Canker-resistant. Medium-sized, semierect and broad. Grows slowly after fruiting age.
Murphy	Late. Large berries, fairly good quality.	Canker-resistant. Bush medium to low, spreading.
Scammell	Late. Small, dark, firm berries. Good dessert quality.	Somewhat canker-resistant. Erect bush.
Wolcott	Early. Large, well-shaped berries, medium color.	Semiupright.
Rabbiteye		
Bluegem	Early. Remains on bush for a long time while remaining firm.	Moderately spreading. Makes limited number of suckers.
Brightblue	Large berries, light blue color, firm. Excellent shipper.	Moderately spreading, vigorous.
Delite	Medium-large, round berries, firm.	Upright canes.
Homebell	Large, light blue berries. Good flavor.	Upright.
Menditoo	Late midseason. Large round berries, dark blue color, medium firm, sweet.	Spreading habit, medium vigor.
Southland	Firm berries, light blue color. Skin becomes tough late in the season.	Vigorous with dense foliage.
Tifblue	Late midseason. Large round berries, light blue color, firm, sweet.	Vigorous. Excellent in South due to high resistance to heat and drought.
Woodard	Early. Large berries, light blue color, medium firm, sweet.	Medium-sized. Produces many suckers.

pearing every year for the rabbiteye, which has been in cultivation for just 40 years.

The highbush, the usual blueberry of the supermarket, grows naturally from Florida to Maine and Michigan, wherever the soil is highly acid and well drained, and commercial growers have extended its range as far as Missouri and Arkansas. The rabbiteye is native to the Southeast and tolerates heat and dry soil better than the highbush. It also grows on less acid soil than the highbush. Though several other species of blueberries are sold, they are all undomesticated and gathered from the wild.

Both the highbush and the rabbiteye are woody deciduous bushes with smooth grayish bark and small, glossy, dark green leaves. The highbush is the smaller, growing to 15 feet in height, while the rabbiteye may reach 30 feet. The highbush needs more winter chilling than the rabbiteye, and though more hardy, will grow only as far north as the peach will.

Pollination: Blueberries have somewhat self-sterile flowers, those of the rabbiteye being more self-sterile than those of the highbush, in general. At least two varieties should be planted together to help cross-pollination.

Soil Requirements: The highbush must have acid soil. It prefers a pH just below 5. The rabbiteye will tolerate a higher pH than the highbush—to 5.5 or more. Both need well-drained soil, but tolerate heavy clay and sandy soil provided they contain a good deal of organic matter. Given good, acid soil, both are relatively pest and disease-free.

Propagation: Blueberries can be propagated from dormant cuttings. Prune 4-inch pieces from the lower end of year-old shoots, in spring before budding. Try to get pieces with no fruit buds—these are round and fat. To root the cuttings, keep them moist and the air around them saturated. Expect to lose many cuttings. Blueberries can also be propagated by mound-layering. Cut back the bush to stubs and cover it with earth. Shoots will appear and take root. When they are well rooted they may be cut free of the parent bush and set out as new plants.

Planting and Culture: Both rabbiteye and highbush are planted in the spring, usually as two-year-old plants. Adding peat moss and leaves, bark or sawdust from oaks will lower pH slowly, and in a year or two make most soil acid enough for blueberries. They also supply good drainage, which blueberries demand. But if the soil pH is 6.5 or above, it can be made acid enough only with a great deal of labor. Give the plants an acid mulch, like oak bark or leaves, and be sure to keep the soil moist. The mulch will be enough food for the plants. Highbush plants should be at least 6 feet apart, and rabbiteye plants 7 to 8 feet. It's a good idea to plant at least two varieties together and make sure they ripen at different times.

Pruning: Pruning begins at planting. The new plants should be cut back by one-fourth and any low, bushy growth near the base of the plant pruned away. After two or three years of growth, regular pruning can begin. On upright bushes, one goal of pruning is to open the center of the bush. On spreading bushes, one goal is to remove the low, shaded branches. But the main goal of pruning is to keep the bush well supplied with young, fruitful branches. Blueberries bear fruit on wood that formed during the previous season, and they bear best on young branches which are sending out vigorous fruitful twigs each season. By the time a branch is six years old it has lost its vigor, grown twiggy, and has few fruit buds. Prune these old canes and see that they are replaced with new growth coming from the roots. For thinning, take twiggy branches off newer canes. If shoots appear late in the summer, prune them.

Pests and Diseases: The blueberries in home plantings have few pests and diseases. If the fruitfly appears, rotenone in several applications between June and harvest will help keep the fruit free of maggots. Other pests are cherry fruitworm (a ¼-inch-long red worm), plum curculio, and cranberry fruitworm, which encloses a cluster of berries with its web. If these pests reach damaging numbers, it will help to remove the mulch and keep the soil cultivated for a season. Give blueberries a dormant oil spray to control scale.

Harvest and Storage: Depending on the region and the variety, the highbush ripens from as early as late May in North Carolina to as late as mid-September in Michigan. The berries change from green to red to blue as they ripen. The berries ripen over several weeks and continue to grow larger after they have turned blue. It is best to pick several times, starting six days after the berries turn blue.

The rabbiteye ripens later than the highbush wherever the two grow together. The season starts as early as May in Florida and extends as late as August in North Carolina. Often berries in the same cluster ripen at different times, and the harvest can extend over several weeks. Begin picking one to two weeks after the first blue color appears.

CAROB

Locust bean, St. John's bread, swine's bread
Ceratonia siliqua
Leguminosae

The evergreen carob grows to 50 feet in height, with a round habit, rather like an apple tree.

The fruits are 1 foot long, flat, leathery brown edible pods which contain seeds and sweet pulp. They ripen in the early fall.

Pollination: Most carob trees are either male (pollen-producing) or female (pod-producing), although some are hermaphroditic. To ensure a good crop, plant both a male and a female tree.

Soil Requirements: Carob trees are not demanding. They thrive in dry, slightly alkaline soil where there is good drainage. The secret of the carob tree's success in stressful areas is its long, central taproot, which penetrates deeply into the subsoil and allows the tree to flourish without surface water or special care.

In the United States, carob will grow best in California and Florida where there is little danger of severe frost. It prefers a low 14 to 23 inches of rainfall yearly, with a rainless autumn. Heavy autumn rains cause molding, fermentation, and worm infestation of the pods.

Nutritionally, carob contains B vitamins, calcium, iron, phosphorus, and magnesium. Unlike chocolate it is free of caffeine, and its flavor is naturally sweet.

Planting: Plant when danger of frost is past. The carob tree will not grow where winter temperatures often fall below 32°F or where summer temperatures exceed 113°F. In areas that are very hot in summer, plant the trees far enough up on slopes to compensate for the high temperatures. A site near the sea, but away from fog or damp ocean breezes, will allow the tree to produce more pods.

To plant, dig a hole about 5 feet deep and wide. Fill the hole with good, lime-rich soil and top-dress with manure. Allow each tree a space of 30 feet in diameter for expansion.

Pests and Diseases: Surround seedlings with poultry netting in the first year to deter rabbits and gophers. The tree's only serious enemies are the noctuid moth, the larvae of which can burrow into the wood and kill the tree within a few years, and wood rots.

Harvest and Storage: Carob will begin to produce in its sixth year. The yield may be 5 pounds in the first year of bearing and up to 100 pounds by the twelfth year. The tree tends toward alternate bearing, and yields will be highest when the soil is relatively dry.

Harvesting takes place in late fall. The best time to collect the pods is ten days after the first dry pods drop from the tree. Choose a dry day to shake down the pods and gather them from the ground. After harvesting, continue to dry them indoors or in the sun, then store them in rodentproof sacks or bins. Pods that are stored while still damp may be attacked by microfungi, some of which can cause mycotoxicosis in humans and animals. Dry pods will keep indefinitely.

Uses: Carob is used as a substitute for cocoa powder and chocolate.

Fine-milled, the flour can be mixed with other grains for baking.

CERIMAN

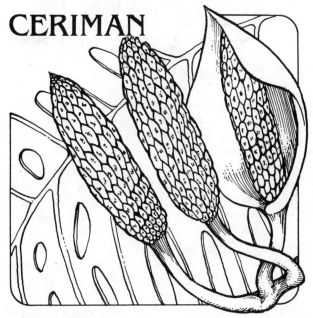

Mexican breadfruit
Monstera deliciosa
Araceae

Ceriman is the fruit of the spectacular evergreen climber, *Monstera deliciosa,* a popular house plant in North America which is native to Mexico and Central America. *Monstera* has a vigorous, vining growth habit, climbing 8 or more feet tall using its aerial roots as support. Its large, glossy leaves are heart-shaped and solid when young; as they mature, they become perforated near the center and deeply cut at the edges.

The flowers look like huge arum lilies on short, thick stalks. They produce the characteristic inflorescence of all Araceae, a fleshy, rodlike spike of flowers called a spadix.

As the fruit matures, it turns from green to yellow and the outer rind of scales drops off. Its shape is similar to a large ear of corn, 8 to 10 inches long and 2 to 3 inches in diameter. The creamy, white pulp inside has a sweet and pleasant flavor that has been likened to a mixture of strawberry, banana, and pineapple. The fruit reaches maturity 14 months after flowering.

Monstera will grow outdoors only in areas that are completely frost-free, but will often bear fruit in greenhouses farther north. Root cuttings in pots of light, loose soil or set them directly in their outdoor location during early summer. The plant benefits from applications of compost, especially when grown indoors.

Ceriman's ripening process begins at the base of the fruit and moves up gradually in an uneven pattern. To encourage even ripening, cut fruit from the stem when partially ripened and place it in the refrigerator for 24 hours, then leave it at room temperature until soft. Eat only ripe portions of the fruit or store them in the refrigerator. Crystals of calcium oxalate are present in the fruit when it is not fully ripe and they can cause a burning irritation in your mouth and throat. If this occurs, rinse your mouth with vinegar to dissolve the crystals.

CHERRY

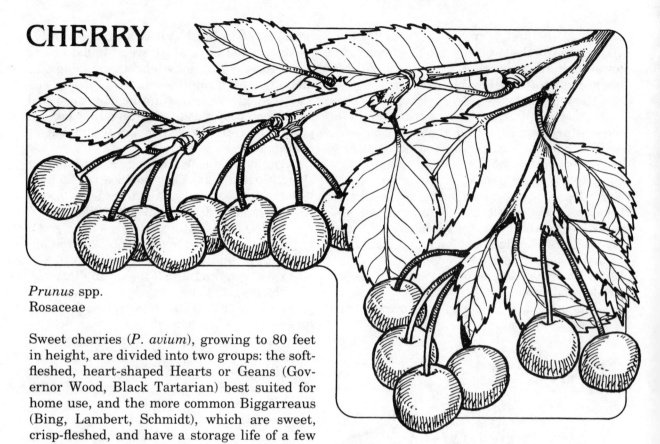

Prunus spp.
Rosaceae

Sweet cherries (*P. avium*), growing to 80 feet in height, are divided into two groups: the soft-fleshed, heart-shaped Hearts or Geans (Governor Wood, Black Tartarian) best suited for home use, and the more common Biggarreaus (Bing, Lambert, Schmidt), which are sweet, crisp-fleshed, and have a storage life of a few weeks.

Sour cherry (*P. cerasus*) trees seldom exceed 35 feet in height and are more bushy and slightly more tolerant of insects and diseases than sweets. Though fewer varieties are available, they also fall into two groups; the red-skinned, yellow-fleshed amarelles (Montmorency) and the more acid, dark-skinned morellos (English Morello) that grow as a large bush rather than a tree.

Duke cherries (*P. effusa*) are the offspring of crossing sours and sweets. They are still a small group and not very productive, but they taste delicious.

Bush types thrive in northern regions where winters are too severe for the major cherries to grow. Their fruit is too tart to eat fresh, but it makes fine preserves. Bush types include: pin cherry (*P. pensylvanica*), chokecherries (*P. virginiana*), Western sand cherry (*P. bes-*

seyi), and others. The last species has been the subject of some breeding efforts and has yielded the improved bush varieties that produce their purplish red, tart fruits as far north as Alaska (Hanson, Brooks) and the extreme northern regions of the United States (Amber, Sioux, Black Beauty).

Sweet cherries produce their first crop 3 or 4 years after planting; sours 2 or 3 years after planting. Crops increase for the next 10 to 15 years as the tree grows. A mature sweet cherry will yield 3 to 4 bushels, amarelles 2½ to 3, and a healthy morello 2 bushels.

Site and Soil Requirements: Though as blossom-hardy as peaches, cherries may bloom a few days earlier and can get caught in spring frosts. To delay bloom, site them where they'll warm slowly in the spring; a north hillside is a good choice. Avoid low areas that tend to be frost pockets. If winter-damaged, cherries recover very slowly. Sweets are very intolerant of heavy, poorly drained soils and a hardpan in the upper 4 feet will cause shallow rooting with poor fruit size and tree vigor in dry seasons. Otherwise, the suggestions for a good peach site will satisfy any cherry.

Bush types can be grown on a wider range of soils, from clay to gravelly loams, with a pH of 6 to 8. High levels of organic matter will greatly benefit any site and should be added if the soil is deficient.

Pollination: Sour cherries are self-fruitful and will set full crops on lone trees, but should not be relied on to pollinate sweets since the bloom periods seldom overlap. Cherries are possibly the only fruit with more complex pollination guidelines than the plum, and volumes have been written on the pollination of sweet cherries. All varieties, except Stella, are self-unfruitful; single trees will bloom profusely but set no fruit. The obvious solution is to plant some other variety, thus providing viable pollen for cross-pollination. This solution is complicated by the presence of incompatability groups. For example, Bing/Lambert/Napoleon/Emperor Francis all have viable pollen, but will not pollinate each other—probably due to common ancestry in breeding programs. Other incompatible groups are: Windsor/Abundance; Black Tartarian/Black Eagle/Knight's Early Black/Early Rivers; Napoleon/Centennial; Elton/Governor Wood/Stark's Gold; Van/Venus/Windsor; Vic/Hedelfingen; Hudson/Giant/Schmidt/Ursula; Vega/Vista/Seneca; and Schmidt/Orelund. For successful pollination, varieties from different groups must be planted and they must have overlapping bloom periods. Consult nursery catalogs or your local extension office for more information on suitable local varieties.

Ordering Stock: With a slightly longer chilling requirement (1,100 to 1,300 hours) than peaches, most cherries will grow best in the northern parts of peach-producing regions. The hotter, more humid summers to the south favor the brown rot fungus which can ruin an entire

crop in a few days. Sweets are about as winter-hardy as the hardier plums, while sours can be grown farther north, well into apple country. One-year-old nursery stock 4 to 5 feet tall and ¾ inch thick just above the bud-union is best for planting. If two-year-old stock is available, it should have several branches indicating vigor and health, while whips of this age should be left in the nursery.

Propagation: For sweets or sours to be planted in heavier soils, the best means of propagation is by budding onto rootstocks of *P. avium,* the Mazzard cherry. Budding on *P. mahaleb* produces a larger, less hardy tree which performs well on wet ground and will have a long, productive life. The Mazzard cherry is nematode-resistant, tolerant of oak root fungus, and will be less affected by borers, gophers, and mice. Most sour cherries are budded onto *P. mahaleb* rootstock, which will produce a bushier, earlier-bearing, though shorter-lived tree than the Mazzard cherry, but may form a poor union with sweet cherry scions. In areas where the soil is light or drought conditions are likely, use *P. mahaleb.* If you have room for only one cherry tree, another variety can be budded onto the main variety while the tree is young. Tag the pollinator limb to save it from inadvertent pruning.

Planting and Culture: Cherry buds open very early in the spring and moisture-demanding foliage develops soon after. If the newly planted tree has not grown enough roots to meet the demand for water, the tree may die quickly. In warmer areas, fall planting is suggested, while in more northern climes where severe cold could damage the young tree, early spring planting on ground prepared the previous fall is best. Follow planting guidelines for peaches, spacing the trees 15 to 18 feet apart for morellos, 22 to 25 feet for other sours and dukes, and 35 to 40 feet for sweets. If possible, plant cherries where no peaches or cherries have grown before to avoid nematode problems. Cut the newly planted tree back to a height of 3 feet to induce branching to form scaffolds.

Cherry

Variety	Fruit	Tree
Sweet Cherries		
Bing	Large; nearly black, dark flesh. Firm, sweet, aromatic. Superb fresh. May crack severely in East. Susceptible to brown rot. Late.	Very productive, but buds are winter-tender. Susceptible to bacterial and Cytospora canker.
Black Russian	Black-red skin, dark firm flesh. Resists cracking. Excellent fresh. Midseason.	Moderately hardy, productive.
Black Tartarian	Very large; purplish black skin, dark flesh. Very good dessert quality. May crack in rainy weather. Early.	Vigorous, upright growth, hardy, productive. Good pollinizer. Susceptible to bacterial canker.
Emperor Francis	Large; yellow with pink blush. Firm, light flesh, very sweet. Resists cracking. Midseason.	Moderately hardy, productive.
Giant	Extremely large; black-red with firm, dark flesh. Very good tree-ripe. Slight cracking. Midseason.	Fairly productive, medium hardy.
Gold	Medium-small; yellow with firm, light flesh. Very sweet for dessert use, not troubled by birds. Late.	Extremely hardy, very productive. Good pollinizer.
Hedelfingen	Large; nearly black, firm, dark flesh. Sweet, excellent fresh or canned. Resists cracking. Late.	Hardy, very productive, but may be biennial. Good pollinizer, resists bacterial canker.
Lambert	Large; purple-red, firm, pale flesh. Very sweet and juicy, possibly the best for fresh use. Cans well, may crack. Late.	Vigorous, hardy, bears heavily every year.
Napoleon (Royal Ann)	Large; yellow skin with bright red cheeks. Very attractive. Sweet, firm flesh, excellent for canning or fresh. Less troubled by birds. May crack. Midseason.	Very productive, but bud-tender.
Rainier	Yellow cherry with pink blush. Large, firm, keeps well. Resists cracking, excellent quality. Early.	Very hardy, productive; flower buds frost-hardy. Good pollinizer.
Schmidt	Large; almost black skin, firm red flesh. Excellent fresh, canned, or frozen. Moderately acid. May crack. Susceptible to brown rot.	Medium hardy, tends to be shy bearer. Susceptible to bacterial and Cytospora canker.
Stella	Large; black, heart-shaped Lambert type. Sweet, very good quality. Midseason.	Moderately hardy, productive. The only self-fruitful sweet cherry.

If treated like a peach tree, though fed less, cherries will thrive. Sweets and dukes are very drought-sensitive, with the transpiring leaves of a water-stressed tree actually removing water from the fruit. All cherries respond well to watering, but in the eastern and midwestern U.S., the water needs of this early-maturing crop are usually satisfied by winter and spring rains.

Bare, cultivated ground under the trees may help counter the effects of spring frost by soaking up heat during the day and slowly ra-diating it back at night. Heavy mulching with any coarse organic material is highly recommended, but wait until all danger of frost is past and keep the mulch a foot or two away from the trunk to discourage mice.

Use the length of a season's shoot growth to determine the tree's vigor: 12 to 24 inches is good for sours; 26 to 36 inches for sweets before bearing begins. When trees are beginning to bear but are still growing, 8 to 12 inches of growth is enough, dropping to 4 to 8 inches when trees are in full bearing. In humid areas,

Variety	Fruit	Tree
Sweet Cherries *(continued)*		
Ulster	Cross of Schmidt and Lambert. Large; dark, high quality. Very crack-resistant. Midseason.	Good hardiness, fairly productive.
Van	Dark red skin, hard dark flesh. Very good dessert quality. Midseason.	Vigorous, very hardy, productive. Resists Cytospora canker, susceptible to bacterial canker. Good pollinizer.
Vista	Large; dark red skin, firm, dark flesh. Good early cherry. Slightly susceptible to brown rot.	Medium hardy, moderately productive. Bears early. Resists Cytospora canker.
Windsor	Dark red, firm flesh. Very good fresh or processed. Resists brown rot. Midseason.	Hardy and productive, grows rapidly. Good pollinizer. Resists Cytospora canker.
Sour Cherries		
Early Richmond	Small, acid fruit. Old variety, good quality. Late.	Moderately productive, hardy.
English Morello	Black skin, dark flesh and juice. Excellent acidic tang for cooking. Freezes well. Late.	Hardy, productive. Susceptible to cherry leaf spot and powdery mildew. Large (10-ft.) bush.
Meteor	Pale red skin, yellow flesh. Good quality, larger than North Star. Late.	Natural spur-type, semidwarf. Heavy annual bearer, very hardy.
Montmorency	The finest pie cherry; tart, moderately acid. Bright red skin, yellow flesh. Long ripening season. Late.	Vigorous, hardy, very productive on fertile soils. Spur-type tree available that is 75% full size.
North Star	Similar to Montmorency, but not as high quality. Late.	Natural full dwarf, very hardy, productive. Mature tree is 8–10 ft. tall. Tolerant to cherry leaf spot fungus.
Dukes		
Late Duke	Large; dark red, good quality. Late.	Hardy, moderately productive.
May Duke	Red skin, dark red flesh; good flavor. Early.	Medium hardy and productive.
Reine Hortense	Large; amber, red skin. Fair quality. Midseason.	Hardy, moderately productive.
Royal Duke	Dark red skin, light soft flesh. Best flavor of the dukes. Midseason.	Hardy and most productive of the dukes.

where cherries are grown on lighter soils, deficiencies of magnesium (indicated by chlorotic, stunted leaves) and/or potassium (scorching of leaf edges, older leaves first) may occur, although a manuring program should be adequate. If not, spread 10 pounds of dolomite lime for magnesium or 1 gallon of wood ashes for potassium around the drip-line.

Those varieties of sweet cherries that taste best are also most prone to cracking. Only a problem when rains occur within a week or so of harvest, the cracking is not caused by the tree taking up too much water through its roots, but by direct absorption into the fruit of the rainwater in the stem cavity. Unable to contain the extra volume, the skin bursts. If heavy rains are predicted near harvest, you can reduce the amount of cracking by applying a solution of ½ cup liquid dishwashing soap to 10 gallons of water.

Pruning: More than other tree fruits, sweet and sour cherries will grow into a productive shape with little pruning. Prune sweet cherries only to remove dead or broken limbs, to thin out shoots to allow sunlight to penetrate, and to eliminate cross limbs. Spreaders may be needed to bend young branches down to form a wider crotch angle.

Sour cherries have a more spreading growth habit and are easily trained to the modified central leader shape described under Apricot. Avoid heading cuts and heavy pruning on sours which will stunt the tree and delay bearing. Don't attempt to thin the crop. It will not affect size.

Pests and Diseases: Insects and disease can be troublesome, though slightly less so with sour cherries than with other stone fruits. The biggest challenge to harvesting a crop of red sweet cherries is birds. Not content to eat a whole cherry, they take a few pecks and can ruin the crop as fast as it ripens. The holes they leave are perfect infection sites for brown rot. See chapter 11 for information on controls.

Curled leaves on shoot tips will reveal the black cherry aphid when unrolled. More of a problem on sweets, where a heavy infestation can stunt a young tree, it can be kept under control with rotenone until the predators move in. Tent caterpillars, though they will eat other fruits, prefer cherry foliage and can strip a branch or young tree in a few days. In the spring, remove any of the egg masses, found as a hardened, gray foam surrounding small twigs. Other insect problems are borers, cherry maggot, and scale.

Brown rot fungus, the bane of stone fruit orchards, can be a very serious problem in cherries, especially sweets. Another fungal disease, cherry leaf spot, attacks the leaves, producing ⅛-inch purplish red spots that develop a pink cushion of infecting spores on the lower leaf surface. Heavily spotted leaves drop from the tree and total defoliation can occur before harvest. Both diseases can be retarded by a light sulfur spray. Sour cherries may develop a condition known as "yellows," a virus-induced speckling of the leaves. Increasing the nitrogen fertilizer to affected trees will help.

Harvest and Storage: When the fruit reaches its full skin color, pick a few of the best colored by pinching and slightly twisting the cluster of stems. If they're sweet, juicy, and a bit firm, keep picking those of similar color. If you like them sweeter, try again the next day. There is no standard for picking once full color is reached and, like other stone fruits, cherries get sweeter and larger the longer they hang on the tree, until they begin to soften.

They will keep several weeks in a moisture-tight container in the refrigerator, but are best right off the tree.

Uses: Sweet cherries are best when eaten out of hand, but they also make a good addition to fruit salads and assorted desserts, and may be canned. Sour cherries make tasty preserves, are unsurpassed in pies, and can be frozen.

CITRUS FRUITS

Citrus spp.
Rutaceae

There are about 130 genera in the botanical family that includes edible citrus, the Rutaceae. Most are trees or shrubs that grow in the warm, or tropical, regions of the world. Though varying in chemical composition and nutritional value, all edible citrus are rich in ascorbic acid.

Most citrus have a single taproot, with lateral roots providing a surface mat of feeder roots. Root growth alternates with stem growth in cycles. Stem wood is very hard. Some species have thorns adjacent to leaf axil buds. Fruit takes 7 to 14 months from pollination to maturity, and only a small proportion of the flowers produce mature fruits. Both flowers, before opening, and fruits, when young, have a tendency to drop off. Most cultivars have seeds with several embryos, most of them asexual.

Pollination: Most citrus are self- and cross-compatible, though grapefruit tend to self-pollination rather than cross-pollination. To encourage self-pollination, orchard keepers sometimes bag flower branches. In artificial pollination, anthers are removed at the bud stage before the flowers are bagged.

Soil Requirements: Latitude and altitude are more important than soil type for citrus. Though for some species wide variations of soil type are possible, light, loamy soil of good fertility is generally preferred. The pH should be between 5 and 7, and the soil well drained and free of alkaline salts like boron and sodium.

Most citrus are grown from 45° North to 35° South latitude and from sea level to 6,000 feet. In order of hardiness from tender to most frost-hardy the citrus species are: citron, lime, lemon, grapefruit, sweet orange, sour orange, mandarin orange, kumquat (not a true citrus), and trifoliate orange. Citrus will stand temperatures well over 100°F, but growth is reduced under 55°F. Mandarins tolerate wetter, and grapefruit drier and windier, conditions than do the other species.

Citrus fruits of commercial importance fall into five groups: oranges, mandarins, pummelos, grapefruits, and common acid fruits. The latter group includes citrons, lemons, and limes.

Oranges include the common orange, the sugar orange, the pigmented or blood orange, and the navel orange. Among the sour oranges are the bitter orange, most used for rootstock; the bittersweet orange, which has less acid; and the variant bitter oranges used principally as ornamentals.

Mandarins include satsumas, King mandarins, Mediterranean mandarins, common mandarins, and small-fruited mandarins. Mandarin hybrids include Temple oranges, some tangelos, Ugli, and the calamondins including Otaheite and Rangpur.

Grapefruit and pummelos closely overlap in their cultivars, including some synthetic tangelos, the Seville, and some orangelos.

Ordering Stock: It is important to select citrus stock that is free of virus disease and true to variety. Many nursery trees, especially oranges, grapefruit, and lemons, are certified. Look for well-grown, vigorous stock with deep green leaves, straight trunks, and clean bark. The root system should also be well developed, with many lateral and feeder roots. If the nursery tree has been balled, probe inside the ball for the feeder roots and examine the main root for lesions, a sign of *Phytophthora*. The bud-union should be 4 to 12 inches above the ground.

The best nursery trees are one year past grafting or budding. Nurseries, however, sometimes sell two-year-old trees that were very small when budded. These should be rejected unless they were grown under excellent conditions. One-year-old trees may be identified by the leaves growing out of the trunk below the main stem. The diameter of the trunk 1 inch above the bud-union should be between ¾ and 1¼ inches depending upon the mature size of the species.

Balled trees are preferable, but some nurseries sell bare-rooted, sphagnum-packed, or potted trees. If possible, buy nursery trees before they are dug.

Propagation: Citrus trees are often budded onto seedling rootstocks in commercial nurseries. The most common rootstocks grown from seed for citrus budding in the United States are sweet orange, sour orange, grapefruit, shaddock, rough lemon, trifoliate orange, Cleopatra mandarin, and Sampson tangelo. These rootstocks are chosen for hardiness, resistance to disease, tolerance of salinity, compatibility with the intended scion, and their effects on fruit size and other factors.

There are several other frequently used propagation techniques for citrus trees. Cuttings ranging from 3 to 6 inches long can be made from recently matured terminal growth of healthy trees in early summer. Remove basal leaves before setting the cuttings in rooting medium. Newly transplanted cuttings require protection. Citrus can also be started from leaf-bud cuttings. In this method a bud with a single leaf attached is set in bottom-heated rooting medium with the bud shield barely covered.

In twig grafting, two leafy twigs are grafted together by means of a whip graft and the lower one is rooted. This produces plants with the desired rootstock/scion combination. Sometimes a three-part graft is done with the third part serving as interstem. The two or three cuttings must be of equal diameter. This method is particularly useful for dwarf trees.

Planting and Culture: In tropical and semi-tropical areas planting may be done at any season of the year with reasonable success. In Florida, the best time to plant is late winter or early spring when the trees are most dormant.

The best site for a citrus orchard is a warm, sunny, protected spot, preferably on a gentle, south-facing slope with good air and water drainage. If possible, avoid soil that has grown citrus before. High water tables and salinity due to irrigation may cause poor tree growth.

The most frequent planting pattern for land other than hillsides, where contour planting or artificial terraces are employed, is the rectangular system with trees planted at intersections of lines parallel and perpendicular to the field boundaries. The distance between trees should assure room for growth to maturity and range between 20 and 35 feet in each direction, the distance depending on the species and variety. Wide spacing tends to reduce pro-

duction per acre when the trees are young, but it produces the heaviest production when trees are from 15 years old to full maturity. Closer planting may be used if weaker trees are culled as they age.

It is wise to incorporate phosphate rock and granite dust into the soil before planting.

Newly planted trees demand much attention. In California, they require water every four or five days in desert areas, and every two to three weeks in wetter areas. In Florida trees are watered every two to five days until they become established.

Young trees also require protection against sunburn and cold damage. Check them frequently for signs of disease and pests.

Citrus trees have a relatively high nitrogen demand, so top-dressing with compost or well-rotted manure will benefit them. Take care to protect trunks from the rotting compost or mulch. Citrus also requires potassium and phosphates which may be added in the form of greensand or granite dust and phosphate rock. Light applications of compost and rock powders may be spread under citrus trees during the growing season.

Pruning: Although pruning is less essential for citrus trees, with the exception of lemon trees, than it is for most other fruit trees, it does have some value in citrus growing. It establishes a strong, well-balanced framework of scaffold branches that support a large amount of foliage and fruit. During the early life of the trees, especially lemon trees, all entangled and broken branches should be removed. As maturity approaches, prune for maintenance only, and to achieve a balance for tree vigor and maximum fruit production. Citrus sets and ripens best in full light, and pruning lets light in to interior branches. Pruning is also done on old, increasingly unproductive trees to rejuvenate them by improving the balance between taproot and top growth. Pruning should be done during the period of greatest dormancy, usually December to February.

Pests and Diseases: In Texas the major pests

of citrus are brown soft scale, California red scale, cottony-cushion scale, Florida red scale, purple scale, rust mite, and the Texas citrus mite. Of lesser importance are ants, aphids, Baker's mealybugs, citrus whitefly, false spider mites, flatid plant hoppers, and termites. Common diseases are foot rot, greasy spot, melanose fungus, psorosis, Rio Grande gummosis, and other virus diseases.

In California both pests and disease prevalence depend on local climatic conditions. In coastal areas pests are black citrus aphids, black orangeworms, black scale, California red scale, citrus bud mites, citrus red mites, cotton aphids, green peach aphids, leafrollers, pink scavenger caterpillars, purple scale, and spirea aphids. In the interior valleys of southern California, they are black scale, California red scale, citricola scale, citrus red mites, citrus thrips, orange tortrix, purple scale, spirea aphids, and yellow scale. Interior valleys of central California have California red scale, citricola scale, citrus thrips, cottony-cushion scale, potato leafhoppers, and yellow scale. In desert areas there are California red scale, citrus thrips, cottony-cushion scale, leafrollers, and Yuma spinning mites. The major diseases are Armillaria fungus, exocortis, foot rot, psorosis, stubborn, tristeza, and xyloporosis. Nematodes and rodents also do extensive damage.

In Arizona major pests include cottony-cushion scale, mites, and thrips. Diseases include black rot, dry root rot, exocortis, psorosis, stubborn, tristeza, and xyloporosis. Fungus diseases are of lesser importance because the climate is dry.

In Florida the major pests are Florida red scale, purple scale, purple mites, rust mites, six-spotted mites, snow scale, spreading decline (caused by nematodes), and whiteflies. Aphids, grasshoppers, and mealybugs are minor pests. Major citrus diseases include Armillaria root rot, brown rot, citrus scab, Clitocybe root rot, exocortis, gummosis, melanose fungus, tristeza, and xyloporosis.

Harvest: Home growers should allow fruit to ripen on trees whenever possible for improved flavor and nutrition. Much commercial citrus fruit is harvested immature or underripe and ripened artificially.

COCONUT

Cocos nucifera
Palmae

Coconut palms grow to 100 feet tall. The trunk, either leaning or erect, is slender and tapering from base to crown. It is smooth, light grayish brown in color, sturdy and wind-resistant with a terminal crown of about 20 large feathery leaves.

The large fruit is roughly egg-shaped and a thick fibrous husk surrounds the nut with a hard, hairy shell. The nut has three eyes at one end, which are actually sunken holes of softer tissue. Inside the shell of the nut is the "meat" (endosperm), ½ inch of thin, white flesh surrounding the watery, white milk. In immature coconuts, the meat is jellylike and the milk abundant. As the fruit matures, the meat becomes firm and the milk is absorbed by the ripening process. The meat when dried is known as copra, and contains 60 to 68% oil.

The fruit turns from green or yellow to brown as it matures, depending on the variety. Trees of dwarf varieties begin to bear 3 to 5 years after the seed is planted; taller varieties take 6 to 10 years to come into bearing. Full production is not reached until the tree is 15 to 20 years old. The fruit takes a year to develop, with a yield of 50 to 200 coconuts per tree constant throughout the year.

Soil Requirements: Salt spray and brackish soil are hospitable to the coconut palm. While it flourishes near tropical beaches, it will do well inland, too. It can tolerate a wide range of soil types, if well drained, and a pH range from 5 to 8.

Propagation: The whole coconut is considered one seed, and it is always used for propagation. Choose a large, ripe nut from a tree that is producing an abundance of good fruit. Place it on its side, and bury it about halfway in the soil in a semishaded seedbed or in a pot. The shoot and root will emerge through one of the eyes. Transplant it after six months, or continue to grow it in a pot in a greenhouse.

Planting and Culture: Plant the tree in full sun anytime in the year and at any period in its growth. Dig a hole 3 feet wide and 3 feet deep, and set the tree in at the same depth as it was in the container. Mix peat with soil removed from the hole before replacing it, to assist water and nutrient retention.

Water immediately after planting and frequently during the first five months. Thereafter, the tree will need an inch of water a week. Mulch is helpful. Space trees 25 feet apart.

Minimum average temperature for coconut palms is 72°F. Temperatures below 32°F will cause injury, and temperatures around that level will hamper flowering and fruiting. Trees require full sunlight, high humidity, and annual rainfall of at least 40 to 60 inches, evenly spaced throughout the year. Wind and flooding do not affect them.

In the United States, the coconut palm will fruit in only a few warm subtropical areas, including in Florida the area from Stuart on the east coast and Punta Gorda on the west coast, south to Key West. Hawaii is on the northern border of the coconut zone.

Pests and Diseases: In Florida, lethal yellowing (also called telephone pole syndrome) and palm bud rot are the most important diseases. Coconut scale is occasionally damaging, as are other pests, including caterpillars, mealybugs, mites, palm aphids, and palm weevils.

Harvest: Harvest throughout the year by using a knife attached to a long pole. Nuts can be harvested for their milk at 7 months, and for copra when fully ripe at 12 months.

Varieties: In Florida, plant Malayan Dwarf or Maypan. Malayan Dwarf takes three forms: either green, yellow, or golden in its petiole and fruit. The tree, a semidwarf, grows 40 to 60 feet high, and seems to resist lethal yellows.

CRABAPPLE

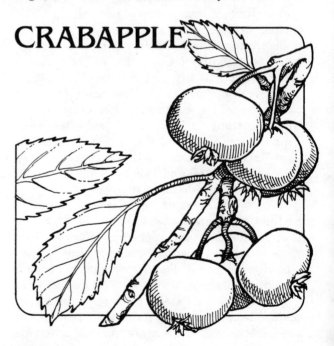

Malus spp.
Rosaceae

Crabapple trees, or crab trees, are closely related to the common eating apples, but their fruits are much smaller and their flowers more

Crabapple

Variety	Area of Best Growth	Fruit	Tree
Adams	All apple-growing areas	Carmine red fruit, ½ in. diameter. Good for jellies.	Pink flowers, hardy. Resistant to scab, fireblight, mildew, rust. Rounded and dense growth habit.
Centennial	Central to northern U.S.	Fruit good for processing. Red over yellow. Approximately 2 in. in diameter.	Hardy. Resistant to scab, fireblight, mildew, cedar apple rust, and frog-eye leaf spot. White flowers.
Chestnut	All apple-growing areas	Yellow with red blush. Large-fruited, makes deep pink jelly.	Very hardy. Fairly resistant to common apple diseases.
Dolgo	All apple-growing areas	Small, red fruit. Jells easily if picked before full ripeness.	Very hardy. White to pink blossoms. Open, vigorous, large.
Katherine	All apple-growing areas	Small fruit, but makes jelly. Red over yellow. Fruits in alternate years.	Hardy, small, grows to 15 ft. White to pink flowers. Fairly disease-resistant.
Montreal Beauty	All apple-growing areas	Green- and red-striped fruit, good for jellies.	Very hardy. Fairly resistant to common apple diseases. Grows to 25 ft.
Robinson	All apple-growing areas	Red fruit, ⅝-in. diameter. Good for processing to jellies, sauces, etc.	Hardy. Crimson blossoms. Resistant to scab, fireblight, mildew, rust.
Whitney	All apple-growing areas	Large-fruited. Good for fresh eating, jelly, preserves, apple butter, or spiced apples.	Very hardy. Old variety. Fair disease resistance and reliable. Grows to 25 ft.
Young America	All apple-growing areas	Large, red fruit, good for jelly.	Hardy and vigorous.

showy. They are usually grown for their blossoms rather than for their fruit, although some varieties do produce fruit of good eating quality. Crabapple's growth habit and size depends on the variety, ranging from low, moundlike shrubs to upright or pendulous trees 10 to 25 feet tall. Large trees tend to produce larger fruit than small trees.

The fruits, which ripen in fall, are usually only slightly larger than marbles, but may grow as large as walnuts, and vary in color from shades of yellow to various shades of red.

Grow and harvest crabapples just the same as other apple trees. Crabs, though, are gen-erally hardier, Dolgo being among the hardiest of all fruit trees. Crabs also suffer from the same diseases as other apple trees, but there are varieties available for humid climates which are resistant to scab and fungal diseases. Ornamental crabs are particularly susceptible to scab.

See the chart for a listing of varieties with good-tasting fruit, some disease resistance, and ornamental qualities.

Fruits can be turned to good use as spiced crabapples, or in jelly. All crabapples make excellent wildlife food, even when they are not satisfactory food for people.

CRANBERRY

Vaccinium macrocarpon
Ericaceae

A low, trailing plant, the cranberry has woody stems that run along the ground and give rise to numerous upright shoots. The stems may reach 6 feet in length and will root readily if covered with soil. The shoots may reach 2 feet in length, but curve upward at their tips, which stand 6 to 12 inches tall. In commercial cranberry bogs, the shoots are grown so thickly that they support one another, forming a dense, erect stand that produces big crops—as much as 300 bushels per acre.

The plants bloom in spring or early summer. Berries are bright green at first, but turn bright red by harvest in October. A good source of vitamin C, the berries are tart and rarely eaten raw.

The cranberry grows on sandy or peaty acid bogland. Having no root hairs, the plant depends on a symbiotic fungus to provide food and water from the soil, and does not tolerate dry conditions in the top 6 inches of soil. Most commercial bogs are leveled and diked on the sites of natural bogs of leather leaf, brownbush or

peat, with water at hand for flooding (a practice used to control insects at certain times), to protect the plants from frost, drying winter winds and summer heat, and sometimes to help in harvesting. The water is also used for irrigation. Some West Coast growers, however, use sprinkler irrigation to give the plants the moisture they need, and grow their plants in ordinary acid soil rather than natural bogs. A heavy peat mulch protects these plants during winter.

The cranberry is relatively untried as a garden plant. It may be a useful dual-purpose groundcover for acid northern sites, provided the soil can be kept moist.

Pollination: The flowers are self-pollinating, but when honeybees and bumblebees visit the plants, there is an increase in the size of the crop and the berries.

Propagation: Six- to 8-inch cuttings are taken from upright shoots in the spring, before the terminal buds begin to sprout. The cuttings are set in the soil on 18-inch centers, with only an inch of each cutting aboveground.

Planting and Culture: Cuttings are planted on 18-inch centers in peaty or sandy acid soil (pH 5). The ground must be kept weed-free for several years, until the stems cover it and upright shoots have made a thick stand. The plants use only the top 6 inches of soil, which must be kept constantly moist. When the soil is frozen, the plants, being semievergreen, can be dried and killed by winds. To counteract drying, bogs are often flooded in winter.

The main commercial cranberry varieties are Early Black, Howes, Searles Jumbo, McFarlin, Ben Lear, Crowley, and Stevens. There are local favorites in New Jersey, Wisconsin, and Oregon.

Pests and Diseases: False blossom, a virus disease spread by leafhoppers, nearly destroyed the commercial cranberry industry in the 1920s. Three varieties of cranberry, Beckwith, Stevens, and Wilcox, seem less attractive to the leafhopper than other varieties and so escape false blossom more often than other varieties.

The cranberry is subject to several fungal diseases, like red leaf spot, but they are rarely damaging to the crop.

The cranberry fruitworm, which bores into the fruit, eats the seeds and then exits the fruit, can cause the loss of as much as one-third of the crop in some years. The black-headed fireworm, a small, brownish leaf-feeder, causes leaves to brown as though singed. Flooding is the main natural control for these pests.

Uses: Cranberries are made into jam, jelly, condiment, and sauce, and they are also pressed for juice. Fresh berries keep only three weeks or so, but they freeze well.

CURRANT

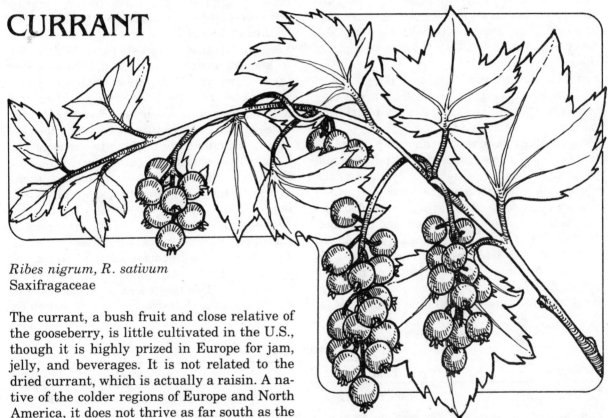

Ribes nigrum, R. sativum
Saxifragaceae

The currant, a bush fruit and close relative of the gooseberry, is little cultivated in the U.S., though it is highly prized in Europe for jam, jelly, and beverages. It is not related to the dried currant, which is actually a raisin. A native of the colder regions of Europe and North America, it does not thrive as far south as the gooseberry. The currant is an alternate host for a serious disease, white pine blister rust, and its cultivation is restricted in many states to protect white pines. The black currant is more susceptible to the disease than the red and yellow currants, and may not be sold or grown in most of the U.S. A reputable nursery will furnish a growing permit, where one is needed, and sell only certified disease-free stock. Planting should be at least 900 feet from white pines to prevent the spread of rust.

The red currants are the best varieties, with erect, vigorous bushes and large, easily picked clusters of fruit. Red Lake and Minnesota 71 are two of the best all-around red currants, and Perfection, Wilder, and Red Cross are also widely planted.

Besides being highly susceptible to white pine blister rust, as well as illegal to grow in most of the U.S., the black currants have an unpleasant odor in their foliage, and, to some noses, in their fruit (but they are highly prized in Europe, and the source of some renowned beverages).

Though the yellow currant, which is often called the white currant, is usually a poor yielder, a new variety from the New York State Fruit Testing Cooperative, Imperial, which is said to be better than the old standard White Grape, may be worth a try.

Pollination: Most currants are readily pollinated by bees, but some black currant varieties, because of the shape of their flowers, are difficult to pollinate and may produce disappointing crops.

Soil Requirements: Currants, like gooseberries, grow on a variety of soils, from heavy clay to sandy loam, and tolerate a range of pH from mildly acid to mildly alkaline.

Propagation: Currants can be propagated from cuttings, like grapes, from tip-layers and by mound-layering, which entails cutting back all branches to 3 inches after growth starts in the spring and then covering the stubs with earth. Many shoots will appear and take root; they can be cut free and set out as new plants.

Planting and Culture: Currants need good drainage and moist soil, which is a combination easier for the gardener to provide if a permanent mulch is used. They are susceptible to powdery mildew and though they will grow in slight shade they are less troubled by mildew in full sun.

Currants may be planted in the fall or the spring. Set the plants at least 5 feet apart, 6 feet apart for black currants, which grow larger than the red and yellow currants. With the usual year-old nursery stock, prune the plant back to stand about 5 inches tall. A planting should be productive for 10 to 20 years.

Pruning: The object of pruning currants is to keep the plant open to help fight mildew, and to keep replacing branches that have passed their third year with new branches. Begin pruning after the third year from planting, and aim to have nine main branches eventually, three of them new branches, three of them one season old, and three of them two seasons old. Take out the oldest canes after the third season and leave three new ones to replace them. Prune during the dormant season, in late winter.

Pests and Diseases: Currants are prone to attacks by aphids, currant sawflies, and fruit-fly maggot. The imported currant worm and currant aphid, which attacks the undersides of leaves and causes them to blister, should be picked off and destroyed or they can quick-

Currant

Variety	Fruit	Bush
Fay	Large, dark red berries. Easy to pick.	Very spreading habit. Canes break easily.
Minnesota 71	Large berries on large clusters. Good quality.	Vigorous, spreading, productive bush.
Perfection	Large red berries on compact clusters. Will scald in hot weather if allowed to hang after ripening. Good dessert quality.	Small spreading bush. Heavy yielder. Canes break easily.
Red Cross	Large, firm berries, light red.	Clusters of fruit easily picked.
Red Lake	Fruit large on large clusters with long stems. Good quality. Lighter color than most varieties.	Vigorous, hardy, and productive. Upright.
White Grape	Large, pale yellow berries. Mild flavor.	Very productive.
White Imperial	Large berries, pale yellow. Nearly sweet. Excellent dessert quality.	Spreading, productive.
Wilder	Large, dark red berries. Large compact clusters.	Very large, upright. Long-lived.

ly damage the bushes. If a wilting shoot betrays the presence of a borer, it should be pruned and destroyed. If fruitfly maggots infested the fruit the previous season, rotenone sprayed at blossom wilt will keep their numbers down.

Currants are susceptible to anthracnose, European currant rust and powdery mildew, all diseases that are more severe in wet springs. Keeping the bush open, so air may circulate and keep it dry, helps combat these diseases.
Harvest and Storage: Currants can be picked green, like gooseberries, and used for jam and jelly, or they can be allowed to ripen and eaten fresh.

DATE

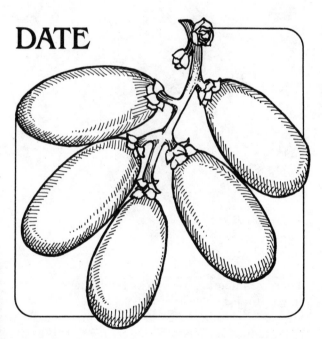

Phoenix dactylifera
Palmae

The date is a desert palm. It is subtropical—growing nowhere in the tropics but only where there are high temperatures and low humidity. Date palms usually grow to about 50 feet high, but may attain as much as 100 feet.

The date is usually dioecious. The inflorescence in both male and female consists of a long, thick bract which opens to reveal branchlets of crowded white male flowers or greenish female flowers. Male flowers can be identified through their characteristic odor, by their wider, thicker spathe, and their more intense crowding on the branches.

The fruit is hard and green when immature, and later turning deep yellow or red. The flesh is thick and very sweet, averaging 54% sugar. Dates usually ripen in October when grown in warm parts of the United States.
Pollination: Date palms have been hand-pollinated for at least 3,000 years and that is still the favored method. Using a newly opened inflorescence of a staminate (male) flower, cut two or three strands that are each 3 to 6 inches long. Invert these strands between the strands of pistillate flowers which have opened within the previous three days. Use string to tie around the cluster and hold the flowers in place. Loosen the string as the flowers grow. Another method is to let the staminate flowers shed their pollen on paper, dip small cotton balls into the pollen, and insert the balls in the female inflorescence.
Soil Requirements: A variety of soil types will do, but heavy-to-sandy soil is best. While date palms are tolerant of salt and brackish water and need the least water of any crop, they cannot tolerate drought. Abundant subsurface moisture is very important.

Cultivating date palms has been called "an exciting art," necessitating just the right mix of hot summer days and nights, low humidity, and an absence of rain during fruit setting in spring and fruit ripening in autumn. The date's cultural requirements are aptly summarized in an old Bedouin saying: "The date must have its head in the fire and its feet in the water."
Propagation: Propagate by offshoots that are four to five years old. Offshoots grow laterally at the base of young palms. Cut rooted offshoots (the ones that are near the ground) and plant immediately in the permanent location. Off-

shoots reproduce the sex and type of the parent.
Planting and Culture: Dig a hole 3 feet across
and 1 to 1½ feet deep. Fill the hole with composted manure and rich topsoil to nourish the
young tree. Water frequently and mulch new
offshoots. Protect the palm during the first winter by wrapping the trunk with paper or old
fronds. Space plants 25 to 30 feet apart.

Date palms will withstand temperatures
down to 20°F, if the frost is of short duration.
Below that temperature fronds may be killed.
The terminal growing point, however, is safe
to 8° to 10°F. Hawaii, southwestern Arizona
and the Coachella Valley of southeastern California are the prime date-growing areas in the
United States. These areas have long hot summer days and nights. If days are warm and
nights are cool, the date palm will not flourish.

Date palms should fruit after 4 years and
live for a century. Annual yields of 100 to 200
pounds of fruit per tree can be expected after
10 to 15 years.
Pruning: In late summer, remove old fronds
as the leaf pinnae begin to brown. Remove the
sharp thorns at the base of the leaves to facilitate pollination and harvesting. Keep fruit
production down to 8 to 12 clusters by removing
new clusters when they appear.
Harvest and Storage: Fruit ripens at different times on the same bunch, making it necessary to pick several times. Harvest the fruit
as it reaches the preripe pink, yellow, or red
stage, starting in October. Fruit will then
soften naturally to its brown and slightly wrinkled fully ripe state. Store at 30° to 32°F for a
year, and at 0°F for longer.
Uses: The semidry and soft dates that are preferred in this country are eaten fresh or dried,
added to cereal or oatmeal, used in baked goods,
jams, and confections.
Varieties: Over 1,000 varieties of date are
grown. The varieties fall into three classes: dry,
semidry, and soft. Dry dates, whose sugar content is mainly in the form of sucrose, are not
commonly available in the United States.
Thoory is one of the best Algerian dry dates.

Deglet Noor, the leading variety in the
United States, and Zahidi are semidry dates.
They are used commercially because they pack
well.

Soft dates have very little fiber and are of
the best quality. Their sugar is in the form of
glucose and fructose. Varieties include Barhee,
Halawy, Khadrawy, Medjhool, and Saidy.

ELDERBERRY

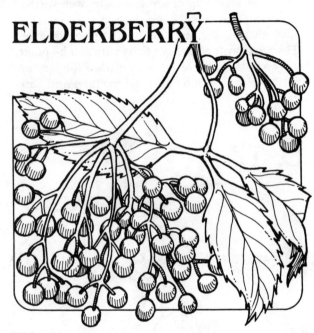

Elder
Sambucus spp.
Caprifoliaceae

There are about 20 species of elderberry growing around the world. Some produce edible berries, while others are only ornamental. The
American elderberry, *S. canadensis,* thrives in
fencerows and brushland throughout the colder
climates of eastern North America. One of the
hardiest of fruits, elderberries grow well into
northern Canada. Two varieties of *S. caerulea,*
blue elder, are native to the Pacific coast.

An elderberry bush can grow to a height
of 20 feet in some species, but commonly
reaches about 10 feet or less. Huge clusters of
creamy blossoms appear in late June and early

July, sending out a sweet, honeysucklelike fragrance. In August and September, the tiny, buckshot-sized berries of *S. canadensis* ripen to a lustrous black. They are round and smooth, and grow in clusters.

Pollination: Elderberry is said to be self-unfruitful, but a clump at some distance from other plants will often bear heavily. To ensure good fruit set, it is best to plant at least two different varieties together.

Propagation: Easily propagated by softwood, hardwood, and root cuttings.

Planting and Culture: Follow commonsense rules of planting. Plant in a moist site, in full sun or partial shade, and keep well watered for at least the first year. Elderberries do not like dry weather. Rich, well-drained soil with a pH of 6 to 7 is best. Plant 5 feet apart, closer together for a hedge. Bushes will thrive if mulched and fertilized with manure every year, but they are reasonably hardy and persistent even if neglected.

Pruning: Bushes sucker profusely and are best planted as a hedge so their rampant growth is less obvious. Prune out old and dead canes at ground level after they have borne fruit for three years, in order to leave room for new, vigorous shoots to grow. Canes over three years old are less productive than younger ones. To contain the bush, cut off new shoots growing too far out.

Pests: Birds like elderberries, and occasionally borers and mites are a nuisance, but generally elderberries are the most pest-free of all berries.

Harvest, Storage, and Uses: Harvest the berries in late summer by picking whole clusters into baskets. Freeze them as is, or strip off the berries from the twigs for immediate use in canning, jelly, pie, or elderberry wine.

Varieties: Improved varieties, with berries somewhat larger than those found in the wild, are available from nurseries. Adams, Johns, Kent, Nova, and York are readily available. Nova sets especially heavy yields, and York has a particularly small number of suckers.

FIG

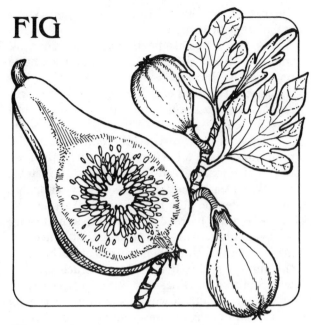

Ficus carica
Moraceae

The edible fig is one species in a large genus of tropical evergreen or deciduous trees, shrubs, or vines which includes the rubber plant and weeping fig that are popular house plants. The fig tree can reach 30 feet tall in its native habitat, but tends to grow smaller the farther north it is planted. Common figs have both male and female flowers, as do the inedible caprifigs, but Smyrna varieties have only female flowers.

Most fig trees bear two crops during the growing season. The first is in the early summer, and the second, heaviest-bearing crop is in the late summer or fall.

Figs are moderately difficult to grow depending upon the type of pollination required. They are always more difficult if caprification is necessary. Figs are susceptible to a number of insect and disease pests.

Pollination: The fruits develop either of two ways, depending upon the variety: without pollination, or only when their tiny flowers are pollinated.

Caprifigs are inedible wild figs that supply

the pollen for the pollination of other types, called caprification.

Common figs are parthenocarpic, meaning that their fruits enlarge even though they have not been pollinated and have developed no fertile seeds. The bulk of edible figs on the market and those popular for home cultivation fall into this category.

Smyrna figs, on the other hand, must be pollinated with pollen from the caprifig in order to produce fertile seeds and enlarge the fruits.

When caprification is necessary, caprifigs must be planted near the receiving trees so that the pollen can be readily transferred by the fig wasp. Southern areas are the best places to grow varieties that need caprification because the fig wasp can live and reproduce only in warm climates. Since the climate that favors fig culture is not always congenial to the fig wasp, many growers now use hormones which cause the fruits to mature without pollination.

Soil Requirements: Figs grow best in a rich, fertile, sandy or clay loam with a good percentage of humus. The soil must be very well drained but with a high moisture content. Figs prefer a pH of 5.0 to 6.5 but will tolerate high levels of lime and high concentrations of salts.

Propagation: Figs are normally propagated by cuttings, but layering, seeds, budding, and grafting also may be used.

Take cuttings in winter or early spring from firm wood one to three years old that is about ¾ inch in diameter. Make the cuttings from 3 to 12 inches long, slicing below a node at the base and above a node at the top. Set the cuttings deeply in the soil with only up to 1½ inches exposed. Keep the soil moist and by the following spring cuttings should be rooted enough to be replanted in their permanent locations.

To propagate figs by layering, bend down a low-growing branch and cover it with soil, except for the tip. When the branch is rooted, sever it from the parent tree and plant it.

Planting and Culture: Figs should be planted during the winter months when their growth has slowed down. Plant them in any area where the soil is moist and well drained, and the temperature does not drop below 20°F.

Dig a hole 3 to 4 feet deep and wide and mix the soil with sand, peat moss, and compost. Set the tree a couple of inches lower in the soil than it grew in the nursery and carefully spread out the roots. Fill the hole with soil, pack it down solidly and water well. Top-dress with an organic fertilizer high in nitrogen, plus phosphate rock and wood ash. Mulch with 3 to 4 inches of wood chips. Depending upon the size of the variety, space trees from 8 to 25 feet apart if you are planting them solidly in an orchard arrangement.

Pruning: Figs need very little pruning except to train them when young to grow strong and healthy so that they will be able to bear heavily.

Prune young trees only during their dormant period so that only three to four of the best-placed branches remain on each tree. As they grow older, cut out any dead wood and extra shoots each spring. Occasionally pinch off the tops of limbs to encourage branching; new shoots produce the highest-quality fruits.

Different varieties of figs are pruned as follows:

Adriatic: Prune back drooping branches to encourage the production of new wood.

Brown Turkey: Pruning after the first crop in the early summer stimulates new growth for the second crop and new wood for the next year's fruit.

Brunswick: Prune lightly after harvesting the first crop in the early summer.

Calimyrna: In the summer pinch back the tips of branches to stimulate lateral growth. Then in the winter cut back long, upright branches to give good shape to the tree.

Caprifigs: Not much pruning is required except to thin suckers and unnecessary branches.

Celeste: Remove extra shoots growing out of the base of the tree.

Dottato: Train a young tree by allowing

Fig   421

only three to five scaffold branches to develop. Every winter cut new branches back to short stubs and thin out the central or inside branches. Keep the topmost branches short for maximum fruiting.

Mission: Select wide-angled scaffold branches when the tree is young, since many of its branches tend to grow at acute angles that split under the weight of the fruit.

Pests and Diseases: Figs in a home garden attract fewer pests and diseases than when they are planted in an orchard. Major pests and diseases are: birds, fig mites, gophers, Mediterranean fig scale, red spider mites, root knot nematode, *Botrytis* dieback, fruit drop, internal rot, mosaic, rust, smut, souring, split.

Winter Protection: In areas of the country where winter temperatures drop below 10°F, train the branches to droop close to the ground. Then, in the winter, bend the branches down to the ground and cover them with soil, along with the lower trunk.

Figs can also be grown in tubs or pots, then moved to a cool, moist cellar or garage during the winter.

Harvest and Storage: Fig trees normally start bearing after three years. Pick fresh-eating figs when they are fully ripe and their necks

Fig

Variety	Area of Best Growth	Fruit	Tree
Adriatic common fig	Cool coast of eastern U.S.	Will produce fruit without caprification. Two crops—June and Aug. Bears around the 10th year. Fruits greenish. Excellent quality for drying.	Hardy tree of 30 years' productivity. Leafs out early so is subject to frost.
Brown Turkey (Black Spanish, San Piero) common fig	Southeastern U.S., Gulf states, Pacific states	Will produce fruits without caprification. Two crops—June and Aug. First crop good quality. Fruits coppery brown. Good for eating fresh.	Prolific when pruned heavily. Can be grown as far north as Zone 5 with winter protection.
Brunswick (Magnolia) common fig	Southeastern U.S., Gulf states, Pacific states	Will produce fruit without caprification. Two crops—June and Aug. Fig bronze or purple-brown. Fair eating quality. Good for canning and preserving.	Can be pruned back sharply. Will produce fruit on new wood.
Calimyrna (Lob Injir) Smyrna fig	California	Needs caprification or hormone spray to set fruit. Fruits tend to split. Color yellow. Grown for drying and eating fresh.	Tree takes 10 years to mature.
Celeste common fig	Southeastern U.S., Delta states, southern plains	Will produce fruit without caprification. One crop in the late summer. Fruits resistant to spoilage. Fruits bronze-purple. Grown mainly for drying.	Hardy tree, but will not bear for 1 year after freezing to the ground. Most commonly grown fig in the southeastern U.S.
Kadota (Dottato) common fig	Southeastern U.S. and California	Will produce fruits without caprification, but they are larger when pollinated. Two crops—June and Aug. Bears around the 8th year. Fruits yellow. Good for drying, canning, and eating fresh.	Prolific when pruned back sharply. Produces best over 15 years.
Mission common fig	Pacific states	Will produce fruits without caprification. Two crops—June and Aug. Fruits black. Good for drying, making jam, and eating fresh.	Old variety from the mid-1700s. Unproductive when pruned heavily. Makes a fine shade tree.

are bending over. They must be handled with great care when picked because their delicate skins are easily damaged. If even a small break is made in the skin, the flesh will sour and break down. Wear gloves while picking figs to protect your hands from contact with the irritating white sap produced by the tree. Figs for drying should be left on the tree until they drop, then gathered and dried further in the sun.

Drying is the most common method of storage but figs can also be preserved frozen in syrup at 0°F. The fruits are highly perishable upon thawing.

Uses: Because fresh figs are so perishable, they are usually preserved rather than eaten fresh. Preserved figs can be suspended in syrup, spiced, pickled, candied, or made into jam. Figs have been used since ancient times as a natural laxative.

GOOSEBERRY

Ribes rusticum, R. hirtellum, R. grossularia
   and others
Saxifragaceae

Though there are many native species of gooseberry, whose ranges overlap to cover most of the U.S., the named, cultivated gooseberries are mainly derived from a few native species and from crosses of native species with the European gooseberry, *R. grossularia*. The cultivated gooseberries are extremely hardy and do best in the northern half of the U.S., though at least one named variety, Glendale, is grown as far south as Arkansas. They are grown commercially from southern Michigan to New York, and from San Francisco to Oregon. In areas where white pine blister rust might attack valuable stands of white pine, there are restrictions on importing gooseberries, which are an alternate host for the rust, and a permit may be required to grow them.

The gooseberry is a 3- to 4-foot deciduous shrub, with woody branches armed with stout, ½-inch spines. The small, pale green flowers appear early in the spring, and the fruit, which is globe- or egg-shaped and sometimes slightly fuzzy, is a translucent green until it ripens in August and September, when it turns red or purple in some varieties.

Soil Requirements: The gooseberry grows on almost any neutral to slightly acid soil, including heavy clay and sandy loam. It is shallow-rooted and needs moist soil, but it will not stand poor drainage. It does best when permanently mulched.

Propagation: Gooseberries may be propagated by hardwood cuttings, like grapes, or by tip-layers. They may also be mound-layered—cut back to 3-inch stubs in spring after growth has started and then covered with earth. As many as 100 shoots will appear and take root. Cut from the parent plant, they may be set out to start new bushes.

Planting and Culture: Gooseberries may be planted in the fall or the spring, though spring is a better choice where cold, dry winters might harm the fall-planted stock. Set the plants at least 5 feet apart and prune them back to stand 5 inches tall. Planting on a northern slope will help delay budding in the spring, a good idea for gooseberries, which bud early and can be damaged by frost, especially in the southern part of their range.

Pruning: Gooseberries, being upright bushes, tend to have crowded branches. Pruning helps keep the shape open. The other object of pruning gooseberries is to have one-third of the branches be new, one-third be one season old, and one-third be two seasons old. Usually, nine branches in all are kept on a bush, and when the oldest three reach the end of their third season they are pruned and three new branches are allowed to remain to replace them. This system of pruning keeps the bush productive, since branches older than three years tend to produce less fruit. Gooseberries are pruned in late winter, before they begin to bud.

Pests and Diseases: Check with a reputable nursery about white pine blister rust before deciding to plant gooseberries, and obtain a permit when one is needed. Avoid planting the bushes within 900 feet of white pines to reduce the risk of spreading the rust. Pruning to keep the bushes open will help fight powdery mildew, a disease that is encouraged by wet weather and that is especially apt to attack English varieties of the gooseberry. Use a dormant spray in late winter before budding to control scale, and handpick and destroy imported currant worms before the population grows numerous. Bluish green, with a black head and black spots, the imported currant worm is ¾ inch long.

Harvest and Storage: Gooseberries ripen over a period of four to six weeks in August and September and may be picked green or ripe, although in the U.S. they are usually picked green. Most pickers wear gloves out of respect for the gooseberry's thorns, and strip the berries from the plant by running each branch through one hand. The berries keep up to three weeks at temperatures just above freezing. Picked green, the gooseberry's tart, sweet flavor is much-loved in pies, jam, and jelly. The berry is also good fresh and is often eaten this way when ripe, especially in Europe.

Gooseberry

Variety	Fruit	Bush
Chautauqua	European type. Fruit is pale green. Larger fruit than American types.	Highly susceptible to powdery mildew, especially when grown in partial shade. Small.
Downing	Older type. Large, pale green fruit. Midseason. Good for canning.	Large, abundant bush.
Fredonia	European type. Plum-sized fruit, dark red when ripe. Late. Good quality.	Highly susceptible to powdery mildew. Bushes vigorous and open. High yielder.
Houghton	Fruit small, dark red.	Large, productive bush. Drooping habit.
Pixwell	Oval fruit, medium-sized. Picks easily.	Few thorns, very hardy. Canes slender and somewhat drooping on older plants. Very hardy.
Poorman	Large fruit, red when mature. Good for eating raw.	Vigorous, productive, large bush. Short thorns.
Welcome	Dull red fruit with pink flesh. Medium-sized. No spines on the fruit.	Nearly thornless.

GRAPE

Vitis spp.
Vitaceae

The grape is a woody vine that climbs by means of tendrils. Though some species, given suitable climate and soil, can grow many feet or even yards in one season, in arid regions the grapevine grows slowly and assumes the appearance of an erect shrub.

The pulp in most grapes is sweet when ripe, although the degree of sweetness or acidity varies with the species and variety. In general, native American species contain tough pulp which is easily separated from the skin (hence the term "slipskin") but harder to separate from the seeds, while European species contain more tender pulp which adheres to the skin but not to the seeds.

Grapevines are usually winter-hardy in the temperate zone (labrusca types more so than viniferas) and may live as long as 50 years. Leaves and flowers, needing heat, appear late in spring, long after fruit trees bloom. Grapes grow rapidly, and some don't stop growing in time to harden up before the first frost, and so are frequently injured. Most American grapes mature in about 165 frost-free days if the summer heat is adequate. *V. vinifera* requires 175 days and hybrids fall between these two, while some varieties related to *V. riparia*, the frost grape, ripen in a shorter period.

"American grapes" describes a group composed of several species, *V. labrusca* being the most notable. Mixed parentage of some of them with *V. riparia* assures their survival in shorter seasons and colder temperatures than those required for *V. vinifera*. They are also distinguished for slip skins and relatively large bunches. Most of these varieties grow well in the United States from New England to the southern plains and from coast to coast (see chart).

Southern or Muscadine grapes are descended from several native species, among them *V. bourquiniana*, *V. champini*, *V. lincecumi*, *V. rotundifolia*, and *V. rupestris*. Unlike

V. labrusca varieties, Muscadines seldom survive temperatures below 5°F. Muscadine fruit clusters are small and contain few fruits. Vines are rangy and so are usually spaced widely, pruned lightly, and trained to high arbors. Some require two varieties for pollination (see chart).

Because a Mediterranean grape was used in breeding American seedless varieties, their winter hardiness is less than that of their labrusca parent. This is not true for the Thompson Seedless, which is a vinifera and is not winter-hardy at all (see chart).

Varieties of *V. vinifera,* the Old World grape, are the principal grapes of world production, comprising about 72% of the European crop. They grow best in semiarid, irrigated areas of the warm temperate zone and in subtropical areas with daily mean temperatures of 35° to 50°F in winter and 70° to 85°F in summer, and 20 to 25 inches of rain a year. Most varieties of vinifera grapes are now grown on American stock in phylloxera-affected areas of the world. All viniferas have non-slip skins.

Most viniferas, due to their lack of winter hardiness, are grown in California, though limited acreages have been planted in Pennsylvania, New York, and Maryland. Varieties yielding a white wine include French Colombard, Rieslings (Grey, White, and Johannisburg), Chardonnay (a white burgundy), and Gewurtztraminer, a pink grape that is fermented without the skins. Red wines are produced from Zinfandel, Cabernet Sauvignon, Salvador, Pinot Noir, and Gamay (see chart).

The French hybrids originated in France by crossing *V. vinifera* with wild American species in order to provide both high quality and disease resistance. All French hybrids are produced for wine, often in blends of juice from more than one variety. These hybrids require less protection from weather, fungi, and pests than vinifera varieties and will thrive farther north. French hybrids are being grown in Kentucky, Michigan, Ohio, Pennsylvania, New York State, and other relatively cold areas.

Pollination: Since most cultivated grapes are bisexual, self-pollinating, and self-fruitful, pollination is seldom a problem. Among the commonly grown varieties that require a vine of another variety nearby for cross-pollination are Brighton, Worden, and several of the Muscadines.

Soil Requirements: *V. vinifera* and its many hybrids do well in light loams which are moderately rich in organic matter, and hold the warmth of the sun. American stocks, now widely used with vinifera grafts, are more adaptable. Either clays or loams will do for them, provided drainage is superior. Grapes will not grow in soggy soils. Slightly acid to neutral soils are best, pH 5.5 to 5.7. The quality of soil affects the flavor and sugar content of the grape. Grapes also do well on rocky, flinty, or chalky soil which holds warmth.

Ideally, a grape-growing soil is rich, cultivated deeply—from 9 to 12 inches—easily drained, alluvial, and built up gradually over centuries from the runoff of a hillside. The rule of thumb is that "poor vines produce the finest grapes." That is, rich loamy soils produce beautiful vines with large crops of late-maturing, low-sugar fruit. Though the crops will be lighter on vines growing in lighter soils they will mature sooner and have significantly higher sugar levels.

Given the proper temperature range and length of growing season, adequate moisture and good drainage, culture of labrusca grapes is comparatively easy, especially when using disease-resistant American stock. Viniferas, however, can be very difficult to grow.

Ordering Stock: Home and commercial growers prefer one-year-old, number 1 plants, well grown and healthy with good, strong roots. Plants should be about 14 inches long. Some nurseries sell two-year-old plants, but these may be of questionable quality. Buy fresh stock from a nursery in your immediate locality that is appropriate to your climate and topography. French hybrid vines, however, are only gradually becoming available in local nurseries and must usually be ordered by mail, keeping local conditions in mind.

Propagation: Propagate canes by selecting mature wood cuttings the size of a pencil. In early winter set bunches of cuttings upside down and cover them with 3 inches of soil to help them produce tip calluses during their dormant period. A cool cellar may be used for this treatment. In spring, set cuttings right side up, 6 inches apart in loose but firmed soil with the top bud exposed. The strongest vines can be planted in place the following spring. Vines also reproduce by layering. A vigorous cane is bent from a vine and covered with 3 inches of soil, leaving three tip buds exposed. Roots form from nodes in a few months. New plants may then be severed from the cane and set out.

Viniferas and other tender varieties are often grafted to more hardy rootstock. Grafts are usually made below the level of the ground since the wood there is most flexible. A simple cleft graft is most common. Late winter is the best time for grafting because scions must be dormant.

Planting and Culture: Set plants out as late in winter or as early in spring as possible in northern areas. Prepare the ground the fall before, digging deeply, and enriching it with compost or rotted manure, phosphate rock, and granite rock. On very acid soil add a small quantity of dolomite lime to bring pH to between 6 and 7. In southern areas where winter injury is not a problem, plant in the fall, making sure that vines are dormant when planted. Buds are easily damaged when their growth has started.

Choose a southern slope if possible, or provide some form of protection from northwesterly winds. Dig holes 1 foot in diameter, or wide enough to allow for full spreading of all roots once they have been trimmed to 6 inches. Remove entirely all damaged roots. Spread the lowest whorl of roots over the hole bottom, first making sure the lowest bud on the trunk is even with the soil surface. Tamp fine soil over the lower whorl, then spread and cover the up-

per whorl and tamp the soil again. Flood the hole with water to wash soil around the roots, and then fill the hole with soil, allowing for some settling.

Remove all but the two or three strongest canes on the vine top and cut those back until they show only two to four buds each. Space the plants 8 feet apart in rows 6 feet apart for moderately vigorous growers like Delaware, and 12 to 20 feet apart in rows 9 to 10 feet apart for Muscadines. Muscadines are often grown on 7-foot arbors, which allows them to be spaced closer.

Posts or trellises for any variety of grape may be added up to the second or third growing season, but if adding a trellis is to be delayed, some support may be necessary.

Vines are adapted to dry areas and seldom need watering except in early spring while shoots are developing and during midsummer droughts before canes begin to harden for winter. Grape leaves look conspicuously droopy when the vines need water. Well-rotted manure is the best fertilizer for grapevines, but over-fertilizing or feeding too late in the season can cause rapid growth, an abundance of low-quality fruit, and increased susceptibility to frost damage.

Most grape species need mulching for winter protection in cold areas. Spread compost, or rotted manure, or a coarse mulch over the soil in a 3-foot circle an inch deep around the vine trunk. If not mulching, be sure to cultivate the vines to remove weeds. Rake back the mulch in early spring when more compost is applied.

Proper location of vineyards is an important factor in winter protection. In very cold areas vines can be bent to the ground and layered over with earth or straw during winter. Fiberglass fence windbreaks provide a sun-reflecting surface and block wind. Some vine growers in cold regions use plastic tents over their trellises. Some smaller vines can be grown in large pots and trained to the rafters in greenhouses.

Pruning: Grapes are pruned in order to reduce

the amount and proportion of woody growth, to limit the quantity of fruit so as to improve its quality and reduce strain on the vine, to keep the vines off the ground and of manageable size for harvesting, and to permit sunshine to reach all portions of the vine and fruit. Fruit is always borne on woody growth of the present season. Wood of previous seasons, out of which present-season growth has emerged, is itself unproductive. The rate of bearing and the quality of fruit is enhanced when growers practice selection in developing their vines. This means preventing vines from developing too many fruit clusters and too much wood by choosing the one or two growth buds which are judged to have the best production potential, while removing all possible competitors. Fruit grows best on a hard, well-ripened cane the size of a man's small finger.

Unless careful pruning is done, grapes are borne farther and farther from the main trunk each year on the ends of long canes. As sustenance from the roots must travel longer distances each year, the quality of grapes on a poorly tended vine tends to decline. One important goal in pruning is to keep the site of fruit clusters as near the main trunk wood as possible. This is achieved by either first developing a relatively high trunk and then selecting shoots and guiding them outward from the trunk in an umbrella or fan formation, or by selecting, developing, and training arms which grow laterally from the trunk at a relatively low height and from which bearing shoots will be grown. There are many variations on these two basic systems.

Head pruning, often used for viniferas, develops a 5-foot trunk with a ring of arms at the summit and spurs at the ends of the arms. Cane pruning also uses a long-trunk system, but develops a fan shape with two arms, one on each side of the head, and with fruiting canes up to 5 feet long retained at the ends of arms and wrapped around a supporting trellis wire. Cordon pruning, used for both viniferas and American grapes, develops a 3-foot trunk, branching to horizontal sections from which arms are developed at 8- to 12-inch intervals with spurs coming from them. Cordon pruning is suitable for use with a vine trellis, while the other types require a stake or post for each vine.

Prune between February and April when vines are dormant and will not bleed. During the first year after planting four shoots should develop from the two buds left on each of the two original spurs which were cut back after planting. When they are 2 to 3 inches long, remove all but the strongest one. By the end of the first year this trunk stem should be up to 6 feet tall. Before the second growing season, remove all side branches of the trunk and construct a support or trellis system. Tie the trunk cane to the lowest wire on the trellis, usually a yard or more from the ground, and anchor the trunk tip to the top wire, trimming it to no more than 3 inches above the wire. Most trellises have two or three wires at 2½-foot intervals.

By the third year a vine can carry 25 buds. Select four strong canes, two near each wire level, and prune away the rest, leaving one short renewal stub near the base of each cane. This stub should have two buds. The two canes on the upper level should have four or five buds and the two on the lower level should have six. (For this example, we are using the popular four-arm Kniffen system for American grapes.) On each level one cane is trained to the left and one to the right. Each is tied loosely with twine and then wrapped in a spiral around the wire. These trained canes will be the arms. Fruiting canes which grow from them during the following season will also be trained to the two wire levels.

In commercial plantings, vinifera grapes are usually head or cane pruned and trained to a post, but they can be trained to an arbor or to an umbrella- or fan-shaped system like the Munson trellis system. Muscadines are most often arbor trained, but will respond to a four-arm system. American hybrids are most often trained to a two-, four-, or six-arm Kniffen

Four-arm Kniffen system

system or to the Munson system. Agricultural extension offices can provide more detailed information about pruning, training, and support building.

Pests and Diseases: Though less subject to pests and diseases than other fruits, grapes are frequently damaged by birds and require protection from them. Insect pests include Japanese beetles and grapeberry moth; worst diseases are mildews. On most varieties other than Concord, powdery mildew and downy mildew are serious problems. Grape phylloxera can be a problem on some viniferas and hybrids.

Harvest and Storage: Harvest time for grapes ranges from late summer to midfall in most vine-growing areas, with time of harvest depending on the variety grown and the use that is to be made of the crop. Grapes do not continue to ripen after picking, so the ability to gauge ripeness is crucial to full harvests. Signs of ripeness are sweet and mellow taste (in most varieties), browning and slight shriveling of the stem, brownish red color of ripe wood, ease of picking clusters and berries, brownness of ripe berry seeds, and, in most varieties, ease with which pulp is freed from seeds.

Cut grapes from the vine with a sharp knife or shears and handle carefully, particularly those intended for table use. To preserve as much of the powdery bloom on the berries as possible, handle the vines, not the berries. To prevent crushing of the first-picked bunches, use baskets holding no more than 4 quarts.

Pick berries for storage in the coolest part of the day, if vines are dry. Select only the most perfect and firm fruit for storage. Cool storage grapes to 50°F as soon as possible, and spread them in single layers, keeping them spread out until the stems shrivel slightly. Then stack the trays 4 inches deep in a cool (30° to 40°F) cellar where humidity is 87 to 92% for viniferas and 80 to 85% for Eastern varieties. Many varieties stored in this way will last several months, but they should be checked frequently for spoilage. Grapes can also be canned or frozen.

Grapes for wine are usually harvested all at one time at various degrees of ripeness unless especially fine wine of assured sugar content is desired. For jelly and jam, grapes should be picked somewhat early so that bunches contain some underripe berries that are full of pectin and prevent crystals from forming in processed jelly. When using grapes for juice, allow them to reach full maturity.

Grape

Variety	Fruit	Season and Cold Hardiness	Special Characteristics
Eastern or American Types			
Beta	Black. Small fruit and clusters. Fruit high in acid and sugar.	Very cold-hardy, to −35°F.	Vigorous, productive. Used for juice and jelly. Self-sterile, requires pollination by another variety.
Blue Jay	Blue-black. Must be fully ripe to be eaten.	Hardy to −15°F, but needs protection from wind.	Requires pollination by another variety.
Buffalo	Black. Dessert quality; juicy, sweet.	Ripens 3 weeks before Concord. Hardy to −15°F.	Good early table grape. Moderately susceptible to downy and powdery mildew.
Catawba	Red. Medium-sized berries and clusters.	Ripens 2 weeks after Concord. Late-bearing. Hardy to −15°F.	Productive but subject to fungal disease. Needs 10–12 ft. spacing. Used for wine, juice. Stores 5–8 weeks.
Concord	Deep purple to black. Aromatic. Large clusters. Medium sugar content.	Late-bearing. Growing season 170 days. Hardy to −15°F.	10–12-ft. spread. Most common Eastern grape. Disease-resistant and productive. Used for jelly and dessert. Stores 4–7 weeks.
Delaware	Red. Small berries; small clusters.	Ripens 2 weeks before Concord. Hardy to −15°F.	Susceptible to downy mildew. Good yields. Not for heavy soils. Small vines need 6–8 ft. Used for white wine. Stores 4–7 weeks.
Fredonia	Black. Large clusters of medium size.	Ripens 2–3 weeks before Concord. Hardy to −15°F.	Vigorous, productive. Susceptible to downy mildew. Makes good jelly.
Moore Early	Black. Similar to Concord. Moderately large.	Ripens 2 weeks earlier than Concord. Hardy to −15°F.	Less vigorous vine than Concord. Fruit often cracks. Needs fertile soil and heavy pruning. Stores 3–6 weeks.
Niagara	White. Medium to large berries; large clusters. Acid, foxy.	Ripens few days before Concord. Hardy to −5°F.	Moderately susceptible to disease. Most popular white variety. Stores 3–6 weeks. Excellent yields.
Senaca	White. Non-slip skin. Firm, tender.	Ripens 3 weeks before Concord. Hardy to 5°F. Not very winter-hardy.	Very susceptible to powdery mildew.
Sheridan	Black. Medium-sized, compact bunch.	Ripens 1 week after Concord. Hardy to −5°F.	Stores well. Requires much pruning, good location.
Steuben	Blue-black. Sweet and spicy. Large bunches.	Ripens few days after Concord. Hardy to −15°F.	Promising as a wine grape. Stores 8 weeks. Excellent dessert grape.
Van Buren	Black. Medium-sized fruits and clusters. Less aromatic than Concord.	Ripens 1 month before Concord. Very early. Hardy to −15°F.	Vigorous and productive. Susceptible to downy mildew.
Worden	Black. Sweet. Large berries and clusters.	Ripens 2–3 weeks before Concord. Hardy to −15°F.	Needs another variety for pollination. Moderately resistant to mildew. Wet fruit cracks. Stores 3–5 weeks.

(continued)

Grape—*continued*

Variety	Fruit	Season and Cold Hardiness	Special Characteristics
Southern or Muscadine Types			
Creek	Red-purple. Thin skin.	Late.	Good quality. Very vigorous. High yield.
Dulcet	Dark red. Small berries.	Early.	Vigorous. Good quality.
Higgins	Bronze. Large berries.	Midseason.	Good quality. Large.
Hunt	Black. Thin skin.	Early.	Excellent quality. High yield.
Magoon	Medium red.	Early to midseason.	Vigorous vine. Self-pollinating.
Scuppernong (a wild variety)	Green to bronze.	Early.	Rich in vitamin C.
Tarheel	Black. Thin skin. Small berries.	Midseason.	Self-pollinating.
Topsail	Light red.	Late.	High sugar content. Very vigorous. Excellent quality.
Yuga	Reddish amber. Thin skin.	Late.	Very good flavor.
American Seedless Types			
Canadice	Red, large compact clusters, medium fruit.	Ripens 3 weeks before Concord. Good hardiness.	Much like Delaware Slipskin. Stores well.
Concord Seedless	Blue-black. Very small berries and clusters.	Ripens same as Concord. Very good hardiness.	Very poor yields. Flavor and vine characteristics like Concord.
Glenora	Blue-black. Large clusters, medium berries. Delicate flavor.	Ripens 2 weeks before Concord. Fair hardiness.	Phylloxera-resistant.
Himrod	Yellow. Large, loose clusters; medium fruit.	Ripens 4 weeks before Concord. Good hardiness.	Excellent dessert quality. Moderate mildew susceptibility.
Interlaken	Golden yellow. Medium, compact clusters; medium fruit.	Ripens 3 weeks before Concord. Fair hardiness.	Bird protection needed. Moderate mildew susceptibility.
Lakemont	White. Large, compact clusters; medium berries.	Ripens 1 week before Concord. Good hardiness.	Moderately susceptible to downy, but not powdery, mildew. Excellent table grape.
Romulus	Yellow-white. Medium to large compact clusters; small berries.	Ripens same as Concord. Good hardiness.	Moderate mildew susceptibility. Similar to Thompson Seedless, but better eating quality.
Suffolk Red	Red. Loose, medium clusters; large berries.	Ripens 3 weeks before Concord. Good hardiness.	Moderate mildew susceptibility. Possibly the best Eastern seedless table grape.
Viniferas			
Emperor	Red. Large berries, large clusters.	Early.	Highest in production in California. Keeps 1–2½ months. Used for raisins, wine, table.

Variety	Fruit	Season and Cold Hardiness	Special Characteristics
Viniferas *(continued)*			
Flame Tokay, Tokay	Red. Large berries.	Midseason.	Similar to Malaga, but for cooler areas. Table.
Muscat of Alexandria	White. Large berries. Sweet and flavorful.	Midseason.	Keeps 1–1½ months. Raisins and wine.
Red Malaga (also called Castiza)	Red. Large berries.	Midseason.	Good for hot areas. Keeps 2–3 months. Table use.
Ribier (Alphonse Lavallee)	Black. Very large berries. Medium-sized bunches.	Early to midseason.	Keeps 3–5 months. Table.
Thompson Seedless (Sultanina)	White to light green. Large bunches.	Early.	Highest in production in California. Keeps 1–2½ months. Used for raisins, wine, table.
French Hybrids			
Aurora (Siebel 5279)	White, amber or pinkish white.	Early-maturing. Winter-hardy in southern grape-growing areas.	Excellent grape. Heavy-bearing. Susceptible to powdery mildew. Needs heavy pruning and cluster thinning. Makes delicate white wine. Also used for table.
Baco Noir (Baco 1)	Blue. Long, compact cluster. Medium-sized berries.	Ripens 1 month before Concord. Moderately winter-hardy.	Very vigorous vine, attractive on trellis. Makes excellent red table wine; much used commercially.
Cascade (Siebel 13053)	Deep red to blue.	Ripens 1 month before Concord. Medium vine hardiness.	Heavy-bearing. Very disease-resistant. May have problems with soilborne viruses. Red wine banned in France as possible liver damage cause. Makes superior rosé. Often blended with Baco Noir.
Chelois (Siebel 10878)	Blue.	Matures shortly after Aurora. Medium hardy.	Often overbears. Needs heavy pruning. Tendency to winter damage. Makes good red wine.
DeChaunac (Siebel 9549)	Blue.	Ripens 10 days before Concord. Early-blooming. Moderately hardy.	Heavy-producing vines, grown in New York and Michigan. Vines need heavy pruning and well-drained, frost-protected site. Excellent red wine.
Foch (Kuhlmann 188-2)	Blue-black.	Ripens 1 month before Concord. Cold-hardy. Midseason.	Some disagreement over vine vigor. Burgundy-type wine.
Seyval Blanc (SV 5-276)	Green. Large clusters. Medium berries.	Needs long growing season. (Ripens in October in south of England.) Medium-hardy. Poor vine vigor.	Low sugar, high acid content. Heavy-bearing. Cluster thinning recommended. Makes dry white wine.
Swenson Red (Cross of Siebel 11803 and Minnesota #78, an American hybrid)	Red. Medium to large compact clusters. Large round berries.	Ripe in Minnesota by early September. Midseason.	Vigorous, productive. Susceptible to mildew. Makes white wine, or if fermented in skins, a fruity rosé.

(continued)

Grape—*continued*

Variety	Fruit	Season and Cold Hardiness	Special Characteristics
French Hybrids *(continued)* Veeblanc (Cross of two French hybrids produced in Ontario)	White. Larger bunches and berries than Concord.	Matures earlier than Concord. Medium-hardy in Ontario.	Resistant to mildew. Excellent for dry white wine.
Villard Blanc (SV 12-375)	Green or greenish yellow.	Late-blooming and ripening. Needs long growing season. Medium winter-hardy.	Vigorous, productive vine. Needs heavy pruning. Good table grape when fully ripe. Good white wine.

GRAPEFRUIT

Citrus ×paradisi
Rutaceae

The grapefruit is a large, round-topped, vigorous, spreading tree with dense foliage. It grows 33 to 50 feet high, one of the largest of the citruses. Flowers are large, white, and pungent in fragrance. Fruits are round or slightly oval, yellow or pinkish yellow, and larger than oranges. Grapefruit can be up to 6 inches in diameter.

The tree is particularly resistant to heat and to drying winds and can tolerate cold as well as the orange. At least nine to ten months are needed to mature grapefruit on the tree. The limiting factor in the growing of grapefruit is the heat required and the length of the growing season. Grapefruit grows best in hot desert valleys.

Pollination: Grapefruit will set fruit without pollination or fertilization and several grapefruit varieties are seedless. Unlike other citrus, grapefruit has a tendency to self-pollination. Grapefruit flowers attract bees with their strong perfume and abundant nectar. Usually, grapefruit is artificially pollinated only when a specific cross is sought. When pollination is artificially prevented by removing anthers from the buds, some grapefruit, like the Marsh variety, will produce seedless fruit.

Soil Requirements: The most favorable soil for grapefruit, as for other citrus, is acid with a pH of from 5.0 to 6.5, though it will grow at 7.0. Most feeder roots occur in the top 3 feet of soil, although grapefruit taproots can penetrate 17 feet or more. Therefore, it is important that the upper part of the soil be well enriched. Subsoil should be loose and as rich as possible.

Vetch, clover, and hairy indigo are frequently used as cover crops in grapefruit orchards to increase soil organic content, for grapefruit requires more organic enrichment than oranges do. Cover crops must be used with care in dry areas where heat is used in winter, for they may, untended, present a fire hazard. Grapefruit trees are quite sensitive to some salts such as boron.

Propagation: When planting grapefruit from seed for the home orchard, use large flats, cold frames, or containers. Give seedlings frequent, light waterings and remove all weeds. Grapefruit is more difficult to root from cuttings than lemons or limes, but easier than mandarins.

Planting and Culture: In tropical and semi-tropical areas, planting may be done at any season of the year with reasonable success. In Florida the best time to plant is late winter or early spring when the trees are most dormant. If grapefruit trees are planted in December, they should be banked with soil for protection against cold. In the Rio Grande Valley of Texas, an important grapefruit area, December to January is considered the best time to plant. Plant grapefruit like other citrus (see Citrus Fruits), but allow maximum spacing. After the initial period has passed, grapefruit requires less frequent watering than other citrus.

Grapefruit trees, while less easily wind damaged than many other citruses, are sometimes given protection from strong or cold winds by means of windbreaks. In desert areas the trees must sometimes be protected from blowing sand. At times when cold nights follow warm days, ripe grapefruit should be given protection from frost at 26°F and green or half-ripe fruit at 27°F. If days have been cold (under 59°F) ripe fruit should be protected at 27°F and half-ripe at 27.5°F. Damp nights are more dangerous than dry.

Pruning: Pruning of grapefruit trees is not essential either for growth or for fruit production. This is especially true where land is fertile and well drained. Since grapefruit tends to an upright habit with terminal buds dominant, sometimes too few lateral limbs may grow to make the tree easy to pick. When fruit weighs the upright branch down to a lateral position, lateral buds start to develop. One of these becomes a new upright branch, while others become fruiting shoots. As this process goes on, year after year, the lower interior portions of the tree become filled with dense, weak wood. Pruning of this wood is sometimes necessary.

Shoot growth is less vigorous in the grapefruit than in other citrus, so generally less pruning must be done. In desert valleys, shoot vigor is greater than in coastal areas. Young grapefruit trees sometimes grow unevenly and require pruning to force the tree to correct its irregular growth habit.

Pests and Diseases: See Citrus Fruits.

Harvest and Storage: Grapefruit can be left on the tree for storage in dry areas, and this is the recommended storage method for home growers.

Grapefruit

Variety	Area	Description
Duncan (many descendants called Florida Common)	Florida, South, and Southeast	Common. Pale color. Rich, juicy flavor. Seeds. Used for canning and processing. Early.
Foster	Florida, South, and Southeast	Pigmented. Pale to light, or blushed pink. Medium-large. Good flavor. Many seeds. Medium-early.
Marsh (Marsh Seedless, White Marsh)	California	Common. Pale to light yellow. Medium-sized. Less rich than Duncan. Seedless. Best variety for eating fresh. Ships well. Late.
Red Blush	California	Pigmented. Crimson blush on rind. Medium-sized. Good flavor. Seedless. Midseason.
Thompson (Pink Marsh)	California	Pigmented. Light pink flesh. Medium-sized. Good flavor. Seedless. Midseason.
Triumph	California	Common. Pale to light yellow. Medium-sized. Juicy, excellent flavor. Very seedy. Midseason.

If tree-storing ripe grapefruit, water or irrigate the trees frequently to maintain the juice content of the fruit. Seedless forms work better for tree storage, as seeds sometimes sprout inside mature seedy varieties.

Like most citrus, grapefruit is picked by clipping. Thin-skinned varieties must be handled with care because they bruise easily.

Uses: Grapefruit is most often eaten fresh, as a breakfast fruit or in fruit salads. Grapefruit juice, rich in vitamin C, is the other major use.

JUNEBERRY

Sarviceberry, serviceberry, shadblow,
  shadbush
Amelanchier spp.
Rosaceae

There are about 25 species of *Amelanchier* in the north temperate areas of the world, many of which are native to the U.S. and Canada. Most of the species have separate common names, but they all answer to the general name of juneberry. Juneberries are grown for their delicate white flowers that bloom profusely in May, and for their edible fruits. *A. laevis* and

A. alnifolia are the most commonly grown species in North America.

Species of *Amelanchier* are either large shrubs or small trees that reach an average of 15 to 20 feet tall. The leaves turn an attractive yellow and red in the fall. The "berry" is really a small pome fruit—a tiny apple—averaging about ⅜ inch in diameter. It is usually deep blue, but some varieties, especially those of *A. alnifolia,* are not. Planting two varieties together ensures better pollination. The plants are adaptable to a wide range of soil types, and are extremely hardy. As *A. alnifolia* becomes more of a commercial crop in the northwest plains and Canada, a number of varieties are being developed. Three are most often recommended. Smoky has large, fleshy, round, very sweet but mild-flavored fruit on a spreading bush. It reaches a height of 6 to 8 feet and suckers freely. Pembina has large, slightly oval, sweet, full-flavored fruit on an upright vigorous bush that grows to about 10 feet. It does not sucker as much as Smoky. Forestburg has very large fruit, but not quite the quality of Smoky or Pembina. It fruits later than these two varieties.

Propagation: Juneberries can be propagated by seed, cuttings, or by transplanting root sprouts or suckers. The latter is easiest and surest. Plants grown from seed may not come true to the parent form. When digging up a root sprout to move it, try to keep intact its fibrous root system. Transplant in spring.

Planting and Culture: Plants of *A. alnifolia* are usually grown as hedgerows with plants set 6 feet apart, although they can be grown in rows 8 feet apart both ways for cross-cultivation to control weeds. A grass-legume sod between rows can be maintained where moisture is sufficient, with mulch to control weeds around the plants. In dryland climates, the rows are often kept cultivated with a cover crop of oats or barley sown between the rows after harvest to catch snow for moisture. *A. laevis* should be planted as single trees with space enough to catch the sun and flourish on all sides. On any average garden soil, extra fertilizer should rarely be necessary.

A vigorous bush, one or two years old and 6 to 12 inches high, is best to start out with. Set the plant a little deeper than it was in the nursery bed. Be very particular with the roots. Drying and exposure to sunlight will quickly kill them. Plants begin to bear in two to four years, and increase in production for about ten years.

Pruning: Prune bushes in early spring after the coldest weather has passed. Keep the bushes at about 6 feet high. Thin out old center growth, and all weak or diseased canes. Fruiting takes place in the second year on older growth, decreasing on a cane as it grows older.

Pests and Diseases: Pests are not a serious problem. Common junipers (red cedar) can transfer rust to juneberries, as to apples. The fruit maggot is sometimes a problem. The more humid the weather, the greater the chance for fungal diseases. Juneberries in their natural habitat seldom have critical pest problems, although they are subject to the same ills as any pome fruit.

Harvest, Storage, and Uses: Juneberries ripen in early to midsummer. For highest vitamin C content and easier jelling, pick fruit when not quite fully ripe. It freezes and preserves better at this stage, too. For wine, allow fruit to ripen fully for highest sugar content. Two juneberry trees usually provide all the jelly and pies a family can use, if the birds don't get them first. The trees are also useful to draw birds away from other summer fruit.

KIWIFRUIT

Chinese gooseberry, yangtao
Actinidia chinensis
Actinidiaceae

A. chinensis is one of 40 species in this genus of woody vines that entwine themselves around whatever support is available. It can grow up to 30 feet long. Kiwifruit varieties currently in cultivation need 235 frost-free days for the fruit to grow and mature. These conditions exist in southern, western, and southeastern border states, including eastern Virginia, Alabama, Florida, Louisiana, southernmost Texas, and large parts of California. *A. chinensis* is one of the less hardy species of the genus, but will grow in temperate to semitropical areas that meet its climatic needs. New growth and fruit can tolerate 30° to 105°F. Fully dormant vines can tolerate temperatures as low as 10°F, but vines partially dormant in the fall can tolerate only 24°F.

The fruit is an oval berry the size and shape of a lemon or slightly smaller, with fuzzy, reddish brown skin covering emerald green flesh that is embedded with many small, soft, black seeds. The fruit grows on the vine in clusters like grapes, usually appearing around June. The skin is thin, but firm enough to protect the fruit over long-distance travel.

The flesh has a firm, melonlike texture, and a delicious, fresh, sweet taste that has been described as a blend of banana, lime, strawberry, and melon. It contains as much as twice the vitamin C of oranges, with the greatest concentrations just under the skin. It takes about 150 days for fruit to develop its mature taste and texture once it has become full-grown. All the fruit on a single vine ripens simultaneously in the fall in California. Despite the vigorous growth habit of the vine, it takes four to five years to bloom and eight years to fruit.

Pollination: Since the plants are unisexual, plant a male close to a female in order for wind or bees to effect cross-pollination. Plant one pollinator for every eight or nine fruit-bearing plants.

Soil Requirements: Soil should be well drained, loamy sand to loam, and 4 to 8 feet deep to allow for root growth. Kiwifruit will grow well on land that accommodates almonds, avocados, or peaches. Soil should be low in sodium and chloride, and neutral to acid in pH. Cultivation is not difficult in the proper soil and climate.

Propagation: Plant named varieties only; planting seedlings may yield fruit inferior in size and quality. Also, half of the seedlings will be males that cannot be identified until they flower, and which will be far in excess of the number required for pollination. To root cuttings, use wood ½ inch in diameter with two or three nodes, taken in midsummer.

Planting and Culture: Plant in a sunny or shady location in soil finely prepared to accommodate the vine's mass of shallow fibrous roots. Space plants 15 to 20 feet apart in the rows and space rows about 15 feet apart. Work in compost, well-rotted manure, and other soil amendments at the end of the growing season to keep the soil rich in organic matter and nutrients.

In early spring, the growth is vulnerable to damage from wind and frost. If the first tender shoots bearing the flower buds freeze or break, the whole crop is lost for the season because any later growth will be only vegetative. Hard frosts in the fall can also damage immature fruit. For these reasons, plant vines only in areas bordered by windbreaks and protected from the possibility of frost.

Pruning: Pruning and training are crucial to a successful crop. At the time of planting, build trellises or arbors that will support the rapidly growing plants. The framework can be similar to, but much stronger than, a grape trellis in order to accommodate the great weight of the fully grown vines.

To construct a trellis: use posts 4 to 6 inches in diameter and 6 to 9 feet long. Position one post at each plant, set 2 to 3 feet into the soil. Space one or more galvanized steel wires (8- to 12-gauge size) at the top, with a second wire midway below it. Stretch the wires to 300 pounds of tension. In the first season, train each vine to grow vertically to the top of the post as a single trunk. Once it reaches the top, head it back so that two permanent arms or cordons develop from the trunk along the center wire. From these arms will grow the branching vines from which flowers and fruit develop. Tie leaders loosely with twine, rather than twisting them around wires.

Prune the vines every winter when they are dormant. Remove about a third of the limbs growing from the permanent arms, choosing limbs that have already fruited for two years, as well as removing damaged wood and the most twisted of the current year's growth. Shorten the remaining current year's limbs sufficiently to prevent the next crop of fruit from bending to the ground. Shorten older spurs back to within two or four buds beyond last season's fruiting wood.

Prune again in summer by rubbing off basal suckers, and vertical growth when it is a few inches long. To prevent the plant from weakening, shorten the ends of the current season's branches from the permanent arms back to seven or eight buds from their base.

Kiwifruit

Variety	Area Where Growth Has Been Tested	Description	Pollinating Needs
Monty	New Zealand		Female; grow with Tomuri.
Abbott	New Zealand	Early flowering.	Female; grow with Matua.
Bruno	New Zealand	Early flowering.	Female; grow with Matua.
Hayward	New Zealand	Has large fruit size and keeps well; favorite variety in New Zealand.	Female; grow with Tomuri, Chico-male, Matua.
Chico-male	California		Favorite pollinator in California; grow with Hayward.
Matua	California		Male; grow with Abbott and Bruno.
Tomuri	California		Male; grow with Hayward and Monty.

Pests and Diseases: Pests of kiwifruit include omnivorous leafroller worms, root knot and lesion nematodes, and salt marsh caterpillars. Diseases include crown rot and oak root fungus.

Harvest and Storage: Though fruit is full-sized by midsummer, do not pick it until the texture and flavor mature. Fruit picked too soon will wither before it softens. Fruit picked when almost soft will have a peculiar taste. To check if fruit is ready to harvest, pick one, let is soften for a few days, then taste it. If it's sweet, pick all the fruit at once and refrigerate. Remove from the refrigerator a few days before needed to allow for final softening and development of flavor. All the fruit should be picked before frost, but if no frost danger exists, fruit can remain on the vine throughout the dormant season.

Fully ripe fruit can be frozen in slices for up to six months. Thawed slices retain their texture and color but lose some sweetness. Canned fruit has a mild, pleasant flavor, even though it changes in color and texture.

Because it is acidic, kiwifruit is excellent for blending with bland juices, or used as a breakfast drink by itself. Add fresh kiwifruit to salads, ice cream, cakes and tarts, mix it with yogurt, and add it to sandwiches. It is too delicate to cook.

KUMQUAT

Fortunella japonica
Rutaceae

The kumquat is an evergreen shrub or small tree, fine-stemmed and bushy. The fruit is very small, round or oval. Its color is golden orange to reddish orange. The rind surface is smooth and the flavor is sweet and spicy.

The kumquat has been reclassified in the genus *Fortunella,* rather than the genus *Citrus.*

It is closely related to the calamondin and to some mandarins. Since it is very cold-resistant, it can be grown in Florida as well as in California where it ripens midseason. Kumquats can also be container-grown in warm greenhouses.

The kumquat requires rich organic soil for good production.

In addition, because of its cold hardiness, the kumquat has been used in Florida for crosses producing limequats, orangequats, and citrangequats. The most well known orangequat variety is Nippon, which makes good marmalade, but is not widely grown. In Florida, Nagami is the kumquat variety commonly grown.

The shrubs are usually grafted onto other rootstocks suitable for dwarfing, including trifoliate orange. They can be purchased from nurseries.

Ripe kumquats hold well on the tree with little loss in quality.

The taste of the kumquat is too tart to be widely appreciated for fresh eating. It is used in syrup, candying, and making marmalade, but its greatest commercial use is in Florida where it is used in gift packaging of other citrus and as decoration. The tree is much used as an ornamental for terraces, patios, and house decorating.

LEMON

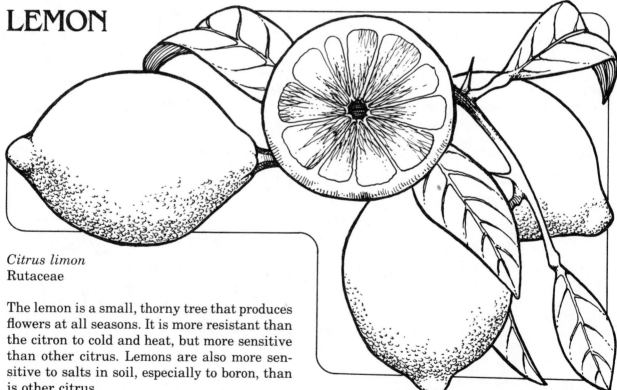

Citrus limon
Rutaceae

The lemon is a small, thorny tree that produces flowers at all seasons. It is more resistant than the citron to cold and heat, but more sensitive than other citrus. Lemons are also more sensitive to salts in soil, especially to boron, than is other citrus.

Pollination: Many lemon blossoms are sterile due to pistil abortion and many lemon varieties regularly produce seedless fruit.

Culture: Lemon trees are most often propagated by budding onto rough lemon rootstock.

To be safe from frost, lemons need at least 28°F temperature if ripe, and 30°F when underripe. Ice on underripe lemons can damage the rind. In central California, lemons become more cold-resistant during the winter months when they are partly dormant. Windbreaks, lath shelters, water spraying, and heating devices protect lemons from cold.

Pruning: Lemon trees, unlike other citrus, require pruning to maintain the life of the tree. Unpruned lemon trees become so choked with inner branches that fruit becomes small and scarred. Pests are also more difficult to combat on unpruned trees, and harvesting becomes difficult or impossible. Shoot growth is more vigorous on the lemon than on other citrus trees. The more humid the growing area, the more rapid the growth.

Lemon trees are open and irregular in their growth habit. Their shoots tend to be spindly and easily broken. Weak shoots should be pruned back to the lateral. The trees also tend to grow strong horizontal branches in all directions through the center of the trees, which in turn send out tangled interior limbs. They also grow strong upright branches that bend when laden with fruit. Careful and frequent pruning helps to establish a good framework without crossing branches. Lightly pruned lemon trees produce more fruit than either unpruned or heavily pruned ones. Dead wood should always be removed to prevent disease. Top wood is sometimes pruned to permit the entry of light which assists ripening.

Prune lemon trees once or twice a year throughout their life. The purpose of moderate pruning is to produce a low, spreading tree of compact form which is easy to harvest. Pruning also hastens the development of fruit to picking size.

Pests and Diseases: See Citrus Fruits.

Harvest and Storage: Lemons are harvested year-round in southern California. They may be kept for six to eight months after picking if they are cured during dry weather. Keep the fruit at a temperature of 50° to 60°F. During storage the rind loses moisture and becomes tougher and more resistant to injury.

Fall and winter fruits usually store and ship better than spring and summer ones. In humid, semitropical or tropical regions, rind

Lemon

Variety	Where Grown	Fruit	Tree
Berna (Vernia, Bernia, Verna)	California	Holds on tree into summer, but becomes large and loses quality. Winter.	
Dorshapo (Citron Doux is similar)	California	Sweet lemon. Like Eureka, but more ribbed and with more prominent nipple. Flesh amber yellow, insipid, lacking in acid and flavor.	Like Eureka, but less productive.
Eureka (clonal relatives are: Allen, Cascade, Cook, Thornton; also Ross, which is often given variety status)	Southern coastal California	Medium-small with few seeds. Flesh greenish yellow, juicy, highly acid. Mostly spring and early summer, but some in late winter.	Smallest lemon tree, thornless with few leaves. Less cold-resistant, more everbearing.
Lisbon (clonal relatives: Limmeira 8A, Monroe, Prior, Strong; also Galligan and Rosenberger, which are often given variety status)	California	Inconspicuous neck and large nipple. Flesh greenish yellow and very acid. Winter and spring.	Very vigorous, with many thorns. Dense foliage.
Villafranca (some clones attributed to Eureka and Lisbon may belong to it instead)	Southern California	Similar to Eureka. Winter and early spring.	Between Eureka and Lisbon in hardiness and size.

diseases prevent storage and consequently limes are more used than lemons in the tropics. **Uses:** Lemons are grown primarily for their juice. They are used in lemonade, as a garnish for fish or meats, and in pies, cakes, sauces, candies, jams, and jellies. The peel is candied or used in marmalade. Lemons are also useful for pectin.

LIME

Citrus aurantiifolia
Rutaceae

The two main groups of limes are sour limes and sweet limes. The West Indian lime, a sour type, has smaller, paler leaves than the Tahitian lime, and is thorny. It is also much more frost-sensitive. In fact, this type is as sensitive to frost as the citron.

Limes and lemons, which can substitute for one another in use, seldom grow well in the same place.

The lime tree is small with many branches and many sharp, stout spines. Flowers, produced over a long period, have four to five white petals. The fruits are small and oval or round with a thin and clinging peel that is greenish yellow when ripe. Pulp is greenish and very acid.

Limes are rich in ascorbic acid, though they have less than lemons. Citric acid is in 7 to 8% concentration in limes, the highest for any citrus. Limes ripen the year round if grown in warm areas.

Soil Requirements: The West Indian, Mexican, or Key lime is particularly suited to the alkaline, rocky soil of the Florida Keys, though it will also grow in deep, acid, sandy soil such as is found in southern Florida. On the acid soil, however, it produces less fruit and fruit with less juice, though fruits are larger.

The Persian lime is suited to alkaline, rocky soil and to sandy, acid soil. Home gardeners often mix shell rock in their acid, sandy soil to improve it before planting lime trees. The Rangpur lime can be grown in almost any soil and will withstand flooding. When grown from seed, it grows best on low, wet soils.

Propagation: Throughout the world, most limes are grown from seedling stock or from seeds without requiring rootstock or budding. Trees come fairly true from seed, but varieties are sometimes difficult to classify.

Planting and Culture: A spineless form of Mexican or West Indian lime tree is widely sold in nurseries in the southern United States. It has a compact growth and dark green leaves and is used as an ornamental as well as for its fruit crop. It can be used near patios or in tubs or pots, but it must be fertilized with compost or well-rotted manure occasionally. This form is more cold-resistant than most West Indian limes and it also resists disease. Sweet limes are also planted in home gardens, but they are harder to find in nurseries.

When planting West Indian limes in the home garden, it is wise to set them in isolated corners of the yard. They require less soil enrichment than other plants and will grow in sandy soil, but they also require very little water and may be hurt by being watered by sprinkler along with the rest of the yard. Young flowers, foliage, and fruits are susceptible to anthracnose fungus which may develop when the trees are inadvertently sprinkled.

Limes, and especially West Indian limes, need protection from cold winds. Use screens or windbreaks.

Pruning: Most limes are pruned like other citrus, very lightly, but a few share the lemon's tendency to produce tangled interior growth, and these need frequent pruning. The Rangpur lime tends to top-heaviness and needs pruning to maintain balance in growth.

Harvest and Storage: Most limes grown commercially are picked immature and, like lemons, cured. Most varieties remain fresh on the tree, but the Tahitian keeps less well than the West Indian. The West Indian will drop from the tree when fully mature. The Tahitian improves in flavor when it is tree-ripened and this method is best for home growers to use. Acid limes are harvested all year, but mainly in winter. Sweet limes bear only once, in winter.

Uses: Limes are made into ade, juice, and marmalade, and used with soft and hard drinks. Lime oil is made from the peel. Because they ship poorly, limes are usually either eaten fresh in the tropics, or made into frozen or bottled juice.

Lime

Variety	Where Grown	Fruit	Tree
Bearss (possibly identical to Persian)	Florida, southern California	Seedless, very similar to Tahiti.	
Rangpur (possibly not a true lime)	Southern Florida	Ripens in November or December and stays on tree until spring. Hardier than other limes; fruit resembles tangerine in size, shape, and color, but is very acid; holds on tree well; peels easily.	Spreading habit, but is inclined to top-heaviness and needs pruning.
Tahiti (Tahitian, Persian) (probably a cross of West Indian and citron or lemon)	Florida	Medium-sized—about like small lemon fruit—oval; few seeds; thin rind; pale greenish yellow flesh; juicy and very acid. Stores poorly.	Somewhat everbearing, but chiefly winter, vigorous, broad-spreading, drooping, nearly thornless with dense foliage; flowers bloom all year, but mostly in spring; more cold-resistant than West Indian.
West Indian (Mexican, Key)	South Florida and the Keys	Small and round; moderately seedy; greenish yellow; very cold-sensitive and needs protection from wind; juicy and highly acid; drops from tree when mature.	Medium-sized with many fine-stemmed branches; leaves have blunt ends; blooms all year but mostly in late summer; usually grown from seed.

MANDARIN ORANGE

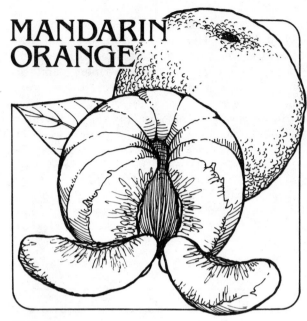

Tangerine
Citrus reticulata
Rutaceae

The mandarin tree, with a few varieties as exceptions, is the hardiest of all citruses, but the fruit is damaged by cold. Mandarins are also remarkably heat-resistant, comparing favorably with the grapefruit.

The terms "mandarin" and "tangerine" are used interchangeably, but mandarin is more often used for yellow-fruited cultivars and tangerine for those with a deep orange rind. Some of the many subgroups are closely related to natural tangelos, which both trees and fruits resemble.

The mandarin tree is small and frequently has spines. Fruits are yellow-orange or reddish orange when ripe. The peel is thin and loose and the core usually open and hollow. Mandarin pulp is sweet, juicy, and orange. The fruits more closely resemble the orange than any other citrus, but the flavor and aroma are distinctive.

The development of good, juicy, mild flavor in mandarin oranges requires a period of relatively hot weather and humidity during the latter part of the growing season. Fruit size and form are also favored by high heat and humidity. This means that in the United States the best mandarins are grown in Florida and in the hottest portions of California and Arizona.

Mandarins are also much influenced by the rootstock on which they are grown. Rough lemon rootstock, for example, may make the flavor of mandarins insipid and shorten the time they will hold ripe on the tree. Trifoliate orange and sour orange rootstocks enhance the flavor of mandarins. Light-textured soils accentuate the undesirable effects of using rough lemon rootstock for mandarins.

Pollination: Unlike most citrus, some mandarins, including Clementine, along with several tangelos, require cross-pollination to assure fruitfulness and seeds. The practice of interplanting such mandarins with suitable pollinators is common. In two varieties of Satsuma mandarins, self-pollination and no pollination obtain the same results. Generally, but with many exceptions, it is the hybrids that require cross-pollination.

Culture: Most mandarins require some protection from cold at temperatures below 26°F. Culture is like that of other citrus fruits.

Pruning: One of the main problems in growing mandarins comes from their tendency to produce poor crops in alternate years. The tendency is especially pronounced in Dancy and in some Mediterranean varieties. It can be controlled to some extent by thinning during years of heavy bearing.

Harvest and Storage: The time of harvest depends on the maturing time of the variety, and on whether or not the fruit holds well on the tree. Many mandarins have a tendency to puff around the rind and to lose flavor if left on the tree. Some varieties have either a strong or a weak tendency to alternate-year bearing. Some store well and some poorly.

Uses: Most mandarins are either eaten fresh as a dessert fruit, or used for marmalade. Some are particularly suitable for canning in segments, and some are used for juice.

Mandarin Orange

Variety	Where Grown	Fruit	Tree
Satsuma			
Ishikawa	Northern Florida, Gulf states	Late (mid-December). One of the largest satsumas; rind finely pitted; high sugar and acid content; stores very well.	
King or King of Siam	In hottest parts of California; central and northern Florida	Late to very late; stores well on tree. Largest mandarin and more like orange than others; high heat requirements for production of mature fruit; markedly affected by rootstock and soil.	Vigorous, medium-high, has few branches and upright habit; does best on heavy soil and sour orange rootstock.
Owari	Northern Florida, Gulf states		Upright. Requires cold weather dormancy to send up shoots and mature fruit. Also needs cool autumn and winter to ripen fruit.
Satsuma, Wase, Matsuyama, Miho, Iseki	Northwest Florida, Alabama, Mississippi, Louisiana, East Texas, and the San Joaquin Valley of California	Very early; holds poorly on tree, but stores well; most cold-tolerant citrus; survives at 15°F. Medium-small, seedless. Loose, thin rind.	Slow-growing, small, spreading.
Sugiyama	Southern United States	Early (November). Large for satsuma; seedless; juicy, excellent quality; sweet; most widely grown satsuma; ships well.	
Common Mandarin			
Clementine (seed parent for mandarin-tangelo crosses and for tangelos)	California	Early; holds on tree only when certain rootstocks used; very early in hot areas. Medium-small to medium; rind medium-thick, firm, easily peeled; flesh tender, juicy, deep orange.	Willowlike, nearly thornless, fine-stemmed; medium-vigorous, strongly cold-resistant. Needs cross-pollination in most areas; low total heat requirements.
Dancy (the variety most often called tangerine)	Florida; humid areas of California and Arizona	Midseason; loses quality rapidly on tree and puffs; stores well. Medium-sized; flesh deep orange, fairly juicy; tender, flavorful; some alternate-bearing tendency; recommended for home planting; good for eating fresh, or for juice or sherbet.	Cold-resistant, but fruit is not; large, spreading, pendulous, thornless; leaves dark green, glossy.
Fortune (Clementine–Dancy cross)	Desert areas of California and Arizona	Exceptionally late; fruit holds well on tree. Medium to medium-large; rind medium-thin, reddish orange; flesh orange, firm; juicy with rich flavor; seeds numerous; often needs cross-pollination.	Vigorous, dense, spreading.
Kinnow (King–Willowleaf cross; Wilking is sister cross grown in	California, Arizona	Midseason (about like Dancy); holds on tree. Medium-sized with flat apex; rind thin, more adherent than most mandarins,	Vigorous, columnar with many branchlets, cold-resistant. *(continued)*

Mandarin Orange—*continued*

Variety	Where Grown	Fruit	Tree
Kinnow (*continued*)			
Morocco, Brazil and is similar)		yellow-orange; flesh deeper yellow-orange, very juicy; many seeds; strong alternate-year tendency.	
Murcott	Florida	Medium-late; ships exceptionally well. Very cold-sensitive for mandarin; flesh orange, tender, juicy; tendency to alternate-year bearing.	Medium-vigorous, medium size, upright with long, willowy branches.

MANGO

Mangifera indica
Anacardiaceae

In the family Anacardiaceae, the mango is related to the cashew, the pistachio nut, and poison ivy. The mango tree is an evergreen with a dome-shaped canopy that may be low and dense or upright and open. It can range between 30 and 130 feet tall, and may live for over 100 years.

The small, sweet-scented flowers appear between December and April.

The fruit varies in size between 1 inch and 12 inches long. It has the same range of shapes as the avocado, from rounded to ovoid-oblong. Color may be greenish, yellow, or red, or some combination of all these colors. It ranges in weight from a few ounces to over 5 pounds. The skin is usually tough and smooth, and the flesh is yellow to deep orange with a delightful aroma and a rich, delicious flavor that has been compared to the very best peaches. Each fruit contains a stone. The fruit ripens during the summer.

Mangoes have a strong tendency to biennial bearing with a good crop, depending on cultivar, only every three or four years.

There are two types of mango: the Indian race, and the Philippine type. The Indian race has monoembryonic seeds, like most plants, with each seed producing one plant that does not grow true to type. This race is susceptible to anthracnose disease. It has a stronger flavor and fragrance and higher color than the Philippine race.

The Philippine race is polyembryonic; each seed produces several plants which are all true to type. This group is relatively resistant to anthracnose disease.

Mango growing in the U.S. is confined to southern Florida and the mildest parts of southern California and Hawaii. Warm weather year-round, night and day, is important, with best temperatures for growth 75° to 80°F. Temperatures of 25°F will kill large trees, and young trees cannot survive 30°F. The embryo of young fruit is even more highly susceptible to cool weather than the rest of the plant and will abort if temperatures stay in the high 30s and 40s for a long period of time.

Pollination: Trees are usually self-compatible and flowers are sometimes self-fertile. The fruit takes two to five months to reach maturity after fertilization. Pollination and fruit set are reduced if there is rain or high humidity at the time of blossoming.

Soil Requirements: Mango will grow in many kinds of soil without difficulty, tolerating drought as well as some flooding. Poor soil, as long as it is well drained, will suffice, but sandy soil with a pH of 5.5 to 7.5 is best.

Propagation: Some types come true from seed, which should be planted within a month of removing from ripe fruit. Remove the endocarp to speed germination, which will then take about two weeks. Vegetative propagation is usually by veneer grafting and chip budding, using strong mango seedlings as rootstock.

Planting and Culture: Site trees away from strong winds and rain. A site with continuous sunlight will produce greater yields than partial shade. Elevations below 2,000 feet are best.

Irrigate the soil before transplanting to avoid having the roots dry out and slow the tree's growth by several months. Dig a hole three times the width and twice the depth of the container. Roots should be covered to the same depth as in the container and irrigated immediately. Water newly planted trees once or twice a week. You can plant grafted trees with mature leaves or well-swollen buds at any time, but during the rainy season is best.

In Florida, plant trees 20 to 30 feet apart, and in Hawaii plant trees 35 to 40 feet apart.

Because mangoes make several growth flushes during the year, the soil around their roots must be maintained in a highly fertile condition. Several applications a year of well-rotted manure, compost, or a mixture of organic sources of nitrogen, phosphorus, and potassium are needed.

Pruning: Prune only to remove dead branches. Cut back the top and sides of trees that have fruited for several years in order to lessen storm damage and facilitate harvesting. Prune in the summer after the harvest.

Pests and Diseases: Anthracnose is a major problem for mangoes. In Hawaii, sooty mold, stem rot, and tip burn can also be troublesome. In Florida, mango scab and powdery mildew are a minor problem. Mites, scales, and thrips may attack trees.

Harvest and Storage: Pick the fruit when it has softened slightly and its color has begun to turn slightly to yellow. Mangoes do not store well and should be eaten right away. But if the fruit is harvested while still firm and allowed to ripen at room temperature for a few days it will taste even better. If possible, pick fruits with an inch of stalk remaining. Speckled skin is another indication of ripening. Refrigerate before peeling.

Uses: Mangoes can be used at any stage of their development. Use any windfall fruit for pickles and chutney. Tender green fruits, chopped up, can substitute for tamarind in dishes requiring an acidic ingredient. Green fruit can be used in jelly, and more mature fruit in pies, puddings, and sauces. Eat ripe mango from the half shell or slice and serve it with cream. It also makes an excellent ice cream.

MELON

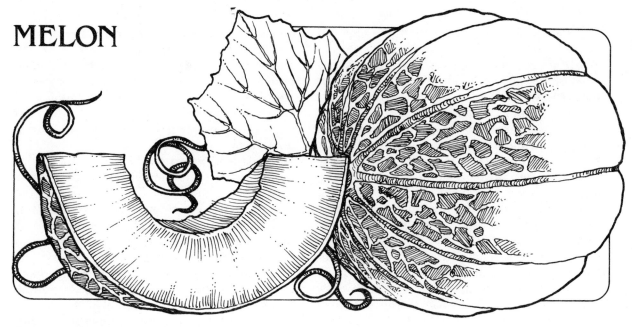

Cucumis melo
Cucurbitaceae

Melons that grow in the U.S. include the musk-melon or American cantaloupe *(C. melo* var. *reticulatus),* the European true cantaloupe *(C. melo* var. *cantalupensis),* and winter melons *(C. melo* var. *inodorus),* including honey-dew and casaba. Melons can be netted or smooth-skinned, ribbed or furrowed, and green, light brown, pale orange, or yellow, with inside flesh ranging from white to green and through every shade of orange and yellow. Some melons have a pronounced musky scent, while others are scentless. Some are sweet, some bitter in taste, and many insipid.

Melons also vary in nutritional value. The American cantaloupe is particularly rich in vitamin A. It also contains vitamins B and C, and iron, calcium, and phosphorus. Winter melons, including honeydew melon, supply a larger quantity of vitamin C, as well as vitamin A.

Melons bear for one season only and must be replanted annually in temperate areas. The fruit ripens from mid to late summer or early autumn, depending on variety.

In northern temperate areas melons are not an easy crop. They are susceptible to all the many diseases and afflictions of the Cucurbitaceae, including rots, mildew, and mosaics. Their seedlings are easy prey for aphids, damping-off fungus, and squash bugs, and insects can devastate mature plants. Melons need delicate handling, they must be protected from contact with damp ground, and they need large quantities of space and nutrients to grow well.

The crucial factor in growing melons is soil warmth. Winter melons prefer a cool period for ripening, but American cantaloupe needs tropical conditions from as soon as possible after it is planted from seed or set out as a seedling, on through harvest. On the other hand, most varieties of cantaloupe ripen faster than winter melons. Seed germinates at 80°F and vines grow fastest at daytime temperatures in the 80s and do well even at over 100°F. In spite of all their difficult cultural demands, melons, most gardeners agree, are well worth raising.

Pollination: Melons are self-fertile and self-polilnating. Melons cross easily between varieties and all crossings remain fertile. If you want to save melon seeds, don't plant the crop near any other melons.

Soil Requirements: Light, fertile sandy or loamy soils that are rich in organic matter and have a pH of 6 ot 8 are best for melons. They do poorly in heavy, poorly drained clays, but will stand light clay if it is well drained.

Ordering Stock: Melons are usually planted from seed, either directly in the plot, or in seedling trays or flats. They transplant poorly and are too delicate to ship as plants. In ordering seed, the most important consideration is your growing season. Count the days with proper growing temperature in your area and choose varieties on this basis. A week or two may be cut from the season by starting seed indoors, but muskmelons will not finish ripening in the fall if night temperatures fall consistently below 50°F.

Planting and Culture: In cool areas that offer fewer than 80 to 100 warm days for muskmelons, or 105 to 125 for winter melons, start seeds indoors in individual peat pots or deep, spacious flats, 10 to 30 days before outdoor planting time. Seedlings can then be transferred to a prepared plot before they have developed more than three leaves. More fully developed plants are easily root-damaged in transplanting. Plant the seedlings pot and all. Transplanting is done when the soil temperature has reached 50°F and daytime temperatures have reached 80°F or, in many northern areas, early June. Hotcaps, plastic tents, and mulch can protect seedlings from rapid temperature change, but do not delay planting too long, or the season will not be long enough for the melons and they will also be susceptible to the various diseases that strike when the ground becomes warm.

In warmer areas, melons can be started from seed in the plot.

The melon patch should be in a sunny spot, protected from winds, with good drainage and good air circulation. A southern slope or south-facing hill is ideal. Avoid spots with high water tables. Break up compacted soil and double-dig if possible.

Melons are usually planted in hills 3 to 5 feet apart in beds at least 5 feet wide. This method allows growing areas to be prepared by digging a pit the size of a bushel basket, working in manure, and heaping up soil over the dug-out area. Set six to eight seeds or three or four plants in each hill. Cover seeds ½ inch with fine soil. As they develop, thin seedlings to three per hill.

Another method is to space plants equidistantly at 3 to 5 feet, to allow better root spreading. But distance in planting should always be related to the vine size and habit of the variety.

Melons require heavy watering, especially when bearing flowers and small fruits, but they use less water when ripening. In extremely dry areas, a clay flower pot sunk into the melon hill and filled with water each day, will provide a constant water supply. In other areas, water for about half an hour, or until thoroughly soaked, in weeks in which no rain has fallen. A mulch will conserve water, but should not be applied until the ground is thoroughly warm.

Since melons are heavy feeders, applying manure to a whole melon patch in fall or adding rotted manure to hills in spring two weeks before planting is beneficial.

Feed plants with fish or seaweed emulsion or compost tea on planting, at time of fruit set, and about two weeks after fruit set. An excess of nitrogen can produce soft, odd-shaped fruit. High levels of potassium and phosphorus are, however, necessary, and the trace elements magnesium and boron, elements lacking in many soils, are essential to melons. Melon patches should be shifted in the garden every year for pest control and soil recovery.

Pests and Diseases: The chief pests of melons are melon aphids, squash bugs, and striped and spotted cucumber beetles. Cucumber beetles spread fusarium wilt fungus, while aphids spread cucumber mosaic.

Harvest and Storage: Handle melons, especially muskmelons, carefully at all stages of ripeness. When the vines go beyond the edges of a bed, lift the fruit gingerly and set it back in the bed center, rather than flipping it. Heap mulch under fruit to protect it from rot. Do not allow the mulch or ground under fruit to remain damp.

Melon

Variety	Days to Maturity	Fruit	Vine
Muskmelons			
Burpee Ambrosia	86	Medium-sized, firm, sweet, juicy. Edible to rind. Small seed cavity.	Mildew-resistant.
Burpee Hybrid	82	Heavy netting, orange flesh.	Vigorous.
Delicious #51	86	Medium-sized, round. Coarse netting, gray rind, orange flesh.	Resistant to fusarium wilt.
Fordhook Gem	82	Lime green flesh, tinted orange around cavity. Medium-sized. Green skin, fine, silvery netting.	Grows well in North.
Hale's Best	90	Small, round with heavy netting. High quality. Salmon flesh.	Susceptible to mildew.
Hale's Best, Jumbo	88	Large, round with heavy netting. Flesh salmon-orange.	
Harvest Queen	95	Medium-sized, oval, sparce netting, orange flesh.	Resistant to fusarium wilt.
Hearts of Gold	85–90	Small to medium, green netted rind, orange flesh. Sweet, juicy.	
Queen of Colorado	88	Good flavor. Soft rind.	Vigorous.
Short and Sweet	70	Orange flesh, netted skin.	Compact. Nonvining.
Sweet and Early	75	Salmon flesh, round to oval. Corky netting.	Resistant to mildew. 6–8 fruits per plant.
Winter Melons			
Burpee Early Hybrid Crenshaw	90	Salmon pink flesh, oval fruit, pointed at stem end. Up to 14 lb. Green skin, no netting. Turns yellow-green when ripe.	Vigorous.
Crenshaw Casaba	110–125	Smooth, pear-shaped fruit. Thin pale yellow to tan skin. Flesh light salmon-orange, sweet.	Susceptible to powdery mildew.
Golden Beauty Casaba (Casaba melon)	110–125	Globular, pointed at stem end. Yellow skin with lengthwise wrinkles. Flesh white and sweet.	Large, vigorous. Needs cool weather before harvest. Susceptible to mildew.
Haogen	85	Small, green-fleshed, ribbed. Skin tinged orange when ripe.	Small vine developed in Israel.
Honeydew	110–125	Heavy, round-to-oval melon with cream white skin, no ribbing, and sweet, green flesh.	Stem remains attached at maturity.
Honey Drip (honeydew)	90–110	Silvery, smooth skin. Green flesh. Fragrant.	Less rangey than Honeydew. Will not slip stem.
Persian	105–120	Large melon with dark green netted skin, orange flesh, sweet.	Vine subject to mildew, but vigorous.
European True Cantaloupes			
Charantais	75–90	Extremely fragrant when ripe. Orange flesh. Scaly skin. Easily bruised.	Very long vine. Releases stem when ripe. Resistant to mosaic and fusarium wilt.
Vedrantais	90	Extremely fragrant, orange flesh.	Resistant to mosaic and fusarium wilt.

The first muskmelons begin to ripen 35 to 45 days after pollination, depending on the variety. Winter melons take somewhat longer. Each vine produces three or four fruits, although there are sometimes more in the true cantaloupes and in muskmelons. Ripeness is evidenced by the odor which permeates the garden where true cantaloupes or most varieties of muskmelons are grown. In some varieties, the skin color of muskmelons becomes yellow behind the netting. The best test for ripeness is to examine the stem for cracks. If the stem separates when pushed gently with the thumb, the fruit is ripe. Home gardeners who will eat the melon immediately can wait for the stem to crack and separate from the fruit naturally. The sugar content declines rapidly after slipping, however, so daily examination of melons during ripening season is essential. Refrigerate them immediately upon picking.

Some winter melons will not show stem cracks when ripe. Honeydew fruit must be cut from the vine when the blossom end is slightly springy. At this stage the fruit has reached normal size, has changed from green to white, and has lost much of its waxy look. A dull sound made when a honeydew or winter melon is thumped is also a sign of ripeness. To test an early picked or accidentally slipped muskmelon for ripeness, smell the stem end.

The ideal storage temperature for muskmelons is 45° to 55°F, but muskmelons seldom keep over a week or two after ripening. Honeydews will store three to four weeks and casabas four to seven in a humid place, kept slightly cooler than for muskmelons. Mold can be inhibited by dipping melons in 135°F water for 30 seconds before chilling.

Uses: A good melon harvest will last two weeks. With a late and an early variety, a plot will supply melons for a month. Melons can be frozen in segments of flesh, but they are best eaten fresh as dessert, appetizers, or in salads. They are also sometimes made into preserves or pickles, or used for their juice.

MULBERRY

Morus spp.
Moraceae

There are many species and subspecies of mulberry grown worldwide, but *M. alba* and *M. rubra* are the two most common. *M. alba,* native to China, is the species whose leaves are the principal diet of Chinese silkworms. It was introduced into the United States to perform a similar service, but the silkworm industry did not succeed here. *M. alba,* the white mulberry, often produces berries that are black or red. Most of the "black" mulberries growing in the South are, in fact, *M. alba,* though they are often mistaken for *M. nigra.*

M. nigra, the true black mulberry, is not hardy and is rarely grown in the U.S., except occasionally in California and Hawaii. *M. rubra* is a very hardy native American mulberry. It grows from Massachusetts to Florida, west to Michigan, Nebraska, Kansas, and Texas.

Mulberries are deciduous and can reach 50 to 60 feet high, though species used for silkworm production are more shrubby.

Greenish, inconspicuous blossoms appear

in spring. Berries are the size and shape of blackberries, with many seeds. They ripen in late June and July and have a rather insipid taste. They are, however, high in vitamin C, and are a fair source of vitamin A.

Pollination: Most trees are self-pollinating.

Soil Requirements: Mulberries will adapt to any soil as long as it is not extremely wet, including barren and stony sites.

Propagation: Propagate from cuttings, which transplant easily if plenty of moisture is applied to the soil. The trees attract birds, who eat the berries, drop the seeds, and thus start new trees.

Planting and Culture: In orchards, plant trees 25 to 30 feet apart, closer in border plantings. Mulch during the first year of growth. No fertilization is usually necessary.

Pruning: Prune upright trees to shape them. Prune mulberries with a weeping growth habit to accentuate the weeping branches, to discourage upright growth, and to keep branches from crowding each other.

Pests: Scale and other pests attack mulberry trees, but they are not a serious problem.

Harvest and Storage: Spread a light-colored sheet under the tree and shake the branches until ripe berries fall. Fresh berries will not keep and should be frozen if not used immediately.

Uses: Combine with more tart fruit and use in pies and jelly. Mulberries used to be planted in barnyards to provide berries for hogs and chickens. The wood makes good fence posts.

Varieties: Downing grows to about 15 feet tall, and can be grown in sun or shade. It requires little maintenance, and its big, sweet berries can be used for pies and jams. The true Downing is not hardy in the northern U.S. or Canada, but the hardier New American has been sold under this name. The best varieties for northern areas are New American, Trowbridge, and Thornburn's. Another variety, Wellington (which may be New American renamed) produces heavy crops of long, slender, cylindrical fruit with a good flavor.

OLIVE

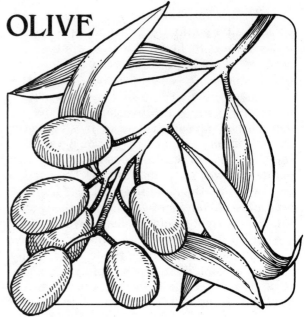

Olea europaea
Oleaceae

The olive is a subtropical tree, beautiful, sturdy, and symmetrical. Its branches bend downward, giving it a thick, bushy, and round-headed appearance. The base of an old tree looks like many trunks gathered together. Among cultivated fruit trees, only the mango tree lives as long as the olive, with its life span ranging from 300 to 600 years. It usually grows to 15 to 20 feet tall, but can reach 35 feet when mature and well tended.

Olive trees bear the most flowers of any fruit tree. A fruit set of 1 percent or less will yield a heavy crop, although in cultivation a 5 percent fruit set is more desirable. The fragrant flowers are cream-colored to white, and bloom in May and June.

The fruit is a drupe, produced on the new wood of the previous year's growth. Its color changes from green, when immature, to straw color to pink to red to black when ripe. Olives are oval, with thin, smooth skin. They have one elongated seed. The fruit is very bitter when fresh due to its tannin content, and is cured in brine before eating.

In the United States, olives are grown in the interior valleys of California, the warmest areas of Arizona, and other parts of the southwest.

Temperatures of 28°F will injure flowers and fruit, 15°F will injure the tree, and 10°F will kill it. Olives will not grow above 2,000 feet. The trees like hot, dry areas with a winter chilling period of two months when temperatures average 50°F.

Pollination: Most cultivars are self-fertile, but some are self-sterile or intermediate. Cross-pollination increases fruit set.

Soil Requirements: Olive trees will grow in almost any kind of soil, but will be much more productive in good soil, like sandy loam. Avoid poorly drained or highly alkaline soil. The trees like soil high in calcium and boron.

Planting and Culture: Nursery trees come in gallon containers or as field-grown bare-rooted stock. Set out bare-rooted trees in December, January, or February. Plant container-grown trees anytime. Site in full sun. Dig a hole only large enough to hold the roots. Prune very long

roots and cut off broken ones. Set in the tree at the same depth as in the nursery. Firm the soil around the roots as you fill in the hole. Thoroughly soak the soil and keep it moist when the tree is newly planted. Mulch with 2 to 3 inches of sawdust, straw, or sand to prevent surface drying.

Protect the trunks of newly planted trees from sunburn by coating with whitewash or wrapping in impervious white paper or newspaper. Give each tree 35 feet of space all around to allow for maximum exposure to sun.

Olive trees are very drought-resistant, needing a minimum of only 8 to 10 inches of water annually. The tree's long taproot can reach down to the water table to get its own moisture. For best growth, however, olives should be watered like other evergreen trees. Also, water stress during the blooming period or when buds are developing will sharply reduce fruit set.

In fall, apply a thick layer of composted manure.

Container Culture: Site in a sunny position

Olive

Variety	Harvest	Fruit	Tree	Disease Resistance
Ascolano	Late Sept.–early Oct.	Large. High flesh/pit ratio and good quality makes it a fine table olive. Tender at maturity, bruises easily.	Very resistant to winter cold injury.	Fairly resistant to olive knot and peacock spot.
Barouni	Oct.–early Nov.	Medium to large. Used for pickling.	Somewhat spreading, easy to harvest. Bears better in northern than in southern Calif.	Susceptible to olive knot.
Manzanillo	Oct.	Medium. Pickling and oil extraction.	Relatively low and spreading; easy to hand harvest. Susceptible to winter cold injury.	Susceptible to olive knot, resistant to peacock spot.
Mission	Late Oct.–early Nov.	Small. Has lowest flesh/pit ratio. High oil content. Used for oil and pickling.	Tall unless pruned. Most resistant to cold.	Susceptible to peacock spot. Resistant to attacks of olive knot.
Sevillano	Mid–late Oct.	Very large. Used for pickling. Oil content relatively low. Quality lower than Mission and Manzanillo.	Properly trained trees do not grow tall, making fruits easy to pick.	Susceptible to olive knot, resistant to peacock spot.

in a greenhouse. Keep in a large pot, using sandy loam as a growing medium. Give the tree as much light as possible, and keep the branches pruned to control the size of the tree.

Pruning: In the first three years of growth, shape to produce four or five strong scaffold branches, removing all other branches. Allow new laterals on scaffold branches to grow. Prune bearing trees to confine tree to available space and to stimulate production of new fruiting wood.

Propagation: Propagate from cuttings of any size except for the soft tip cuttings. Use subterminal cuttings, removing all but the terminal leaves.

Pests and Diseases: Olive trees are subject to nematodes, olive knot and peacock spot, scales, split pit, and verticillium wilt.

Olive knot, a bacterial disease, appears as swellings or galls, sometimes 2 inches or more in diameter. The disease occurs on twigs, branches, trunks, roots, and often on leaf petioles and fruit stalks. It is most prevalent during long periods of rain which aids in the spreading of the disease. The fungal disease peacock spot occurs in years with above-average rainfall. The infection appears on leaf blades, beginning as small sooty patches that enlarge into dark lesions. The area surrounding the lesions becomes yellow, leading to premature leaf drop.

Harvest and Storage: Pick green olives usually in September; black olives are picked in November. Oil olives, which are black olives left on the tree, are picked in January. Freezing temperatures do not affect oil content. Pick carefully by hand to avoid bruising when picking olives to pickle. To harvest olives to press oil in January, beat the branches with poles and gather the fallen olives from tarpaulins spread out on the ground around the tree.

Uses: Olive trees are highly ornamental. Their wood is beautiful and close-grained. Green olives are pickled to dispel their bitter taste; ripe olives are cured in brine. Olive oil, of course, is of worldwide importance in cooking.

ORANGE

Citrus sinensis
Rutaceae

The sweet orange tree is 20 to 40 feet high at maturity with upright to slightly spreading habit. It is hardier than the lime or lemon, but less hardy than the mandarin and sour orange. The branches often have stout spines. The flowers are extremely fragrant.

Pollination: Cross- and self-pollination produce no notable differences in Valencias and no changes in fruit set. Cross-pollination does, however, sometimes increase the seediness. There have been small increases in yield of Washington Navel oranges when they were cross-pollinated. Navel oranges produce parthenocarpic (seedless) fruit regularly without pollination. Valencia oranges, on the other hand, set some seedless fruit only when pollen is excluded from them.

Soil Requirements: Oranges grown in home yards, especially on dry, sandy soil, often do poorly because they lack soil minerals. Irrigation or sprinkling and organic enrichment should be provided on such soils. On low, wet soils, drainage must be provided to prevent waterlogging, and trees are often planted on

Orange

Variety	Where Grown	Fruit	Tree
Butler	Central Arizona	Early midseason. Medium-large, oblong; color light orange; moderately seedy; flesh juicy, flavorful.	Large, vigorous, productive.
Hamlin	Texas, Florida (major variety there because of hardiness); in subtropical, dry areas fruit is small.	Medium-small, round to oval, well-colored at maturity; few seeds; flesh tender, sweet, juicy. Very early (Oct. through Dec.).	Moderately vigorous, medium-large, cold-tolerant.
Jaffa (Florida Jaffa)	Florida	Midseason; stores poorly on tree, but ships well. Medium-sized; furrows around base; flesh light orange, medium-tender, juicy; few seeds; good flavor; has alternate-bearing tendency. Susceptible to alternaria infection.	Vigorous, medium-sized, cold-resistant.
Joppa	Texas	Midseason, earlier than Jaffa. Medium-sized, round to oblong; few seeds; flesh light-colored, medium-tender, juicy, flavorful.	Vigorous, upright with stiff, thornless branches, prolific.
Parson (Parson Brown)	Florida	Very early, possibly earliest. Medium-large, moderately seedy, well-colored; flesh dull orange, firm, juicy.	Vigorous, large, productive.
Pineapple	Florida, Louisiana	Principal midseason variety in Florida. Holds poorly on tree, but processes well. Medium-sized, round with depressed base; moderately seedy; flesh light orange, tender, juicy; flavor sweet, rich.	Moderately vigorous, medium-large, thornless, productive; more sensitive to frost than most oranges.
Queen	Florida	Midseason; holds better than Pineapple on tree. Less reddish in color than Pineapple and richer in flavor; less seedy.	More vigorous and cold-resistant than Pineapple, but very similar and equally productive.
Valencia (Valencia Late, Hart, Hart Late; has many clones probably including Luc Gim Gong, widely used in Florida)	Rio Grande Valley in Texas, in desert areas of California and Arizona, Florida	Holds very well on tree; ships and stores well; matures in February in hot areas; overlaps next bloom in cooler areas; summer ripening on California coast. Medium-large, well-colored at maturity, few or no seeds; juicy; acid but good flavor; excellent for processing.	Most important common variety; vigorous, upright, prolific; alternate-bearing tendency; wide range of adaptability.
Navel Oranges			
Australian	California	Late; flavor remains tart until very late in season. Smaller than Washington and flatter; flesh soft, juicy.	More vigorous and hardy than Washington, upright to spreading.
Baianinha Piracicaba (produces many clones)	California	Small; navel closed; oval; rind thin.	Small, less productive than Washington.
Dream	Florida	Early; holds on tree in Florida. Medium; navel medium-large; rind smooth, medium-thick; flesh soft, sweet, rich in flavor.	

(continued)

Orange—*continued*

Variety	Where Grown	Fruit	Tree
Navel Oranges *(continued)*			
Gillette	Interior of California	Very early, 10 days before Washington; holds well on tree. Larger than Washington and more spherical; rind thick; flesh color and texture similar to Washington, but fruit less susceptible to sunburn.	Vigorous with erect branches and thick, cupped leaves.
Robertson	California	Early; young fruits develop more rapidly than in other varieties. Very similar to Washington, but tend to grow in bunches and become distorted.	Lacking in vigor and markedly dwarfed; a good patio tree. Heat-resistant and prolific. Grows well in containers.
Summerfield	Most-grown Florida variety	Very early. Similar to Washington, but smaller and with smaller navel; flavor sweet with little acid.	Productive.
Texas	More satisfactory in Texas than California	Fairly early. Similar to Washington, but smaller and seedier.	Similar to Washington.
Thomson	California	Very early; holds on tree poorly. Medium-large; navel large and open; less well-colored than Washington; rind medium-thin; flesh firm, flavorful, medium-juicy.	More compact, less vigorous than Washington; semidwarfed; less heat- and cold-resistant than others.
Washington (Bahai, Riverside, Baiana; has many clones including Robertson, Thomson, Gillette, and possibly Florida variety, Glen)	California	Moderately early; holds well on tree; processes poorly; ships well. Round, large; navel medium large, sometimes protruding; flesh deep-colored and firm.	Round-topped, drooping, medium in size and vigor, sensitive to heat and dryness during fruit set.

mounds to keep feeder roots above the water table level. Home growing is relatively difficult, but may be done successfully with reasonable care and if proper rootstocks are used.

Sour oranges are planted, cultivated, and harvested much like sweet oranges. The tree is somewhat smaller and hardier than the sweet orange. Its major use is as a rootstock for lemon, sweet orange, and grapefruit trees. The fruit has a thick, rough peel and sour or bitter pulp that makes good marmalade.

Most sour orange varieties have deep taproots and are not susceptible to drought or easily damaged by damp, heavy soil or by hurricanes. Growth is slow in the early years, but the tree produces high yields after it matures. The rootstock is resistant to gummosis, but when used with sweet orange or grapefruit, it is susceptible to scab and tristeza.

Pigmented oranges or blood oranges are varieties that under certain conditions exhibit pink or red rind and flesh color and distinctive flavor. They have been grown successfully in interior valleys in California. Among principal varieties are Doublefina, Doublefina Ameri-orée, Entrefina, Maltaise Sanguine, Moro, Ruby, Spanish Sanguinello, Tarocco, and Vaccaro.

Navel oranges have as their chief characteristic the development of a rudimentary secondary fruit embedded in the apex or interior cavity of the primary fruit. Pollen is lacking in navel orange flowers, and the fruits are always seedless. The flesh texture is usually crisp, and these oranges separate into segments more easily than do common oranges. The trees are less vigorous than common orange trees and more difficult to grow in poor environments. They adapt poorly to many areas including humid tropics and hot deserts.

Propagation: Oranges are usually grown from budded rootstocks.

Ordering Stock: Dwarfed varieties for indoor and patio growing may sometimes be found in nursery catalogs, but dwarfed trees seldom bear well indoors. In tropical areas local nurseries sell budded trees for home planting. These are almost always dependable.

Planting and Culture: Orange trees grown on high, dry land in Florida benefit from mulch spread under the trees to the extent of their canopies. Late-maturing varieties on sandy soil need some irrigation or heavy watering in order to hold the juice content of the fruit. At the first sign of new growth in the spring, fertilize trees with compost, fish emulsion, or well-rotted manure, and water well. This will allow them to bloom evenly. Water less heavily in the growing season, but the trees should always be watered when there are long dry periods in midsummer. This prevents tough, dry skins which may split when the rains come in autumn.

In central California valleys, orange trees become partly dormant by late November, and during a period which lasts through January, the fruit can stand more cold than it can at other times. By late November, small Navels and partly ripe Valencias should be protected at 26°F. Larger Navels need protection at 25°F. By mid-February when trees come out of dormancy, the danger point rises about 1 degree. In southern California and Florida, dormancy is of shorter duration. Freezing begins for green oranges at 28.5°F, for half-ripe oranges at 28°F, and for ripes ones at 27°F.

Harvest: In Texas, Valencias are harvested from January to May, and in California from March to November. In Arizona, they are harvested immature in December and January and mature from March to May. In Florida, they are harvested March through June.

Navel oranges are harvested in central California from November to April, in southern California from January through May, and in northern California from December through February.

Uses: Sweet oranges are widely eaten as dessert and breakfast fruit, and, of course, are valued for their juice. Oranges are also used in flavoring and marmalade.

PAPAYA

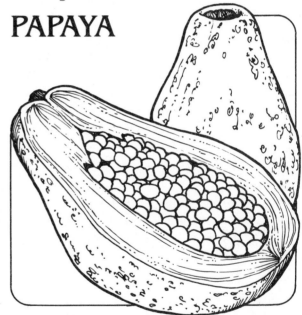

Carica papaya
Caricaceae

The papaya may grow to 33 feet tall or more in fertile soil. Its leaves, spirally arranged near the apex of the plant, grow up to 2 feet across. The papaya plant is either male, female, or hermaphroditic, but these categories are clouded by the fact that plants may produce more than one kind of flower. Flowers may also change and become more male or more female depending on temperature and drought conditions. The female flowers are bell-shaped and waxy, and grow directly from the main stem of the plant. Male flowers grow from the end of dangling stems growing from the top of the plant.

The large fruit has a thin, smooth skin changing in color from deep green to golden orange as it ripens. The pulp is a rich yellow to almond color, with a very pleasant flavor.

A papaya seed will germinate in 10 to 15 days, flower in five months, and yield fruit for harvesting in eight to ten months. After three or four years, trees are considered to have outlived their usefulness and are cut down because the fruit is smaller and is being produced higher and higher up the tree. Plants set in the field in February or March will be ready for harvest in October or November.

In the United States, only Hawaii, southern Florida, parts of Texas, and the protected desert valleys and southern coast of California are suitable growing areas. Temperatures below 30°F cause severe damage, and recovery from leaf or root damage is very slow.

Pollination: Papaya is polygamous. Male plants do not fruit, female plants need the presence of a male, and hermaphroditic trees are self-pollinating. Hand pollination is sometimes necessary. Cover unopened female or bisexual flowers with a paper bag until they open, then transfer the pollen onto a receptive pistil. A female plant as much as 800 yards from a male plant can set fruit.

Soil Requirements: Papaya thrives in well-drained, fertile soil with a pH of 6.0 to 6.5. Good drainage is crucial because stagnant water around the stem will kill the roots.

Propagation: Propagation can be from seed, which germinates in 10 to 15 days. Wash seeds to remove their gelatinous envelopes and plant two or three to a pot, preferably a small peat pot which can then be planted directly in the soil when the strongest seedling is 6 to 8 inches tall. For potting soil, use equal parts well-rotted manure, coarse sand, and loam. Plants can also be propagated by grafting or cuttings.

Planting and Culture: Site plants in full sun,

preferably on a hillside site. The heavy fruit, soft stem, and large leaves are also vulnerable to strong winds, so a windbreak may be needed. Space plants 8 to 10 feet apart.

Because plants grow so fast, nutrients are important. Starting two weeks after planting, fertilize biweekly with blood meal, cottonseed meal, or fish emulsion. Increase the amount of fertilizer as the plants grow larger, and spread the material carefully over the entire root area.

Papayas need constant moisture, especially when the blossoms have opened, or they will not set fruit. If the soil is dry or drains quickly, papayas should be watered every five or six days during dry weather.

Pests and Diseases: Pests include papaya fruitfly, papaya webworm, and papaya whitefly. Diseases include anthracnose, powdery mildew, and virus diseases, including distortion ringspot. Nematodes can be very damaging to papaya.

Harvest and Storage: Pick when fruit is half-ripe and then keep at 60°F for a few days to ripen fully. Ripening starts at the stem and the golden color gradually travels down the whole of the fruit. Harvest by cutting with a knife or twisting off by hand.

Uses: Papaya has many uses. In its immature state, cook it like squash. Sweetened, the immature fruit can be cooked in pies, preserves, and sauces. The ripe fruit is eaten fresh for breakfast or dessert, made into juice, jam, ice cream, and crystallized fruit, or canned in syrup. Young leaves can be eaten like spinach.

Papain, a milky juice obtained by incising the rind of the unripe fruit while still on the tree, is particularly effective in aiding digestion. Papain digests proteins and starches contained in most foods and is a very effective meat tenderizer. Even papaya leaves, wrapped around fresh meat, have a tenderizing effect.

Before eating the fruit fresh, it is a good idea to "milk" it. Cut the skin and let the fruit sit for a day. The latex will drain out and the fruit will taste sweeter.

PASSION FRUIT

Passiflora edulis
Passifloraceae

There are two forms of *P. edulis;* purple passion fruit *(P. edulis* var. *edulis)* and yellow passion fruit *(P. edulis* var. *flavicarpa).* It is thought that the yellow passion fruit originated as a mutation from the purple passion fruit. The purple passion flower is also known as the purple granadilla or lilikoi, its Hawaiian name.

Both forms have woody, fast-growing stems that reach 50 feet long, with tendrils in the axils of the leaves that anchor the stems as they climb. Vines grow all year, stopping only once just after the winter crop. Growth is rapid, progressing from seed to flower to fruit in less than a year, although in commercial cultivation no crop is harvested the first year.

Passion flowers are beautiful and exotic. Flowers of the purple form open at dawn and close at noon, while those of the yellow form open at noon and close at the end of the day. In Hawaii, flowering is in early spring and early fall.

Fruit of the purple form is round or egg-shaped, and has many small, blackish seeds, each enclosed in pulp that is juicy and yellowish. The rind is wrinkled and leathery.

Fruit of the yellow form, which is also called yellow granadilla, is a golden color when ripe. It has a more acidic flavor and a higher percentage of juice to pulp. Its seeds are dark brown. Both forms are high in vitamins A and C. Fruit matures in midsummer and again in midwinter.

Passion fruit requires a subtropical climate without extremes of heat and cold. Frost will damage the vines. Rainfall should be between 30 and 50 inches annually. Passion fruit is hardy in southern Florida, grows well in frost-free areas of California, and in Hawaii.

Pollination: In both purple and yellow passion fruit cross-fertilization between flowers of different vines is necessary. Hand pollination increases fruit set significantly. Rain inhibits pollination; pollen grains cannot stand water.

Soil Requirements: A variety of soil types will do, as long as soil is well drained. Vines do not like to be waterlogged. Apply lime to strongly acid soils.

Propagation: To propagate from seed, plant unwashed seeds immediately in flats of soil. Germination from seeds treated this way takes two to four weeks. Seed can be kept at room temperature for a month, and at 55°F for two months. Seedlings of 2 inches can be transplanted to a container, and at 12 inches be set in the field.

Root cuttings in a porous rooting medium using material from actively growing, somewhat woody vines taken from the part of the stem from the first mature leaf back to the fully extended branch. Make a 2- to 3-node cutting the thickness of a pencil. Bury two-thirds of the cutting in the rooting medium. Rooting starts in a month.

Air layering is also possible. Cuttings and air layers should be transferred to containers, and carefully set out when well established.

Planting and Culture: Plants require a strong fence or trellis if they are to climb properly. Yellow passion fruit is extremely vigorous and requires strong trellis wire that reaches at least 7 feet from the ground. Site in full sunlight against a wall or to provide shade on an arbor. It can also grow as a groundcover.

Dig a hole 18 inches wide and 18 inches deep. Leave a ring around the hole to retain water. Add compost before planting. Fertilize mature vines at the start of spring growth. Provide ample moisture. Space plants 6 to 10 feet apart; rows 10 feet apart.

Passion fruit will also grow in a large pot or tub in a greenhouse with winter temperatures of 55°F and summer temperatures of 85°F. Pot up in February or March and keep in a moist and shady spot (though it grows in sun outdoors). Starting in a 7-inch pot, pot up to an 18- or 24-inch pot, where the vine will grow for years if compost is added to the topsoil every spring. Water only lightly until well rooted. Train the vine to grow along wires.

Pruning: Prune after winter harvest only to remove growth that would trail on the ground and to reduce the weight of the vine on the trellis. Heavy pruning will adversely affect plant growth and productivity. The yellow form does not produce as well when pruned, but the purple form can take more vigorous pruning.

Pests and Diseases: In Florida, nematodes and crown disease may be a problem. In Hawaii, brown spot and root rot are the most troublesome diseases. Pests in Hawaii include aphids, barnacle scale, broad mites, oriental fruitfly, Mediterranean fruitfly, melon fruitfly, red spider, spider mites, and thrips.

Harvest and Storage: Harvest the ripe fruit when it falls to the ground. Fruit picked from the vines when it is partially ripe will taste unpleasant. Pick up the fallen fruit promptly, within a day or so after it falls; it is highly perishable.

Uses: Eat fresh or use juice extracted from the pulp with a sieve. The juice is more often used than the pulp, being commonly added to iced drinks, cake icing, ice cream and sherbet, pie, jam, jelly, barbecue sauce, and gelatin. The rind is a good source of pectin.

PAWPAW

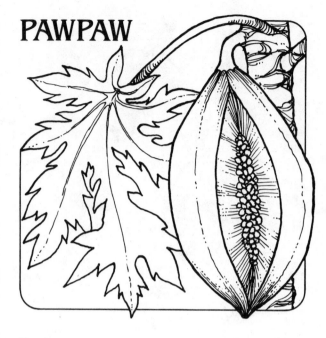

Papaw
Asimina triloba
Annonaceae

The pawpaw grows in both tropical and temperate climates as far north in the United States as central Michigan. The tree is slender, grows to 30 feet tall, and is most often found on rich valley soil along creeks and rivers in wooded areas, and occasionally on hillsides in Appalachia. Pawpaw is easily identifiable by its exceedingly long green leaves, 9 or more inches long. With its purple blossoms in early spring, the pawpaw makes a delightful ornamental.

The fruit is pear-sized, 5 inches long, turning yellow and then brown when ripe. Its two or three seeds are not quite as large as plum seeds. The fruit is preferred by some devotees when it is not quite ripe and not yet so cloyingly sweet. Others like it dead ripe or even two weeks overripe. The fruits ripen in early fall, but sometimes a few ripen later from blossoms that developed after the usual early spring blooming. The seeds are high in protein but contain an alkaloid that is mildly poisonous.

Pollination: Because pawpaws blossom early, sometimes before bees are active, serious pawpaw growers place small, dead animals or other rotting meat under trees to lure the large, blue-headed flies which help with early pollination. Otherwise, you can hand-pollinate.

Planting and Culture: Plant trees in soil that is deep, moist, fertile, and slightly acid at the same depth they grew in the nursery bed. If grafted trees are unavailable plant seeds, since transplanted suckers, stolons, or seedling trees (except very young ones) seldom survive.

Seeds extracted from the fruit must be kept moist if not planted immediately. Store them in the refrigerator in a plastic bag over winter. Seeds planted in spring may not germinate until July or sometimes not until the second year. The best way is to plant the whole pawpaw fruit barely under the soil surface, then thin out to the strongest seedling that grows. Partial shade is good for young trees, and older trees will tolerate it.

Not much pruning is necessary. Clean out dead and broken limbs. Keep suckers cut off around the tree unless you want to start a pawpaw thicket. No pest or disease seems to affect the trees seriously.

Harvest and Use: Pick pawpaws a little sooner than dead ripe and either eat them then or allow to ripen further. If left on the tree, they become mushy, and may fall and get dirty before you can pick them up. Pawpaws will not store fresh. The pulp makes pies and other desserts.

Varieties: Most pawpaw trees sold by nurseries are seedlings, good for ornamental purposes. But occasionally grafted trees of selected varieties are available from small nurserymen. Davis, Overlease, Sunflower, Taylor, and Taytwo are varieties with flavorful fruit.

PEACH AND NECTARINE

Prunus persica
Rosaceae

Peaches are grown in most of the major apple-producing regions, though they can tolerate hotter weather and require less cold to break dormancy. Nectarines, the bald cousins of the peach, are nearly identical to peaches in the general appearance of the tree, growth habits, and bearing characteristics. An interesting horticultural oddity, it is possible for peach trees to grow from nectarine pits and vice versa and for a peach tree to sprout a limb bearing nectarines or the reverse. Their culture is so similar that all practices described here for peaches are also suitable for growing nectarines. Like peaches, there are white- and yellow-fleshed nectarines.

A yellow-fleshed peach, about the size of a baseball, contains vitamin A, vitamin C, small amounts of many minerals including calcium, phosphorus and iron, and traces of B vitamins. White-fleshed varieties have comparable nutrient levels, but almost no vitamin A.

Most varieties produce a small, inconspicuous, ½-inch bloom which has little landscape value. Some varieties, however, produce shocking pink, large-petaled flowers resembling a primrose. These include Loring, Redskin, Rio-oso-gem, Velvet and Early RedFre—all excellent landscaping trees. They have an attractive spreading shape with dark, glossy foliage and reddish brown bark.

Peaches, as a rule, are limited in their northern range by their inability to survive sustained temperatures below −20°F. Northern New England, the heart of the Great Plains, Alaska, and higher elevations in mountainous regions are unsuited for peach growing. In these areas, the tree itself will usually survive if the first winter or two after planting is relatively mild, but the blossom buds will be frozen probably five years out of six so no crop will be harvested.

Pollination: Most peach varieties are self-fruitful and will set full crops without another variety for pollination, except for J.H. Hale, June Elberta, and Halberta.

Soil Requirements: Peaches will grow well on any deep, well-drained, loamy soil with a pH of 6 to 8. Presence of a hardpan within a foot or so of the surface, unless it can be broken and a good subsoil exposed below, will prevent healthy growth by preventing water drainage from the root zone in wet years. In a dry year, with such a shallow root system, the tree will quickly wilt and the fruit, if any remains, will be barely larger than the pits.

Excessively well-drained sandy soils can be a problem in dry years due to their low moisture-holding capacity. Before planting, the soil should be tested so deficiencies or imbalances in pH and nutrients can be corrected.

Ordering Stock: Most garden centers will have a few peach varieties available, but at a large mail-order nursery the selection may include up to 75 varieties. There have been hundreds of varieties developed over the past century, probably several for any conceivable site, taste, or use.

Choose one-year-old stock that is intermediate in size, about 4 to 5 feet tall and ½

inch in diameter (some catalogs may refer to the diameter as "caliper"). Avoid the very small seedlings, since they may be genetically weak, runts of a sort, and may never develop into strong, healthy trees.

Propagation: Choices of rootstocks for peaches are limited. If you live along the northern fringe of the peach-growing region, where winter arrives suddenly and freezing/thawing cycles are rare, Siberian C is a good choice. It has a high degree of winter hardiness and is able to increase the hardiness of the scion variety. Trees on Siberian C will be 10 to 15% smaller than standard and the fruit of a given variety will mature a few days earlier than on other rootstocks. Where winters commonly have a "January thaw" or similar warming followed by a return to winter's deep freeze, this rootstock may break dormancy early, resulting in substantial bud damage.

Halford and Lovell are the other commonly available rootstocks. Halford is a tried-and-true workhorse of the major peach regions. Lovell is a more recent offspring of Halford possessing a higher degree of disease resistance than its parent. Nemaguard, a nematode-resistant rootstock, has performed poorly with low tree vigor and winter hardiness, though it does seem to tolerate higher nematode populations than the others. Very little is available in dwarfed peaches, though some nurseries have introduced a genetic dwarf of Red Haven and seedlings of other varieties treated chemically to induce dwarfing are available on a limited basis. The *P. tomentosa* rootstock will produce a dwarfed tree, but is not compatible with many scion varieties. Western sand cherry, *P. besseyi*, has had limited acceptance as a dwarfing rootstock.

Site Selection: The question of whether a north- or south-facing slope is best for peaches is complex. In colder areas, where the weather in the spring warms gradually (rather than a week of very balmy days followed by three weeks of freezing temperatures), a southern slope is best since the trees will bloom relatively early and will have a longer growing season before autumn frosts. Where spring temperatures fluctuate widely, a northern exposure is best. Because a north slope warms more slowly than the surrounding area, the trees will not blossom as soon as on a southern slope where the opening buds may get caught by a spring freeze. An hour of 25°F temperatures can destroy a peach crop. Of course, during much of the winter a north slope may be exposed to severe winds that can dry and kill buds on the dormant trees, resulting in no blossoms at all. East and west slopes, obviously, are between these two extremes. Ideally, trees should bloom as early as possible to increase your growing season, but not so early as to risk a freeze.

On the northern fringes of the peach regions you should take advantage of microclimates that are substantially warmer than the surrounding region; maybe the south side of a barn or hill, or just below a heavy, windbreaking treeline. In these pockets the tree can overwinter without exposure to harsh winds and can bloom in relative safety. If there is a large body of water nearby, its temperature-moderating effect may be enough to allow for peach production.

Peaches require a chilling period, between 700 and 1,100 hours of temperatures below 45°F for most varieties. Breeding programs have produced peaches for warmer regions that need as little as 50 hours. In areas where there is insufficient chilling, even though blossom buds are present the tree will not bloom and will have very sparse foliage.

The best tree site is in full sun all day, where the somewhat sensitive buds and flowers will not be exposed to extremely cold temperatures, but also one where the buds don't break too early in the spring and chance freezing. Not too cold or hot, not soggy or bone dry, enough weight to the soil but not a raw material for ceramics; a site that is intermediate in all these conditions. Nectarines should not be planted in areas with very humid, muggy summers, as

brown rot will likely ruin most, if not all, of the crop.

Planting and Culture: As with most tree fruits, the best time to plant is in very early spring except in southern areas where fall planting is recommended. Plant trees that are fully dormant or just beginning bud-swell when the ground is moist, but not wet. Space the holes 20 to 25 feet apart depending on the fertility of the soil. Peaches planted in old peach orchards may do very poorly and, in many cases, die after several listless years. It is thought that a nematode-transmitted virus is responsible, though this problem may be less serious where no herbicides are used and the level of organic matter and beneficial fungi in the soil is maintained through mulching, manuring, or adding compost.

A leaf and/or soil analysis, usually available through the county extension office, will help determine nutrient needs. Peaches require little phosphorus or potassium, but show dramatic responses to nitrogen applications. If you are using a concentrated nitrogen source such as dried blood, tankage, or cottonseed meal, apply it in the spring when buds swell. Manures provide nitrogen but it is available at a lower rate over a longer period and should be applied in the fall after the trees are dormant. This allows rains and melting snow to leach the nutrients down to the root zone where they'll be available in the spring. Wood ashes may be spread with the manure.

Peach trees require 1 ounce of actual nitrogen annually for every year of tree age up to 12 years, when it levels off. This ounce may be found in 10 to 12 pounds of cow manure, 4 pounds of poultry manure, 10 ounces of fishmeal, 8 ounces of dried blood, or 14 ounces of cottonseed meal. Nectarines require slightly more nitrogen than peaches.

Weed control is necessary for producing large, sweet peaches, especially when the fruit begins to ripen and can't compete for water. Mulch heavily to keep the area under the tree weed-free, or cultivate by hand or with a rotary tiller. Be careful not to penetrate deeper than an inch or two to avoid damage to the roots.

If allowed to ripen all the fruit it sets, the tree will yield baskets of small peaches that are little more than a pit with a thick skin, and the tree may not be fully hardened for winter. Some varieties need thinning more than others, but nearly all need it despite claims to the contrary in some nursery catalogs. In mid-June when the "June drop," the shedding of unpollinated or abnormal fruits, is nearly finished, pick off enough cherry-sized peaches so that only one fruit remains on every 6 to 8 inches of branch. Distribute the load by dividing it between both sides of the limb. A well-thinned tree will yield much larger fruit. If fruit-laden branches begin bending severely as the fruit ripens, it may be necessary to use props under the sagging limbs. A 1 × 3 with a notch cut in one end to hold the limb will do.

If a dry spell should develop, fruit will not size well and may become mealy, as the tree will withdraw the fruit's water for its own needs. Watering every other day with 25 gallons per tree will help until the rains return.

Pruning: Train trees to an open-center form. Peach limbs need exposure to sunlight to remain healthy and will die if shaded for a season or two. Cut back the leader or main stem of the newly planted tree to 24 to 30 inches above the ground in order to encourage branching. Trim off close to the trunk any weak, dead, or broken branches that remain on the trunk. At this point the tree will look like no more than a stick but it will very quickly leaf out and you can begin selecting the scaffold limbs. Let a foot or so of growth push out, then in the middle of the first summer, carefully select three or four shoots spaced evenly around the tree and cut off the rest. If there are insufficient shoots to make the scaffolds, fill in the empty spots the next summer. Don't remove any growth from those chosen shoots, allowing them to grow vigorously all summer. Pruning off shoots is better than rubbing off unopened buds, which unnaturally forces all of the tree's vigor into the re-maining buds and causes excessive growth.

Pruning in following years can be done anytime during the winter in warmer areas and to reduce possible winter damage, late winter or early spring farther north. Though the tree may set a few peaches the year after planting, concentrate on developing the open-center shape and a strong framework to bear later crops. Remove any shoots arising from the trunk and select several on each of the young scaffolds to form laterals. Since peaches bear fruit on the previous season's wood, develop as much bearing surface as possible from which fruit-bearing shoots can grow. Leave some shoots in the center of the tree, but head them back to 12 to 15 inches. Remove any vertical growth or cut it back to an outward growing shoot, since the idea is to keep the tree low, 8 feet but spreading.

Before the tree begins to bear heavily in the third or fourth year, it should be making 18 to 24 inches of new growth each year. If there is less than this, remove more wood during pruning and fertilize lightly; if more, then you're probably pruning too heavily and forcing all the tree's energy into the few remaining shoots. Once full cropping begins, 10 to 12 inches each season is considered a good indicator that the tree is healthy, but not overly vigorous.

Once bearing begins, thin the crop to control shoot growth and tree vigor.

Pests and Diseases: The peach tree and lesser peach tree borers (PTB) are probably the most persistent insect pests, while Japanese beetles, oriental fruit moths, and plum curculio may be occasional local problems. The adult female borer is a 1-inch clear-winged moth with a metallic blue body banded with one orange stripe, active from June through September with peak egg-laying in August. Eggs are deposited in crevices on the bark on the lower trunk and in the soil immediately around the trunk, and the larvae tunnel into the trunk to spend a year munching tunnels. They will reveal their presence with small bits of sawdust mixed with their droppings around a hole in the trunk near the ground. A heavy infestation can seriously weaken or kill a tree. Lesser peach tree borer, a smaller version of the PTB, attacks the scaffold limbs, though seldom causes serious damage. The best medicine against borers is preventive; keeping your trees healthy and avoiding damage to the trunk where pieces of bark are torn away (favored egg-laying sites). When pruning don't leave stubs or allow branches to grow with narrow crotch angles where lesser PTB will lay eggs. Moth crystals (naphthalene) around the trunk may act as a repellent, and a band of Tanglefoot around the trunk down to the soil line will gum up any moth attempting to lay eggs, though it may cause some bark shedding, especially on younger trees.

As the fruit is sweetening just prior to harvest, watch for Japanese beetles and handpick into soapy water when necessary. Oriental fruit moths will lay eggs in the growing shoot tips early in the season, causing them to wilt, while the later generation attacks the fruit, causing it to drop prematurely. If these get to be a problem, *Bacillus thuringiensis* will help.

Brown rot fungus heads the list of disease problems. Brown rot infections on twigs, flowers, and/or fruit must be removed as soon as they are noticed. "Mummies," dried infected fruits that remain in the tree over the winter, must be removed before the buds swell, and a light cultivation under the trees just before bloom will destroy any overwintering infections. Sanitation is critical in brown rot control, though powdered sulfur applied to the trees as a dust or spray will retard the growth of the fungus. To prevent bacterial leaf spot, plant varieties that are not susceptible to this disease. Cytospora or Valsa canker is a fungal infection of the wood which blocks the tree's circulatory system, causing sticky, brown sap to ooze from the bark. Delay pruning until bud swell so the cut surfaces can heal and avoid breaking the bark. When canker is found, prune it out.

Nectarines are more susceptible than peaches to brown rot and, possibly due to their lack of fuzz, to damage from plum curculio and thrips.

Harvest and Storage: As a peach begins the last phase of ripening, it rapidly expands and the size may increase 50% in the last three weeks. When it's first ready for picking the flesh at the end away from the stem will give slightly to thumb pressure. This is considered firm-ripe. Peaches at firm-ripe will store in a refrigerator for two weeks and, brought out, will ripen to excellent flavor and texture at room temperature.

A peach will continue to grow and sweeten the longer it is left on the tree until it is tree-ripe, when the flesh near the stem end yields to thumb pressure. These can be held in the refrigerator, at best, only a few days and if left on the tree will, depending on the variety, begin to dry out or drop. The flavor and melting quality of a tree-ripe peach is a real delicacy and worth the extra few days' wait.

To pick a peach without bruising it or damaging the tree, cup it in your hand and lift with a slight twist. The short stem will separate cleanly rather than tearing as it would if you were to pull it straight off.

Uses: Peaches may be preserved, canned, frozen, dried, or made into an excellent fruit leather. They make delicious pies, preserves, butters, and a multitude of desserts and salads.

Peach

RedHaven is a widely grown variety and its ripening date in your area can be used as the standard to gauge ripening times of other varieties. Ripening times for varieties in this chart are listed as number of days before (+) or after (−) RedHaven.

Variety	Ripening Days	Fruit	Tree
Harbinger	+30	Small–medium; yellow clingstone. Soft flesh.	Vigorous, hardy, upright. Needs heavy thinning.
Springcrest	+24	Small–medium; firm yellow flesh. Semifreestone, good flavor.	Moderately vigorous, susceptible to bacterial spot. Needs 650 hrs. of cold.
Waverly	+19	Medium; white, semifreestone. Bright red skin.	Vigorous, bears early, hardy.
DesertGold	+18	Medium; yellow, semifreestone. Soft flesh, good flavor.	Vigorous, productive, for warmer regions, blooms early. Needs 350 hrs. of cold.
Maybelle	+18	Medium; white, semiclingstone. Freezes well, susceptible to brown rot.	Vigorous, must be thinned, very bud-hardy
Dawne	+16	Medium; excellent eating quality. Earliest yellow freestone.	Vigorous, bears early and heavily, must be thinned. Showy blossoms, brown rot-susceptible. Bud-hardy.
Stark Earliglo	+14	Large; yellow, freestone when fully ripe. Dessert quality.	Vigorous, must be thinned, bud-hardy. Needs 900 hrs. of cold.
Dixired	+11	Medium; yellow freestone. Fair eating quality, freezes well.	Very productive, bud-hardy, resistant to bacterial canker and leaf curl. 1050 hrs. of cold.
Garnet Beauty	+10	Medium; yellow, semifreestone. Seldom has split pits.	Vigorous, very hardy buds.
SunHaven	+10	Large; round, yellow, semifreestone. Sweet, good flavor.	Moderately vigorous, susceptible to canker.
Early RedFre	+7	Medium; white, semifreestone. Excellent for freezing.	Moderately productive, self-thinning, resistant to bacterial spot. 850 hrs. of cold.
Sentinel	+7	Medium; white, semifreestone. Good dessert quality.	Resistant to bacterial spot. 950 hrs of cold.
Sunshine	+5	Large; yellow, freestone. Firm, good flavor.	Vigorous, resistant to leaf curl, must be thinned.
Babcock	+1	Medium; white, semifreestone. Good dessert peach.	Moderately vigorous, low chilling requirement.
Jerseyland	+1	Very large; yellow, semifreestone. Excellent fresh.	Bears early, susceptible to bacterial spot, very hardy.
RedHaven	0	Medium-large; yellow, freestone when ripe. Nearly 100% red. Very firm, nonbrowning, dessert peach. Most widely planted variety.	Spreading, vigorous, very productive, must be thinned heavily. Very bud-hardy. 950 hrs. of cold.
Com-Pact RedHaven	0	Identical to RedHaven.	Half to ⅔ size of standard tree. Bears heavily, should be thinned. Dense foliage, tolerant to bacterial spot and leaf curl.

Variety	Ripening Days	Fruit	Tree
Harken	−2	Large; yellow, freestone. Very attractive, superb flavor.	Moderately vigorous, very bud-hardy, productive. Very resistant to bacterial spot.
Norman	−2	Large; yellow, freestone. Firm, excellent dessert quality.	Medium vigor, productive, hardy flower buds, bacterial spot tolerant. Must be thinned. 850 hrs. of cold.
Raritan Rose	−3	Large; white, freestone. Freezes well, excellent fresh. Susceptible to brown rot.	Productive, resistant to leaf curl, upright growth. 950 hrs. of cold.
Delp EarlyHale	−6	Very large; fine-textured, yellow, freestone. Very good fresh or canned.	Medium vigor, moderately winter hardy.
Velvet	−7	Medium-large; firm, yellow, freestone. Superb dessert peach, good for canning.	Spreading growth, productive. Slightly susceptible to bacterial spot. Showy bloom. 750 hrs. of cold.
Golden Jubilee	−8	Medium; yellow, freestone. Strong flavor, very old and popular.	Very productive, spreading, hardy. Produces best when fertilized.
Ranger	−8	Medium; firm, yellow, freestone. Very good fresh, canned or frozen.	Vigorous, productive, very resistant to bacterial spot. 950 hrs. of cold.
Cumberland	−9	Medium; white, oval, semiclingstone. Mild flavor. Brown rot-susceptible.	Medium vigor and productivity. Very hardy flower buds.
Triogem	−10	Large; yellow, freestone. Superb fresh, canned or frozen. Peachy flavor.	Medium vigor, hardy, bears heavy crops. Requires good soil and care. Some bacterial spot tolerance. 850 hrs. of cold.
Reliance	−11	Medium; round, yellow, freestone. Fair dessert quality.	Extremely bud-hardy (to −25°F). Good for northern areas.
Topaz	−11	Very large; round, yellow, freestone. Excellent flavor and quality. Red color.	Medium vigor, very productive.
Washington	−13	Large; firm, yellow, freestone for fresh use or canning. Fine texture.	Vigorous and productive. Very hardy, tolerant of spring frosts. 950 hrs. of cold.
Burbank July Elberta	−14	Old favorite. Large; firm, yellow, freestone. Excellent fresh or canned. Developed by Luther Burbank.	Strong, moderately vigorous, productive. Somewhat susceptible to bacterial spot. 750 hrs. of cold.
Sunhigh	−15	Large; red skin, firm yellow freestone. Premium dessert peach, sweet and flavorful.	Productive, must be thinned. Very susceptible to bacterial spot. Spreading, bud-hardy. 750 hrs. of cold.
GloHaven	−15	Large; yellow freestone. Superb fresh, frozen or canned. Nonbrowning flesh.	Very vigorous, productive. Slight bacterial spot resistance; susceptible to leaf curl. Bud-hardy. 850 hrs. of cold.
Loring	−18	Large; round, yellow freestone. Sweet, flavorful. Freezes and cans well.	Very vigorous, sturdy, heavy cropper. Must be thinned; very showy bloom. Resistant to leaf curl and bacterial spot. Bears early. 800 hrs. of cold.
Winblo	−21	Large; firm, yellow freestone. Fine dessert quality, cans well. Nonbrowning.	Buds, flowers and wood are very hardy. Must be thinned. 850 hrs. of cold.

(continued)

Peach—*continued*

Variety	Ripening Days	Fruit	Tree
Culinan	−24	Large; firm yellow freestone. Good quality.	Vigorous, productive, bacterial spot-resistant.
Madison	−24	Firm-fleshed, yellow freestone; tender skin. Cans well, very good fresh.	Medium vigor, bears heavily every year. Spring frost tolerant. 850 hrs. of cold.
Cresthaven	−25	Very large; yellow freestone. Tough skin, firm, nonbrowning flesh. Good for canning and freezing. Excellent flavor.	Strong, moderately vigorous, productive. Wood and buds hardy. 850 hrs. of cold.
Yakima Hale	−25	Large; round, yellow freestone. Very flavorful; very good fresh or canned.	Vigorous, productive. Though a Hale type, is self-fruitful.
Blake	−28	Large; highly colored, firm, yellow freestone. Good dessert quality and for canning.	Very productive, must be thinned; vigorous, very bud-hardy. 750 hrs. of cold.
Biscoe	−30	Large; round, firm yellow freestone. One of the best canning varieties, rich flavor.	Moderately vigorous, very hardy flower buds. Bacterial spot-resistant. 800 hrs. of cold.
Redskin	−30	One of the most popular late peaches. Aromatic, sweet, firm yellow freestone. Large fruits, excellent fresh or canned.	Vigorous, willowy growth, must be thinned. Large tree, showy blossoms, resistant to bacterial spot. 750 hrs. of cold.
Elberta	−31	Most popular peach worldwide. Large; yellow freestone for all uses. Slight bitterness around pit preferred by some. Susceptible to brown rot.	Productive, medium vigor, upright growth. Susceptible to canker. 900 hrs. of cold.
J.H. Hale	−32	Very large; golden yellow, firm, delicious. Keeps well for a peach. Excellent flavor.	Moderately productive, upright, medium vigor. Susceptible to bacterial spot. Self-sterile, needs a pollinator. 900 hrs. of cold.
Belle of Georgia	−34	Large; aromatic, firm white freestone. Susceptible to brown rot. Excellent fresh.	Very productive, vigorous, hardy. Susceptible to canker and leaf curl, resistant to bacterial spot. 850 hrs. of cold.
Havis	−35	Large; high-quality yellow freestone. Flavorful. Brown rot-tolerant.	Vigorous, moferately productive and hardy. Long chilling period.
Stark Autumn Gold	−35	Very large; yellow freestone. Excellent flavor for all uses.	Vigorous, moderately productive and hardy. Long chilling period.
Rio-oso-gem	−38	Very large; aromatic yellow freestone of the highest quality. Excellent fresh, cans very well.	Low vigor, but productive. Susceptible to canker, leaf curl, and bacterial spot but worth the trouble. Tender buds, so should be planted on the best site. 900 hrs. of cold.
Monroe	−44	Large; firm, yellow freestone. Very good flavor and texture for canning or fresh use.	Generally light bud set, spring frost-tolerant, moderately vigorous. Long chilling period.
Marsun	−55	Large; yellow freestone. Excellent dessert quality, cans and freezes well.	Best for southern areas where frosts are late in autumn. Vigorous, moderately productive. 850 hrs. of cold.

Nectarine

Ripening times for varieties in this chart are listed as number of days before (+) or after (−) the RedHaven peach.

Variety	Ripening Days	Fruit	Tree
Stark Earliblaze	+5	Medium; bright red skin, soft, yellow clingstone. Mild flavor. Susceptible to brown rot.	Vigorous, productive, medium-hardy. Must be thinned.
Cherokee	−1	Medium, yellow, semifreestone. Fair quality, some brown rot tolerance.	Medium vigor, productive. Large showy bloom, resists spring frosts.
Hardired	−7	Medium, yellow freestone. Average quality.	Healthy, productive, tolerant to bacterial spot and brown rot. Very bud-hardy.
Nectared #6	−10	Medium; yellow freestone. Very red skin. Good, sweet flavor.	Very productive, thinning required.
SunGlo	−12	Very large; deep yellow, orange-blushed freestone. Excellent fresh, may be canned or frozen. Brown rot-susceptible.	Vigorous, hardy, somewhat self-thinning.
RedChief	−20	Medium-large; white-fleshed freestone. Soft, aromatic, sweet.	Low vigor, but productive; some brown rot resistance. Spring frost-tolerant.
Stark Sunburst	−21	Medium; yellow clingstone. Good flavor, juicy.	Genetic dwarf only 5–6 ft. high at maturity. Dense foliage, thinning a must. Good air drainage required.
Lafayette	−25	Large; white freestone. Sweet; some brown rot tolerance.	Vigorous, bears heavily every year.
RedGold	−27	Medium-large; yellow freestone. Bright red skin. Very aromatic, distinctive flavor. Crack-resistant, stores well.	Strong-growing, heavy-bearing, disease-tolerant. Very winter-hardy, resists spring frosts.
Stark LateGold	−41	Large; firm, yellow freestone. Excellent, mild flavor.	Vigorous, spreading. Must be thinned. Slight brown rot tolerance.
Cavalier	−46	Medium, yellow freestone. Fragrant, sweet, firm flesh.	Productive, hardy, spreading; early bloom.

PEAR

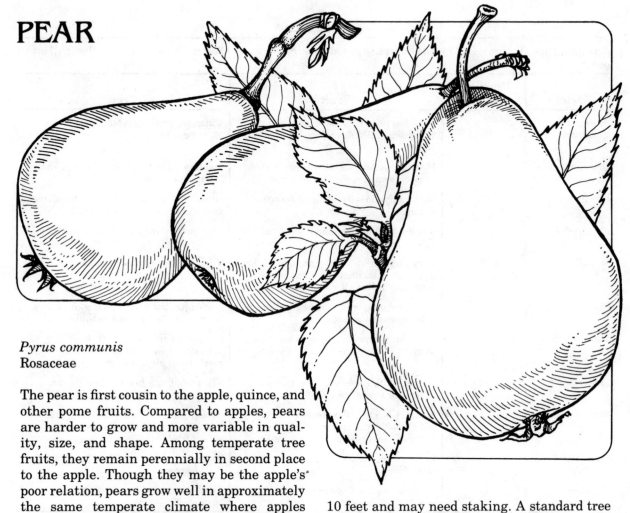

Pyrus communis
Rosaceae

The pear is first cousin to the apple, quince, and other pome fruits. Compared to apples, pears are harder to grow and more variable in quality, size, and shape. Among temperate tree fruits, they remain perennially in second place to the apple. Though they may be the apple's poor relation, pears grow well in approximately the same temperate climate where apples thrive, and in general are nearly as hardy.

Pear trees grow more upright than apples, and sometimes even taller, though standard sizes can usually be maintained at about 20 feet tall. Average size is that of an elongated apple, with some varieties, like Seckel, being half the average size. Characteristic color is green ripening to yellow, though some varieties are red, and the yellows are often russeted and blushed with red or pink.

Dwarfing of pears has not progressed as rapidly as for apples, but commercial nurseries now sell many varieties dwarfed onto quince rootstocks, with an Old Home pear interstem for graft compatibility. These trees grow to only 10 feet and may need staking. A standard tree can be expected to produce 5, 10, or more bushels of fruit in a year; a dwarf, 1½ bushels.

Pollination: Most pear trees need cross-pollination for good fruit set, and although there are exceptions, it is best to plant two varieties, in some cases three. Seckel and Bartlett will not, for instance, pollinate each other. But pear trees do not always react consistently. Some Seckels are self-fruitful, some are not. Duchess, Clapp's Favorite, and Flemish Beauty are good pollinators, and, reportedly, self-fruitful.

Soil Requirements: Pears, more than apples, prefer a heavier loam, but will grow on any well-drained soil.

Propagation: Trees can be grown from seed,

Pear

Variety	Best Growing Area	Fruit	Tree
Anjou	Pacific Coast and Great Lakes—northeastern commercial fruit-growing areas	Large, greenish with pink blush. Good flavor, texture. Midseason.	Medium-hardy. Needs a pollinator.
Aurora	Northeast and northwest U.S.	Early, large pear, high dessert quality.	Susceptible to fireblight. More spreading growth habit than most pears.
Bartlett	Originally an English pear, adaptable to all but the coldest pear-growing regions	Midsized to large, yellow. High dessert quality. Medium-early.	Medium-hardy. Very susceptible to fireblight. Needs a pollinator.
Bosc	Northeast and Pacific Northwest	Large, tapering neck. Russet color. Keeps well. High dessert quality. Late.	Not too hardy. Quite susceptible to fireblight. May need pollinator.
Clapp's Favorite	All pear-growing regions	Yellow. Poor keeper. Early.	Very hardy. May need pollinator.
Comice	Coastal areas with climate like Pacific Northwest coast	Roundish. Some greenish yellow, some strains red. Highest quality.	Not too hardy. Quite susceptible to fireblight. Self-fertile.
Devoe	All pear-growing areas	Large, midseason.	Bears early.
Duchess	Northern temperate regions	Large, yellow, midseason.	Hardy. Self-fertile.
Dumont	European variety. Not much tested in U.S.	Winter pear. Firm but juicy, flavor sweet. Good quality for winter pear. Late.	Tends to alternate bearing.
Flemish Beauty	Northern temperate regions	Large, yellow, with red blush. Good quality and taste. Will ripen to high quality on tree.	Very hardy. Very susceptible to fireblight. Self-fertile.
Gorham	Normal pear-growing areas	A Bartlett-type pear but ripens later. Keeps well in storage.	Susceptible to blight.
Kieffer	Everywhere, from coldest fruit-growing regions to warmest	Winter pear. Softens only in winter storage. Low quality. Cooking pear.	Extremely hardy. Somewhat resistant to fireblight.
Magness	Adaptable to all pear-growing regions	Oval in shape, tough skin but soft, juicy and aromatic. Medium-sized, russeted. Keeps well. Midseason.	Very blight-resistant. Needs a pollinator. Bears in 6 years. Branches sometimes thorny.
Maxine	Northeast and central U.S.	Large. Coarse flesh but good flavor. Midseason.	Hardy; blight-resistant.
Monterey	Will bear in the South. All areas of U.S. except the extreme north.	Fair quality. Good canning pear. Midseason to late.	Blight-resistant.
Moonglow	All pear-growing regions	Yellow. Pick 5–10 days before dead ripe. Early.	Hardy; blight-resistant.

(continued)

Pear—*continued*

Variety	Best Growing Area	Fruit	Tree
Seckel	Everywhere but deepest southern U.S.	A small—half-sized—pear, very sweet. High dessert flavor. Midseason to late.	Very hardy. Resistant to fireblight. Will not pollinate Bartlett (or vice versa). May or may not be self-fruitful. Best for backyard.
Tyson	New England	High flavor, grainy at core. Early.	Somewhat blight-resistant. Late-bearer. Productive and vigorous. Good for home gardens.
Winter Nelis	Northern ⅔ of U.S.	Medium-sized, roundish, yellow to russet. Winter pear, keeps well, better quality than Kieffer. Very late.	Somewhat resistant to fireblight. Needs a pollinator.

but are better purchased as varieties grafted onto quince or Farmingdale-Old Home rootstock.

Planting: Follow the general rules for planting described in chapter 7. Set in the tree at approximately the same depth as it grew in the nursery bed, with the graft bulge above ground level. Then cut back the top so it roughly equals the amount of root. A yearly mulch of straw, hay, or light strawy manure with a cup of bone meal and several cups of wood ashes should suffice. Do not feed pear trees too much soluble nitrogen, because the lush growth such feeding can cause is especially susceptible to fireblight. Plant dwarf varieties 12 feet apart. Plant standard varieties 16 to 20 feet apart.

Pruning: Prune pears as little as possible. They seldom respond well to corrective pruning and it may, especially in summer, invite the lush growth that encourages fireblight. A pear tree's upright growth habit makes it necessary to head back side branches that want to overtake the central leader, but head back only cautiously and in the dormant season since the cuts too may induce lush growth. It's better to train branches out with spreaders or weights, or wait for a heavy crop of pears to bow the branches over. Prune off and burn branches affected with fireblight.

Pests and Diseases: Fireblight, a bacterial disease, is the worst enemy of pears, and there is no cure. The best program to follow is to plant resistant varieties and avoid heavy fertilization. Pear psylla are the worst insect pests, having become resistant to many sprays. A late spray of water and dormant oil has been found to be effective in orchards where other psylla predators are active. But this spray must be timed exactly; you need a trained entomologist to predict just when the female psylla are going to emerge for egg-laying. Pear slug is another pest, a soft-bodied, dark green worm that feeds on leaves.

Harvest and Storage: The harvest season for pears generally runs from early August through September. For highest quality, pick pears by hand about two weeks before dead ripe and allow them to ripen slowly in a cool room. This practice eliminates some of the graininess that is characteristic of many tree-ripened pears. When it is green and firm, lift the fruit and the pedicel should separate from the twig.

To store for up to three months, keep pears at temperatures just above freezing in their preripened state, then thaw and keep at room temperature for a few days until ripe. Winter pears, which are still hard and inedible when they fall from the tree, can be put in any common storage where they will soften during the winter and can be canned or used for other processed foods.

Uses: Pears are excellent for eating out of hand, in a variety of desserts, and for canning.

PERSIMMON

American persimmon
Diospyros virginiana
and
Japanese persimmon, kaki
Diospyros kaki
Ebenaceae

The American persimmon and the Japanese persimmon or kaki belong to the only cultivated genus of the ebony family, Ebenaceae. The persimmon is mainly a tropical tree, and its existence in a temperate climate is a sort of horticultural accident; do not expect much cold hardiness from persimmons. *D. kaki* grows in California, Florida, and the Gulf Coast. It is best adapted to the cotton belt. *D. virginiana* grows from New England to southern Florida and westward to eastern Iowa, Kansas, Oklahoma, and east Texas.

On rich riverbottom soil, the American persimmon may grow to 80 feet tall or more, but usually trees are only half that height at most.

Fruit is golden orange, tough-skinned, and may have no seeds or as many as eight. American persimmons are about an inch in diameter and the Japanese about 3 inches in diameter. Flavor is similar to a plum but not quite as tart. Unripe fruit is very astringent, except in some varieties, which are nonastringent (see Varieties).

Pollination: American persimmon trees may be male, female, or bisexual, making some self-fruitful and some not. Some of the best *D. virginiana* varieties, like Meader, are female but can produce fruit without a male tree, in which case the tree will bear seeded fruit. Japanese persimmons are more or less self-fruitful, but bear better if two varieties are planted.

Varieties: Named varieties (grafted trees) of *D. virginiana* available include Early Golden, Garretson, John Rick, and Meader. Supply of good grafted varieties is very limited. Mail-order nurseries normally offer seedling trees which may not have quality approaching that of selected varieties.

D. kaki varieties are divided between astringent and nonastringent types. Included in the former, which become nonastringent when fully ripe, are Eureka, Great Wall, Peiping, Pen Saijo, Sheng, Tamopan, and Tecumseh. Nonastringent kakis are Fuyu, Gosho, Jiro, and Smith's Best.

Propagation and Planting: Persimmon trees have long taproots and are difficult to transplant. Trying to transplant a sucker or stolon from an established tree is even more difficult because of the lack of fibrous roots on the sucker. Only very small trees, just sprouted, transplant easily. The best method is to plant seeds and later graft on a good variety if the seedling fruit is not of good quality. Don't allow the seed to dry out before planting. Store in plastic in the refrigerator over winter or plant as soon as the fruit is harvested. For grafting on, wait till the seedling has grown a year or two, and graft only after the tree has begun to leaf out. A simple splice graft works quite well.

If planting a purchased grafted tree, set it in the ground at about the same height as it grew in the nursery. Mulch around the tree, as you would other fruit trees, and no other fertilizer should be necessary. The site should be well drained, but persimmons will persist fairly well on poorer ground.

Pruning: American persimmons in climates favorable to them are pioneer plants. That is, they will spread by suckering on poorer land where they have no competition from other trees, and therefore can be a "weed" tree in pastures. Some regular pruning off of suckers is therefore necessary to keep them in bounds. No other pruning, except cutting out dead branches, is necessary. Prune kaki trees similarly.

Pests: Persimmons are relatively pest-free, although raccoons will steal fruit if given a chance. A tin collar, 1 foot wide, wrapped around the tree trunk during fruiting season will keep raccoons out of the tree.

Harvest and Storage: It is not true that frost ripens American persimmons. Good ones may ripen before frost, and poor ones may remain slightly astringent even after frost. Harvest is usually accomplished by picking American persimmons off the ground after they fall. Some will hang on the tree until well into winter. Sweet, unripe, or astringent persimmons can be dried and eaten like figs and dates. Store in a cool place or freeze them.

Uses: Eat fresh when fully ripe and soft to the touch. Persimmons also are pulped and used for puddings, pies, cookies, and a very delicious ice cream.

PINEAPPLE

Ananas comosus
Bromeliaceae

The pineapple plant is an herbaceous perennial that reaches 3 feet tall and spreads its stiff, spiny leaves out 4 to 5 feet. The short stem of the pineapple is hidden by the leaves that grow around it in a spiral, each leaf 3 to 5 inches long and about 1½ inches wide. The leaves of some cultivars have marginal spines.

When the plant is over a year old it sends up reddish flower clusters. Over a period of 20 days the flowers, as many as 150, open. Each flower produces a single fruitlet. The fruitlets all merge into the collective fruit which is the pineapple. The fruit is mature and ready to harvest 6 to 8 months after the flowers die.

Fruits vary in size from 1 to 10 pounds, in shape from oval to cylindrical, and in color from yellow to orange. Each fruit is topped by a crown of small leaves which grows while the fruit is developing, and becomes dormant when the fruit is mature. About 60% of the fresh fruit is edible, apart from the rind or shell and central core. It is a good source of vitamins A, B, and C, as well as containing fiber, minerals, and the enzyme bromelain which aids in the digestion of protein.

Pineapples require a uniformly warm tropical or subtropical environment. In Florida, they will survive 28°F with extensive leaf damage. Below that temperature, they will die. Temperatures that remain in the low 40s or that are too consistently hot will ruin the fruit; leaves and roots will not grow below 60°F or above 108°F. In the United States, pineapples grow in Hawaii and southern Florida.

Pollination: Cross-pollination is necessary.

Soil Requirements: Sandy loam that is mildly acid and well drained provides the best growing medium.

Propagation: Vegetative, using offsets or crowns. Offsets, most often used, are shoots or branches which originate from buds present in the leaf axils. Crowns form on the top of the fruit. Offsets continue to grow on the plant after the fruit is cut. To use them for propagation, remove the slip from the mother plant after harvest, dry it from a week to a month, then plant in the permanent location.

Planting and Culture: Pineapple culture is somewhat difficult, considering that each plant produces only one fruit and much hard labor is involved. Plant the crown, offset, or sucker in summer, in a dibbled hole 4 to 6 inches deep. Plants should be 10 to 18 inches apart.

Mulch to keep down weeds and conserve moisture, and water frequently. Coffee grounds, worm castings, and compost make good fertilizers and should be applied four times a year before fruiting. In Florida, a seaweed nutritional supplement or fish emulsion may be applied monthly. Hand weeding is necessary during early growth.

Pineapple can also be grown in containers. Cut off the crown from a ripe pineapple, leaving an inch of fruit attached. To prevent rot, turn the cut end up to air dry for five to ten days, until the base becomes somewhat firm.

Plant in a light, rich potting medium, such as a mix of equal parts of leaf mold and sharp sand, in a 5-gallon container. Set the crown in firmly and cover to the base of the leaves. Keep soil moist but not soggy with evenly warm temperatures of 75° to 85°F. The plant takes about two years to flower and six months more for the fruit to ripen. If fruit does not appear after two years, enclose a ripening apple and the plant in a clear plastic bag for a week. The ethylene gas given off by the apple may stimulate bloom.

Pests and Diseases: Mealybugs and nematodes are the most troublesome pests in Florida. Scale and thrips can be a problem, as can various fungal diseases and the yellow spot virus.

Harvest and Storage: Pineapples are ripe when they are golden in color, richly fragrant, and when a leaf from the crown can be pulled easily from the fruit. Harvest by severing the stalk with a sharp knife about 2 inches below the fruit. The fruit ripens from the base up and is always sweeter at the base. For maximum sugar content, let fruit ripen fully before harvesting. Allow the crown to stay on the fruit to prolong its keeping qualities.

Uses: Eat fresh as a dessert fruit, sliced, crushed, or cubed. Make into jam, juice, crystallized and glacé fruit.

Pineapple

Variety	Where Grown	Description
Abakka (Abacaxi)	Florida	Sweet flavor; 3–6 lbs.
Natal Queen	Florida	Golden flesh, delicate flavor, 2–3 lbs.; good keeping qualities. Plant has spiny leaves.
Pernambuco	Florida	White flesh, sweet flavor, 2–4 lbs. Spiny leaves.
Red Spanish	Florida, Hawaii	Sweet, pale yellow to white flesh, 2–4 lbs. Spiny leaves. Mainly used in fresh fruit trade.
Smooth Cayenne	Major cultivar in Hawaii; Florida	Yellow flesh, high in sugar and acid, 5 lbs. Spineless leaves. Accounts for 95% of world's commercial crop.

PLUM

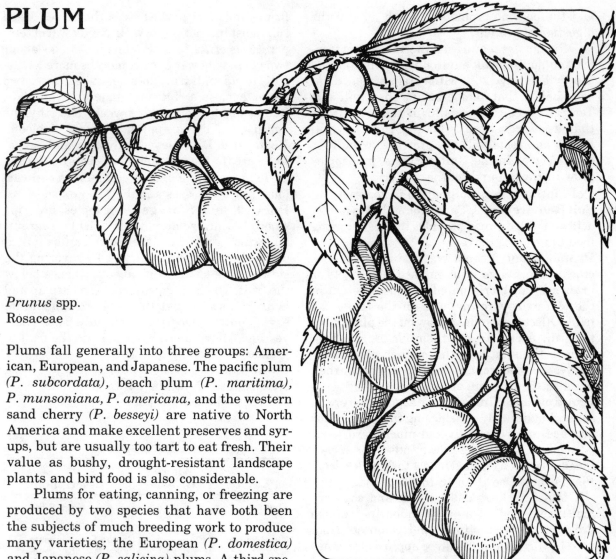

Prunus spp.
Rosaceae

Plums fall generally into three groups: American, European, and Japanese. The pacific plum *(P. subcordata)*, beach plum *(P. maritima)*, *P. munsoniana, P. americana,* and the western sand cherry *(P. besseyi)* are native to North America and make excellent preserves and syrups, but are usually too tart to eat fresh. Their value as bushy, drought-resistant landscape plants and bird food is also considerable.

Plums for eating, canning, or freezing are produced by two species that have both been the subjects of much breeding work to produce many varieties; the European *(P. domestica)* and Japanese *(P. salicina)* plums. A third species, *P. institia,* the Damson plum, should be considered as a special case; though its fruit is too tart to eat fresh, Damson preserves are of a quality that is in a class apart.

To clear up any confusion between prunes and plums: A prune is a dried European plum, which has a very high sugar content. It can be dried whole without fermentation around the pit. A plum that is split and dried with the pit removed is a dried plum, not a prune. All prunes are plums; not all plums are prunes.

A mature Japanese plum will produce an average of 1 to 1½ bushels of fruit. European types will yield twice that amount.

Soil Requirements: Plums do well on any deep, well-drained soil, though they will tolerate heavier soils better than most tree fruits. European plums root deeply and can penetrate a slight hardpan. For other considerations in choosing a site, see Peach.

Pollination: Pollination in the plum world is a complex operation and bears careful consideration when choosing varieties. To start with, most plums require a second variety for cross-pollination, though a few, mostly European, types are self-fruitful. Some plums have sterile pollen, making a third variety necessary if all trees are to bear. For pollination to occur the bloom periods of the varieties must, obviously, overlap. This is the main problem with relying on late-blooming European plums to pollinate the generally early-blooming Japanese types or vice versa. Neither should you depend solely on a particular variety for pollination if it tends to be biennial (such as Beauty, Formosa, or Sugar) because its flowerless years will leave your other trees plumless, too.

Ordering Stock: As a rule European plums are similar in hardiness to apple and slightly more hardy than the Japanese type, though some Japanese hybrids are quite hardy. They also make a much larger, more upright tree that blooms later, often avoiding damage from spring frosts. Japanese types with their often severely spreading habit can be a striking landscape addition, especially when the branches are covered with small white blossoms in spring. Chilling requirements are similar to those of peaches.

Propagation: Most plum varieties do not come true from seed, so are purchased as selected varieties budded onto one of several rootstocks. By far the most popular and useful is myrobalan plum; it is hardy, deep-rooted, long-lived and tolerant of drought and a wide range of soils including those that are heavy and poorly drained. Its only drawback is a slight lack of vigor. Peach rootstock, best suited for lighter soils and used commercially on the West Coast, has a degree of nematode tolerance and causes the fruit to ripen a few days earlier than on other roots. Where soils remain wet or Armellaria oak root fungus exists, peach rootstock is not suggested. Western sand cherry is a dwarfing rootstock for European plums and will make a very small tree when used with Japanese types.

Planting and Culture: Plant a plum much as you would a peach, leaving a space 18 to 24 feet in diameter for Europeans, 14 to 16 feet for Japanese, and 10 to 14 feet for the native species, which tend to be large bushes rather than trees. It is important that the area around the tree (1 to 2 feet at planting, increasing to 4 to 6 feet) be kept weed- and grass-free to avoid competition for nutrients and water with the tree's subsurface feeder roots. Mulch is a good idea. A good soaking and a tree guard or wire mesh to stymie the mice are the final planting chores.

Requiring less fertilizer than peaches, a plum tree can be kept adequately fed with annual applications of barnyard manure 1 to 2 inches deep under the drip-line. Spread it in late winter to allow the nutrients to begin leaching into the root zone and be largely consumed by late summer, when the tree must begin hardening for winter. A bucket of wood ashes, spread with the manure, will supply important mineral nutrients.

As with peaches, if you want to pick full-sized fruits rather than thousands of marbles, plums should be thinned after the "June drop" to a 2-inch spacing or so none are touching. A few varieties (such as Santa Rosa and Climax) will self-thin reasonably well.

Water is very critical to growing plums. Don't allow the trees to wilt or they may jettison the entire crop. Use the weeds near the tree as soil moisture indicators. When they're wilted early in the morning it's time to add 25 gallons of water per tree, twice a week.

Boron deficiencies may develop in some areas and can be recognized by dry, hard, sunken pockets in the flesh. Spreading ½ pound of borax under the tree every third year will prevent this disorder.

Pruning: One-year-old European trees are usually sold as unbranched whips and should be trained to the modified central leader form as described for Apricot, though they will form a sound tree capable of bearing heavy crops

Plum

Variety	Fruit	Tree
Japanese Types		
Abundance	Purple blush on yellow flesh. Good quality but softens quickly. Early midseason.	Excellent pollinizer, tends to biennial bearing.
Burbank	Large, purple-red skin. Very meaty and firm, cans well, very good flavor. Late midseason.	Vigorous, hardy, prolific, droopy growth. Thinning a must. Methley pollinates well.
Duarte	Large; red skin and flesh. Fair flavor. Early.	Needs pollination.
Early Golden	Yellow skin and flesh, fair quality. Very early.	Very strong-growing, needs thinning. Biennial tendency.
Elephant Heart	Very large, purple-red skin. Blood red flesh. Very juicy, flavorful. Late.	Hardy, productive, vigorous. Grows very large. Needs pollination.
Elliot	Large; red, firm flesh. Good for cooking. Late midseason.	Productive, hardy, should be thinned. Showy bloom.
Formosa	Large; gold-orange skin with red blush. Fragrant, amber flesh. Freeze fairly well, superior dessert quality. Midseason.	Medium vigor, poor set some years. Blooms early, needs pollination.
Frontier	Large, blue-black skin, red, firm flesh. Almost freestone, excellent flavor. Midseason.	Vigorous, productive, needs pollination.
Methley	Small-medium, reddish purple with red flesh. Juicy, sweet, slightly sour skin. Ripen over several weeks. Very early.	Vigorous, upright, large. Hardy, self-fruitful. Fruit borne heavily along all limbs.
Monitor	Very large; reddish skin. Clingstone, sweet with sour skin.	Medium vigor and productivity. Excellent pollinizer.
Omaha	Speckled red and yellow. Excellent flavor, very juicy. Late.	Very hardy, productive.
Ozark Premier	Large; bright red skin; yellow, juicy flesh of fair quality. Clingstone, ripens over a long period. Midseason.	Hardy, productive, vigorous. Fairly resistant to bacterial spot, needs pollination.
Santa Rosa	Large, dark red skin, yellow flesh. Very fragrant, flavorful. Midseason.	Large, vigorous, partially self-fruitful. Better crops with pollinator. Moderately bud-hardy.
Satsuma	Large, round; dark red skin. Sweet, purple, firm flesh excellent for canning or preserves. Semifreestone.	Moderately hardy, vigorous, early bloom. Needs pollination.
Shiro	Small-medium, yellow skin and flesh. Good flavor when fully ripe. Early midseason.	Very productive, hardy, vigorous. Needs pollination. Burbank will not pollinate.
Starking Delicious	Medium; purple-red skin; coarse red flesh. Very juicy, good flavor. Midseason.	Vigorous, long-lived, hardy. Productive, very disease-resistant, needs pollination.
Superior	One of the largest plums. Red skin can be peeled like a peach. Good flavor. Early midseason.	Fast-growing, hardy, needs pollination.
European Types		
Blufre	Very large; blue freestone. Yellow flesh, prone to split pits in some areas. Hangs on the tree long after ripening. Late.	Bears early and heavily, vigorous. Pollinizer helps.

Variety	Fruit	Tree
European Types *(continued)*		
Bradshaw	Medium; purple, semifreestone. Good flavor, prone to brown rot. Midseason.	Medium vigor, sets a heavy crop.
Burbank Grand Prize	Very large; oval, purplish freestone. Yellow, sweet, juicy flesh. Excellent dessert quality. Midseason.	Medium vigor, hardy. Thin heavily. Pollination by Stanley or Blufre will greatly increase crop.
Earliblue	Medium; Stanley type, soft flesh. Excellent freestone. Early midseason.	Vigorous, hardy, but slow to begin bearing. Self-fruitful.
Fellenberg	Large; long purple freestone. Excellent dessert plum, very sweet. Cans very well. High in vitamin A. Old European variety also known as Italian or German prune. Late midseason.	Medium vigor, hardy, self-fruitful, blooms late.
Mount Royal	Good eating quality; round, blue; medium freestone. Cans well. Midseason.	Medium vigor, productive. Slightly dwarfed tree is extremely hardy.
Reine Claude Conducta	Gage type. Blushed red skin, green flesh. Excellent for fresh use, very fragrant. Midseason.	Productive, hardy, vigorous. Self-fruitful.
Shropshire Damson	Small; oval, dark clingstone. Too tart for eating; the finest plum for jam. Late.	Heavy crops on vigorous, very hardy trees. Self-fruitful.
Stanley	Medium; purple-blue skin. Firm yellow flesh. Sweet, excellent for eating, canning, freezing. Most popular freestone prune type. Late midseason.	Vigorous, hardy, productive. Bear early and annually, partially self-fruitful, though a pollinizer helps.
Sugar	Large; purple-red; yellow flesh. Very sweet, not for processing. Early midseason.	Medium vigor, very productive. Must be thinned.
Tragedy	Medium; purple skin. One of the best dessert varieties. Early midseason.	Moderately hardy, strong-growing. Needs pollination.
Valor	Large, dark purple, semifreestone. Superior flavor, greenish flesh. Cans and freezes well. Late.	Vigorous, productive, medium-hardy. Needs pollination.
Yellow Egg	Large; golden yellow; thick skin. Juicy, mild flavor. Late.	Very productive, hardy, good vigor. Self-fertile.
Hybrid Types		
Pipestone	Medium; red skin with golden blush. Juicy, very sweet. Very early.	Very hardy and productive.
Toka	Medium; salmon-orange; fine texture; excellent flavor.	Very hardy for northern areas. Pollinator for Pipestone.

with little help from the pruner. Japanese plum seedlings are usually branched and with their spreading habit work best in the open-center shape with four or five main scaffolds (see Peach). Prune trees lightly for the first few years; heavy pruning will delay fruiting and promote more vegetative growth that must only be removed. Japanese plums begin bearing in three to four years, the Europeans a year or two later.

To assess the vigor of your tree examine new shoot growth. If there is 16 to 24 inches on a young, nonbearing tree consider it in balance; you've neither removed too much nor too little in pruning and the tree is not overfed or underfed. Once fruiting begins, 10 inches is plenty of shoot growth with the rest of the tree's energy going into fruit production.

To rejuvenate a tired, shy-bearing plum tree, remove a large limb that has borne several crops as shown by the numerous fruit spurs on it. Develop a new limb by selecting a young shoot growing in the desired direction and favor it during later prunings. Plums bear on one-year-old shoots and spurs on older wood. The object of pruning is to maintain seasonal growth of the one-year wood and to keep the center of the tree open to sunlight, without which the spurs will die. Plums, as a rule, are pruned more lightly than most fruits, except cherries. To reduce possible winter damage, prune in the early spring before the buds swell.

Pests and Diseases: Birds, borers, plum curculio, and scale all prey on plum trees. They are also affected by brown rot. But the biggest enemy of the plum tree is black knot, a fungus known by the characteristic black, gnarled swellings it produces on affected shoots and limbs. Although black knot doesn't affect the fruit, if left unchecked it can girdle and kill major limbs, eventually killing the tree. Black knot can be eliminated over the winter, when its dark color makes it obvious. Cut the cankers out, removing 6 inches of unaffected wood below the cut to prevent reappearance, and burn the prunings.

Harvest and Storage: Plums are green until just before ripening when the green gives way to red, purple, or yellow depending on the variety. Picked when firm-ripe, when the flesh is beginning to soften to thumb pressure, a plum can be held several weeks at 35°F, slightly cooler than a household refrigerator. But if you're going to the trouble of growing them, restrain your urge to harvest, give the plums another week, and pick them when tree-ripe, soft as a fresh blister and sweeter and more fragrant than possible otherwise. A tree-ripened plum, like a tree-ripened peach, is a rare treat that's only available if you grow it yourself, since they don't ship well.

Japanese plums are best eaten fresh, losing some of their flavor and most of their aroma and texture when canned or frozen. The Europeans, while not having the exotic fragrance or melting texture of the premier Japanese types, can and freeze very well and may be dried for nutritious winter snack.

POMEGRANATE

Punica granatum
Punicaceae

The pomegranate is a bushy shrub that reaches up to 20 feet in height. Its pink to orange-red flowers are large and ornamental, and bloom in spring through midsummer.

The fruit is 2½ to 5 inches in diameter and is classified as a leathery berry. The rind is hard, brownish yellow to deep red, and forms a protective ball that is filled with chambers containing many seeds, each covered with juicy red pulp. Fruit ripens from late July to September. It is sweet-acid in flavor and high in phosphorus.

The trees are injured by temperatures below 12°F. Pomegranate likes cool winters and hot, dry summers but will grow in a range of climatic conditions. In humid areas the fruit is of inferior quality.

Pollination: Pomegranate trees are self-pollinating.

Soil Requirements: Pomegranates will grow in a surprisingly large variety of soils from sand to clay, but prefer deep, heavy loam with a pH of 5.5 to 7.0. Sandy soil produces lower yields and clay has an adverse effect on fruit color. Trees prefer well-drained soil, but will tolerate slow drainage.

Propagation: Hardwood cuttings provide the easiest method. Use cuttings 8 to 10 inches long, 1/4 to 1/2 inch in diameter, cut in late winter from the previous season's shoot or sucker growth. Plant vertically in nursery rows 6 to 8 inches apart, with the top node exposed. Leave for up to two years, then transplant bare root in winter or early spring to permanent location. Layering is also possible.

Planting: Plant in early spring after danger of frost is past; site in full sun. Work the soil loosely. Space trees 15 to 18 feet apart.

Pomegranates require less fertilizing than other fruit trees. Water as you would citrus. While the trees have substantial drought resistance, good soil moisture as harvest approaches in early fall reduces the quantity of split fruit. Trees require 50 to 60 inches of water per year. An excess of water or fertilizer increases young trees' tendency to drop fruit.

Container Culture: Nana is a dwarf variety of pomegranate that will grow easily from seed. Both Nana and full-sized pomegranate cultivars can be grown in tubs if they are given plenty of direct sunlight. Multiflora is another dwarf variety that will grow from seed very readily, but its fruit is inedible. Pot pomegranates in a well-drained mix of pasteurized potting soil, vermiculite, perlite, or sand. Nana attains a shrublike size, but Multiflora remains small enough to rest on a windowsill. Pomegranates in containers need to be kept constantly moist.

Pruning: To train young trees to grow with only one trunk, remove all other suckers as they appear. To develop a multiple-trunk system, allow five or six vigorous suckers to grow into permanent trunks, a process that may take three years or more, and remove all other suckers in summer and during dormant pruning. Multiple-trunk trees come into bearing sooner than one-trunk trees and have an increased chance of surviving frost damage.

In the first winter after planting shorten branches by 40%. Tying with ropes for support may also be necessary in the first few years until trunks are strong enough to support the new top growth. Flowers develop on short spurs on two- or three-year-old wood that is primarily on the outer edge of the tree. Prune lightly once a year to encourage new fruit spurs to grow. Remove interfering or crossing over branches and thin out crowded bearing areas.

Pests and Diseases: In California, pests include flat mites (*Brevipalpus lewisi*) and omnivorous leafroller (*Platynota stultana*), while the only serious disease is heart rot. In Florida, trees may develop leaf blotch and fruit spot. Scale mites may also be a problem.

Harvest and Storage: Harvest the fruit with clippers, beginning in August, when the fruit is yellowish brown. If there is a detectable sound of grains cracking inside when you press the fruit lightly, it is ready to pick. Skin color darkens once picked, but it will last many weeks at room temperature. Flavor actually improves with age and the seeds will become softer and more edible.

Uses: Eat the fruit fresh, either sucking the flesh off the seeds and discarding the seeds, or crunching and swallowing pulp and seeds together.

Pomegranate juice, extracted by squeezing kernels in a cloth bag or pressing on an orange reamer, is used in wine making and as the base for punch. Grenadine, a syrup made from pomegranate juice, is used in flavoring drinks, desserts, and as an ice cream topping. Pomegranate jelly is particularly good. Be careful when working with the juice because it stains easily.

Varieties: Wonderful, the largest and most brilliantly colored pomegranate, is the cultivar most commonly grown commercially in California. Other California cultivars include Foothill Early, Granada, Ruby Red, and Spanish Sweet. In Alabama, Wonderful is the recommended cultivar. In Florida, Purple Seed and Spanish Ruby are recommended.

QUINCE

Cydonia oblonga
Rosaceae

The quince belongs to the same subfamily as the pear. Its fruit, though, is rather unpalatable and rarely eaten fresh. Native to Asia, quince is hardier than the peach and less hardy than the pear. Generally, it will grow wherever pears grow in temperate climates.

Orchard quince, *C. oblonga,* is not to be confused with flowering quince, *Chaenomeles japonica* or *C. speciosa.* Flowering quince is much hardier and, while it does produce fruit, it is of inferior quality and usually remains green. Flowering quince grows to only 6 feet tall and produces lavish flowers in white to bright red. The fruit of both orchard quince and flowering quince can be used for preserves.

Orchard quince is usually small and suckers enough so that it can be maintained as a tall bush. Otherwise, a single trunk can be developed that grows to about 20 feet tall.

Flowers bloom in late spring (after apples). Fruit is either pear- or apple-shaped, with a hard, yellow flesh that is fragrant, but tart and chewy. It ripens in late October and November.

Pollination: Quince are self-fertile.

Soil Requirements: A moist, well-drained soil is best.

Propagation: Propagate by root cuttings or by scraping a bit of bark at the bottom of a young sucker and heaping soil around it. Roots will form at the bark injury. One year later, cut the sucker loose from the mother tree and plant it.

Pruning: Prune in winter or early spring to maintain a tree form. Quince grown as a bush needs little or no pruning.

Pests and Diseases: Quince is bothered by the same problems that attack pears, particularly fireblight. It is also troubled by an assortment of apple worms.

Harvest and Storage: Fruit is yellow when ripe, shading to orange. It will hang on the tree until cold weather, but is best picked a little before maturing, and then stored. Stored in a shallow tray, where the easily bruised fruit will not harm each other, it will keep for two or three months. Do not keep in the refrigerator or near apples or pears, which will absorb the quince's tangy aroma.

Uses: Use quince in jelly, preserves, marmalade, or as a sauce mixed with applesauce. Fruit can also be canned or spiced. With its high pectin content, it is useful combined in jellies with berries or grapes that are low in pectin.

Varieties: Orange, Pineapple, and Smyrna are good choices, when available.

RASPBERRY

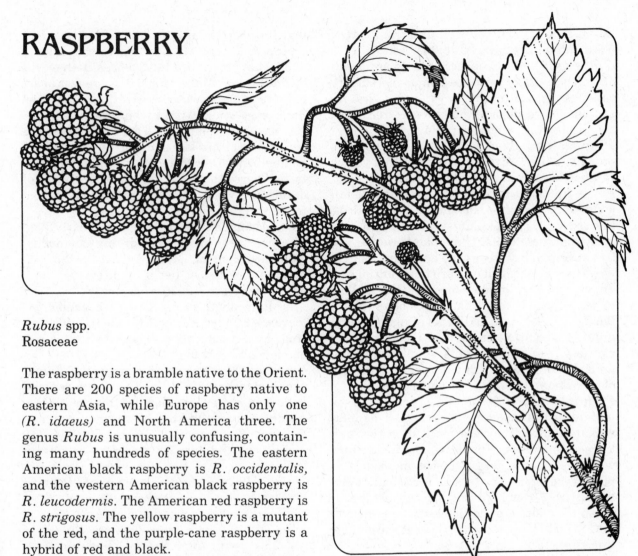

Rubus spp.
Rosaceae

The raspberry is a bramble native to the Orient. There are 200 species of raspberry native to eastern Asia, while Europe has only one (*R. idaeus*) and North America three. The genus *Rubus* is unusually confusing, containing many hundreds of species. The eastern American black raspberry is *R. occidentalis,* and the western American black raspberry is *R. leucodermis.* The American red raspberry is *R. strigosus.* The yellow raspberry is a mutant of the red, and the purple-cane raspberry is a hybrid of red and black.

The raspberry bush usually grows to a height of 5 to 8 feet. Red raspberries have erect canes, while black raspberries have canes that arch or trail. Canes (or stalks) vary in color: pale purple on blacks and purples; greenish yellow on yellows; red to brown on reds. All canes turn brown when mature and all have thorns. Canes vary in size from the diameter of a pencil to the diameter of a finger.

Flowers are white and bloom in late spring on summer-bearing varieties. Flowers bloom in early spring and again in late summer on summer and fall (everbearing) varieties.

The berries or caps are shaped like thimbles, and range in size from ⅜ inch to 1 inch. Each berry is composed of small drupelets tightly clustered around a central core. When the fruit is picked it pulls away from a white cylinder which remains attached to the plant. The raspberry's hollowness distinguishes it from the blackberry, which it otherwise closely resembles.

Pollination: Plants are self-fertile.

Soil Requirements: Raspberries can tolerate both light and heavy soils, but cannot tolerate wetness. Soil should be well drained. A pH of 5.5 to 7.0 is adequate, but 6.0 is best.

Ordering Stock: Raspberry plants are available in a choice of varieties from many nursery catalogs. Because of the prevalence of viral infections in raspberries, buy virus-free stock even though it is more expensive.

Propagation: Black and purple raspberries propagate themselves one way; red and yellow raspberries another. The black and purple varieties tip-root: the canes bend over in late fall and plunge their tips back in the ground. Rooting occurs and new plants grow up the next year from these roots. These plants can be easily cut from the mother cane and transplanted.

The red and yellow varieties multiply by growing suckers or new canes from the shallow roots spreading out from the mother plant. Sucker growth is usually very vigorous and difficult to control, but it does facilitate propagation. To start new plants, simply pull or dig up a sucker after it has put down a few roots of its own, and it will transplant easily.

Planting and Culture: Raspberries can be maintained in hedgerow plantings or as individual clumps. They are most often tied and trained to trellises, the designs of which vary with the grower. The simplest method is to plant raspberries in rows with a single overhead wire 3 feet high and set between posts. Wrap the canes around the wire or tie them to it. Cultivate the soil a whole year ahead of time, if possible.

Plants received from a nursery have a short length of cane above the roots and crown. Spread the roots out in the planting hole with the crown just barely under the soil surface. Press soil firmly down around the plant. New shoots will grow from the crown. Once they start growing well enough to mark the row, cut off the short length of old cane, even if it is sending out buds. It's new growth you want to encourage. Those first new canes will probably not produce fruit, but they will get the plant well established so that the next season's shoots will produce the first crop the year after plant-

ing. Raspberries are biennial. Shoots bear in their second year, then die. Space the plants 2 to 3 feet apart in the row. Eventually they will fill in the row. Make rows 6 or more feet apart to leave ample space for cultivating or for mowing a grass walkway between rows.

Raspberry plants need a lot of water in the period just before late summer. In August and September, however, too much water this late in their growth period may delay maturity of developing wood. This immaturity could lead to winterkill.

Add mulch or compost in May or early June to prevent the roots from drying out during fruit development. Mulching may make irrigation unnecessary, but if conditions are very dry, water from 1 to 2 inches a week.

Mulch in fall as well, using grass clippings, leaves, straw, or manure. Raspberries like nitrogen, used sparingly. Phosphate rock is recommended every four years.

Pruning: Different varieties require different pruning techniques. In addition, the red and yellow varieties are handled differently depending on whether they bear in summer only, or bear in both summer and fall.

Blacks and purples: Tip prune to prevent the canes from rooting new plants and to increase the crop the following year. Pruning black raspberries is very simple and makes sense, unlike some pruning measures. Keep in mind that blacks bear on canes produced the previous year. After picking, cut out those canes at ground level, giving the new growth more room and sunlight. When the rapidly growing current season's canes reach 2½ to 3 feet tall, tip them to encourage laterals to develop. This, in turn, will increase the bearing wood/cane for the following year.

Once tipped, the laterals may grow 2 to 5 feet, depending on the vigor of the particular plant. If the laterals seem determined to tip-root, nip off a few inches. Otherwise, no pruning is necessary after the tipping. In the spring following tipping, and before growth begins, cut back the laterals to 10 inches. On less vigorous

Pruning Black Raspberries:
(1) New canes grow among fruiting canes (above, left)
(2) Fruiting canes are cut back after harvest; new canes are thinned (above, right)
(3) Next spring, prune laterals back to 10 inches (left)

canes, cut back the laterals to only 6 to 8 inches. It's on these stubs that flowers, and later berries, will be borne.

If you have allowed some canes to root to fill in gaps in the row, cut the mother cane loose from the new plant or leave it to produce berries low on the hedgerow. After berry harvest, cut out all the old fruiting canes. Thin the new canes, which will fruit the following year, to about four of the healthiest per foot of row if the row is maintained 2 feet wide. If the row is very narrow, thin more vigorously to one cane every 6 inches. Trial and error will reveal how many vigorous canes your particular soil can support.

Red and yellow summer bearers: Immediately after berry harvest, cut out all the old bearing canes to make room for the new canes growing amidst them. Thin the new canes as described above. Since reds and yellows spread by suckering, they are much harder to keep within the row bounds than are blacks. Despite all efforts they usually grow so thick by the end of five years that it is better to tear up the row and start again someplace else. Figure high production and big berries from a row for only that long, although by vigorously digging out extra suckers and old decayed roots, it is possible to keep a bed or row going until virus disease renders it unproductive. In spring pruning, thin out the canes, leaving only the heaviest spaced 6 inches apart and cut them back to about 40 inches tall, being sure to cut off all winterkilled ends. Less vigorous canes should be headed at 36 inches.

Red and yellow summer and fall bearers: After summer harvest, cut out the old canes that have fruited. The new canes coming on will fruit in the fall, and then again the following spring. Thin out the weak ones nonetheless. After the fall crop has been picked (or more than likely, after frost has stopped the fall production), there are two possible ways to proceed. The first is to prune off the bearing tops of the canes, leaving about 3 feet of cane, which will grow out and produce a summer crop the next year. The second method avoids having to cut out old canes in the heat of summer; cut the whole hedge right down to the ground. Do not use a rotary mower for this chore. It will spread virus, if any is present, and infect the whole bed. A scythe or weed chopper is best. Remove and burn cut canes. There will be no summer crop the next year but the new canes that grow next spring will produce a better crop without the competition of the summer-bearing canes.

Pests and Diseases: Red raspberries are more disease-resistant than black and purple varieties. The black sap or juice beetle, often called the picnic bug, is the worst insect pest of raspberries. Virus disease and anthracnose fungus present the most difficult disease problems. The best defense is to cut out old canes promptly after they have fruited. Moving healthy young plants to start a new row on a regular schedule is also helpful (every five years).

Blacks are not as hardy as reds, but no raspberries need winter protection. To avoid winterkill do not fertilize or water in fall, which would encourage lush growth into winter.

Harvest and Storage: Harvest gently with thumb and forefinger. Place berries in a shallow bowl to avoid crushing and bruising them. Keep them out of the sun. Pick every other day during the ripening season. Washing raspberries tends to make them lose texture, and is not necessary if they are grown without toxic chemicals and are picked with clean hands. To help them retain their texture during freezing, put unwashed berries on waxed paper, freeze, and then package and store in freezer.

Uses: Raspberries are best eaten fresh, but also make fine jam, jelly, and wine.

Raspberry

Variety	Area of Best Growth	Fruit	Bush
Black Hawk	Midwest	Black, firm berry, very good quality.	Vigorous grower, anthracnose-tolerant. Susceptible to powdery mildew.
Bristol	North to mid-South	Black, very large, excellent quality. Midseason.	Vigorous, hardy, extremely productive. Very susceptible to anthracnose.
Cumberland	North to mid-South	Black, fair quality, reliable, good bearer.	Susceptible to fungal and viral diseases.
John Robertson	North	Black, fair quality. Good for jam and jelly.	One of the hardiest of the blacks.
Logan	North to mid-South	Black, modest bearer. Early.	Resistant to disease, especially mosaic. Vigorous.
Boyne	Upper Midwest	Red, summer bearer	Vigorous. Canes shorter than normal.
Heritage	North to mid-South	Red, summer and fall bearer, excellent quality.	Requires no support. Performs very well when moved for fall crop. Vigorous in most soils.
Latham	North to mid-South	Red, fair to good quality, summer bearer. The old reliable.	Full of virus now. Buy only virus-free stock.

Variety	Area of Best Growth	Fruit	Bush
Scepter	Middle Atlantic states	Red, summer and fall bearer, good quality.	Adapted to fluctuating winter temperatures.
Southland	Developed for South, good in North too	Red, summer and fall bearer, good taste quality.	Disease-resistant.
Willamette	West, North	Red, very good quality, summer bearer.	Not top-hardy.
Brandywine	North to mid-South	Purple, very tart, firm, large. Very late.	Vigorous and very productive.
Clyde	North to mid-South	Purple, soft, large, tart. Best for jams and jellies. Late.	Very vigorous and disease-resistant. Moderately hardy.
Amber	North to mid-South	Yellow, with pink bloom. Excellent taste, summer bearer.	Prone to disease.
Fallgold	North to mid-South	Yellow, not tinged with pink. Poor to fair quality. Poor producer. Only fall bearer readily available.	Prone to virus infection.

STRAWBERRY

Fragaria spp.
Rosaceae

Strawberry is a low-growing perennial herb. Wild species of strawberry, native to both Europe and America, are small, extremely delicious and aromatic fruits that grow in woodland environments. In flavor and texture, they are more than the equal of cultivated strawberries. The large domestic berries developed from them are now grown throughout temperate regions. There is, for instance, at least one strawberry variety adapted to every state of the United States. Many varieties are, in fact, so regionalized that they do not perform well elsewhere.

A few odd varieties have white fruit, but almost universally, the strawberry is red. Fruit forms in clusters on stems that grow from the crown of the plant.

Pollination: Strawberries are self-pollinating.

Propagation: Most varieties propagate themselves by runnering. The mother plant, soon after producing fruit, sends out runners, in quantities that vary with the cultivar, that tiproot about a foot away. These new plants in turn send out their own runners. If left unchecked, plants will soon form a dense mat or bed. In the case of wild strawberries new runners move constantly away from the old, established bed, the new plants producing berries, and the old ones becoming less productive, until eventually they become barren and die. The wild patch moves slowly but constantly to new territory to renew its vigor and health.

In the first bearing year, young plants will bear heavily, as will their first runner plants, which root early in the summer. The next year, the runners that rooted later will bear heavily, the old mother plants only moderately. By the third year the old plants bear only a few small berries, and the patch will become so crowded that the new plants can find little space to root and grow vigorous. In these conditions, they may become infected with a disease the old plants contracted, and they might have to compete with a weed buildup. A partial solution to this kind of deterioration is to continually dig out old plants. Better still is to rotate the strawberry patch every other year or every third year. Another possibility is to allow a strawberry row to "move" across the garden, letting runners root on one side of the row, and then the next year tilling under the old plants left behind. Or simply dig up year-old plants in the spring, and transplant them, intact in a clump of dirt, to a new planting.

If an old bed is to be held over for a second bearing year, renew it mechanically and it will bear reasonably well again. Immediately after harvest, mow off the tops with a lawn mower. Then use a tiller to cultivate strips through the bed, leaving rows of plants about a foot wide. Cultivate the old plants, leaving the current season's well-rooted runners to bear the next year's crop.

Planting: Plants come from the nursery tightly wrapped in plastic. Store them in the refrigerator or some equally cold place until ready to plant. At planting time, place them unwrapped in a bucket of water so the roots won't dry out. Make a little cone of soil with your fist and set the plant on the cone. Fan out the roots over the cone, pull in dirt, pat it down firmly, and water to settle the earth around the roots. It is very important that the crown of the plant be right at the soil surface, neither so high that roots are exposed, nor so low that it is buried. Good nurseries send along detailed instructions on this point. If the roots are very thick and long, prune them to about 5 inches long with a scissors before planting. Healthy young roots are brown to cream-colored. Black, wiry roots may indicate an old plant.

Spacing rows, like training runners, can be done in a number of ways. The way rows are spaced, however, depends on the method used to train runners. You can plant rows 4 to 5 feet apart and plants 2 feet apart in the row, and by allowing only four runners to set around each mother plant, have two well-defined rows producing very large berries the next year. Or you can allow the runners to form a matted bed.

Everbearing types cannot be treated as above, since they produce berries a second time in the fall. Everbearers are satisfactory only in those few climates where cool weather in late summer prevails.

Plants are set in the spring in the north, for the next year's crop. Farther south, plants can be set out in fall, for next spring's crop. To extend the harvest season, use a combination of early, midseason, and late varieties.

After the plants start growing, cultivate

around them once or twice to destroy early weeds, then mulch in June. Strawberries are shallow-rooted but need ample moisture. Keep the mulch fairly shallow immediately around the crown. Thick mulch discourages rapid drying after rains or dew and may increase berry rot. On small beds, you can usually set early runners down through the mulch so they root rapidly for better production next year. Or use a very fine mulch material that the runner tips can easily root down through. Once the ground has frozen apply clean straw or similar clean material over the berry plants to inhibit frost heaving and possible plant damage. Wait till after freezeup, so mice do not take up winter quarters under the straw. When warm weather returns pull the straw off the plants into the row spaces or along the sides of the bed, where it will cushion the berries and keep them clean.

If the first mulch put around the plants (in the first year when no berries are harvested) is a barn manure, the plants will get all the nutrition they need in a normal soil. Even straw alone is useful. Overfertilizing berries increases yields at the expense of flavor. That's also true of irrigating. In areas of adequate rainfall, mulch will provide adequate moisture for a backyard crop except in drought years. If soil is poor or in need of fertilizer, the prospective bed should be worked up a year before planting and treated with manure or a balanced mixture of organic amendments. Preworking the soil can also help minimize weeds and destroy certain soil grubs that can be harmful to the berry plants.

Pests and Diseases: Slugs and birds present the most serious problems. In rotated backyard patches, insect pests are common but not unusually troublesome. Buy disease-free stock to avoid verticillium wilt and red stele.

Harvest, Storage, and Uses: Strawberries ripen about a month after blossoming. Pick by pinching the stem between the thumbnail and forefinger, avoiding pulling on the berry itself. Berries do not keep well for more than a day or two. The sooner eaten after picking, the better. Fresh strawberries make wonderful jams and pies. Frozen, they hold a considerable portion of their nutritional value. Freeze strawberries immediately after harvesting.

Strawberry

Variety	Best Growing Area	Fruit	Plant
Albritton	Southeast	Late; good freezer.	Not very hardy in North.
Apollo	Southeast, South	Late.	Not recommended for North.
Armore	Midwest	Late midseason; fair freezer.	Very hardy.
Atlas	Southeast	Midseason; firm.	Not very hardy.
Badgerglow	Upper Midwest	Midseason.	
Blakemore	All U.S.	Early, firm; good shipper.	Runners make heavy growth that may decrease yield if not controlled.
Catskill	North, Central, Northeast	Midseason; good dessert quality.	Resists spring frosts.
Cyclone	Midwest	Early; good freezer.	Hardy.
Darrow	East	Early; very firm.	Very resistant to red stele and verticillium wilt.
Delite	Central	Late.	Plants are vigorous, making runners freely. High resistance to disease.
Dixieland	Southeast, South Central	Early; good freezer.	Susceptible to leaf scorch.

(continued)

Strawberry—*continued*

Variety	Best Growing Area	Fruit	Plant
Dunlap	North and far North	Early to midseason.	One of oldest varieties still grown.
Earlibelle	South	Early; very firm; good for jams.	Will adapt to sandy soil vigorously.
Earlidawn	All areas	Very early; good freezer.	Resists spring frosts.
Earliglow	East, Central	Early; good quality.	Very resistant to red stele.
Empire	North	Midseason.	Commercial berry.
Fairfax	North, Central, Northeast	Early to midseason. Very deep red when ripe. Very high taste quality.	Hardy.
Fletcher	North, East	Late.	Very hardy.
Florida 90	South	Midseason.	Not productive in North.
Fort Laramie	Central and West	Everbearer.	Abundant runner production.
Guardian	East	Midseason; firm.	Very resistant to diseases. Fruit stems do not snap loose freely.
Holiday	East	Midseason, very firm; tough skin.	
Jerseybelle	East	Late. Tough skin. Maintains large size through season.	Vigorous. Fairly productive the second bearing year.
Lassen	Pacific Coast	Midseason.	Resistant to red stele.
Marlate	East	Late.	Easy to pick, stem snaps free.
Marshall	Pacific Coast	Early midseason; excellent flavor.	Old patches may contain virus.
Midway	Central, East	Midseason.	Prolific runner maker.
Ogallala	Northern plains	Everbearer.	Very hardy and somewhat drought-tolerant.
Ozark Beauty	Eastern half of U.S.	Everbearer.	
Pocahontas	Northeast to mid-South, west to Mississippi River	Midseason.	Thrives in mild winters and hot summers.
Premier	North to mid-South, coast to coast	Early.	Resistant to spring frosts.
Quinault	West, Pacific Coast	Everbearer.	Produces only a limited amount of larger-than-usual berries in East.
Raritan	East	Midseason to late.	High disease resistance.
Redchief	East	Midseason.	Good disease resistance.
Redglow	East	Early.	Resistant to red stele.
Robinson	North	Late; very large.	Resistant to verticillium wilt.
Scott	East, eastern Midwest	Midseason.	Resistant to red stele.

Variety	Best Growing Area	Fruit	Plant
Shasta	West, Pacific Coast	Midseason.	
Sparkle	Midwest	Midseason, prolific. One of the best freezers.	Good disease resistance.
Sunrise	East	Early; fair taste.	Good disease resistance.
Superfection	Eastern U.S., especially northern half	Everbearer.	Very hardy.
Surecrop	Midwest, Central Appalachia	Midseason; fair quality.	Good disease resistance.
Tennessee Beauty	Mid-South	Midseason.	Fairly resistant to leaf disease.
Vermillion	Midwest and Northern Plains	Midseason.	Very hardy.
Vesper	East	Very late; large.	

TANGELO

Citrus × tangelo
Rutaceae

The tangelo is a cross between a grapefruit (or pummelo) and a mandarin orange. The best commercial varieties of tangelos more closely resemble the mandarin than the grapefruit. The cross creating the tangelo is probably the most successful and satisfactory of all citrus crosses. Less successful crosses bear more resemblance to the grapefruit. Culture, planting, and propagation are similar to that of the mandarin. Tangelo trees are not everbearing and the time of harvest varies with the variety.

For regular production, some tangelos require cross-pollination because they benefit from the presence of seeds and they cannot produce them without cross-pollination. The variety Sampson is an exception, because its seeds have several embryos and will produce trees from seed.

Natural tangelos are fruits that resemble the grapefruit/mandarin crosses, but have unknown origins. Among these are the Ugli of Jamaica. The Temple may be either a grapefruit/mandarin or an orange/mandarin natural cross, but is usually considered a tangor.

For more information on planting and harvesting, see Citrus Fruits. Also see general characteristics of Mandarin Orange.

Tangelo

Variety	Where Grown	Fruit	Tree
Allspice (cross of Imperial grapefruit and Willowleaf mandarin)	Florida	Midseason; loses quality if left on tree. Small, rich, tart. Flesh tender and juicy.	Similar to mandarin.
Clement (Duncan grapefruit crossed with Clementine mandarin)	Florida	Medium-early. Large fruit; few seeds. Mild, sweet flavor.	Productive.
K-Early	Florida	Very early. Fruit medium-sized, yellow-orange, seedy. Fewer mandarin characteristics.	
Minneola (Duncan grapefruit and Dancy tangerine cross)	Florida, California	Medium-late. Fruit large with few seeds. Tender, juicy, tart.	Less cold-resistant than Orlando; vigorous; needs cross-pollination with Dancy, Clementine, or Kinnow mandarin; cross-incompatible with Orlando.
Orlando (Duncan grapefruit and Dancy tangerine cross)	California, Florida	Early. Medium-large, seedy; flesh juicy, orange, sweet.	More cold-resistant than Minneola; vigorous; needs cross-pollination with Dancy, Clementine, or Kinnow mandarins or Temple tangor; most commercially significant of tangelos.
Pearl	Florida	Medium-early; loses flavor if held on tree. Medium-small with yellow color; seedy; rind smooth; flesh tender and sweet. Fewer mandarin characteristics.	Vigorous.
Sampson	Florida, California	Late midseason. Medium-sized, orange-yellow; seedy; smooth clinging rind; semihollow center; flesh dull orange; flavor acid with bitter tang. Fewer mandarin characteristics.	
Seminole (Duncan grapefruit and Dancy tangerine cross)	Florida	Later than Minneola. Medium-sized, deep reddish orange, seedy; rind pebbled and thin, moderately adherent.	Vigorous and productive; self-fruitful; leaves cupped.
Wekiwa (Pink Tangelo; cross of grapefruit and Sampson tangelo)	Florida	Early. Medium-small, pale yellow; few seeds; flavor sweet and mildly acid, but unpleasant when overripe. Rind pink blushing under favorable conditions; flesh amber pink. Fewer mandarin characteristics.	Less vigorous with small leaves.

WATERMELON

Citrullus lanatus
Cucurbitaceae

The large family to which watermelons belong includes squash, pumpkin, gourd, and other melons. The long-trailing annual vine has green stems that turn brown and woody when the fruit is ripe. At maturity it can occupy as much as 36 square feet of space. Both male and female flowers are borne on the same plant, making it monoecious.

The fruit of the watermelon is globe-shaped, oblong, or cylindrical, with mottled or striped green skin. The sweet-tasting flesh is red, orange, yellow, or white, depending on the variety and its degree of ripeness.

Watermelons can be cultivated in the southeastern United States, from Virginia to the Gulf of Mexico, wherever the long-leaf pine grows. The new short-season varieties, some requiring as little as 70 days to mature, will grow as far north as New York State. A site protected from wind and in full sun will help lengthen the growing season for watermelons.

Pollination: Vines are usually self-pollinating or pollinated by insects. The new Japanese-developed seedless watermelon, however, which has been genetically rendered larger and infertile by colchicine treatment and selective crossing, must be planted near a small watermelon variety like Sugar Baby for pollination. Since most watermelons are hybrids, the seeds, unless purchased, seldom breed true. There is an unusually large number of watermelon cultivars. To avoid crossbreeding, most growers plant just one variety.

Soil Requirements: Watermelons prefer a light, fertile, deep loam or sandy soil. Soil should be well drained and have a pH of 5.5 to 6.5. Because they are a tropical fruit, watermelons generally require a long, dry growing season with temperatures ideally between 70° and 80°F during the day and 60° to 70°F at night. This fact, along with their need for fertile soil and abundant space, is the chief limitation to success in growing them.

Prepare the soil of the watermelon plot the fall before planting by digging deeply and adding well-rotted manure or compost, turning it under to a depth of 6 inches or more so that deep roots may make use of it. If the soil is clay, add a half bucket of coarse sand to every hill or circle. Watermelons are heavy feeders. Phosphate rock or bone meal and greensand or granite dust should be added to watermelon hills using one handful per hill. Watermelons also need a supply of trace minerals.

Ordering Stock: Watermelon seeds are widely available. One packet will plant eight hills. Seed should be selected on the basis of length of the growing season and disease resistance.

Propagation: In southern areas, start watermelons from seed planted outdoors no more than two months before the date of the last anticipated frost. Seed for most varieties will not germinate until the soil reaches 70°F, but seeds of short-season varieties will sprout at lower temperatures.

In areas farther north, where the last frost date comes in late spring, it is common practice to start watermelons indoors or in warm greenhouses or bottom-heated cold frames where soil temperatures will reach 75° to 80°F. Plant seeds in individual peat pots a month to six weeks before they are to go in the garden, which should be when all danger of frost is past. Put three or four seeds in each pot. Thin the seedlings to one per pot. Keep the soil moist, but make sure seedlings do not become leggy from too much watering and too little sunlight. Neither should they develop too large a root system, for this will interfere with transplanting them. Set whole peat pots in the ground with their tops even with the soil level.

Planting and Culture: When planting seeds directly in the garden, poke them into hills. Hills provide seeds with added warmth to aid germination. Make the hills or circles 13 inches in diameter, then heap up the soil to a depth of 2 or 3 inches. The higher the mound the warmer it will be, but also the drier it will become in hot weather. Poke eight to ten seeds into each hill and cover with an inch of soil.

After the true leaves develop, thin out all but three or four strong plants per hill. If seedling plants are used, set out three or four plants per hill. When the vines have grown 1 to 2 feet long, thin them to allow only one or two vines per hill.

Spacing of the plants depends on the variety planted and fertility of the soil. Some small varieties adapt to container or circle bed planting, or to trellising, with slings used for fruit support. Field-grown watermelons, however, require 6 to 12 feet per vine. As vines advance, set them gently back into rows or onto hills.

Water seedlings as you set them out, and provide ample water during germination. After this point, water more sparingly. A half-hour soaking when no rain has fallen for a week is sufficient. At midsummer when the fruit has set, a feeding with manure tea or fish emulsion keeps plants thriving.

Mulch, if used, should be applied after a rain and only when the ground is thoroughly warm. Until the mulch is laid, keep weeds down by shallow hoeing. Straw, hay, and chopped leaves make good mulches when laid 6 inches deep and heaped at the base of the vine. To prevent fruit rot, take care that ripening fruit does not sit on ground or mulch that is wet.

Watermelons also benefit from fruit or flower thinning to speed ripening and to help them produce larger and more uniform fruit. In home gardens, thinning is not necessary until the season is waning. When nights grow colder, remove all blossoms before they develop in order to send energy to ripening fruit.

Pests and Diseases: Watermelons are bothered by anthracnose, fusarium wilt, mosaic, aphids, cucumber beetles, and other melon and squash pests and diseases.

Harvest and Storage: Small, short-season varieties produce fruit by midsummer as far north as South Carolina, and in the interior valleys of California. Harvest time for larger watermelons is mid to late summer.

There are many ways to gauge ripeness.

The most popular is to strike the melon with your knuckles and listen for a dull, deep, muffled "punk." According to Mark Twain if the sound you hear is "pink" or "pank" the melon is not yet ripe. If a melon is ripe, the tendril nearest the stem turns dry and brown, the two other nearby tendrils die, and the stem becomes brittle. Some varieties, when ripe, turn from white to yellow on their underside. You can take a plug sample from a watermelon you believe is ripe, but this practice leaves the melon vulnerable to bacterial rot.

Uses: Cold watermelon is an old American remedy for summer heat, especially when eaten by the slice and within pit-spitting distance of a lake. The flesh will freeze well if packed in a honey-based syrup, or sprinkled with lemon juice. Don't waste the rind—pickle it.

Watermelon

Variety	Days to Maturity	Fruit	Vine
Black Diamond	90	Large, round. Dark green skin. Flesh red and sweet. Seeds stippled black.	Vigorous.
Charleston Gray	85	Red flesh, little fiber. Skin greenish gray. Fruit 24 in. long and weighs 28 lb.	Resists anthracnose, fusarium wilt, sunburn. Climate adaptable.
Crimson Sweet	80	Round melon. Light green with dark green stripe. Weighs 25 lb. Flesh dark red.	Vigorous vine. Resists anthracnose and fusarium wilt. Good for northern areas.
Dixie Queen	85	Medium-sized. Oval, light green with dark stripe. Flesh red, crisp, and very sweet. Small white seeds.	Resistant to wilt.
Fordhook Hybrid	74	Round fruit. Bright red flesh. Small seeds. Weighs 12–14 lb.	Productive, vigorous vine, hardy in north.
Garrison	85	Large, long, light green with dark stripe. Red, flavorful flesh. White seeds.	
Irish Gray	95	Large, long, gray-green. Red, firm flesh. White seeds.	
Klondike R-7	85	Oblong, solid green. Medium-sized.	Resistant to wilt.
New Hampshire Midget	70	Small, oval, medium green. Red flesh. Small black seeds.	Small-sized. Hardy in north.
New Shipper	75	Firm-textured, flavorful red flesh. 8–16 lb.	Vigorous, disease-resistant.
Sugar Baby	75	Midget. Round, dark green. Red, flavorful flesh. Small, dark tan seeds.	Small-sized. Grows well in the North.
Sugar Bush	80	Oval, icebox type. Bright scarlet flesh. Rind medium green.	Compact vine takes 6 sq. ft. and is 3–3½ ft. long.
Yellow Baby Hybrid	70	Icebox type. Oval to round, 7 in. across. Bright yellow flesh. Small seeds. Light green rind with dark stripe.	Small but vigorous vine.
Seedless Varieties			
Seedless Hybrid	80	Sweet, red flesh.	
Seedless Sweety	75	Oval, 8 lb.	Small vine.
Triple Sweet Seedless	80	Oval. Bright red, sweet, solid, flesh.	Small vine.

Glossary

Annual: a plant that completes its life cycle in one growing season.

Berry: a simple multi-seeded fleshy fruit with a skinlike covering; examples are grapes and tomatoes.

Biennial: a plant that completes its life cycle in two growing seasons, making vegetative growth the first season, then flowering, fruiting, and dying the second season.

Bolting: premature flowering of a plant at the expense of its vegetative development; generally, a plant at this stage is no longer edible.

Budstick: the bud and surrounding wood which are inserted into the shoot in the process of budding.

Bud-union: the junction of the rootstock and scion (bud) on a grafted plant.

Cambium: the thin layer of tissue located between the bark and wood of a tree, which is capable of dividing and forming new cells.

Cane: a long, slender, woody biennial stem usually rising from perennial roots; the characteristic stem of the bramble fruits.

Central leader: the topmost vertical branch on the framework of a tree, usually the trunk.

Cole crops: species of the genus *Brassica* that are known collectively as cole crops, brassicas, or the cabbage family. Includes broccoli, Brussels sprouts, cabbage, cauliflower, Chinese cabbage, collards, kale, kohlrabi, mustard, rutabaga, and turnips.

Cotyledons: specialized seed-leaves which are the first leaves to appear on a seedling.

Crown: the area on woody and herbaceous plants where the stem(s) and roots meet.

Determinate: a plant growth habit in which flowers and fruits form from terminal buds on the main axis; an example of this growth habit is corn.

Drupe: a fleshy fruit with a skinlike covering and one seed enclosed in a hard, stony casing; cherries, plums, and peaches are all drupes.

Espalier: a plant trained to grow flat next to a support such as a wall, fence, trellis, or horizontal wires.

Forcing: encouraging plants to grow faster than they normally would by providing warmer growing temperatures.

Grafting: a method of propagation in which parts of plants are joined together so they will unite and grow as one plant.

Graft-union: see Bud-union.

Hardening-off: the process of gradually acclimatizing young plants grown indoors to the outdoor environment.

Hardy: a term used for plants which are able to withstand temperatures at or below freezing.

Hill: a mound of soil which provides a well-drained, warm environment ideal for the germination and growth of warm-season crops like squash and corn.

Humus: a dark-colored, amorphous substance derived from the decomposition of organic matter carried out by bacterial action. The end product of composting.

Indeterminate: a plant growth habit in which flowers form from lateral buds; cucumbers exhibit this type of growth.

Interstem: a piece of stem which is inserted between the scion and stock, forming two graft-unions.

Interstock: see Interstem.

Latent bud: a small, inconspicuous, dormant bud common on old branches of woody plants; usually produces water sprouts.

Lateral bud: a bud growing on the side of a branch or stem.

Leaching: the process by which nutrients are carried down through the soil by percolating rainwater, often out of the reach of plant roots.

Nutrient availability: a term indicating that the nutrients in the soil are present in a form that plants are able to use; natural fertilizers break down over a period of time, so their nutrients become available gradually.

Perennial: an herbaceous plant which lives for three or more years.

pH: a numerical representation expressing both the acidity and alkalinity of the soil on a scale from 1 to 14; soils with a pH of 7 are neutral, those with a pH less than 7 are acid, and those with a pH greater than 7 are alkaline.

Pistil: the female organ of a flower which consists of a stigma, style, and ovary.

Pollinator variety: a compatible fruit tree capable of pollinating neighboring trees of different variety.

Pome: a fleshy fruit with a dry, paperlike core containing several to many seeds; examples of this type fruit are apples and pears.

Raised bed: a growing area in which the soil is well dug and fortified with organic matter, thereby raising it above the level of the adjacent ground; plants are concentrated within these specially prepared beds and are accessible from all sides so there is no need to step into the bed and compact the soil; this general term encompasses growing beds, Chinese mounds, and structured-side beds.

Rootstock: the lower part of a grafted plant which provides the root system for the plant.

Runner: a specialized stem which develops from the crown of a plant and forms new plants which then root; strawberry plants spread by runners.

Scaffold: the supporting framework of a tree; consists of a main trunk and radiating branches.

Scion: the upper part of a grafted plant, consisting of a detached shoot with several dormant buds which develop into stems or branches or both.

Self-fruitful: a plant that is able to pollinate itself and bear fruit.

Self-unfruitful: a plant which can only produce fruit by cross-pollinating with another variety.

Spur: a short, compact, woody stem with very little annual growth that appears laterally on branches; the place where the fruit is borne on many fruit trees.

Stamen: the male organ of a flower, consisting of an anther and filament.

Stock: see Rootstock.

Stolon: a modified stem which grows horizontally; it takes root intermittently and plants develop after the root growth forms.

Stone fruits: see Drupe.

Subsoil: the layer of soil below the topsoil; usually not as fertile as topsoil and unable to support plant life.

Sucker: extra growth in the form of a shoot that appears on a plant; generated by buds below the ground, usually on roots.

Sunscald: tissue damage on the trunks of trees caused by hot sun and fluctuating temperatures in both summer and winter; causes the bark to split and come off.

Tender: a term used for plants which are sensitive to freezing temperatures.

Terminal bud: a bud growing at the tip of a branch or stem.

Topsoil: the top layer of soil in the garden, which is suitable for plant growth.

Top-working: technique of grafting used to change the variety of an established fruit tree to a more desirable variety.

True leaves: the leaves characteristic of the mature plant, which appear after the cotyledons.

Water sprout: a shoot on a plant which arises from latent buds on older stems growing off trunks or main branches.

Whip: a young, unbranched tree.

Bibliography

Bartholomew, Mel. *Square Foot Gardening.* Emmaus, Pa.: Rodale Press, 1981.

Branch, Diana S., ed. *Tools for Homesteaders, Gardeners, and Small-Scale Farmers.* Emmaus, Pa.: Rodale Press, 1978.

Bubel, Mike and Nancy. *Root Cellaring.* Emmaus, Pa.: Rodale Press, 1979.

Bubel, Nancy. *The Seed-Starter's Handbook.* Emmaus, Pa.: Rodale Press, 1978.

Carr, Anna. *Rodale's Color Handbook of Garden Insects.* Emmaus, Pa.: Rodale Press, 1979.

Chan, Peter. *Better Vegetable Gardens the Chinese Way.* Portland, Ore.: Graphic Arts Center, 1977.

Childers, Norman. *Modern Fruit Science,* 7th ed. New Brunswick, N.J.: Rutgers University Horticultural Publications, 1976.

"Container Gardening." Agriculture Canada, Publication No. 1653, 1978. (Write Information Services, Canada Department of Agriculture, Ottawa, K1A 0C7.)

Editors of *Organic Gardening* magazine. *Getting the Most from Your Garden.* Emmaus, Pa.: Rodale Press, 1980.

Halpin, Anne Moyer. *Gourmet Gardening.* Emmaus, Pa.: Rodale Press, 1981.

Hertzberg, Ruth; Vaughan, Beatrice; and Greene, Janet. *Putting Food By,* 2d ed. Brattleboro, Vt.: Stephen Greene Press, 1975.

Hill, Lewis. *Fruit and Berries for the Home Garden.* New York: Alfred A. Knopf, 1977.

———. *Pruning Simplified.* Emmaus, Pa.: Rodale Press, 1979.

"Home Storage for Fruits and Vegetables." Agriculture Canada, Publication No. 1478, 1978.

Johnson, Mary. *Tub Farming.* Charlotte, Vt.: Garden Way Publishing, 1978.

Larkcom, Joy. *Vegetables from Small Gardens.* London: Faber & Faber, 1976.

Logsdon, Gene. *Organic Orcharding.* Emmaus, Pa.: Rodale Press, 1981.

———. *Successful Berry Growing.* Emmaus, Pa.: Rodale Press, 1974.

Lorenz, Oscar A. and Maynard, Donald N. *Knott's Handbook for Vegetable Growers,* 2d ed. New York: John Wiley & Sons, 1980.

McCullagh, James C., ed. *The Solar Greenhouse Book*. Emmaus, Pa.: Rodale Press, 1978.

Milne, Murray. "Residential Water Conservation." California Water Resources Center, Report No. 35, University of California/Davis, March 1976.

———. "Residential Water Re-Use." California Water Resources Center, Report No. 46, University of California/Davis, Sept. 1979.

"Minigardens for Vegetables." USDA Home and Garden Bulletin No. 163, 1978. (Write Superintendent of Documents, Government Printing Office, Washington, D.C. 20402.)

Minnich, Jerry; Hunt, Marjorie; and the editors of *Organic Gardening* magazine. *The Rodale Guide to Composting*. Emmaus, Pa.: Rodale Press, 1979.

Popenoe, Wilson. *Manual of Tropical and Subtropical Fruits*. New York: Hafner Press, 1974.

Seymour, John. *The Self-Sufficient Gardener*. Garden City, N.Y.: Doubleday, 1979.

Shoemaker, James S. *Small Fruit Culture,* 5th ed. Westport, Conn.: Avi, 1977.

"Soil Drainage Affects—You, Your Home, and Your Plants—Parts 1 and 2." Bulletin published by Cooperative Extension Service, College of Agriculture and Environmental Science, Rutgers University, New Brunswick, N.J.

Stoner, Carol Hupping, ed. *Stocking Up*. Emmaus, Pa.: Rodale Press, 1977.

"Storing Vegetables and Fruits in Basements, Outbuildings and Pits." USDA Home and Garden Bulletin No. 110, 1978.

"Trickle Irrigation Guidelines for the Home Garden." Research Report No. 285, Michigan State University Agricultural Extension Service, July 1, 1975.

Tukey, Harold B. *Dwarfed Fruit Trees*. New York: Macmillan, 1964

Weygers, Alexander G. *The Recycling, Use, and Repair of Tools*. New York: Van Nostrand Reinhold, 1978.

Wolf, Ray. *Solar Growing Frame*. Emmaus, Pa.: Rodale Press, 1980.

Yepsen, Roger B., ed. *Organic Plant Protection*. Emmaus, Pa.: Rodale Press, 1976.

Metric Conversion Chart

Area

square inches × 6.5 = square centimeters
square feet × 0.09 = square meters
square yards × 0.8 = square meters

Length

inches × 2.5 = centimeters
feet × 30 = centimeters
yards × 0.9 = meters

Temperature

Subtract 32 from degrees Fahrenheit; multiply the difference by 0.56 to find degrees Centigrade.

Volume

tablespoons × 15 = milliliters
fluid ounces × 30 = milliliters
cups × 0.24 = liters
pints × 0.47 = liters
quarts × 0.95 = liters
gallons × 3.8 = liters
cubic feet × 0.03 = cubic meters
cubic yards × 0.76 = cubic meters

Weight

ounces × 28 = grams
pounds × 0.45 = kilograms

Index

Page numbers in **boldface** indicate an entry in the Guide to Vegetables or the Guide to Fruits section.

A

Abelmoschus esculentus. See Okra
Acerola, **384–85**
 diseases, 385
 growing of, 384–85
  soil for, 384
  spacing requirements, 384
 ordering stock, 384
 pests, 385
 propagation, 384
 pruning, 385
 storage of, 385
 time to harvest, 385
 uses for, 385
Acid soil, ix
 raising pH and, ix–x
Actinidia chinensis. See Kiwifruit
Agaricus bisporus. See Mushroom
Air drainage, 293
Alkaline soil, ix
 lowering pH and, ix–x
Alligator pear. *See* Avocado
Allium ampeloprasum. See Leeks

Allium cepa. See Onions and Scallions; Shallots
Allium sativum. See Garlic
Amaranth, **160–61**
 diseases, 161
 growing of, 160–61
  range for, 161
  soil for, 161
 pests, 161
 storage of, 161
 time to harvest, 160–61
 varieties of, 161
Amaranthus tricolor. See Amaranth
Amelanchier spp. *See* Juneberry
Ananas comosus. See Pineapple
Apium graveolens var. *dulce. See* Celery
Apium graveolens var. *rapaceum. See* Celeriac
Apple, 296, 303, 327, **385–89**
 container culture, 306
 diseases, 389
 growing of, 388–89
  soil for, 388
 ordering stock, 388
 pests, 389
 pollination, 385, 388
 propagation, 388
 pruning, 389
 storage of, 389
 time to harvest, 389
 varieties of, 386–87
 winter protection, 389

Apple tree, 313
Apricot, 306, 327, **390–92**
 diseases, 462–63
 growing of, 390–91
  spacing requirements, 390
 pests, 462–63
 pollination, 390
 propagation, 391
 thinning fruit, 390
 time to harvest, 392
 varieties of, 391
Arachis hypogaea. See Peanuts
Armoracia rusticana. See Horseradish
Artichoke. *See* Globe Artichoke; Jerusalem Artichoke
Asexual reproduction, plants and, 330–31
Asimina triloba. See Pawpaw
Asparagus, 88–89, 157–58, **161–64**
 diseases, 164
 growing of, 162–64
  range for, 162
  soil for, 162
  spacing requirements, 163
 mulch for, xiii, 163–64
 pests, 164
 storage of, 164
 time to harvest, 164
 trench method, 162
 varieties of, 164

498